The Canterbury and York Society

GENERAL EDITOR: PROFESSOR R.L. STOREY

ISSN 0262-995X

TWELFTH-CENTURY ENGLISH ARCHIDIACONAL AND VICE-ARCHIDIACONAL ACTA

Twelfth-Century English

Archidiaconal and Vice-Archidiaconal Acta

EDITED BY

B. R. KEMP

The Canterbury and York Society

The Boydell Press

2001

First published 2001

A Canterbury and York Society publication
published by The Boydell Press
an imprint of Boydell & Brewer Ltd
PO Box 9, Woodbridge, Suffolk IP12 3DF, UK
and of Boydell & Brewer Inc.
PO Box 41026, Rochester, NY 14604–4126, USA
website: http://www.boydell.co.uk

ISBN 0 907239 62 5

A catalogue record for this book is available
from the British Library

Details of previous volumes are available from Boydell & Brewer Ltd

This publication is printed on acid-free paper

Typeset by Joshua Associates Ltd, Oxford
Printed in Great Britain by
Antony Rowe Ltd, Chippenham, Wiltshire

CONTENTS

FOR CHRISTOPHER BROOKE

PREFACE

A work of this kind could not be accomplished without incurring numerous debts of gratitude, which I am pleased to acknowledge. I am especially grateful to the all owners or custodians of manuscripts for their kindness in granting permission to publish material in their collections, namely His Grace the Duke of Buccleuch and Queensberry; His Grace the Duke of Rutland, Belvoir Castle, Leicestershire; the Most Honourable the Marquess of Bath, Longleat House, Wiltshire; the Most Honourable the Marquess of Tavistock and the Trustees of the Bedford Estate; the Lord Vestey; the Lord Bishop of Chichester; the Executors of the late Miss M. L. A. Strickland; Mr C. H. Bagot, Levens Hall, Cumbria; Mr J. R. Thistlethwayte; the Trustees of the British Library; the Bodleian Library, Oxford; the Syndics of Cambridge University Library; Durham University Library; Glasgow University Library (Department of Special Collections); the Guildhall Library, Corporation of London; the Huntington Library, San Marino, California; Lambeth Palace Library, London; the Spalding Gentlemen's Society; the Whitby Literary and Philosophical Society (at Whitby Museum); the Deans and Chapters of the Cathedrals of Carlisle, Durham, Exeter, Gloucester, Hereford, Lichfield, Lincoln, Peterborough, St Paul's London, and Salisbury; the Dean and Chapter of Westminster; the Master and Fellows of Corpus Christi College, Cambridge; the Master and Fellows of St John's College, Cambridge; the Master and Fellows of Trinity College, Cambridge; the Master and Fellows of Balliol College, Oxford; the Governing Body of Christ Church, Oxford; the President and Fellows of Corpus Christi College, Oxford; the Warden and Fellows of New College, Oxford; the President and Fellows of St John's College, Oxford; the President and Fellows of Trinity College, Oxford; the County Archivists of Buckinghamshire, Cumbria, Devon, Essex, Hampshire, Kent, Lincolnshire, Norfolk, Northamptonshire, Shropshire, West Sussex, and Wiltshire and Swindon; and the Public Record Office, Kew. Duchy of Lancaster copyright material in the Public Record Office is reproduced by permission of the Chancellor and Council of the Duchy of Lancaster. I am equally grateful for access to materials held by the Bibliothèque nationale, Paris; the Bibliothèque municipale of Rouen; and the Archives départementales of Caen and Rouen. I am also very grateful to Mrs Mary Cheney and to the Bedfordshire Historical Record Society for permission to reprint the late Professor Christopher Cheney's text of an actum for Harrold priory (no. 67). I am in addition greatly indebted to the many librarians, curators and county archivists who have been so generous in making their knowledge available to me and in facilitating the consultation of documents in their care.

I have received much kindness, help and advice from the many friends and fellow scholars with whom I have discussed individual points, including Dr Nicholas Bennett, Dr Julia Boorman, Dr Martin Brett, Professor Christopher Brooke (who also generously drew some archidiaconal acta to my attention), Dr

Michael Franklin, Professor Diana Greenway, Dr David Johnson, Dr Dorothy Johnstone (who was instrumental in my gaining access to material at Belvoir Castle), Professor Simon Keynes, Mr Lowinger Maddison, Mr Alan Piper, and Professor Nicholas Vincent. I am much indebted to Professor David Smith, who has kindly read and commented on the Introduction, and I warmly acknowledge the unstinting help and understanding I have received from Professor Robin Storey, General Editor of the Canterbury and York Society, who has not only read the entire text but has made a number of useful suggestions for its improvement. I am alone responsible for any remaining faults and errors.

In dedicating this edition to Christopher Brooke, whom I am proud to be able to claim as a friend, I should like not only to acknowledge the enormous contribution his life's work has made to the study of the medieval church in general and, not least, of archdeacons in particular, but also to record my deep sense of gratitude for the encouragement, support and advice which he first showed to me as a young research student and which have continued unabated ever since.

MANUSCRIPT SOURCES CITED

Aylesbury, Buckinghamshire Record Office, Boarstall cartulary: *172*
Belvoir Castle, Additional mss: 71: *137–8, 276*
—, —, 105: *289*
Caen, Archives dép. Calvados, H non classé 8(1): *210*
—, —, H non coté 25/1: *254*
Cambridge, Corpus Christi Coll. Lib., ms 111: *259*
—, St John's Coll. Lib., ms S. 25: *203*
—, Trinity Coll. Lib., ms O. 2. 1: *106*
—, University Lib., Additional ms 3020: *32, 113, 115*
—, —, Additional ms 3021: *114*
—, —, Ely, D. & C. Muniments, EDC 1: *106*
—, —, Peterborough, D. & C. Lib., ms 1: *251*
Carlisle, Cumbria Record Office, Carlisle D. & C. Muniments, Holm Cultram
    cartulary: *7*
—, —, —, Wetheral cartulary: *8, 9*
—, —, ms DZ/1: *12*
Chelmsford, Essex Record Office, D/DP T1/693: *App. I, no. 6*
Chichester, West Sussex Record Office, Ep. VI/I/6: *14*
Durham, University Lib., Durham Cathedral Muniments: 2. 1. Arch. Dunelm.
    16: *30*
—, —, —, 2. 4. Ebor. 6: *267*
—, —, —, 2. 4. Ebor. 8: *285*
—, —, —, 3. 2. Spec. 9: *31*
Exeter, D. & C. mss: 814: *36*
—, —, 3672: *36*
—, Devon Record Office, ED/PP/10: *44*
—, —, W 1258 M/G 5/22: *37*
Glasgow, University Lib., ms Hunter 215 (U. 2. 6): *202*
Gloucester, D. & C. Lib., Register A: *App. I, no. 12*
—, —, Muniments, Register B: *256*
Hereford, Cathedral Archives, HCA 784: *241*
Levens Hall, Cumbria, ms Box A/18: *6*
Lichfield, Cathedral Lib., Magnum Registrum Album: *26, 29*
Lincoln, Lincolnshire Archives, D. & C. Muniments, A/1/6: *41, 128*
—, —, —, Dij/62/1/1a: *301*
—, —, —, Dij/73/2/18a: *41*
—, —, —, Dij/90/3/20: *128*
—, —, —, Dij/90/3/21: *128*
London, BL, Additional charters: 22002: *163–4*
—, —, —, 28325: *103*
—, —, —, 28334: *195*
—, —, —, 28336: *App. I, no. 7*

Spalding, Gentlemen's Society, Crowland cartulary: *104–5, 120–22, 214–15, 290–1*

Trowbridge, Wiltshire and Swindon Record Office, mss: D1/1/1: *150–1, 235, 238, 248*

—, —, —, D1/1/2: *234, 236*

—, —, —, D1/1/3: *234, 236*

—, —, deeds: 9/15/5: *245*

Westminster Abbey, Muniments: 371: *255*

—, —, 381: *255*

—, —, 2492: *75*

—, —, 2496: *96*

—, —, 2573: *94*

—, —, 2583: *76*

—, —, 3042: *74*

—, —, 7259: *231*

—, —, 13167: *207*

—, —, 16737: *3*

—, Muniment Books: 1: *3*

—, —, 10: *74–5, 94–6*

—, —, 11: *109, 204–5, 255, 264*

Whitby, Literary and Philosophical Society, Whitby cartulary (on loan): *6*

Winchester, Hampshire Record Office, 1M54/1: *252*

PRINTED BOOKS AND ARTICLES CITED, WITH ABBREVIATED REFERENCES

AASRP	*Associated Architectural Societies' Reports and Papers*, 42 vols. (1850–1935).
Ancient Charters	*Ancient Charters, royal and private, prior to A.D. 1200*, ed. J. H. Round, PRS, 10 (1888).
Ann. Mon.	*Annales Monastici*, ed. H. R. Luard, 5 vols., RS, 1864–9.
Arch. Cant.	*Archaeologia Cantiana*, Kent Archaeological Society, 1858–.
Arnulf of Lisieux	*The Letters of Arnulf of Lisieux*, ed. F. Barlow, Camden 3rd ser. 61 (1939).
Baddeley, W. St Clair	*A History of Cirencester*, Cirencester 1924.
Baddeley, W. St Clair	'The early deeds of St Peter's, Gloucester', *Transactions of the Bristol and Gloucestershire Archaeological Society* 37 (1914), 221–34; 38 (1915), 19–46.
Barlow, F	*The English Church 1066–1154*, London 1979.
Barlow, F.	*Thomas Becket*, London 1986.
Basset Charters	*Basset Charters c. 1120–1250*, ed. W. T. Reedy, PRS, new ser. 50 (1995).
Bateson, M.	'The Huntingdon song school and the school of St Gregory's, Canterbury', *EHR* 18 (1903), 712–13.
Beverley Fasti	R. T. W. McDermid, *Beverley Minster Fasti*, Yorkshire Archaeological Society, Record Series 149 (1993).
BIHR	*Bulletin of the Institute of Historical Research.*
Blair, J.	*Early Medieval Surrey*, Stroud 1991.
Blythburgh Cartulary	*The Cartulary of Blythburgh Priory*, ed. C. Harper-Bill, 2 vols., Suffolk Records Society, Suffolk Charters 2–3 (1980–1).
BM Cat. Seals	W. de G. Birch, *Catalogue of Seals in the Department of Manuscripts in the British Museum*, 6 vols., London 1887–1900.
Boarstall Cartulary	*The Boarstall Cartulary*, ed. H. E. Salter, Oxford Historical Society 88 (1930).
Bracton's Note Book	ed. F. W. Maitland, 3 vols., London 1887.
Bradenstoke Cartulary	*The Cartulary of Bradenstoke Priory*, ed. V. C. M. London, Wiltshire Record Society, 1979.
Brett, M.	*The English Church under Henry I*, Oxford 1975.
Bridlington Cartulary	*Abstract of the Charters . . . of Bridlington Priory*, ed. W. T. Lancaster, Leeds 1912.
Brooke, C. N. L.	'The archdeacon and the Norman Conquest', in

	Tradition and Change: Essays in honour of Marjorie Chibnall . . ., ed. D. Greenway, C. Holdsworth and J. Sayers, Cambridge 1985, 1–19; repr. in Brooke, *Churches and Churchmen in Medieval Europe*, London 1999, 117–37.
Brooke, Z. N. and C. N. L.	'Hereford cathedral dignitaries in the twelfth century', *Cambridge Historical Journal* 8 (1944–6), 1–21, with supplement, 179–85.
Bruton and Montacute Cartularies	*Two Cartularies of the Augustinian Priory of Bruton and the Cluniac Priory of Montacute*, ed. Anon., Somerset Record Society, 8 (1894).
Buckland Cartulary	*A Cartulary of Buckland Priory in the County of Somerset*, ed. F. W. Weaver, Somerset Record Society, 25 (1909).
Bucks Place-Names	A. Mawer and F. M. Stenton, *The Place-Names of Buckinghamshire*, EPNS 2 (1925).
Burton Abbey Muniments	*Descriptive Catalogue of the Charters and Muniments belonging to the Marquis of Anglesey . . .*, ed. I. H. Jeayes, *SHC*, 3rd ser., 1937.
'Burton chartulary, The'	ed. G. Wrottesley, in *SHC*, 5 (1884), 1–101.
Burton, J.	*The Monastic Order in Yorkshire, 1069–1215*, Cambridge 1999.
Cal. Chart. R.	*Calender of the Charter Rolls preserved in the Public Record Office* (1226–1516), 6 vols., HMSO, 1903–27.
Canonsleigh Cartulary	*The Cartulary of Canonsleigh Abbey*, ed. V. C. M. London, Devon and Cornwall Record Society, new ser. 8 (1965).
Canterbury St Augustine's Cartulary	*The Register of St Augustine's Abbey, Canterbury, commonly called the Black Book*, ed. G. J. Turner and H. E. Salter, 2 vols., British Academy, 1915–24.
Carisbrooke Cartulary	*The Cartulary of Carisbrooke Priory*, ed. S. F. Hockey, Isle of Wight Records Series 2 (1981).
Cartae Antiquae Rolls 11–20	*The Cartae Antiquae Rolls 11–20*, ed. J. Conway Davies, PRS, new ser. 33 (1960).
Cat. Anc. Deeds	*A Descriptive Catalogue of Ancient Deeds in the Public Record Office*, 6 vols., HMSO, 1903–27.
CDF	*Calendar of Documents preserved in France, illustrative of the History of Great Britain and Ireland, I, A.D. 918–1201*, ed. J. H. Round, HMSO, 1899.
Chatteris Cartulary	*The Cartulary of Chatteris Abbey*, ed. C. Breay, Woodbridge 1999.
Cheney, C. R.	*English Bishops' Chanceries 1100–1250*, Manchester 1950.
Cheney, C. R.	*From Becket to Langton*, Manchester 1956.
Cheney, C. R.	'Harrold Priory: a twelfth-century dispute', Bedfordshire Historical Record Society 32 (1951), 1–26; repr. in idem, *Medieval Texts and Studies*, Oxford 1973, 285–313.
Cheney, M. G.	*Roger of Worcester 1164–1179*, Oxford 1980.

Chichester Acta	*The Acta of the Bishops of Chichester 1075–1207*, ed. H. Mayr-Harting, CYS 56 (1964).
Chichester Cartulary	*The Chartulary of the High Church of Chichester*, ed. W. D. Peckham, Sussex Record Society 46 (1946).
Chronicle of Jocelin of Brakelond, The	ed. and transl. H. E. Butler, NMT, 1949.
Church and Government	*Church and Government in the Middle Ages: Essays presented to C. R. Cheney on his seventieth birthday*, ed. C. N. L. Brooke, D. E. Luscombe, G. H. Martin and D. Owen, Cambridge 1976.
Cirencester Cartulary	*The Cartulary of Cirencester Abbey, Gloucestershire*, ed. C. D. Ross and M. Devine, 3 vols., Oxford 1964, 1977.
Clay, 'Archdeacons'	C. T. Clay, 'Notes on the early archdeacons in the church of York', *YAJ* 36 (1944–7), 269–87, 409–34.
Clay, 'Deans of York'	C. T. Clay, 'Notes on the chronology of the early deans of York', *YAJ* 34 (1938–9), 361–78.
Clay, C. (T.)	'Master Aristotle', *EHR* 76 (1961), 303–8.
COD	*Conciliorum Oecumenicorum Decreta*, ed. G. Alberigo and others, 3rd edn, Bologna 1973.
Colchester Cartulary	*Cartularium monasterii S. Johannis Baptiste de Colecestria*, ed. S. A. Moore, 2 vols., Roxburghe Club, 1897.
Coll. Top. et Gen.	*Collectanea Topographica et Genealogica*, ed. J. G. Nichols, 8 vols., London 1834–43.
Colvin, *White Canons*	H. M. Colvin, *The White Canons in England*, Oxford 1951.
Complete Peerage	G. E. C(ockayne), *The Complete Peerage*, revised edn V. Gibbs, H. A. Doubleday, Lord Howard de Warden, G. H. White and R. S. Lea, 13 vols. in 14, London 1910–59.
Constable, *Monastic Tithes*	G. Constable, *Monastic Tithes from their Origins to the Twelfth Century*, Cambridge 1964.
CRR	*Curia Regis Rolls . . . preserved in the Public Record Office* (Richard I–Henry III), in progress, HMSO, 1922–.
Cumberland Place-Names	A. M. Armstrong, A. Mawer, F. M. Stenton and B. Dickins, *The Place-Names of Cumberland*, 3 vols., EPNS 20–2 (1950–2).
CYS	Canterbury and York Society.
Danelaw Charters	*Documents illustrative of the Social and Economic History of the Danelaw*, ed. F. M. Stenton, British Academy, 1920.
Darley Cartulary	*The Cartulary of Darley Abbey*, ed. R. R. Darlington, 2 vols., Kendal, for The Derbyshire Archaeological Society, 1945.
Daventry Cartulary	*The Cartulary of Daventry Priory*, ed. M. J. Franklin, Northamptonshire Record Society 35 (1988).
Davis, *Medieval Cartularies*	G. R. C. Davis, *Medieval Cartularies of Great Britain*, London 1958.

Davis, R. H. C.   'The College of St Martin-le-Grand and the Anarchy, 1135–54', *London Topographical Record* 23 (1974), 9–26.

Denton, J. H.   *English Royal Free Chapels 1100–1300*, Manchester 1970.

Devonshire Studies   W. G. Hoskins and H. P. R. Finberg, *Devonshire Studies*, London 1952.

Diceto, *Opera Historica*   *Radulfi de Diceto decani Londoniensis opera historica . . .*, ed. W. Stubbs, 2 vols., RS, 1876.

Dickinson, *Austin Canons*   J. C. Dickinson, *The Origins of the Austin Canons and their Introduction into England*, London 1950.

Dodwell, 'Bacton Charters'   'Some charters relating to the honour of Bacton', ed. B. Dodwell, *Misc. D. M. Stenton*, 147–65.

Duckett, G.   'Charters of the Priory of Swine in Holderness', *YAJ* 6 (1879–80), 113–24.

Dunstable Cartulary   *A Digest of the Charters preserved in the Cartulary of the Priory of Dunstable*, ed. G. H. Fowler, Bedfordshire Historical Record Society 10 (1926).

Durham Seals   W. Greenwell and C. Hunter Blair, *Catalogue of the Seals in the Treasury of the Dean and Chapter of Durham*, 2 vols., London 1911–21.

Early Charters of St Paul's   *Early Charters of the Cathedral Church of St Paul's*, ed. M. Gibbs, Camden 3rd ser. 58 (1939).

Early Yorkshire Charters   vols. 1–3, ed. W. Farrer (1914–16); vols. 4–12, ed. C. T. Clay, and index to vols. 1–3 by C. T. and E. Clay, Yorkshire Archaeological Society Record Series, extra ser. (1935–65).

EEA   *English Episcopal Acta*, published by the British Academy; vols. cited:

     I   *Lincoln 1067–1185* and IV *Lincoln 1186–1206*, ed. D. M. Smith (1980, 1986)

     II   *Canterbury 1162–1190* and III *Canterbury 1193–1205*, ed. C. R. Cheney with E. John and B. Jones (1986)

     V   *York 1070–1154*, ed. J. E. Burton (1988)

     VI   *Norwich 1070–1214*, ed. C. Harper-Bill (1990)

     VII   *Hereford 1079–1234*, ed. J. Barrow (1993)

     VIII   *Winchester 1070–1204*, ed. M. J. Franklin (1993)

     IX   *Winchester 1205–1238*, ed. N. Vincent (1994)

     X   *Bath and Wells 1061–1205*, ed. F. Ramsey (1995)

     XI   *Exeter 1046–1184* and XII *Exeter 1186–1257*, ed. F. Barlow (1996)

     14   *Coventry and Lichfield 1072–1159*, 16 *Coventry and Lichfield 1160–1182*, and 17 *Coventry and Lichfield 1183–1208*, ed. M. J. Franklin (1997, 1998)

     15   *London 1076–1187*, ed. F. Neininger (1999)

     18   *Salisbury 1078–1217* and 19 *Salisbury 1217–1228*, ed. B. R. Kemp (1999, 2000)

     20   *York 1154–1181*, ed. M. Lovatt (2000).

EHR	*The English Historical Review.*
Ekwall, *English Place-Names*	E. Ekwall, *The Concise Oxford Dictionary of English Place-Names*, 4th edn, Oxford 1960.
Emden, *Biog. Reg. Oxford*	A. B. Emden, *A Biographical Register of the University of Oxford to 1500*, 3 vols., Oxford 1957–9.
EPNS	English Place-Name Society.
Epp. Cant.	*Epistolae Cantuarienses*, ed. W. Stubbs, RS, 1865.
Essex Place-Names	P. H. Reaney, *The Place-Names of Essex*, EPNS 12 (1935).
EYC	*Early Yorkshire Charters* (q.v.).
Eye Cartulary	*Eye Priory Cartulary and Charters*, ed. V. Brown, 2 vols., Suffolk Records Society, Suffolk Charters 12–13 (1992, 1994).
Eynsham Cartulary	ed. H. E. Salter, 2 vols., Oxford Historical Society 49, 51 (1907–8).
Facsimiles of Royal and other Charters in the British Museum	ed. G. F. Warner and H. J. Ellis, London 1903.
Fasti	John le Neve, *Fasti Ecclesiae Anglicanae 1066–1300*, compiled by D. Greenway, in progress, London 1968–: I, *St Paul's, London* (1968); II, *Monastic Cathedrals* (1971); III, *Lincoln* (1977); IV, *Salisbury* (1991); V, *Chichester* (1996); VI, *York* (1999); VII, *Bath and Wells* (2001).
Feet of Fines, Henry II and Richard I	*Feet of Fines of the reign of Henry II and of the first seven years of the reign of Richard I, A.D. 1182–A.D. 1196*, PRS 17 (1894).
Finberg, H. P. R.	'A vice-archdeacon's legacies', *Devon and Cornwall Notes and Queries* 22 (1942–6), 285–7.
Fisher, *History of Masham*	J. Fisher, *The History and Antiquities of Masham and Mashamshire*, London 1865.
Fisher, 'Petre Documents'	J. L. Fisher, 'The Petre Documents', *Transactions of the Essex Archaeological Society*, new series 23 (1942–5), 66–97.
Flaxley Cartulary	*The Cartulary and Historical Notes of the Cistercian Abbey of Flaxley . . .*, ed. A. W. Crawley-Boevey, Exeter 1887.
Foliot Letters and Charters	*The Letters and Charters of Gilbert Foliot*, ed. A. Morey and C. N. L. Brooke, Cambridge 1967.
Foster, C. W.	'Institutions to Benefices in the Diocese of Lincoln', *AASRP* 39 (1928–9), 179–216.
Fountains Cartulary	*Abstracts of the Charters and other Documents contained in the Chartulary of the Cistercian Abbey of Fountains*, ed. W. T. Lancaster, 2 vols., Leeds 1915.
Furness Coucher Book	*The Coucher Book of Furness Abbey*, ed. J. C. Atkinson and J. Brownbill, 2 vols. in 6 parts, Chetham Society, new ser. 9, 11, 14, 74, 76, 78 (1886–1919).
Gallia Christiana	16 vols., Paris 1715–1865.

Gesta (Benedict)	*Gesta regis Henrici secundi Benedicti abbatis* . . ., ed. W. Stubbs, 2 vols., RS, 1867.
Gesta Abbatum	*Gesta Abbatum monasterii Sancti Albani*, ed. H. T. Riley, 3 vols., RS, 1867–9.
Gilbertine Charters	*Transcripts of Charters relating to the Gilbertine Houses of Sixle, Ormsby, Catley, Bullington and Alvingham*, ed. and transl. F. M. Stenton, Lincoln Record Society 18 (1922).
Gir. Camb.	*Giraldi Cambrensis Opera*, ed. J. S. Brewer, J. F. Dimock and G. F. Warner, 8 vols., RS, 1861–91.
Gloucester Cartulary	*Historia et cartularium monasterii sancti Petri Gloucestriae*, ed. W. H. Hart, 3 vols., RS, 1863–7.
Gloucestershire Place-Names	A. H. Smith, *The Place-Names of Gloucestershire*, 4 vols., EPNS 38–41 (1964–5).
Godstow English Register	*The English Register of Godstow Nunnery*, ed. A. Clark, 3 vols., Early English Text Society, original ser. 129, 130, 142 (1905–11).
Golding, *Gilbert of Sempringham*	B. Golding, *Gilbert of Sempringham and the Gilbertine Order c.1130–c.1300*, Oxford 1995.
Gorham, *Hist. Eynesbury and St Neot's*	G. C. Gorham, *The History and Antiquities of Eynesbury and St Neot's* . . ., 2 vols., London 1824.
Green, J. A.	*The Government of England under Henry I*, Cambridge 1988.
Green, *English Sheriffs*	J. A. Green, *English Sheriffs to 1154*, PRO Handbooks 24, London 1990.
Guisborough Cartulary	*Cartularium Prioratus de Gyseburne*, ed. W. Brown, 2 vols., Surtees Society 86, 89 (1889, 1894).
Haines, R. M.	*The Administration of the Diocese of Worcester in the first half of the Fourteenth Century*, London 1965.
Harmer, L.	*The Parish of St Giles-in-Reading*, Reading 1946.
Harvey, P. D. A. and McGuiness, A.	*A Guide to British Medieval Seals*, London 1996.
Hatton's Book of Seals	*Sir Christopher Hatton's Book of Seals*, ed. L. C. Loyd and D. M. Stenton, Oxford 1950.
Haughmond Cartulary	*The Cartulary of Haughmond Abbey*, ed. U. Rees, Shropshire Archaeological Soc. and Univ. of Wales Press, Cardiff 1985.
Heads	*The Heads of Religious Houses, England and Wales, 940–1216*, ed. D. Knowles, C. N. L. Brooke and V. C. M. London, Cambridge 1972.
Heales, A.	*The Records of Merton Priory*, London 1898.
Henry, Archdeacon of Huntingdon	*Historia Anglorum*, ed. and transl. D. Greenway, OMT, Oxford 1996.
Heslop, T. A.	'English seals from the mid-ninth century to 1100', *Journal of the British Archaeological Association* 133 (1980), 1–16.
Heslop, T. A.	'Twelfth-century forgeries as evidence for earlier seals: the case of St Dunstan', in *St Dunstan, his Life,*

	Times and Cult, ed. N. Ramsay, M. Sparks and T. Tatton-Brown, Woodbridge 1992, 299–310.
Historians of the Church of York	*The Historians of the Church of York and its Archbishops*, ed. J. Raine, 3 vols., RS, 1879–94.
Hist. Northumberland	*A History of Northumberland*, issued under the direction of the Northumberland County History Committee, 15 vols., Newcastle-upon-Tyne 1893–1940.
HMCR	*Royal Commission on Historical Manuscripts, Reports*, HMSO, 1870–.
HMCR Rutland	*The Manuscripts of His Grace the Duke of Rutland, G.C.B., preserved at Belvoir Castle*, 4 vols., 1888–1905.
HMCR Wells	*Calender of the Manuscripts of the Dean and Chapter of Wells*, 2 vols., 1907–14.
Hodgson, J., and Hinde, J.	*A History of Northumberland*, 3 parts in 7 vols., Newcastle-upon-Tyne 1827–58.
Holy Trinity Aldgate Cartulary	*The Cartulary of Holy Trinity Aldgate*, ed. G. A. J. Hodgett, London Record Society 7 (1971).
Hope, W. H. St John	'The seals of archdeacons', *Proceedings of the Society of Antiquaries of London*, 2nd ser. 15 (1893–5), 26–35.
Howden	*Chronica Rogeri de Houedene*, ed. W. Stubbs, 4 vols., RS, 1868–71.
Innocent III's Letters	*The Letters of Pope Innocent III concerning England and Wales*, ed. C. R. and M. G. Cheney, Oxford 1967.
Jackson, S.	'Savaric, Bishop of Bath and Glastonbury', *Proc. Somerset Archaeological and Natural History Society* 12 (1865), 158–60.
Jeayes, *Derbyshire Charters*	*Descriptive Catalogue of the Derbyshire Charters in public and private libraries and muniment rooms*, compiled by I. H. Jeayes, London 1906.
Kemp, B. R.	'Archdeacons and parish churches in England in the twelfth century', in *Law and Government in Medieval England and Normandy: Essays in honour of Sir James Holt*, ed. G. Garnett and J. Hudson, Cambridge 1994, 341–64.
Kemp, B. R.	'Informing the archdeacon on ecclesiastical matters in twelfth-century England', in *Medieval Ecclesiastical Studies in honour of Dorothy M. Owen*, ed. M. J. Franklin and C. Harper-Bill, Woodbridge 1995, 131–49.
Kemp, B. R.	'Monastic possession of parish churches in England in the twelfth century', *Journal of Ecclesiastical History* 31 (1980), 133–60.
Kemp, B. R.	'Towards admission and institution: English episcopal formulae for the appointment of parochial incumbents in the twelfth century', *Anglo-Norman Studies* 16 (1994), 155–76.
Kennett, *Parochial Antiquities*	W. Kennett, *Parochial Antiquities attempted in the History of Ambrosden, Burcester, and other adjacent parts*

in the Counties of Oxford and Bucks., new edn, 2 vols., Oxford 1818.

Knowles and Hadcock D. Knowles and R. N. Hadcock, *Medieval Religious Houses, England and Wales*, 2nd edn, London 1971.

Lancashire Pipe Rolls and Charters *Lancashire Pipe Rolls 1130–1216 and early Lancashire Charters*, ed. W. Farrer, Liverpool 1902.

Landboc Winchelcumba *Landboc sive Registrum monasterii . . . de Winchelcumba . . .*, ed. D. Royce, 2 vols., Exeter 1892–3.

Landon, L. *The Itinerary of King Richard I*, PRS, new ser. 13 (1935).

Lanercost Cartulary, The ed. J. M. Todd, Surtees Society 203 (1997).

Later Letters of Peter of Blois, The ed. E. Revell, British Academy, Auctores Britannici Medii Aevi XIII, Oxford 1993.

Launceston Cartulary *The Cartulary of Launceston Priory*, ed. P. L. Hull, Devon and Cornwall Record Society, new ser. 30 (1987).

Leiston Cartulary and Butley Charters *Leiston Abbey Cartulary and Butley Priory Charters*, ed. R. Mortimer, Suffolk Records Society, Suffolk Charters 1 (1979).

Lewes Cartulary, iii *The Chartulary of Lewes Priory: the portions relating to counties other than Sussex*, ed. W. Budgen and L. F. Salzman, Sussex Record Society, Additional volume, 1943.

Liber Eliensis ed. E. O. Blake, Camden 3rd ser. 92 (1962).

Luffield Charters *Luffield Priory Charters*, ed. G. R. Elvey, 2 vols., Buckinghamshire Record Society 15, 18 (1968, 1975); Northamptonshire Record Society 22, 26 (1968, 1975).

Madox, *Formulare* *Formulare Anglicanum*, ed. T. Madox, London 1702.

Magnum Registrum Album *The Great Register of Lichfield Cathedral, known as Magnum Registrum Album*, ed. H. E. Savage, *SHC*, 3rd ser. 14 (1926).

Mason, E. 'The Mauduits and their Chamberlainship of the Exchequer', *BIHR* 49 (1976), 1–23.

Materials *Materials for the History of Archbishop Thomas Becket . . .*, ed. J. C. Robertson and J. B. Sheppard, 7 vols., RS, 1875–85.

Miller, E. *The Abbey and Bishopric of Ely*, Cambridge 1951.

Milne, J. G. 'Muniments of Holy Trinity Priory, Wallingford', *Oxoniensia* 5 (1940), 50–77.

Misc. D. M. Stenton *A Medieval Miscellany for Doris Mary Stenton*, ed. P. M. Barnes and C. F. Slade, PRS, new ser. 36 (1962).

Missenden Cartulary *The Cartulary of Missenden Abbey*, ed. J. G. Jenkins, 3 vols., Buckinghamshire Record Society 2, 10, 12 (1938–62).

Mon. Ang. W. Dugdale, *Monasticon Anglicanum*, rev. edn, J. Caley, H. Ellis and B. Bandinell, 6 vols. in 8, London 1817–30.

Moore, N. *The History of St Bartholomew's Hospital*, 2 vols., London 1918.

Morey, A., and Brooke, C. N. L. *Gilbert Foliot and his Letters*, Cambridge 1965.

Mowbray Charters *Charters of the Honour of Mowbray, 1107–1191*, ed. D. E. Greenway, British Academy, 1972.

Newington Longeville Charters ed. H. E. Salter, Oxfordshire Record Society 3 (1921).

Newnham Cartulary *The Cartulary of Newnham Priory*, ed. J. Godber, 1 vol. in 2, Bedfordshire Historical Record Society 43 (1963–4).

Nichols, *Leicestershire* J. Nichols, *The History and Antiquities of the County of Leicester*, 4 vols. in 9, London 1795–1815.

NMT Nelson's Medieval Texts (later Oxford Medieval Texts).

Noble, W. M. 'The cartulary of the priory of St Mary, Huntingdon', *Transactions of the Cambridgeshire and Huntingdonshire Archaeological Society* 4 (1915–30), 89–280 *passim*.

Northants Charters *Facsimiles of Early Charters from Northamptonshire Collections*, ed. F. M. Stenton, Northamptonshire Record Society 4 (1930).

Norwich Cathedral Charters *The Charters of Norwich Cathedral Priory*, ed. B. Dodwell, 2 vols., PRS, new ser. 40, 46 (1974, 1985).

'Notes from the Chartulary of the Abbey of St Bertin' *Archaeologia Cantiana* 4 (1861), 203–19 (no editor given).

Offler, H. S. 'The early archdeacons in the diocese of Durham', *Transactions of the Architectural and Archaeological Society of Durham and Northumberland* 7 (1962), 189–207.

Oliver, *Mon. Exon.* *Monasticon Dioecesis Exoniensis*, ed. G. Oliver, Exeter 1846; *Additional supplement*, London 1854.

OMT Oxford Medieval Texts.

Original Acta of Gloucester *The Original Acta of St Peter's Abbey, Gloucester c.1122 to 1263*, ed. R. B. Patterson, Bristol and Gloucestershire Archaeological Society, Gloucestershire Record Series 11 (1998).

Oseney Cartulary *Cartulary of Oseney Abbey*, ed. H. E. Salter, 6 vols., Oxford Historical Society 89–91, 97–8, 101 (1929–36).

Oxford Charters *Facsimiles of Early Charters in Oxford Muniment Rooms*, ed. H. E. Salter, Oxford 1929.

Oxon Place-Names M. Gelling and D. M. Stenton, *The Place-Names of Oxfordshire*, 2 parts, EPNS 23–4 (1953–4).

Owen, D. M. *Church and Society in Medieval Lincolnshire*, London 1971.

Petri Blesensis . . . Opera Omnia *Petri Blesensis Bathoniensis in Anglia Archidiaconi Opera Omnia*, in *PL* 207.

Pinchbeck Register, The ed. Lord F. Harvey, 2 vols., Brighton 1925.

PL	*Patrologiae Cursus Completus, Series Latina*, ed. J.-P. Migne, 221 vols., Paris 1844–64.
Pleas before the King	*Pleas before the King or his Justices, 1198–1202*, ed. D. M. Stenton, 3 vols., Selden Society 67–8, 83 (1953–67).
PRS	Pipe Roll Society.
PUE	*Papsturkunden in England*, ed. W. Holtzmann, 3 vols., Berlin 1930–36, Göttingen 1952.
Quarr Charters	*The Charters of Quarr Abbey*, ed. S. F. Hockey, Isle of Wight Records Series 3 (1991).
Ramsey Cartulary	*Cartularium monasterii de Rameseia*, ed. W. H. Hart and P. A. Lyons, 3 vols., RS, 1884–93.
Ramsey Chronicle	*Chronicon abbatiae Rameseiensis . . .*, ed. W. D. Macray, RS, 1886.
Reading Abbey Cartularies	ed. B. R. Kemp, 2 vols., Camden 4th ser., 31, 33 (1986–7).
Records of Templars	*Records of the Templars in England in the Twelfth Century*, ed. B. A. Lees, British Academy, 1935.
Red Bk Exch.	*The Red Book of the Exchequer*, ed. H. Hall, 3 vols., RS, 1896.
Redvers Charters	*Charters of the Redvers Family and the Earldom of Devon, 1090–1217*, ed. R. Bearman, Devon and Cornwall Record Society, new ser. 37 (1994).
Reg. Antiquissimum	*The Registrum Antiquissimum of the Cathedral Church of Lincoln*, ed. C. W. Foster and K. Major, 10 vols. and 2 vols. of facsimiles, Lincoln Record Society 27–9, 32, 34, 41–2, 46, 51, 62, 67–8 (1931–73).
Reg. Bronescombe	*The Register of Walter Bronescombe, Bishop of Exeter 1258–80*, ed. O. F. Robinson, in progress, 2 vols. published, CYS 82, 87 (1995, 1999).
Reg. Bronescombe and Quivil	*The Registers of Walter Bronescombe and Peter Quivil, bishops of Exeter, with some records of the episcopate of Bishop Thomas de Bytton . . .*, ed. F. C. Hingeston-Randolph, London and Exeter 1889.
Reg. Halton	*The Register of John de Halton, Bishop of Carlisle*, ed. W. N. Thompson and T. F. Tout, 2 vols., CYS 12–13 (1913).
Reg. Hamonis Hethe	*Registrum Hamonis Hethe, diocesis Roffensis*, ed. C. Johnson, 2 vols., CYS 48–49 (1948).
Reg. Holm Cultram	*The Register and Records of Holm Cultram*, ed. F. Grainger and W. G. Collingwood, Cumberland and Westmorland Antiquarian and Archaeological Society, Record Series 7 (1929).
Reg. Malmesburiense	*Registrum Malmesburiense*, ed. J. S. Brewer and C. T. Martin, 2 vols., RS, 1879–80.
Reg. S. Osm.	*Vetus registrum Sarisberiense alias dictum registrum S. Osmundi episcopi*, ed. W. H. R. Jones, 2 vols., RS, 1883–4.
Reg. Wetheral	*Register of the Priory of Wetheral*, ed. J. E. Prescott,

	Cumberland and Westmorland Antiquarian and Archaeological Society, Record Series 1 (1897).
Regesta, ii, iii	*Regesta Regum Anglo-Normannorum, 1066–1154*: ii, *1100–35*, ed. C. Johnson and H. A. Cronne, Oxford 1956; iii, *1135–54*, ed. H. A. Cronne and R. H. C. Davis, Oxford 1968.
Regesta Regum Scottorum, i	*Regesta Regum Scottorum 1153–1424*: i, *The Acts of Malcolm IV*, ed. G. W. S. Barrow, Edinburgh 1960.
'Register of Gloucester Churches'	'A Register of the Churches of the Monastery of St Peter's, Gloucester', ed. D. Walker, in *An Ecclesiastical Miscellany*, Bristol and Gloucestershire Archaeolgical Society, Records Section 9 (1976), 1–58.
Registrum Roffense	ed. J. Thorpe, London 1769.
Rievaulx Cartulary	*Cartularium abbathiae de Rievalle*, ed. J. C. Atkinson, Surtees Society 83 (1889).
Robinson, J. Armitage	'Early Somerset archdeacons', in idem, *Somerset Historical Essays*, London 1921, 73–99.
Rot. Chart.	*Rotuli Chartarum in Turri Londinensi asservati* (1199–1216), ed. T. D. Hardy, Record Commission, 1837.
Rot. de Dominabus	*Rotuli de Dominabus et Pueris et Puellis in XII Comitatibus, 31 Henry II, 1185*, ed. J. H. Round, PRS 35 (1913).
Rot. Hug. de Welles	*Rotuli Hugonis de Welles Episcopi Lincolniensis*, ed. W. P. W. Phillimore and F. N. Davis, 3 vols., CYS 1, 3, 4 (1907–9).
RS	Rolls Series.
St Bees Register	*The Register of the Priory of St Bees* [ed. J. Wilson], Surtees Society 126 (1915).
St Benet of Holme	*St Benet of Holme, 1020–1210*, ed. J. R. West, 2 vols., Norfolk Record Society 2–3 (1932).
St Denys Cartulary	*The Cartulary of the Priory of St Denys near Southampton*, ed. E. O. Blake, 2 vols., Southampton Records Series 24–5 (1981).
St Frideswide's Cartulary	*Cartulary of the Monastery of St Frideswide at Oxford*, ed. S. R. Wigram, 2 vols., Oxford Historical Society 28, 31 (1895–6).
St Mark's Cartulary	*Cartulary of St Mark's Hospital, Bristol*, ed. C. D. Ross, Bristol Record Society, 21 (1959).
St Thomas's Chartulary	*Chartulary of the Hospital of St Thomas the Martyr, Southwark*, ed. L. Drucker, Southwark 1932.
Salisbury Charters	*Charters and Documents illustrating the history of the cathedral, city and diocese of Salisbury in the twelfth and thirteenth centuries*, ed. W. (H.) R. Jones and W. D. Macray, RS, 1891.
Salter, *EHR* 34 (1919)	H. E. Salter, 'Geoffrey of Monmouth and Oxford', *EHR* 34 (1919), 382–5.
Salter, H. E.	*Medieval Oxford*, Oxford Historical Society 100 (1936).

Saltman, *Theobald*   A. Saltman, *Theobald, Archbishop of Canterbury*, London 1956.

Salzman, L. F.   'Some Sussex Domesday tenants, II: the Family of Dene', *Sussex Archaeological Collections* 58 (1916), 171–89.

Sanders, *English Baronies*   I. J. Sanders, *English Baronies: a study of their origin and descent, 1086–1327*, Oxford 1960.

Sawyer , *AS Charters*   *Anglo-Saxon Charters: An annotated list and bibliography*, ed. P. H. Sawyer, Royal Historical Society, Guides and Handbooks 8 (1968).

Sayers, J.   'Monastic archdeacons', in *Church and Government* (q.v.), 177–203.

Scammell, G. V.   *Hugh du Puiset, Bishop of Durham*, Cambridge 1956.

Scammell, J.   'The rural chapter in England from the eleventh to the fourteenth century', *EHR* 86 (1971), 1–21.

Selby Coucher Book   *The Coucher Book of Selby*, ed. J. T. Fowler, 2 vols., Yorkshire Archaeological Society, Record Series 10, 13 (1891–3).

Select Canterbury Cases   *Select Cases from the Ecclesiastical Courts of the Province of Canterbury c.1200–1301*, ed. N. Adams and C. Donahue, Selden Society 95 (1981).

SHC   *Staffordshire Historical Collections*, William Salt Archaeological Society, now Staffordshire Record Society; volumes cited: 3 (1882); 5 (1884); new ser. 13 (1923); 3rd ser. (1937).

'Shenstone Charters'   ed. H. E. Savage, *SHC*, new ser. 13 (1923), 257–77.

Shropshire Place-Names   M. Gelling and H. D. G. Foxall, *The Place-Names of Shropshire*, in progress, 2 parts published, EPNS 62–3, 70 (1990, 1995).

Smith, 'Officialis'   D. M. Smith, 'The "Officialis" of the bishop in twelfth- and thirteenth-century England: problems of terminology', in *Medieval Ecclesiastical Studies in Honour of Dorothy M. Owen*, ed. M. J. Franklin and C. Harper-Bill, Woodbridge 1995, 201–220.

Southwick Cartularies   *The Cartularies of Southwick Priory*, ed. K. A. Hanna, 2 vols., Hampshire Record Series 9–10 (1988–9).

Stenton, F. M.   'Acta Episcoporum', *Cambridge Historical Journal* 3 (1929–31), 1–14.

Stogursey Charters   ed. T. D. Tremlett and N. Blakiston, Somerset Record Society 61 (1949).

Stoke-by-Clare Cartulary   *Stoke-by-Clare Priory Cartulary*, ed. C. Harper-Bill and R. Mortimer, 3 vols., Suffolk Records Society, Suffolk Charters 4–6 (1982–4).

'Tavistock charters'   'Some early Tavistock charters', ed. H. P. R. Finberg, *EHR* 62 (1947), 352–77.

Taxatio   *Taxatio Ecclesiastica Angliae et Walliae auctoritate P. Nicholai IV*, ed. J. Caley, Record Commission, 1802.

Thame Cartulary, The ed. H. E. Salter, 2 vols., Oxfordshire Record Society 15–16 (1947–8).

Thompson, A. Hamilton 'Diocesan organization in the middle ages: archdeacons and rural deans', *Proceedings of the British Academy* 29 (1943), 153–94.

Thompson, A. Hamilton 'The registers of the archdeaconry of Richmond, 1361–1442', *YAJ* 25 (1920), 129–268.

Thompson, *Welbeck Abbey* A. Hamilton Thompson, *The Premonstratensian Abbey of Welbeck*, London 1938.

Thompson, *Women Religious* S. Thompson, *Women Religious: the Founding of English Nunneries after the Norman Conquest*, Oxford 1991.

van Caenegem, R. C. 'Public prosecution of crime in twelfth-century England', in *Church and Government* (q.v.), 41–76.

VCH *The Victoria History of the Counties of England*; counties cited: *Bedfordshire, Buckinghamshire, Dorset, Essex, Hampshire, Hertfordshire, Huntingdonshire, Lancashire, Leicestershire, Northamptonshire, Oxfordshire, Staffordshire, Surrey, Warwickshire, Wiltshire.*

Vodola, E. *Excommunication in the Middle Ages*, California University Press, Berkeley etc. 1986.

Walker, D. 'Some charters relating to St Peter's abbey, Gloucester', in *Misc. D. M. Stenton*, 247–68.

Walker, 'Earldom of Hereford charters' 'Charters of the earldom of Hereford, 1095–1201', in *Camden Miscellany XII*, Camden 4th ser. 1 (1964), 1–75.

Waltham Charters *The Early Charters of Waltham Abbey, 1062–1230*, ed. R. Ransford, Woodbridge 1989.

Wardon Cartulary *Cartulary of the Abbey of Old Wardon*, ed. G. H. Fowler, Bedfordshire Historical Record Society 13 (1930).

Warwickshire Place-Names J. E. B. Gover, A. Mawer and F. M. Stenton, with F. T. S. Houghton, *The Place-Names of Warwickshire*, EPNS 13 (1936).

Westminster Abbey Charters 1066–c.1214 ed. E. Mason, London Record Society 25 (1988).

Wethered, F. T. *Lands and Tythes of Hurley Priory, 1086–1535*, Reading 1909.

Whitby Cartulary *Cartularium abbathiae de Whiteby*, ed. J. C. Atkinson, 2 vols., Surtees Society 69, 72 (1879–81).

Worcester Cartulary *The Cartulary of Worcester Cathedral Priory*, ed. R. R. Darlington, PRS, new ser. 38 (1968).

Wrottesley, G., ed. 'Staffordshire chartulary', *SHC* 3 (1882), 178–231.

YAJ *Yorkshire Archaeological Journal.*

York Minster Fasti ed. C. T. Clay, 2 vols., Yorkshire Archaeological Society, Record Series 123–4 (1958–9).

Yorks E. Riding Place-Names A. H. Smith, *The Place-Names of the East Riding of Yorkshire and York*, EPNS 14 (1937).

Yorks N. Riding Place-Names A. H. Smith, *The Place-Names of the North Riding of Yorkshire*, EPNS 5 (1928).

OTHER ABBREVIATIONS

A-D	Archives départementales
Add.	Additional
App.	Appendix
archbp	archbishop
archdn	archdeacon
archdnry	archdeaconry
BL	British Library
Bodl.	Bodleian Library, Oxford
bp	bishop
cal.	calendar, calendared
Ch.	Charter
D. & C.	Dean and Chapter
dep.	dependent
fo(s).	folio(s)
Lib.	Library
m.	membrane
Mr	Master (*magister*)
ms(s)	manuscript(s)
om.	omitted
pd	printed
PRO	Public Record Office, London
R.O.	Record Office
s.	century
s. -ex.	late-century
s. -in.	early-century
s. -med.	mid-century
ser.	series
transl.	translated, translation

INTRODUCTION

This is believed to be the first attempt to bring together the surviving acta of English archdeacons in the twelfth century. It extends to archdeacons the interest that has been so profitably focused on episcopal acta since the late Sir Frank Stenton's call for their systematic publication over sixty years ago.[1] While making no claim to completeness, this collection nevertheless manages to assemble no fewer than 285 archidiaconal acta of the period, mainly full texts or nearly so, but in a minority of cases references to lost acta. In addition to those which certainly belong to the twelfth century, acts are included whose dating range straddles the turn of the century and which may possibly therefore date from no later than 1200; conversely, acts issued after 1200 by archdeacons whose tenure of office began before 1200 are excluded. Archdeacons' letters, as distinct from acta, including the voluminous correspondence of Peter of Blois, archdeacon of Bath and of London,[2] are omitted. Also generally omitted from the main sequence of acta are those of archdeacons acting with other ecclesiastics as papal judges-delegate. These very important indications of archidiaconal participation in ecclesiastical justice, along with an act of an archdeacon serving as a delegate of the archbishop of Canterbury, are given in calendar form in an appendix.[3] Finally, this edition includes twenty-one acta of English vice-archdeacons of the twelfth century.

Most English archdeaconries are represented in this collection, some more richly than others, and none more so than those of the enormous diocese of Lincoln, which, apart from considerations of size, suffered in the second half of the century periods of vacancy or virtual vacancy in the episcopal see which threw increased responsibilities on the archdeacons.[4] It is notable by contrast that six archdeaconries – Barnstaple, Bath, Wells, Shropshire (Hereford diocese), Chester and York – have yielded no surviving archidiaconal acta in any form. Of the remaining archdeaconries, four – Chichester, Lewes, Hereford and Nottingham – appear to have left acta only of a personal or private character not involving the exercise of archidiaconal authority as such; we therefore have no official archidiaconal acta from the diocese of Chichester, made up of the archdeaconries of Chichester and Lewes, nor, if we build in the omissions noted in the first list, from that of Hereford, comprising the archdeaconries of Hereford and Shropshire. We may note, too, that the single act surviving from the diocese

---

[1] F. M. Stenton, 'Acta Episcoporum', *Cambridge Historical Journal* 3 (1929–31), 1–14. The call is being answered by the British Academy's ongoing series of *English Episcopal Acta*.
[2] See *Petri Blesensis . . . Opera Omnia*; *Later Letters of Peter of Blois*.
[3] See below, App. I. Also omitted is an act of Jocelin, archdn of Lewes (Chichester), as an itinerant justice with two others in 1187 × 1188 (*EYC*, iii, no. 1682).
[4] See Kemp, 'Archdeacons and parish churches', 357–8; for episcopal vacancies at Lincoln and Geoffrey Plantagenet's period as unconsecrated bp-elect, see *Fasti Lincoln*, 2–3.

of Bath, for Taunton archdeaconry, leaves that diocese largely unrepresented, while acts from the two archdeaconries of Winchester diocese, Surrey and Winchester, begin to occur only very late in the twelfth century, none in fact dating unequivocally before 1200. Why there should be such a paucity of acta surviving for some archdeaconries is difficult to determine. To some extent absenteeism on the part of archdeacons may be the reason, but it is hardly likely to explain the lack of acta from an archdeaconry as a whole throughout the century.[5] It may perhaps be connected with whether or not there was a tradition of the local archdeacon issuing written documents to record his actions. It certainly cannot be assumed that lack of archidiaconal documentation means lack of activity. Many cases are known of an archdeacon's involvement in a transaction being recorded only in another person's charter. For example, although I have found no administrative or judicial act for Herbert Poore, archdeacon of Canterbury, and only one private act, we know that in 1176 he was present in the 'chapter of priests' of Ospringe, meeting in St Mary's church, Canterbury, and confirmed the settlement there reached between the abbey of Saint-Bertin and Henry de Insula over the parochial jurisdiction of Throwley church, the sort of business that might well have yielded an archidiaconal act, but which is here mentioned only in the abbot's charter.[6] We should also note that, within the territorial extent of an archdeaconry, the archdeacon's authority might be limited by the existence of episcopal peculiars, episcopal manors, exempt monasteries, notably where there were recognised monastic arch-deacons, and parish churches attached to cathedral prebends, as exemplified in this collection at Lyme Regis and Halstock (Dorset).[7]

DIPLOMATIC OF THE ACTA

The range of archdeaconries and the large number of individual archdeacons represented in this collection, many of them with only one or a handful of surviving acta to their name, render a detailed analysis of the diplomatic of the acta as a whole impossible, but a few general observations may usefully be made. Firstly, as to the name and style of the archdeacon, by far the commonest in all periods apart from the very earliest is the form 'N. archdeacon of Y.', to which the overwhelming majority of the acta printed here conform. The rare form 'N. archdeacon', without naming the archdeaconry, is found in the earliest

---

[5] See, for example, the archdns of Hereford diocese (Hereford and Shropshire), all of whom after the mid-12th century witnessed episcopal acts frequently enough, and none of whom are known to have been regularly absent from the diocese before Ralph Foliot, archdn of Hereford from *c.* 1180, entered royal service as a justice in 1186 (Brooke, 'Hereford cathedral dignitaries', 14–18; *EEA* VIII, index *sub nominibus*; *Pleas before the King,* iii, pp. cviii ff.).

[6] 'Notes from the chartulary of the abbey of St Bertin', *Archaeologia Cantiana* 4 (1861), 212–13. See also the same archdn's involvement in another case, of 1178 × 1188, similarly yielding no archidiaconal actum (*EEA* VIII, no. 173).

[7] Haines, *Administration of the Diocese of Worcester,* 13–15, 17, 24–5; J. Sayers, 'Monastic archdeacons', in *Church and Government,* 177–203; below, no. 238. The four major monastic archdnries in England were Bury St Edmunds, Glastonbury, St Albans and Westminster (Sayers, 177).

document in the collection, dating from *c.* 1115 × 1129,[8] a period when, even in dioceses containing more than one archdeacon, territorial designations for each were not yet normally in use.[9] It also occurs rather later in dioceses containing one archdeaconry only, although this was not standard practice in such dioceses, or where the archdeacon combined his archidiaconal office with another dignity in the cathedral, but again this circumstance did not necessarily result in the omission of the territorial name.[10] Rather strangely, and for no apparent reason, the simple form was employed at relatively late dates by two archdeacons in Salisbury diocese, Reginald fitzJocelin in Wiltshire archdeaconry in 1167 × 1173 (no. 240) and Azo in Salisbury archdeaconry in *c.* 1185 × 1193 (no. 239), and exceptionally late by Burchard du Puiset, archdeacon of Durham, in 1195 (no. 30). One must remember, too, that, although an archdeaconry may apparently be given a name, that name might still, at a very late date in the century, be that of the diocese rather than of the local archdeaconry concerned.[11] Thus, for example, 'Robert archdeacon of Bath' (no. 1) was in fact archdeacon of Taunton in that diocese, 'Jocelin archdeacon of Chichester' (no. 14) was archdeacon of Lewes, and 'John archdeacon of Durham' (no. 31) was archdeacon of Northumberland.[12] Sometimes the fact that the diocese is being named is made a little clearer by referring to the archdeacon as 'of the church (i.e., cathedral or diocese) of Y.' For instance, Roger of Calne and Steingrim, described as archdeacons 'of the church of Norwich', held the archdeaconry of Norfolk in succession,[13] while Ralph de Diceto, 'archdeacon of the church of London', and Ralph Baro, 'archdeacon of the church of York', were archdeacons respectively of Middlesex and Cleveland.[14] Among other variations in title the slightly affected form 'N. called (*dictus*) archdeacon of Y.', following apparently some monastic and episcopal precedents, occurs three times under different archdeacons in different archdeaconries.[15] Again, from as early as 1140 × 1148, but mostly later, the archidiaconal style is augmented in sixteen cases by the addition of *dei gratia*. It seems to have been favoured particularly in the diocese of Norwich, where it was employed by three archdeacons of Norwich between *c.* 1150 × 1161 and ?1186 × 1187, and by one archdeacon of Norfolk in 1146 × 1173.[16]

In some fifty of the acta the full name of the archdeacon is given. This is so, for instance, in all four acts of Peter de Ros, archdeacon of Carlisle (1189/90–1196/7),[17] and most other examples belong to the last quarter of the century.

[8] No. 221.

[9] For this point in general, see Brooke, 'The archdeacon and the Norman Conquest', 13–15.

[10] Compare, e.g., nos. 190 and 191.

[11] Brooke, 'The archdeacon and the Norman Conquest', 13. To illustrate the difficulties of identification that might arise, see Robinson, 'Early Somerset archdeacons', esp. 79 ff., corrected by *EEA* X, 219–20 (Bath and Wells diocese); Clay, 'Archdeacons', 269–87, 409–34 (York diocese).

[12] Durham diocese had two archdns by *c.* 1127, but they were not known by separate territorial titles until after 1174 (Offler, 'Early archdeacons in Durham', 204–6).

[13] Nos. 214–16.

[14] Nos. 208, 268.

[15] Nos. 57 (Nicholas, of Bedford), 135 (Baldric, of Leicester), 259 (Godfrey, of Worcester).

[16] Nos. 217–19, 214–15.

[17] Nos. 8–11.

The earliest cases, however, are an act of Hugh du Puiset, treasurer of York and archdeacon of the East Riding (*c.* 1143–53), followed by that of Ralph Baro, archdeacon of Cleveland, in ?1157 × 1158,[18] and some others may also be relatively early but cannot be precisely dated within a longish date-range. In a number of instances, however, the use of the full name is uncommon among a particular archdeacon's acta; thus Robert of Burnham, archdeacon of Buckingham, is so called in but three of his nineteen acts,[19] appearing in others simply as 'Robert archdeacon of Buckingham', while Nicholas de Sigillo, archdeacon of Huntingdon, similarly occurs as such in no more than six of his twenty-two acta.[20]

In a majority of the acta archdeacons refer to themselves in the plural, but in about eighty cases the singular is used and a dozen acta mix singular and plural. One of the problems here, as in other aspects of diplomatic, is that so many texts survive only as later copies, which may conceal minor alterations such as the substitution of a plural verb, adjective or pronoun for others that were originally singular. Nevertheless, the main trend, as one might have expected by comparison with developments in episcopal acta, was for the singular to be superseded over time by the plural, save that in some cases, where the business was of a private nature or where the archdeacon was addressing an ecclesiastic of senior or at least equivalent rank, the singular continued to be preferred. This collection contains several exceptions to this general pattern, however, revealing in particular that the use of the singular might survive in some straightforwardly administrative or legal acts to the end of the twelfth century and even beyond.[21]

Most acta have a general address, the overwhelmingly most common form of which is some form of 'to all sons of holy mother Church'. This appears in over 100 acta as *omnibus* (or *universis*) *sancte matris ecclesie filiis*, with or without an addition such as *tam presentibus quam futuris*, or *ad quos presens scriptum pervenerit*, or *literas has visuris et audituris*. In six of these cases the reference is to the 'catholic' rather than to 'holy mother' Church, and in a seventh case to 'holy and catholic Church'.[22] Thirteen acta are addressed to 'the faithful of holy (mother) Church', a form favoured by Walter, archdeacon of Oxford, and two (both from the same archdeacon, Godfrey of Worcester) to 'the sons and faithful of holy mother Church'.[23] There are in addition twenty-six addresses to 'the faithful of Christ', with one to 'the faithful of God'.[24] Some twenty-one have other kinds of general address, eight, for example, in the form *presentibus et futuris* or its equivalent, a characteristic of the acta of Nicholas, archdeacon of Bedford.[25] Twenty-five have a specific address to one or more named

---

[18] Nos. 272, 268.

[19] Nos. 78, 87, 88.

[20] Nos. 107, 114, 115, 117, 123, 126.

[21] E.g., nos. 1, 30, 81, 224, 252.

[22] Nos. 72, 83–5, 159–60 ('catholic'); 74 ('holy and catholic').

[23] See nos. 166–9 (Walter, of Oxford); 258, 260 (Godfrey, of Worcester).

[24] Addresses to 'the faithful of Christ' seem to have been particularly favoured in the dioceses of Norwich (nos. 219–20, 224), Rochester (nos. 225–6), and Salisbury (nos. 229–32, 238, 242, 244); for an address to 'the faithful of God', see no. 73.

[25] Nos. 48–9, 51, 53–4.

individuals,[26] and several have a limited address restricted to the clergy, or the clergy and faithful, of a diocese, archdeaconry or, in one case, a rural chapter.[27] Among these, the twelve addressed to the clergy (in one case *dilecti*) of his archdeaconry by Nicholas de Sigillo, archdeacon of Huntingdon, indicate this as a favoured formula in the diplomatic of his acta.[28]

Twenty-nine acta have an *arenga*, or pious statement at the beginning of the main text explaining the wider context and motives of the archdeacon's action, imitating in this respect contemporary developments in episcopal acta.[29] In twenty-four cases the *arenga* consists of an independent sentence (or sentences), but in five cases it forms the opening, subordinate clause of the first main dispositive sentence of the act. The earliest known is a semi-*arenga* of this sort in the act of David, archdeacon of Buckingham, recording the settlement before him in 1140 × 1148 of a dispute over two churches in his archdeaconry, which reads: *Quoniam ea que ad utilitatem ecclesie spectant diligenter providere et efficaciter implere, credita nobis dispensatione, debemus, ideo ego David . . .(etc.).*[30] Almost all the other *arenge*, however, belong certainly or probably to the second half of the century. Half a dozen of them harp on an aspect of the archdeacon's authority as the reason for his action, like *mutatis mutandis* a number of episcopal examples. Mr Robert of Burnham, archdeacon of Buckingham, has notably three of these, including the semi-*arenga*: *Quoniam ad nostrum spectat officium veritati testimonium perhibere, . . .*; and the *arenga*: *Quod in nostra presentia rationabiliter actum est, nos ratum habere et auctoritate nostra munire nostri postulat officii sollicitudo.*[31] Nicholas de Sigillo of Huntingdon provides another example, lengthy and elevated in tone: *Que a pia matre nostra sancta Romana ecclesia statuta sunt et ordinata tenemur ex iniuncto nobis officio quantum possumus attentius providere, ut illesa et inconcussa perpetuo permaneant, et ut dispensationes quas, gratia pietatis et intuitu sancte religionis, indulserit cum omni integritate sua firmiter observentur.*[32]

The main dispositive clauses of acta, making up the *narratio et dispositio*, covered too wide a range of business to be adequately summarised here. It is worth noting, however, that in the second half of the century (and especially in its last quarter) and in certain dioceses (especially Lincoln), archidiaconal confirmations of churches, institutions to benefices, and other acts concerning spiritualities, might be qualified by a saving clause reserving the rights of the cathedral church or of the bishop and the cathedral. In Lincoln diocese, for instance, the phrase *salva in omnibus Lincoln(iensis) ecclesie dignitate*, or the shorter *salva Linc(olniensis) ecclesie dignitate*, occurs in nine acta from the archdeaconries of Bedford, Huntingdon, Northampton, Oxford and Stow,[33] while the reservation of Lincoln episcopal as well as cathedral customs and dignities is specified

---

[26] E.g., nos. 5 (prior Herbert and the monks of St Martin, Richmond), 22 (Hubert archbp of Canterbury), 66 (three named abbots), etc.

[27] E.g., nos. 21 (clergy of Scarsdale chapter), 44 (parsons and vicars of Totnes archdnry), 139 (archdns of Lincoln diocese), and 236 (clergy of Bridport chapter).

[28] Nos. 107, 110–12, 114, 118–19, 121–3, 126–7. He addressed another act to 'all clergy of Huntingdonshire' (no. 113).

[29] Cheney, *English Bishops' Chanceries 1100–1250*, 71–3.

[30] No. 70.

[31] Nos. 84, 92.

[32] No. 117.

[33] Nos. 63–4, 107, 117, 127, 159–60, 185, 190.

in a further two acta (from Bedford and Lincoln archdeaconries).[34] The right (*ius*) of Lincoln cathedral is reserved in two acts from Northampton archdeaconry (in one of which the archdeacon of Berkshire was acting for the local archdeacon) and in a third from the archdeaconry of Oxford.[35] In other dioceses the right (*ius*) of the bishop and his officials is cited, this being coupled in Carlisle with that of the archdeacon,[36] while, in a powerful demonstration of the authority of the archdeacon of Richmond at a date before Innocent III's final ruling on its privileges in 1202, two acts of successive archdeacons, Godfrey de Lucy and William de Chemillé, contain the phrase *salvis in omnibus antiquis consuetudinibus archidiacono Richem(und') debitis*, and another of William de Chemillé's has *salvo iure archidiacono Richemund'*.[37]

In the great majority of cases the archdeacon does not state by what authority he is acting. Mostly, however, this must be assumed to be the authority of his office, as is in fact made specific on a few occasions. Thus, in ?1157 × 1158 Ralph Baro, archdeacon of Cleveland, forbade *pro nostro officio* the breaking of a tithe settlement; in 1177 × 1186 Robert of Burnham, archdeacon of Buckingham, confirmed a gift of tithes *auctoritate officii [?nostri]*; and in 1182 × 1183 Walter of Coutances, archdeacon of Oxford, confirmed the gift of a church *ex officio archidiaconatus nostri*.[38] More grandly, in 1175 × 1192 Savaric, archdeacon of Northampton, confirmed another gift of a church *auctoritate archidiaconatus qua fungimur*;[39] and in three other cases archdeacons stated that they were acting *auctoritate qua fungimur*, which looks like a shorthand version of Savaric's phrase.[40] It is striking, by contrast, that one archdeacon of Lincoln diocese, Robert of Burnham in Buckingham, in five appointments to benefices or confirmations of churches, cited 'the authority of the church of Lincoln', on two of these occasions coupling it with his own;[41] Laurence, archdeacon of Bedford, did the same in the appropriation of a church to a priory.[42] Use of this formula almost certainly indicated a vacancy in the episcopal see and implies devolution of episcopal authority in these circumstances to the cathedral. However, this sort of expression is not found outside Lincoln diocese, where, at least in some dioceses (Bath, Carlisle, Salisbury and Worcester), we know that other practices obtained which played down the cathedral's rights.[43] Lastly, in a

---

[34] Nos. 62, 143.

[35] Nos. 162, 228 (Northampton); 183 (Oxford).

[36] Nos. 8–10 (Carlisle); 211 (London diocese).

[37] Nos. 275, 279, 283. For Innocent III's ruling, see A. Hamilton Thompson, 'The registers of the archdeaconry of Richmond, 1361–1442', *YAJ* 25 (1920), 130–5; Kemp, 'Archdeacons and parish churches', 356.

[38] Respectively, nos. 268, 78, 183.

[39] No. 160.

[40] Nos. 189–90, 210. Against that, two archdns, in employing the phrase *quantum ad officium meum* (or *nostrum*) *pertinet* when confirming churches or tithes to monasteries, appear to express doubt as to the extent of their authority in this respect (nos. 172, 242; and cf. *EEA* 18, no. 169).

[41] Nos. 83, 86, 88, 90–1.

[42] No. 64.

[43] For Bath, see *Bruton and Montacute Cartularies*, 25, Bruton no. 105, recording that when the see was vacant (after bp Robert of Lewes' death in 1166) R(obert), archdn of Wells, 'had the episcopal place in the institution of churches' (the Latin, from BL, Egerton 3772,

small number of acta an archdeacon will cite a more specific authority, such as an instruction from the diocesan bishop.[44]

In common with contemporary episcopal acts, corroborative clauses do not become common in those of archdeacons before the third quarter of the century, although the absence of such a clause cannot be taken as evidence that a seal was not used. None of the eleven surviving full texts of acta issued by Nicholas, archdeacon of Bedford (1140s–*c.* 1181), for example, contains such a clause, although one of them refers to his 'letters' and seal.[45] The same is true of six acta of Baldric de Sigillo, archdeacon of Leicester (*c.* 1161–*c.* 1187), even though one surviving original evidently once had a seal and we know that his seal was affixed to a composition over tithes in 1177.[46] Other similar cases could be cited. The earliest known instances of corroborative clauses in archidiaconal acts are those of Henry, archdeacon of Huntingdon, dating *c.* 1135 × 1148; Hugh du Puiset, treasurer of York and archdeacon of the East Riding, of *c.* 1143 × 1153; and Robert Foliot, archdeacon of Oxford, in 1151 × 1152.[47] All of these refer to the archdeacon's seal, its affixing or attestation, and the same is true of the great majority of corroborative clauses, but occasionally the document alone is stated to be the instrument of corroboration, as, for example, in no. 101 (*presentis scripti testimonio communimus*).

The concluding clauses of an act (*eschatocol*) could consist of one or more elements, including a witness-list, valediction, or date. No fewer than 183 of these archidiaconal acts originally had witness-lists, which in nearly all cases brought the text to an end, but some of the acts which survive only as copies have truncated lists and as many as forty-one lack the names altogether, breaking off after *Hiis testibus* or *Testibus*. Alternatively the act might end with a valediction, usually *Valete*, which occurs twenty-eight times, sometimes in the augmented form *Valete in domino*, which is found five times, or yet more elaborately with the further addition of *semper* or *karissimi*. Other variants include *Bene valete*, *Vale* (when a single individual is addressed), or a whole sentence in the subjunctive mood, such as *Valeat universitas vestra semper in domino*.[48] In almost every case an actum will have either a witness-list or a valediction, not both, but very occasionally (four times in the present collection) the two elements appear together, in one case in an original innocent of any

fo. 48v, reads 'in ecclesiarum institutionibus vices episcopales gerebat'); for Carlisle, see *Whitby Cartulary*, i, no. 36 (at p. 42), where Bernard, bp of Carlisle (1204–14), refers to Robert, archdn of Carlisle, 'ad quem, tunc temporis vacante sede Karleolensi, ecclesiarum spectabat institutio'; for Salisbury, see *EEA* 18, no. 158, showing that bp Jocelin de Bohun (d. 1184) had committed institutions in the succeeding vacancy to the archdn of Berkshire (and probably to the other archdns); for Worcester, see Cheney, *Roger of Worcester*, 99–100, showing a division of authority between the archdn(s) and the prior of Worcester while bp Roger was away, although below, no. 264, shows that institutions in the diocese in 1184–6 *sede vacante* were committed on that occasion to the archdn(s) by Baldwin, archbp of Canterbury, formerly bp of Worcester.

[44] Nos. 232, and cf. no. 262.

[45] No. 47.

[46] BL, Lansdowne 415, fo. 23r: 'Hec compositio facta est assensu Baldrici tunc temporis archidiaconi Legrec' cuius etiam sigillo confirmata est.'

[47] Respectively, nos. 100, 272, 172.

[48] Nos. 250 (*Bene valete*); 106, 200, 261 (*Vale*); 209 (*Valeat . . .*); with the last, cf. no. 259.

suspicion of copyist's error.[49] Usually in these cases *Valete* rounds off the text, but in one early and archaic example (no. 274) a reference to witnesses follows the valediction. There is often no evident reason determining whether an act should conclude with a witness-list or with a valediction, and, while a certain tendency can be detected for the latter to be characteristic of acts addressed to one or more individuals or to a limited group, a significant proportion appear in acts of general address. Only four of the acta bear a dating clause, in every case in company with witness-lists, inserted before the witnesses in the three examples from the last quarter of the century, but after them in a relatively early original of 1150 × 1151.[50] Finally regarding the *eschatocol*, as many as twenty-nine texts lack it entirely, concluding after the final dispositive clause. It is tempting to surmise that, since twenty-five of these survive only as cartulary copies, the *eschatocol* may have been left out by copyists who no longer saw it as containing anything of relevance, but such a view, though possibly true in some cases, must be treated with extreme caution, for some of the copies date from not many decades later than the acts themselves, and four of the acta which lack an *eschatocol* exist as originals, all of which are to be dated after 1160 and one as late as 1189 × 1200.[51]

SEALS

Sixteen originals among the present collection have remains of seals, to which we may add a seventeenth act with its seal which is now known only from a photograph taken before its destruction in 1944.[52] Two of these are so fragment-ary that no details are accessible.[53] Against that, however, seals of three of the archdeacons represented here (Edmund of Coventry, Nicholas of London and Jeremy of Cleveland) survive on other documents,[54] while in addition the seals of Peter of Waltham, archdeacon of London, and Geoffrey, archdeacon of Suffolk, occur on their acts as judges-delegate, and a rough drawing exists of Hugh du Puiset's seal as treasurer of York and archdeacon of the East Riding.[55] Furthermore, casts exist of the seals of two of our archdeacons, Nicholas de Sigillo and Robert of Hardres, both archdeacons of Huntingdon,[56] and there are cartulary references to the seals of Savaric of Northampton and Amicius of Surrey.[57]

From this sigillographic evidence some general conclusions on twelfth-

---

[49] Nos. 126, 168 (original), 169, 274.

[50] Nos. 79, 103 (date after the witnesses), 216, 231. The date in no. 69 is not certainly part of the text, and that in no. 123 has clearly been mistakenly added to the text.

[51] Nos. 136, 188, 220, 225.

[52] No. 284.

[53] Nos. 103 (Henry, archdn of Huntingdon), 168 (Walter, archdn of Oxford).

[54] For these seals, see below, notes 66, 60, 61, respectively.

[55] For the seal of Peter of Waltham, archdn of London (App. I, no. 6), see Chelmsford, Essex R.O., D/DP T1/693; for that of Geoffrey, archdn of Suffolk (App. I, no. 15), see BL, Harley Ch. 43 I. 18; pd, *Leiston Cartulary and Butley Charters*, no. 130. For Hugh du Puiset's seal, see below, no. 272n.

[56] *BM Cat. Seals*, i, nos. 1824, 1825.

[57] See below, nos. 150–1, 248 (all from Salisbury cathedral's 'Register of St Osmund').

century archdeacons' seals may usefully be drawn.[58] Although most are broadly similar to one another in shape, size and iconography, there is on the whole more diversity within the group than among episcopal seals of the period. The overwhelming majority are, like those of bishops, pointed-oval or vesica-like in shape, though generally of rather smaller dimensions than their episcopal counterparts. Some, mostly among the earliest, are rather broader in relation to their length than tended to become standard in the later twelfth century. The only exceptions to the pointed-oval outline comprise the lozenge-shaped seal of Ivo of Cornwall, archdeacon of Derby, a rather beautiful if much damaged piece of the later twelfth century,[59] and two rounded-oval seals of Nicholas, archdeacon of London, on a document of *c.* 1182 × 1186, and of Herbert Poore, archdeacon of Canterbury, on a quitclaim of 1191 × 1194.[60] Both these last, however, seem to incorporate an antique gem, depicting in the first case a male untonsured head in profile, in the second a scene with figures in a landscape. Both are also smaller than most other archidiaconal seals. It may well be that they are counterseals (perhaps in the form of signets) used on occasions instead of the archdeacon's larger and more usual seal of dignity. A clue that this might be the case is provided by the two quite distinct seals that survive for Jeremy, archdeacon of Cleveland (*c.* 1170–89), their legends both unequivocally declaring themselves to be his seals.[61] One is a typical archidiaconal seal, pointed-oval in shape and bearing on the obverse a frontally standing ecclesiastical figure; the other, though also pointed-oval in form, is much smaller and utterly different in design, showing the profile of a male head similar to that on Nicholas of London's seal mentioned above. Neither of the documents concerned is in the name of archdeacon Jeremy, but both record settlements involving Byland abbey which he had helped to bring about. There is no obvious reason, however, why one seal rather than the other should have been used on either of them. No archidiaconal seal of the twelfth century that I have seen bears a counterseal, but the evidence adduced above strongly suggests that at least some archdeacons possessed additional seals which were on occasion preferred over their larger seals of dignity.

[58] We are able greatly to expand the account of such seals given by W. H. St John Hope in 1893 in what is still the best starting point for archidiaconal seals: 'The Seals of Archdeacons', *Proc. Soc. Ants.*, 2nd ser. 15 (1893–5), 26–35; see also P. D. A. Harvey and A. McGuiness, *A Guide to British Medieval Seals*, 73–5.

[59] No. 21. Other lozenge-shaped archdns' seals are known from Exeter diocese, whence Ivo presumably came: Walter fitzDrogo, archdn of Cornwall ?1177–1216, had one in the early 13th century, depicting, like Ivo's, a frontally seated figure (Exeter, D. & C. muniments, Medieval deeds, Exeter 284), and that of Henry of Melhuish, archdn of Exeter *c.* 1204–?1221, survives in two impressions on documents of Cowick priory (Exeter, Devon R.O., ED/M/28; W 1258 M/G 6/47), one fragmentary, the second fine and virtually complete, showing an angel rising in profile to the left and bearing in a napkin a soul, whose arms are raised in prayer.

[60] The seal of Nicholas of London survives on London, St Bartholomew's Hospital, Archives, HC 1/1444, pd with facsimile in N. Moore, *The History of St Bartholomew's Hospital*, i, 147n.; also pd with description of the seal, *Foliot Letters and Charters*, no. 416. For the seal of Herbert Poore, archdn of Canterbury, see below, no. 3.

[61] BL, Add. Ch. 70693; *HMCR Rutland*, iv, 75–6 (with a description of the seal), of which charter an 18th-century copy with a drawing of the seal is in BL, Add. ms 4937, fo. 6r–v.

As to the iconography of seals, by far the commonest device was an image of the archdeacon himself, in most cases (though not all) clothed in deacon's vestments and usually standing frontally, but in one early case seated frontally and in a late example seated in profile reading at a desk.[62] Frontally standing figures fall into three main categories: (a) those with both arms outstretched, perhaps in a gesture of prayer; (b) those with arms similarly outstretched and holding an object in one hand (commonly a book, sometimes a cross) or different objects in their two hands; and (c) those clasping a book with both hands to their chest.[63] Alongside these, however, were other seals whose designs departed radically from this theme. Two, possibly three, have religious imagery, depicting respectively the Virgin and Child with a diminutive suppliant (presumably the archdeacon), Noah's Ark with a dove descending upon it, and possibly a nimbused figure of unknown identity.[64] The seal of Richard of Ely, archdeacon of Colchester, on a settlement of 1200 may also have a religious meaning, bearing as it does a nimbused lion standing on a scroll, although the indistinct lettering on the scroll seems not to allude to St Mark, as the lion would suggest.[65] One further seal, that of Edmund, archdeacon of Coventry, resembles a secular seal in its imagery, for it depicts two birds of different types and sizes, the smaller standing upon the breast of the larger, whose head and neck are bent back.[66]

CONTENTS OF THE ACTA

The acta give us a very limited and incomplete picture of archidiaconal activity. We see none of the aspects of their authority which made archdeacons unpopular, nothing of the moral coercive power that came to exercise the concern even of Henry II in the Constitutions of Clarendon, nothing of the enforcement of canonical rules against clerical marriage and concubinage, and only the most incidental glimpses of archidiaconal visitations with their enquiries into the state of the clergy and church buildings and into the sins and failings of the laity in their archdeaconries.[67] The subject matter of the acta

---

[62] Nos. 267, 44.

[63] For examples of each category, see nos. 97, 31, 284. The seal of Geoffrey, archdn of Suffolk (see n. 55), is distinctive in that he is shown holding two objects, a book and a short staff, but his arms are set close to his body and not outstretched.

[64] Respectively, no. 255 (William of Northolt, archdn of Gloucester); *BM Cat. Seals*, i, no. 1824 (Nicholas de Sigillo, archdn of Huntingdon); no. 30 (Burchard du Puiset, archdn of Durham).

[65] *Newington Longeville Charters*, 45 n. 1.

[66] A substantial portion of the seal is attached to BL, Add. Ch. 48303, but a drawing of the complete seal, made in 1836 from a now lost original, formerly at Caen, makes the design and legend fully clear (PRO, PRO 31/8/140B, part 3, p. 434); see also *EEA* 16, no. 90.

[67] For accounts of archdns and the archidiaconal office, see Barlow, *English Church 1066–1154*, 134–7, 154–6; Brett, *English Church under Henry I*, 199–211; Cheney, *From Becket to Langton*, 145–6; A. Hamilton Thompson, 'Diocesan organization in the middle ages: archdeacons and rural deans', *Proceedings of the British Academy* 29 (1943), 153–94; R. C. van Caenegem, 'Public prosecution of crime in twelfth-century England', in *Church and Government*, esp. 66–70; and see also J. Scammell, 'The rural chapter in England from the eleventh to the fourteenth century', *EHR* 86 (1971), 1–21.

is overwhelmingly concerned with parish churches. Out of the 285 archidiaconal acta, the huge total of 211 are devoted to such business as the confirmation of gifts of churches to beneficiaries, the appointment of incumbents (individual or corporate), pensions payable from churches, privileges and obligations of churches, or settlements over their rights and status. When to this group are added a further thirty-three acts concerned with tithes, and three others relating to ecclesiastical privileges of monasteries or to Peter's Pence, we reach the staggering total of 247 acts dealing with spiritualities. Some twenty-six of the remaining acta have to do with lands or, in one case, with mills,[68] most of these being private acts of archdeacons, but even in two of the public acts in this group the land concerned belonged to a parish church and so could also be counted with the other 'spiritual' acts.[69] There is in addition a small clutch of about fourteen acts containing material of a very miscellaneous character.

It is evident that the primary purpose behind the acquisition and preservation of these acts was the provision of written title to support the claims and rights of those who held the churches, tithes and lands concerned, and, since the main repositories of the documents now surviving were monastic or other ecclesiastical treasuries and muniment rooms, it is hardly surprising that spiritual matters should predominate. It is most instructive to note, moreover, that it was considered desirable in so many cases to seek archidiaconal acts for this purpose in addition to, or often in place of, episcopal acts. Particularly striking is the increase in the second half of the century in the number of acts recording the appointment of incumbents to churches, either individual clerks or religious communities, in the latter case probably involving an appropriation process.[70] The formulae employed by archdeacons in these contexts were varied, far from standardised and sometimes confusing to modern readers familiar with later medieval forms. In general, developments in archidiaconal diplomatic mirrored, where appropriate, those in episcopal acts, which themselves underwent change in the course of the twelfth century.[71] In archidiaconal acts, however, the precise action being described is often less than entirely clear. For example, 'investiture' in no. 27 (?1172 × 1175) is clearly equivalent to 'induction', since the archdeacon, having been required by papal judges-delegate to induct (*introducere*) the canons of a priory into a church, describes his action as investiture, but in no. 149 (1175 × 1185) the word seems to mean (or at least to encompass) 'institution'. The issue is complicated by archdeacons' assumption of the power of instituting to benefices (or the equivalent), whether *sede vacante* or not, and by the fact that the act of 'institution' could in certain circumstances signify induction.[72]

Many of the straightforward confirmations of churches or appointments of incumbents, though valuable for the specific information they contain, hold comparatively little additional interest, but the acta recording disputes,

---

[68] For the mills, see no. 213.

[69] Nos. 19, 133.

[70] This phenomenon is also found in episcopal acta of the period; see, e.g., Kemp, 'Towards admission and institution', 157.

[71] For developments in episcopal acta, see Kemp, 'Towards admission and institution', esp. 157–70.

[72] Kemp, 'Archdeacons and parish churches', 355–64; for 'institution' meaning 'induction', see below, no. 289n.; *EEA* II, no. 234n.

agreements or settlements frequently reveal illuminating details, not only about the points at issue themselves, but also about the assemblies in which the transactions took place. It is among this category of documents that occasionally the veil is lifted on a fascinating sequence of events and proceedings of a kind usually lost to us because they were (understandably) omitted from the final settlement. Among the best examples is the letter written to the bishop of London in 1141 × 1150 by Richard de Belmeis II, archdeacon of Middlesex, concerning a dispute over the chapel of Bonhunt (Essex).[73] The story has been well told by the late Professor R. H. C. Davis,[74] but some aspects are worth highlighting again here. What is particularly fascinating about the letter is the information it preserves concerning two rural chapters presided over by archdeacons of Colchester of which we should otherwise know nothing, permitting us, as it were, to catch a fleeting glimpse of a whole corpus of similar activity that has for the most part vanished without trace. Richard de Belmeis records not only that he was present in the chapter at Saffron Walden presided over by Ailward, archdeacon of Colchester (an interesting enough fact in itself), but also that, in listening privately to witnesses in a case before the chapter, he learnt of an earlier judgement made in a chapter held in Wenden church before archdeacon Cyprian, who first occurs in 1115 and had been succeeded as archdeacon by *c.* 1136 × 1138 at the latest; the latter chapter could easily, then, have taken place well back in Henry I's reign.[75] Richard de Belmeis also explains that he agreed to listen to the witnesses at their request when the presiding archdeacon, Ailward, had refused to hear them in open court, and is now informing the bishop of what he has discovered. Difficult though it is to see how his actions could be legally justified, he presents a precious record of the determination of one party to the dispute, which felt driven to enlist his support against their opponent.

This sort of case illustrates in general the fact that archdeacons, or in their absence their deputies (as sub- or vice-archdeacons, later as officials) or even rural deans, were available to help in the settlement of ecclesiastical disputes that might otherwise have been in danger of remaining unresolved.[76] A structure of local and fundamentally delegated jurisdiction, based on the rural and archidiaconal chapters or synods, provided both the context and the means of resolving many of these disputes, and it was important that it was able to do so at this particular time. The twelfth century was a period of dynamic progress and development, of course, and yet the more elaborate structure of diocesan courts and officers of the later middle ages, especially the jurisdiction of the bishop's official, had barely begun to make its appearance by the end of the twelfth century.[77] The bishops of larger dioceses, even the most conscientious, would

---

[73] No. 207.

[74] R. H. C. Davis, 'The College of St Martin-le-Grand and the Anarchy, 1135–54', *London Topographical Record* 23 (1974), 17–18.

[75] For Ailward and Cyprian, see *Fasti St Paul's*, 18.

[76] This is not to say, of course, that they were always successful in resolving disputes; see, e.g., the difficulties encountered in settling a dispute over the parochial affiliation of Smithfield, London, between the 1120s and the 1160s, in which three successive archdns of London were involved (*Holy Trinity Aldgate Cartulary*, nos. 964–71).

[77] For the bp's official, see Cheney, *English Bishops' Chanceries*, 20–21; idem, *From Becket to Langton*, 147–8; Smith, 'Officialis', 201–20. For the effect on archidiaconal jurisdiction

clearly have found it impossible to handle all cases themselves, but even in comparatively small dioceses there were probably too many issues, including relatively minor ones, for the bishop to be able to deal with unaided. The age was a litigious one, and increasing definition was required in such matters as tithe-rights, parochial boundaries, and the like. It was clearly part of the archdeacon's office to provide an additional or alternative forum, and the present collection yields plenty of evidence of their acting as facilitators of agreements. They seem mainly to have been resorted to in this respect, however, not by the very grandest monasteries and individuals, but by religious houses of lesser pretensions, incumbents of parish churches, knights and gentry, and so on. Although such a distinction must not be pressed too far, it does appear that the greatest or wealthiest religious communities, like the abbeys of Bury St Edmunds or Reading, and the higher nobility had normally no need of the archdeacon. For the settlement of a dispute between a parish priest and a lesser monastery, on the other hand, his participation might well be more appropriate, especially if the knowledge of the local rural chapter could be made available. So, for example, in *c.* 1164 × 1189 the archdeacon of Huntingdon presided over and confirmed a settlement over Holy Trinity church, Huntingdon, between Roger, the incumbent, and St Neots priory; in 1198 × 1205 the archdeacon of Middlesex settled a dispute between Stoke-by-Clare priory and the parson of Harefield church over the demesne tithe of Harefield; and in 1151 × 1174 the archdeacon of Oxford recorded the settlement in his presence in the chapter at Stoke Lyne deanery of the conflict between the priories of St Frideswide's and Cogges over certain demesne tithes in Fritwell.[78]

Disputes over parish boundaries or over the parochial affiliation of chapelries might also usefully come before archdeacons and their chapters. An act by William I, archdeacon of Norwich, dating from *c.* 1150 × 1161, reveals that a parish boundary dispute between the churches of St Mary Magdalene and St Peter in Wiggenhall that had been basically settled by Everard, bishop of Norwich (d. 1145), and confirmed by Theobald, archbishop of Canterbury, needed further definition.[79] Other comparable cases concerned the chapelry of Acton Reynald (Salop), partly in dispute between Haughmond abbey and the parson of Stanton-upon-Hine-Heath, in ?*c.* 1160 × 1182; the chapelry of Akeley (Bucks), claimed as a dependency by the incumbent of Leckhampstead, but denied by the monks of Longueville, in 1151 × 1174; and a cemetery at St Sepulchre's priory, Warwick, within the parish of St Mary's collegiate church, this last case being settled by Gilbert Foliot, bishop of Hereford, and Godfrey, archdeacon of Worcester, as papal judges-delegate, probably in 1161 × 1162.[80] It seems, too, that archdeacons were particularly useful in resolving difficulties created for parish churches by the foundation or substantial endowment of Cistercian monasteries within their parishes. Cistercian exemption from paying tithes on their land, modified though it was from time to time, and though much prized by the monks,

---

of the rise of episcopal officials, see the appeal by Peter of Blois to Innocent III, in 1199 × 1200 or 1203 × 1206, to protect the archdn's office (*Later Letters of Peter of Blois*, no. 8).

[78] Nos. 116, 212, 174.

[79] No. 217.

[80] Nos. 23, 179, 260.

operated to the disadvantage of the secular clergy, who were thus deprived of what they considered their rightful spiritual income from lands in their parishes.[81] The usual solution to this problem, often worked out by, or with the authority of, the local archdeacon, was to maintain Cistercian exemption but to require instead an annual payment to the parish church. A fine and relatively early example is provided by the agreement confirmed in ?1157 × 1158 by Ralph Baro, archdeacon of Cleveland, that Rievaulx abbey would pay 12d annually to Scawton church (Yorks N.R.) in lieu of certain tithes.[82] The cartulary of the Cistercian abbey of Garendon (Leics) contains the texts of four agreements, made with the assent of Baldric de Sigillo, archdeacon of Leicester, providing for annual payments to be made to two parish churches for the tithes on the abbey's lands in their parishes; and in *c.* 1170 × 1181 Jeremy, archdeacon of Cleveland, witnessed and sealed an agreement that Byland abbey would pay 20s annually to Hawnby church (Yorks N.R.) for the tithe of Murton.[83] In a slightly different process Peter, archdeacon of Cornwall, who held the church of Colyton (Devon), reached a similar settlement with Quarr abbey regarding its land of Farwood within his parish.[84] An alternative arrangement, involving an exchange of land, resolved the dispute between the parson of Camerton church (Cumberland) and the Cistercians of Holm Cultram in *c.* 1176 × *c.* 1178.[85]

Only rarely do archidiaconal acts survive which confer no title to ecclesiastical or lay possessions, mainly because such acts served an essentially ephemeral purpose and there was usually no reason to preserve them. A small number are nevertheless found in this collection, but there can be no doubt that such documents were originally far more numerous. In one, dating from ?*c.* 1180 × 1193, Azo, archdeacon of Salisbury, notifies the master of the Templars in England that the wife of a knight who has chosen to become a Templar has promised to preserve her own chastity.[86] Although for much of this period, late 1184–1193, the see of Salisbury was either vacant or occupied by the mainly absent Hubert Walter, the archdeacon might in any case have been approached to issue such a testimony. Most remarkable of all, however, is the pair of archidiaconal acta of the 1190s drawn from a dossier of documents which was produced in the king's court in 1208 by a certain Jordan son of Avenell in the suit brought against him by Alice Clement.[87] Alice had been a nun of the small Benedictine priory of Ankerwyke (Bucks), from which she had absconded, most probably in order to press her claim to a share of her father's inheritance. Her case depended essentially on whether or not she had become a fully professed nun at Ankerwyke, since, if she had, she would have forfeited

[81] For Cistercian tithe exemption and reactions to it, see Constable, *Monastic Tithes,* esp. 241–2, 270–1; Burton, *Monastic Order in Yorkshire,* 264–5.

[82] No. 268.

[83] See below, no. 133n.; BL, Add. Ch. 70693, the latter confirmed by archbp Roger of York (*EEA 20,* no. 9).

[84] No. 36.

[85] No. 7 and n.

[86] No. 239.

[87] *CRR,* v, 171, 183–6. For the complicated history of this case, see Vodola, *Excommunication in the Middle Ages,* 102–110.

her ability to inherit land. By 1204, when her case first came into the royal court,[88] it had already been before various ecclesiastical authorities for nearly twenty years, including in the 1190s no less a figure than Hubert Walter, archbishop of Canterbury. It was his reaction that triggered our two acta: on receipt of his letters, the dean of Lincoln and the archdeacon of Leicester ordered the archdeacons of Lincoln diocese to denounce Alice as excommunicate;[89] and, in response to the archbishop's mandate to compel Alice to return to the cloister, the archdeacon of Derby and another wrote to inform him that, having failed in this, they had excommunicated Alice and her supporters, whereupon Alice had appealed to the archbishop's audience.[90] These two documents again allow us a brief glimpse of a type of archidiaconal activity which must presumably at this time have been common but which we usually do not see.

SYNODS AND CHAPTERS

The acta throw considerable light on the nomenclature and location of ecclesiastical assemblies within archdeaconries and rural deaneries, at least for some dioceses, although how systematic the terminology was in the English church as a whole is a matter of some uncertainty. It seems generally to have been the case in the large diocese of Lincoln that an assembly of the clergy of an archdeaconry, with some laity present as well, was usually termed a 'synod', although we cannot demonstrate this with certainty outside the diocese. The term 'synod' is found in the Lincoln archdeaconries of Bedford, Buckingham (held at Aylesbury), Huntingdon (at Huntingdon), Leicester (at Leicester), Northampton (in St Peter's, Northampton), and Oxford (at Oxford).[91] We also hear of a 'general' synod in the diocese and archdeaconry of Carlisle in *c.* 1176 × *c.* 1178, and references to 'chapter or synod' occur in an act of a former archdeacon of Ely in ?1151 × 1161 (where the synod is called a senate) and in an act of an archdeacon of Stafford in 1176 × 1191, but in these cases 'synod' may represent an episcopal assembly.[92] On one occasion the assembly of an archdeaconry is termed a 'provincial chapter',[93] reflecting the contemporary and potentially confusing use of the term 'province' for an archdeaconry, which is well-attested in the twelfth century and is used, for example, for the

---

[88] *CRR*, v, 79–80.

[89] No. 139.

[90] No. 22.

[91] See nos. 50, 52 (Bedford); 70, 88 (Buckingham); 100, 113, 125a–b (Huntingdon); 136; *Foliot Letters and Charters*, no. 126 (Leicester); 155 (Northampton); 181, 299; PRO, E164/20, fo. 143r; *Gir. Camb.*, i, 259, 263–4 (Oxford). The distinction, in this diocese, between the 'synod' of an archdnry and the 'chapter' of a rural deanery within it, is nicely brought out in an act of 1204, just after the turn of the century, in which Reimund, archdn of Leicester, records the testimony before him in the 'full synod held in St Martin's church at Leicester' concerning the earlier hearing of a case in the 'full chapter held at Melton [Mowbray]' (BL, Cott. ms Nero D iii, fo. 65v).

[92] Respectively, nos. 7n., 32, 28.

[93] No. 194.

archdeaconries of Lincoln and of Wiltshire in 1160 × 1166 and ?*c.* 1155 × 1165, respectively.[94]

More generally, the term 'chapter' was employed to describe an assembly held by an archdeacon for the clergy either of his archdeaconry as a whole or of a rural deanery within it. When such chapters were held under the presidency of a rural dean, they were normally meetings simply of the deanery concerned, but in the case of those presided over by the archdeacon the extent of the constituency of those present (archdeaconry or deanery) is not always clear. It may be that the addition of some such qualifying epithet as 'full', 'general' or 'universal' refers, at least sometimes, to the archdeaconry as a whole, especially perhaps outside the diocese of Lincoln; and clearly the 'chapter of the province' held by Adelelm, archdeacon of Dorset, in Longbridge Deverill church (Wilts) in ?*c.* 1155 × 1165 concerned the whole archdeaconry of Wiltshire.[95] Archdeacon Godfrey of Worcester's chapter held at an unstated place in 1144 × 1168 may similarly refer to his archdeaconry.[96] The word 'general', however, cannot be taken necessarily to indicate the archdeaconry rather than the deanery, as is evident in an act by a vice-archdeacon of Berkshire in 1174 × 1184 recording an institution carried out *in generali capitulo Abendunie apud Cingest(un')*, for this meeting, held at Kingston [Bagpuize], was clearly drawn from no more than the rural deanery of Abingdon.[97] Moreover, an unqualified reference to a 'chapter', especially where a distinctly local assembly is implied, probably often indicates a ruridecanal chapter, even when presided over by the archdeacon. Unqualified notices of chapters held by archdeacons occur relatively frequently, many of them giving the location of the meeting and clearly pointing to chapters of the relevant rural deaneries. In addition to 'the chapter of the deanery of Stoke [Lyne]', Oxford archdeaconry, in 1151 × 1174, about which there can be no doubt, they include the following: 'the chapter of Buckingham at Stowe', Buckingham archdeaconry, in ?1190 × ?1202, and 'the chapter of Buckingham at [Maids] Moreton' in ?1202; 'the chapter of priests' held in Melton [Mowbray] church, Leicester archdeaconry, in 1161 × *c.* 1187; and 'the chapter of Bere [Regis] at Puddletown', Dorset archdeaconry, in ?*c.* 1180 × 1184.[98] Despite the pitfalls involved in identification, however, the information

---

[94] Nos. 73, 235. This is closely related to the use of 'province' to mean 'county' (e.g., 'Hertfordensis provincia', used in *Gesta Abbatum*, i, 130, 162), for in several places (though not in Hertfordshire) the county was coterminous with the archdnry. I am indebted to Dr Julia Boorman for help on this point.

[95] No. 235.

[96] No. 258. It should be noted, however, that 'our chapter at Chesham' presided over by the archdn of Buckingham in 1189 (no. 79) was most probably the chapter of the deanery, since the Buckingham synod usually met in Aylesbury; and that *toto capitulo de Cliveland'*, witnessing with the archdn of Cleveland in *c.* 1170 × 1189, refers not to the archdnry of Cleveland but to the rural deanery of the same name (BL, Add. Ch. 70693; cf. *Taxatio*, 324).

[97] No. 303.

[98] Nos. 174, 94, 96n., 133, 237, respectively; and cf. 'the full chapter of the clergy of Cirencester', Gloucester archdnry (*Godstow English Register*, i, no. 149; the Latin text (PRO, E164/20, fo. 40v) reads *in pleno capitulo clericorum de Syrecest'*). On the other hand, the 'full chapter' held at Aylesbury (Wendover deanery) in 1177 × 1194 may have been

contained in these acta, particularly when combined with the numerous and as yet uncollated references to chapters in other twelfth-century charters, etc., will undoubtedly help to reveal more of the network and vitality of archidiaconal and ruridecanal activity in the localities.

ARCHDEACONS' HOUSEHOLDS AND STAFF

As befitted their station archdeacons needed to maintain households. It is easy to forget that archdeacons were, and many no doubt considered themselves to be, quite grand figures in the twelfth-century church. Despite their needing to be in no higher orders than those of deacon,[99] they were the most senior officers in the secular church after the archbishops and bishops, charged with a formidable array of administrative, inquisitorial and judicial powers. While some of them were certainly not active in their archdeaconries, plenty of evidence survives, of which the texts in this volume are but a part, to show that most of the others were deeply involved in the fabric of their local society and were familiar figures in the lay and ecclesiastical life of the local county or regional community. Moreover, some of them were high-born or were related to bishops,[100] and a surprising number of them were elevated to the episcopate in their turn.[101] Much of this was to change in succeeding centuries, with the increasing elaboration of diocesan administrative machinery and to some extent with the rising absenteeism of archdeacons, but that should not make us blind to the high profile they enjoyed in the twelfth century. Even after the number of mounted attendants for whom they could demand procurations on visitations was regulated by the papacy at the Third Lateran Council (1179), they were permitted to have as many as five or seven mounted followers.[102] There is usually insufficient evidence to throw any light on the composition of an archdeacon's staff and household, but occasionally enough acta survive for an individual archdeacon to enable us to glimpse the group of assistants and attendants who normally served and accompanied their master, even if the significance of some of them may need to be deduced from other documents.

The most spectacular case is Nicholas de Sigillo, archdeacon of Huntingdon

---

an assembly of the archdnry, since it dealt with a tithe dispute in Mursley, in the deanery of that name (no. 76; *Taxatio*, 33, 33b).

[99] *COD*, 190 (Lateran I, canon 6), 199 (Lateran II, canon 10), 212 (Lateran III, canon 3); Brooke, 'The archdeacon and the Norman Conquest', 3–4.

[100] Among the grandest was Savaric, archdn of Northampton, to whom the Emperor Henry VI referred as *consanguineus noster* and who was related to the imperial family through his mother, Estrangia (*Epp. Cant.*, 350; *Hatton's Book of Seals*, no. 434n.).

[101] Barlow, *English Church 1066–1154*, 221, 275: 'the archdeacon who got a bishopric was usually specially well connected'. The promotion of archdns to bprics can be demonstrated in many archdnries, especially in the second half of the century; see, e.g., Oxford archdnry in Lincoln diocese, where three archdns in succession, Robert Foliot, Walter of Coutances and John of Coutances, left for bprics between 1174 and 1196 (*Fasti Lincoln*, 35–6).

[102] *COD*, 213 (Lateran III, canon 4); to put these figures into context, the same canon prescribes up to 40 or 50 mounts for archbps, 20 or 25 for cardinals, 20 or 30 for bps, and 2 for [rural] deans.

(*c.* 1164–*c.* 1190), of whose twenty-two known acta no fewer than thirteen retain their witness lists in a more-or-less complete state. Nicholas de Sigillo's household appears from this evidence to have been predominantly clerical in nature, as one might expect for this archdeacon in particular, individual lay witnesses never occurring more than once in each case. Among his acta, no. 111, dating from 1166 × 1190, provides an excellent example of a group of household witnesses comprising, in first place, one of the archdeacon's chaplains, Benedict, followed by two of his *magistri*, Simon of Histon and Hamo of Winchester, then by Adam de Aumeri, who we know from no. 125 (a and b) was the archdeacon's nephew and held the church of Warboys (Hunts), and another presumably clerical witness, Ralph de Amblia, after whom come five named clerks and finally three possibly lay attendants, making a total of thirteen. If we study all this archdeacon's acts together, it is clear that his chaplains were, as usual elsewhere, among the most senior members of his household. We know of four of his chaplains: Benedict, already mentioned, who in addition to no. 111 witnesses a further six times; Humphrey, who witnesses on five occasions and always takes precedence when the two appear together (in nos. 118, 127, 128); Richard, who seems earlier to have had the lesser status of one of the archdeacon's clerks and who witnesses twice as chaplain; and Geoffrey, who seems similarly to have been promoted from the position of clerk to that of chaplain, in which capacity he occurs twice.[103] *Magistri* were important in any well established household and, though often not holding any particular office, would be available for specialised advice and counsel. There is enough evidence in this collection to suggest that most, if not all, archdeacons in the second half of the century would have had at least one, and that therefore archidiaconal households were another possible route for advancement for gifted clerks alongside episcopal, royal and other households. What became of many of them, however, is unknown, including the Mr Bernard who appears in three of the four witness-lists of Baldric de Sigillo's acta as archdeacon of Leicester.[104] Nicholas de Sigillo relied particularly on three: Mr Jordan, who witnessed four times and who, though perhaps not as regularly in attendance as some others, evidently served Nicholas throughout virtually the whole of his time as archdeacon, occurring both as early as *c.* 1164 × 1166 and as late as 1185 × *c.* 1190; less easy to date precisely were two other *magistri* who attended more assiduously, Mr Simon of Histon, a witness on eight occasions, and Mr Hamo of Winchester (or simply Mr Hamo), who occurs in this capacity nine times, a frequency greater than that of any other of Nicholas de Sigillo's known witnesses.[105] A fourth *magister*, Mr Hugh, appears once only, in *c.* 1164 × 1166, and may have been an early member of the household who soon moved away.[106] Then there were the archdeacon's clerks, of whom we know the names

---

[103] Richard and Geoffrey both witness nos. 114, 126.

[104] Nos. 131–3, and see BL, Cotton Ch.xi.10.

[105] Nos. 109, 125b, 127–8 (Jordan); 111–12, 114, 121, 123, 125–7 (Simon of Histon); 111–12, 114, 118, 123, 125–8 (Hamo of Winchester). Mr Hamo of Winchester, along with the chaplains Benedict, Richard and Geoffrey (see above), also witnessed a lay charter issued by Nicholas de Sigillo without archidiaconal title (*St Denys Cartulary*, i, no. 37b). Hamo became a canon of Lincoln (*Fasti Lincoln*, 126).

[106] No. 109.

of five, Geoffrey and Richard, who, as we have seen, were later promoted as chaplains, Laurence and William, who each appear twice, and Daniel, who makes a single appearance.[107] In addition, Adam de Aumeri, Nicholas's nephew (though never so described in witness-lists), witnesses four times;[108] two other apparently senior clerics in the household, Ralph de Amblia and William son of Richard, witness in high positions on four and three occasions respectively; and a variety of (rural) deans appear from time to time, some more frequently than others, including Ralph (three times) and Albrict (twice).[109]

Among other archdeacons whose acta have survived in some numbers, a useful case for comparison is that of Mr Robert of Burnham, archdeacon of Buckingham (*c.* 1177–*c.* 1194), for whom nineteen acts survive, thirteen with witness-lists, although one of the latter has been truncated by the copyist after the first witness. Here it is striking that, being himself a *magister*, he appears to have had fewer *magistri* regularly in his household than Nicholas de Sigillo, possibly because, unlike the latter, he was able in part to supply the expertise himself. Three *magistri* occur once only in each case, Osbert in 1177 × 1186, Richard of Aylesbury (later vice-archdeacon of Oxford) in 1186, and Eustace in 1190 × 1194,[110] but their service is entirely eclipsed by that of the archdeacon's brother, Mr Alard of Burnham (or Mr Alard), later archdeacon of London and dean of St Paul's, who witnessed eight times (once not designated Mr, in a late copy) and, assuming him to be the 'Mr Alard the official', on a further occasion in 1189.[111] Three chaplains occur, Walter and Thomas (once and twice respectively), and Richard, who occurs once, in the company of Thomas the chaplain, from whom he is particularly differentiated as *Ricardus capellanus archidiaconi*.[112] Clerks, so described, are much less in evidence, but two (rural) deans, John of Preston [Bissett] and Peter of Whitchurch, witness in high positions on five and four occasions respectively.[113] Among laymen Ralph of Weedon, who gave his demesne tithes of Chesham to St Albans abbey, witnessed twice, firstly an agreement concerning these tithes in 1189 and secondly the institution of a clerk to Amersham church (not many miles distant) in 1190 × 1194.[114]

It seems often to have been the case that, among a particular archdeacon's chaplains, one of them was regarded as his principal chaplain. Thus, to judge from the frequency of their attestations, Humphrey and Benedict among Nicholas de Sigillo's chaplains may have fulfilled this role at different times, while the description of 'Richard chaplain of the archdeacon' in Buckingham archdeaconry, just mentioned, suggests something comparable. The phenomenon is clear in other archdeaconries. For example, among the witnesses to an

---

[107] Nos. 111, 118, 127 (Geoffrey); 111–12, 118, 125 (Richard); 111, 126 (Laurence); 111, 125 (William); 111 (Daniel). In 1164 × 1166 the archdn granted the perpetual vicarage of Datchworth to Elias, his clerk, but it is not certain that Elias was his rather than the bp's clerk (no. 109 and n.).

[108] Nos. 111, 114, 118, 126. He is called the archdn's nephew in no. 125.

[109] Nos. 114, 123, 125 (Ralph); 114, 128 (Albrict).

[110] Respectively, nos. 78, 88, 81.

[111] Nos. 77, 79 (as official), 81, 83–6, 88–9.

[112] Nos. 89 (Walter); 81, 89 (Thomas); 81 (Richard).

[113] Nos. 74–5, 84–6 (John); 79, 84–5, 89 (Peter).

[114] Nos. 79, 81.

act of Hugh Barre, archdeacon of Leicester, in the 1150s is *Ricardus capellanus Hugonis archidiaconi,*[115] while the status of Richard the chaplain who witnessed two acta of Edmund, archdeacon of Coventry, in 1160 × 1176 is made clear in a layman's charter of gift to Combe abbey (Warks) addressed to the bishop of Coventry, the witness-list of which begins: *His testibus, scilicet magistro Edmundo archidiacono et Ricardo capellano eius . . .*[116] Similarly, Achard the chaplain, the first witness of an act of archdeacon Baldric de Sigillo of Leicester (no. 134) and occurring in three other of Baldric's acts as Achard or Achard the priest, witnessed with Baldric's son a non-archidiaconal document as *A. capellano archidiaconi Legrecestrie.*[117]

VICE-ARCHDEACONS

In the twelfth century the main deputy of the archdeacon was an officer whose title was normally vice-archdeacon, but in two dioceses might have the alternative form of sub-archdeacon.[118] Sub-archdeacons apparently occur very early, in ?1133 × 1136, in Exeter diocese, although the text which names them is possibly not genuine;[119] in 1177 × 1184 they occur in two archdeaconries of the same diocese, Cornwall and Exeter, in unquestionably genuine contexts.[120] At roughly the same time and also a little earlier two sub-archdeacons are found in the archdeaconry of Cleveland in York diocese.[121] Mostly such officers are called vice-archdeacons, however, the earliest reference so far found being to one Angot in York diocese in *c.* 1119 × *c.* 1138,[122] perhaps slightly earlier than the first (probably spurious) occurrence of sub-archdeacons; and indeed one each of the sub-archdeacons of Cornwall, of Exeter, and of Cleveland, respectively John, Ralph and Robert, used both titles on different occasions.[123] It is clearly safe and convenient to consider all users of either title together under the single title of vice-archdeacon.

Though widespread in the English church, the distribution of known vice-archdeacons is very uneven, both as between dioceses and in some cases within dioceses.[124] The dioceses of Carlisle, Durham, Ely, Norwich, Rochester and Winchester have yielded no references to vice-archdeacons, and elsewhere the occurrence is patchy. In Lincoln diocese I have found none for the arch-deaconries of Bedford and Buckingham, while a vice-archdeacon occurs in only one of the five archdeaconries of Coventry diocese (the archdeaconry of Coventry itself), and there is virtually none in London diocese apart from the

---

[115] No. 130.
[116] Nos. 17–18; Stratford-upon-Avon, Shakespeare Birthplace Trust R.O., DR 10/193; see also *EEA* 16, nos. 22, 90, and cf. 4.
[117] Nos. 131–3; *Danelaw Charters,* no. 320.
[118] Cheney, *English Bishops' Chanceries,* 143.
[119] *EEA* XII, no. 15.
[120] Ibid., nos. 95, 97.
[121] *EYC,* i, no. 577; ix, no. 131.
[122] *EYC,* ii, no. 1073; the date depends on the abbacy of Geoffrey, abbot of St Mary's, York (*EYC,* vi, 81, n. 6), for which see *Heads,* 84.
[123] See App. II, pp. 199–202.
[124] For a provisional list of known occurrences in England, see App. II.

single, difficult reference in Colchester archdeaconry to Robert, dean of [West] Bergholt, *qui . . . archidiaconi vices gerebat.*[125] On the other hand, in some archdeaconries which lack any reference to vice-archdeacons we find in the later twelfth century 'officials', either in the plural or as individual officials serving as witnesses or performing an ecclesiastical act of one sort or another. The individuals were evidently equivalent to vice-archdeacons elsewhere. For example, in 1188 'Geoffrey, bishop's chaplain and official of the archdeaconry of Ipswich (i.e., Suffolk)', witnessed an act by John of Oxford, bishop of Norwich, to Dodnash priory; in 1189 'Mr Alard official' witnessed a tithe settlement reached before the archdeacon of Buckingham; and in 1189 × 1197 Thomas de Thorp, official of Carlisle, witnessed three parochial institutions by the arch-deacon.[126] Before December 1181 the official of the archdeacon of Bedford passed on a mandate from his superior to the local rural dean to invest and induct a priory in a church;[127] and in *c.* 1186 × 1189 the archdeacon of London's official, acting for his master, inducted the new parson of a church.[128] In other places, where the title of vice-archdeacon was well-known, it was gradually superseded by the newer title of official in the later twelfth and early thirteenth centuries. This can be seen in the archdeaconries of Northampton from 1173 × 1182 and Leicester in the 1190s, for instance,[129] but the transition from the one title to the other is made particularly explicit in those cases where the same individual employs both terms to describe his office, including Richard of Aylesbury (*alias* Grim) and Adam of Chinnor in Oxford archdeaconry, Alexander in Stow archdeaconry, Vincent in Wiltshire archdeaconry, and Roger of Melsonby in Richmond archdeaconry.[130] I have found no evidence to counter, but on the contrary much to reinforce, Professor Cheney's rather tentative conclusion in 1950 that 'it is preferable to suppose . . . that his [the vice-archdeacon's] title was in process of changing, in the last quarter of the twelfth century, to the title [of official] which was becoming common in episcopal administration'.[131]

It seems likely that the title of vice-archdeacon was derived originally from the notion of a subordinate clerk or other representative exercising the *vices archidiaconi* on his behalf, a form which in fact is found occasionally until quite late in the century.[132] Caution is needed, however, in interpreting these cases as necessarily indicating a vice-archdeacon. For example, two

---

[125] *Colchester Cartulary*, ii, 540.

[126] *EEA* VI, no. 211; below, no. 79; below, nos. 8–10.

[127] No. 57n. A later official, Warin, in *c.* 1180 × 1189 carried out an induction on behalf of the archdn, and in 1186 × 1188 witnessed an episcopal act (no. 61; *EEA* IV, no. 72).

[128] No. 205.

[129] For vice-archdns, see App. II, p. 201, and for officials cf. nos. 155, 162; *Eynsham Cartulary*, i, no. 58 (Northampton); BL, Add. Ch. 47644 (Leicester).

[130] For Richard of Aylesbury, see below, nos. 296–9; PRO, E164/20, fo. 115r–v. For Adam of Chinnor, see Cheney, *English Bishops' Chanceries*, 144 and 145 n. 6; *EEA* III, no. 489; below, no. 186. For Alexander, see below, no. 300n. For Vincent, see *Reg. Malmesburiense*, i, 444; *Salisbury Charters*, 46. For Roger of Melsonby (*alias* of Richmond), see below, no. 306; *Beverley Fasti*, 59–60; *Fasti York*, 48, n. 122.

[131] Cheney, *English Bishops' Chanceries*, 146; and see the positive conclusion in Smith, 'Officialis', 208.

[132] See App. II, p. 203.

archdeacons themselves use a form of this expression when deputising for another archdeacon, clearly without becoming vice-archdeacons.[133] On the other hand, two vice-archdeacons, who unequivocally occur as such, describe themselves on other occasions as *vices gerens* or *vicem tenens* of their respective archdeacons.[134] The present edition includes only those acts of vice-archdeacons who use precisely that term to designate their office.

A great deal of work remains to be done on the vice-archdeacon. As the late Christopher Cheney remarked as long ago as 1950, 'the man's precise functions seem to be nowhere defined [and] no commission is known'.[135] His competence and responsibilities have to be deduced from the acts he has left behind or in which he is said to have played a part. The present collection runs to twenty-one items, including four originals, of which two retain their seals, one very fragmentary, the other circular in form and bearing an image of a frontally seated tonsured figure with a legend describing itself as a 'sigillum secretum'.[136] The largest number of acta surviving for one individual is the eight of Robert of Hardres, vice-archdeacon of Lincoln under the largely absent archdeacon, Peter.[137] Many of the other vice-archidiaconal acts were probably also produced during periods when their superiors were absent, and we know this for certain in the case of two acts of Richard of Aylesbury, vice-archdeacon of Oxford, issued by the authority of the archdeacon, John of Coutances, who was away in the schools,[138] and of two acts of Richard of Shrivenham, vice-archdeacon of Berkshire, acting for Geoffrey de Vernun, absent overseas.[139] The subject-matter of vice-archidiaconal acta is entirely concerned with churches and tithes, including the institution of individual or corporate incumbents[140] and on occasions involving the settlement before vice-archdeacons of conflicting claims to churches or tithes.[141] Although the witness-lists, even of Robert of Hardres' eight acta, provide very little evidence on vice-archdeacons' households, small though these probably were, or on their life-styles in general, there is the pure gem of an archidiaconal document (no. 37) which throws exceedingly rare and valuable light on the possessions of John, vice-archdeacon of Cornwall, and on his relationship with a great religious house of the diocese of Exeter.

ARRANGEMENT OF THE EDITION AND EDITORIAL METHOD

The acta are arranged by the dioceses of the medieval English church in alphabetical order and, within each diocese, by archdeaconries in alphabetical order (if more than one) and not by the order of precedence of archdeacons in the diocese. So, for example, whereas the order of precedence in Salisbury

[133] Nos. 73 (David of Buckingham acting for Robert of Lincoln, 1160 × 1166); 228 (Geoffrey of Berkshire for Savaric of Northampton, 1175 × 1185).
[134] Below, no. 302 (Richard, of Berkshire); App. II, p. 203 (William, of Richmond).
[135] Cheney, *English Bishops' Chanceries*, 145.
[136] The four originals are nos. 295, 300, 302–3; the seals are, respectively, nos. 302, 300.
[137] Nos. 286–93.
[138] Nos. 296–7.
[139] Nos. 302–3.
[140] Nos. 286, 289–93, 300, 303.
[141] Nos. 294–5, 304.

diocese was settled in the early thirteenth century as Dorset, Berkshire, Salisbury, Wiltshire, the archdeaconries are given here, for convenience's sake, in the order Berkshire, Dorset, Salisbury, Wiltshire.[142] The vice-archidiaconal acta, though far less numerous, are arranged according to the same principles. Under each archdeacon or vice-archdeacon the principle has been in general to arrange acta in roughly chronological order, except that, where more than one act by the same archdeacon relates to the same beneficiary, it has been thought desirable to group them together rather than to scatter them through a chronological sequence.

The acta have been edited in accordance with the principles established for the British Academy's *English Episcopal Acta* series. In the citing of manuscripts the siglum A indicates an original actum, the sigla B, C (etc.) indicating copies in approximate chronological order. The text printed in each case is that of the first manuscript cited, significant variant readings in other copies being given in the textual notes. With regard to spelling, 'i' and 'j' have been standardised as 'i', the consonantal 'u' and 'v' as 'v', and, except in originals, 'c' and 't' as 't' where appropriate (i.e., in such words as 'pertinentiis'). The normal medieval spelling of 'michi' has been adopted throughout in expansions of that word. Expansions of abbreviations are not in general indicated unless any doubt might exist as to the form of an expansion, in which case it appears in round brackets. In headings round brackets are used to identify names that are given in the text only as capitals. Square brackets generally indicate an addition supplied by the editor; in the acta themselves, they indicate also the supply of words lost by damage or omitted from the text being printed and available from another copy or copies. Punctuation and the use of capital letters in the edited texts, including all originals, is in accordance with modern practice.

Those acta about whose authenticity there is any degree of doubt are marked with a dagger (†). Lost acta, known only from other sources, are marked with an asterisk (*), the relevant part of the source in each case being printed. In descriptions of the sealing of original acta where the seal is affixed to a tag passing through a turn-up at the foot of the document, the expressions 'method 1' and 'method 2' are used, the former meaning that the tag is threaded through a single pair of slits cut in the turn-up, the latter through two sets of parallel slits. Each actum has been assigned a date. This appears without brackets in the case of the few documents which are themselves dated, but in square brackets where a date, or a date-range, has been supplied by the editor. All county designations are in accordance with boundaries as they were before the changes introduced in 1974.

---

[142] See *Fasti Salisbury*, 25–37; *EEA* 18, xxxi n. 8.

ARCHIDIACONAL ACTA

DIOCESE OF BATH AND WELLS

Archdeaconry of Taunton

Mr Robert of Guildford

1. *As archdeacon of Bath, notification that Nicholas of Merriott has, in his presence in the full chapter of Ilminster at Ashill, given to Bruton priory as much as pertained to him in the chapel of Lopen.* [?1186 × 12 Sept. 1204]

> B = BL, Egerton ms 3772 (Bruton cartulary), fo. 73r (p. 145), copy (1840) of transcript (1719) from fo. 69 of original 13th-century text.[1]
> Pd (calendar), *Bruton and Montacute Cartularies*, 39, Bruton no. 172.

Universis Cristi fidelibus &c, Robertus Bathon' archidiaconus, salutem. Ad universitatis vestre notitiam pervenire volo quod Nicholaus de Meriet in pleno capitulo de Ilmenistre apud Aishell congregato in presentia mea protestatus est se capellam de Lopene ecclesie beate Marie de Briueton' quantum ad eum pertinebat in perpetuam elemosinam cum omnibus pertinentiis suis dedisse &c. Testibus Ricardo vicearchidiacono de Spaxt'[a], W. decano de Ilmenistre &c.

> *a Ms* Spart; *for amended reading see note*

Robert's predecessor in the archdnry, Ralph of Lechlade, occurs in in the mid-1180s and perhaps in 1186, but had evidently ceased to be archdn before 29 Sept. 1188; Robert first occurs as archdn before late 1189 (but how long before is uncertain), and his own successor in the archdnry, William of Wrotham, was in office by 12 Sept. 1204 (*Fasti Bath and Wells*, 36–7). For Nicholas of Merriott's gift of the chapel, see *Bruton and Montacute Cartularies*, 39, no. 171. The first witness occurs in another charter of roughly similar date-range (*Stogursey Charters*, no. 51 (8)) and is to be identified with the Richard of Spaxton, [rural] dean, who occurs a number of times and witnessed with the archdn in 1195 (ibid., nos. 3, 25; *EEAX*, no. 169; *Buckland Cartulary*, no. 150); he was perhaps incumbent of Spaxton.

---

[1] Egerton 3772 comprises, from fo. 77, the surviving part of the original cartulary and, preceding it, a copy (1840) of George Harbin's extracts from that part of the cartulary that was subsequently lost.

DIOCESE OF CANTERBURY

ARCHDEACONRY OF CANTERBURY

Thomas Becket

2. *As king's chancellor and archdeacon of Canterbury, mandate and advice to the burgesses of Dover to pay their tithes to Dover priory as fully as is contained in the pope's privilege, the king's charter and their chirograph.* [Jan. 1155 × 3 June 1162]

> B = London, Lambeth Palace Library, ms 241 (Dover cartulary), fo. 35r–v (34r–v). s. xiv ex.
> Pd, Saltman, *Theobald*, 539, no. C. 1.

Thomas regis cancellarius et Cant' archidiaconus burgensibus Dovorr', salutem. Mando vobis et consulo ut priori et ecclesie Dovorrensi decimam vestram ita plenarie reddatis sicut in privilegio domini pape et in carta regis et in cirographo vestro continetur. Quod si facere nolueritis, iusticia regis meo adiutorio et fortasse [fo. 35v] non sine vestro dampno faciet fieri. Insuper et ego ecclesie et monachis in iusticia ecclesiastica deesse non potero. Valete.

After Thomas became royal chancellor, being already archdn, and before his consecration as archbp of Canterbury (F. Barlow, *Thomas Becket*, 42; *Fasti Monastic Cathedrals*, 4). The tithes in question were the burgesses' fish tithes or their commutation, as is made clear in their own grant to the priory (presumably the 'chirograph' here) and in Henry II's confirmation (Saltman, *Theobald*, 539–41, nos. C. 2–3). The grant was also confirmed by archbp Theobald and, later, by Thomas Becket as archbp (ibid., 313, no. 90; *EEA* II, 6, no. 9).

Herbert Poore

3. *Quitclaim to the abbot and convent of Westminster of all the land at Staines, called New Court, which his father occupied of their demesne against their will, and which he himself has held of them for ten shillings.* [13 Oct. 1191 × 29 Apr. 1194]

> A = Westminster Abbey Muniments, no. 16737. Endorsed: Quiet' Clam' Herberti Cant' archidiaconi de terra in Stanes que dicitur Nova Curia (s. xiii ex.); [?] ecclesie Wst' concess' (ss. xiii–xiv); iiii. (s. xiii). Size 191 × 101 + 18 mm. Seal in white wax on tag (method 2), rounded oval (28 × 23 mm); obverse, kneeling figure at left offering cup to seated figure at right, trees to left, right and in background (?antique gem); legend: + SVM CVSTOS . . . TEST . . . SIGILLI.
> B = Ibid., Muniment Book 1 (Liber Niger Quaternus), fos, 12v–13r. s. xv ex. C = London, College of Arms, Young ms 72 (Westminster register), fo. 14r. s. xv ex.
> Pd from A, B, C, *Westminster Abbey Charters*, 293, no. 457.

Herebertus*a* dei gratia Cant' archidiaconus omnibus ad quos presentes littere pervenerint, salutem in domino. Noverit universitas vestra me reddidisse et in perpetuum omnino clamavisse*b* abbati et conventui Westm' totam terram*c* quietam de Stanes, que dicitur Nova Curia, quam pater meus extraxit et occupavit de proprio dominio abbatis et monachorum Westm' contra voluntatem et assensum eorum, quam scilicet tenui de predicto abbate et conventu pro

decem solidis. Et *d*nunc, quia*d* amplius contra rationem et voluntatem predictorum monachorum terram prefatam et Novam Curiam tenere nolo, eis sicut
iustum est supradictam terram et curiam in pace et cum bona voluntate, etiam
voluntarie, pro liberatione anime patris mei reddo. His*e* testibus: Osberto filio
Hervei, Othone filio Willelmi, magistro Iohanne de Brideport, magistro Thoma
de Husburne,*f* Teobaldo*g* senescallo abbatis, Andrea de Scacario,*h* Albino
clerico, Rogero Enganet, et multis aliis.

a [H]enricus *B,C*	*b* clamasse *B,C*	*c Om. in B,C*	*d–d* quia nunc *B,C*
e Hiis *B,C*	*f* Husbourne *C*	*g* Theobaldo *C*	*h* Scaccario *B*

During the abbacy of William Postard, whose steward Theobald of Feering was (*Heads*, 7;
Westminster Abbey Charters, nos. 312–13), and before Herbert's election as bp of Salisbury
was confirmed and he received the temporalities (*Fasti Salisbury*, 3). Herbert's father was
most probably Richard of Ilchester, bp of Winchester, who died in Dec. 1188.

Henry de Castilion

4. *Gift in perpetual and free alms to St Mary's abbey, Valmont, of twenty shillings
annual rent in the land which he has of the escheat of Robert his brother in the forest of
Lillebonne, which land Robert de Stuteville gave to his said brother.*

[Nov. 1195 × ?1208]

A = Rouen, A-D Seine-Maritime, 19HP, carton 1. Endorsed: donacio Henrici de
Castelione (s. xiii); Lillebonne (? s. xix). Size: 161 × 76 + 27 mm. Seal and tag
missing (method 1).

Sciant omnes quod ego Henricus de Castellione archidiaconus Cantuariensis
pro salute anime mee et pro salute patris mei et matris mee et predecessorum et
successorum meorum dono deo et abbatie sancti Marie de Walem(on)t in
perpetuam et liberam elemosinam viginti solidatas annui redditus in terra quam
habeo de escaeta Roberti fratris mei in foresta Lindebonie, quam terram
dominus Robertus de Estotevill' donavit dicto Roberto fratri meo pro servicio
suo. Et ut hoc firmum permaneat, presenti carta mea et sigilli mei munimine
confirmo. Testibus: Iohanne Pelerin, Willelmo clericis meis, Ricardo de
Omvill', Alano anglico, Nicholao dignoc, Rogero carpent(ario), et aliis.

The dates of Henry's archidiaconate are uncertain; his predecessor was elected bp of
Durham in Nov., 1195 (though not consecrated until Apr. 1197), and Henry first occurs
as archdn 3 June 1196; the date of his death is unknown and, although his last certain
occurrence is Apr. 1206, he was probably still alive in June, and possibly as late as 1208 or
later (*Fasti Monastic Cathedrals*, 14). For the Lillebonne possessions of Robert de Stuteville
(or d'Estouteville), a member of the Norman branch of the family who died not later than
1185, see *EYC*, ix, 54.

DIOCESE OF CARLISLE

ARCHDEACONRY OF CARLISLE

Robert

5. *With W(alter), prior of Carlisle, notification to prior Herbert and the monks of St Martin's, Richmond, that Nisan son of Other testified in their presence before the general chapter that he gave to St Agatha's church, Richmond, tithes of land at* Thornedale *and of a quarry at Aske near* Ruchedic *before the death of Henry I and for fifteen and more years after his death; they should therefore permit the brethren of that church [i.e., the canons of Easby abbey] to possess them in peace.* [? late Dec. 1154 × 1158]

> B = BL, Egerton ms 2827 (Easby cartulary), fo. 289v. s. xiii ex.
> Pd, *EYC*, v, 72–3, no. 169.

G. dictus prior Karl' et Rodbertus Carliolensis archidiaconus Herberto priori sancti Martini de Richem' et fratribus ibidem deo servientibus, salutem. Significamus vestre dilectioni Nysanum filium Other in presentia nostra coram generali capitulo sub veri testimonio testatum esse se de terra de Thornedale et de subpetrario apud Asck' iuxta Ruchedic omnes decimas dedisse absque retentatione vel participio ecclesie sancte Agate de Richem' ante obitum regis Henrici senioris et post eius decessum xv. annis et eo amplius. Vestrum itaque intererit predicte ecclesie fratribus permittere ut in pace possideant quod notum est eos ratione mediante contingere.[a] Valete.

> *a* Ms contigere

This act dates from after the foundation of Easby abbey in 1151 (Colvin, *White Canons*, 57–8), despite C. T. Clay's suggestion that it dates from before the foundation on the grounds that, as he thought, 'brethren' referred to the pre–existing collegiate establishment in the church (*EYC*, v, nos. 169n.; this interpretation was supported by Colvin, 57, and has recently been reiterated by J. Burton, *Monastic Order in Yorkshire,* 89, but Burton had correctly rejected it in *EEA* V, no. 112n.; Premonstratensian canons were not infrequently referred to as 'brethren' in this period: see, e.g., Colvin, 337, 341–4). The date has usually been assumed to be not long after the period specified in the text (more than 15 years after Henry I's death), but, if the reference to King Henry I as *senior* can be accepted as an original part of the text and not a later insertion, it presumably cannot be before Henry II's coronation, 19 Dec. 1154, and might conceivably be a few years later. A date early in Henry II's reign would help to explain why the prior and archdn of Carlisle were acting in respect of a place within the archdnry of Richmond, since judicial proceedings were then in progress against the local archdn, Osbert of Bayeux, on suspicion of having murdered William Fitzherbert, archbp of York (died 8 June 1154), and Osbert was probably deposed in 1157, to be succeeded as archdn before the end of 1158 by (probably) Bartholomew (Saltman, *Theobald,* 122–5; *EEA* V, 127; Clay, 'Archdeacons', 409–10, 424; *Fasti York,* 47–8); it may also be relevant that the see of Carlisle was vacant after the death of Æthelwulf in May 1156 or May 1157 (*Fasti Monastic Cathedrals,* 19). The address, in this act, to the prior and brethren of St Martin's, Richmond, a dependency of St Mary's abbey, York (Knowles and Hadcock, 74), and the final clause of the act suggest that the priory had somehow acquired an interest in the tithes in question.

6. *Notification that, on a precept of Roger, archbishop of York, he has canonically seised the abbot and monks of Whitby of the church of Crosby Ravensworth, as the church was confirmed by the charters of the archbishop, Æthelwulf, late bishop of Carlisle, and Torphin son of Uthred, which were read in general chapter at Carlisle.*
[25 May 1156 × ?22 Nov. 1181; ? × 1164]

B = Whitby Literary and Philosophical Society, Whitby Museum (on loan from the Estate of the late Miss M. L. A. Strickland), Whitby cartulary, fos. 9v–10r. s. xiii med.   C = Levens Hall mss (in possession of Mr C. H. Bagot), Box A/18 (exemplification[1] of charters relating to Crosby Ravensworth church), no. 5. s. xiii ex.
Pd from B, *Whitby Cartulary*, i, 38–9, no. 33; (calendar) from C, *HMCR, 10th Report*, Appendix IV, 321.

Robertus dei gratia Karl' archidiaconus omnibus sancte matris ecclesie filiis, salutem. Sicut in uno corpore diversa membra diversa sibi vendicant officia, nec tamen aliqua diversitatem illam perturbat dissonantia, ita et in ecclesia discreta quidem sunt graduum et dignitatum ministeria, omnia tamen ad universitatis pacem conservandam distributa. Unde et ego qualiscumque Karl' archidiaconus, ministerium meum honorificare desiderans et religiosorum quieti et paci invigilans, denuntio me precepto domini Rogeri Ebor' archiepiscopi, iuste et canonice saisiasse abbatem de Wyteby et monachos ibidem deo servientes de ecclesia [fo. 10r] de Crosseby Ravenswart et omnibus pertinentiis eius, secundum quod carte domini Rogeri archiepiscopi Ebor' predicti et beate memorie Adelwoldi episcopi nostri atque Thorphini filii Uchetredi,[a] que in generali capitulo apud Karl' lecte sunt, concedunt atque confirmant. Hiis testibus: Waltero[b] priore Karl', Willelmo decano, Radulfo clerico de Burg,[c] Willelmo filio Utradi, Rogero Brudos, W. clerico, immo universis clericis qui in eodem capitulo nobis assederunt et affuerunt.

a *Preceded in B by* Uc *marked for deletion*   b Watero *C*   c Burg' *C*

After the probable earliest date for bp Aethelwulf of Carlisle's death (*Fasti Monastic Cathedrals*, 19), and before the probable date of archbp Roger de Pont l'Evêque of York's death (*Fasti York*, 4), but perhaps not long after the latter's confirmation of the gift in 1157 × 1164 (*EEA* 20, no. 107). The archbp's precept appears not to survive. Bp Aethelwulf's confirmation of the gift is *Whitby Cartulary*, i. no. 34. The present act is referred to in the confirmation of his father's gift by Alan son of Torphin (ibid., no. 30); also in an act by Bernard, bp of Carlisle (1204–1214), where the process is described as 'institution', and in another by bp Hugh (1219–1223), where it is said to have been 'induction' (ibid., nos. 36, 39).

[1] By the abbots of Rievaulx and Byland and the priors of Guisborough, Bridlington, Newburgh and Marton.

7. *Notification that, at Carlisle in his presence and that of his clerks and the canons of Carlisle and many other clergy and laity, Adam son of Cospatrick son of Orm, parson of the church of Camerton, quitclaimed to the monks of Holm [Cultram] the chapel of Flimby with appurtenances and all things belonging to the mother church of Camerton, viz., tithes and the chapel's appurtenant land in Flimby, in exchange for which he received other land in Seaton in his parish from his father, Cospatrick, who gave Flimby in perpetual alms to the monks.*
[c. 1176 × c. 1178]

B = Carlisle, Cumbria R.O., Carlisle D. & C. Muniments, Holm Cultram cartulary, fo. 20v (p. 36). s. xiii ex. C = BL, Harley ms 3911 (Holm Cultram cartulary), fo. 37v. ss. xiii ex.–xiv in. D = BL, Harley ms 3891 (Holm Cultram cartulary), fo. 51v. s. xiv med.
Pd (calendar) from B, *Reg. Holm Cultram*, 23, no. 53.

Omnibus sancte matris ecclesie *[a]*filiis tam presentibus quam futuris*[a]* Robertus archidiaconus de Karl(eol)o,*[b]* salutem. Sciat universitas vestra quod Adam clericus filius Cospatricii filii Ormi, persona ecclesie de Camertona,*[c]* concessit et clamavit quietam deo et sancte Marie et monachis de Holm' in perpetuum, apud Karl(eolu)m*[b]* in presentia mea et clericorum meorum et canonicorum sancte Marie*[d]* Karl(eol)i*[b]* et aliorum multorum litteratorum*[e]* et laicorum, capellam de Flemingby cum omnibus*[f]* pertinentiis et omnibus que de ipsa terra de Flemingbi pertinebant ad matrem ecclesiam de Camertona, decimas videlicet et terram quam habebat*[g]* ipse Adam in Flemingby ecclesie sue predicte adiacentem, pro qua terra aliam in excambium a patre suo Cospatricio recepit in Setona in eiusdem ecclesie sue parochia, quando prefatus*[h]* Cospatricius concessit et dedit predictis monachis in perpetuam elemosinam eandem Flemingby per divisas suas, sicut *[i]*ipsius carta*[i]* testatur.*[j]* Testes sunt Udardus decanus, et c'.

a–a et c' *B,C* b Karl' *C* c Camberton' *C* d *Insert* de *D*
e literatorum *C* f *Om. in* D g habet *C* h *Insert* pater eius *D*
i–i carta ipsius *C* j *C,D end with* et c'

The date is based on that suggested in *Reg. Holm Cultram* (*c.* 1174) on the ground that Cospatrick's gift of Flimby with land near Camerton church (ibid., no. 49) was made in the county court before Robert de Vallibus, king's justice, but the date is amended since the latter was an itinerant justice in Cumberland in 1178 and perhaps in 1176–7, but not in 1174 (*Pleas before the King*, iii, pp. lvii–lx; Howden, ii, 88); I am grateful for help on this point to Dr Julia Boorman. Adam's own charter, quitclaiming to Holm Cultram the chapel of Flimby and its appurtenances, reveals that the transaction was made, in general synod at Carlisle before William the official, in settlement of a dispute between Adam and the abbey over the tithes of Flimby, evidently those arising on the abbey's land there (BL, Harley 3891, fo. 51v; *Reg. Holm Cultram*, no. 53a); the settlement was clearly designed to preserve the Cistercian abbey's exemption from tithe-paying in accordance with the privileges of the Order and parallel to different arrangements, involving annual money payments, made for other houses in similar circumstances (Constable, *Monastic Tithes*, 296–9; Burton, *Monastic Order in Yorkshire*, 264–5; below, nos. 36, 133n., 268). In confirming Flimby chapel and the exchange of land to Holm Cultram in 1190, Pope Clement III referred to the archdn as having been at this time *diocesanus vacante episcopatu* (*Mon. Ang.*, v, 600; *Reg. Holm Cultram*, no. 268).

Peter de Ros

8. *As archdeacon of Carlisle and custodian of the bishopric, notification to all clergy and laity of the diocese that, in his presence, Robert son of Bueth of Bewcastle conveyed the advowson of [Nether] Denton church to the abbot and convent of St Mary's, York, and the monks of Wetheral, and seised the abbot of the right of patronage; the archdeacon has therefore canonically admitted and instituted in the vacant church William, clerk, presented anew by the abbot and by the monks of Wetheral.* [Feb. 1189 × Apr. 1197]

B = Carlisle, Cumbria R.O., Carlisle D. & C. Muniments, Wetheral cartulary, fos. 78v–79r (63v–64r), no. 130. s. xiv in. C = BL, Harley ms 1881 (transcript of same), fo. 66r (p. 127). s. xviii in.
Pd from C, *Reg. Wetheral*, 216–17, no. 120.

Petrus de Ros archidiaconus Karl' et custos episcopatus eiusdem universis clericis et laicis per episcopatum Karleoli constitutis litteras has visuris vel audituris, in domino salutem. Quoniam ea que coram nobis gesta sunt ad presentium et posterorum memoriam volumus pervenire, noverit universitas vestra Robertum filium Buet*[a]* de Buthcastre*[b]* [fo. 79r] in presentia mea et aliorum multorum fidedignorum advocationem ecclesie de Dentona abbati et conventui sancte Marie Ebor' et monachis de Wederh(al') carta sua contulisse*[c]* et confirmasse, et eundem abbatem de iure patronatus eiusdem ecclesie coram nobis saisisse. Unde ad huius rei evidentiorem firmitatem Willelmum clericum, per predictum abbatem et monachos de Wederh(al') de novo nobis presentatum, ad dictam ecclesiam de Dentona canonice admisimus et eundem in dicta ecclesia, tunc vacante, cum omnibus pertinentiis suis instituimus. Unde dictam collationem et institutionem presenti carta confirmavimus, salvo iure episcopali et archidiac(onali) et officialium nostrorum. Hiis testibus: Thoma de Thorp officiali Karl', Willelmo de Kirkebride decano Karleoli, Adam de Levigton',*[d]* Gilberto de Cambo, Ricardo de Haitona,*[e]* Alano de Raveneswic, Thoma fratre eius, Rogero sacerdote de Buthcastre,*[f]* et aliis multis.

a Buec *C*   *b* Buchcastre *C*   *c* concessisse *C*   *d* Levington *C*
e Mss Hartona *(cf. no. 9)*   *f* Buchecastre *C*

Peter first occurs, without title, 1 Feb. 1189; and as archdn of Carlisle 17 June 1190. He died 1196 × 1197, and his succesor in the archdnry was appointed before Apr. 1197 (*Fasti Monastic Cathedrals*, 23). Wetheral was dependent on St Mary's abbey, York (Knowles and Hadcock, 80). Robert son of Bueth's gift of [Nether] Denton church to the abbey is *Reg. Wetheral*, no. 121, but his father, Bueth Barn, had earlier given the church to Lanercost priory (probably in 1164 × 1174) and the gift had been confirmed by Robert (*Lanercost Cartulary*, nos. 45–6). The resulting dispute was settled before papal judges-delegate in 1199 × 1210 by giving Wetheral and Lanercost each a moiety in the church (ibid., no. A2; *Reg. Wetheral*, no. 119). By 1304 the bp of Carlisle had the advowson of the church, with a pension of 33s 4d to Lanercost (*Reg. Halton*, i, 226). The Wetheral cartulary was lost after 1812 and found in a private library at Castletown, Cumberland, in 1897, the year in which the 18th-century transcript in BL, Harley 1881 was published (Davis, *Medieval Cartularies*, no. 1025).

9. *As archdeacon of Carlisle and custodian of the bishopric, notification to all clergy and laity of the diocese that, at the presentation of Robert son of Bueth of Bewcastle, he has received William, clerk of Denton, in the church of [Nether] Denton, vacant, and canonically instituted him into the same.*   [Feb. 1189 × Apr. 1197]

B = Carlisle, Cumbria R.O., Carlisle D. & C. Muniments, Wetheral cartulary, fos. 79v–80r (64v–65r), no. 133. s. xiv in. C = BL, Harley ms 1881 (transcript of same), fo. 67r (p. 129). s. xviii in.
Pd from C, *Reg. Wetheral*, 219, no. 123.

Petrus de Ros archidiaconus Karl', custos episcopatus eiusdem, universis clericis et laicis per episcopatum Karl' constitutis litteras has visuris vel audituris, in domino salutem. Sciatis nos recepisse Willelmum clericum de Denton' in ecclesia de Denton', vacante, ad presentationem Roberti filii Buet^a de Buthe-castre,^{b} ad quem ius patronatus de iure spectare dinoscitur, et eum in ^{c}ipsa ecclesia^c cum omnibus pertinentiis suis canonice instituisse, et institutionem ipsius presenti carta nostra confirmasse, salvo iure episcopali et nostro et officialium nostrorum. Hiis testibus: Thoma de Thorp' officiali Karl', Willelmo decano Karl', Adam de Levigton',^{d} Gilberto de Camboc, Ricardo de Haiton', Alano de Ravenwic, Thoma fratre eius, Rand(ulfo) [fo. 80r] de Raveswic, Thoma diacono de Warthwic, et multis aliis.

a Buec *C*	*b* Buchcastre *C*	*c–c* ipsam ecclesiam *C*
d Levington *C*		

The witness-list indicates that this was issued on the same occasion as no. 8.

10. *As archdeacon of Carlisle and custodian of the bishopric, notification that, at the presentation of Gilbert Pipard, he has received and instituted Ralph, clerk, as parson in the church of Dearham.*   [Feb. 1189 × Apr. 1197]

> B = Bodl. ms Dodsworth 70 (transcripts of original charters), fo. 67v. s. xvii med.

Universis sancte matris ecclesie filiis literas has visuris et audituris Petrus de Ros archidiaconus Carl', custos episcopatus eiusdem, in domino salutem. Noverit universitas vestra nos, ad presentationem domini Gilberti Pipard, recepisse Radulfum clericum in ecclesia de Derham et ipsum in eadem ecclesia personam instituisse, et institutionem suam presenti carta nostra confirmasse, salvo in eadem ecclesia iure episcopali et nostro. Hiis testibus: Thoma de Thorp officiali nostro, Roberto de Helmesl' decano, Martino capellano, Willelmo capellano, Bartholomeo de Trineres,^{a} Waltero de Brigham, Roberto de Cave, Symone de Bildesdale, Sim'^{a} de Yrebi, et multis aliis.

> *a Reading uncertain*

Date as for no. 8.

11. *Notification that, when he was at York as a justice in 1 Richard I, a charter of Watton priory, concerning twelve bovates in Hutton [Cranswick] from William de Vesci, was torn by accident while in his hands when he was quelling a tumult; and testimony, with that of certain of his fellow justices, that [before the accident] the charter was entire in all respects.*   [1190, ? summer × 2 Sept.]

> B = Bodl. ms Dodsworth 7 (transcripts of charters formerly in St Mary's Tower, York, 1644), fo. 188v. s. xvii med.
> Pd, *EYC,* ii, 402–3, no. 1105.

Cunctis Cristi fidelibus Petrus de Ros archidiaconus de Karliel', salutem. Noverit universitas vestra, me apud Ebor' ad assisas primo anno coronationis regis R. iusticiario existente, infortunio quodam in manu mea cartam quandam domus de Wattun, videlicet de xii. bovatis^a in Hotun de Willelmo de Vesci, ex parte fractam fuisse, dum ad sedendum quandam contumeliam quorundam satellitum me in turba transferre.^{b} Ne igitur in posterum carta ipsa notari ex aliqua infidelitate valeat propter resarciamentum quod in eadem habetur, testimonium perhibeo presenti scripto et sigilli mei appositione me cartam predictam domus de Wattun integram^c ex omni parte invenisse, et testimonium huic perhibent mecum tunc coniusticiarii mei, quorum hic sigilla apponuntur, videlicet Simon de Kymba, et Hern' de Novill', et his testibus: Osberto de Longo Campo, Willelmo de Stutevill', Gaufrido Haget, magistro R. Harundel.

a Followed in ms by illegible deletion   *b Sic; ? for* transferrem   *c Ms* integrum

The first year of Richard I ran from 3 Sept. 1189 to 2 Sept. 1190, but the eyres of that year appear to have been sent out in the summer of 1190 (*Pleas before the King*, iii, page lxxviii; the present document is cited, ibid., page lxxxiii). For the identification of Hutton Cranswick, see *EYC*, ii, no. 1105n.

Aimeric

12. *Grant and confirmation to the prior and canons of Lanercost, at their request, that, on the deaths of the parsons and vicars holding the churches of Irthington, Brampton, Walton, Farlam, Lazonby and Grinsdale, they may serve the churches in their own persons or by their own chaplains, and convert* in proprios usus *the lands, tithes, obventions and proceeds of the churches, provided that they meet all episcopal, archidiaconal and other burdens; also confirmation to the canons of three marks annually in the church of Burgh-by-Sands, and of all lands and pastures conveyed to them by Robert de Vallibus or others.*   [1197 × ? 10 Jan. 1204]

B = Carlisle, Cumbria R.O., ms DZ/1 (Lanercost cartulary), fos. 55v–56r. s. xiii med.
Pd, *The Lanercost Cartulary*, ed. J. M. Todd, Surtees Soc. cciii (1997), 204–5, no. 173.

Omnibus sancte matris ecclesie filiis ad quos presens scriptum pervenerit Americus archidiaconus Karl', salutem in salutis auctore perpetuam. Religiosorum virorum petitionibus que iuri consonant favorem quantum in nobis est prebere tenemur et assensum. Quocirca, venerabilium virorum prioris et canonicorum sancte Marie Magdalene de Lanrecost' piis postulationibus permoti, divini amoris instinctu et religionis eorundem obtentu, eisdem concedimus et hac presenti carta nostra confirmamus ut, decedentibus personis et vicariis ecclesias de Yrthington', de Brampton', de Walton', de Farlam, de Leisingby, de Grenesdale in presentiarum tenentibus, liceat eisdem canonicis in predictis ecclesiis cum eas vacare contigerit in propriis personis vel per proprios capellanos, si maluerint, ministrare, et omnes earundem ecclesiarum terras, decimationes, obventiones et proventus in proprios usus convertere; ita tamen quod predicti canonici tam de synodalibus et episcopalibus quam de auxiliis et hospitiis nostris et successorum nostrorum et omnibus aliis oneribus ad predictas ecclesias spectantibus diocesano episcopo, nobis et successoribus nostris pro ipsis ecclesiis respondebunt. Preterea confirmamus eisdem canonicis tres marcas annuas in ecclesia de Burgo iuxta Karl' et omnes terras et pasturas quas Robertus de Vall(ibus) vel alii quicumque in illos con[fo. 56r]tulerunt. Et ut hec nostra concessio et nostre concessionis confirmatio illibate et inconcusse in perpetuum habeantur, eas presentis scripti patrocinio et sigilli nostri appositione coroboramus.*ᵃ* Hiis testibus: Iohanne priore Karl', magistro Gilberto officiali de Norhumb', magistro A. officiali Karl', Rogero capellano archidiaconi, et aliis.

a Sic

While Aimeric was archdn, and perhaps before royal assent was given to the translation to Carlisle of Bernard, the first bp for nearly fifty years (*Fasti Monastic Cathedrals*, 23,19), since the grant makes no reference to the similar confirmation made by bp Bernard (*Lanercost Cartulary*, no. 174), although both are witnessed by John, prior of Carlisle. However, the act may be later, since Aimeric continued as archdn until at least after 1208, and John's successor as prior of Carlisle was not elected until June × Aug. 1214 (*Fasti Monastic Cathedrals*, 23, 22). Robert de Vallibus had founded Lanercost priory in *c.* 1166 (Knowles and Hadcock, 162). For Burgh-by-Sands, see *Cumberland Place-Names*, i, 126.

DIOCESE OF CHICHESTER

ARCHDEACONRY OF CHICHESTER

Mr Seffrid II

13. *As archdeacon of Chichester and parson of Bloxham, gift in perpetual alms to Robert of Porchester, his chaplain, of the* cantaria *of Bloxham church, viz., the altar with all oblations and bequests belonging to it, and the tithe of flax with the lesser tithes of silver, with half* digesarum. [*c.* 1175 × 10 July 1176]

> B = PRO, E164/20 (Godstow cartulary), fo. 28v (15v). s. xv in. C = Bodl. ms Rawlinson B. 408 (Godstow cartulary, English calendar), fo. 26v.[1] s. xv ex.
> Pd from C, *Godstow English Register*, i, 226–7, no. 305.

Universis sancte matris ecclesie ad quos littere iste pervenerint Seffridus archidiaconus Cicestrie et persona ecclesie sancte Marie de Bloxham, salutem. Noverit universitas vestra me pro amore dei et beate virginis Marie dedisse cant(ar)iam de ecclesia beate Marie de Bloxham in perpetuam elemosinam Roberto capellano meo de Porecestria, scilicet altar'[a] cum omnibus oblationibus suis et divisis ad altare pertinentibus et decimam lini cum decimis minutis argenti cum medietate digesarum. Et ut hec presens carta firma et rata habeatur,[b] sigilli mei impressione[c] confirmavi. Testibus hiis: magistro Waltero archidiacono Oxonefordie, et Galfrido et Nicholao et Rogero capellanis domini regis, et Willelmo capellano meo, et Godwino[d] decano, et Symone et Waltero et Radulfo hominibus meis.

> *a Possibly to be expanded* altaragium   *b Ms* habeat   *c Ms* impresione
> *d Ms* Gowino

After Walter of Coutances became archdn of Oxford and before Nicholas, king's chaplain, became archdn of Coventry (below, no. 182n.; *EEA* 16, 113–14); Seffrid II became dean of Chichester by probably Dec. 1178 (*Fasti Chichester*, 21). The word *cantaria* is very difficult to translate in this context, but it clearly means the spiritual revenues assigned to the service of the church. The meaning of *digesarum* is unclear, and the word is left untranslated in the English calendar. Bloxham church was granted to Godstow abbey in 1182 × 1183 (below, no. 183).

[1] The calendared text lacks witnesses.

ARCHDEACONRY OF LEWES

Mr Jocelin

14. *As archdeacon of Chichester, gift in pure and perpetual alms to Chichester cathedral, for the soul of his uncle, Bishop Hilary, of specified lands within and outside the town of Chichester; and, with the chapter's consent, grant of these lands to John Precaz and his heirs, to be held of the cathedral for specified annual services on the anniversary of Bishop Hilary, as set out in the chapter's charter.*

[*c.* 1177 × 16 Nov. 1180]

B = Chichester, West Sussex R.O., Ep. VI/1/6 (Chichester cathedral cartulary, Liber Y), fo. 142r (85r). s. xiii med.
Pd (translation), *Chichester Cartulary*, 100–1, no. 385.

Omnibus sancte matris ecclesie filiis magister Ioscelinus archidiaconus Cyc(estrensis), salutem in domino. Sciatis me pro anima domini avunculi mei felicis memorie Hilarii episcopi in puram et perpetuam elemosinam donasse ecclesie Cyc' in urbe Cyc' terram que fuit Nicholai Avenel, et terram que fuit Turstani prepositi cum edificiis et iiii.^{or} acris ad terram illam pertinentibus, et quintam acram que fuit Leticie emptam de filia sua Anneis, et terram cum edificiis que sunt inter terram Iordani Trentemars et terram que fuit Salomonis iudei. Has autem terras assensu capituli concessi Iohanni Precaz pro servitio suo et heredibus suis tenendas de ecclesia in feudo et hereditate pro servitiis expressis in carta capituli annuis, scilicet pro terra Nicholai Avenel duos cereos duarum librarum cere in anniversario predicti episcopi Hilarii, et pro aliis terris in urbe et extra in eodem anniversario panem trium quarteriorum frumenti et unius quarterii ordei distribuendorum pauperibus per manum Iohannis vel heredis sui et per visum distributoris panis ecclesie. Easdem terras tenebunt Iohannes et heredes sui per hec servitia libere et quiete, salvis servitiis dominorum predictarum terrarum. Teste et auctore capitulo Cyc'.

These arrangements were confirmed by dean Seffrid II and the chapter of Chichester (*Chichester Cartulary*, 101, no. 386), whose charter was clearly issued at approximately the same time as the archdn's. The date is determined by the facts that Seffrid II first occurs as dean probably in Dec. 1178, his predecessor occurring as late as *c.* 1177, and that Seffrid himself was consecrated bp of Chichester 16 Nov. 1180 (*Fasti Chichester*, 8, 3). Jocelin had become archdn of Lewes by 6 Oct. 1174 and was certainly dead by Sept. 1203 (ibid., 24). Bp Hilary died *c.* 13 July 1169 (ibid., 3). (For an act by Jocelin as an itinerant justice, see *EYC*, iii, no. 1682.)

DIOCESE OF COVENTRY AND LICHFIELD

ARCHDEACONRY OF COVENTRY

Richard Peche

* 15. *Confirmation to [Monks] Kirby priory of its lands, tithes and obventions, and all its liberties and free customs which it had in the time of King Henry [I].*
[? *c.* 1136 × 1160; prob. × 19 Dec. 1154]

> Mentioned only, in the confirmation of this act (and another by Walter Durdent, bishop of Coventry) by Archbishop Richard of Canterbury in ?Aug. 1174 × Sept. 1175: (1) original: PRO, E210/119 (Ancient Deed D 119); pd, *EEA* II, 140, no. 168; *EEA* 14, 67, no. 68A; (2) partial inspeximus of same by Archbishop Baldwin in 1186 × 1187: PRO, E327/94 (Ancient Deed Madox 94); pd, *EEA* II, 250, no. 296; Madox, *Formulare*, 51, no. 94.

. . . nos [*sc.* the archbishop] presentis carte patrocinio confirmasse ecclesie de Kirkebi omnia tenementa sua in terris, decimis et omnimodis obventionibus ad eam pertinentibus, cum omnibus libertatibus et liberis consuetudinibus quibus tempore Henrici regis melius et liberius tenuit, sicut bone memorie Walterus Coventr' episcopus et dilectus filius noster Ricardus Coventr' archidiaconus ea cartis suis rationabiliter confirmaverunt . . .

After the death of Henry I (1 Dec. 1135) and before the archdn was consecrated bp of Coventry (*EEA* 16, 109), but probably before the coronation of Henry II.

Mr Edmund[1]

16. *Notification that, at the presentation of A(nsketil), prior of St Oswald's [Nostell], and the consent of the convent, he has given and granted the church of Leamington [Hastings] in perpetual alms to Nigel, his clerk, and canonically invested him with the same.*
[1160 × 10 July 1176]

> B = BL, Cotton ms Vespasian E xix (Nostell cartulary), fo. 114v. s. xiii ex.

Edmundus Coventrensis archidiaconus omnibus filiis sancte matris ecclesie, salutem. Noscant tam posteri quam presentes quod nos, presentatione A. prioris de Sancto Oswaldo et concessione conventus eiusdem loci, dedimus et concessimus ecclesiam de Lemingtona cum omnibus pertinentiis suis et libertatibus Nigello clerico nostro in perpetuam elemosinam, et eum inde canonice investivimus. Et ut donatio ista in perpetuum valitura insolubili gaudeat firmitate, eam presentis carte et sigilli nostri attestatione corroboravimus. Hiis, et c'.

Edmund presumably succeeded Richard Peche as archdn when the latter became bp of Coventry; his own successor, Nicholas, was in office by 10 July 1176 (*EEA* 16, 113–14, and references there cited); Ansketil, prior of Nostell, occurs from 1158 × 1159 and died in 1196 (*Heads*, 179). For the prior of Nostell's pension in Leamington [Hastings] church, see also *EEA* 17, no. 120.

¹ For Edmund's title of *magister*, see above, p. lii, and BL, Additional Charters 48137 and 48165.

17. *Notification and confirmation of the grant in perpetual alms made, at his request, by Prior Laurence and the convent of Coventry to the hospital of St John Baptist, Coventry, of the land on which it is sited.* [1160 × 10 July 1176]

> B = Bodl. ms Dugdale 13 (extracts, 1653, from now destroyed Coventry cartulary), p. 117.
> Pd, *Mon. Ang.*, vi (2), 659, no. 2.

Omnibus etc. sancte matris ecclesie filiis Edmundus Coventr' archidiaconus, salutem in domino. Sciant tam presentes quam futuri quod Laurentius prior Coventrie et eiusdem loci conventus concesserunt, ad petitionem nostram, deo et sancto Iohanni in perpetuam elemosinam terram in qua domus hospitalis Coventr' sita est, ad susceptionem pauperum, cum terris et domibus et omnibus aliis rebus ad eandem*a* pertinentibus. Et ut concessio ista perpetuam habeat firmitatem, eam scripto nostro et sigilli nostri impressione confirmamus. Hiis testibus: Roberto de Wulveya, Ricardo capellano, magistro Ricardo medico,*b* magistro Ricardo de Gnoweshale, Elya de Eton, Willelmo*c* de Essex,*d* et multis aliis.

> *a Ms* eundem   *b Ms* medice   *c Ms* Williemo   *d Sic; ? rectius*
> Essess(ia)

Date as for no. 16. For the hospital, which was among the larger in medieval England, see Knowles and Hadcock, 354; *VCH Warks*, ii, 109–11. It was founded by the archdn on land belonging to the cathedral priory with the approval of prior Laurence and the convent (ibid., 109).

18. *Notification that, at the presentation of Prior Laurence and the convent of Coventry, he has given and granted the church of St Laurence, Alspath [now Meriden], to Henry the clerk, son of Peter of Northampton, in perpetual alms, and canonically invested him with it according to the charter of the prior and convent.*

[1160 × 10 July 1176]

> B = Bodl. ms Top. Warwicks. c. 8 (including extracts by W. Reader from now lost Coventry cartulary), fo. 77r. s. xix in.–med.
> Pd (listed) from same lost cartulary, *Mon. Ang.*, iii, 184, n. l, no. 9.

Omnibus sancte ecclesie filiis Edmundus Coventr' archidiaconus, salutem in domino. Sciant tam presentes quam futuri quod nos, ad presentationem Laurentii prioris de Coventr' et eiusdem loci conventus, donavimus et concessimus ecclesiam sancti Laurentii de Alspath cum omnibus pertinentiis suis et libertatibus Henrico clerico filio Petri de Norhamtonia in perpetuam elemosinam, et eum inde canonice investivimus secundum formam carte supramemorati prioris et conventus. Et ut donatio ista firma sit et in perpetuum valitura, eam scripto nostro [et]*a* sigilli [nostri]*a* inpressione communimus. Hiis testibus: Ricardo cappellano, magistro Ricardo de Gnowesale, Liulfo de Coventr',

Nicholao et Simone, Rogero et Alano filio eius, Osberto de Senicarleis,[b] Willelmo marescallo, Elia de Eton, et aliis.

    a Supplied   *b Reading uncertain*

Date as for no. 16. The archdn witnessed both Ivo of Alspath's recognition that the advowson belonged *iure parochie* to Coventry and the confirmation of his grant by Richard Peche, bp of Coventry (*Mon. Ang.,* iii, 194, no. 13; *EEA* 16, no. 22); it is notable that a number of the witnesses are common to all three documents. For the replacement of Alspath, the ancient name of the parish, by Meriden, see *VCH Warks,* iv, 147; Ekwall, *English Place-Names,* 323.

19.   *Confirmation, in the full chapter of Coventry, of the grant by Walter, parson of Bilton, to the monks of Pipewell of two acres within the curtilage of the grange of Dunchurch and nearby, to be held in perpetuity for fourpence annually to the church of Bilton or two cow-hide boots, if the parson prefers; and confirmation of the same Walter's grant concerning all exchanges of the land of Bilton church made between himself and the brothers of the said grange.*   [1160 × 10 July 1176]

     B = BL, Cotton ms Caligula A xiii (Pipewell cartulary), fos. 62v–63r. s. xiii med.

[O]mnibus et c', Edmundus Coventr' archidiaconus, salutem. Notum sit vobis quod nos concessionem Walterii persone de Beltona ratam habemus et robur nostre confirmationis eidem accommodamus, monachis scilicet Pip(ewell') in pleno capitulo factam de duabus acris terre intra curtam grangie de Duneschr' et iuxta in perpetuum tenend(is) per iiii. denarios annuatim reddendos ecclesie de Belton' vel duas botas vaccinas, si persona maluerit. Et [fo. 63r] sub eodem tenore confirmamus concessionem prefati Walterii super omnibus escambiis de terra ecclesie de Beltona factis inter fratres predicte grangie et eundem Walterium prefatis monachis ut in perpetuum illas possideant per easdem escambias. Volumus itaque ut omnia ista in capitulo Coventr' recitata et subscriptarum personarum roborata concessione perpetua gaudeant firmitate, quam presentis carte et sigilli nostri inpressione communimus. Hiis testibus.

Date as for no. 16. The two acres at Bilton are the subject of two charters by Roger de Craft and Beatrice, his wife (cartulary, fo. 62r). The grange at Dunchurch seems to have been later known as Cawston, a place within the parish (Knowles and Hadcock, 129, 130; *VCH Warks,* vi, 81). It was presumably based upon the church of Dunchurch, whose advowson, according to a final concord of 1247 (cartulary, fos. 67r–68v), was given to Pipewell by William Clement in the time of abbot Robert, ?presumably the second abbot, who became abbot of Fountains in 1170 (*Heads,* 139); William Clement's charter of gift is cartulary, fo. 67r, and refers precisely to *universum ius advocationis ecclesie de Duneschr'*, but whether it can be accepted as genuine is not certain (cf. *EEA* 16, no. 87 and n.).

Nicholas

20.   *As archdeacon of Coventry and king's chaplain, notification that, at the presentation of the prior and canons of Kenilworth, and by concession of Robert the clerk of Audley, he has granted the church of [Fenny] Compton to William Frumentyn, clerk, in perpetual vicarage; and has canonically invested him with the same. William will pay annually one mark of silver to the said Robert, and will*

answer for the church as regards the canons of Kenilworth, the bishop and the
archdeacon of Coventry and their officials. [early 1176 × 1182]

B = BL, Additional ms 47677 (Kenilworth cartulary), fo. 328v. s. xvi in.

Nicholaus Coventr' archidiaconus et domini regis capellanus omnibus sacrosancte ecclesie filiis tam presentibus quam futuris, salutem in domino. Notum
sit universitati vestre quod nos concessimus ecclesiam de Compton' cum
omnibus pertinentiis suis et libertatibus Willelmo Frumentyn' clerico, ad
presentationem prioris et canonicorum de Kenell' et concessionem Roberti
clerici de Aldetheleg', in perpetuam vicariam et eundem W. exinde canonice
investivimus. Et iamdictus W. solvet annuatim marcam argenti memorato
Roberto et adquietabit ecclesiam illam erga canonicos de Kenell' et episcopum
et archidiaconum Coventr' et eorum officiales, et c'.

Nicholas's predecessor, Edmund, was still archdn in early 1176, but Nicholas had
succeeded him by 10 July (*EEA* 16, 113–14). The church was included in the general
confirmation to Kenilworth by bp Walter Durdent, who died in Dec. 1159 (*EEA* 14,
no. 60).

ARCHDEACONRY OF DERBY

Mr Ivo of Cornwall

21. *Notification to all clergy of the chapter of Scarsdale that, at the presentation of*
Geoffrey fitzPeter, he has instituted the abbot and canons of Welbeck in St Peter's
church, Duckmanton, and granted them the personatus *in the same, which they*
successfully claimed in the king's court at Westminster.
[late 1189 × Feb. 1198; ? × 1195]

A = BL, Wolley charter I. 46 B. Endorsed: Institucio super appropriacione ecclesie de
Dugmanton' (s. xiv). Size 131 × 89 + 25 mm. Seal in browned white wax on tag
(method 2); lozenge-shaped, fragment only (approx. one half), *c.* 40 × *c.* 33 mm;
obverse, frontally standing ecclesiastic holding a book against his chest; legend:
+. SIGILLM' . . . . CONI. No counterseal.
B = BL, Harley ms 3640 (Welbeck cartulary), fo. 124r. s. xiv med.
Pd from A, Jeayes, *Derbyshire Charters*, 133, no. 1080.

Magister Ivo Cornub(iensis) archidiaconus Dereb'[a] omnibus clericis per capitulum de Scarvesdal'[b] constitutis, salutem. Noverit universitas vestra nos, ad
presentationem Galfridi filii Petri instituisse abbatem et canonicos de Wellebech[c]
in ecclesia sancti Petri de Duchemanetun'[d] et eis personatum prefate ecclesie
concessisse, quam ipsi dirationaverunt in curia domini regis apud Westmonas-
terium coram iusticiis domini regis, scilicet Rann(ulfo)[e] de Glanvill', Hugone
Dunelmensi, Iohanne Norwicensi, Galfrido Heliensi episcopis, Godefrido de
Luci, Gocelino archid(iacono), Ricardo thesaurario domini regis. Testibus:
magistro Ascelino, Hugone de Dranefeld,[f] Stephano de Cestrefeld, Gervasio
filio Roberti, Ricardo de Stafaleg', Roberto de Aumetun, Gregorio de Scardecl-
ive.

a Derb' *B*   *b* Scharvesd' *B*   *c* Well' *B*   *d* Duk' *B*   *e* Rad'i *B*
f Dranfeld *B; B ends*

After Ivo had become archdn, presumably in succession to Godfrey de Lucy, who was elected bp of Winchester, 15 Sept. 1189, and consecrated 22 October; and before Ivo's successor was in office (*EEA* 16, 116–17); however, Ivo does not certainly occur after 30 Sept. 1194 (*EEA* 17, lv n. 215), although C. R. Cheney says that he occurs as late as 1195, without giving a reference (*EEA* III, no. 528n.). The case in the king's court referred to here must have taken place before the death of Geoffrey Ridel, bp of Ely, on 20 or 21 Aug. 1189 (*Fasti Monastic Cathedrals*, 45). For Geoffrey fitzPeter's gift, see Jeayes, no. 1079, and for further discussion of the charters by him and Richard of Wiverton, from whom Geoffrey bought the manor of Duckmanton, see Colvin, *White Canons*, 68–9; Thompson, *Welbeck Abbey*, 48–9. In 1189 × 1198, bp Hugh de Nonant of Coventry granted the church to Welbeck *in proprios usus* (*EEA* 17, no. 61). The church no longer exists, its former parish being now united with Sutton (Scarsdale) to form Sutton cum Duckmanton.

22.   *With G(odfrey) de Insula, letter to H(ubert), archbishop of Canterbury, responding to the latter's mandate to compel Alice, daughter of William Clement, who has absconded from Ankerwyke priory after living there for fifteen years in the monastic habit, to return to the monastery. Having failed to persuade her to return, or to induce her main supporter, W. de Bidun, knight, to abandon her, and being informed by letters of G(ilbert), late bishop of London, a rescript of the prioress and convent of Ankerwyke and the verdict of judges of Lincoln diocese, who had previously excommunicated her, they [the writers] excommunicated Alice and W. de Bidun and their accomplices. The parties later appeared at Coventry on the morrow of Michaelmas, but Alice insisted that she had never been a nun and appealed to the archbishop's audience.*   [7 Nov. 1193 × Feb. 1198; ? × summer 1196]

> B = PRO, KB 26/48, m. 15 (quoted in a dossier of documents produced in the king's court in 1208 by Jordan son of Avenell in the case brought against him by Alice Clement). Badly worn and illegible in places.[1]
> Pd, *CRR*, v, 185–6; see also *EEA* III, no. 331.

Reverendo domino suo H. dei gratia Cant' archiepiscopo totius Anglie primati fideles sui I. Dereb' archidiaconus et G. de Insula, salutem et debitum famulatum. Suscepimus mandatum serenitatis vestre ut A. filiam Willelmi Clementis, que, relicto habitu quem susceperat in ecclesia de Ankerwic et spreta religione, indecenter nimis et irreverenter et temere evagatur, ad monasterium suum per ecclesiasticam censuram redire conpelleremus. Unde et trina commonitione freti sumus ut ipsa ab errore suo resipisceret et [ad]*ᵃ* monasterium suum rediret, ipsumque receptorem suum et fautorem et erroris sui succursorem precipuum W. de Bidun ut ei communicare et errorem suum tenere desisteret frequenter etiam precepimus. Verum ipsa et prenominatus fautor suus, in malitia sua nimis infrunite perseverantes, commonitionibus nostris acquiescere contempserunt. [. . .]*ᵇ* habitoque constanter et plenarie per litteras G. bone memorie Lond' episcopi et per rescriptum priorisse et conventus monialium de Ankerwic et per veredictum iudicum Lincolnienssis*ᶜ* episcopatus, qui eam propter eundem excessum preexcommunicaverant et ab omnibus de episcopatu Lincol' evitari preceperant, quod nobis per eorundem scripta, immo et per famam publicam consentientem quod ipsa ab annis xv. retro habitum monachicum receperat et quod in domo de Ankerwic regulariter vixerat [. . .]

memorie G. Lond' episcopo [. . .], sicut ex ipsius autentico scripto perpendere poteritis, ipsam et fautorem suum W. de Bidun manifeste [. . .] canonice penitentie nominatim suosque complices et erroris sui participes generaliter excommunicavimus. Procedente tamen tempore [. . .] in crastino sancti Michaelis apud Covintr' comparuerunt partes et cum ei beneficium absolutionis et iuramentum parendi [. . .] secundum formam ecclesie [. . .] et iuramentum prestare et absolvi contempsit, proponensque constanter se nunquam monia(-lem) fuisse neque regulariter vixisse ideoque iniuste militem ut eam [. . .] ab hereditate sua defraudaret hoc ei imposuisse, ad audientiam vestram appellavit [. . .] gladio [. . .] a nobis cuiquam iusticiario domini regis quatenus ad reprimendam malitiam ipsius A. et W. militis [. . .] gladium [. . .].

a Supplied   *b Square brackets indicate passages illegible in ms*   *c Sic*

After Hubert Walter's enthronement at Canterbury and before the date by which at the latest Ivo's successor as archdn was in office (*Fasti Monastic Cathedrals*, 5; *EEA* 16, 117), and evidently after below, no. 139, to which it refers; possibly before the hearing of Alice's case by judges-delegate of Celestine III, commissioned 2 Mar. 1196 (*CRR*, v, 183–4), since the latter is not cited here. Godfrey de Insula, a frequent witness of Hubert Walter's early archiepiscopal acts, had become official of Coventry diocese by 1198 (*EEA* III, no. 626). This act, with no. 139, forms part of the documentation in a protracted dispute between Alice Clement, an absconded and excommunicated nun of Ankerwyke, and her brother-in-law, Avenell, and his son Jordan, over her part of her father's lands. The dispute first came into the king's court in 1204 (*CRR*, v, 79–80), but Alice's case had been before various ecclesiastical tribunals since before 1187 (the death of Gilbert Foliot, bp of London, whose letters are mentioned in the present letter; see also *EEA* 15, no. 77), and she had been excommunicated in 1193 × early 1195 (below, no. 139, presumably the 'verdict of judges of Lincoln diocese' mentioned here), an excommunication now renewed. This interesting and instructive case is discussed in detail in E. Vodola, *Excommunication in the Middle Ages*, Berkeley, California, etc. 1986, 102–10.

[1] The reading of some passages is not entirely certain, even under ultra-violet light.

ARCHDEACONRY OF SHROPSHIRE

Roger

23. *Notification of the settlement in his presence, and with his assent, of the dispute between the canons of Haughmond and Roger, parson of Stanton[-upon-Hine-Heath], over the 'parish' of Acton [Reynald]. Roger has surrendered to the canons their portion in the 'parish' in return for an annual pension to his church of half a mark.*

[? *c.* 1160 x 1182]

B = Shrewsbury, Shropshire Records and Research Centre, 2922/15/1 (Dudmaston transcript of part of lost Haughmond cartulary), fo. 8v. ss. xvi ex. − xvii. in. Pd, *Haughmond Cartulary*, 253, App. C, no. 8.

Universis sancte matris ecclesie filiis Rogerus archidiaconus Salopesb', salutem in eo qui est salus omnium. Noverit universitas vestra quod, cum mota esset controversia inter canonicos de Haghem' et ecclesiam de Stantun super parrochia de Actona, quam canonici pro parte possidebant, Rogero qui eiusdem ecclesie de Stantun persona extitit suam proponente querimoniam, hoc tandem fine inter iamdictos canonicos et ecclesiam de Stant', eodem Rogero plenum et voluntarium prebente assensum, domino dante pax reformata est. Memoratus siquidem Rogerus universo iuri, si quod in portione illa quam canonici tenebant ecclesia sua habebat, renuntiavit et ad firmiorem inter canonicos et ecclesiam suam de Stantun pacem statuendam portionem ecclesie sue in memorata parrochia de Actona cum omni integritate canonicis de se et ecclesia sua in perpetuum tenendam in presentia nostra et consensu nostro concessit, sub annua pensione dimidie marce ecclesie sue de Stant' in festo omnium sanctorum persolvenda. Hancque conventionem iuramento corporaliter prestito confirmavit. Ut igitur id quod rationabiliter factum est perpetuum robur obtineat et nullius possit perversitate molari, presentis nostri testimonium duximus adhibendum. Testibus: Reginaldo Extraneo, Ricardo de Sancta Maria, Herberto canonico, Ricardo de Curcun, magistro Nicholao de Hasting', Ricardo filio Pichot, Iohanne fratre eius, magistro Nicholao, Alano de Osbnest', Willelmo de Baschur', Henrico de Hodeneta, Radulfo de Wrocwrthin, Roberto de Pectun, et multis.

This act is difficult to date narrowly. Roger became archdn in or before 1127 and ceased to be so after 1180 × 1182 and prob. in 1182 (*EEA* 16, 116), but Reginald Lestrange (*Extraneus*) in first place among the witnesses also occurs in 1157 × 1172, 1159 × 1179 and *c.* 1186 × 1189 (*Haughmond Cartulary*, nos. 200, 279; below, no. 24), suggesting a fairly late date, after *c.* 1160. For notes on this and other Haughmond mss, see *EEA* 14, no. 23n. Acton Reynald chapel was a dependency of the abbey's church of Shawbury (*Haughmond Cartulary*, nos. 683, 1099, 1100).

24. *Notification of events in the dispute between Walter son of John and Osbert, prior of St Guthlac's, Hereford, over two parts of Walter's demesne tithes of [Waters] Upton. Walter had retained the tithes, which belonged to the priory, until prior Osbert sued him in the archdeacon's presence in full chapter, whereupon Walter recognised the priory's right and surrendered the tithes into the hand of the archdeacon, who consigned them to the prior as a possession of the priory.* [1159 × 1179]

B = Oxford, Balliol College Library, ms 271 (St Guthlac's Hereford cartulary), fo. 76r (59r). s. xiv in.

[O]mnibus sancte matris ecclesie filiis Rogerus Salop' archidiaconus, salutem. Noscat dilectio vestra Walterum filium Iohannis duas partes decimationis dominii sui de Optuna [*blank for approx. 3–6 words*] ad ius Herefordensis ecclesie pertinentes quodam tempore retinuisse. Tempore vero procedente Os[bertus],[a] eiusdem ecclesie prior, cum eo inde in presentia nostra in pleno capitulo litem contesta[batur].[a] Walterus autem ob multitudinem testium et diutinam possessionem ecclesie cause sue diffide[ns],[a] ius eius recognovit et decimationes in manu nostra refutavit. Nos autem easdem ut propriam ecclesie beati Petri Hereford' possessionem priori plene resignavimus. Hiis testibus: R. abbate Salop', W. abbate de Lilushull', Al(ano) de Hideshale, R. decano de Salopesbr', G. decano de Novoburg', W. dapifero, A. et W. et Nigello et Nicholao presbiteris, R. Extraneo, et c'.

a Ms torn and repaired at right side; letters in square brackets supplied

The earlier dating limit is determined by the occurrence of prior Osbert's predecessor in 1159 × 1160; the later by the fact that his successor resigned as prior in 1179 to become abbot of Gloucester (*Heads*, 91). For Waters Upton, see *Shropshire Place-Names*, i, 297. This act may be connected with an unusual and perhaps contemporary document recording that the monks of Gloucester abbey (superior of St Guthlac's) proved their right to two parts of the demesne tithes of Stoke [upon Tern], [Waters] Upton and Higford, and of Forton (?and) Hopley, in the chapter of Newport before R. archdn of Shropshire, War' the dean, A. of Idsall, H. the dean and the whole chapter (cartulary, fo. 72r); there were three archdns R. of Shropshire in sucession in the 12th century: Roger, Richard Peche and Mr Robert (*EEA* 16, 116). For an early 13th-century episcopal confirmation, in full synod at Shrewsbury, of the tithes of Stoke upon Tern, Higford and Montford (presumably Forton), see *EEA* 17, no. 97A. For Stoke upon Tern, Higford (in Stockton parish), Forton (in Montford parish) and Newport, see *Shropshire Place-Names*, i, 283–4, 151, 133–4, 222.

ARCHDEACONRY OF STAFFORD

Elias

25. *Notification that, in his presence and that of many clergy and laity at Stone, Osbert and Osbert, clerks of Swynnerton, recognised that Swynnerton church, over which there had been a dispute between them and the canons of Stone, belonged to the church of Stone, and restored and quitclaimed it to the canons, with the assent of Robert son of Eelen, lord of the vill of Swynnerton.*

[8 January 1152 × 7 December 1159]

B = BL, Cotton Roll xiii. 6 (Stone charter roll), no. 22. s. xii med.
Pd, G. Wrottesley, 'Staffordshire chartulary', iii, 185.

Universis ecclesie filiis Helyas archidiaconus de Staford', salutem. Noverint omnes tam posteri quam presentes quod clerici de Swinvertona, Osbertus et alter Osbertus, in nostra aliorumque multorum tam clericorum quam laicorum presentia apud Stan' recognoverunt quod ecclesia de Swinv(ertona) de iure et pertinentiis est ipsius ecclesie de Stan', unde diu controversia[a] fuerat inter canonicos de Stan' et predictos clericos de Swinv(ertona), et in conspectu nostro idem clerici prefatam ecclesiam de Swinv(ertona) super altare beate Marie in ecclesia de Stan' reddiderunt, et ab omni controversia et impetitione ex toto quietam et liberam in perpetuum clamaverunt. Et hoc fecerunt gratuito assensu Roberti filii Eelen, qui Robertus predicte ville [b]de Swinvertona[b] dominus est. Insuper prefati clerici iuratoriam cautionem in eodem loco prestiterunt quod cum ecclesia et pro ecclesia de Stan' ubique sensum et posse suum impenderent, et nominatim et[c] ad defendendum et retinendum predictam ecclesiam de Swinv(ertona) canonicis de Stan', sicut illam quam de iure et parrochia ipsius ecclesie de Stan' esse constat, nec unquam cum aliquo contra ipsam starent. His testibus: Alexandro decano, Ricardo capellano, Martino de Salopesb', Willelmo filio Iosep, Willelmo de Mortuna, clericis, Roberto de Salopesb', Wimundo de Elvithelega, Theoderico de Mortuna, Geri de Sceldona, et Roberto fratre eius, Willelmo de Estona, et multis aliis.

a Followed in ms by an erasure   *b–b Interlined*   *c Sic*

After the date when Elias's predecessor as archdn was still in office (*EEA* 14, 130), and before the death of Walter Durdent, bp of Coventry, who confirmed the settlement (ibid.,

125, and no. 72). The confirmation reveals that the bp had committed the dispute to Elias for settlement, and that, despite their renunciation, the two priests were to continue in possession of Swynnerton church for an annual pension of 2s (see also Kemp, 'Archdeacons and parish churches', 343).

Ralph of Tamworth

26. *Agreement to the grant and confirmation [made by Richard Peche, bishop of Coventry] to the church of Chebsey of freedom from synodals and all other customs and exactions.*   [1160 × early 1176]

> B = Lichfield, Cathedral Library, Lichfield Magnum Registrum Album, fo. 150r. s. xiv in. Much abbreviated.
> Pd (calendar), *Magnum Registrum Album*, 116, no. 247.

Radulfus Stafford' archidiaconus universis sancte matris ecclesie filiis, et c' ut supra proximo.[a] Testibus:[b] Rogero capellano de Colleshull', Bartholomeo presbitero, Unfrido milite, Gerv(asio), et c'.

> a *Referring to bp Richard's act (see note)*   b *Change of ink for witness-list, but same hand*

After the bp's consecration and before the archdn's death (*EEA* 16, 109, 115). For bp Richard's act exempting the church 'tam a sinodalibus quam a ceteris omnibus consuetudinibus et exactionibus', see ibid., no. 61. The church was later appropriated to Lichfield cathedral's common fund (ibid. n.).

27. *Notification of the settlement reached before Roger, bishop of Worcester, and Hugh, dean of London, judges-delegate of Pope Alexander III, of the dispute over the church of Shenstone between the canons of Osney and himself with William de Bray, lord of the fee; after which he was ordered by the judges to induct the canons, whom they had invested, into corporal possession of the same, and accordingly invested the canons corporally.*   [? Sept. 1172 × c. Apr. 1175]

> B = BL, Cotton ms Vitellius E xv (Osney cartulary), fo. 36v. ss. xii ex.–xiii in.
> Pd, *Oseney Cartulary*, v, 72, no. 578 E; 'Shenstone Charters', ed. H. E. Savage, *SHC*, 1923, 264–5.

Radulfus archidiaconus de Stafford omnibus fidelibus sancte dei[a] ecclesie, salutem. Notum sit vobis omnibus et indubitatum quod dominus papa Alexander tertius causam que vertebatur super ecclesia de Senestan inter canonicos de Osen' eam vendicantes et me eandem ecclesiam tenentem et Willelmum de Brai fundi dominum Rogero Wigornensi episcopo et Hugoni decano Londoniensi delegavit cognoscendam et concordia vel iudicio terminandam. Cumque ad concordiam conveniremus in presentia prefatorum iudicum et eorundem consensu, ipsi iudices michi preceperunt quatinus supradictos canonicos in corporalem possessionem predicte ecclesie de Senest(an) auctoritate apostolica introducerem. Ipsi etiam eadem auctoritate apostolica qua fungebantur, sicut moris est, investierant eos, compositionem inter nos factam in scriptum redigentes. Quod mandatum exequens, auctoritate iamdicta sepedictos canonicos corporaliter investivi, et ad perpetuam huius investiture fidem et commemorationem, hec rerum gesta presenti pagina comprehendens, illam sigilli nostri impressione munivi. His testibus: Roberto monacho de

Bordesl', Waltero et Alexandro canonicis de Osen', Rogero et Henrico et Bartholomeo presbiteris, magistro Rogero de Stafford, Willelmo de Brai et Humfrido militibus, Rogero de Chircham, Helia et Ricardo de Burth', et multis aliis.

a Interlined

The act of the judges-delegate recording the agreement is printed, *Oseney Cartulary*, v, no. 578 D, and calendared, M. G. Cheney, *Roger of Worcester*, 280, no. 49, q.v. for the date. It is clear from this that William de Bray was the advocate (patron) of the church, and that the archdeacon was to continue in possession of the church, paying a pension to the canons. By *c.* Apr. 1175 the dean and chapter of Lichfield had appealed to the pope against the occupancy of Shenstone church by Osney abbey and the archdeacon (*Oseney Cartulary*, v, no. 578 B), resulting in a further settlement in 1176 (ibid., 578 B, 578; *EEA* 16, nos. 84–5).

Alan

28. *Grant to Burton abbey of all its liberties, namely, of rendering no custom for chrism or holy oil or for any episcopal matter or custom, and of not sending to [rural] chapters or synods a chaplain of the abbey or any man or woman from its lands in Burton, [Abbots] Bromley or Ilam, but that the abbot shall maintain justice in his court.* [1176 × Apr. 1191]

B = BL, Loans ms 30 (Burton cartulary), fo. 59v (39v). s. xiii med.
Pd, 'The Burton chartulary', ed. G. Wrottesley, *SHC*, v, part 1 (1884), 54.

Universis sancte matris ecclesie filiis Alanus Stafford' archidiaconus, salutem in domino. Noverit universitas vestra nos concessisse et auctoritate qua fungimur confirmasse matri ecclesie Burth(on') universas libertates suas, has scilicet: quod non reddet ullam consuetudinem pro crismate vel oleo sancto neque pro aliqua re episcopali aut aliqua consuetudine, nec mittet capellanum predicte ecclesie nec aliquem hominem aut feminam de tota terra sua quam habet in manu sua, sive in tenura de Burt' sive in tenura de Bromleia aut Ylum, ad capitula vel sinodos, set abbas ipsius ecclesie teneat rectum in curia sua et habeat curiam suam in omni causa quamdiu in exhibitione iustitie non defecerit. Hiis testibus: magistro Waltero de Bruges, magistro Albino, et aliis.

After the latest possible date for Alan's predecessor as archdn and before the first occurrence of his successor (*EEA* 16, 115–16). These liberties seem first to have been confirmed to Burton abbey by Robert Peche, bp of Chester (1121–6), who stated that the abbey had enjoyed them since its foundation (1002 × 1004); in 1140 × 1147 bp Roger de Clinton, in confirming the liberty in general terms, ordered the then archdn and his ministers not to exact any *redditum vel consuetudinem* from the chaplain of Burton; both acts were confirmed by Theobald, archbp of Canterbury, and the liberties were further confirmed by later bps of Coventry (Chester) and by later archbps (*EEA* 14, nos. 5, 12, 48; Saltman, *Theobald*, 250–1, no. 23; *EEA* 16, no. 10; *EEA* II, no. 63; *EEA* III, no. 360). See also the 13th-century confirmation by Robert, archdn of Stafford (*Burton Abbey Muniments*, 25, no. 44).

Henry of London

29.   *Grant that, when the three prebends in the church of Gnosall held by William Durdent, Mr Richard of Gnosall and Stephen of Worston become vacant, he will give them to clerks of the bishop [of Coventry] at the latter's will.*

[24 Nov. 1190 × 1213; ? × 27 Mar. 1198]

> B = Lichfield, Cathedral Library, Lichfield Magnum Registrum Album, fo. 127v. s.
> xiv in.
> Pd (calendar), *Magnum Registrum Album*, 80, no. 173.

Omnibus Cristi fidelibus H. archidiaconus Staff', salutem. Noverit universitas vestra me concessisse et presenti scripto cum sacramenti religione confirmasse me tres illas prebendas quas in ecclesia de Gnoweshal' possident Willelmus Duredent, magister Ricardus de Gnowesh(al') [et]*ª* Stephanus de Wiveredeston', cum vacaverint, ad voluntatem domini episcopi clericis suis quibus voluerit donaturum. Hiis testibus: magistro Simone de Derbi, magistro Silvestro, magistro Willelmo de Lond', Iohanne de Essington', Thoma de Beverlaco, et multis aliis.

> *a Supplied*

After the last dated occurrence of Henry's predecessor as archdn, 24 Nov. 1190, Henry himself occurring with title in Apr. 1191, and before Henry's consecration as archbp of Dublin (*EEA* 16, 115–16); possibly before the death of bp Hugh de Nonant, who made a life grant to Henry of the gift of these prebends, the gift of which the archdn had claimed as an appurtenance of the fourth prebend in the church, which he himself held (*EEA* 17, no. 37). On Gnosall church, the advowson of whose four prebends properly belonged to the bp, see *EEA* 14, no. 22n.; *VCH Staffs*, iv, 128.

DIOCESE OF DURHAM

ARCHDEACONRY OF DURHAM

Burchard du Puiset

30.   *Notification that he has assented to and confirmed the charter given by Hugh, bishop of Durham, to prior B(ertram) and the convent of Durham concerning their liberties, namely in respect of the* personatus, *institution and free disposition of all their churches, as granted by his predecessors.*   [early Mar. 1195]

> A = Durham University Lib., Durham Cathedral Muniments, 2. 1. Arch. Dunelm.
> 16. Endorsed: Testimonium Burchardi archid' de libertatibus ab Hug' episcopo
> nobis concessis (s. xii ex.); 2ª prime arch'nalium Dunelm' 1, Q (s. xv). Size 198
> × 131 +16 mm. Seal on tag (passing over the top of the turn-up and through
> slits in the turn-up and in the fold at the bottom), in varnished white wax;
> fragment only (obverse *c.* 30 × 23 mm), ?pointed oval, design very unclear;[1]
> legend: . . . . .NA . . . .
> B = Ibid., Cartuarium Vetus, fos. 141v–142r. s. xiii med. C = Ibid., Cartuarium I,
> fo. 72r. s. xv in. D = Ibid., fo. 130v.

Burchardus archidiaconus universis sancte matris ecclesie filiis ad quos presens pagina pervenerit, salutem. Sciatis me assensum prebuisse carte illi quam dominus meus Hugo Dunelmen' episcopus B. priori et conventui Dunelmen' dedit super libertatibus suis, scilicet de personatu et institutione et libera dispositione omnium ecclesiarum suarum sicut a predecessoribus suis eis indultum est, et eam carta mea presenti corroborasse.[a] Hiis testibus: Willelmo archidiacono, Simone[b] camerario, magistro Ricardo de Coldingham, magistro Willelmo Blesen',[c] magistro Angerio, Hugone de Feritate, Radulfo Haranc, et aliis multis.

   a B ends with T'   *b* Dun' *C*; Dunelm' *D*   *c* Blesens' *C*

The charter of bp Hugh du Puiset, to which Burchard refers, was almost certainly that granted to the priory when he was on his deathbed, early Mar. 1195 (Scammell, *Hugh du Puiset*, 259–60, no. 8), five of the witnesses and Burchard being common to both acts; the present act is therefore either of the same date or perhaps just after the bp's death on 3 Mar. 1195 (*Fasti Monastic Cathedrals*, 30); the archdn himself died 6 Dec. 1196 (ibid., 38).

¹ It has been described as 'part of a seated figure with a nimbus' (*Durham Seals*, i, 503).

ARCHDEACONRY OF NORTHUMBERLAND

John

31. *As archdeacon of Durham, notification that, in the presence of German, prior of Durham, and his own, Adam of Dunbar son of Cospatrick admitted that Edlingham church belonged to the right of Robert, abbot of St Albans, and of Tynemouth priory, and promised to pay annually to the abbot and the monks of Tynemouth one mark of silver for the church.*   [? early 1163 × 23 Oct. 1166]

  A = Durham University Lib., Durham Cathedral Muniments, 3. 2. Spec. 9. Endorsed: Testimonium Iohannis archidiaconi Dun'i de confirmatione ecclesie Edeluing' inter nos et Adam de Dunbar (s. xii). Edelingeham (s. xiv). Size 213 × 88 + 17 mm. Seal on tag (method 1), in varnished white wax, pointed oval, broken away at top and bottom, surviving portion 47 × 40 mm; obverse, frontally standing ecclesiastic, holding a book in his left hand; legend: . . SIGILL . . . . ANNIS. D. . . . . . .MENSIS: ARCH . . . .

  B = Ibid., Cartuarium II, fo. 44v. s. xiv ex.

  Pd from A, Hodgson, *History of Northumberland*, vi, 121–2; *History of Northumberland*, vii, 145n.

Iohannes archidiaconus Dunelmi omnibus ad quos littere iste pervenerint, salutem. Notum esse cupimus universitati vestre quoniam Adam de Dumbar[a] filius Cospatric,[b] in presentia venerabilis viri Germani ęcclesię nostrę prioris et nostra, in iure confessus est ęcclesiam de Eduluingeam[c] ad ius Rodberti abbatis Sancti Albani et monasterii Sancti Oswini tanquam propriam pertinere; marcam etiam argenti nomine eiusdem ęcclesię singulis annis abbati et monachis Sancti Oswini se redditurum fide interposita promisit. His[d] testibus: Roberto filio Odardi, Albano filio Gervasii, Ricardo de Bolonia, Gaufrido fratre abbatis, Ricardo de Flamæstede,[e] Rogero Tusart,[f] Alano de Walesende, Radulfo de Werchewrthe, Stephano medico, Salomone de Biwelle, Ricardo de

Wdehorne, Philippo de Appeltune, Radulfo capellano de Tinemutha, Roberto ianitore, Henrico filio Gaufridi de Goram, Gaufrido de Colum.

a Dunbar *B*   b Gospatric *B*   c Edlingeham *B*   d Hiis *B*
e Flamastede *B*   f *B ends with* et c'

After the election of German, prior of Durham (*Fasti Monastic Cathedrals*, 34), and before the death of Robert de Gorron, abbot of St Albans (*Heads,* 67). For St Oswin's priory, Tynemouth, see Knowles and Hadcock, 78–9. There were two archdns in Durham diocese by *c.* 1127, but they were not given separate territorial titles until after 1174; John belonged to the sequence of Durham archdns of the junior line, who were known as archdns of Northumberland (or at first Northumbria) after 1174 (*Fasti Monastic Cathedrals*, 37; Offler, 'Early archdeacons in Durham', 204–6; Brooke, 'The archdeacon and the Norman Conquest', 16). In 1174 St Albans abbey surrendered Edlingham church, *salvo tenemento Ade de Dunbar,* to Durham cathedral priory in return for the latter's renunciation of its claim to Tynemouth priory (*History of Northumberland*, vii, 143–5; Cheney, *Roger of Worcester*, 251–3, no. 18).

DIOCESE OF ELY

ARCHDEACONRY OF ELY

William Brito

32. *As former archdeacon, testification to Theobald, archbishop of Canterbury and primate, that neither in the time of Hervey, bishop of Ely, his uncle, nor in that of bishop Nigel, was Roger the clerk made parson of Whittlesey church, either in chapter or in synod; and that the church has never had any parson other than the abbot and convent of Thorney, although the abbot held it to supply the lights and ornaments of the abbey, and the archdeacon had always demanded from the abbey episcopal customs relating to the church.*   [? 1151 × 18 Apr. 1161]

> B = Cambridge University Lib., Additional ms 3020 (Thorney cartulary, Part 1), fo. 172v. s. xiv in.
> Pd (incompletely), Saltman, *Theobald*, 527.

Reverentissimo domino suo et patri T. dei gratia Cantuar' archiepiscopo et totius Anglie primati Willelmus qui fuit archidiaconus, nepos Hervei Eliensis episcopi defuncti, salutem et dilectionem in domino. Sciat revera paternitas vestra numquam, sive in tempore Hervei episcopi avunculi mei sive sui successoris domini Nigelli episcopi, Rogerum clericum nec in capitulo nec in senatu de ecclesia de Witles' personam factum fuisse, nec breve nec testimonium de datione abbatis et conventus Thorn' unquam accepisse. Vere scio et testimonium perhibeo ecclesiam illam numquam aliam personam preter abbatem et conventum Torneye habuisse, set abbatem in manu propria ad Thornensis ecclesie luminaria et ornamenta emendanda semper illam tenuisse. Nos vero consuetudines episcopales ad ecclesiam illam pertinentes ab abbate et conventu Thorneye omni tempore exegimus. Valete.

After the archdn's deposition, which happened between his probable suspension on

22 Dec. 1150 and 1152, and before archbp Theobald's death (*Fasti Monastic Cathedrals*, 50, 4); this dating assumes that the omission of Theobald's legatine title, which he held from early 1150 to late 1159, is not significant. Theobald's general confirmation to Thorney, given in the time of abbot Robert (de Prunelai), who died in 1151, includes Whittlesey, but does not refer specifically to the church (Saltman, *Theobald*, 525–7; *Heads*, 75). The episcopal customs mentioned in the archdn's act were presumably ecclesiastical customs and not the secular and hundredal jurisdiction over its land at Whittlesey which bp Hervey of Ely had granted to Thorney in Nov. 1128 (Miller, *Abbey and Bishopric of Ely*, 240, 284, no. 6, 288, n. 14; see also confirmation by bp Alexander of Lincoln: *EEA* I, no. 60) and which was also mentioned in Theobald's confirmation.

Richard Fitz Neal

33. *Notification to N(igel), bishop of Ely, of his gift and grant in perpetual alms to the abbey and nuns of Chatteris of one hide of land in Madingley which Robert his brother gave to the abbey, free of all exaction and secular service save Danegeld,* murdrum *and sixpence as sheriff's aid.* [*c.* 1159 × 30 May 1169]

> B = BL, Cotton ms Julius A i (Chatteris cartulary), fo. 110r. s. xv med.
> Pd, *Chatteris Cartulary*, 224–5, no. 109.

Domino suo N. Eliensi episcopo et *ᵃ*omnibus sancte matris ecclesie filiis tam presentibus quam futuris Ricardus archidiaconus,*ᵃ* salutem. Sciatis me dedisse et in perpetuam elemosinam concessisse deo et ecclesie sancte Marie de Chatriz et monialibus ibidem deo servientibus unam hidam*ᵇ* terre in Maddynglee, quam Robertus frater meus eidem ecclesie dedit, libere sine aliqua exactione et omni seculari servitio preter*ᶜ* denegeld' et murd(ro) et vi. den(ariis) ad auxilium vicecomitis. Hiis testibus: domino Salamone priore de Ely, et Hugone priore de Bernewelle, et aliis.

> *a–a Ms is confused, reading* Ric' archid' *(followed by* et *interlined)* omnibus sancte matris ecclesie filiis tam presentibus quam futuris   *b Ms* idam   *c Followed by* dei *marked for deletion (i.e., with a single point under* i)

Richard became archdn in *c.* 1158, but Solomon's predecessor as prior of Ely, Alexander, was still in office after *c.* 1158 (*Fasti Monastic Cathedrals*, 50, 48); *c.* 1159 is therefore the earlier terminus for this act; the later terminus is the death of Nigel, bp of Ely (ibid., 45). The text is followed by: 'Ista carta registratur plenius in registro domini episcopi Eliensis', but, according to *Chatteris Cartulary*, no. 109n., 'no copy has been found in any of the extant records of the bishops of Ely'.

Richard Barre

34. *Notification that William de Longchamp, bishop of Ely and king's chancellor, has received and instituted abbot Walter and the regular canons of Waltham in the* personatus *of the vacant church of Babraham; and that he, at the bishop's mandate, has inducted them into the church and put them into corporal possession of the same by his official, master Geoffrey of Cambridge.* [late July × 8 Oct. 1191]

> B = BL, Harley ms 391 (Waltham cartulary), fos. 101v–102r. s. xiii in. C = BL, Cotton ms Tiberius C ix (Waltham cartulary), fo. 152r. s. xiii med.
> Pd from B collated with C, *Waltham Charters*, 75, no. 123.

Omnibus sancte matris ecclesie filiis ad quos presens scriptum pervenerit

Ricardus Barre Eliensis archidiaconus, salutem in vero salutari. Notum sit vobis omnibus quod dominus meus Willelmus de Longocampo Eliensis episcopus et domini regis cancellarius dominum Walterum abbatem et canonicos regulares de Waltham in personatum vacantis ecclesie de Badburgeham*a* suscepit et eos in eam instituit, et nobis precepit quod eos in corporalem possessionem eiusdem ecclesie mitteremus. Nos igitur, mandatis illius obedientes, predictum abbatem et canonicos in prefatam ecclesiam introduximus et eos in corporalem possessionem prefate ecclesie per manum magistri*b* Galfridi de Cantebrige*c* officialis nostri misimus. Testibus hiis: magistro Galfrido officiali nostro,*d* magistro Michaele persona de Heddenham, et alio magistro Michaele clerico domini [fo. 102r] episcopi nostri, Radulfo capellano nostro, Briano de Scalariis qui fuit persona in eadem ecclesia ante canon' de Waltham, Roberto capellano de Sauseton', Gervasio capellano de Badburgeham, Iohanne clerico de Langeford', Iohanne filio magistri Radulfi, Waltero filio Hamelini, Galfrido Bigot, Symone Ruffo, Radulfo preceptore de Sausetun', Iohanne clerico de Badburgeham, Roberto de Henefeld.

 a Badburham *C*   *b Om. in C*   *c* Cantebrigge *C*   *d C ends with* et c'

After William de Longchamp ceased to use the title of papal legate, and before his dismissal as king's chancellor (Landon, *Itinerary of Richard I*, 218, 216). Babraham church was given to Waltham in 1181 × 1186 by Geoffrey II de Scalers, on the advice of his nephew, Brian, parson of the church, who was about to become a canon at Waltham (*Waltham Charters*, no. 121) and who witnesses the present act.

* 35. *Institution, at the presentation of Ralph de Keynes, of Everard as parson of Barton church, the see of Ely being vacant.* [prob. 31 Jan. 1197 × 8 Mar. 1198]

 Mentioned only, in an assize of darrein presentment in the king's court in Michaelmas term, 1202, between William de Keynes and the prior of Merton: PRO, KB 26/27, m. 5d; pd, *CRR*, ii, 128–9.

... qui Ebrardus venit et dicit se esse persona illius ecclesie [*sc.* Barton] et quod *a*extitit persona xxx. annis transactis per presentationem Radulfi de Kaain' et per institutionem*a* Ricardi Eliensis archidiaconi, qui eum instituit personam vacante sede Eliensi*:b*; et inde producit sectam, scilicet cartam ipsius archidiaconi hoc testantem ...

 a–a Interlined   *b Ms* Elienss'

Most probably during the vacancy at Ely between the death of William de Longchamp and the consecration of Eustace (*Fasti Monastic Cathedrals*, 45).

DIOCESE OF EXETER

ARCHDEACONRY OF CORNWALL

Peter

36. *Agreement with abbot Peter and the monks of Quarr that the latter will possess for ever all tithes, fruits and obventions of their land of Farwood, for which they will pay twelve shillings annually to the archdeacon's church of Colyton, which will continue to have a fardel of land in the fee of Farwood as before. Colyton church is not obliged to serve the chapel of Farwood, but will provide certain services to the abbot's household, if the abbot desires, although he may use another church for this purpose if he prefers.*

[1158 × 7 Sept. 1171]

> A = PRO, E210/3718 (Ancient Deed D 3718). (Very faded and difficult to read at left side; some passages illegible even under ultra-violet light.) Endorsed: De convencione que facta est inter monachos Quarr'(?) et Petrum archidiaconum Cornubie de capella Forawud' (? s. xii ex.). Size 145 × 66 + 8 mm. Seal missing, tag surviving (method 1).[1]
>
> B = Exeter, D. & C. ms 814: quoted in original confirmation by John the Chanter, bp of Exeter, [?1189 × 1190]. C = Ibid., ms 3672 (Exeter cartulary), pp. 50–51, copy of B. s. xv in.
>
> Pd from B collated with C, *EEA* XII, 141, part of no. 151; (calendar) from A and B, *Quarr Charters*, 112, no. 455.

Controversia que vertebatur inter Petrum abbatem de Quarraria et magistrum Petrum archidiaconum Cornubie tali [est]*a* conventione sopita. Abbas et monachi de Quarraria omnes decimas et fructus et universas obventiones terre sue de Forewoda*b* libere et quiete iure perpetuo possidebunt, tali videlicet conditione quod abbas nomine monasterii sui predicto archidiacono nomine ecclesie de Colintonia*c* duodecim solidos ad festum sancti Iohannis Baptiste annuatim persolvet. Et ipsa ecclesia de Colintona*d* habebit unum ferdlingum terre in feudo de Forewoda*b* quod*e* [prius habuit] et sicut prius habuit. Servitio autem capelle de Forewoda*b* non tenebitur, quia ipsa capella [pro abbatis arbitrio] aut [cadet] aut stabit. Verumtamen, si abbati placuerit, prefata ecclesia de Colintona [ipsius] abbatis familie de viatico et sepultura et consimilibus ministrabit. Quod si abbas maluerit, quelibet ecclesia ad ipsum ad libitum eius*f* facere poterit.

> *a Bracketed passages illegible in A, supplied from copies*   *b* Forwud' *B,* Forwode *C*
> *c* Culint' *B,C*   *d* Culint' *B,* Colinton' *C*   *e* quem *B,C*   *f Placed before* libitum *B,C*

Peter, brother of bp Robert II of Exeter, became archdn after 1157 and died 7 Sept. 1171 (*EEA* XII, 310). Farwood lay in the parish of Colyton, whose church belonged to Exeter cathedral (ibid., no. 150n.). After a further dispute between the monks of Farwood and Colyton church this agreement was confirmed in ?1189 × 1190 by John the Chanter, bp of Exeter, who at the same time stated that the monks of Quarr and Farwood had made satisfaction to the church (ibid., nos. 151–2). The agreement is similar to others allowing Cistercian abbeys (including, as here, those of the Savigniac family) to retain their own tithes in return for annual payments to the local parish churches (cf., above, no. 7n.; below, no. 133n.), but the abbot is allowed remarkable freedom in seeking other spiritual services for his household. Quarr's cell at Farwood seems to be otherwise unknown (*EEA* XII, no. 151n.), and in a later settlement over the spiritualities of Farwood between the dean and chapter of Exeter and Quarr abbey in 1239 there is no mention of monks at Farwood (*Quarr Charters*, 114, no. 465; from Exeter D. & C. ms 822).

[1] The document bore one seal only.

Walter fitzDrogo

37. With H(erbert), abbot of Tavistock, agreement with Jordan, William and Reginald, brothers of John, late vice-archdeacon of Cornwall, and the latter's other kinsmen, over the said John's goods, chattels and debts, including the provision that the abbot and monks of Tavistock will have the corn and tithes of Lamerton and all John's silver spoons, and the archdeacon will have a palfrey with harness, etc.

[3 June 1190 × 1 June 1191]

A = Exeter, Devon R.O., W 1258 M/G 5/22. Endorsed: Pyderwyne (? s. xv); also post-medieval. Size 142 × 155 + 23 mm. Seal: originally two on tags (method 1), fragment of one tag only remaining.

Pd (facsimile and translation), H. P. R. Finberg, 'A Vice-Archdeacon's Legacies', *Devon and Cornwall Notes and Queries* 22 (1942–6), 285–6; reprinted (translation only), *Devonshire Studies*, 250–51.

CIROGRAPHVM[1]

Hec est conventio facta inter H. abbatem Tavistoch' et archidiaconum Cornub' et inter Iordanum et Willelmum et Reginaldum fratres Iohannis quondam vicearchidiaconi Corn' et ceteros consanguineos ipsius I. super rebus et catallis et debitis ipsius I. Scilicet quod dictus abbas habebit totum bladum et decimas de Lamerton' ad suum et monachorum de Tavistoch' sustentationem. Habebunt etiam abbas et monachi omnia coclearia ipsius I. argentea. Archidiaconus vero unum palefredum ipsius I. cum hernesio. Et Willelmus frater ipsius I. habebit unum pallium novum de burnet' ad opus cuiusdam neptis sue pro portione que illum contingebat de pannis usitatis et de ceteris utensilibus ipsius I. que neque de auro neque de argento vel de mazero fuerunt. Omnia autem vasa que de auro vel argento sive de mazero fuerint cum ceteris rebus et catallis et debitis que Iohanni debebantur in tres equas partes dividentur, quarum unam habebit abbas, alteram archidiaconus et tertiam fratres et consanguinei sepedicti I. Abbas etiam et archidiaconus, si que debebant ipsi Iohanni, quieti sunt et erunt in perpetuum, set reliqua debita omnia communi labore et consilio et sumptibus inquiri et perquiri debent, et inter eos per tres equas partes dividi. Si qua vero ab abbate vel archidiacono vel ab aliquo fratrum ipsius I. pro his catallis perquirendis ante hanc conventionem promissa sunt, unusquisque pro sua promissione satisfaciet. Et de his omnibus fideliter observandis abbas et archidiaconus et Iordanus et W. et ceteri fratres memorati I. fidem corporaliter prestiterunt. His testibus: Willelmo archidiacono de Dorset', Alardo filio Willelmi tunc vicecomite, Ricardo Flammanc', Roberto de Campellis, Willelmo de Cheinna, Hugone Cofin', Ioele de Buchintun',[a] [mi]litibus,[b] magistris Petro Picot et Aluredo et Henrico de Melewis, Ricardo filio Drogonis, canonicis Exon', Willelmo de Spinevaus, Iohanne Walens', Petro fratre Galteri archidiaconi Cornub', Willelmo de Burdevill', Guidone de Daggevill', Radulfo Gave, et Gilleberto archidiacono Toton', cuius sigillum cum sigillo H. abbatis de Tavistoc' ad maiorem conventionis securitatem presenti pagine est appositum.

   a Reading of end of word uncertain   b First two letters illegible through fading

After Gilbert Basset became archdn of Totnes in 1190, following the death of his predecessor on 3 June (*EEA* XII, 308), and before the death of John the Chanter, bp of Exeter, who confirmed new arrangements concerning the tithes of Lamerton (ibid., 302; Finberg, 'Vice-archdeacon's legacies', 286–7); at this time Walter fitzDrogo was archdn of Cornwall (*EEA* XII, 310). Finberg plausibly suggests that the vice-archdn had been granted for life Tavistock's entitlement to half the tithes of Lamerton, conferred upon it by bp Bartholomew (*EEA* XI, no. 128), and that the settlement recorded in the present agreement reflected the vice-archdn's wishes, which had not earlier been defined in detail. The vice-archdn's relationship with Tavistock is indicated by the fact that he witnessed two lay charters to the abbey ('Tavistock charters', nos. 30, 35).

[1] Written across a straight, not indented, cut.

* 38. *Notification that, at the presentation of the prior and convent of Montacute, he has admitted and instituted James de Siccavilla as parson of Veryan [formerly Elerky], and put him into corporal possession, the see being vacant.*

   [? Dec. 1184 × Oct. 1186 *or* June 1191 × Mar. 1194 *or* Oct. 1206 × June 1214]

Mentioned only, as having been produced in an assize of darrein presentment in the king's court in Trinity term, 1214, between John de Monte Acuto and Montacute priory: PRO, KB 26/58, m. 14r; pd, *CRR*, vii, 200.

. . .et *[a]*inde profert*[a]* [*sc.* the prior of Montacute] cartam G. archidiaconi Cornub'*[b]* in qua continetur quod idem G. archidiaconus ratione sedis vacantis ad presentationem prioris et conventus de Monte Acuto admisit ipsum Iacobum [*sc.* de Siccavill'] ad ecclesiam de Lerky et ipsum in eadem ecclesia personam instituit et in corporalem possessionem*[c]* eum solemniter misit . . .

   a–a Interlined   b Followed by quam profert *deleted   c Followed by* solemniter *deleted*

Walter became archdn after June 1177 and died 23 June 1216 (*EEA* XII, 310); this act dates from one of the vacancies at Exeter between these dates (but before the date of the assize), possibly one of those in the later twelfth century (ibid., 302–3).

* 39. *Notification that, at the presentation of the prior of Montacute and with the assent of James de Siccavilla [the parson], he has admitted and canonically instituted Roger Cola, clerk, as perpetual vicar of Veryan [formerly Elerky], saving a pension of twenty shillings, the see of Exeter being vacant.*

   [? Dec. 1184 × Oct. 1186 *or* June 1191 × Mar. 1194 *or* Oct. 1206 × June 1214]

Mentioned only, as in no. 38.

. . . Profert [*sc.* the prior of Montacute] etiam literas*[a]* eiusdem G. archidiaconi testificantes quod ipse, vacante sede Exon', ad presentationem prioris de Monte Acuto una cum assensu predicti Iacobi de Sicca Villa admisit Rogerum Cola clericum ad perpetuam vicariam ecclesie de Lerky et ipsum in eadem ecclesia canonice instituit, salva pensione xx. solidorum. . . .

> *a Repeated in ms*

Date probably similar to no. 38, but subsequent to it.

ARCHDEACONRY OF EXETER

Henry fitzHarding[1]

* **40.** *?Act concerning the church of Stoke[-in-Teignhead] in his archdeaconry.*
[1161 × 27 Apr. 1162]

> Briefly abstracted in: (1) Bodl. ms Tanner 342 (misc. volume, including extracts from lost Plympton cartulary), fo. 177v. s. xvii ex; (2) BL, Harley ms 6974 (Matthew Hutton's notebook, including extracts copied from the same), fo. 29v. s. xvii ex.

Henricus archidiaconus [in diocesi Exon' in archidiaconatu ubi ecclesia de Stokes][a] tempore Bartholomei episcopi et Ricardi comitis Devon.

> *a Square brackets sic in both mss*

Henry became archdn after 18 Apr. 1161 and before 27 Apr. 1162 (*EEA* XII, 307); Richard de Redvers, 2nd earl of Devon, died 21 or 27 Apr. 1162 (*Complete Peerage*, iv, 313). Plympton priory was patron of the church of Stoke-in-Teignhead (*Reg. Bronescombe and Quivil*, 182, 228, 356; *Reg. Bronescombe*, ii, 130). It is not certain that this text refers to a written act of the archdn.

[1] The supposed act by this archdn, calendared in *Canonsleigh Cartulary*, no. 145, is in fact an act by his (un-named) deputy, 'qui tunc vicem gerebam H. archidiaconi', and refers neither to an episcopal vicar nor to a vacancy in the see (BL, Harley ms 3660, fo. 76r).

John

41. *Notification that, whereas the prebend of the church of Bampton, held by Godfrey de Lucy before he became bishop of Winchester, was afterwards assigned to him (John), he confirms the grant made by Godfrey, when he held the prebend, to Robert de Lucy, his nephew, of a certain prebend in Bampton church, namely, that which Nicholas of Bampton held.* [22 Oct. 1189 × 24 May 1204; poss. late 1189]

> B = Lincoln, Lincolnshire Archives, Lincoln D. & C. Muniments, A/1/6 (The Registrum), fo. 112v, no. 1918. s. xiv med. C = Ibid., Lincoln D. & C. Muniments, Dij/73/2/18a, single leaf with copies of four documents probably from same. s. xiv med.
>
> Pd from B and C, *Reg. Antiquissimum*, iii, 265, no. 923.

Omnibus Cristi fidelibus ad quos presens scriptum pervenerit Iohannes Exon' ecclesie archidiaconus, salutem. Noverit universitas vestra me, cum prebenda ecclesie de Bampton' que fuit domini Godefridi de Luci ante promotionem suam in episcopum Winton' michi postea canonice assignaretur, concessionem et donationem quam idem G. de Luci dum adhuc eandem haberet prebendam fecit Roberto de Luci nepoti suo de quadam prebenda in ecclesia de Bampton' cum pertinentiis, illa scilicet quam Nicholaus de Bampton' tenuit, ratam et gratam habere et presenti carta mea confirmare. Testibus hiis: magistro Alexandro, Hugone de Giherst, Eustachio de Falcoberg' clericis domini G. Winton' episcopi, Iohanne capellano de Bampton', Hugone de Lilleburn', Rogero Doilly.[a]

a Doylly *C*

After the consecration of Godfrey de Lucy to Winchester, and before the first certain occurrence of John's successor in the archdnry (*Fasti Monastic Cathedrals*, 85; *EEA* XII, 307); but possibly shortly after John's presumed succession to the prebend. Bampton church was a decayed Anglo-Saxon minster, which was given to Exeter cathedral in 1153 as two prebends; it was reorganized in the later 12th century into a prebend with two chaplaincies, the latter being converted by the mid-thirteenth century into three portionary vicars (*VCH Oxon*, xiii, 48–9).

42. *Notification that, whereas Peter the clerk of Ottery has resigned his vicarage in Ottery St Mary church into the hands of W(illiam), bishop of Ely, king's chancellor and papal legate, the archdeacon has received, instituted and canonically invested Roger the chaplain in the perpetual vicarage of that church, at the presentation of the chapter of Rouen cathedral.* [July 1190 × late July 1191]

B = Rouen, Bibl. municipale, ms Y. 44 (Rouen cathedral cartulary), fo. 64v. s. xiii in.
C = PRO, PRO 31/8/140A (transcripts from Norman sources), no. 375 (copy from B). 1831–5.
Pd from B, Oliver, *Mon. Exon.*, 263, no. 3; (calendar) from B,C, *CDF*, 16, no. 60.

Omnibus sancte matris ecclesie filiis ad quos presens carta pervenerit I. archidiaconus Exon',[a] eternam in domino salutem. Universitati vestre notum facimus quod, cum nobis plenius constaret Petrum clericum de Oteri vicariam quam habuit in ecclesia beate Marie de Oteri coram W.[b] Eliensi episcopo, domini regis cancellario, totius Anglie legato,[c] abiurasse et eam in manus ipsius W.[d] Eliensis episcopi et apostolice sedis legati resignasse, nos Rogerum capellanum, ad petitionem et presentationem capituli ecclesie beate Marie Roth(omagensis), ad perpetuam vicariam predicte ecclesie de Oteri, quam idem Petrus habuerat, recepimus et instituimus et canonice investivimus. Quod[e] ut ratum de cetero perseveret, presenti carta confirmavimus. Hiis testibus: magistro W. de Axem' tunc vicearchidiacono,[f] Bartholomeo[g] de Karent' clerico, Roberto le beden' et Reginaldo fratribus, Petro de Fonte, et multis aliis.

a Exoniensis *C*   *b* Willelmo *C*   *c* legata *B*   *d* Willelmi *C*
e Quare *C*   *f* archidiacono *C*   *g* Bartholomeus *B*

After William de Longchamp's appointment as legate (5 June 1190) would have become known in England, and before he ceased to use the title (Landon, *Itinerary of Richard I*, 215, 218). Mr William of Axmouth was a canon of Exeter and witnessed a number of episcopal acts of John the Chanter and Henry Marshal (*EEA* XII, index *sub nomine*).

ARCHDEACONRY OF TOTNES

Hugh of Eu

* 43.   *Conferment of the [rural] deanery of Plympton upon Godfrey at the presentation of Richard, prior of Plympton.*   [1160 × 23 May 1162]

> Briefly abstracted in: (1) Bodl. ms Tanner 342 (misc. volume, including extracts from lost Plympton cartulary), fo. 177v. s. xvii ex.; (2) BL, Harley ms 6974 (Matthew Hutton's notebook, including extracts copied from same), fo. 29v. s. xvii ex.; pd, *EEA* XII, no. 169n.

Hugo [de Augo]*ᵃ* archidiaconus [Tottonie] de decanatu [de Plimpton ad presentationem Ricardi prioris] Godefrido tradito.

a All square brackets sic in both mss

After Richard Pilatus became prior of Plympton (*Heads*, 181), and before Hugh of Eu ceased to be archdn (*EEA* XII, 308).

Gilbert Basset

44.   *Notification to the parsons and vicars of the archdeaconry of Totnes that for a long time past the [rural] deanery of Plympton has been in the jurisdiction of Plympton priory, and that he grants the deanery to the priory in perpetuity so that the prior and canons shall present a clerk to the archdeacon of Totnes or his official, from whom he shall receive the cure of the deanery.*   [3 June 1190 × prob. 1191]

> A = Exeter, Devon R.O., Exeter city archives, ED/PP/10. Endorsed: (i) De decanatu Plimton' (s. xiii in.); (ii) Gilbertus Basset arch' Totton' (s. xiii); Carta xxxiii. (s. xiii). Size 200 × 137 + 19 mm. Seal on tag (method 2), in pale reddish-pink wax, pointed oval, missing approx. quarter or third, when complete *c.* 50 × 30 mm; obverse, seated figure facing left and reading at a desk, a star behind his shoulder; legend: . . . . .EBERTI ARCH. T . . .
> Pd, Oliver, *Mon. Exon.*, 138–9, no. 15.

Gillebertus Basset archidiaconus Totton' omnibus ecclesiarum personis et vicariis per archidiaconatum Totton' manentibus, salutem in auctore salutis. Provide posteris providit antiquitas ut quod in iugi et recenti voluit permanere memoria scripture beneficium consignaret. Quamobrem ad omnium tam presentium quam futurorum volumus pervenire noticiam et fieri manifestum quod decanatus Plimton' a multis retro temporibus fuit in iurisdictione Plimton' ecclesie et prioris qui eiusdem regimini preerat. Hoc idem eis testimonio et auctoritate episcopali et archid(iaconi) Totton' testificatum et confirmatum est. Nos vero, libertatem et dignitatem predicte Plimton' ecclesie per omnia conservare et augere volentes, decanatum de Plimton' ecclesie sanctorum apostolorum Petri et Pauli et canonicis ibidem commorantibus concedimus, volentes ut ecclesie Plimton' in perpetuum libere et sine contradictione remaneat, ita scilicet ut clericus per priorem et canonicos Plimton' archidiacono Totton' qui pro tempore fuerit vel eius officiali presentetur, et curam decanatus per eum suscipiat. Et ne temporis processu vel malignitate alicuius decessorum nostrorum et nostra super predicto decanatu eis facta concessio valeat mutari vel infirmari, eam caritatis intuitu presenti scripto cum appositione sigilli nostri concedimus et confirmamus. His testibus: magistro Ivone, magistro Milone, magistro Ricardo de Plimton', Radulfo de Plimton', Radulfo de Cornewda, Rand(ulfo) de Aleinton', Ansgero de Niwaton', Simone de Plimst', Adam de Motberi, Godefrido de Holbohaton', capellanis, Marco de Devenaberi, Roberto de Hiwis, Reginaldo de Uggab', clericis.

Gilbert was archdn from 1190 (after 3 June) to 1207 (*EEA* XII, 308), but this act is almost certainly contemporary with, or soon after, bp John the Chanter's confirmation of the deanery to the priory, in 1188 × 1191 (ibid., no. 169, where the present act is cited). Oliver (*Mon. Exon.*, 139) gives the seal's legend as: SIGILLVM GILLEBERTI ARCH. TOTTON.

DIOCESE OF HEREFORD

ARCHDEACONRY OF HEREFORD

Ralph Foliot

45. *Notification that the prior and monks of St Andrew's, Northampton, have given him their church of Potton in pure and perpetual alms for an annual pension of five marks, which he has promised to pay.* [*c.* 1179 × *c.* 1190]

B = BL, Royal ms 11 B. ix (St Andrew's Northampton cartulary), fo. 35v. s. xiii ex.

Omnibus ad quos presentes littere pervenerint Radulfus Herfordensis archidiaconus, salutem. Ad omnium notitiam cupio pervenire priorem et monachos sancti Andree de Norhamt' dedisse et concessisse michi ecclesiam suam de Pottona cum omnibus pertinentiis suis in puram et perpetuam elemosinam, sub annua pensione v. marcarum, quas eisdem monachis ad duos anni terminos persolvam, sicut presentibus ewangeliis in verbo veritatis me illud fideliter observaturum promisi. Quod ne tractu temporis alicui veniat in dubium, presentis scripti testimonio confirmo et sigilli mei appositione corroboro.

After Ralph became archdn (*EEA* VII, 307) and before the later terminus of his institution in the church by Laurence, archdn of Bedford (below, no. 62).

46. *At the request of prior H(enry) and the monks of St Andrew's, Northampton, for the sake of peace between them and David, earl [of Huntingdon], over the church of Potton, and by the authority of R(obert) of Bedford, precentor of Lincoln cathedral and official, grant to Mr T., the earl's clerk, of an annual pension of two marks out of the monks' pension, saving the archdeacon's vicarage for life.* [1187 × *c.* 1190]

B = BL, Royal ms 11 B. ix (St Andrew's Northampton cartulary), fos. 35v–36r. s. xiii ex.

Sciant universi sancte matris ecclesie filii quod ego R. Herfordensis archidiaconus, ad petitionem H. prioris et monachorum sancti Andree de Norh(am)t' pro bono pacis inter eos et comitem David super ecclesia de Potton', auctoritate magistri R. de Bedeford, Linc(olniensis) ecclesie presentoris*a* et officialis, concessi et hac carta mea confirmavi magistro T. clerico predicti comitis [fo. 36r] annuam pensionem solvendam nomine ecclesie Potton', scilicet unam marcam argenti et Pasca et aliam ad festum sancti Michaelis, de pensione predictorum monachorum, salva vicaria mea in vita mea. Testibus: Willelmo et Henrico capellanis meis, Ricardo Ruffo clerico et senescallo meo, Angero et Germano et Henrico de Rufhale, Iohanne de Ba,*b* et Willelmo servientibus meis, Willelmo de Stoccham, Nicholao de Gelstona, Gilberto de Hales, et multis aliis.

a Sic   *b Reading uncertain; possibly* Ha

After no. 45 and, according to D. M. Smith, shortly after 1186 × 1188 (Smith, 'Officialis', 215). Robert of Bedford and Roger of Rolleston acted as officials for bp Hugh of Lincoln when he was abroad in the later 1180s (ibid.).

DIOCESE OF LINCOLN

Archdeaconry of Bedford

Nicholas

47. *Notification to the clergy of Bedfordshire that he has received and canonically instituted the prior of Dunstable in the* personatus *of Pulloxhill church, so that the prior and convent shall possess it in perpetual alms, at the grant and presentation of Robert de Albini, who much earlier proved his right to the advowson of the church in judgement before the archdeacon.* [1141 × 31 Mar. 1181]

B = BL, Harley ms 1885 (Dunstable cartulary), fo. 22v (21v). s. xiii in.
Pd (calendar), *Dunstable Cartulary*, 47, no. 139.

Nicholaus archidiaconus Bedef' universo clero de Bedefordesyr', salutem in domino. Ut in publicam notitiam veniat quod a nobis caritatis intuitu factum esse recolimus, sane factum litterarum nostrarum curavimus confirmare testimonio et corroborare sigillo, fraternitati et dilectioni vestre significantes nos ad concessionem et presentationem Roberti de Alben' priorem de Dunst(aplia) in personatum ecclesie de Pullokesh(ull') suscepisse et canonice instituisse, ut idem prior cum conventu predictam ecclesiam cum omnibus pertinentiis suis in perpetuam elemosinam liberam et quietam perpetuo possideat. Cuius quidem ecclesie advocationem prefatus Robertus de Alben' coram nobis in iudicio multo ante tempore dirocinavit.*a* Testibus: Radulfo de Barton', magistro Lodewico, et c'.

a Sic; ? for dirationavit

Nicholas' predecessor as archdn last occurs after 1141, and he himself first occurs in 1145 × 1146; he died 31 Mar. *c.* 1180 × 1181, and his successor was in office by Oct. × Dec. 1181 (*Fasti Lincoln*, 41–2; below, no. 61n.). This act may be the 'charter' produced in a case in the king's court in 1212 between the prior of Dunstable and Henry Buniun over a moiety of Pulloxhill church, where the institution was said to have been made *sede episcopatus . . . vacante* (*CRR*, vi, 279).

(?†) **48.** *Declaration that Aspley [Guise] church was never an appurtenance of his prebend of Bedford; he had first known a priest called Aschetil in the church, allegedly as parson, and afterwards a certain clerk; after he became archdeacon, he himself received and canonically invested R(obert),*[1] *clerk of Salford, in the* personatus *of the church at the presentation of R(oger)*[1] *and Stephen, lords of the vill; afterwards he was present when R(obert), bishop of Lincoln, received the prior of Dunstable into the* personatus *at the presentation of R(oger) of Salford; and he himself has recently received Nicholas, clerk, into the perpetual vicarage of the church at the prior's presentation.* [1149 × 31 Mar. 1181; ? × 1166]

B = BL, Harley ms 1885 (Dunstable cartulary), fo. 24r (23r). s. xiii in.
Pd, *Dunstable Cartulary*, 55–6, no. 161.

Nicholaus archidiaconus Bedeford' presentibus et futuris, salutem. Quia intimatum est michi quosdam discordie clanculo[a] dicere ecclesiam de Aspele ad prebendam meam de Bedeford' pertinere, quod inde certissime novi in veritate que deus est diligenter manifestare curavi. Videlicet quod ipsa ecclesia de Aspele nunquam prebende mee de Bedeford pertinens fuit, verum quendam sacerdotem nomine Aschetil' primo vidi in ecclesia illa, ut dicebatur, gerere personatum, postmodum quendam clericum. Tempore vero procedente, cum essem archidiaconus factus, R. clericum de Saleford, presentatione R. et Stephani dominorum ipsius ville, in personatum predicte ecclesie suscepi et canonice investivi. Postmodum autem presens affui ubi dominus R. Linc' episcopus, ad presentationem R. de Saleford, priorem de Dunst' in personatum predicte ecclesie suscepit et in perpetuam elemosinam canonicis de Dunst' concessit et confirmavit. Novissime vero, presentatione prioris, quendam clericum Nicholaum nomine in perpetuam vicariam sepedicte ecclesie suscepi. Testibus: magistro Nigello, Adam clerico de Leiton', et c'.

a Sic; ? for clanculum

After Robert Chesney's consecration as bp of Lincoln, 19 Dec. 1148, and before the latest possible date for the archdn's death (*Fasti Lincoln*, 2; above, no. 47n.), but, if the form of reference to the bp of Lincoln can be trusted, perhaps before the latter's death, *c.* 25 Dec. (prob. 27 Dec.) 1166 (*Fasti Lincoln*, 2). The text may well be a forgery in its present form: see *Dunstable Cartulary*, 287–8 n. 161.

[1] For these expansions, see *Dunstable Cartulary*, no. 161.

49. *Notification that he has canonically received and constituted the prior of Dunstable as parson of the church of Steppingley, at the presentation of Richard of Steppingley, advocate of the church, and in the presence and at the request of William, clerk of Steppingley, whom many years before he had constituted as parson at Richard's presentation.* [? *c.* 1160 × 31 Mar. 1181]

B = BL, Harley ms 1885 (Dunstable cartulary), fo. 24r (23r). s. xiii in.
Pd (calendar), *Dunstable Cartulary*, 54–5, no. 159.

Nicholaus archidiaconus Bedef' presentibus et futuris, salutem. Noverit universitas vestra me priorem de Dunst' in ecclesiam de Steppingel' canonice suscepisse et personam constituisse, presentatione Ricardi de Stepingel' advocati eiusdem ecclesie, Willelmo clerico de Steping' presente et hoc postulante, quem quidem Willelmum multis antea transactis annis predicti R. presentatione prefate ecclesie de Steppingel' personam constitueram. Testibus: Ricardo capellano, Willelmo de Stepingel', et c'.

While Nicholas was archdn and before the latest possible date for his death (above, no. 47n.), but date otherwise uncertain; perhaps after *c.* 1160, since Richard of Steppingley first occurs in 1166 (*Red Bk Exch.*, i, 335).

50. *Notification that he has inducted the prior of Dunstable into corporal possession of the church of St Mary, Bedford, in the presence and with the approval of Osbert, dean, and on a mandate of B(artholomew), bishop of Exeter, before whom by papal commission the dispute between the prior and Osbert has been settled, namely, that Osbert shall hold the church for life for an annual pension to Dunstable priory; Osbert has sworn before the archdeacon in general synod to keep faith with the prior and convent.* [18 Apr. 1161 × 31 Mar. 1181]

> B = BL, Harley ms 1885 (Dunstable cartulary), fo. 22v (21v) (added at foot of folio). s. xiii in.
> Pd (calendar), *Dunstable Cartulary*, 48, no. 144.

Nicholaus archidiaconus Bedef' et c'. Universitati vestre notum facimus[a] me priorem de Dunst' in corporalem possessionem induxisse de ecclesia sancte Marie de Bedef', Osb(erto) decano presente et factum meum approbante, et hoc mandato domini B. Exon' episcopi, cui fuit a domino papa facta commissio cognocesci[b] super controversia que inter predictum priorem et decanum de eadem ecclesia vertebatur, coram quo tandem facta est compositio inter priorem et O., ita quidem quod idem O. ipsam ecclesiam sancte Marie sub annua pensione nomine ecclesie de Dunst' quoad viveret possideat. Ipse etiam O. in presentia mea in generali sinodo super fidelitate priori et conventui observanda super quatuor[c] evangelia iuratoriam exhibuit cautionem. T'.

> *a Sic*   *b Sic; ? rectius* cognoscendi   *c Ms* iiii.[or]

After Bartholomew of Exeter's consecration, which occurred between 18 Apr. and ?25 Dec. 1161 (*EEA* XII, 302), and before the latest possible date for the archdn's death. (above, no. 47n.). No other notice of the bp of Exeter's involvement survives. Osbert was rural dean of Bedford as well as holder of this church (*Dunstable Cartulary*, 53–4, no. 155, and 283 n. 144).

51. *Notification that, at the presentation of Alexander of Studham and at the request of Alexander's son, John the clerk, he has canonically received the prior of Dunstable to the rule of Studham church and constituted him as parson. The prior and convent shall possess the church in perpetuity with all appurtenances and liberties granted to them by Alexander and confirmed by his charter.* [?1167 × 31 Mar. 1181]

> B = BL, Harley ms 1885 (Dunstable cartulary), fo. 19r (18r). s. xiii in.
> Pd (calendar), *Dunstable Cartulary*, 35, no. 99.

Nicholaus archidiaconus Bedeford' presentibus et futuris, salutem. Quod a nobis sane factum est ad vestre notitiam universitatis volumus pervenire, videlicet nos priorem de Dunst' presentatione Alexandri de Stodham ad regimen ecclesie que[a] in honore beate Marie in ipsa villa fundata est canonice suscepisse et personam constituisse, Iohanne clerico filio predicti Alexandri presente et hoc petente et factum nostrum approbante. Quare volumus et concedimus ut prefatus prior et conventus de Dunst' predictam ecclesiam illis intuitu pietatis concessam in perpetuum possideant cum omnibus pertinentiis suis et libertatibus quas predictus Alexander eis concessit et carta sua confirmavit. Testibus: Radulfo de Bartun', Roberto de Wilsamstud', magistro Lodowico de Dunst', Willelmo de Stepping', Ricardo presbitero, Willelmo clerico, Ricardo de Husseburn', Ricardo Raguel, Radulfo presbitero, Adam nepote archidiaconi, Iohanne de Hida, Gileberto de Hida, Ricardo de Hella.

a Interlined

While Nicholas was archdn and before the latest possible date for his death, and perhaps after the death of bp Robert de Chesney in late Dec. 1166 (above, no. 47n.; *Fasti Lincoln*, 2), since the act was confirmed by Hugh of Avallon, bp of Lincoln, in *c.* 1189 × 1193 (*Dunstable Cartulary*, no. 100; *EEA* IV, no. 52).

52. *Notification to Richard, archbishop of Canterbury, at the request of the parties, of what he has learnt in chapter and from laymen concerning the dispute between William son of Fulcher and Alexander the canon of Ruxox over the chapel of Ruxox, which is pending before the archbishop.* [Aug. 1174 × Sept. 1175; ? × June 1175]

B = BL, Harley ms 1885 (Dunstable cartulary), fo. 21v (20v). s. xiii in.
Pd, *EYC*, vii, 102–3, no. 49; (calendar), *Dunstable Cartulary*, 43–4, no. 126.

Dilecto domino suo Ricardo dei gratia Cant' archiepiscopo totius Anglie primati et apostolice sedis legato Nicholaus archidiaconus Bed', salutem et debitam subiectionem. Cum causam que vertitur inter Willelmum filium Fulcheri et Alexandrum canonicum de Rokeshac in vestra presentia tractandam esse acceperimus, ab utraque parte requisitus ut vobis scriberem super capella de Rokeshac, veritatem ex commemoratione et attestatione capituli, a capitulo convocato necnon a laicis discretis et legittimis, didici. Philippus de Sannervill' divina instinctus inspiratione prefatum locum assensu Roberti Linc' episcopi divino assignavit, suamque donationem carte sue attestatione communivit. Unde quidam episcopus de Sancto Asafo, qui tunc temporis prefati Linc' episcopi vices gerebat, capellam cum cimiterio in honorem dei et beati Nicholai ibi constructam dedicavit, et omnes qui ausu sacrilego illum locum invaderent aut everterent excommunicavit. Predicto vero Philippo postmodum defuncto, Gilebertus de Saunervill', illius heres, et Hugo Gubiun, cuius filiam in uxorem duxerat, donationem Philippi in irritum revocare machinantes, sacerdotem quendam Edgarum nomine, qui loco illi preerat, vexare et infestare non destiterunt donec in presentia sepedicti Linc' episcopi receptis xl. solidis memorato loco renuntiavit, et cartas omnes reddidit. Aliquanto autem tempore elapso, prefatus G. lepra tactus in mea et totius synodi presentia voce lacrimabili confessus est se flagellum dei merito sensisse propter loci divino cultui mancipati eversionem, unde et penitentiam sibi iniungi requisivit et in pristinum statum locum eundem reformavit, et sicut carte quas palam produxit attestantur reformationem ac suam donationem corroboravit. Et hoc totum completum est antequam rex Angl(orum) filiam prenominati G. cum hereditate sepememorato W. concessisset. Valete.

After the archbp's arrival in England after his consecration (*EEA* II, lv, and no. 111n.) and before his confirmation of the settlement of the dispute in his presence, not later than Sept. 1175 (*EEA* II, no. 128; *EYC*, vii, 103–4, no. 50); possibly, if the following act dates from the vacancy in the see of Lincoln, before the papal confirmation of Geoffrey Plantagenet's election as bp, 'before July 1175' (*Fasti Lincoln*, 2). On this case, see also Kemp, 'Informing the archdeacon', 142. The chapel at Ruxox (in Flitwick) was in effect a cell of Dunstable priory, to which the site was given in 1148 × 1166 (*EYC*, vii, 98). The place was part of the Sanderville fee in the honour of Skipton (ibid., 87–8, 101–6). William son of Fulcher became involved as the husband of Gilbert de Sanderville's daughter.

53.   *Notification that, on a mandate of Richard, archbishop of Canterbury, and at the request of William son of Fulcher, he has inducted and canonically invested the prior of Dunstable in the churches of Ruxox, Husborne [Crawley] and Flitwick; and by the authority of the church of Lincoln, the authentic deeds produced by the prior having been inspected and read out, he has granted the said churches to the convent in perpetuity.*   [Aug. 1174 × 31 Mar. 1181; ? × Sept. 1175; ? × June 1175]

> B = BL, Harley ms 1885 (Dunstable cartulary), fo. 21r (20r). s. xiii in.
> Pd (calendar), *Dunstable Cartulary*, 42, no. 123.

Nicholaus archidiaconus Bedef' presentibus et futuris salutem. Universitati vestre notum facimus nos, ex mandato domini Ricardi Cant' archiepiscopi et petitione Willelmi filii Fulcheri, priorem de Dunst' in corporalem possessionem induxisse et canonice investisse de ecclesia de Rokeshac cum omnibus pertinentiis suis, et de ecclesia de Hesseburne cum omnibus pertinentiis suis, et de ecclesia de Flittewic cum omnibus pertinentiis suis; et auctoritate Lincolniensis ecclesie conventui de Dunst' predictas ecclesias perpetuo possidendas concessisse et presentis scripti testimonio roborasse, inspectis et recitatis auctenticis instrumentis que prefatus prior in presentia nostra produxit, Alexandro etiam canonico et Ricardo clerico de^a presentibus et factum nostrum^b approbantibus. Hiis testibus: Radulfo de Bartun', Roberto de Wilsam', et c'.

    a Sic, a place-name being presumably omitted   *b Repeated in ms*

After the archbp's arrival in England (see no. 52n.) and before the latest possible date for the archdn's death (above, no. 47n.); but probably following the archbp's settlement of the dispute (above, no. 52n.) and, if the reference to 'the authority of the church of Lincoln' indicates a vacancy in the see, before the papal confirmation of Geoffrey Plantagenet's election as bp, 'before July 1175' (*Fasti Lincoln*, 2).

54.   *Settlement, in the presence of Robert II, bishop of Lincoln, of the archdeacon's dispute with the monks of St Neots over the church of Tempsford: namely, he has surrendered the church to the monks, who have returned it to him to hold of them for life as 'inparsonated' vicar for five shillings annually; if Goisbert the [?rural] dean outlives him, he will then hold the church on the same condition, and after the death or change of life of both of them the church will return to the monks' perpetual possession.*   [19 Dec. 1148 × ?1158]

> B = BL, Cotton ms Faustina A iv (St Neots cartulary), fo. 39v (38v). s. xiii med.
> Pd (calendar), Gorham, *Hist. Eynesbury and St Neot's*, ii, page xii, no. 60.

Notum sit tam presentibus quam futuris quod, post diu habitam controversiam inter Nicholaum archidiaconum Bedeford' et monachos^a Sancti Neoti de ecclesia de Tameseford, taliter pax et finis inter eos facta est. Presente Lincolniencis^b ecclesie episcopo Roberto secundo, Nicholaus archidiaconus apud Sanctum Neotum in capitulo ecclesie monachorum rectum recognovit et per manum eiusdem episcopi ipsam ecclesiam de Tameseford monachis reddidit liberam et quietam et solutam ab omni retroacta calumpnia.*c* Ita sane quod eandem ecclesiam prorsus*d* ei monachi reddiderunt, ut teneat*e* eam de ipsis quasi vicarius inpersonatus omni vita sua per quinque solidos reddendos per annum ad festum sancti Neoti, et post ipsum Goisbertus decanus si ei supervixerit eiusdem predicti conditione. Post mortem vero utriusque vel vite mutationem prefata ecclesia iure perpetuo in propriam monachorum redeat possessionem, exclusa post ipsos omnium hominum calumpnia et reclamatione. Et hoc ab ipso archidiacono fide data coram episcopo firmatum est, quod post dies ipsorum neque per ipsos neque per aliquos ex parte sua ecclesia Sancti Neoti a recto suo elongabitur. T'.

> *a Altered in ms from* monachis   *b Sic*   *c Altered in ms from* calumpna
> *d Altered in ms from* porsus   *e Altered in ms from* teneant

The date is that proposed for the notification of the agreement by bp Robert Chesney (*EEA* I, no. 243). The agreement was also confirmed by archbp Theobald (Saltman, *Theobald*, 460, no. 234). The term *vicarius inpersonatus* is remarkable and represents a most unusual adaptation of the verb *inpersonare* (found in the second half of the twelfth century as apparently equivalent to *instituere* for the institution of parsons) to the status of vicars (see also Kemp, 'Towards admission and institution', 171–2).

* 55. *Admission of the canons of Newnham [sc. St Paul's, Bedford] to the church of [Lower] Gravenhurst, at the presentation of William son of Brian, during a vacancy in the see of Lincoln.*   [prob. 1167 × c. May 1173]

> Mentioned only, in the confirmation of the church to Newnham priory by William of Blois, bp of Lincoln, in 1203 × 1206: BL, Harley ms 3656 (Newnham cartulary), fo. 52r–v (58r–v). s. xv in.; pd, *Newnham Cartulary*, i, 61–2, no. 98; (calendar), *EEA* IV, 169–70, no. 266.

. . . Noveritis nos [*sc.* the bishop] confirmasse . . . canonicis de N. ecclesiam de Gravenhirst' quam ad presentationem dilecti filii Willelmi filii Brien et admissionem Nicholai quondam archidiaconi Bed' vacante sede Linc' adepti [fo. 52v] sunt, prout ex cartis dictorum W. et Nicholai quas inspeximus perpendimus . . .

It seems likely that the admission was made during the vacancy at Lincoln between the death of bp Robert de Chesney at the end of 1166 and the election of Geoffrey Plantagenet, i.e., before the move of the canons to Newnham. For the identity of Lower Gravenhurst, see *VCH Beds*, ii, 338. No other notice of William son of Brian occurs, and the name may be an error for William son of Robert, who gave the advowson of his church of Gravenhurst to the canons of St Paul, Bedford, prob. in *c.* 1166 (*Newnham Cartulary*, ii, no. 938; see also ibid., i, no. 5).

56. *Acknowledgement that the chapel of St Mary, Bedford, with the tithes of Hordelhide, and the school of Bedford, which for some time he held with the assent of his fellow canons, belong to the church of St Paul, Bedford; and resignation of the same to prior Auger and the regular canons of the same church.*   [c. Apr. 1170 × c. 1180]

> B = BL, Harley ms 3656 (Newnham cartulary), fo. 88r (94r). s. xv in.
> Pd, *Newnham Cartulary*, i, 127–8, no. 196.

Universis sancte matris ecclesie filiis Nicholaus archidiaconus Bed', salutem. Noverit universitas vestra quod capellam sancte Marie de Bed' cum decimis de Hordelhida et scolas Bed', quas ego aliquamdiu assensu concanonicorum meorum in manu mea habui, confiteor esse de iure et pertinentia ecclesie sancti Pauli Bed', et ideo eas Augerio priori et conventui canonicorum regularium eiusdem ecclesie sponte mea resignavi. Hiis testibus.

The collegiate church of St Paul, Bedford, became an Augustinian house in *c.* 1165 and moved to Newnham in *c.* 1180 (Knowles and Hadcock, 167). Auger became prior in or shortly before April/May 1170 (*Heads*, 177).

57. *Notification that he has inducted and solemnly invested prior Auger and the canons of St Paul, Bedford, in the church of [Cockayne] Hatley, on a mandate from Walter, abbot of Colchester, and Stephen, prior of Holy Trinity [Aldgate], London, papal judges-delegate, who have settled the dispute over the church between the priory and William the chaplain in favour of the former and have invested the canons. The archdeacon has acted the more readily, having long known the church to belong to the prebend of Ascelin the canon in St Paul's church, Bedford, and having afterwards, at the canons' presentation, received William the priest to the perpetual vicarage of the church for an annual pension to them of two gold pieces.* [17 May 1170 × c. 1180]

B = BL, Harley ms 3656 (Newnham cartulary), fos. 210v–211r (217v–218r). s. xv in. Pd, *Newnham Cartulary*, ii, 390–1, no. 916.

Universis sancte matris ecclesie filiis Nicholaus dictus Bed' archidiaconus, salutem in domino. Noverit dilectio vestra quod Augerium priorem et canonicos sancti Pauli Bed' in corporalem possessionem ecclesie de Hattele induxi et sollempniter investivi ex mandato Walteri abbatis Colecestr' et Stephani prioris Sancte Trinitatis Lond'. Ipsi vero, testantibus literis a sede Romana impetratis, cause cognitionem que vertebatur inter prefatos canonicos et Willelmum capellanum super ecclesia de Hattele a summo pontifice susceperunt, et per legitimos testes iure canonicorum probato illis ecclesiam suam restituentes exinde investierunt et sic ordine iudiciario causam terminaverunt. Hanc igitur executionem ex auctoritate [fo. 211r] Romane sedis tanto libentius et diligentius celebrari quod ab ineunte etate ipsam ecclesiam pertinere vidi ad ecclesiam beati Pauli Bed' et specialiter ad prebendam quam Ascelinus canonicus tenebat. Postmodum vero de presentatione memoratorum canonicorum Willelmum presbiterum ad vicariam perpetuam ecclesie de Hattele suscepi duorum aureorum pensionem eis annuam ad festum sancti Michaelis soluturam,[a] qui propositis sacrosanctis ewangeliis se canonicam fidelitatem eis observaturum affirmavit. T(estibus).

a *Sic; ? rectius* soluturum

After the election of Stephen, prior of Holy Trinity, Aldgate (*Heads*, 174), and before the move to Newnham (Knowles and Hadcock, 167). The archdn is here executing the sentence of the judges-delegate, whose own act states that they have invested and inducted the canons and have ordered the execution of their sentence (*Newnham Cartulary*, ii, no. 917). A later statement by Bodin, parson of [Upper] Stondon and rural dean, shows that it was he who had actually carried out the investiture and induction on the orders of the archdn, transmitted by the latter's official, Robert, parson of Wilshamstead (ibid., no. 923).

58a. *Notification that, in his presence and in that of his chapter, Simon de Bueles has withdrawn his suit against the canons of Newnham and their clerk, Robert of Wilshamstead, over the church of St Mary, [Lower] Gravenhurst, and has surrendered the charter he had from William, lord of the estate of the church. The said Robert has, however, with the assent of the canons, admitted Simon to the church, to be held in his name for an annual pension of twenty shillings for as long as either of them lives out of religion.* [c. 1180 × 31 Mar. 1181]

B = BL, Harley ms 3656 (Newnham cartulary), fo. 88v (94v). s. xv in.
Pd, *Newnham Cartulary*, i, 128, no. 197.

Universis sancte matris ecclesie filiis Nicholaus archidiaconus Bed', salutem. Notum facimus universitati vestre Symonem de Bowel' in presentia nostra et capituli nostri spontanea voluntate recessisse a lite quam moverat adversus canonicos de N(ewenham) et adversus clericum eorum Robertum de Wilshamsted' super ecclesia de Gravenhurst', et reddidisse in manu mea cartam quam habebat de Willelmo domino fundi predicte ecclesie. Ipse autem Robertus supranominatus ipsum Symonem admisit in eandem ecclesiam, tenendam nomine ipsius pro viginti solidis reddendis ipsi Roberto annua pensione quamdiu uterque eorum vixerit extra religionem ad quatuor terminos: ad festum sancti Michaelis quinque solidos, ad festum sancti Andree quinque solidos, ad Anuntiationem sancte Marie quinque solidos, ad festum sancti Iohannis Baptiste quinque solidos. Et hoc fecit Robertus favore et assensu predictorum canonicorum de N. de quibus iamdictam tenet ecclesiam. Et sciendum quod predictus Symon canonicis prenominatis et Roberto prefato prestitit sacramentum corporaliter de indempnitate omnimoda et fidelitate eis servanda. In cuius rei t(estimonium).[a]

a Ending sic

After the move of the canons from St Paul's, Bedford, to Newnham, and before the latest possible date for the archdn's death death (Knowles and Hadcock, 167; above, no. 47n.). For the identity of the church, see above, no. 55n.

(?†) **58b.** *Expanded version of the same, stating that both the canons and Robert have admitted Simon to the church and adding that, if Simon resiles from the agreement, the canons and Robert will retain the church in their hands, and that, if anyone brings a suit against the canons or Robert concerning this church, Simon is to give them aid and counsel.* [c. 1180 × 31 Mar. 1181]

B = BL, Harley ms 3656 (Newnham cartulary), fo. 217r–v (224r–v). s. xv in.
Pd (noted incorrectly), *Newnham Cartulary*, ii, 403, no. 945.

Universis[a] sancte matris ecclesie filiis tam presentibus quam futuris Nicholaus archidiaconus Bed', salutem. Notum facimus universitati vestre Simonem de Bueles in presentia nostra et capituli[b] nostri spontanea voluntate recessisse a lite quam moverat adversus priorem et canonicos de N. et adversus Robertum clericum eorum super ecclesia sancte Marie in Gravenherst', et reddidisse in manu mea cartam quam habebat de Willelmo domino fundi predicte ecclesie. Ipsi autem canonici et Robertus supranominatus ipsum Simonem admiserunt in eandem ecclesiam nomine ipsius Roberti tenendam pro viginti solidis ipsi Roberto solvendis annua pensione quamdiu uterque eorum vixerit extra religionem ad quatuor terminos, scilicet ad festum sancti

Michaelis quinque solidos, ad festum sancti Andree quinque solidos, ad Anuntiationem sancte Marie in Martio quinque solidos, ad Nativitatem beati Iohannis Baptiste quinque solidos.[c] Et si iamdictus S. ab hac conventione resilierit, canonici predicti et predictus Robertus ecclesiam prenominatam in manu sua retinebunt, Simone predicto ab [fo. 217v] eadem ecclesia penitus amoto sine omni contradictione aut reclamatione quam ipse vel aliquis per ipsum eis inde faciat. Et si quis vel canonicis predictis vel Roberto clerico, ipse aut aliquis per ipsum, questionem moverit super hac ecclesia aut super quolibet de pertinentiis suis vel vexationem aliquam inferre presumpserit, Simon totiens nominatus secundum sacramentum eis prestitum de fidelitate obervanda auxilium eis et consilium legitimum prestare tenetur. Hanc autem conventionem fideliter et sine dolo tenendam, et c'. Hiis testibus, et c'.

a *Passages in small type as in no. 58a*   b *Ms* capellani   c *From this point the* text *is entirely different from no.* 58a

Date as for no. 58a. It is possible that the expanded text is a forgery, since it seems so much to Robert's and the canons' advantage, but, on the other hand, it may simply be an additional act issued at the same time as no. 58a, spelling out further details regarding Simon's obligations.

* 59.   *Ratification of the gift by Cecily of Milton and her sons to Beadlow priory of the church of Milton [Ernest], to which she presented the monks to the archdeacon and which, the see of Lincoln being vacant, he confirmed to them by his authority; and notification that, at his request, the monks have granted the church to Mr John of Bedford for life, as long as he remains a secular, for half a mark annually as vicar.*
[prob. 1167 × c. May 1173]

Mentioned only, as having been produced in an assize of darrein presentment in the king's court in Trinity term, 1214, between Robert of Milton and the priors of Beadlow and [Canons] Ashby: PRO, KB 26/58, m. 4r; pd, *CRR*, vii, 135–6.

. . . Profert [*sc.* the prior of Beadlow] etiam cartam Nicholai archidiaconi Bedeford', in qua continetur quod ipse ratam habet donationem quam Cecilia de Middelton' et filii eius fecerunt ecclesie sancte Marie Magdal', ad quam ipsa[a] Cecilia prefatos monachos ei presentavit, et quod ipse, quia sedes Linc' tunc vacavit, auctoritate sua eis confirmavit et quod predicti monachi, precatu eiusdem archidiaconi, concesserunt magistro Iohanni de Bedeford' predictam ecclesiam de Middelton' tenendam de eis tota vita sua, reddendo inde eis annuatim dimidiam marcam argenti nomine vicarii quamdiu vixerit in seculari habitu . . .

a *Interlined*

Probably during the vacancy at Lincoln between the death of Robert Chesney, 27 Dec. 1166, and the election of Geoffrey Platagenet (*Fasti Lincoln*, 2).

* 60.   *Reception, at the presentation of Simon Basset and William Ursel, of Mr John of Bedford to those parts of Milton [Ernest] church which they successfully claimed in King Henry II's court to be of their advowson; and confirmation to them of this institution and presentation.*   [? 1167 × c. May 1173]

Mentioned only, as having been produced in the same case as in no. 59.

. . . Profert [*sc.* the prior of Canons Ashby] etiam cartam Nicholai archidiaconi Bed', in qua continetur quod, ad presentationem*a* Simonis Basset et Willelmi Ursel, recepit magistrum Iohannem de Bedef' ad illas partes ecclesie de Middelton' quas dirationaverunt in curia regis Henrici regis filii inperatricis Matillidis esse de iure sue advocationis, et hanc institutionem et presentationem eis confirmavit . . .

    a Written over confirmationem *deleted*

Perhaps contemporary with no. 59. In 1214 the prior of Canons Ashby was claiming a quarter of the church (*CRR*, vii, 136).

Mr Laurence

61. *Grant to the canons regular of Waltham Holy Cross abbey, at the request of King Henry II, of a moiety of Arlesey church, which William the clerk held, to be converted to their own uses; and notification that, when he had canonically instituted the canons in the said vacant portion, he caused them to be inducted into corporal possession by his official, Mr Warin. In the chapter of Warden.*

Warden [c. 1180 × 6 July 1189]

    B = BL, Harley ms 391 (Waltham cartulary), fos. 97v–98r. s. xiii in. C = BL, Cotton ms Tiberius C ix (Waltham cartulary), fo. 142r. s. xiii med.
    Pd from B, *Coll. Top. et Gen.*, vi, 201; from B collated with C, *Waltham Charters*, 44–5, no. 82.

Omnibus ad quos presens scriptum pervenerit Laur(entius) archidiaconus Bedef', salutem in salutis auctore. Ad vestram universeque posteritatis vestre notitiam presentium inscriptione volumus pervenire nos, caritatis intuitu et domini nostri H. secundi illustris regis Anglorum petitione devota, concessisse canonicis regularibus in ecclesia Sancte Crucis de Wauth(am)*a* deo militantibus medietatem ecclesie de Ailriches*'b* cum omnibus suis pertinentiis, quam Willelmus clericus tenuit, eis cum omni integritate cessuram et propriis eorum usibus omnimodis profuturam, salva in omnibus Linc' ecclesie dignitate. Et cum prefatos canonicos in predicta portione vacante canonice instituissemus, eos per officialem nostrum magistrum Gar(inum)*c* in corporalem eius possessionem fecimus induci. Et ut memorata concessio perpetuis [fo. 98r] maneat illibata temporibus, eam presentis scripti tenore et sigilli nostri appensione*d* confirmavimus. His*e* testibus: magistro *f*Garino, Roberto de Wilshamestede, Bodino et Asketillo decanis, magistro Engelram, Hugone sacerdote de Henlawe, Adeodato de Meperteshale, et magistro Petro clerico nostro, et multis aliis presentibus in capitulo de Waredona.*f*

a Walth' *C*	*b* Alricheseie *C*	*c* Gwarinum *C*	*d* appositione *C*
e Hiis *C*	*f–f* Gwarino et c' *C*		

After the last occurrence of the archdn's predecessor, Nicholas, *c.* 1180 × 31 Mar. 1181, he himself being in office by Oct. × Dec. 1181 (*Fasti Lincoln*, 42), and before Henry II's death. The Augustinian canons were introduced into Waltham abbey, 11 June 1177 (*Waltham Charters*, no. 26 n. 4).

62. *Confirmation to the prior and convent of St Andrew, Northampton, of the church of Potton, and, at their presentation, admission and canonical institution of Ralph Foliot, archdeacon of Hereford, as perpetual vicar in the same for an annual pension to the monks of five marks.* [*c.* 1180 × *c.* 1190]

B = BL, Royal ms 11 B. ix (St Andrew's Northampton cartulary), fo. 36r. s. xiii ex.

Universis Cristi fidelibus ad quos presens scriptum pervenerit Laur(entius) archidiaconus Bedeford', salutem. Noverit universitas vestra me priori et conventui sancti Andree de Norh(am)t' ecclesiam de Potton' cum omnibus pertinentiis suis confirmasse, et ad presentationem illorum Rad(ulfum) Foliot archidiaconum Herfordie ad perpetuam vicariam ecclesie predicte admisisse et ipsum canonice in ipsam *ᵃperpetuum vicariumᵃ* instituisse; ita tamen quod predictus Rad(ulfus) singulis annis predictis monachis v. marcas argenti pro pensione annua persolvet, salvis in omnibus episcopalibus consuetudinibus et Linc' ecclesie dignitatibus.*ᵇ* Quod ut ratum et inconcussum habeatur, presentibus litteris et sigilli mei testimonio predictis monachis confirmavi. Hiis testibus: magistro Petro de Tilen', magistro Alano Linc' canonico, magistro Roberto de Hiboldestou',*ᶜ* magistro Alexandro de Norh(am)t', Ranulpho clerico filio Ran' clerici de Norh(am)t', Henrico decano de Haddon', Willelmo filio Ermenildi, Nicholao decano de Ravenesden', Boid(er)o decano, Hugone persona de Bluham.*ᵈ*

a–a Ms perpetuam vicariam   *b Sic*   *c Ms* Hiboldeston'
d Sic; ? for Blunham

After Laurence became archdn (above, no. 61n.), and before the grant by Ralph Foliot, archdn of Hereford, to the clerk of David, earl of Huntingdon, which has been dated 'shortly after 1186 × 1188' (above, no. 46 and n.).

63. *Confirmation to the regular canons of Dunstable priory of the gift in free, pure and perpetual alms of the church of Harlington made by Ralph Pirot, lord of the fee, and confirmed by his charter, save that Philip the clerk shall possess the church for life, paying the priory and canons two shillings annually.* [*c.* 1180 × 6 June 1199]

B = BL, Harley ms 1885 (Dunstable cartulary), fo. 23r (22r). s. xiii in.
Pd (calendar), *Dunstable Cartulary*, 49, no. 147.

Laurentius dei gratia archidiaconus Bedeford' omnibus ad quos presentes littere pervenerint, salutem. Noverit universitas vestra nos ratam habere donationem quam Rad(ulfus) Pirot fecit deo et ecclesie beati Petri de Dunst' et canonicis regularibus deo ibidem servientibus de ecclesie de Herlinged' cum omnibus appenditiis suis in liberam et puram et perpetuam elemosinam, qui dominus fundi esse dinoscitur, et eisdem carta sua confirmavit, salvo eo quod Philippus clericus tota vita sua predictam possidebit ecclesiam, solvendo annuatim duos solidos nomine ecclesie de Herlingedun' predicte ecclesie de Dunst' et eiusdem loci canonicis. Et ut hec donatio perpetuis debeat illibata observari temporibus, eam presentis scripti patrocinio et sigilli nostri appensione confirmavimus, salva in omnibus Linc' ecclesie dignitate. Hiis testibus: Osberto decano, magistris Guarino et Petro, et c'.

After Laurence became archdn (above, no. 61n.) and before the first occurrence of his successor, Richard, 6 June 1199 (*Fasti Lincoln*, 42).

64. *Notification that in his presence Richard, clerk and vicar of Husborne [Crawley], has resigned and given up all his right in that church, the prior of Dunstable being present and producing authentic writings showing that the church had been properly given to the canons of Dunstable and that the prior had been canonically instituted; and grant of the church to the uses of the canons by the authority of the church of Lincoln.* [1182 × 8 May 1183 or 1185 × 25 May 1186]

B = BL, Harley ms 1885 (Dunstable cartulary), fo. 21v (20v). s. xiii in.
Pd (calendar), *Dunstable Cartulary*, 44, no. 127.

Laurentius archidiaconus Bedef' omnibus sancte ecclesie filiis ad quos littere iste pervenerint, in salutis auctore salutem. Noverit fraternitas vestra Ricardum clericum de Husseburne, qui vicariam in ecclesia ipsius ville habuisse dinoscitur, in presentia nostra cessionem fecisse, et ius universum quod in ipsa ecclesia habuit resignasse, priore de Dunst' presente et auctentica scripta producente in quibus fuit manifeste*ᵃ* expressum canonicis de Dunst' congruam donationem de ipsa ecclesia factam fuisse et priorem canonice institutum fuisse. Unde, scriptorum veritate*ᵇ* et virorum prudentium testimonio indubitanter certificati, predictam ecclesiam predictis canonicis auctoritate Lincoln' ecclesie cum universis pertinentiis eiusdem ecclesie usibus eorum cessuram concessimus et sigillo nostro corroboravimus, salva in omnibus Lincoln' ecclesie dignitate. Hiis testibus: magistro Guarino, Roberto de Wilsam(estede),*ᶜ* et c'.

a Ms repeats fuit *here*   *b Ms* veritati   *c For expansion, see no. 61*

While Laurence was archdeacon of Bedford (*Fasti Lincoln,* 42) and, given the reference to the authority of Lincoln cathedral, during the vacancy in the see following either the resignation of Bishop Geoffrey or the translation to Rouen of Walter of Coutances (ibid., 2–3).

65. *Grant, with the consent of the chapter of York minster, to abbot R(alph) and the convent of Fountains of a toft formerly held by Ulfkil belonging to the archdeacon's prebend in Clifton, to be held in perpetuity for forty pence annually to him and his successors. The abbot and convent have confirmed by their charter that they will not have or occupy any land or pasture in that vill to the detriment of this or any other prebend.* [6 Nov. 1190 × Jan. 1194]

B = BL, Cotton ms Tiberius C xii (Fountains cartulary), fo. 283v. s. xv.
Pd, *EYC*, i, 139, no. 163; (calendar), *Fountains Cartulary*, i, 171.

Omnibus sancte matris ecclesie filiis presentibus et futuris Laurentius archidiaconus Bedeford', salutem. Noverit universitas vestra me consensu capituli sancti Petri Ebor' concessisse et hac carta mea confirmasse domino R. abbati et conventui de Fontibus unum thoftum de prebenda mea iuxta aquam in Clyftona, quod Ulfkil prius tenuit, tenendum in perpetuum libere et quiete, reddendo annuatim pro omni servitio michi et successoribus meis xl. denarios in festo sancti Martini. Et predictus abbas et conventus carta sua confirmaverunt quod nullam terram vel pasturam in prefata villa aliquo modo habebunt vel occupabunt unde ius vel conditio illius prebende vel aliarum prebendarum in aliquo deterioretur. Testibus: Galfrido archidiacono Cliveland', magistro S. Apulie, R. preposito Beverlac', Radulfo archidiacono, W. de Stiandebi,*ᵃ* *ᵇ*W.

fratre P. de Ledes,[b] Willelmo Win capellano, W. de Buthun, Waltero capellano et notario.

a Ms Stiliend'   *b–b Punctuation uncertain*

After the death of Ralph's predecessor as abbot of Fountains, 6 Nov. 1190 (*Heads*, 133), and before Simon de Apulia left for Rome (Jan. 1194), where he was appointed dean of York by the pope in May (Clay, 'Deans of York', 374); Ralph the archdn is Ralph, archdn of York, who was among those who went with Simon of Apulia, and died on the return journey (ibid.). Geoffrey Muschamp, archdn of Cleveland, was consecrated bp of Coventry, 21 June 1198 (*EEA* 16,110). Archdn Laurence held the prebend of Strensall (*York Minster Fasti*, ii, 71).

66.   *Testimony, with the [rural] deans of Bedford, Luton, Langford and Ravensden, to R(ichard), abbot of Grimsby, J(ohn), abbot of Thornton, and W(illiam), prior of Elsham [? papal judges-delegate], that they have made inquiries through all the deaneries as to whether John, whom Walter de Neville claims to have been parson of the church of [Cockayne] Hatley, ever had or acquired any right in the same; and that all declared that John had acquired no such right, and that the prior and canons of Newnham had for many years held the church as parsons as an ancient prebend of the church of St Paul, Bedford.* [? *c.* Jan. 1198]

B = BL, Harley ms 3656 (Newnham cartulary), fo. 212r (219r). s. xv in.
Pd, *Newnham Cartulary*, ii, 393, no. 921.

Venerabilibus amicis suis et dominis R. et I. de Grimesby et de Thorton' abbatibus et W. priori de Ellesham, Laurentius archidiaconus Bed', et W. et R. et A. et H. de Bed' et de Luyton' et de Langef' et de Ravenesdene decani, verum in domino salutare. Testimonium veritati perhibere super beneficiis ecclesiasticis nostre sollicitudini commissis nostri interest officii, et que plena cognitione gesta didicimus publice protestari. Hac igitur ducti ratione, vestre discretioni significandum duximus quod, multa diligentia et attestatione debita, debite ac sollempniter per cunctos decanatus publice tam vicariis quam personis diligenter inquisivimus ea qua decet adhibita sollempnitate utrum I., quem Walterus de Novavilla personam asserit extitisse in ecclesia de Hattele, aliquo tempore ius personatus vel vicarii in memorata ecclesia optinuerit, vel utrum aliquid iuris ex institutione episcopi diocesani vel archidiaconi vel alicuius officialium suorum in eadem ecclesia nactus[a] fuerit. Protestati sunt siquidem singuli et universi memoratum Iohannem omnibus incognitum et nichil iuris penitus alicuius auctoritate optinuisse, priorem vero et canonicos de N(ewenham) ius personatus in eadem ecclesia assecutos eam pluribus annis sicut personas possedisse tanquam ius ecclesie beati Pauli Bed' antiquitus prebendatum. Huius rei testes sumus et in veritate quod[b] deus est protestamur. Valete in domino, et c'.

a Ms nectus   *b Sic*

Dating uncertain, but perhaps close to that of the final concord between Adam de Port and St Paul's, Bedford, 26 Jan. 1198 (*Newnham Cartulary*, ii, no. 912).

67. *Notification to R(oger), dean of Lincoln, that, on receipt of letters of the archbishop of Canterbury, he made inquiry through the archdeaconry of Bedford as to whether Stevington church was correctly adjudged to the nuns of Harrold by papal judges-delegate, and found that it was; when he warned B(aldwin) of Guines and his accomplices to restore the church to the nuns, they refused and were excommunicated by the archdeacon, but have not desisted* [1198 × 6 June 1199]

> B[1] = Private collection (formerly Bristol, Baptist College, ms Z. c. 23), psalter with copies of Harrold charters, fo(s). unknown. s. xiii in.
>
> Pd, C. R. Cheney, 'Harrold priory: a twelfth-century dispute', *Beds Hist. Rec. Soc.* 32 (1952 for 1951), 17, no. 9; repr., idem, *Medieval Texts and Studies*, 303–4, no. 9.

Venerabili domino et amico karissimo magistro R. decano Lincoln' suus L. archidiaconus Bedeford', salutem in vero salutari. Post susceptionem literarum domini Cant' michi denuo transmissarum, diligenti facta inquisitione per archidiaconatum Bedeford' utrum ecclesia de Stiventon' sententia iudicum a domino papa delegatorum monialibus de Harewold' rationabiliter esset adiudicata, assertione multorum michi constitit predictam ecclesiam sententialiter fuisse monialibus adiudicatam et ipsas eam aliquo tempore possedisse; quam cum B. de Ginnes et complices sui iniuste occupassent et detinerent contra iustitiam occupatam, ipsum, ut decuit, commonui ut monialibus predictam ecclesiam restitueret et a[a] tam enormi[b] temeritate desisteret. Quem cum salubres monitus meos contempnere et manifestum et notorium intrusorem viderem, sicut ex mandato domini Cant' et vestro suscepi, ipsum B. et complices suos ob manifestam et notoriam intrusionem sententia excommunicationis innodavi et ab omnibus quasi excommunicatos cautius evitari precepi. Ipsi vero nichilominus ab incepta temeritate [non][c] desistunt.

> *a Interlined*   *b Ms* anormi, *with a deleted*   *c Supplied*

After the probable date of the sentence of the judges-delegate (Cheney, 'Harrold priory', 14–15, no. 4) and before the first occurrence of Laurence's successor as archdn (*Fasti Lincoln*, 42). The archbp's mandate to hold the inquiry had been sent to the dean of Lincoln, who had passed it on to the relevant archdn (Cheney, 'Harrold priory', 7; Kemp, 'Informing the archdeacon', 142–3).

[1] It has not been possible to inspect this ms. The text given here is taken from the printed edition.

Mr Richard

68. *Notification, to all faithful of Christ in the archdeaconry of Bedford, of the settlement in his presence of the dispute between the prior and canons of Newnham and Robert de Broy, clerk, over the tithes of Simon de Beauchamp's assarts at Ravensden; the prior and canons have granted the tithes to Robert for as long as he remains a secular for an annual pension of half a mark of silver.* [1199 × 25 Sept. 1205]

> B = BL, Harley ms 3656 (Newnham cartulary), fo. 123v (129v). s. xv in.
>
> Pd, *Newnham Cartulary*, i, 206, no. 427.

Universis Cristi fidelibus per archidiaconatum Bed' constitutis magister Ricardus archidiaconus Bed', salutem in domino. Rerum gestarum series scripture testimonio solet commendari ne ea que concordia mediante sopita sunt in residivam rursus devocentur contentionem[a] vel tractu temporis in oblivionem deducantur. Eapropter volumus ad communem omnium notitiam pervenisse controversiam inter priorem et canonicos de N(ewenham) et Robertum clericum de Broy super decimis de essartis Symonis de Bellocampo apud Raven' diutius actitatam demum in presentia nostra in hunc modum conquievisse. Videlicet quod prefati prior et canonici concesserunt prescripto Roberto clerico de Broy memoratas decimas quamdiu in seculari habitu vixerit, tenendas de ipsis reddendo inde eis annuatim nomine pensionis dimidiam marcam argenti, videlicet xx. d' ad Natale domini et xx. d' ad Pascha et xx. d' ad festum sancti Iohannis Baptiste et xx. d' ad festum sancti Michaelis; quod idem Robertus sine dolo se facturum tactis sacrosanctis evangeliis coram multis iuravit. Hiis testibus, et c'.

a Ms conventionem

Richard's predecessor as archdn, Laurence, last occurs after late 1198, and Richard was himself archdn by 6 June 1199; his successor was in office at the latest by 25 Sept. 1205 (*Fasti Lincoln*, 42).

ARCHDEACONRY OF BUCKINGHAM

Richard de Urville

* 69.   *Gift to Missenden abbey of one hide of land [in Missenden], for which while he lives the archdeacon, and after his death his brother, Peter, will do the service due to the overlord.*   1140

B = Bodl. ms Willis 5 (transcripts from lost Missenden cartulary), fo. 23r (abbreviated). s. xviii in.
Pd (calendar), *Missenden Cartulary*, i, 241, App. A, no. 13.

Anno D. Inc. M° C° XL° facta carta Ric' archid' de Hida.
Notificetur sancte ecclesie filiis francis et angligenis*a* quod Ricardus de Urvilla archidiaconus de Buchingaham dedit terram suam in elemosinam abbatie de Messendena liberam et quietam ab omni servitio sicut divisa est. Et ipsemet Ricardus tam diu quam vixerit predictam terram adversus dominum deserviet et post obitum Ricardi Petrus frater eius. Et hi sunt testes donationis: Hugo de Messend', Radulfus presbiter, et Galfr(idus) presbiter de al(ia)*b* Messend', Bernardus de Burnea, et Willelmus clericus de Woburna, &c.

a Sic   *b Expansion uncertain*

The transcript by Browne Willis is evidently in part a Latin calendar. The confirmation by King Stephen locates the land in Missenden, and Walter Giffard's confirmation of the abbey's foundation, which is witnessed by archdn Richard, makes reference to the latter's land and wood in Missenden (*Regesta*, iii, no. 586; *Missenden Cartulary*, i, no. 39).

David

70. *Notification that, having established in public synod before him [at Aylesbury] that the churches of Wraysbury and Langley [Marish] had been rightly given to the abbot and monks of Gloucester, and hearing that they had been violently despoiled of them and the intruder had not come to justice, he has adjudged the investiture of the churches to Gloucester and, by judgement of the whole synod, has inducted the abbot into possession of the churches by handing over their keys.* [1140 × 25 Feb. 1148]

B = PRO, C150/1 (Gloucester cartulary), fos. 189v–190r (172v–173r). s. xiii ex.
Pd, *Gloucester Cartulary*, ii, 166–7, no. 706.

Quoniam ea que ad utilitatem ecclesie spectant diligenter providere et efficaciter implere, credita nobis dispensatione, debemus, ideo ego David Bugingham' dei gratia archidiaconus tam presenti etati quam future posteritati quod de causa abbatis et monachorum Gloucestr' in presentia nostra actum est de ecclesiis de Wiretesbir' et Langeleya presenti scripto notificare curavi. Causa igitur hac in pupplica synodo in medium deducta, predictas illas duas ecclesias ecclesie Gloucestr' donatas fuisse rationabiliter tam cartarum confirmatione quam presentis synodi attestatione cognovimus. Unde ipsam per cuiusdam violentam[a] intrusionem iniuste spoliatam[b] audientes, cum intrusum illum sepius ad iusti[fo. 190r]tiam vocavissemus, nec ille nec aliquis pro eo se iustitie presentaverit, investituram earumdem ecclesiarum abbati et ecclesie Glouc' adiudicavimus, et per claves ipsarum ecclesiarum eum in possessionem earundem totius synodi nostre adiudicatione induximus.

a Ms violentiam   *b Ms* spoliatum

After David became archdn, 1140 × Sept. 1142 (*Fasti Lincoln*, 39–40), and, since the case was delegated to him by Alexander, bp of Lincoln (see below), probably before the bp's death (*Fasti Lincoln*, 2). This case is discussed by Kemp, 'Towards admission and institution', 173–4; the testimony of Gilbert Foliot, former abbot of Gloucester, shows that, on receiving the abbey's complaint, Alexander had delegated the case to the archdn, and that the synod was held at Aylesbury (*Gloucester Cartulary*, 168–9, no. 708; *Foliot Letters and Charters*, no. 371).

* 71. *Notification that, at the presentation and gift of William of Sherington, he has canonically inducted the monks of Newport [Pagnell] priory into the church of Sherington.* [1140 × 18 Apr. 1161]

Mentioned only, in an assize of darrein presentment in the king's court in Trinity term, 1229, between John de Carn and the prior of Newport [Pagnell]: PRO, KB 26/102, m. 17r; pd, *CRR*, xiii, 475–6, no. 2228.

. . . Profert [*sc.* the prior of Newport] etiam litteras patentes Davidis quondam archidiaconi Buk' que testantur quod ipse canonice introduxit monachos de Neuport in ecclesiam de Shirinton' ad presentationem et donationem Willelmi de Shirinton' . . .

While David was archdn (*Fasti Lincoln*, 39–40) and before the latest possible date for bp Robert Chesney's general confirmation to the priory, which includes this church (*EEA* I, no. 183).

72. *Settlement, in his presence and that of the whole chapter of Buckingham, of the dispute between Eynsham abbey and the church of Turweston over two-thirds of the demesne tithes of Turweston; Richard, the incumbent, has admitted that his church has no right in the tithes, which had long ago been given to Eynsham abbey by Ralph de Scotville and Emma, his wife.*   [Feb. × 19 Dec. 1148]

  B = Oxford, Christ Church, D. & C. Lib., vi. a. 2 (Eynsham Cartulary), fo. 34v,
    no. 115. s. xii ex.
  Pd, *Eynsham Cartulary*, i, 99–100, no. 115.

David archidiaconus de Bucchingeham omnibus catholice matris ecclesie filiis, salutem. Post multam disceptationem inter monasterium de Egnesham et ecclesiam de Torveston' super duabus partibus decimationis de dominio prefate Torveston', sub nostra presentia et totius Buchehamensis capituli, Ricardus in prefata ecclesia ordinatus confessus est in discussione de iure ecclesiam suam in his duabus partibus nichil iuris habere, set eas antiquitus ex donatione Radulfi de Scotvilla et eius uxoris Emme Egneshamnensi monasterio collatas fuisse; idque nostro et capituli testimonio et iudicio ratum habetur. His testibus: Willelmo priore de Luffeld', magistro Roberto de Burneham, Bern(ardo) de Winesl'.

This settlement occurred during a vacancy in the see of Lincoln (*Eynsham Cartulary*, i, 3); the editor of the cartulary suggested the vacancy following bp Robert Chesney's death (1166), but, since William, prior of Luffield, died in 1164, it was clearly the vacancy between bp Alexander and bp Robert in 1148 (*Heads*, 53; *Fasti Lincoln*, 2).

73. *Notification that, when he was acting in place of the archdeacon of Lincoln, William, clerk of Newton [in Aveland], surrendered the church in his presence; and, with his assent, the monks of [St Andrew's] Northampton were inducted into the same by the hand of Robert, bishop of Lincoln, which he (the archdeacon) has confirmed in perpetual alms, saving the right of Laurence, his clerk, so long as he remains a secular.*
[19 Nov. 1160 × 27 Dec. 1166]

  B = BL, Royal ms 11 B. ix (St Andrew's Northampton cartulary), fo. 35v. s xiii ex. C =
    BL, Cotton ms Vespasian E xvii (St Andrew's Northampton cartulary), fo. 246v
    (231v). s. xv med.

David archidiaconus Buching'*ᵃ* omnibus fidelibus dei, salutem. Noscat*ᵇ* universitas vestra Willelmum clericum Nevent'*ᶜ* ecclesiam de Nevent'*ᶜ* sub presentia nostra, dum vices archidiaconi in provincia Linc' ageremus, omnino refutasse et per manum domini Roberti Linc' episcopi dilectos filios nostros monachos*ᵈ* Norh(am)t'*ᵉ* in eadem introductos esse, nostro interveniente assensu. Eandem itaque eis in perpetuam elemosinam concessimus et auctoritate nostra confirmavimus, salvo iure Laurentii clerici*ᶠ* nostri quamdiu vixerit in habitu seculari. Teste magistro Petro, Stephano de Eccheton', Willelmo Burdon', Roberto Grimbaud.*ᵍ*

  a Boching' *C*   *b* Noverit *C*   *c* Newenton' *C*   *d* monacos *B*
  e North' *C*   *f* canonici *in episcopal act (see note)*   *g* Grimbald' *C*

The dating limits are those of the bp of Lincoln's act concerning the same matter (*EEA* I, no. 196). Why David was acting for the archdn of Lincoln, who was Robert (*Fasti Lincoln*, 25), is unknown, but he was the first witness to the bp's act, heading a list of seven archdns, including six of the diocese, a fact which perhaps suggests that Robert was either abroad or indisposed. The present act makes it very likely that 'Richard archdn of Lincoln', the seventh of the bp's witnesses, was not an otherwise unknown archdn of Lincoln, but Richard de Almaria, archdn of what became known as Stow (cf. *EEA* I, no. 73n.). David also occurs as *locum tenens* of archdn Robert in 1155 × 1160 (*Gilbertine Charters*, Sixle 5).

Mr Robert of Burnham

74. *Notification that Nigel, prior of Bradwell, has in his presence renounced the right which he had in the church of Thornborough, in the presence of Hamo son of Meinfelin, patron of the church; and, at the latter's presentation, canonical institution of John, prior of Luffield, in the same.* [1177 × 1184]

> A = Westminster Abbey Muniments, no. 3042. Endorsed: De Roberto archidiacono Bukinh' (s. xiii); Thorneberg' (s. xiii ex.). Size 143 × 63 + 16 mm. Seal in varnished white wax on tag (method 1), pointed oval (*c.* 43 × 27 mm); obverse: frontally standing ecclesiastic, arms outstretched; legend unclear.
> B = Ibid., Muniment Book 10 (Luffield cartulary), fols. 24v–25r. s. xv ex.
> Pd from A, *Luffield Charters*, i, 43, no. 36 (with facsimile).

Universis sancte et*a* catholice ecclesie filiis Robertus archidiaconus de Buchingeham,*b* salutem. Noscat presens universitas et subsecutura posteritas Nigellum priorem de Bradewell'*c* in nostra presencia constitutum renunciasse iuri quod habebat in ecclesia de Torneberg',*d* presente Hamone filio Meinfelinni qui ius patronatus habebat in ecclesia illa, et me presentacione eius et peticione Iohannem priorem de Luffeld*e* canonice instituisse in eadem ecclesia. His testibus: Alano filio Meinfel', Bertholomeo*f* de Lugton', Rogero vis delue,*g* Iohanne decano, Radulfo filio Berneri, Rogero filio Azeri, Thoma de Torneberg',*d* Alardo de Burneam.

a Om. in B	*b* Bukingeham B	*c* Bradewelle B	*d* Thorneberg' B
e Luffelde B	*f* Spelling sic	*g* vis delue sic	

After the probable date of death of the archdn's predecessor in Jan. 1177 (*Fasti Lincoln,* 40) and before the death of Hamo son of Meinfelin in 1184 (*Rot. de Dominabus,* 38). Bradwell priory had been founded by Meinfelin, lord of Wolverton, as a cell of Luffield in the early 1140s, with William, prior of Luffield (d. 1164), as its first prior (*Luffield Charters,* ii, p. xiv). The present act seems to have followed the settlement by papal judges-delegate of a dispute between Luffield priory and Hamo son of Meinfelin, which entailed Luffield's renunciation of its right over Bradwell and Hamo's gift of Thornborough church to Luffield (*Luffield Charters,* i, no. 39; *EEA* VII, no. 167).

75. *Confirmation to the priory and monks of Luffield of the chapel of Evershaw, in accordance with the tenor of Hugh of Evershaw's charter and the gift of his ancestors.* [1177 × 22 Mar. 1194]

> A = Westminster Abbey Muniments, no. 2492. Endorsed: De capella de Eversawe (s. xiii); Littera Roberti archidiaconi Buck' (s. xiii ex.). Size 153 × 48 mm (36 to tongue). Seal[1] in light brown wax on tongue <u>and</u> wrapping tie, in fine canvas bag (uncoloured), reconstructed from fragments, pointed oval (*c.* 47 × 31 mm); obverse, frontally standing ecclesiastic, arms outstretched, holding ?banner or book in his left hand; legend: + SIGILL' R . . .TI . . . .IA[C]ON[I] . . .
> B = Ibid., Muniment Book 10 (Luffield cartulary), fo. 33r. s. xv ex.

Pd from A, *Luffield Charters*, i, 70, no. 67 (original wrongly cited); from B, *Mon. Ang.*, iv, 350, n. 11.

Omnibus sancte matris ecclesie filiis Robertus archidiaconus de Buchingham,[a] salutem. Noscat universitas vestra me, secundum tenorem carte Hugonis de Eversawe[b] et[c] donacionem antecessorum suorum, capellam de Eversawe[b] cum omnibus pertinenciis liberam et quietam ecclesie sancte Marie de Luffeld[d] et fratribus eiusdem loci deo servientibus confirmasse et sigilli mei munimine roborasse. Testibus his:[e] Michaele decano de Blechesl', et Iohanne decano de Prestona, et magistro Philippo de Lillingston'.

a Buk' *B*   b Evershawe *B*   c in *B*   d Luffelde *B*   e hiis *B*

After the probable date of the death of the archdn's predecessor in Jan. 1177, and before the date by which his successor, Stephen de Swafeld, had ceased to be chancellor of Lincoln (*Fasti Lincoln,* 40). The seal on this act, even allowing for its reconstructed state, differs from that on no. 74, both in size and possibly in some of its detail. Evershaw chapel became a church in the 13th century, but the place decayed in the later middle ages and the chapel/church fell into disuse in the later 16th century; Evershaw is now in Biddlesden parish (*VCH Bucks,* iv, 157; *Bucks Place-Names,* 42).

[1] A nearly complete impression of this seal survives on a chirograph in New College, Oxford, Archive 11991, dated 1182 (*Newington Longeville Charters,* no. 23). It measures 47 × 31 mm, shows a saltire cross on the ?banner or book held by the archdn, and has the legend: + SIGILL' ROBERTI AR . . .IACONI DE BUCKINH'.

76. *Notification of the settlement before him in full chapter at Aylesbury of the dispute between the prior of Luffield and Gilbert of Mursley over two-thirds of the demesne tithes of Salden; viz. that Gilbert has entirely renounced them to the priory.*
[1177 × 22 Mar. 1194]

A = Westminster Abbey Muniments, no. 2583. Endorsed: Saldenne (s. xiii); Littera Roberti archidiaconi Buck' (s. xiii ex.). Size 153 × 38 mm (27 to tongue). Seal missing, tongue and wrapping tie surviving.
Pd, *Luffield Charters*, i, 71, no. 67A.

Omnibus sancte matris ecclesie filiis Robertus archidiaconus de Buchingham, salutem. Sciatis controversiam que vertebatur inter priorem de Luffeld et Gilebertum de Muresle taliter coram nobis apud Ailesbiri in pleno capitulo esse sopitam: quod ipse Gilebertus iuri quod se asserebat habere in duabus partibus decimarum de dominio de Saldene, scilicet de xx. acris et de cotariis, omnino renunciavit et ecclesie sancte Marie de Luffeld integre resignavit. Valete in domino.

Date as for no. 75. Gilbert was presumably the incumbent of Mursley church.

77. *Ratification and confirmation of Walter de Chesney's gift and confirmation to Dunstable priory of the church of Cublington in free, pure and perpetual alms; and 'inparsonation' of the prior in the church.* [1177 × 15 July 1186]

B = BL, Harley ms 1885 (Dunstable cartulary), fo. 23r (22r). s. xiii in.
Pd (calendar), *Dunstable Cartulary*, 50, no. 150.

Robertus dei gratia archidiaconus de Buch' omnibus ad quos presentes littere pervenerint, salutem. Noverit universitas vestra me ratam habere donationem quam Walterus de Kainoto deo et ecclesie beati Petri de Dunst(aplia) et canonicis regularibus ibidem deo servientibus de ecclesia sancti Nicholai de Cublint(on') fecit et carta sua confirmavit cum omnibus pertinentiis suis in liberam et puram et perpetuam elemosinam. Et ut hec donatio in posterum illibata et integra observetur, predictam elemosinam predictis canonicis de Dunst' in perpetuum possidendam presentis scripti patrocinio et sigilli nostri appositione confirmavimus, et priorem de Dunst' de predicta ecclesia inpersonavimus. Hiis testibus: magistro Alardo, Petro capellano de Cestresham, et c'.

After the death of David, Robert's predecessor in the archdeaconry (*Fasti Lincoln*, 40), and before the final concord over this church between the prior of Dunstable and another party (*Dunstable Cartulary*, no. 152).

78. *Ratification and confirmation of Ralph of Weedon's gift to St Albans abbey of the tithes of his demesne of Chesham.*
[1177 × autumn 1186; poss. Nov. 1180 × Mar. 1182]

B = BL, Cotton ms Julius D iii (St Albans sacrist's cartulary), fo. 122r. ss. xiv ex.–xv in.

Universis sancte matris ecclesie filiis presentibus et futuris Robertus de Burneham archidiaconus Buchingeh', salutem. Nosse[a] volumus universitatem vestram nos ratam habere donationem et concessionem quam Radulfus de Wedduna fecit deo et ecclesie Sancti Albani de decimis dominii sui de Cestresham, secundum formam carte quam monachi ecclesie Sancti Albani de eodem Radulfo optinuerunt. Et ut hec concessio stabili gaudeat firmitate, eam auctoritate officii[b] roboramus et sigilli nostri munimine confirmamus. Teste[a] Rodberto priore Sancti Edmundi, Benedicto monacho eius, magistro Osberto, Symone de Merstoun', et multis aliis.

    a Sic   *b ?Insert* nostri

While Robert was archdn (*Fasti Lincoln*, 40) and before the agreement, dated autumn 1186, by which the prior of Dunstable was to hold the tithes of the sacrist for seven years (cartulary, fos. 122v–123r); possibly during the vacancy in the abbacy of Bury St Edmunds following abbot Hugh I's death, when Robert the prior was in charge of the abbey and Benedict was a senior monk there (*Heads*, 32; *Chronicle of Jocelin of Brakelond*, 8–9, 16). Ralph of Weedon's charter of gift to St Albans abbey, *ad luminaria in predicta ecclesia invenienda*, is cartulary, fo. 122r–v. The Weedon family's estate in Chesham was held of the earls of Oxford, i.e., within the parish of the moiety of Chesham church held by Woburn abbey (*VCH Bucks*, iii, 213, and cf. 206, 216; see also below, no. 79n.).

79. *Notification of the settlement before him in his chapter at Chesham, on the morrow of St Bartholomew next after the death of King Henry II, of the dispute between the monks of St Albans and of Woburn over certain tithes* de novalibus *of Ralph of Weedon [in Chesham], which the monks of St Albans claimed to have held for a long time through farmers until they were deprived by lay power, complaining that the monks of Woburn have collected the tithes for some time and presumed to convert them to their own uses; the tithes were adjudged to belong to the monks of St Albans, whom the archdeacon has put in possession.* Chesham, 25 August 1189

B = BL Cotton ms Julius D iii (St Albans sacrist's cartulary), fo. 121r–v. ss. xiv ex.–xv in.

Omnibus ad quorum notitiam presens scriptum pervenerit Robertus archidiaconus de Buching', salutem. Veritatis assertio libera et sine offensione solet
procedere quotiens certis rerum nititur argumentis et celeberime opinionis
attestatione vallatur. Hac igitur consideratione inducti, hoc quod in nostra
presentia in capitulo nostro apud Cestresham, cui in crastinum sancti Bartholomei proximum post mortem domini nostri regis Henrici secundi deo auctore
presedimus, inter monachos Sancti Albani et de Woburne super quibusdam
decimis de novalibus Radulfi de Wedon' actum est in publicam deferre notitiam
congruum iudicamus. Conquerebantur quidem nobis monachi Sancti Albani se
absque iure et ratione per violentiam laice potestatis decimis de essartis Radulfi
de Wedon' spoliatos fuisse, quas monachi de Woburn' in detrimentum iuris
ecclesie Sancti Albani colligere aliquandiu et irrationabiliter possidere et in usus
suos convertere invitis monachis Sancti Albani presumpserunt, quas etiam
monachi Sancti Albani per tempora longa et dies multos ecclesie sue pertinuisse
et se illas cum omni integritate aliquando per interpositam personam, videlicet
per firmarios suos illarum decimarum, percepisse constanter asserebant, donec
per laicam potestatem eis possessio [fo. 121v] decimarum predictarum pertur-
baretur, et ad hoc docendum totius capituli et confinii*a* testimonium audacter
flagitabant. Monachi de Woburn' nichil in contrarium probare potuerunt, set
aliquando decimas illas se percepisse dicebant et eas sibi in pace permitti
postulabant. Nos vero, qui veritatis et iustitie servi sumus, veritatis et iustitie
tramitem prosequi desiderantes ut iusticia utrique partium quod suum erat
rationabiliter exiberet, iudicium capituli fecimus exinde in commune proferri;
iudicantes vero monachis Sancti Albani decimas pretaxatas libere de cetero
percipiendas et possidendas adiudicaverunt. Sententia vero sicut intelleximus
legitime et iuste prolata, monachos Sancti Albani in possessionem decimarum
illarum misimus, sicut iuris ordo postulabat. Qui postquam decime celebri
sententia eis adiudicate fuerunt, ne quid in preiudicium ecclesie sue super
decimis illis aliquid mollirentur, audiente toto capitulo solempniter appellaver-
unt.*b* Hoc in presentia nostra die supradicto et loco actum fuisse testamur, et
ideo scriptum sigilli nostri testimonio roboramus. His testibus: Anketillo
quondam priore de Messenden', magistro Alardo officiali, Laurentio decano,
Petro de Witecherche, Willelmo capellano prioris de Dunestaple, et Willelmo
capellano, Ricardo Barre et Thoma capell' de Aumodesham, Radulfo de
Wedon', Ricardo de Broch, et multis aliis.

  a Reading uncertain   *b Reading uncertain; ms* appella

The rubric locates the tithes in Chesham. Before 1194 Woburn abbey acquired the
moiety in Chesham church that was originally appurtenant to the manor of Chesham
Higham, held of the earls of Oxford, from which manor Ralph of Weedon held an estate
(*VCH Bucks*, iii, 216). Mr Alard, the archdn's official, is probably Mr Alard of Burnham,
the archdn's brother, later archdn of London and dean of St Paul's (*Fasti St Paul's*, i, 32,
10, 6). The prior of Dunstable's chaplain probably appears among the witnesses because
the priory had leased Ralph of Weedon's demesne tithes from St Albans for seven years in
1186 (BL, Cott. Julius D iii, fos. 122v–123r). Among the other witnesses, Peter of
Whitchurch witnessed a further settlement between St Albans and Woburn, to be dated
1189 × 1195, as dean of Whitchurch, Laurence did so as dean of Chesham, and William
as chaplain of Chesham church (ibid., fos. 123r–124r).

80. *Grant to the monks of Walden of an annual pension of five marks in the church of Amersham, to be paid by the clerk who shall hold the church.*

[1177 × 22 Mar. 1194]

B = BL, Harley ms 3697 (Walden cartulary), fo. 61r, no. 1. s. xiv ex.

Universis sancte matris ecclesie filiis Robertus archidiaconus, salutem. Noverit universitas vestra nos monachis de Waleden' pro amore dei et pietatis intuitu concessisse quinque marcas argenti in ecclesia de Aumondesham sub pensione annua illis reddenda per manum clerici qui prefatam ecclesiam tenuerit. Et ut ratum et inconcussum permaneat, prefatis monachis istud beneficium sigilli nostri appositione roboravimus.

Date as for no. 75.

81. *Notification that, at the presentation of the abbot and convent of Walden, he has canonically instituted John the clerk in the church of Amersham, under an annual pension to the monks of five marks.* [1 Aug. 1190 × 22 Mar. 1194]

B = BL, Harley ms 3697 (Walden cartulary), fo. 61r, no. 2. s. xiv ex.

Universis sancte matris ecclesie filiis Robertus archidiaconus, salutem. Noverit universitas vestra me, ad presentationem abbatis et conventus de Waleden', instituisse Iohannem clericum canonice in ecclesia de Aumodesham sub pensione quinque marcarum predictis monachis annuatim reddenda ad duos terminos, ad Natale domini duas marcas et dimidiam, ad Nativitatem sancti Iohannis Baptiste duas marcas et dimidiam. Testibus istis: magistro Alardo fratre archidiaconi, Roberto de Burneham, Ricardo capellano archidiaconi, Thoma capellano, magistro Eustachio, Radulfo de Wedun', Radulfo de Hide, Adam de Stocca,[a] Waltero de Broch', Waltero clerico, Galfrido scriptore, Angorth le Corp, et multis aliis.

a Reading uncertain

After Walden priory became an abbey (*VCH Essex,* ii, 114) and before the date by which the archdn had left office (see above, no. 75n.).

82. *Notification that he has instituted the canons of Missenden in the church of Chalfont [St Peter] and confirmed it to them, at the presentation of Richard de Turville, the lord of the fee to whom the right of patronage belonged, in the presence of, and with the assent of, Ralph, rector of the church, who resigned it into the archdeacon's hands.* [1177 × Sept. 1193]

B = Bodl. ms Willis 5 (transcripts from lost Missenden cartulary), fo. 62r (abbreviated). s. xviii in.

Notum sit &c. quod ego Robertus archidiaconus Bukinh' institui dilectos fratres nostros canonicos de Messend' in ecclesia de Chalfhunta et eam cum omnibus pertinentiis suis eis presenti carta confirmavi, ad presentationem Ricardi de Turvilla domini fundi ad quem ius patronatus eiusdem ecclesie de iure spectabat, presente Radulfo presbitero eiusdem ecclesie rectore et assensum prebente, qui et prefatam ecclesiam cum omnibus pertinentiis suis et omne ius quod in ea habebat spontanea voluntate in manus nostras resignavit. Test' Iohanne priore de Messend'.

After the death of the archdn's predecessor (*Fasti Lincoln,* 40), and before the date of bp Hugh of Lincoln's confirmation of the gift (*Missenden Cartulary,* i, no. 23; *EEA* IV, no. 121, q.v. for the date); the final concord of 31 May 1196 by which Geoffrey de Turville quitclaimed the advowson of the church to Richard (*Feet of Fines, Henry II and Richard I,* no. 171) must have postdated the latter's grant to Missenden, since Robert of Burnham had certainly ceased to be archdn by then. This transcript is evidently somewhat selective, not only at the beginning, but most likely in the truncation of the witness-list. (The mixture of singular and plural references for the archdn is probably not significant.) Richard de Turville's gift of 'the church of St Peter of *Chalfunda*' is witnessed by Robert, archdn of Buckingham (Bodl. ms Willis 5, fo. 62r). The Chalfont section is missing from the surviving cartulary of Missenden (BL, Harley 3688), but that cartulary's table of contents lists what is presumably Richard de Turville's charter, in the form: *De advocatione ecclesie de Chalfhunte* (*Missenden Cartulary,* ii, 175); no other reference to the archdn's act is known.

83.   *Confirmation, on his own authority and that of the church of Lincoln, of the settlement, in the presence of Richard, archbishop of Canterbury, of a dispute between the abbot and canons of Missenden and William de Turville and Geoffrey the clerk, his brother, over the church of Weston [Turville]. Geoffrey and his successors in the church of Taplow will pay annually to the said canons sixty shillings, with the approval of William de Turville, patron of the church, saving to him and his heirs the right of patronage. Furthermore, the canons will continue to hold the chapel of Lee as before, under an annual pension of six shillings to the mother church of Weston [Turville].*
[? 17 Nov. 1184 × 21 Sept. 1186; ? × 25 May 1186]

B = BL, Harley ms 3688 (Missenden cartulary), fos. 59v–60r. s. xiv in. C = Bodl. ms Willis 5 (transcripts from lost Missenden cartulary), fos. 61r, 62r (abbreviated). s. xviii in.
Pd from B, *Missenden Cartulary,* i, 222–3, no, 249.

Robertus dei gratia archidiaconus Bukingham universis catholice ecclesie filiis, salutem. Notum sit universitati vestre causam que vertebatur inter *ª*abbatem et*ª* canonicos de Messend' et Willelmum de Turvilla et Gaufridum clericum fratrem eius super ecclesia de Weston' mediante concordia in hunc modum esse*ᵇ* sopitam. Prefatus siquidem G. et successores sui *ᶜ*in ecclesia de Tappelawa*ᶜ* predictis canonicis singulis annis solvet*ᵈ* sexaginta solidos sterlingorum in ecclesia de Tappellawa pro bono pacis, scilicet viginti solidos in Natali domini, xx. s' ad Pascha, xx. solidos ad festum sancti Michaelis; ita quod, nisi predicti lx. solidi ad primam exactionem canonicorum ad predictos terminos soluti fuerint, *ᵉ*pretaxatus clericus et eius successores in ecclesia de Tappellawa eos deferent infra octavas eorundem terminorum usque Messend' et ibi eos predictis canonicis persolvent. Accessit autem ad hec voluntas et assensus predicti Willelmi de Turvilla eiusdem ecclesie patroni, salvo tamen in omnibus ipsi W. et heredibus suis iure patronatus in prefata ecclesia; ita quod predicti canonici nichil iuris umquam in ecclesia ipsa sibi poterunt vendicare preter predictos lx. s'; set, persona eiusdem ecclesie decedente, clericus ad presentationem predicti W. vel heredum suorum institutus prefatum redditum de ecclesia illa canonicis annuatim iuramenti religione interposita persolvet. Preterea canonici, sicut capellam de Lee prius pacifice possederunt sub annua pensione sex solidorum matrici ecclesie de Westona annuatim persolvenda, ita eam decetero pacifice et sine controversia sub eadem pensione infra Natale domini persolvenda possidebunt in perpetuum.*ᵉ* Hanc autem conventionem se firmiter observaturum tam prelibatus abbas quam sepedictus G. clericus necnon et predictus Willelmus de Turvilla in presentia domini Ricardi Cantuar' archiepiscopi*ᶠ* iuravit; ita quod abbas pro se et conventu suo iuravit quod super ecclesiis spectantibus ad donationem memorati W. et heredum suorum nichil umquam sibi iuris vendicabunt, nisi de voluntate ipsius W. vel heredum suorum. Ut autem hec conventio firma et stabilis in perpetuum permaneat, sigillis abbatis et conventus de Messend' ex una parte cirographi et sigillis predictorum Willelmi de Turvilla et G. clerici fratris sui ex alia parte pendentibus corroboratur et confirmatur. Ego quoque predictam compositionem ratam habeo et predictos lx. solidos et prefatam capellam de Leia sub predicta pensione tenendam canonicis de Messend' in perpetuum possidenda Lincoln' ecclesie auctoritate et mea confirmo. Testibus: Alardo fratre meo,*ᵍ* Bartholomeo et Radulfo decanis, A. et P. canonicis de Messend', Nigello presbitero de Riseburgh', Ricardo presbitero de Eilesbir', Radulfo capellano de Wendover', Luca clerico de Stanes, Benedicto clerico de Hertwella, Willelmo milite de la Merse, Ricardo milite de Kenebella, et Willelmo [fo. 60r] milite fratre eius, et multis aliis.

    a–a Om. in C   *b* fuisse C   *c–c Om. in* C   *d* persolvet C
    e–e ut supra &c C *(referring to the preceding text of the agreement)*   *f* episcopi B
    g C ends

The settlement was reached in the archbp's presence probably mid-Aug. × 25 Sept. 1183 (*EEA* II, no. 167 and n.), but the reference here to the church of Lincoln's authority probably points to the next vacancy at Lincoln after that time, i.e., between the papal confirmation of Walter of Coutances' election to Rouen, 17 Nov. 1184, and the consecration of Hugh of Avallon, 21 Sept. 1186, or possibly his election, 25 May 1186 (*Fasti Lincoln*, 2–3). Large sections of this confirmation follow the text of archbp Richard's act (*Missenden Cartulary*, i, no. 246).

84. *Notification that the chapel of Dorton, which is dependent upon the church of Chilton, from which it obtains chrism and oil, is and ought to be free of synodals, exactions and episcopal customs.*   [1177 × 22 Mar. 1194]

    B = Oxford, Christ Church, Archives, Notley Charter Roll, m. 21. s. xvi med.

Universis catholice ecclesie filiis R. archidiaconus de Buckingham, salutem. Quoniam ad nostrum spectat officium veritati testimonium perhibere, ad omnium volumus pervenire notitiam quod capella de Dorton, que ad matricem ecclesiam de Chilt(on') pertinet, de qua crisma et oleum tenetur accipere, ab omnibus sinodalibus est et debet esse libera et ab omnibus exactionibus et episcopalibus consuetudinibus immunis et exonerata. Ne igitur quod universitati presentium [? constat]*ᵃ* posteritati subsequentium possit in dubium venire vel aliquis adversantium veritati valeat in posterum obviare, placuit nobis hanc veritatem litteris nostris testificari et sigilli nostri appositione communire. Hiis testibus: A. fratre archidiaconi, Willelmo Baligan, Petro decano Whitchirche, Martino de Hill'don', Iohanne decano de Prest', A. clerico de Essend', Willelmo clerico de Wottesdon, Iohanne capellano de Crendon.

    a Conjecturally supplied to complete the sense

Date as for no. 75. A. the archdn's brother was Alard of Burnham, later archdn of

London, from 1196, and dean of St Paul's, from 1200 × 1201 (*Fasti St Paul's*, 10, 6). A charter by William son of Payn of Dorton and Rose his mother makes various gifts to Dorton chapel, including certain tithes, and records the grant by Notley abbey, to whom the mother church of Chilton belonged, of *plenarium servitium et sacerdotem residentem in villa et sepulturam in cimiterio capelle* and the quittance of all demand and custom *qua tenebatur matrici ecclesie de Chilton excepto quod crisma et oleum ad baptizandos pueros et ungendos infirmos capella cum indiguerit a matrice ecclesia postulabit* It is witnessed by Robert of Burnham, archdn of Buckingham, and four of the others in the present witness-list (Notley Charter Roll, m. 21).

85. *Notification that, whereas the chapel of Dorton has frequently been burdened in the past by unjust exaction of synodals, he has freed it from its debts at the request of the canons of Notley.*   [1177 × 22 Mar. 1194]

    B = Oxford, Christ Church, Archives, Notley Charter Roll, m. 21. s. xvi med.

Universis catholice ecclesie filiis R. archidiaconus de Buckingham, salutem. Quia ad nostrum spectat officium errantibus lumen veritatis providere[a] non solum verbo sed etiam exemplo ut ad tramitem iustitie possint redire, que in nostro archidiaconatu acta sunt perperam et contra iuris ordinem curamus corrigere et ad rectitudinis statum redigere. Inde est quod capellam de Dorton' aliquibus retro diebus indebitis exactionibus oneratam nomine sinodalium et frequenter gravatam, pietatis intuitu et religiosorum fratrum de Parco interventu, quietam ab omnibus debitis absolvimus. Et ut hoc pro certo habeat presens universitas et subsecutura posteritas, sigilli nostri attestatione communimus. Hiis testibus: A. fratre archidiaconi, Willelmo Baligan, P. decano de Witechirch', Iohanne decano de Preston', A. clerico de Essend', Willelmo clerico de Wotteston'.

    a Suggested reading: ms ou'dere

Date as for no. 75.

86. *Notification that Martin, clerk of Hillesden, has resigned the church of Hillesden, which he had held of the abbot and canons of Notley for an annual pension, into the hands of the [rural] dean by the archdeacon's authority; and that the archdeacon, by the authority of the church of Lincoln, has inducted the abbot and canons into corporal possession of the same and has, at their presentation, received a chaplain to the administration of the same.*
[? *either* Jan. 1182 × 3 July 1183 *or* 1185 × 21 Sept. 1186]

    B = Oxford, Christ Church, Archives, Notley Charter Roll, m. 1. s. xvi med.

Universis ad quos littere iste pervenerint Robertus archidiaconus de Buchingham, salutem in domino. Noverit universitas vestra Martinum clericum de Hildesdon' ecclesiam de Hildesdon, quam de abbate et canonicis de Parco sub annua pensione tenuerat, in manus decani nostri auctoritate nostra resignasse; et nos auctoritate Lincolnensis ecclesie prefatum abbatem et canonicos in corporalem possessionem prelibate ecclesie per donum nostrum induxisse; nos[a] etiam ad eorundem canonicorum presentationem capellanum ad administrationem iamdicte ecclesie suscepisse. Et ne istud alicui de cetero in dubium veniat, et ut firmum illibatumque permaneat, quod in presentia nostra et auctoritate nostra rationabiliter factum est scripto nostro et sigilli nostri

attestatione communivimus et confirmavimus. Hiis testibus: Alardo de Burn',
Iohanne decano de Preston', Elia clerico de Hynton', Waltero de Broch,
Roberto canonico de Parco.

a Ms nec (*in error*)

Reference to the authority of Lincoln cathedral probably indicates the vacancy in the see,
either after Geoffrey Plantagenet's resignation or after Walter of Coutances' translation to
Rouen (*Fasti Lincoln*, 2–3). The first witness, though not called Mr, is no doubt the
archdn's brother, Mr Alard of Burnham.

87. *Testimony that the abbot and canons of Osney granted to him for life two parts
of the demesne tithes of Iver, which belonged to St George's church, Oxford, of which
they are rectors; and that, after many years' possession of the tithes in their name, he
has voluntarily resigned the tithes to them.*

[21 Mar. 1178 × 22 Mar. 1194; ? × 1188]

> B = BL, Cotton ms Vitellius E xv (Osney cartulary), fo. 157r. ss. xii ex.–xiii in.
> Damaged by fire. C = Oxford, Christ Church, D. & C. Lib., vi. a. 1 (Osney
> cartulary), fo. 266r–v. s. xiii ex.
> Pd from B and C, *Oseney Cartulary*, v, 327, no. 807.

Omnibus ad quos presens scriptum pervenerit magister Robertus de Burneham
archidiaconus de Bukingeham,[a] salutem in domino. Cum due partes decimationum de dominio de Evra ad ecclesiam sancti Georgii de Oxenef'[b] de antiquo
iure pertineant, dilecti fratres nostri abbas et canonici de Osen', eiusdem
ecclesie rectores et predictarum decimarum possessores, eas nobis tanquam[c]
personale beneficium in vita nostra de ipsis tenendas misericorditer concesserunt. Quas cum nomine eorum per multos annos pacifice percepissemus, ne
liberalitas quam nobis impenderunt ipsis postmodum in dispendium converta-
tur, memoratas decimationes cum omni integritate sua eis sponte resignavimus,[d]
eos in plenaria illarum possessione relinquentes. Et ne hoc in dubium posteris
veniat, presentibus litteris attestari curavimus.

a Bukingham *C*   *b* Oxon' *C*   *c* tamquam *C*   *d* Corrected from
regnavimus *C*

After the letter to Robert from Richard of Ilchester, bp of Winchester (*Oseney Cartulary*, v,
no. 806; *EEA* VIII, no. 170, q.v. for the date), and before Robert's successor had ceased to
be chancellor of Lincoln (*Fasti Lincoln*, 40), but possibly before, or soon after, the death of
Richard of Ilchester, 22 Dec. 1188 (*Fasti Monastic Cathedrals*, 85). Richard of Ilchester's
letter reveals that it had been at his request that the canons of Osney had granted the
tithes to Robert. St George's church, Oxford, was the free chapel in Oxford Castle, which
was given with its possessions to Osney abbey in 1149 (J. H. Denton, *English Royal Free
Chapels*, Manchester 1970, 119–21).

88. *Notification that he had been present when Alexander, bishop of Lincoln,
admitted and instituted Wigod, abbot of Osney, in the church of Stone at the
presentation of William de Braci. Afterwards, in the archdeacon's presence in synod at
Aylesbury, Gilbert de Braci confirmed his father's gift and the archdeacon admitted
Abbot Hugh of Osney anew to the church by the authority of the church of Lincoln; in
the same synod Gilbert also confessed that he had given to the abbot and canons one*

hide of land, over which he had subsequently brought a case against them before the royal justices, which gift the archdeacon has confirmed by the same authority.

[9 May × 21 Sept. 1186]

B = BL, Cotton ms Vitellius E xv (Osney cartulary), fo. 41v. ss. xii ex.–xiii in. Damaged by fire. C = Oxford, Christ Church, D. & C. Lib., vi. a. 1 (Osney cartulary), fos. 209v–210r. s. xiii ex.
Pd from B and C, *Oseney Cartulary*, v, 144–5, no. 624.

Robertus de Burnham archidiaconus de Buchingeham*ᵃ* omnibus ad quos iste littere pervenerint, salutem. Noverit vestra presens universitas et tota futura posteritas nos presentes fuisse ubi Alexander Lincolniensis episcopus [Wygo]-dum*ᵇ* abbatem Oseneie admisit in ecclesia de Stanes et instituit ad presentationem Willelmi de Braci. Postea vero, cum essent in [nostra] presentia in sinodo apud Ailesberi Hugo abbas Osen' et Gillebertus*ᶜ* de Braci, idem Gilebertus donationem patris sui Willelmi quam fecerat de predicta [ecclesia de] Stanes abbati et canonicis de Osen' viva [voce] confirmavit et ratam habuit et exinde cartam suam eis dedit. Nos igitur in memorata sinodo confirmationem memorati Gileberti [ratam] habuimus, et auctoritate Lincoln' ecclesie confirmavimus et abbatem Hugonem in iam dicta ecclesia [de] Stanes de novo admisimus. Et preterea, cum iam dictus Gilebertus prefatis abbati et canonicis controversiam movisset super una hida terre [quam] ipsi possederant, et diutius coram iusticiariis domini*ᵈ* regis [causa] esset v[entilata, in eadem] sinodo [confessus] est se dedi[sse eis dictam terram et in auctoritatem sue donationis cartam] suam eis dedit. Unde et nos eandem donationem auctoritate Lincoln' ecclesie confirmavimus. Hiis testibus:*ᵉ* Roberto priore de Neuport, Radulfo monacho de Heddenham, magistro Alardo, Roberto de Burneham, Ricardo canonico de M[es]send', Roberto Walingef' canonico Sancte [Fri]deswide, Radulfo decano de Horewude, Iohanne capellano de Stowe, Roberto capellano de [ ]indune, Philippo clerico de Osen', magistro R. de Ailesberi, Benedicto persona de Her[twella].*ᶠ*

a Buchingham *C* except in witness-list
b *B damaged by fire; words in square brackets supplied from C,*
c Gilebertus *C*
d *Om. in C*
e *C ends with* et cetera
f *For this reading, see no. 83*

After the date of the final concord between the abbey and Gilbert de Braci (*Oseney Cartulary*, v, no. 623) and, given the reference to the authority of Lincoln cathedral, before the consecration of Hugh of Avallon (*Fasti Lincoln*, 3). No *actum* of admission and institution by bp Alexander survives, but William de Braci's gift to prior Wigod (as he then was) and the canons of Osney is *Oseney Cartulary*, v, no. 620; Osney was raised to abbatial status in 1154 during Wigod's time as head of the house (*Heads*, 179).

89. *Notification that, at the presentation of Agnes de Munchensy, he has canonically instituted the abbess and convent of Godstow in the church of Dinton.*

[1177 × 1190]

B = PRO, E164/20 (Godstow cartulary), fo. 39v (26v). s. xv in. C = Bodl. ms Rawlinson B. 408 (Godstow cartulary, English calendar), fo. 37r (36r).¹ s. xv ex.
Pd from C, *Godstow English Register*, i, 65, no. 54.

Universis sancte matris ecclesie filiis Robertus archidiaconus Buchingh', salutem in domino. Noscat presens universitas et subsecutura posteritas me ad petitionem et presentationem Agnetis de Munchanesi canonice instituisse abbatissam de Godestow et totum conventum eiusdem loci in ecclesia de Donyngton' et in omnibus pertinentiis suis. Et ut illa institutio rata sit et firma, literis meis presentibus et sigilli mei munimine confirmavi. Hiis testibus: priore Sancte Frideswyde, Alardo de Burneh', Petro decano, magistro A. de Burneham, Waltero et Thoma capellanis, Bartholomeo, et pluribus aliis.

Agnes, daughter and coheir of Payn fitzJohn, married (firstly) Warin de Munchensy (d. *c.* 1162) and died in 1190 × 1191 (Sanders, *English Baronies*, 144; *Hatton's Book of Seals*, no. 405n.). Their eldest son, Ralph, who confirmed his mother's gift of the church to Godstow, died before her, in 1185 × 1190 (ibid.; *Godstow English Register* , no. 55). This act can therefore be dated after the probable date of the death of the archdn's predecessor, in Jan. 1177 (*Fasti Lincoln*, 40), and before Ralph de Munchensy's death; there seems to be no evidence in favour of a date 'about 1180', as suggested in *Godstow English Register*. The gift of the church was for the benefit of the infirmary, and Agnes originally intended that, after the death of Bartholomew the clerk, who was to hold the church *in perpetuam vicariam*, a daughter house of Godstow should be established in Dinton church if the abbey agreed (ibid., nos. 52–3; PRO, E164/20, fos. 38v–39r), but nothing came of it.

¹ The calendared text lacks witnesses.

90. *Notification that, at the presentation of the prior of Kenilworth with the consent of the convent, he has admitted Richard the clerk to the vicarage of the church of Hughenden, under an annual pension of ten marks, and, by the authority of the church of Lincoln, he has canonically instituted him in the same.*

[? *either* Jan. 1182 × 3 July 1183 *or* 1185 × 21 Sept. 1186]

B = BL, Additional ms 47677 (Kenilworth cartulary), fo. 297v. s. xvi in.–med.

Universis et c' Robertus archidiaconus de Bukingham, salutem. Noverit tam presens universitas quam subsequenta posteritas me Ricardum clericum, presentatione prioris de Kenell' et consensu conventus eiusdem loci, in vicaria ecclesie de Hugendon' sub annua pensione decem marcarum admisisse et eum in eadem auctoritate Lincoln' ecclesie canonice instituisse, et hanc institutionem hac presenti mea carta confirmasse, et c'.

The reference to the church of Lincoln suggests one of the two vacancies in the see while Robert was archdn (see above, no. 86n.). The use of *admittere* would also suggest a relatively late date.

91. *Testimony to all deans in the archdeaconry of Buckingham that the monks of Longueville are religious men of good living; and mandate, by the authority of the church of Lincoln and his own, to protect them and their possessions within their deaneries and to enforce the payment to them of tithes or other alms.*

[?*either* Jan. 1182 × 3 July 1183 *or* 1185 × 21 Sept. 1186]

B = Oxford, New College, Archive 9744 (Liber Niger), fo. 37r. s. xvi in.
Pd, *Newington Longeville Charters*, 8–9, no. 4.

R. archidiaconus de Bukingeham*ᵃ* omnibus decanis per archidiaconatum de Bukingeham*ᵃ* constitutis, salutem in vero salutari. Noverit discretio vestra dilectos fratres nostros monachos de Longavill' viros religiosos et bone conversationis esse. Inde est quod vobis auctoritate Linc' ecclesie et nostra precipiendo mandamus quatinus et ipsos et eorum possessiones ubicumque fuerint in parochiis vestris custodiatis et pro posse vestro protegatis et, si quis ausu temerario eis in aliquo in decimis aut aliis elemosinis aut eventionibus obstiterit, districte compellatis eos supradictis fratribus omnia integre persolvere aut eos sub vinculo anathematis innodetis.[b] Valete.

a Ms Bukinqueham   *b Ms* ignodetis

Date as for no. 90. [It is possible, but unlikely, that the archdn is not Robert but Roger, who occurs Sept. 1202 × May 1206 (*Fasti Lincoln*, 40).] The use here of the word *parochie*, apparently to signify the rural deaneries, is noteworthy and would on balance favour a 12th-century date.

92. *Notification to all faithful of Christ in the archdeaconry of Buckingham that, in his presence, Roger son of William, parson of Moulsoe, has resigned to the monks of Longueville all the demesne tithes of Moulsoe, which he had possessed by their grant for an annual pension of five shillings.* [Apr. 1185 × Sept. 1191]

B = Oxford, New College, Archive 9744 (Liber Niger), fo. 66r–v. s. xvi in.
Pd, *Newington Longeville Charters*, 51, no. 57.

Omnibus Cristi fidelibus per archidiaconatum de Bukingham constitutis Robertus de Burneham archidiaconus de Buk', salutem. Quod[a] in nostra presentia rationabiliter actum est, nos ratum habere et auctoritate nostra munire nostri postulat officii sollicitudo. Quapropter universitati vestre dignum duximus innotescere quod Rogerus filius Willelmi [fo. 66v] persona de Molesho omnes decimas dominii de Moleshou, quas de monachis de Longvill' sub annua pensione quinque solidorum ex eorundem monachorum concessione in pace possederat,[b] prefatis monachis coram nobis cum omni decimarum integritate dimisit, et iuri quod in eisdem decimis habebat solenniter et spontanee renuntiavit. Et ne alicuius malignitate de cetero valeat revocari, scripti nostri firmitate et sigilli nostri appositione quod in presentia nostra factum est roborare curavimus.

a Ms Quoniam   *b Ms* possiderat

After the settlement before Baldwin, archbp of Canterbury, when the tithes were granted by Longueville to Roger for 5s annually (*Newington Longeville Charters*, no. 55; *EEA* II, no. 297, q.v. for the date), and before Roger's death (*Fasti Lincoln*, 142). Roger was a canon of Lincoln as well as parson of Moulsoe (ibid.; *Newington Longeville Charters*, nos. 55–6, 58).

Mr Stephen de Swafeld

93. *Notification that, at the presentation of the prior and convent of Nostell, Mr William son of Fulk of Lincoln has been received and instituted in the church of Cheddington, vacant, by H(ugh), bishop of Lincoln, and put into corporal possession of the same by the archdeacon.* [? *c.* 1190 × 16 Nov. 1200]

B = BL, Cotton ms Vespasian E xix (Nostell cartulary), fo. 113r. s. xiii ex.

Universis sancte matris ecclesie filiis tam presentibus quam futuris Stephanus archidiaconus de Buchingeham, salutem. Quoniam temporalia facta lapsu temporis a memoria labuntur hominum nisi pagine mandentur et scripto, volentes notum esse quod factum est nec tempore labi, ad omnium vestrum volumus pervenire notitiam quod magister Willelmus filius Fulconis de Lincoln', ad presentationem prioris et conventus Sancti Oswaldi de Nostl', ad ecclesiam de Chettend' que est in Buchinghamsire, tunc temporis vacantem, a domino H. Lincoln' episcopo est receptus et institutus, et per nos in corporalem possessionem predicte ecclesie missus. Huius rei cum multis aliis testes sumus et sigillum nostrum apposuimus.

After the latest occurrence of the archdn's predecessor, Robert of Burnham, 25 Aug. 1189, and before the death of bp Hugh of Avallon (*Fasti Lincoln*, 40, 3). Stephen de Swafeld was previously chancellor of Lincoln, to which dignity he was appointed 18 Oct. 1188 × 24 Mar. 1190 and in which he had been succeeded by 22 Mar. 1194 (*Fasti Lincoln*, 16), but for how long he remained chancellor before becoming archdn of Buckingham, in which office he first occurs *c.* 1194 (ibid., 40), is unknown. No equivalent *actum* by bp Hugh is known, although the church is included in what is probably a confirmation by him to Nostell (*EEA* IV, no. 137).

94. *Notification that William son of William of Stratford, patron of [Water] Stratford church, has granted the church in pure alms to the monks of Luffield, whom he has presented to the church before the archdeacon in his chapter of Buckingham at Stowe, and has caused his charter of confirmation to be read before the archdeacon.*

Stowe. [? *c.* 1190 × ?1202]

A = Westminster Abbey Muniments, no. 2573. Endorsed: De ecclesia de Strafford (s. xiii). Littera Stephani archidiaconi Buck' (s. xiii ex.). Size 145 × 57 mm (45 to tongue). Seal missing, tongue remaining (no trace of wrapping tie).
B = Ibid., Muniment Book 10 (Luffield cartulary), fo. 26v. s. xv ex.
Pd, *Luffield Charters*, i, 49, no. 43.

Universis sancte matris ecclesie filiis Stephanus archidiaconus Bukinham',[a] salutem in domino. Noverit universitas vestra Willelmum filium Willelmi de Stratfort,[b] patronum ecclesie de Stratfort,[b] concessisse monachis de Luffeld[c] et fratribus ibidem deo famulantibus ecclesiam de Stratfort[d] cum omnibus pertinentiis in puram et perpetuam elemosinam; quos coram nobis in capitulo nostro ad eandem ecclesiam presentavit, cartamque suam qua ipsis ecclesiam illam confirmaverat in audientia nostra legi fecit. Nos autem, ad ipsius et illorum petitionem, in huius facti testimonium hoc scriptum concipi fecimus, cui sigillum nostrum apposuimus. Teste capitulo de Bukinham apud Stowe.

a Bukingham *B*   *b* Stratford *B*   *c* Luffelde *B*   *d* Stratforde *B*

For the uncertain date of the start of Stephen's archidiaconate, see above no. 93n.; his last certain occurrence is Sept. 1202, but the exact dates of his immediate successor, Roger, are unknown, although the latter had certainly ceased to be archdn before 10 May 1206 (*Fasti Lincoln*, 40).

95. *Notification, at the request of the parties, that the dispute between the prior and monks of Luffield and John son of William of Rollright over the chapel of Evershaw has been settled by agreement before him. John has renounced all right he had claimed in the chapel and has voluntarily sworn never to bring a suit over this against the prior and monks.*   [? *c.* 1190 × ? 1202]

    B = Westminster Abbey Muniments, Muniment Book 10 (Luffield cartulary), fo. 35r.
    s. xv ex.
    Pd, *Luffield Charters*, i, 77, no. 75.

Universis sancte matris ecclesie filiis S. archidiaconus Bukingham, salutem. Noverit universitas vestra quod in presentia nostra controversia que vertebatur inter priorem et monachos de Luffelde et Iohannem filium Willelmi de Rolledric*ᵃ* super capella de Evershawe finem accepit per concordiam. Ita quod predictus Iohannes iuri quod proposuerat in predicta capella se habere penitus renuntiavit, et de sponte sua sine omni coactione iuramenter interposuit se decetero nullam umquam questionem super hoc contra predictos priorem et monachos moturum. In cuius rei testimonium scriptum hoc fecimus ad petitionem utriusque partis, cui appositum est sigillum nostrum. Valete in domino.

    a Sic; ? rectius Rollendric

Date as for no. 94. For the former chapel of Evershaw, now in Biddlesden parish, see above, no. 75n.

96. *Notification to the abbots of Garendon and Combe and the prior of Daventry, papal judges-delegate, that, an inquest having been made in his chapter at Buckingham concerning the chapel of Evershaw, which is in dispute between the prior and monks of Luffield and Robert, rector of Shalstone church, it was asserted by all that the chapel belongs to Luffield priory and has always done so.*
[*c.* Mar. 1198 × *c.* Oct. 1201]

    A = Westminster Abbey Muniments, no. 2496. Endorsed: De capella de Eversawe (s.
    xiii); Littera S. archidiaconi Buck' (s. xiii ex.). Size 154 × 44 mm (38 to tongue).
    Seal missing; tongue and wrapping tie remaining.
    B = Ibid., Muniment Book 10 (Luffield cartulary), fo. 35v. s. xv ex.
    Pd from A, *Luffield Charters*, i, 79, no. 79 (original wrongly cited).

Viris venerabilibus de Gerunden' et de Cumbe abbatibus et priori de Daventr' S. archidiaconus Bukingh',*ᵃ* salutem in domino. Noscat vestra discretio quod facta est in capitulo nostro apud Bukingh'*ᵃ* diligens inquisitio super capella de Eversau',*ᵇ* super qua vertitur causa inter priorem et monachos de Luffeld'*ᶜ* et Robertum rectorem ecclesie de Saldeston', que vobis ut dicitur a domino papa est commissa, et a singulis et universis pro vero et constanter assertum est*ᵈ* predictam capellam pertinere ad monasterium de Luffeld'*ᶜ* et ab olim pertinuisse, ita ut nec mentio habita sit prius questionis alicuius super ea facta. Istud scribimus ne prudenciam ipsam circumveniat alicuius suggestio vana vel scrupulosa. Valete in domino.

    a Bukingham *B*   *b* Evershawe *B*   *c* Luffelde *B*   *d Followed by*
    erasure of one word in A

The judges were commissioned by Innocent III, who was elected 8 Jan. and crowned

22 Feb. 1198; the earliest possible time by which a commission issued by him could have arrived in England would be Mar. 1198; since a new commission to fresh delegates was issued on 2 Mar. 1202, it is likely that the appeal from the first group of delegates would have been made not later than Oct. 1201 (see *Innocent III's Letters*, nos. 351, 389). The settlement reached before the second panel of judges, possibly late 1202, was brought to the archdn sitting in the chapter of Buckingham at [Maids] Moreton by the prior of Luffield, and by the archdn's order was publicly read in the chapter (*Luffield Cartulary*, i, no. 76).

97. *As archdeacon of Buckingham and canon of the prebend of Sutton, gift to Gilbert Ruffus and his heirs of one virgate of land in Horley for an annual rent of two shillings, in exchange for Gilbert's quitclaim of half a hide of land in Hornton, for which he had a charter, which he has returned to the archdeacon.*

[? *c.* 1190 × ? 1202]

A = BL, Harley Charter 84 F. 30. Endorsed: De Hornel' (ss. xv–xvi). Size 131 × 127 + 41 mm. Seal on tag (method 2), pointed oval in white wax, nearly complete (*c.* 51 × 35 mm); obverse: frontally standing figure of an ecclesiastic, bare-headed, with both arms outstretched; legend: [ST]EPHANV[S] AR[C]HIDIA[CON]VS DE BUCKINGH.

Sciant omnes presentes et futuri quod ego Stephanus archidiaconus Bukinham', canonicus prebende de Suttun', dedi et concessi Gileberto Ruffo et heredibus suis unam virgatam terre in villa de Hornel', videlicet dimidiam virgatam quam Willelmus Whirtop tenuit cum tofto et aliam dimidiam virgatam quam Galfridus palmarius tenuit sine toffto,[a] ut unam habeat plenam virgatam cum pertinenciis libere et quiete, reddendo inde michi et successoribus meis annuatim duos solidos ad duos terminos, vidilicet[a] ad Pascha xii. denarios et ad festum sancti Michaelis xii. denarios. Hanc donationem ei feci in exscambium dimidie hide terre quam Ricardus cocus olim tenuit in villa de Horningtun', in qua prefatus G. ius sibi vendicabat et de qua cartam habuit, quam michi reddidit. Ita quod eam[a] terram quietam clamavit et in perpetuum abiuravit in plena curia, ipse et heredes sui. Et in huius facti testimonium hanc meam cartam ei tradidi. Hiis testibus: Roberto filio sacerdotis, Henrico filio eius, Ricardo Flement, Waltero de Porz,[b] Galfrido filio Alani, Baldewino de Soteswill', Roberto filio eius, et multis aliis.

a Sic   *b Reading of last two letters uncertain*

Date as for no. 94. The archdn's prebend was Sutton-cum-Buckingham, which included the church of King's Sutton, Northants, and land at Horley, Oxon (*Fasti Lincoln*, 99); Hornton is very near Horley.

* 98. *Ratification of the confirmations by Bishops Robert and Hugh of Lincoln of a moiety of the church of Chesham to the abbot and canons of Leicester, and notification that he has put the canons into corporal possession.* [? *c.* 1190 × ? 1202]

Mentioned only, as having been produced in an action of *quare non permittit* brought by Richard de Sifrewast against the abbot of Leicester in the king's court in Hilary term, 1214: PRO, KB 26/59, m. 15d; pd, *CRR*, vii, 72.

. . . Profert [*sc.* the abbot of Leicester] etiam cartam archidiaconi Buck'[a] Stephani qui[b] testatur quod ipse quantum in eo est ratam et gratam habet

confirmationem quam Robertus et Hugo episcopi Linc' eis fecerunt de
medietate ecclesie de Cestreham, et protestatur missionem eorum in corporalem possessionem illius ecclesie . . .

　　a Interlined　　　　*b* Sic

Date as for no. 94. Neither of the episcopal charters survives (see *EEA* I, no. 144; *EEA* IV,
no. 88).

ARCHDEACONRY OF HUNTINGDON

Henry of Huntingdon

* 99.　*At the presentation of Hamo de St Clair, canonical institution of J(ohn) the
clerk as parson of Walkern.*　　　　　　　　　　　　[1120 × 1155; ? × c. 1150]

> Mentioned only, in a letter by Gilbert Foliot, bishop of London, to Pope Alexander III
> in 1163 × 1181 concerning a dispute, committed to him by the pope, between John
> the clerk and William de Lanval' over the church of Walkern, *Foliot Letters and
> Charters*, 319–21, no. 248; (calendar of relevant parts), Henry, Archdeacon of
> Huntingdon, *Historia Anglorum*, 832, App. 1, Lost acts.

> . . . partibus evocatis, I(ohannes) se in iam dicta ecclesia, presentatione
> Hamonis de Sancto Claro . . ., per manum H. archidiaconi Huntedon'
> personam canonice institutum fuisse asseruit . . . cartam proferens Hamonis,
> a quo fuerat archidiacono presentatus, cartam etiam archidiaconi per quem
> fuerat institutus . . .

> After Hamo de St Clair acquired the barony of Walkern and certainly before it had
> passed to his son, Hubert (Sanders, *English Baronies*, 92), although he is not recorded
> after 1143 and may have died *c.* 1150 (Green, *Government of England under Henry I*, 272;
> Henry, Archdeacon of Huntingdon, 832). If the archdn's act referred specifically to
> anything approximating to 'canonical institution', it is most likely to have been later
> rather than earlier in the dating range (Kemp, 'Towards admission and institution',
> esp. 172–3).

100.　*Notification that, in his presence, Godric Gustard offered himself to the abbey
of Bec and the priory of St Neots on the altar of St Neots, along with the church of
Holy Trinity, Huntingdon, and all his land in Huntingdon; and that afterwards, in
the synod at Huntingdon, he resigned the church into the hands of the archdeacon,
who, at his presentation, received and instituted the monks of St Neots into the church.*
　　　　　　　　　　　　　　　　　　　　　　　[? c. 1135 × 20 Feb. 1148]

> B = BL, Cotton ms Faustina A iv (St Neots cartulary), fo. 42r (41r). s. xiii med.
> Pd, Henry, Archdeacon of Huntingdon, *Historia Anglorum*, 827, App. 1. no.1;
> 　　(calendar), Gorham, *Hist. Eynesbury and St Neot's*, ii, p. xiii, no. 76.

Omnibus sancte matris ecclesie filiis ad quos presens scriptum pervenerit
Henricus archidiaconus Hunt', salutem. Noverit universitas vestra Godricum
Gustrad*a* de Huntend' nobis presentibus seipsum obtulisse deo et ecclesie
sancte Marie Becci et ecclesie Sancti Neoti super altare Sancti Neoti et cum
seipso ecclesiam sancte Trinitatis in Hunt' et quicquid iuris in*b* eadem ecclesia
habuit cum tota terra sua de Huntend' et cum omnibus pertin(entiis) predicte

ecclesie. Postea vero in sinodo apud Huntend' congregata predictus Godricus in manus nostras resignavit prefatam ecclesiam, et nos, ad ipsius concessionem et presentationem, monachos Sancti Neoti ad predictam ecclesiam sancte Trinitatis recepimus*c* et ipsos instituimus. Et ut hoc ratum et inconcussum*d* permaneat, scripto nostro sigilli nostri apositione roborato predictam ecclesiam cum omnibus pertin(entiis) suis prenominatis monachis concessimus et confirmavimus. Hiis testibus.

a *Corrected in ms from* Gustad   b *Interlined, replacing* de *deleted*   c *Corrected in ms from* recipimus   d *First syllable interlined*

Dating problematical: the later terminus is provided by bp Alexander of Lincoln's confirmation of the church as having been given 'by the hand of Henry archdn of Huntingdon' (*EEA* I, no. 54), but the earlier terminus is uncertain, although Dr Brett suggests a date for this act of possibly as early as 1135 (Brett, *English Church under Henry I*, 208). The church was also confirmed to Bec and St Neots by archbp Theobald as a gift by King Henry II (Saltman, *Theobald*, 461–2, no. 236). It is possible, given certain anachronistic elements in the present text, that it was revised at the time of the priory's dispute with Roger, clerk of Huntingdon, over this church under archdn Nicholas de Sigillo, whose act refers to an 'authentic writing' of archdn Henry (see below, no. 116; Henry, Archdeacon of Huntingdon, App. 1, no. 1n.).

101. *Notification to all faithful of Huntingdonshire of the settlement before T(heobald), archbishop of Canterbury, of the dispute between St Neots priory and the church of [Great] Gransden over the tithes of* Kingesfeld, *namely, that Gerinus through his proctor gave up his claim to the tithes, which were adjudged to the monks of St Neots, and which the archdeacon has confirmed to them in perpetuity.*

[8 Jan. 1139 × 1164]

B = BL, Cotton ms Faustina A iv (St Neots cartulary), fo. 43v (42v). s. xiii med.
Pd, Henry, Archdeacon of Huntingdon, *Historia Anglorum*, 828–9, no. 3; (calendar), Gorham, *Hist. Eynesbury and St Neot's*, ii, p. xiv, no. 87.

H. archidiaconus Huntundonensis omnibus sancte matris ecclesie fidelibus per Huntendusiram constitutis, salutem. Significetur universitati vestre controversiam que vertebatur inter ecclesiam Sancti Neoti et ecclesiam de Grantendena super decimationibus de Kingesfeld iuxta Offordeslawa coram domino T. Cant' archiepiscopo sopitam esse hoc modo. Gerinus, qui decimationem illam sibi vendicabat, per*a* procuratorem suum iamdictam decimam in integrum et solidum cessit ecclesie et monachis Sancti Neoti. Nos itaque prenominatam decimam, ecclesie Sancti Neoti adiudicatam, ecclesie et fratribus confirmamus pleno iure perpetuo possidendam et presentis scripti testimonio communimus, sub anathemate prohibentes ne quis decetero eos super predicta decima vexare et inquietare presumat. Valete.

a *Ms* pro

After Theobald became archbp of Canterbury (*Fasti Monastic Cathedrals*, 4) and before the latest possible date for the archdn's death (Henry, Archdeacon of Huntingdon, lvii). Virtually the whole of this text is *mutatis mutandis* identical with that of archbp Theobald's settlement, which is addressed to the archdn (Saltman, *Theobald*, 458, no. 231), the common passages being given in italics in Henry of Huntingdon, 829; whether, therefore, the anathema should apply to the archdn as well as to the archbp is unclear. Gerinus was evidently the incumbent of Great Gransden, but neither act says so specifically.

102.   *Restoration to the canons of Huntingdon of their song school of Huntingdon.*
[1149 × 1164]

B = BL, Cotton ms Faustina C i (Huntingdon priory cartulary), fo. 17r. s. xiv med.
Pd, M. Bateson, 'The Huntingdon song school and the school of St Gregory's, Canterbury', *EHR* 18 (1903), 713; Henry, Archdeacon of Huntingdon, *Historia Anglorum*, 829, App. 1, no. 4; (transl.), W. M. Noble, 'The cartulary of the priory of St Mary, Huntingdon', *Trans. Cambridgeshire and Huntingdonshire Archaeol. Soc.*, iv (1915–30), 257–8, no. 72.

Universis sancte dei ecclesie filiis Henricus archidiaconus Hunt', salutem in Cristo. Quia negotiis et commoditati, maxime eorum qui renuntiaverunt seculo et militant Cristo, omnimoda eorum indempnitate sollicite providere et, ne dampnosa temporum interiectio antiquet et obnubulet, si quid misit in dubium quod eorum ad veri fidem trahi possit, assertione in lucem evocare pia et honesta curatio est, vestram dignum duximus non latere notitiam nos canonicis de Hunt' scolas de cantu de Hunt', quas ad ius eorum dinoscitur pertinere, in perpetuum reddidisse et super altare obtulisse. Valete.

After the mandate from bp Robert Chesney to suppress the unlicensed schools which were being maintained to the prejudice of the canons of Huntingdon (*EEA* I, no. 134) and before the latest possible date for the archdn's death (Henry, Archdeacon of Huntingdon, lvii). For discussion of this act, and the possibility that the archdn himself may have been guilty of infringing the canons' rights, see ibid., xlii–xliii.

103.   *Notification to all clergy of Huntingdonshire that Ansered the priest has recognised in chapter before him that the abbey of St Melaine [Rennes] ought to have two thirds of the lesser tithes of Payn the sheriff's demesne of Hemingford [Grey], as it has of the corn; and that the monks have leased these corn and lesser tithes to Ansered for seven years for an annual rent of seven shillings.*   1150 × 1151

A = BL, Additional Charter 28325. Endorsed: Hemyngforth' (s. xv). Size 143 × 74 mm. Seal on tongue (with tie above), featureless fragment in brown wax.
Pd, Henry, Archdeacon of Huntingdon, *Historia Anglorum*, 828, App. I, no. 2.

Henricus archidiaconus Hunt' omnibus clericis de Hunted'sir' tam presentibus quam futuris, salutem. Sciatis quia Anseredus presbiter recognovit in capitulo coram me quod ecclesia Sancti Melani debet habere minutarum decimarum duas partes, scilicet de agnis et lana et caseis et aliis rebus que solent decimari, de dominio Pagani vicecomitis de Hemmingeford' sicut habent de segetibus, et dimiserunt ei monachi ipsas decimas tenendas,*a* segetem scilicet et alia, usque ad vii. annos per redditionem vii. solidorum ad Pentec(osten) per annum. Post septem vero annos facient inde monachi libitum suum. His testibus: magistro Rogero,*b* Osmundo de Brant', Reg' decano, Radulfo de Godmet', Iohanne*c* de Brant', Willelmo decano, Cunano, Iocelino de Stivecl'. Hoc*d* autem factum est anno gratie M.° C.° Q.*oe* Valete.

> *a Altered in ms from* tenandas   *b Ms* Rog's   *c Ms* Joh'es   *d Altered in ms from* Hec   *e The final digit is not certainly* Q, *resembling more the Arabic numeral 4*

There is uncertainty as to when the year was reckoned to begin at this time. The monks of St Melaine were those in the priory of Hatfield Regis (or Hatfield Broad Oak), which was founded as a dependency of the parent abbey by Aubrey de Vere in *c.* 1135 (Knowles and

Hadcock, 54, 67). Payn the sheriff's gift to 'the monks of St Melaine in Hatfield Regis' of his tithes of Hemingford and Yelling, as his ancestors had given them to the monks, is BL, Add. Ch. 28337.

104. *Notification that Gilbert of Folksworth, Guy his son and heir, and Elias, Guy's brother, have given in the archdeacon's presence the church of Folksworth to the monks of Crowland in perpetual alms, saving the* personatus *which Adam, clerk, of Stukeley has in the same.* [? c. 1150 × 1164]

B = Spalding Gentlemen's Society, Crowland cartulary, fo. 200r. s. xiv med.
Pd, Henry, Archdeacon of Huntingdon, *Historia Anglorum*, 830–1, App. I, no. 6.

Universis sancte matris ecclesie filiis Henricus Huntyndon' archidiaconus, salutem. Sciat universitas vestra Gilbertum de Folkesworth' et Wydonem filium et heredem eius, Elyam quoque fratrem eiusdem Wydonis donasse in presentia nostra ecclesiam de Folkesworth' cum omnibus pertinentiis suis deo et sancto Guthlaco Croiland' et monachis deo ibidem servientibus in perpetuam elemosinam, salvo tamen personatu quam habet Adam clericus de Stivecle in eadem ecclesia; quod nos presentis sigilli munimine corroboramus. Hiis testibus et c'.

Before the archdn's death (see no. 101n.) the gift was confirmed by bp Robert Chesney of Lincoln (died 1166), his act being witnessed by Martin, treasurer of Lincoln, who may have become so in the early 1150s (*EEA* I, no. 101 and n.; *Fasti Lincoln*, 2). Guy's own charter says that the gift was made before Henry the archdn in the chapter of Coppingford (cartulary, fo. 200r). Adam of Stukeley was the archdn's son (Henry, Archdeacon of Huntingdon, *Historia Anglorum*, xxvii; see also below, nos. 107–8). Diana Greenway regards this act and no. 105 as suspicious (ibid., 831, no. 7n.), but, although the church was in dispute in 1201 (*CRR*, i, 3), there is no clear reason to reject them.

105. *Notification that Gilbert of Folksworth and his sons, Guy and Elias, have given to the monks of Crowland in perpetual alms thirty acres of land of their demesne, free and quit of all secular services and exactions.* [? c. 1150 × 1164]

B = Spalding Gentlemen's Society, Crowland cartulary, fo. 200v. s. xiv med.
Pd, Henry, Archdeacon of Huntingdon, *Historia Anglorum*, 831, App. I, no. 7.

Omnibus universe sancte matris ecclesie filiis Henricus Huntygdon' archidiaconus, salutem. Universitati vestre notificamus Gilbertum de Folkesworth' et filios eius Wydonem et Elyam dedisse deo et sancto Guthlaco Croiland' et monachis ibidem deo servientibus in perpetuam elemosinam triginta acras terre de dominio suo liberas, solutas et quietas ab omnibus secularibus servitiis et exactionibus; quod presentis*^a* sigilli testimonio premunimus. Hiis testibus et c'.

a Ms presens

Date as for no. 104, as this gift was included in the same confirmation by bp Robert of Lincoln (*EEA* I, no. 101).

106. *Notification to Alexander, prior of Ely, that neither Nicholas, archdeacon of Cambridge, nor his predecessors exercised any power in, or received anything from, an accused person having undergone trial by ordeal of water or fire in the Isle of Ely.*
[*c.* 1150 × 1163]

B = Cambridge, Trinity College Lib., ms O. 2. 1, fo. 61r. s. xii ex. C = Cambridge University Lib., Ely D. & C. muniments, EDC 1 (Ely cartulary), fo. 60v (59v). s. xiii in.

Pd from B and C, *Liber Eliensis*, 125; Henry, Archdeacon of Huntingdon, *Historia Anglorum*, 830, App. 1, no. 5.

Venerabili domino et amico karissimo Alexandro priori Elyensi Henricus archidiaconus Huntedunie,[a] salutem. Noverit dilectio vestra nunquam Nicholaum archidiaconum[b] Cantebrigie aut predecessores eius potestatem exercuisse vel quicquam accepisse ab aliquo reo qui subisset aquam vel ignem infra insulam Elyensem, sicut mea fert memoria et ab illis, quos diligenter super eadem re conveni et eiusdem rei scientes, didici. Vale.

a Huntendunie *C*   b archidianum *(sic) B,C*

After Alexander became prior of Ely and before his successor, Solomon, was in office (*Fasti Monastic Cathedrals*, 48). Nicholas, archdn of Cambridge (or Ely), was probably Henry of Huntingdon's father (*Fasti Lincoln*, 27). For the customs of the archdn of Ely (Cambridge) in the Isle of Ely, see *Liber Eliensis*, 402–4.

Nicholas de Sigillo

107. *Notification to all clergy of his archdeaconry that, [? by the authority] of Robert, bishop of Lincoln, at the presentation and gift of Walter de Neville and the concession of his lord, Geoffrey de Valoynes, and at the presentation and gift of Alban Hayrun, he has instituted the canons of Malton in the church of [King's] Walden, saving the right of Adam of Stukeley in the church.*   [*c.* 1164 × 27 Dec. 1166]

B = BL, Cotton ms Claudius D xi (Malton cartulary), fo. 226v (222v). s. xiii med.

Nicholaus de Sigillo archidiaconus Huntend' omnibus clericis per archidiaconatum suum constitutis salutem. Universitati vestre constare volumus nos [? auctoritate][a] Roberti Linc' episcopi, ad presentationem et donationem Walteri de Nevill' et concessionem domini sui Galfridi de Valoniis, et ad presentationem et donationem Albani Hayrun, instituisse in ecclesiam de Waldena cum omnibus ad eam pertinentibus canonicos de Malt' sine omni reclamatione et contradictione alicuius, salvo iure Ade de Stiveclea in ipsa ecclesia, salva etiam Linc' ecclesie dignitate. Hiis testibus, et c'.

a *Supplied conjecturally, but not certainly correct*

After the probable earliest date for the archdn's appointment (*Fasti Lincoln,* 27) and before the date of no. 108. Walter de Neville and Alban Hayrun were the patrons of the two moieties in the church (Golding, *Gilbert of Sempringham*, 368). Bp Robert Chesney of Lincoln confirmed the church to Malton as the gift of Walter de Neville, but did not mention Alban Hayrun (*EEA* I, no. 168). For Adam of Stukeley, the incumbent, see above, no. 104n., and below, no. 108n.

108. *Notification of the settlement of the dispute between Mr G(ilbert) of Sempringham and the canons of Malton and Adam, clerk, of Stukeley, and Walter de Neville over the church of [King's] Walden: at the gift and presentation of Mr G(ilbert) and the canons and by the gift and grant of Walter de Neville, the archdeacon has 'ordained' Adam as parson of [King's] Walden church for an annual pension of four marks, namely, one mark to the canons of Malton and three marks to Walter son of the said Walter; however, because Adam lives a long way from Malton, he will hand the said mark to the prior or canons of Chicksands; if Walter junior dies or changes his life before Adam, Adam will pay the four marks to the canons of Chicksands for the use of the canons of Malton; if Adam does so before Walter, the latter will pay the one mark to the canons of Malton; after the deaths of both, the canons of Malton will possess the church free and quit.* [c. 1164 × 27 Dec. 1166]

B = BL, Cotton ms Claudius D xi (Malton cartulary), fo. 226v (222v). s. xiii med.

Nicholaus archidiaconus Huntend' omnibus tam presentibus quam futuris, salutem. Innotescat universitati vestre quod super lite que vertebatur inter magistrum G. de Sempingh' et canonicos de Malton' et Adam clericum de Stiveclai et Walterum de Novill' de ecclesia de Walden iuxta tenorem presentis pagyne transactio facta est. Ex[a] donatione et presentatione magistri G. de Sempingh' et canonicorum de Malt' et Walteri de Novill', quantum ad laycam personam spectat, concessione et donatione, ordinavimus personam Adam de Stiveclay ecclesie de Waldene. Adam vero annuam inde solvet pensionem iiii. marcarum argenti, canonicis scilicet de Malt' i. marcam et Waltero filio dicti Walteri iii. marcas, ad hos terminos: ad Pascha dimidiam ita ut persolvat infra oct(abas) Pasche; ad festum sancti Michaelis dimidiam ita ut persolvat infra oct(abas) sancti Michaelis. Set quia regio ubi canonici de Malt' degunt[b] procul sita est a loco ubi Adam manet, Adam tradet marcam predictam ad terminos superius constitutos priori vel canonicis de Schikesand. Quod si Walterus filius Walteri de Novill' antequam Adam decesserit vel vitam mutaverit, Adam persolvet has iiii. marcas ad terminos predictos canonicis de Schikesand ad opus canonicorum de Malt'. Quod si Adam prius obierit vel vitam mutaverit, Walterus filius Walteri de Novill' de eadem ecclesia solvet i. marcam canonicis de Malt'. Post utriusque vero obitum, possidebunt canonici de Malt' ecclesiam illam liberam et quietam. Adam vero canonicis et Waltero filio iamdicti Walteri cautione fidei interposita se fore promisit fidelem.

a Ms Et   b Placed in ms before de Malt' and marked for transposition

After the probable earliest date for the archdn's appointment (*Fasti Lincoln,* 27), and before the death of Robert Chesney, bp of Lincoln, who confirmed the settlement and who 'ordained' Adam as parson *per manum Nicholai archidiaconi Hunted'* (ibid., 2; *EEA* I, no. 169). The bp's and archdn's acts are very similar, either because one is based on the other or perhaps because both were written together. On this case, see also Golding, *Gilbert of Sempringham,* 368. In 1187 × c. 1191 papal judges-delegate settled a later dispute between Malton priory and Adam the clerk of Stukeley over a higher render of 6 marks annually from Walden church, to which he was found liable and which he agreed to pay (cartulary, fo. 227v). Adam of Stukeley was the son of Henry, archdn of Huntingdon, and probably father of Mr Aristotle, a royal justice (Henry, Archdeacon of Huntingdon, *Historia Anglorum,* xxvii; C. Clay, 'Master Aristotle', *EHR* 76, 305). Aristotle was himself instituted as perpetual vicar of [King's] Walden in 1206 × 1209 (ibid., 307–8).

109.   *Grant to his clerk, Elias, of the perpetual vicarage of the church of Datchworth in perpetual alms, at the request of Abbot Laurence of Westminster and of Richard [of Ilchester], archdeacon of Poitiers, parson of the church; Elias shall pay two gold pieces annually to Richard or, if he leaves the church or dies, to Westminster abbey.*

[*c.* 1164 × 27 Dec. 1166]

B = Westminster Abbey Muniments, Book 11 (Westminster Abbey Domesday), fo. 380v (404v). s. xiv in.
Pd, *Westminster Abbey Charters*, 302–3, no. 468.

Nicholaus Huntend' archidiaconus omnibus ad quos littere presentes pervenerint, salutem. Dilecto clerico nostro Elie utiliter in posterum providere cupientes, venerabilium amicorum nostrorum Laurentii abbatis Westm' et domini Ricardi Pictav' archidiaconi petitione, perpetuam ecclesie*ᵃ* de Dachwrth vicariam in perpetuam elemosinam ei concedimus et presentis scripti testimonio confirmamus. Ita scilicet quod predictus Elyas ecclesiam illam possideat cum omnibus pertinentiis suis et cum omni integritate fructuum, et reddet annuatim predicto Ricardo Pictav' archidiacono, qui eiusdem ecclesie persona constitutus est, duos aureos tantum. Si vero Ricardus Pict(av') archidiaconus eidem ecclesie cesserit vel decesserit, prescripto tenore et conditione idem Elias ecclesie Westm' annuatim reddet illos duos aureos, et ecclesiam illam habebit cum omnibus pertinentiis suis et cum omni illa fructuum integritate quam prius eam possidebat, et ita quod ab eo quamdiu vixerit nichil preter hos duos aureos de iure exigi possit. Hec itaque conventio scripto et sigillo abbatis et conventus Westm' confirmata est. Hiis testibus: Willelmo filio Martini, magistro Iordano, magistro Hugone, et Thoma clerico, et Tornat(o), et Radulfo clerico Exon'.

a Ms ecclesiam *(in error)*

After the probable earliest date for the archdn's appointment (*Fasti Lincoln,* 27) and before the death of bp Robert of Lincoln, who made and confirmed the same grant in very similar terms (*EEA* IV, App. I, no. 20; *Westminster Abbey Charters*, no. 222). Both texts describe Elias as 'our clerk', but it seems on balance likely that he was the bp's clerk rather than the archdn's. For the type of perpetual vicar holding all the fruits of a church and paying a relatively modest pension, see Kemp, 'Monastic possession', 150–2.

110.   *Notification to all of his archdeaconry that, at the presentation and request of Roger and Alan de Somery and Ralph Chenduit, he has received the prior and monks of Walden in the* personatus *of the church of Shenley.*   [*c.* 1164 × Sept. 1179]

B = BL, Harley ms 3697 (Walden cartulary), fo. 41r (24r), no. 25. s. xiv ex.

Nicholaus archidiaconus Hunted' omnibus dilectis per archidiaconatum suum constitutis, salutem. Universitati vestre constare volumus nos, tam presentatione quam petitione Rogeri et Alani de Sumeri et Radulfi Chendeduit, suscepisse priorem et monachos de Waledena in personatu*ᵃ* ecclesie de Senleia. Testibus hiis : Alveredo de Hamelhamsted, Augustino decano, Henrico decano, Willelmo de Trumeta, Fulcho*ᵃ* de Aldeberia, Ricardo Ruffo canonico London', Ricardo fratre eius.

a Sic

After the probable earliest date for the archdn's appointment (*Fasti Lincoln,* 27) and before the death of Ralph Chenduit, whose son William sold the land of Shenley, held of Roger de Somery, with the advowson of the church, to Richard son of Reiner of London before Michaelmas 1179 (*Hatton's Book of Seals,* no. 158 and n.; *VCH Herts,* ii, 265). How this sale affected the position of Walden in the church is not clear. For the various members of the Somery family in the early 13th century, see *Hatton's Book of Seals,* no. 79n.; and for Richard Ruffus (II), canon of St Paul's, and his brother Richard, see *Fasti St Paul's,* 81.

111. *Notification to the clergy of his archdeaconry that, at the request and presentation of John de Rochella, he has received the prior and monks of Walden into the* personatus *of the church of Digswell.* [prob. 1166 × 1 Aug. 1190]

B = BL, Harley ms 3697 (Walden cartulary), fo. 65v (50v), no. 3. s. xiv ex.

Nicholaus archidiaconus Huntend' omnibus clericis per archidiaconatum suum constitutis, salutem. Universitatem vestram latere nolumus nos pio caritatis affectu, ad petitionem et presentationem Iohannis de Rochella, suscepisse[a] priorem et monachos de Waledena in personatum ecclesie de Dygeneswell' sine alicuius reclamatione et contradictione. Ne autem hec nostra institutio dierum vetustate a memoria defacili[b] laberetur, eam scripto nostro et sigilli nostri appositione munire curavimus. Hiis testibus: Benedicto capellano, magistro Simone de Histon', magistro Hamone de Wintonia, Adam de Aumeri, Radulfo de Amblia, Willelmo clerico, Ricardo clerico, Galfrido clerico, Laurentio clerico, Daniele clerico, Radulfo de Hamtona, et Ricardo filio Willelmi, Rocell' de Camera.

a Ms suscipisse   *b Sic*

The witness-list is sufficiently similar to that of no. 112 to suggest that both acts passed in the same period.

112. *Notification to the clergy of his archdeaconry that, at the presentation of Prior Reginald and the convent of Walden, he has instituted Hugh, clerk, as perpetual vicar in the church of Digswell under an annual pension of one mark.*

[1166 × 1 Aug. 1190]

B = BL, Harley ms 3697 (Walden cartulary), fo. 65v (50v), no. 4. s. xiv ex.

Nicholaus archidiaconus Hunt' omnibus clericis per archidiaconatum suum[a] constitutis, salutem. Universitati vestre notum facimus nos, ad presentationem Reginaldi prioris de Waleden' et totius eiusdem loci conventus, constituisse Hugonem clericum perpetuum vicarium in ecclesia de Dygeneswell' sub pensione unius marce eis annuatim persolvende. Hiis testibus: Humfr(ido) capellano, magistro Simone de Huston', magistro Hamone, Willelmo filio Ricardi, Radulfo de Amblia, Ricardo clerico.

a Interlined

After the appointment of Reginald as prior of Walden, and before he and the monastery were raised to abbatial status (*Heads,* 75–6).

113. *Notification to the clergy of Huntingdonshire that Godfrey, clerk, has acknowledged before him in synod at Huntingdon that the five acres of land lying adjacent to the croft of Woodstone church, which Anketil, former parson of the church, held as lay fee of the monks of Thorney for fourteen pence annually, in no way belong to the church of Woodstone; neither Godfrey nor any future parson can claim any right in the five acres save by the grace of the abbey.* [8 Sept. 1164 × 15 Mar. 1185]

> B = Cambridge University Lib., Additional ms 3020 (Thorney cartulary, part 1), fo. 114r. s. xiv in.

Nicholaus archidiaconus Huntend' omnibus clericis de Huntendoneschire, salutem. Noverit universitas vestra Godefridum clericum recognovisse coram me in sinodo celebrata apud Huntend' quod v. acre terre iacentes iuxta croftam*a* pertinentem ad ecclesiam de Wodestone, quas Anketillus dudum eiusdem ecclesie persona de monachis Thorn' sicut laicum feodum tenuit annuatim pro xiiii. d', nequaquam pertinent*b* ad predictam ecclesiam de Wodeston'; et quod nec ipse Godefridus nec quisquam alius futurus eiusdem ecclesie persona ius aliquod vendicare sibi poterit in predictis v. acris terre, nisi ex sola gratia et voluntate capituli Thorn' monasterii. Testibus hiis: Pagano abbate de Saltr', Ger' priore de Hunt', Bereng' de Paxton', Ada de Stivecle, Roberto de Iak', Waltero de Stangr', Iohanne de Moreburn', et c'.

> *a Ms* croftum   *b Ms* pertinet

The date is determined by the attestation of Payn, abbot of Sawtry, whose predecessor was still in office at the earlier terminus, and his successor in office at the later (*Heads*, 142).

114. *Confirmation to Thorney abbey, after diligent inquiry, of its ecclesiastical possessions in his archdeaconry, viz., pensions payable by the churches of Yaxley, [Water] Newton, Woodstone, Haddon, All Saints' Huntingdon, and Stibbington; certain tithes in Stanground; and two sheaves of the demesne tithes of Guy de Odre in Chesterton, of Eustace de Oy in Sibson, and of Gilbert of Grafham in Grafham.* [1167 × ? *c.* 1190; ? 1169 × 1176]

> B = Cambridge University Lib., Additional ms 3021 (Thorney cartulary, part 2), fo. 400r–v. s. xiv ex.

Nicolaus de Sigillo archidiaconus Huntend' omnibus clericis per archidiaconatum suum constitutis, salutem. Ad iuris enodationem nichil hostilius esse novimus veritatis ignorantia. Circa id enim, cuius notitia et certitudo necessaria et perutilis est, erroris fomitem inducit et universos hesitare compellit. Unde frequentius accidit res interdum ab antiquo possessas sub huius occasionis pretextu non modice turbari cum de illarum titulo questionem fieri contigit et possessionis qualitate. Ne igitur venerabile monasterium de Thorneia veritate minus evoluta consimili quandoque fatigetur dispendio, diligenti et exquisita investigatione accepimus loci prefati ecclesias in archidiaconatu nostro sitas a diebus venerabilium patrum A. et R. Lincoln' ecclesie episcoporum eidem monasterio pensionarias extitisse. Habet enim plurimorum assertio virorum ecclesiam de Iachesleia religionis pretaxate loco duas marcas nomine pensionis annuatim solvisse, ecclesiam de Neutone xxix. solidos et viii. denarios, ecclesiam de Wodestona dimidiam marcam, ecclesiam de Heddona v. solidos, ecclesiam omnium sanctorum in villa Huntend' x. solidos, ecclesiam de Sthibenton' unam marcam, ecclesiam de Stangrond' omnium frugum decimam quam persona ecclesie de Stangrond' percipit de decimis eiusdem ville, decimas etiam terre ipsius persone quam ipse vel alius eius nomine excolit. In omnibus autem prefatis ecclesiis curiarum decime ab hac prestatione et solutione excipiuntur, quoniam ab antiquo monachi loci sepius nominati eas in proprios convertunt usus. Preterea in Cestretona duas garbas decime de dominio Wydonis de Odre, in Sibestona duas garbas decime de dominio Eusthachii de Oy, in Grafham duas [fo. 400v] garbas de dominio Gileberti de Grafham percipiunt et percipere consueverunt. Et quoniam his omnibus tanta dierum vetustas cum longevo pastorali assensu auctoritatis munimen prestare dinoscitur, ea litterarum nostrarum auctoritate cum sigilli nostri appositione roborare curavimus. Hiis testibus: Benedicto, Ricardo, Gaufrido, capellanis, magistro Simone de Histona, Ada de Ameri, magistro Hamone de Wint', Radulfo decano, Albritto decano, Gileberto decano, Alketillo*a* decano, Iohanne de Wistowa, Rogero persona, Anselmo clerico, Godefrido de Hospitali, Rogero de Sancto Iohanne, Odone de Chambas, Serlone persona de Stangrond', Hugone clerico.

   a Sic; ? rectius Asketillo

Evidently after the death of bp Robert Chesney, 27 Dec. 1166, and before Nicholas de Sigillo ceased to be archdn, his successor being in office by 4 Apr. 1192 (*Fasti Lincoln*, 2, 27), but, in the absence of reference to an abbot, possibly during the long abbatial vacancy of 1169–76 (*Heads*, 75).

115. *Notification that he was present when Robert son of Thomas, heir of Richard of Dunham, gave in perpetual alms to the convent of Thorney the land of Alan of Rippingale which Walter* Fluri *holds at Scothern, namely seven bovates, so that Walter will hold it for seven shillings annually to the convent of Thorney. Robert has offered this gift by his charter on the altar, and at his request the prior and convent have excommunicated those who despoil the abbey of it.* [1169 × 1176]

   B = Cambridge University Lib., Additional ms 3020 (Thorney cartulary, part 1), fo. 252v. s. xiv in.

Nicholaus de Sigillo archidiaconus Huntend' omnibus filiis sancte ecclesie, salutem. Universitati vestre notum facimus nos interfuisse ubi Robertus filius Thome, heres Ricardi de Dunham, dedit deo et sancte Marie et sancto Botulpho et conventui de Thorn' terram Alani de Reppinghala quam Galt(erus) Fluri tenet, scilicet vii. bovatas, in perpetuam elemosinam libere et quiete possidendam. Ita quod idem Galt(erus) eandem terram teneat reddendo singulis annis conventui de Thorn' vii. s', dimid' ad Pascha et dimid' ad festum sancti Michaelis, et similiter heredes eius post eum. Hanc itaque donationem iamdictus Robertus per cartam suam super altare optulit et, petitione ipsius, prior et conventus Thorn' omnes spoliantes ecclesiam suam hac elemosina excommunicaverunt. Huic rei testimonium perhibemus et plures alii nobiscum. Terra autem hec est in Scotsterne.

Since no abbot of Thorney is mentioned, and it was the prior and convent who pronounced the excommunication, this gift must date from the long vacancy in the abbacy, 1169–76 (*Heads*, 75). Scothern was in the archdnry of Stow, which at this time was held by Richard de Almaria (*Taxatio*, 75; *Fasti Lincoln*, 45). Nicholas de

Sigillo is not acting here in an official capacity, but merely testifies to the gift of the land.

116. *Notification of the settlement in his presence of the dispute between the monks of St Neots and Roger, clerk of Huntingdon, over Holy Trinity church, Huntingdon. Roger acknowledged that the church belonged to the monks and that he had received it at their presentation. He then resigned his right in the same to the prior and monks through the archdeacon's hand, and swore to return their charter. Afterwards, in the archdeacon's presence, the prior and convent granted the church to Roger for life as long as he remained a secular; and the archdeacon, taking into account the confirmation of King Henry [II], the authentic writing of Henry his predecessor as archdeacon, and the testimony of reliable men, confirmed this act and the monks' right in the church.*

[*c.* 1164 × 6 July 1189]

B = BL, Cotton ms Faustina A iv (St Neots cartulary), fos. 41v–42r (40v–41r). s. xiii med.

Pd (calendar), Gorham, *Hist. Eynesbury and St Neot's*, ii, page xiii, no. 75.

Universis sancte matris ecclesie filiis tam presentibus quam futuris Nicholaus archidiaconus Huntend', salutem in domino. Ad vestram volumus pervenire notitiam qualiter in presentia nostra sopita sit controversia que fuit inter monachos Sancti Neoti et Rogerum clericum de Huntendon' super ecclesia sancte Trinitatis in Huntendon'. Predictus vero R., in nostra et aliorum quamplurium presentia constitutus, prefatam ecclesiam ad ius predictorum*a* monachorum confessus est pertinere, et eum ecclesiam ipsam ad presentationem prioris et monachorum Sancti Neoti recepisse. Et postea quicquid iuris in eadem ecclesia sancte Trinitatis habuerat per manum nostram priori et monachis Sancti Neoti resignavit et cartam quam de predicta ecclesia a predictis monachis habuit, tactis sacrosanctis ewangeliis, se eis redditurum coram nobis iuravit, ne carte illius auctoritate in posterum contra ius monachorum per eum vel per alium quicquam iniuriose de predicta ecclesia sancte Trinitatis posset attemptari. Postea vero prior et conventus nobis presentibus ecclesiam sepedictam de ipsis quam diu viveret vel in habitu seculari consisteret prenominato R. concesserunt tenendam. Nos siquidem cum carta et confirmatione domini regis Henrici, cum auctentico scripto predecessoris nostri Henrici archidiaconi, cum proborum virorum testimonio predictos monachos iamdictam ecclesiam canonice adeptos fuisse perpendentes, et utramque partem tam monachorum quam Rogeri indempnem conservare volentes, factum istud et ius monachorum predictorum quod in predicta ecclesia ipsos habere [fo. 42r] cognovimus hoc scripto nostro confirmavimus et sigilli nostri appositione communivimus. Hiis testibus.

a Altered in ms from predicto

After the probable earliest date for the archdn's appointment (*Fasti Lincoln*, 27), and before the death of Henry II. For archdn Henry's act, see above, no. 100. The church was confirmed to St Neots by archbp Theobald as a gift by King Henry II in 1154 × 1161 (Saltman, *Theobald*, 461–2, no. 236).

117. *Notification that, in accordance with an indult of Pope Lucius III to the monks of St Neots that they might retain in their hands their parish churches after the deaths of the incumbents, for the support of the monks and the reception of guests and the poor, provided that vicars be chosen and presented to the archdeacon, the archdeacon has confirmed to the monks the church of St Mary in the vill of St Neots, assigned to the said uses, the said monks having, as parsons, free disposition of all fruits of the church.* [Sept. 1181 × c. 1190]

B = BL, Cotton ms Faustina A iv (St Neots cartulary), fo. 37r (36r). s. xiii med.
Pd (calendar), Gorham, *Hist. Eynesbury and St Neot's*, ii, page x, no. 44.

Omnibus sancte matris ecclesie filiis ad quos presentes littere pervenerint Nicolaus de Sigillo archidiaconus Huntedon', salutem in domino. Que a pia matre nostra sancta Romana ecclesia statuta sunt et ordinata tenemur ex iniuncto nobis officio quantum possumus attentius providere, ut illesa et inconcussa perpetuo permaneant, et ut dispensationes quas, gratia pietatis et intuitu sancte religionis, indulserit cum omni integritate sua firmiter observentur. Unde universitati vestre dignum duximus intimandum venerabilem dominum nostrum Lucium papam tertium hoc misericordie beneficium indulsisse monachis de Sancto Neoto, ut ecclesias parochiales ad eos pertinentes decedentibus clericis in manu sua libere possint retinere, et earum beneficia ad sustentationem fratrum et hospitum ac pauperum susceptionem integre percipere, electis ab eis vicariis qui nobis et successoribus[a] nostris debeant presentari, sive fuerint perpetui sive temporales. Inde est quod, paternis vestigiis inherentes, predictis monachis ecclesiam beate Marie de villa Sancti Neoti cum omnibus pertinentiis suis ad prenominatos usus deputatam concessimus et carte nostre attestatione confirmavimus. Et ne in posterum tam pia dispositio ab aliquibus malitiose possit perturbari, eam sigilli nostri appositione ipsis communivimus, statuentes ut predicti monachi sicut persone de ipsa ecclesia et omnibus fructibus eius iure personali libere et integre valeant ordinare, salva in omnibus Lincolniensis[b] ecclesie dignitate. Hiis testibus.

a Ms suscessoribus   *b Ms* Lincolnienc'

After the coronation of Pope Lucius III, 6 Sept. 1181, and before Nicholas ceased to be archdn (see no. 114n.).

118. *Notification to the clergy of his archdeaconry that, at the presentation of Richard son of Galo, he has instituted the prior and canons of [Canons] Ashby as parson of the church of Puttenham, in the presence of Richard, parson of the same church, who will pay them annually twelve pence.* [c. 1164 × c. 1190]

A = PRO, E326/2967 (Ancient deed B 2967). Endorsed: Nichl' archid' de(?) Horfod' (? s. xii ex.). Size 138 × 100 mm (to cut for tongue 72 mm). Seal and tongue missing; wrapping-tie remaining.
B = BL, Egerton ms 3033 (Canons Ashby cartulary), fo. 51r (p. 95). s. xiii ex.
Pd from A, Cheney, *From Becket to Langton*, 190, App. III, no. 7 (b).

Nicholaus archidiaconus Hunt' omnibus clericis per archidiaconatum suum constitutis, salutem. Noverit universitas vestra nos, ad presentationem Ricardi filii Galonis, instituisse priorem et canonicos de Assebi[a] personam ecclesie de Puteham cum omnibus pertinentiis suis, presente Ricardo eiusdem ecclesie persona; ita tamen quod Ricardus solvet annuatim nomine predicte ecclesie prefatis canonicis xii. denarios in festo Nativitatis beate Marie. His[b] testibus:[c] Humfrido capellano, Benedicto capellano, Adam de Ameri, magistro Hamone de Wint', Radulfo de Amblia, Willelmo filio Ricardi, Ricardo clerico, Gaufrido clerico, Waltero de Triaingnel.

a Esseby *B*   *b* Hiis *B*   *c B ends*

After the probable earliest date for the archdn's appointment and before he ceased to be archdn (*Fasti Lincoln*, 27; above, no. 114n.).

119. *Notification to the clergy of his archdeaconry that, at the presentation of the prior and canons of [Canons] Ashby, he has instituted Richard of Tring, clerk, as perpetual vicar of the church of Puttenham, paying them an annual pension of twelve pence.* [*c.* 1164 × *c.* 1190]

> B = BL, Egerton ms 3033 (Canons Ashby cartulary), fo. 51r (p. 95). s. xiii ex.
> Pd, Cheney, *From Becket to Langton*, 190, App. III, no. 7 (a).

Nicholaus archidiaconus Huntind' omnibus clericis per archidiaconatum[a] suum constitutis, salutem. Universitati vestre constare volumus nos, ad presentationem prioris et canonicorum de Esseby, instituisse Ricardum de Trininge[b] clericum perpetuum vicarium ecclesie de Putteham, solvendo eis annuatim nomine pensionis xii. denarios in festo Nativitatis beate Marie. Hiis testibus.

a Ms archideaconatum   *b Reading uncertain: Cheney read* Trimuge *(suggesting for* Triunge)

If Richard of Tring, who is here instituted as perpetual vicar, is identical with Richard the parson in no. 118, then both acts are probably of the same date and together represent an attempt to turn the existing parson's tenure into that of a perpetual vicar by means of a new institution (see Cheney, 191).

120. *Notification that, coming into his presence, Roger Malarteys declared before all who were present in the chapter that he had given to the monks of Crowland in pure and perpetual alms the church of Washingley; and that he, at the request of both Roger and the monks, has confirmed the gift and instituted the monks into the church, assigned to the uses of the poor, saving the right of Simon the priest for life, who has given his assent and will pay an annual pension.* [*c.* 1164 × *c.* 1190]

> B = Spalding Gentlemen's Society, Crowland cartulary, fo. 202r. s. xiv med.

Nicholaus archidiaconus Huntyngdon' omnibus sancte matris ecclesie filiis, salutem. Vestre innotescat universitati quod, veniens in presentiam nostram, Rogerus Malarteys se concessisse et dedisse et carta sua confirmasse deo et sancto Guthlaco de Croiland' et monachis ibidem deo servientibus in puram et perpetuam elemosinam ecclesiam de Wassingle cum pertinentiis coram omnibus qui capitulo interfuerunt protestatus est. Quocirca, tam ipsius Rogeri quam predictorum fratrum iuste petitioni annuentes, donationem illam nostra duximus confirmatione roborandam, iam dictos monachos in prefatam ecclesiam pauperum usibus assignatam nemine aliquatenus contradicente instituentes, salvo in omnibus iure Simonis sacerdotis quoad vixerit, huic donationi assensum prebentis et pensionem annuam persolventis. Hiis testibus, et c'.

Date as for no. 118. The donor's charter precedes this act in the cartulary, fo. 202r. Under Abbot Henry (1190–1236) Croyland surrendered all right in the church to Richard of Washingley and his heirs (cartulary, fo. 202r). The church no longer exists; it was reported ruinous in 1447 and had been united to the adjacent Northants church of Lutton (*VCH Hunts,* iii, 229; *VCH Northants,* ii, 585).

121. *Notification to all clergy of his archdeaconry that, at the presentation and request of Abbot R(obert) and the convent of Crowland, he has received Richard, clerk, to the rule of the church of Morborne, under an annual pension of two marks; Richard will acquit the church in all things.* [8 July 1175 × 24 Mar. 1190]

B = Spalding Gentlemen's Society, Crowland cartulary, fo. 196r. s. xiv med.

Nicholaus archidiaconus Huntingdon' omnibus clericis per archidiaconatum suum constitutis, salutem. Noverit universitas vestra nos, ad presentationem et petitionem R. abbatis de Croiland' et eiusdem loci conventus, recepisse Ricardum clericum ad regimen ecclesie de Morbourne cum omnibus pertinentiis suis sub annua pensione duarum marcarum ad hos terminos reddendarum, scilicet ad Purificationem beate Marie dimidiam marcam, ad festum sancti Guthlaci dimidiam marcam, ad festum sancti Both(ulf)i dimidiam marcam, et ad festum sancti Michaelis dimidiam marcam. Ipse vero Ricardus acquietabit ecclesiam predictam in omnibus. Hiis testibus: Iohanne monacho de Croiland', Wyberto priore de Bruiera,[a] Benedicto capellano, Reginaldo capellano de Heddona, magistro Simone de Histona, et aliis.

a Reading uncertain; ? Briuera

The dating limits are those of Abbot Robert of Crowland, who became abbot after the abbey was reported as vacant, 1–8 July 1175, and who died 17 Mar. or 24 Mar. 1190 (*Heads*, 42).

122. *Notification to all clergy of his archdeaconry that, at the presentation and request of Abbot R(obert) and the convent of Crowland, he has instituted Aristotle, clerk, as parson of the church of Folksworth, under an annual pension of half a mark; Aristotle will acquit the church in all things.* [8 July 1175 × 24 Mar. 1190]

B = Spalding Gentlemen's Society, Crowland cartulary, fo. 200r–v. s. xiv med.

Nicholaus archidiaconus Huntygdon' omnibus clericis per archidiaconatum suum constitutis, salutem. Noverit universitas vestra nos, ad presentationem et petitionem R. abbatis de Croiland' et eiusdem loci conventus, instituisse Aristotilem clericum personam ecclesie de Folkesworth' sub annua pensione dimidie marce, quam solvet ad duos terminos, scilicet ad festum sancti Michaelis quadraginta denarios et ad Pascha quadraginta denarios. Predictus vero Aris[fo. 200v]totiles acquietabit ecclesiam in omnibus. Hiis testibus.

Date as for no. 121. For Aristotle, see C. Clay, 'Master Aristotle', *EHR* 76, 303–8. Since Aristotle was probably the son of Adam of Stukeley, former parson of the church (above, no. 104), the case provides another example of hereditary succession to a benefice in the 12th century (see Henry, Archdeacon of Huntingdon, *Historia Anglorum*, 831, no. 6n.).

123. *Notification to all clergy of his archdeaconry that, at the request and grant of Prior Robert and the convent of Merton, he has received Eusebius of Wistow, clerk, into the vicarage of the church of Godmanchester, which John of Brampton held of them, with the addition of four acres of land acquired by Roger the canon. Eusebius will pay the canons six pounds annually and will acquit the church as regards the bishop and the archdeacon and their officials concerning episcopal customs and aids. [The text is possibly partly conflated with a later document.]*　　[c. 1164 × c. 1190]

> B = BL, Cotton ms Cleopatra C vii (Merton cartulary), fos. 183v–184r (180v–181r). s. xiv ex.

Nicolaus de Sigillo archidiaconus Huntendon' omnibus clericis per archidiaconatum suum constitutis, salutem. Universitati vestre constare volumus nos, ad petitionem et concessionem Roberti prioris de Merton' et eiusdem loci conventus, recepisse Eusebium de Wistowa clericum in vicariam ecclesie de Gomecestre perpetuo de eis tenendam, quam Iohannes de Brant' de illis tenuit [　　]*a* in terris et decimis et oblationibus et aliis obventionibus. Et preterea concesserunt ipsi Eusebio ad augmentum vicarie iiii. acras terre quas Rogerus canonicus adquisivit. Solvet autem idem Eusebius predictis canonicis annuatim vi. libras argenti [fo. 184r] ad quatuor terminos principales per equales portiones. Et acquietabit ecclesiam illam erga episcopum et archidiaconum et offic(iales) eorum tam de episcopalibus consuetudinibus quam de donis et auxiliis et omnibus rebus. Honeste etiam procurabit ecclesiam illam ut in ea honorifice divina celebrentur. Ipse vero Eusebius promisit se hanc conventionem fideliter servaturum, et quod vero per se nec per alium eis de predicta vicaria nec de memorato redditu aliquod faciet impedimentum nec aliquod dampnum de decimis que ad illos pertinent. Hiis testibus: magistro Simone de Hist', magistro Hamone de Wint', Radulfo decano, et c'. Dat' anno incarnationis domini M° CC° xviii°, vi° idus Martii et c'.*b*

> *a There appears to be a break in the syntax here*　　　*b Dating clause sic*

Date as for no. 118 (the date given in the text is clearly impossible). Although the witnesses are right for Nicholas de Sigillo, the text may be partially a conflation of two documents, the second being a taxation of the vicarage, dated 1218. The latter may be somehow connected with the grant of the vicarage on the same date by Prior Walter and the convent of Merton, and with the undated taxation of the vicarage by R(obert of Hailes), archdn of Huntingdon, J(ohn), prior of Huntingdon (acting for the bp), and Prior Walter of Merton, although the details are different from those given here (cartulary, fos. 90r, 183r–v; A. Heales, *The Records of Merton Priory*, London 1898, 74–5). It is possible, however, given the witnesses, that the date has mistakenly been added to the present text, to which it does not belong. (For another not dissimilar case in the cartulary, see *EEA* VIII, no. 159.)

* 124. *Act concerning an institution [in the church of Wistow], and a pension and portion of the same; and a note that the pension is to provide a candle before the altar [? of Ramsey abbey].*　　[c. 1164 × c. 1190]

> Listed only, in the inventory of charters of Ramsey abbey: PRO, E164/28 (Ramsey cartulary), fo. 27v (18v). s. xiv; pd, *Ramsey Cartulary*, i, 94, no. 294.

Item institutio Nicholai de Sigillo archidiaconi, de pensione eius et portione; et pensio est pro cereo ante altare.

Date as for no. 118. The preceding item in the list reads: 'Concessio Roberti abbatis de ecclesia de Wystowe'; perhaps, but not certainly, referring to Robert Trianel, 1180–1200 (*Heads*, 62).

125a. *Notification that, in synod at Huntingdon, he has received Alan, almoner of Ramsey, into the church of Warboys, and put him into corporal possession, so that he and his successors shall hold the church as Walter, late abbot of Ramsey, lord of the fee, and Robert, late bishop of Lincoln, granted it to the almonry, and the pope and Theobald, archbishop of Canterbury, confirmed it. Adam de Aumari, clerk, the archdeacon's nephew, who will hold the church of the almoner for life, or until he changes his life, will acquit it in all things as regards the archbishop, bishop and archdeacon, rendering to the almoner an annual pension of forty shillings.*

[1167 × c. 1190]

A = BL, Additional Charter 34175. Endorsed: Carta Archidiaconi Huntingdon' (s. xiv). Size 137 x 114 + 22 mm. Seal missing, tag surviving (method 2). Pd, cf. no. 125b.

Nicolaus archidiaconus Huntend' omnibus ad quos littere iste pervenerint, salutem in domino. Noverit universitas vestra quod ego recepi fratrem Alanum Ram(esie) elemosinarium in ecclesiam de Wardeb' et in corporalem possessionem misi, ut tam ipse quam quicumque sit elemosinarius post eum eandem ecclesiam optineat, sicut bone memorie*a* Walterus quondam abbas Ram', dominus fundi, et Robertus quondam Lincoln' episcopus eandem ecclesiam elemosinarie Ram' concesserunt et cartis suis confirmaverunt, et dominus papa postmodum auctoritatis sue privilegio et dominus Theob' Cant'*b* archiepiscopus eandem concessionem carta sua ad noticiam posterorum et ad robur firmitatis munierunt. Hoc autem addere curavimus quod Adam clericus de Aumari nepos noster, qui eandem ecclesiam de elemosinario Ram' quam diu vixerit vel vitam [non]*c* mutaverit tenebit, eam in omnibus tam versus archiepiscopum quam versus episcopum et archidiaconum adquietabit, reddendo memorato elemosinario Ram' ad duos terminos pensionem annuam xl. solidorum, medietatem scilicet ad festum sancti Michaelis et medietatem ad Pascha. Hoc actum est in sinodo apud Huntend', his testibus: Hunfr(ido) capellano, magistro Simone de Hist', magistro Hamone, Willelmo et Ricardo clericis nostris, et Radulfo decano.

a Ms memoire *b Ms* Cart' *c Supplied*

After the death of bp Robert Chesney of Lincoln, 27 Dec. 1166, and while Nicholas was archdn (*Fasti Lincoln*, 2, 27). This is a rather unprepossessing document, which may have been superseded by the version copied into the abbey's registers (below, no. 125b).

125b. *Another version of the same, with some textual variation and a longer witness list.* [1167 × c. 1190]

B = Bodl. ms Rawlinson B. 333 (Ramsey chronicle), fo. 52r. s. xiv in. C = PRO, E164/ 28 (Ramsey cartulary), fo. 186v (162v). s. xiv. Pd from B (collated with above, no. 125a), *Ramsey Chronicle*, 315–16, no. 394; from C, *Ramsey Cartulary*, ii, 173–4, no. 294.

[N]icholaus*a* archidiaconus Huntend'*b* omnibus ad quos littere iste pervenerint, salutem in domino. Noverit universitas vestra quod ego recepi fratrem Alanum Ram(esie)*c* elemosinarium in ecclesiam de Wardebois[d] et in corporalem possessionem misi, ut tam ipse quam quicumque sit elemosinarius post eum eandem ecclesiam optineat, sicut bone memorie Walterus quondam abbas Ram(esie), dominus fundi, et Robertus quondam Linc'[e] episcopus eandem ecclesiam elemosinario Ram(esie) concesserunt et suis cartis confirmaverunt, et dominus papa postmodum auctoritatis sue privilegio et dominus Theodbaldus[f] Cant' archiepiscopus eandem concessionem carta sua ad notitiam posterorum et ad robur firmitatis munierunt. Hoc autem addere curavi quod Adam clericus [de Amauri][g] nepos noster, qui eandem ecclesiam de elemosinario Rameseie tenebit, reddet annuatim eidem elemosinario xl. solidos, xx. solidos[h] ad festum sancti Michaelis et xx. ad Pascha. Idem etiam Adam memoratam ecclesiam de omnibus rebus adversus episcopum et episcopales ministros adquietabit. Cum autem obierit vel vitam mutaverit, eadem ecclesia ad dispositionem elemosinarii Ram(esie) libere revertetur. Hoc actum est in sinodo apud Hunted'.[i] Hiis testibus: Humfrido[j] capellano, magistro Symone de Hist', magistro Hamone, Willelmo et Ricardo clericis nostris, Radulfo decano, magistro Iordano, magistro Herberto de Ram(esia), Roberto[k] clerico, magistro Alexandro, Waltero de Therefeld,[l] Yvone de Burew'.[m]

a Passages in small type as in no. 125a	*b* Huntingdon' *C*	*c (and subsequently)*
Rames' *C* *d* Wardeboys *C*	*e* Lincoln' *C*	*f* Theobaldus *C*
g Om. in B, supplied from C	*h Om. in C*	*i* Huntingd' *C*
j Hunfrido *C* *k* Rodberto *C*	*l* Terfeld' *C*	*m* Bery *C*

Date as for no. 125a. The inventory of charters of Ramsey abbey calls this act 'Item inductio Nicholai de Sigillo archidiaconi Huntingdonie de eadem [referring to Warboys church], et admisit monachum in possessionem corporalem' (*Ramsey Cartulary*, i, 202, no. 448). Nicholas had himself held the church before becoming archdn (ibid., ii, 171–2; *EEA* I, no. 226; Saltman, *Theobald*, 431, no. 209).

126. *Notification to the clergy of his archdeaconry that, [?at the presentation of] Jordan de Ameville he has instituted the abbot of St James [Northampton, in the church] of Little Gaddesden.*	[? *c.* 1170 × *c.* 1190]

B = BL, Cotton ms Tiberius E v (St James Northampton cartulary), fo. 207v (193v). s. xiv in. Badly damaged by fire; lost or supplied passages in square brackets.

Nicholaus de Sigillo archidiaconus Huntind' omnibus clericis per [archidiaconatum suum consti]tutis, salutem. Universitati vestre constare nos[a] volumus, [? ad presentationem] Iordani de Amevill', instituisse abbatem Sancti Iacobi [? Norh(am)t' in ecclesia] de Parva Gadesdena. Ut autem hec institutio [   ], eam literarum nostrarum autoritate et signi nostri app[ositione] [   ]. Hiis testibus: Alexandro priore de Asseby, Benedicto, Ricardo, Galfrido, [? capellanis,[b] magistro Simone] de Histon', Adam de Aumeri, magistro Hamone de Win[ton'   ], Laurentio clerico, Hamone clerico. Valete.

a Interlined		*b For this suggestion, cf. above, no. 114*

Dating very uncertain: Nicholas was archdn, *c.* 1164–*c.* 1190 (above, no. 118n.), but Alexander, prior of Canons Ashby, occurs from *c.* 1181 × 1185 to 1197 × 1205 and 1198 × 1201 (*Fasti Lincoln*, 27; *Heads*, 157).

127. *Notification to the clergy of his archdeaconry that, at the presentation of Robert de Valoynes, he has received and instituted the canons of Waltham Holy Cross into the church of All Saints, Hertford.* [11 June 1177 × 3 Mar. 1185]

B = BL, Harley ms 391 (Waltham cartulary), fo. 97v. s. xiii in. C = BL, Cotton ms Tiberius C ix (Waltham cartulary), fo. 141r. s. xiii med.
Pd from B collated with C, *Waltham Charters*, 210, no. 312.

Nicholaus archidiaconus Hunt' omnibus clericis [suis]*ᵃ* per archidiaconatum suum constitutis, salutem. Noverit universitas vestra nos, ad presentationem Roberti de Valoniis, recepisse canonicos Sancte Crucis de Walth'*ᵇ* in ecclesiam omnium sanctorum de Hertford' et in eadem*ᶜ* eos instituisse,*ᵈ* salva Linc' ecclesie dignitate. His*ᵉ* testibus:*ᶠ* magistro Iordano, Hunfrido capellano, Benedicto capellano, magistro Symone de Huston', magistro Hamone, Radulfo de Amblia, Willelmo filio Ricardi, Ricardo clerico, Galfrido clerico, Rogero de Hamt' constabulo.

a Om. *in B*	*b* Waltham *C*	*c* eandem *C*	*d* constituisse *C*
e Hiis *C*	*f C ends*		

After the introduction of Augustinian canons at Waltham (*Waltham Charters*, 16 n. 4), and before Walter of Coutances, bp of Lincoln, confirmed the church to the canons with the stipulation for a vicarage (ibid., no. 313; *EEA* I, no. 323).

128. *Notification that, at the presentation of the abbot and canons of Holyrood, Edinburgh, he has instituted Mr Peter as parson in the church of [Great] Paxton under an annual pension of six marks to them as parsons, whom R(obert), late bishop of Lincoln, instituted, as his charter testifies.* [1185 × c. 1190]

A1 = Lincoln, Lincolnshire Archives, Lincoln D. & C. Muniments, Dij/90/3/20. Endorsed: none. Size 205 × 119 + 20 mm. Seal missing, tag remaining (method 2).
A2 = Ibid., Dij/90/3/21. Endorsed: De ecclesia Paxton' (s. xii). iiiᵃ (s. xiv). Size 149 × 104 + 25 mm. Seal missing, tag remaining (method 2, modified). A few words illegible, probably from damp.
B = Ibid., A/1/6 (The Registrum), fo. 49r–v, no. 290. s. xiv med.
Pd from A1 (collated with B) and A2, *Reg. Antiquissimum*, iii, 159–60, nos. 814–15, with facsimile of A1 opposite 198.

Omnibus sancte matris ecclesie filiis N. archidiaconus Huntedon',*ᵃ* salutem. Que*ᵇ* provida deliberatione agimus scripti nostri attestatione*ᶜ* corroboranda*ᵈ* censuimus. Universitati igitur vestre innotescat nos, ad presentacionem abbatis et canonicorum Sancte Crucis de Edeneburg', instituisse magistrum Petrum personam in ecclesia de Paxton' sub pensione vi. marcarum persolvendarum illis annuatim *ᵉ*tanquam personis, quos R. bone memorie quondam Lincoln' episcopus instituit, sicut carta eius testatur, ad festum sancti Botulfi.*ᵉ* Hanc autem conventionem tactis sacrosanctis ewangeliis se fideliter observaturum *ᶠ*predictus P. affirmavit.*ᶠ* Hiis testibus: Waltero subpriore*ᵍ* Huntedon',*ᵃ* magistro Iordano, Hunfrido*ʰ* capellano, Benedicto capellano, Iohanne de Branton',*ⁱ* Ailbrytto*ʲ* decano, magistro Hamone, Stephano de Echeton'*ᵏ* iuniore, Helia*ˡ* Tailebois, Ricardo de Draiton',*ᵐ* Michaele, Gaufrido diacono, Adam,*ⁿ* Michaele de Paxton',*ᵒ* Henrico de Winton', Roberto.

a Huntendon' *B*	*b* Quod *A2*	*c First part of this word illegible in A1, A2*

d corroborandum *A2*   *e–e* ad festum sancti Botulfi tanquam personis quos R.
bone memorie quondam Lincoln' episcopus instituit sicut carta eius testatur *A2*
f–f promisit prefatus Petrus *A2*   *g* suppriore *B*   *h* Humfr' *B*
i Brampton' *B*   *j* Ailbritto *A2;* Albritto *B*   *k* Eketon' *A2;* Ccheton' *B*
l Elia *B*   *m* Drayton' *B*   *n Add* de Hele *A2*   *o* Paxtona *A2*

Probably after King Malcolm IV's gift of Great Paxton church to Holyrood (prob. late
1161 × 24 Jan. 1162) was confirmed by David, his brother, who succeeded to the earldom
of Huntingdon in 1185 (*Reg. Antiquissimum,* iii, no. 813), since the preceding earl, Simon
de St Liz, had given the church to Peter in an attempt to alienate the advowson from
Holyrood (ibid., no. 812); and before Nicholas ceased to be archdn (*Fasti Lincoln,* 27).
The only known charter by bp Robert of Lincoln to Holyrood, dated Oct. 1162, simply
confirms Malcolm IV's gift of the church (*Reg. Antiquissimum,* iii, no. 807; *EEA* I, no. 111);
if this is the charter cited here by the archdn, its failure to mention 'institution' of the
abbot and canons is very instructive. An earlier proposal to establish a house of regular
canons in Great Paxton church, approved by archbp Theobald, had not been fulfilled
and the church was given to Holyrood, although a small staff of clergy continued to serve
its extensive parish, including the chapelries of Little Paxton and Toseland (*Reg. Antiq.,*
iii, nos. 800–4; Saltman, *Theobald,* 420, no. 198; Knowles and Hadcock, 158; *VCH Hunts,*
ii, 331–2; *Regesta Regum Scottorum,* i, no. 197).

ARCHDEACONRY OF LEICESTER

Hugh Barre

129. *Notification to dean Ralph [of Langford] and the chapter of St Paul's,
London, that he has given in perpetual alms to Godstow abbey the land which Hugh
son of Jordan holds of him, namely, the shop in Westcheap which Bernard Caldebuf
held of Osbert, his father, and of Richard son of Osbert, his brother, as Richard gave it
to him.*   [*c.* 1149 × *c.* 1154]

> B = PRO, E164/20 (Godstow cartulary), fo. 2r. s. xv med.
> Pd (calendar), *Godstow English Register,* i, 185, no. 243.

Radulfo decano et capitulo Sancti Pauli Lonnd' Hugo Legr(ecestri)e*ᵃ* archidiaconus, salutem. Noscat vestra dilectio me dedisse et in perpetuam elemosinam
concessisse ecclesie de Godestowe et sanctimonialibus in eadem ecclesia deo
servientibus terram illam quam Hugo filius Iohannis de me tenet, sopam illam
in Wescheap' quam Bernardus Culdebuf' de Osberto patre meo et de Ricardo
filio Osberti fratre meo tenuit, sicut predictus Ricardus frater meus illam michi
dedit et libere concessit. Testibus: Willelmo Lund' archidiacono, et Walchei
monachi,*ᵇ* et Radulfo de Monemuta, et Ricardo capellano, et magistro Rogero
de Seis.

a First two letters apparently erased   b Sic

The donor first occurs as archdn of Leicester in *c.* 1150, in succession to Robert de
Chesney, consecrated bp of Lincoln, 19 Dec. 1148 (*Fasti Lincoln,* 33). William [de
Belmeis], archdn of London, had been succeeded by *c.* 1154, and Ralph of Langford,
dean, last occurs in 1152 × *c.* 1154 and in *c.* 1154 (*Fasti St Paul's,* 15, 5). The gift of the
shop was included in Henry II's general confirmation to Godstow in 1182 × 1188
(*Godstow English Register,* ii, 663).

130. *Notification that, by order of Bishop R(obert) of Lincoln, he was appointed judge in the case brought in the bishop's presence against the monks of St Andrew's, Northampton, by William the priest over the church of Brafield[-on-the-Green]; and that it has been established that William brought an unjust plea against the monks, and that therefore they ought to hold the church in peace.*

[*c.* 1149 × 1159; ? × *c.* 1157]

B = BL, Royal ms 11 B. ix (St Andrew's Northampton cartulary), fo. 35r–v. s xiii ex.
C = BL, Cotton ms Vespasian E xvii (St Andrew's Northampton cartulary), fo. 64r (58r). s. xv med.

H. archidiaconus Legrecestr' universis filiis sancte matris ecclesie, salutem. Notum sit omnibus tam presentibus quam futuris me, precipiente domino R.[a] Linc' episcopo, destinatum [?esse][b] iudicem inter monachos sancti Andree de Norh(am)t[c] et Willelmum presbiterum, qui eos in presentia domini episcopi in causam duxerat de ecclesia de Bragefeld.[d] Assertione autem quorundam testium conpetentium [fo. 35v], Willelmi scilicet archidiaconi, Edwini decani, Giraldi presbiteri aliorumque qui testimonium suum sacramento confirmaverunt,[e] certificatum est predictum Willelmum iniustam apud[f] monachos habuisse querelam. Unde exigente ratione a nobis et a clero[g] qui interfuit indicatum[h] est monachos in pace debere tenere predictam ecclesiam de Bragefeld,[i] Willelmo penitus abiudicato. Ad maiorem vero huius rei confirmationem, isti testes subscripti sunt: Willelmus scilicet archidiaconus, magister Robertus, Edwinus decanus, magister Walefridus, magister Thomas, magister Radulphus[j] de Britollio, Ricardus capellanus Hugonis archidiaconi, Giraldus presbiter, Ailbrictus presbiter, Willelmus presbiter de Pittesford',[k] Willelmus presbiter de Adrinth', Haimo de Siwell',[l] Aluredus presbiter de Hardinstor',[m] Ricardus de Oxend',[n] Rand(ulfus) clericus.

a Roberto *C*	*b Om. in both texts; supplied to make the sense*		*c* North' *C*
d Brachafeldie *C*	*e* confinaverunt *B*	*f* adversum *C*	*g For* a clero
B has adero		*h B has* in disicatum *with* si *marked for deletion*	
i Brachafeldia *C*	*j* Radulfus *C*	*k* Pitesfordia *C*	*l* Siwellia *C*
m Hardyngystou *C*	*n* Oxendona *C*		

The dating limits are those of Hugh's archidiaconate (*Fasti Lincoln*, 33). William the archdn seems most likely to have been Hugh's contemporary in the archdnry of Northampton (ibid., 30), where the church concerned was situated; in this case the diocesan has committed the settlement of a dispute that had arisen in one archdnry to a neighbouring archdn.

Baldric de Sigillo

131. *Notification that, coming freely into his presence in Garendon abbey, Ralph of Dishley, son of Roger, has, in the hearing of many, remitted his right in the land of Dishley and renounced it into the archdeacon's hand, undertaking never to bring an action for it against the monks of Garendon abbey. Ralph has solemnly vowed before Abbot T(hurstan) to become a monk at Garendon.* [*c.* 1161 × *c.* 1187]

B = BL, Lansdowne ms 415 (Garendon cartulary), fo. 21r (20r). ss. xii–xiii.
Pd, Nichols, *Leicestershire*, iii (ii), 819.

B. archidiaconus Legrec' universis filiis sancte matris ecclesie, salutem. Sciatis quod Radulfus de Dixel' filius Rogeri, accedens sponte ad presentiam nostram in abbatiam Gerold', sub multorum virorum audientia quicquid iuris unquam habuit in terra de Dixel' remisit, et in manu nostra in perpetuum refutavit, adiciens[a] sub fidei interpositione se nunquam monachis de Gerold' inde moturum questionem vel illaturum calumniam. Et ut abbatia Gerold' maiori gauderet securitate, T. abbati predicti loci se reddidit, sollemniter vovens se in habitu religionis in predicta domo pro salute anime sue fore permansurum. His testibus: magistro Bernardo, Ger(ardo) filio archidiaconi Legrec', Acardo presbitero, Nicholao capellano de Lucteb'.

a Ms aditiens

After Nov. 1160, when Baldric was not yet archdn, and before *c.* 1187, when he was probably dead (*Fasti Lincoln,* 33). Ralph's son's confirmation was made on the same occasion (below, no. 132). At the foot of the folio is the following note: Hoc quod Rad' de Dixeleia et Rog' filius eius fecerant coram archidiacono, fecerunt iterum in curia com(itis) apud Legrec', et affidaverunt in manu Willelmi de Chyrai tunc temporis dapiferi, presentibus Willelmo Burdet et Willelmo de Widevill' et Herveo Marescallo et Rad' filio [?, *corner of folio broken away*].

132. *Notification that, coming to him in Garendon abbey, Roger son of Ralph of Dishley has, in the presence of many, renounced to his father his right in the latter's land of Dishley, and granted and confirmed it in perpetuity to the monks, saving the agreement made between the monks and Ralph.* [*c.* 1161 × *c.* 1187]

B = BL, Lansdowne ms 415 (Garendon cartulary), fo. 21r (20r). ss. xii–xiii.
Pd, Nichols, *Leicestershire,* iii (ii), 819.

B. archidiaconus Legr' omnibus filiis sancte matris ecclesie, salutem. Sciatis quod Rogerus filius Radulfi de Dixl', ad nos veniens in abbatiam de Gerold', multis presentibus, si quid iuris unquam habuit in terra illa de Dixel' que fuit Radulfi patris eius, ei sponte renuntiavit, et terram illam monachis de Gerold' absque querela ab eo eis movenda quiete in perpetuum tenendam concessit, et sub fidei interpositione se hoc firmiter observaturum firmavit, servata conventione inter memoratos monachos et iamdictum Radulfum[a] facta. His testibus: magistro Bernardo, Ger(ardo) filio archidiaconi Legr', Acardo presbitero, Nicholao capellano de Lucteb'.

a Ms Robertum

This clearly passed on the same occasion as no. 131.

133. *Confirmation of the exchange, made in the chapter of priests in Melton [Mowbray] church, between Garendon abbey and the church of Goadby [Marwood] by Walter the priest and Nicholas the clerk, parsons of the church, of one acre of land which the monks have before the gate of their grange in exchange for the acre in* Langfurlanges *and* Salt(er)hou *which Goadby [Marwood] church holds by gift of* Luke de Quatremars. [*c.* 1161 × *c.* 1187]

B = BL, Lansdowne ms 415 (Garendon cartulary), fo. 21v (20v). ss. xii–xiii.
Pd, Nichols, *Leicestershire,* ii (i), App., 133–4, no. 4.

Universis sancte matris ecclesie filiis Bald' archidiaconus Legr', salutem. Sciatis me confirmasse excambium quod factum est inter ecclesiam de Gerold' et ecclesiam de Goutebi per Walterum sacerdotem et Nicholaum clericum, personas eiusdem ecclesie, videlicet de una acra terre que adiacet ante portam grangie monachorum quam habent in excambio illius acre quam predicta ecclesia de Goutebi obtinet in Langfurlanges et in Salt(er)hou, donatione et confirmatione Luce de Quatremars. Hanc igitur commutationem inter predictas ecclesias in capitulo sacerdotum in ecclesia de Meultonia ratam et inconcussam in perpetuum permanere, communi assensu sacerdotum et clericorum, concessimus et confirmavimus. Hii sunt testes: magister Bernardus, magister Durandus, Achardus, Robertus sacerdos de Chaldewel.

Date as for no. 131. For the abbey's grange at Goadby, see *VCH Leics*, ii, 5. The main manor was acquired late in Henry III's reign by the Maureward family, one of whom confirmed the abbey's grange there (Nichols, *Leicestershire*, ii (i), 194; iii (ii), 791, no. 59). The Garendon cartulary also contains four interesting agreements, reached with Baldric's assent, concerning annual payments to be made by the abbey to the parish churches of Ibstock and Prestwold for the tithes arising on its lands in their parishes: cartulary, fos. 21r–v, 21v, 23r (1176), 23r (1177), the last being confirmed by the archdn's seal; pd, Nichols, *Leicestershire*, iii (ii), 819, 821. These provide further instances of preserving Cistercian freedom from tithes (cf. Burton, *Monastic Order in Yorkshire*, 264–5; above, no. 7n.).

134. *Gift in pure and perpetual alms to the abbey and monks of Kirkstead of eight acres of his meadow in Freiston.* [*c.* 1161 × *c.* 1187]

B = BL, Cotton ms Vespasian E xviii (Kirkstead cartulary), fo. 180r (p. 333). s. xiii med.

Universis sancte matris ecclesie filiis Baldricus archidiaconus Legrecestrie, salutem in domino. Sciatis me concessisse,*a* dedisse et hac mea carta confirmasse deo et ecclesie sancte Marie de Kirke(stede)*b* et monachis ibidem deo servientibus in puram et perpetuam elemosinam, pro salute anime mee et parentum meorum, octo acras de prato meo in Frestunenges per perticam decem et pedum,*c* a prato Alani de Roches versus orientem in latum et a fossato comitis versus austrum in longum usque ad divisam prati rusticorum meorum de Frestun(enges), et libertatem ingrediendi et exeundi in idem pratum sicut ego unquam melius vel liberius habui. Quare volo ut predicti monachi habeant et teneant predictum pratum honorifice, libere et quiete ab omni seculari servitio et consuetudine et exactione. Et ego et heredes mei warentizabimus eis predictum pratum erga*d* omnes homines in perpetuum. Testibus: Achardo capellano, Girardo filio*e* archidiaconi, Iohanne clerico, Nicholao clerico.

a Followed in ms by de *(redundant)*   *b Expansion from other texts on this folio*
c et pedum *sic*   *d Ms* ergo   *e Ms* filius

Date as for no. 131. The first witness, occurring in other acts as 'Achard' or 'Achard the priest', was the archdn's chaplain, as is made clear in a grant of Sharnford church (Leics) to Monks Kirby priory made in Baldric's presence in *c.* 1161 × 1177, in which 'Achard the chaplain' appears among the witnesses *ex parte domini archidiaconi* (BL, Cotton Ch. XI, 10), and in an agreement over Claybrooke church (Leics) in 1167 × 1187, which is witnessed by 'A. chaplain of the archdn of Leicester', along with Baldric's son, Mr Gerard (BL, Add. Ch. 47559).

135. *Notification to the abbots, priors, parsons and clergy of the archdeaconry of Leicester that, ratifying the grant by Erenburga, mother of William de Hastings, to the nuns of Polesworth concerning the church of Barwell, he canonically receives them into the church in the presence of the parson, Richard de Hastings, who has first surrendered the church into the archdeacon's hand.* [c. 1161 × c. 1187]

> B = Bodl. ms Dugdale 12, p. 9 (transcript of now lost original, then in possession of Thomas Corbin of Hall End, in Dordon, Warks). 1637. C = Bodl. ms Dodsworth 65, fo. 44r (copy of B). s. xvii med.

Baldricus dictus archidiaconus Legr(ecestri)e universis abbatibus, prioribus, personis [et]^a clericis per archidiaconatum Legr(ecestri)e constitutis, salutem. Quamvis omnium iuste petitiones promto et benevolo favore prosequende sunt, earum tamen voto studiosius exequemini que^b in iugi dei servitio existunt assidue, et in ecclesia sancta digne sunt beneficia consequi potiora. Inde est quod, ratam habentes concessionem et representationem Erenburg' matris Willelmi de Hastinges factam monialibus de Polleswrtha super ecclesiam de Barwella, eas in iamdictam ecclesiam^c canonice recipimus, presente utique persona^d eiusdem ecclesie Ricardo de Hastings et memoratam ecclesiam prius in manu nostra sponte refutante. Ne vero hec que gesta sunt temporis diuturnitate venirent in dubium, presentium attestatione rem gestam communivimus. Valete.^{e}

> a *Supplied*   b qui *B, C*   c ecclesie *B, C*   d parsona *C*
> e Vale *B, C*

Date as for no. 131.

136. *Notification of the agreement made before him in the synod of Leicester between the monks of Thetford and Hugh the priest over two parts of the demesne tithes of William son of Herbert of Twycross; Hugh will hold the said tithe of the monks for three shillings annually.* [c. 1161 × c. 1187]

> A = Bodl. Essex charter 31. Endorsed: none. Size 90 × 95 + 30 mm (turn-up folded out). Seal and tag missing; signs of slits (? method 1).
> Pd, *Danelaw Charters*, 331, no. 451; *Oseney Cartulary*, v, 120, no. 606A.

Bald' archidiaconus Leircest' omnibus fidelibus sancte ecclesie, salutem. Notum sit vobis quod hec est conventio facta inter monachos Tetfort et Hugonem presbiterum super duabus partibus dec(ime) de dominio Willelmi filii Herberti de Tuicros in sinodo Leircestrie coram me: scilicet quod predictus Hugo tenebit predictam decimam de monachis Tetf' pro tribus solidis annuatim reddendis eis[dem]^a infra octabas sancti Luce [evan]geliste fide sua interposita in presentia mea coram multis.

> a *All letters in square brackets not now visible owing to ink loss*

Date as for no. 131. These tithes – and others at Wharton (Herefs) – were granted by Thetford priory to Osney abbey in 1189 in exchange for the latter's church of Hockham (Norfolk): *Oseney Cartulary*, v, 109 and nos. 602–3. This is a very small and unprepossessing act, which evidently makes use of recycled parchment, since a line of upper-case characters is cut through at the bottom of the folded-out deed and would have been out of sight when the turn-up was in position.

* 137. *At the presentation of Hugh de Boby, institution of Croxton abbey into a third part of the church of Sproxton, and induction into corporal possession.*
[1162 × *c.* 1187]

Mentioned only, in an account of Croxton abbey's acquisition of Sproxton church, in Belvoir Castle, Add. ms 71 (Croxton Abbey Register), fo. 84v. s. xiii med. (whence BL, Additional ms 4934, fo. 172v, being a transcript by F. Peck, 1731; BL, Stowe ms 928, fo. 72r, being a transcript by Dr Vernon, 1755); pd from Peck, Nichols, *Leicestershire*, ii (i), App., 82, no. 14 (2).

Baldricus archidiaconus Leyc'*ᵃ* ad presentationem Hugonis predicti [*sc.* de Boby] nos in dictam tertiam partem ecclesie [*sc.* de Sproxton'] instituit et in corporalem possessionem induxit, *ᵇ*ut patet*ᶜ* per script(um) suum,*ᵇ* sed nullam habemus confirmationem episcopi.

a Leycestrie *Add. 4934*   *b–b Interlined in Add. 4934*   *c* pateat *Add. 4934*

After the formal foundation of Croxton abbey (Colvin, *White Canons*, 92) and before the archdn's death (*Fasti Lincoln*, 33).

* 138. *?Notification that, in his presence and that of the [rural] chapter, Roger de Hotot conveyed to Croxton abbey the right of advowson of [a moiety of] the church of South Croxton with four bovates of land.*
[1162 × *c.* 1187]

Mentioned only, in an account of Croxton abbey's acquisition of a moiety of South Croxton church, in Belvoir Castle, Add. ms 71 (Croxton Abbey Register), fo. 84v. s. xiii med. (whence BL, Additional ms 4934, fo. 172v, being a transcript by F. Peck, 1731; BL, Stowe ms 928, fo. 72v, being a transcript by Dr Vernon, 1755); pd from Peck, Nichols, *Leicestershire*, ii (i), App., 82, no. 14 (3).

Predictus vero Rogerus de Hotot' ius advocationis eiusdem ecclesie [*sc.* de Suthcroxt'] nobis contulit in presentia domini*ᵃ* Baldrici tunc archidiaconi Leyc'*ᵇ* et capituli cum quatuor bovatis terre, ut patet*ᶜ* per literam*ᵈ* predicti B.

a Interlined in Add. 4934   *b* Leycestrie *Add. 4934*   *c* pateat *ibid*
d cartam *ibid*

Date as for no. 137. The preceding passage in the text shows that the abbey had only a moiety of the church, and the archdn is recorded as having instituted to a moiety under the abbey's patronage (*Rot. Hug. de Welles*, i, 256). Some time after *c.* 1170 the other half of the fee of South Croxton, presumably with its tithes, was given to the Gilbertines and was by 1184 administered by Malton priory (Golding, *Gilbert of Sempringham*, 257–9); in 1181 × 1187 it was settled before papal judges-delegate that Croxton and Malton would each have a moiety of the church (BL, Add. ms 4934, fo. 173r; BL, Cott. Claud. D xi, fo. 218v), and until the mid-13th century the two houses presented to the whole church alternately (Golding, 259 and n. 291).

Mr Roger of Rolleston

139. *With Hamo, dean of Lincoln, mandate to the archdeacons of Lincoln diocese, on episcopal authority and on receipt of letters of the archbishop of Canterbury, that A(lice), daughter of William Clement, who has absconded from Ankerwyke priory after dwelling there in the monastic habit for fifteen years, as the bishop has been informed by L(etia), prioress of Ankerwyke, is to be denounced as an excommunicate throughout Lincoln diocese.* [7 Nov. 1193 × early 1195]

> B = PRO, KB 26/48, m. 15 (quoted in a dossier of documents produced in the king's court in 1208 by Jordan son of Avenell in the case brought against him by Alice Clement).
> Pd, *CRR*, v, 185; see also *EEA* III, no. 330.

Karissimis amicis suis omnibus archidiaconis per episcopatum Linc' constitutis Hamo Linc' ecclesie decanus, R. de Rolveston' archidiaconus Leyc', salutem. Cum domino episcopo tam viva voce L. priorisse de Ankerwic quam litteris eiusdem L. et conventus sui plene innotuerit quod A. filia Willelmi Clementis habitum [religi]onis in domo sua de Ankerwic suscepisset et in eadem domo in habitu suscepto per xv. annos moram fecisset, et quod prefata A. habitum susceptum postea derelinquens irregulariter evagetur, vobis auctoritate domini episcopi mandamus quatinus predictam A. per totum episcopatum Linc' excommunicatam denuntiari et tanquam excommunicatam cautius ab omnibus evitari faciatis, presertim cum litteras domini Cant' super hoc receperimus. Valete in domino semper.

After Roger of Rolleston became archdn of Leicester, i.e., after 1192 × Sept. 1193, and therefore after Hubert Walter's enthronement as archbp (*EEA* IV, no. 188A n.; *Fasti Monastic Cathedrals*, 5), and before the archdn became dean of Lincoln, probably shortly after Mar. 1195 (*Fasti Lincoln*, 9–10). For further discussion, see above, no. 22, which apparently refers to this act.

ARCHDEACONRY OF LINCOLN

Robert

140. *Testimony that it has been attested before him by Thorald, [rural] dean [of Tathwell], Hamelin [rural dean] of Yarburgh, Robert [rural dean] of Hannah and others that Amfred of Legbourne gave in alms to the nuns of Alvingham the church of [Little] Cawthorpe, as his charter testifies, which the archdeacon concedes to them.* [c. 1142 × 22 Jan. 1155]

> B = Bodl. ms Laud misc. 642 (Alvingham cartulary), fo. 136r. s. xiii ex.

R. archidiaconus Lincoln' omnibus fidelibus sancte matris ecclesie, salutem. Testimonium perhibeo quod atestatum est coram me per Thoraldum decanum et Hamelinum de Ierburc et Robertum de Haneya et aliis quod Amfredus de Lekeburn*ᵃ* concessit et dedit sanctimonialibus de Al(vingham)*ᵇ* ecclesiam de Calethorp in elemosinam cum ei pertinentibus, ut carta sua testatur; et ego illis predictam ecclesiam quantum ad me attinet concedo. Walete.

a Followed in ms by et *marked for deletion*   *b Expansion from entries on first folios of cartulary*

After Robert became archdn (*Fasti Lincoln,* 25) and before the date when the successor of Abbot Gervase of Louth Park, who confirmed Amfred of Legbourne's gift, was in office (*Gilbertine Charters,* 105; *Heads,* 137). The witness-list of Amfred's charter identifies Thorald and Hamelin as deans of Tathwell and Yarburgh, respectively, and gives in second place Robert dean *del Alnei,* who is no doubt to be identified with Robert *de Haneya* of the present act. Little Cawthorpe church was confirmed to the nuns by bp Robert Chesney in 1148 × 1166 (*EEA* I, no. 67).

141. *Notification to all clergy and laity of Lincolnshire that, before him and the chapter of the church of Lincoln, Reingot of Hagworthingham has given to Bardney abbey the church of [Hagworthingham] and all his right in the same.*

[*c.* 1142 × 27 Dec. 1166]

B = BL, Cotton ms Vespasian E xx (Bardney cartulary), fo. 106v (101v). s. xiii ex.

Robertus archidiaconus Linc' omnibus clericis et laicis Linc'sire, salutem. Notifico vobis Reingotum de Hagwrdingham dedisse deo et sancto Oswaldo de Bard' [ecclesiam de Hagwrdingham]*a* et omnia que in eadem ecclesia sui iuris erant, coram me et capitulo Linc' ecclesie et sub testificatione horum clericorum: Walteri presbiteri de Bard', Radulfi decani de Hillewapp', et c'.

a Bracketed passage conjecturally supplied, the act being associated with other deeds of this place

Presumably after the earliest possible date for bp Alexander of Lincoln's general confirmation to Bardney, which does not mention the church, and before the death of bp Robert Chesney, whose general confirmation includes it, although it is there said to have been given by Walter de Gant (*EEA* I, nos. 17, 72). Walter de Gant had given to Bardney six bovates in Hagworthingham, but apparently not the church, although it existed on that land (cartulary, fo. 55v); by 1186 × 1190, however, Robert de Gant included in his general confirmation to Bardney 'six bovates in Hagworthingham which Reingot held and the church of the vill' (ibid., fo. 56v). It appears, therefore, that Reingot, as tenant of the land, has here formally given the church to the abbey. The last witness was presumably dean of Hill wapentake, later called simply Hill deanery.

142. *Notification that, in his presence and before many men of authority, Robert the clerk of Scamblesby has resigned to Prior G(arinus) and the convent of Spalding what right he had in the demesne tithes of Roger de Maletoft in Scamblesby and in two parts of the corn tithes of Simon of Scamblesby, which belong to the church of Spalding.*

[1152 × ? 15 Jan. 1171]

B = BL, Additional ms 35296 (Spalding cartulary, part 1), fo. 398v. s. xiv med.

Robertus Linc' ecclesie archidiaconus omnibus sancte matris ecclesie filiis, salutem. Noverint universi quod totam querimoniam et reclamationem, si quid etiam iuris unquam habuit Robertus clericus de Samelisbi super decimis que sunt de dominio Rogeri de Maletoft in eadem villa manentis et super decimis duarum garbarum Simonis de Scamelisbi que ex toto pertinent ad ecclesiam de Spald', G. priori eiusdemque loci conventui sponte et absque omni coactione vel reluctatione in presentia nostra et coram multis precepte auctoritatis hominibus precise penitus et in perpetuum concessit et resignavit. Eapropter, ne in posterum de cetero pretaxatus Robertus suo voto et voluntati vel huic et confessioni et concessioni aliquando possit occurrere vel refragari, rei geste veritatem scripti nostri et signi testimonio dignum duximus posteris illuminare. T'.

The predecessor of Garinus, prior of Spalding, did not leave office before 1152 (*Heads*, 109); the archdn probably died 15 Jan. 1171 (*Fasti Lincoln*, 25). Although Scamblesby church was confirmed to Spalding priory by bps Alexander and Robert Chesney of Lincoln, in *c.* 1142 × 1148 and ?1152 × 1166, respectively, the church in fact belonged to Lincoln cathedral, of which it formed a prebend (*EEA* I, nos. 56 and n., 253). The present document may perhaps represent the priory's salvaging of some interest in the parish, despite losing the church.

Peter

143. *Notification that, whereas it is clear to him from inspection of the charters of the monks of Spalding and from a declaration made in the chapter of Bolingbroke that the monks have had the churches of Sibsey and Stickney* in proprios usus *for a long time, and that Rannulf the chaplain, deceased, held them at farm from the monks, he has allowed the churches to them* in proprios usus.

[*c.* 1175 × 1218; ? late 12th × early 13th cent.]

B = BL, Additional ms 35296 (Spalding cartulary, part 1), fo. 372v. s. xiv med.

Omnibus Cristi fidelibus P. Linc' archidiaconus, eternam in domino salutem. Quoniam michi constat, tam inspectione instrumentorum et cartarum quas monachi de Spald' habent super ecclesiis*a* de Cibeseia et*b* Stikeneia quam ex asseracione*c* virorum fidedignorum, facta coram eis in capitulo de Bolingbroc super eisdem ecclesiis diligenter inquisitione,*d* prefatos monachos dictas ecclesias in proprios usus diutius habuisse, et Ranulphum capellanum qui decessit ipsas de eisdem monachis ad*e* firmam tenuisse, sepefatis monachis nominatas ecclesias pietatis et caritatis intuitu in proprios usus pacifice dimisi, tenendas sicuti eas antea in pace possederunt, salvis in omnibus episcopalibus et Linc' ecclesie dignitatibus. T' et c'.

a Ms ecclesie   *b Ms* de   *c Sic; ? for* assertione   *d Ms* inquisicioni
e Ms et

Dating very uncertain; the outside limits are the widest possible for Peter's tenure of the archdnry (*Fasti Lincoln*, 25), but records of his being active in this office are confined mainly to the 1190s and the first decade of the 13th century, particularly the vacancy at Lincoln following the death of bp Hugh of Avallon, 16 Nov. 1200 (see *Reg. Antiquissimum*, vii, 205–8). The churches concerned here had been confirmed to Spalding priory by bp Robert Chesney of Lincoln in 1148 × 1161 (*EEA* I, no. 249).

* 144. *Confirmation of a settlement between the monks of Kirkstead and W(illiam), brother of Helto, concerning tithes of Westlaby, Snelland and Swinthorpe.*

[*c.* 1175 × 1218; ? late 12th × early 13th cent.]

Mentioned only, in a list of 'perpetual chirographs', BL, Cotton ms Vespasian E xviii (Kirkstead cartulary), fo. 108r. s. xiii med.

Confirmatio Petri archidiaconi de predicta transactione decimarum [*sc.* facta inter nos et W. fratrem eius (Heltonis) de decimis de Westl', Snell' et Suntorp].

Date as for no. 143. Other chirographs listed include William's settlement with the monks; for William brother of Helto see also *Danelaw Charters*, nos. 216, 220–1.

* 145. *At the presentation of Guy de la Valle, admission and canonical institution of William of Hogsthorpe as parson of the church of Skegness.*

[*c.* 1175 × summer 1212; ? late 12th cent. × summer 1212]

Mentioned only, as having been produced in a case in the king's court in Trinity term, 1212, between William Wibian and the Crown over the advowson of Skegness church: PRO, KB 26/56, m. 4r; pd, *CRR*, vi, 308.

. . . et profert [*sc.* William de Baivill', whom the king presented to the church] cartam P. archidiaconi Linc', in qua continetur quod ipse ad presentationem Widonis de la Val' admisit eum ad ecclesiam illam et canonice instituit eum personam . . .

Date in general as for no. 143, but before the hearing in the king's court. There is no reason to date this act to the time of bp William of Blois (1203–6), as stated in *Reg. Antiquissimum*, vii, 207, which seems to derive from a misreading of the plea roll. For an original charter by Guy de Valle, dated by F. M. Stenton to 'Henry II', see *Danelaw Charters*, no. 534.

ARCHDEACONRY OF NORTHAMPTON

Herbert Poore

146. *Confirmation to the canons of Cirencester of the churches of Oxendon and Glendon, which Henry of Oxendon granted to them in free and perpetual alms in the presence of the archdeacon's whole chapter, having resigned them into the hand of Richard, archbishop of Canterbury.* [7 Apr. 1174 × 1175]

B = Bodl, ms Dep. C. 392 (Cirencester cartulary, Registrum A), fo. 175v (165v, p. 350). s. xiii med.
Pd, *Cirencester Cartulary*, ii, 585–6, no. 705.

Omnibus sancte matris ecclesie filiis tam presentibus quam futuris Herbertus Norhamth' archidiaconus, salutem. Noverit universitas vestra me ecclesias de Oxend' et de Clamd' canonicis Cir' confirmasse, quas Henricus de Oxend' eisdem canonicis in presentia totius capituli mei in liberam et perpetuam elemosinam pro sua et suorum predecessorum salute, cartis suis mediantibus, libere concessit et quiete, resignatis etiam eisdem ecclesiis et ab eodem fide sua media concessis in manu domini nostri Ricardi Cant' archiepiscopi. Hoc autem, ut robore perpetuo et firmitate fulciatur, scripti mei testimonio et sigilli impressione confirmare et corroborare curavi. Hiis testibus: Nicholao de Lindent', Hugone Ridel decano, Alexandro de Cranesleia, Henrico presbitero de Lodinton', Willelmo presbitero de Rowll', Teobaldo de Clamdon', Simone clerico de Harintun' et Nicholao fratre eius, Osberto et Ricardo de Rowll' diaconibus.

After archbp Richard's consecration (*Fasti Monastic Cathedrals*, 4) and before Herbert became archdn of Canterbury (ibid., 14); the latter's appointment as archdn of Northampton was presumably made by bp-elect Geoffrey, but he does not occur in this role before *c.* 1 Dec. 1174 (*Fasti Lincoln*, 30). The gift of Oxendon church by Henry son of Richard of Oxendon is *Cirencester Cartulary*, ii, no. 709.

Savaric

147.   *Grant and confirmation to Abbot Godfrey and the convent of Eynsham of the church of Whitfield, granted to them by Gilbert de Monte, patron of the church.*

[1175 × c. 1177; prob. c. 1177]

> B = Oxford, Christ Church, D. & C. Lib., vi. a. 2 (Eynsham Cartulary), fo. 24r–v, no. 57. s. xii ex.
> Pd, *Eynsham Cartulary*, i, 68, no. 57.

Noverint omnes ad quos presens scriptum pervenerit quod ego Savaricus archidiaconus Norhamton' concessi et presenti carta confirmavi ecclesiam de Witefeld' Godefrido abbati de Egnesham et [fo. 24v] conventui eiusdem loci secundum concessionem et confirmationem quam optinent a Gilleberto de Monte patrono iamdicte ecclesie. Quod ut ratum sit et stabile, presenti scripto et sigilli nostri^a munimine duxi roborandum. His testibus: magistro Bartholomeo, et magistro Wiardo, Martino presbitero, et Gaufrido presbitero, Waltero scriba, Roberto scriba, Henrico Banastre, Prothasio, Adam pincerna, Rogero coco, Roberto coco, Osmundo et Radulfo pistore fratre eius, Gill(eberto) Grant, Waltero Noch'.

> *a Plural sic*

After Savaric became archdn (*Fasti Lincoln*, 31), and before Gilbert de Monte entered the abbey of Eynsham, that is, eight years before the composition of 'Rotuli de Dominabus' (1185), i.e., in 1177 (*Rot. de Dominabus*, 29); and probably c. 1177, if Gilbert gave Whitfield church on that occasion (*Eynsham Cartulary*, i, 118 and n.).

* 148.   *At the presentation of William of Clapton, grant to the prior and convent of St Neots of the church of Clapton, and canonical collation to them of the* personatus *of the same church.*

[1175 × 9 Oct. 1182]

> Mentioned only, in a confirmation by Richard, archbishop of Canterbury, in 6 Jan. × 9 Oct. 1182: (B) Northampton, Northants R.O., Montagu (Boughton) mss, 'Old' box 25, no. 6; (C) BL, Cotton ms Faustina A iv (St Neots cartulary), fo. 40v (39v). s. xiii med.; pd from B, with facsimile, *Northants Charters*, 68–9, no. XXIV (a); from B and C, *EEA* II, no. 206.

. . . Inspeximus [*sc.* the archbishop] quoque cartam dilecti filii nostri Savarici archidiaconi Noramt'^a ex qua intelleximus quod ipse, ad presentationem Willelmi de Clotton', ecclesiam de Clotton' eisdem priori et conventui [*sc.* St Neots] concessit, et quod eis eiusdem ecclesie canonice contulit personatum.

> *a Noranton' C*

After Savaric became archdn (*Fasti Lincoln*, 31) and before the date of the archiepiscopal confirmation (see *EEA* II, no. 206n.).

149. *Notification that Henry, dean of [East] Haddon, has resigned into his hand the church of Guilsborough, in the fee of William de Diva of Nortoft [in Guilsborough], of which church he was parson, and has renounced all right which he had in the same; and that the archdeacon, at the presentation and grant of William de Diva, has invested Prior Ralph de Diva and the Hospitallers with the said church and granted them a perpetual* personatus *in the same.* [1175 × 1185]

B = BL, Cotton ms Nero E vi (Hospitallers cartulary for England), part 1, fo. 115r. s. xv med.

Savaricus archidiaconus Norhampton' universis sancte matris ecclesie fidelibus ad quos presens scriptum pervenerit, salutem in domino. Venit ad nos Henricus decanus*ᵃ* [de]*ᵇ* Heddona, et ecclesiam de Gildesburghe, que ecclesia est in feodo Willelmi de Diva de Nortoft, cum omnibus pertinentiis suis, cuius persona extitit, in manu nostra resignavit et omni iuri quod in eadem ecclesia habebat penitus renuntiavit. Nos ergo, ad presentationem et concessionem nobilis viri predicti Willelmi de Diva domini fundi, investivimus Radulfum de Diva priorem et fratres Ierl'm hospitalis de predicta ecclesia de Gildesburgh' cum omnibus ad eam pertinentibus, et eis in eadem ecclesia personatum perpetuum concessimus et presentis scripti testimonio confirmavimus. Hiis testibus: magistro Gregorio, magistro Galfrido, magistro Iohanne de Beodeford', domino Franc(one) fratre arch(idiaconi), Roberto decano Norhampton', Willelmo de Berihebi,*ᶜ* Warino de Sanford' canonico Sar', Waltero canonico, Osb(erto), presbiteris, Radulpho de Chapem', Rad(ulph)o de Forda clerico prioris, Hugone Picot.

a Ms deaconus   *b Supplied*   *c Sic; ? for* Berchebi

This act represents in effect a confirmation of that by Geoffrey, archdn of Berkshire, who was then acting for the archdn of Northampton, possibly Savaric (below, no. 228). Its date is after Savaric became archdn (*Fasti Lincoln*, 31) and before the death of William de Diva (son of Hugh), which had occurred by 1185 (*Rot. de Dominabus*, 14). By further charters William de Diva also gave land in Nortoft and the church of East Haddon to Sulby abbey, Northants (*Hatton's Book of Seals*, no. 152; *Mon. Ang.*, vi (2), 904). The first witness here may be the Gregory, official of the archdn of Northampton, who 'inparsonated' the abbot of Eynsham in Whitfield church, perhaps in *c.* 1177 (*Eynsham Cartulary*, i, no. 58). For Franco, the archdn's brother, see *Ann. Mon.,* ii, 248.

150. *Grant to Richard son of Richard of the church of Chiddingfold with the chapel of Peper Harow, for an annual pension of one pound of wax and two marks payable to Mr Ralph of Lechlade.* [1175 × 1186]

B = Trowbridge, Wiltshire R.O., D1/1/1 (Register of St Osmund), fo. 43r (p. 85). s. xiii in.
Pd, *Reg. S. Osm.*, i, 301.

Omnibus Cristi fidelibus ad quos presens scriptum pervenerit Savaricus archidiaconus Norhamton', salutem in domino. Noverit universitas vestra me concessisse Ricardo filio Ricardi ecclesiam de Chidingefaud' cum capella de Piperham et aliis pertinentiis suis sibi libere et quiete perpetuo possidendam per annuam pensionem unius libre cere et duarum marcarum magistro Radulfo de Lechelad' annuatim*ᵃ* solvendarum. Quod ut firmum et stabile perpetuis debeat manere temporibus, presentis scripti patrocinio et sigilli mei appositione communivi. *Addition:* Sigillum habens formam clerici. Et nota quod sigillum illud suspectum est, eo quod constat de duabus ceris, una veteri et altera nova.

a Interlined

After Savaric became archdn (*Fasti Lincoln*, 31) and before Ralph of Lechlade became archdn of 'Bath' (i.e., Taunton), by *c.* 1184 × 1186 (*EEA* X, 219), since he was already in possession of the church and chapel before becoming archdn (*Reg. S. Osm.*, i, 268). Richard son of Richard, as he is also called in Ralph of Lechlade's grant (ibid., 303), was evidently *alias* Richard of Chiddingfold, the name he bears in the confirmations of the present act by Jocelin, bp of Salisbury, and the Salisbury chapter (ibid., 302–3; *EEA* 18, no. 56).

151. *Gift and grant in perpetual alms to his clerk, R(ichard) of Chiddingfold, of the vicarage of his church of Godalming, saving an annual pension of twenty shillings.*
[1175 × 22 Dec. 1188; prob. × 1186]

B = Trowbridge, Wiltshire R.O., D1/1/1 (Register of St Osmund), fo. 42v (p. 84). s. xiii in.
Pd, *Reg. S. Osm.*, i, 298–9.

Noverint ad quos presens scriptum pervenerit quod ego Savaricus archidiaconus Norhamton' concessi et dedi dilecto clerico meo R. de Chidingef(aud') vicariam ecclesie mee de Godelm(ing') cum omni iure et pertinentiis suis in perpetuam elemosinam possidendam sicut aliquis vicarius liberius et melius dinoscitur possedisse, salva pensione xx. s' annuatim solvendorum ex debito vicarie. Quod ut ratum sit et stabile et c'. Hiis testibus et c'. *Addition:* Sigillum Savarici.

While Savaric was archdn and before the death of Richard, bp of Winchester, who collated the vicarage to Richard at Savaric's presentation (*Fasti Lincoln*, 31; *Fasti Monastic Cathedrals*, 85; *Reg. S. Osm.*, i, 299; *EEA* VIII, no. 169); probably, since Richard of Chiddingfold appears to have been identical with Richard son of Richard, not later than 1186, by which time Ralph of Lechlade had become archdn of Taunton (see no. 150 and n.). In addition to his archdnry of Northampton, Savaric was treasurer of Salisbury and held the prebend of Heytesbury in Salisbury cathedral, to which Godalming church belonged (*Fasti Salisbury*, 20–1, 73–4). Chiddingfold was a chapelry dependent upon Godalming church, where Richard of Chiddingfold lived and was still living in 1220 (*Reg. S. Osm.*, i, 297; J. Blair, *Early Medieval Surrey,* 133, 154).

152. *Notification that he has confirmed to the canons of [Canons] Ashby the liberty which they have long enjoyed, namely, that their church of [Canons] Ashby and its chapel of Adstone be quit of* cathedraticum *and of all exaction and custom, except Peter's Pence of two shillings to be paid annually from the same as in the times of preceding archdeacons.*
[1175 × 19 Sept. 1192]

B = BL, Egerton ms 3033 (Canons Ashby cartulary), fo. 10r (p. 18). s. xiii ex.
Pd, Cheney, *From Becket to Langton*, 191, App. III, no. 8.

Omnibus ad quos presens scriptum pervenerit Savaricus archidiaconus[a] Northampton', salutem. Noverit universitas vestra me intuitu pietatis et favore religionis concessisse et presenti carta confirmasse canonicis de Esseby hanc libertatem qua ipsi diu gavisi sunt, scilicet ut eorum ecclesia de Essebya et capella de Attiniston',[b] que est de parochia eiusdem ecclesie, libera sit et quieta a cathedratico et ab omni exactione et consuetudine excepto quod annuatim solvent pro denario beati Petri quod solvere solebant tempore archidiaconorum[c] predecessorum meorum, scilicet tantum duos solidos de parochia predicte ecclesie et capelle. Hiis testibus.

a Ms archideaconus   *b Cheney read* Atteniston'   *c* Ms archideaconorum

After Savaric became archdn (*Fasti Lincoln*, 31) and before his consecration as bp of Bath (Diceto, ii, 105–6). For *cathedraticum* and the possible abuses associated with it, see Cheney, 151, 153 and n. 9.

153. *Ratification of the gift which Henry of Oxendon made to the canons of Cirencester of the churches of Oxendon and Glendon, and of the confirmation of the same by Herbert the archdeacon, Savaric's predecessor.* [1175 × 19 Sept. 1192]

> B = Bodl. ms Dep. C. 392 (Cirencester cartulary, Registrum A), fo. 175v (165v, p. 350). s. xiii med.
> Pd, *Cirencester Cartulary*, ii, 585, no. 704.

Universis sancte matris ecclesie filiis tam presentibus quam futuris Savr' archidiaconus Norhamt', salutem in domino. Noverit universitas vestra me ratam habere donationem quam fecit Henricus de Oxendon' canonicis Cir' de ecclesiis de Oxendon' et de Clend(on') et confirmationem a predecessore meo Hereberto archidiacono predictis canonicis super hiisdem ecclesiis factam, sicut in carta ipsius Henrici et confirmatione iamdicti archidiaconi continetur. Et ne hoc de cetero in dubium vocari possit, presentis scripti patrocinio et sigilli mei munimine duxi roborandum. Hiis testibus: magistro Ricardo vicearchidiacono, Ricardo de Dudeford, Iohanne capellano, Iohanne clerico, Rogero filio Hugonis, Gernagot. Valete.

Date as for no. 152. For archdn Herbert's confirmation, see above, no. 146.

154. *Ratification and confirmation of the agreement made in the presence of the abbot of Evesham and the prior of Kenilworth, papal judges-delegate, between the convent of Cirencester and the clerks Hugh of Benefield and John de Hospitali, over the chapels of Slipton and [Little] Oakley pertaining to the church of Brigstock.* [1177 × 1183; ? × 1181]

> B = Longleat, ms 38B (Cirencester cartulary fragment), p. 16a, no. 9. s. xii ex. C = Bodl. ms Dep. C. 392 (Cirencester cartulary, Registrum A), fo. 179v (169v, p. 348). s. xiv in.
> Pd from C, *Cirencester Cartulary*, ii, 598, no. 723; (calendar, inaccurate) from B, Baddeley, *History of Cirencester*, 113, no. 9.

Universis sancte dei matris ecclesie filiis ad quos presens scriptum pervenerit Savaricus archidiaconus Norhamt',[a] salutem in domino. Noverit universitas vestra nos transactionem in presentia abbatis de Evesham et prioris de Kenelingwrthe[b] inter conventum Cirecestrie[c] et clericos Hugonem de Benefeld et Iohannem de Hospitali super capellis de Slipton'[d] et Aclaia[e] ad ecclesiam de Brikestoch'[f] pertinentibus, auctoritate litterarum domini pape[g] sicut ex litteris ipsorum iudicum perpendere poteritis factam, ratam habuisse et confirmasse necnon et sigilli nostri munimine corroborasse. Hiis testibus: magistro Ricardo de Leicestria,[h] Wiberto clerico, Iohanne clerico, Willelmo scriptore.

a Northampton' *C*   b Kenillewrth' *C*   c Cyr' *C*   d Slipeston' *C*
e Acleya *C*   f Brikestok' *C*   g Erased in *C*   h Leycestr' *C*

The Longleat text of the letters of the judges-delegate names the abbot of Cirencester as
Adam (see *Cirencester Cartulary*, ii, no. 720n.), who was appointed in 1177 and died in 1183
(*Heads*, 160); these provide the outside dating limits for this act, but it may be before the
news of the death of Pope Alexander III (30 Aug. 1181), who commissioned the delegates,
arrived in England.

155. *Notification that in his synod at St Peter's church, Northampton, he heard
John de Hospitali ratify the agreement touching the annual payment at Easter of one
bezant from the church of [Little] Oakley to the abbey of Cirencester, as contained in
the letters of the judges-delegate, A(dam), abbot of Evesham, and R(obert), prior of
Kenilworth.*   [1177 × 1183; ? × 1181]

> B = Longleat, ms 38B (Cirencester cartulary fragment), pp. 15b–16a. s. xii ex. C =
> Bodl. ms Dep. C. 392 (Cirencester cartulary, Registrum A), fo. 179v (169v, p. 348).
> s. xiv in.
> Pd from B, Baddeley, *History of Cirencester*, 113, no. 8; C. Jackson, 'Savaric, Bishop of
> Bath and Glastonbury', *Proc. Somerset Archaeol. and Nat. Hist. Soc.* xii (1865), 160;
> from C, *Cirencester Cartulary*, ii, 598, no. 724.

Omnibus Cristi fidelibus ad quos presens scriptum pervenerit Savaricus
archidiaconus Norhamt',*a* salutem in domino. Noverit universitas vestra nos
in sinodo nostra apud ecclesiam sancti Petri de Norhamt'*b* audisse ab ore
Iohannis de Hospitali ipsum ratam habere conventionem illam de bisantio
annuatim reddendo nomine ecclesie de Haccle*c* abbatie *d*de Cirencestr'*d* in die
Pasche, sicut in litteris delegatorum iudicum, A. scilicet abbatis de Evesham et
R. prioris de Kinigwrtha,*e* continetur. Et ut*f* ratum permanere debeat et
inconcussum, presentis scripti attestatione communimus. *g*Testibus hiis:*g*
abbate sancti Iacobi Norhamt',*b* Radulfo de Wacher' officiali, Roberto decano
de Norhamt',*b* Henrico decano de Heddon', Willelmo decano de Berwebi,*h*
Umfrido*i* de Broc, [p. 16a] et Ricardo de Wacherl', et aliis infinitis.

a Northampton' *C*   b Norhampton' *C*   c Acleya *C*   d–d Cyr' *C*
e Kinigwriha *B*; Kenillewrth' *C*   f Om. in *C*   g–g Hiis testibus *C*
h Borewgby *C*   i Hunfr' *C*

Within the same date range as no. 154, but probably later than it, since none of the
witnesses is common to both acts. The settlement had included Cirencester's grant to
John de Hospitali of the church of Oakley for the annual render of one bezant at Easter
(*Cirencester Cartulary*, ii, no. 720).

156. *Notification of the settlement in his presence of the dispute between the prior
and monks of Daventry and William, their chaplain of Welton; William has resigned
into the archdeacon's hand the cure and right that he had in the chapel, and ceded it to
the prior and monks, who will give him annually for life, for his food and clothing, six
loads of wheat and six of rye, and half a mark at Michaelmas and at Easter. Both
parties have safeguarded this agreement in the archdeacon's hand and in his presence.*
                                                  [1175 × 19 Sept. 1192]

> B = BL, Cotton ms Claudius D xii (Daventry cartulary), fo. 83r (79r). s. xiv ex.
> Pd, *Daventry Cartulary*, 161, no. 501.

Savaricus*ᵃ* archidiaconus Norh(am)t' omnibus filiis sancte matris ecclesie, salutem in domino. Sciant omnes ad quos presentes littere pervenerint quod controversia que vertebatur inter priorem et monachos de Daventre et Will-elmum capellanum suum de Weltona in hunc modum in presentia nostra est terminata. Videlicet quod prefatus Willelmus sponte et sine coactione resignavit omnem curam et ius quod habebat in predicta capella in manu mea et totum cessit priori et monachis. Predicti vero prior et monachi eidem Willelmo annuatim quamdiu vixerit dabunt vi. summas frumenti et vi. siliginis, dimidiam marcam argenti ad festum sancti Michaelis et dimidiam ad Pascha ad victum et ad vestitum. Hanc autem conventionem tenendam tam prior quam Willelmus in manu nostra et presentia cavit. Hiis testibus: magistro Gaufrido archidiacono Barrocsire, magistro Rogero de Derby, magistro Gaufrido Testard', magistro Roberto Temprenoise, magistro Gauberto, magistro Herveo, et multis aliis.

a Ms Simon

Date as for no. 152. In 1141 × 1143 Richard, bp of St Asaph, acting for the bp of Lincoln, dedicated the chapel of Welton as a (parish) church, and William its priest undertook to hold it of the monks of Daventry as before he had held it as a chapel (*Daventry Cartulary*, no. 503); he may be the William of the present act.

157. *Notification of proceedings in his presence in the full chapter at Northampton concerning the claim by the prior and monks of Daventry to exemption from episcopal customs from the chapel of Welton.* [1175 × 19 Sept. 1192]

B = BL, Cotton ms Claudius D xii (Daventry cartulary), fo. 83v (79v). s. xiv ex.
Pd, *Daventry Cartulary*, 163–4, no. 505.

Savaricus*ᵃ* archidiaconus Norh(am)t' omnibus sancte matris ecclesie filiis clericis [et]*ᵇ* laycis, salutem in domino. Noverit universitas vestra questionem super statu capelle de Welton' adversus priorem de Daventre et monachos eiusdem loci iam pridem motam denique ventilatam in presentia nostra apud Norh(am)t' in pleno capitulo mediante sententia esse terminatam. Cum enim a predictis monachis episcopales consuetudines pro predicta capella de Welton' frequenter exigerentur, monachis vero instanter solvere renitentibus, die tandem statuto testibus sufficienter productis capellam predictam ab omni consuetudine et exactione ante dedicationem liberam et quietam fuisse, deinde testimoniis et litteris sigillo inpressis Ricardi episcopi de Sancto Asaph', qui predictam capellam vices agens Alexandri Linc' episcopi dedicavit, ex illa dedicatione nichil libertati vel munitati*ᶜ* matrici ecclesie de Daventre vel capelle prefate esse derogatum seu diminutum probaverunt neque in aliquo debere fieri duriorem vel deteriorem capelle conditionem. Sicque prenominati monachi a questione quam diu sustinuerunt per sententiam finitivam meruerunt absolvi. Ne ergo in posterum ex dubietate *ᵈ*finita eam suscitetur,*ᵈ* sententiam in presentia nostra pro monachis latam sigilli nostri testimonio corroboramus.

a Ms Mavaricus   *b Supplied*   *c Daventry Cartulary reads* immunitati
d–d Sic in ms, but evidently garbled or incomplete

Date as for no. 152. The first clause in the final sentence (printed incompletely in *Daventry Cartulary*, no. 505) is obscure, although its purpose is clear enough; the text may be corrupted or possibly an omission has occurred.

* 158. *At the instance and request of Richard son of Wale, institution of the abbot and canons of Leicester in the church of Eydon.*   [1175 × 19 Sept. 1192]

> Mentioned only, as having been produced in an assize of darrein presentment in the king's court in Michaelmas term, 1219, between Richard son of Wale [junior] and the abbot of Leicester: (B) PRO, KB 26/71, m. 18r; (C) BL, Additional ms 12269, fo. 11v; pd from B, *CRR*, viii, 118; from C, *Bracton's Note Book*, ii, 64, no. 72.

. . . et inde profert [*sc.* the abbot of Leicester] cartam Savarici archidiaconi Norhamt' que testatur quod, ad instantiam et petitionem Ricardi filii Walonis, instituit abbatem et canonicos Leic' in ecclesiam de Eyndon', et c' . . .

Date as for no. 152.

159. *Ratification of the gift by Robert Grimbald, with the assent of his wife, Matilda, and his heirs, to the priory of St Andrew's, Northampton, of the church of Hardwick; and confirmation of the church in perpetual alms to the priory and monks by the authority of his archdeaconry.*   [1175 × 19 Sept. 1192]

> B = BL, Royal ms 11 B. ix (St Andrew's Northampton cartulary), fo. 35r. s. xiii ex. C = BL, Cotton ms Vespasian E xvii (St Andrew's Northampton cartulary), fo. 196v (183v). s. xv med.

Universis catholice ecclesie filiis Savaricus dei gratia archidiaconus de Norh(am)t',[a] salutem. Ratam habentes donationem quam Robertus Grimbaud[b] assensu uxoris sue Matildis et heredum suorum fecit monasterio sancti Andree de Norh(am)t', de ecclesia scilicet de Herdewik,[c] auctoritate archidiaconatus qua fungimur eandem ecclesiam cum omnibus suis pertinentiis monasterio beati Andree Norh(am)t' et dilectis fratribus nostris monachis ibidem domino[d] famulantibus in perpetuam elemosinam confirmamus et sigilli nostri attestatione communimus, salva in omnibus Linc' ecclesie dignitate. Teste[e] Galfrido archidiacono de Bairucscire,[f] magistro Alexandro, Roberto capellano sancti Thome.

> a *(and later)* North' C   b Grymbald C   c Herdwyc C   d deo C
> e *Sic in* B,C   f Bayrucshira C

Date as for no. 152. The text is very similar to that of the confirmation by Robert Chesney, bp of Lincoln, in 1148 × 1166 (*EEA* I, no. 190), and was evidently based upon it.

160. *Ratification of the gift by Matilda, for the soul of her late husband, Robert Grimbald, and her other predecessors, with the assent of her heirs and the confirmation of Richard de Pek her second husband, to the priory of St Andrew's, Northampton, of the church of [Little] Houghton; and confirmation of the church in perpetual alms to the priory and monks by the authority of his archdeaconry.*   [1175 × 19 Sept. 1192]

> B = BL, Royal ms 11 B. ix (St Andrew's Northampton cartulary), fo. 35r. s. xiii ex. C = BL, Cotton ms Vespasian E xvii (St Andrew's Northampton cartulary), fos. 67v–68r (61v–62r). s. xv med.

Universis catholice ecclesie filiis Savaricus dei gratia archidiaconus Norh(am)t',[a] salutem. Ratam habentes donationem quam Matildis, assensu heredum suorum et confirmatione Ricardi de Pek[b] secundi mariti sui, pro anima Roberti Grimbaud[c] quondam mariti sui et aliorum predecessorum suorum fecit monasterio beati Andree de Norh(am)t', de ecclesia scilicet de Hocton', auctoritate archidiaconatus qua fungimur eandem ecclesiam cum omnibus pertinentiis suis monasterio beati Andree de Norh(am)t' et dilectis fratribus nostris monachis ibidem deo^d famulantibus in perpetuam elemosinam confirmamus et sigilli nostri attestatione communimus, salva in omnibus Linc' ecclesie dignitate. Teste Galfr(id)o archidiacono de Barrucsire,^{e} magistro Alexandro, Roberto capellano sancti Thome.

a (and later) North' *C*   *b* Pec *C*   *c* Grimbald *C*   *d Followed by*
servientibus *deleted C*   *e* Barrucsira *C*

Date as for no. 152. The text is very similar to that of the confirmation by Robert Chesney, bp of Lincoln, in 1148 × 1166 (*EEA* I, no. 191); both *EEA* I, nos. 190–1, and the present nos. 159–60 are very similar to one another, and all may perhaps have been composed in St Andrew's.

161. *Notification that, at the presentation of the prior and convent of St Andrew's, Northampton, he has admitted their clerk, Henry son of Peter, to the church of St Giles, Northampton, and canonically instituted him as perpetual vicar in the same, so that he will pay fifteen marks annually to the prior and convent.*

[Sept. 1180 × 19 Sept. 1192]

B = BL, Royal ms 11 B. ix (St Andrew's Northampton cartulary), fo. 34v. s. xiii ex.

Savaricus archidiaconus Norh(am)t' omnibus Cristi fidelibus ad quos presens carta pervenerit, salutem. Noverit universitas vestra nos, ad presentationem prioris sancti Andree de Norh(am)t' et conventus eiusdem loci, ^{a}Henricum filium Petri clericum suum^a in ecclesia beati Egidii de Norh(am)t' admisisse, ipsumque in eadem vicarium perpetuum solempnitate canonica instituisse, ita quod priori et monachis prefatis nomine eiusdem ecclesie xv. marcas annuatim persolvet ad terminos inter eos statutos. Ut autem hec institutio firma et illibata permaneat, presentis scripti et sigilli nostri appositione et testium subscriptione corroboravimus. Testes sunt: Walkelinus abbas sancti Iacobi de Norh(am)t', magister Ricardus prior eiusdem loci, magister Ricardus de Eifordeby, Henricus decanus de Haddon', magister Reginaldus de Cantebrigia, magister Robertus de Burtonia, Rad(ulphu)s de Wakerele, Ricardus frater eius, Umfridus clericus archidiaconi, magister Willelmus filius Ermenild, magister Ricardus de Billing', ' Hugo capellanus, Herbertus capellanus, Rad(ulphu)s clericus, Henricus de Armenterers, Radulphus Teyssun, Godefridus clericus, Adam et Willelmus filii Hugonis capellani.

a–a Reading uncertain: ms Henricum filium suum clericum Petri *with marks for transposition after* Henricum *and* suum

After Walkelin became abbot of St James's, Northampton, his predecessor having died 17 Sept 1180 (*Heads*, 178), and before the archdn's consecration as bp of Bath (Diceto, ii, 105–6). This act is referred to in *Rot. Hug. de Welles*, i, 142.

162. *Mandate to all his officials and [rural] deans in the archdeaconry of Northampton that, when any church of the prior and monks of St Andrew's, Northampton, becomes vacant, they are to receive and put into corporal possession a suitable clerk at their presentation; and, in accordance with the privilege of pope Lucius III, their churches and their possessors shall answer to the archdeacon in spirituals, but to the monks in temporals.*   [6 Sept. 1181 × 19 Sept. 1192; ? × 1185]

B = BL, Royal ms 11 B. ix (St Andrew's Northampton cartulary), fos. 34v–35r. s. xiii ex.

Savaricus archidiaconus Norh(am)t' universis officialibus et decanis suis in archidiaconatu Norh(am)t' constitutis, salutem in domino. Mandamus vobis atque precipimus quatinus [fo. 35r], cum aliquam ecclesiam prioris et monachorum sancti Andree de Norh(am)t' vacare contigerit, ad petitionem et presentationem eorundem clericum idoneum absque contradictione vel dilatione suscipiatis*a* et in corporalem possessionem mittatis; et prout in privillegio memoratorum monachorum a domino Lucio tertio impetrato*b* continetur, ecclesie eorundem monachorum et earum possessores nobis de spiritualibus, ipsis vero monachis de temporalibus, respondeant, salvo in omnibus iure Linc' ecclesie et nostro.

a Ms susci   *b Ms* impetrata

After the consecration of Lucius III, and before the archdn's consecration as bp of Bath (Diceto, ii, 105–6), but perhaps during the pontificate of Lucius III, who died 25 Nov. 1185. The latter's privilege appears not to have survived.

* 163. *At the presentation of Mary de Muschamp, institution of the abbot of Sulby as parson of [Great] Harrowden church.*   [1175 × 19 Sept. 1192]

Mentioned only, in a letter concerning this church by Hugh, bishop of Lincoln, to the barons of the Exchequer and other royal justices in 21 Sept. 1186 × 16 Nov. 1200, quoted in an inspeximus by Oliver Sutton, bishop of Lincoln, 3 Oct. 1288: BL, Additional Charter 22002; pd, *EEA* IV, 128, no. 192.

. . . Abbas vero de Suleby . . . asserebat se eiusdem ecclesie [*sc.* de Harwedon'] personam esse per presentationem Marie de Muschamp' et a Savarico archidiacono Norham' institutum fuisse. . . . Die igitur assignata abbas cartam M. de Muschamp' et cartam Savarici archidiaconi protulit in medium quibus testimonium perhibuerunt. Hii qui testes in carta archidiaconi conscripti erant qui tunc interfuerunt. . . .

Date as for no. 152.

* 164. *At the presentation of the abbot of Sulby, institution of Elias, clerk, as vicar of [Great] Harrowden church.*   [1175 × 19 Sept. 1192]

Mentioned only, in the same letter of Hugh, bishop of Lincoln, as in no. 163.

. . . Affuit etiam clericus quidam Helias nomine qui se eiusdem ecclesie de Harwedon' vicarium esse proponebat, presentatum videlicet a prefato abbate [*sc.* de Suleby] et a prenotato archidiacono similiter institutum. . . . H. clericus nichilominus cartam archidiaconi S. de institutione sua exhibuit. . . .

Date as for no. 152.

* 165. *At the presentation of Alnath Papillun, admission of the abbot of Sulby to the church of [Little] Addington.* [21 Sept. 1186 × 19 Sept. 1192]

Mentioned only, as having been produced in an assize of darrein presentment in the king's court in Michaelmas term, 1233, between Richard de Waterville and the abbot of Sulby: (B) PRO, KB 26/113, m. 28d; (C) BL, Additional ms 12269, fo. 119r; pd from B, *CRR*, xv, no. 831; from C, *Bracton's Note Book*, ii, 628, part of no. 820.

. . . Profert [*sc.* the abbot of Sulby] etiam cartam Savarici quondam archidiaconi Norht' que testatur quod ipse admisit abbatem de Suleby ad ecclesiam illam [*sc.* Addington] ad presentationem predicti Alnathi . . .

After the earliest terminus for the grant of appropriation of the church by Hugh, bp of Lincoln, also produced in this case (*EEA* IV, no. 193), and before the archdn's consecration as bp of Bath (Diceto, ii, 105–6).

ARCHDEACONRY OF OXFORD

Walter

166. *Gift in alms to Godstow abbey of the tithe of his land in his lordship of Cutteslowe, which he placed on the altar at the dedication of the church before Alexander, bishop of Lincoln, and the other bishops who dedicated it.* [Jan. 1139]

B = PRO, E164/20 (Godstow cartulary), fo. 99r (96r). s. xv in. C = Bodl. ms Rawlinson B. 408 (Godstow cartulary, English calendar), fo. 95r. s. xv ex.
Pd from C, *Godstow English Register*, i, 321, no. 436.

Walt(erus) Oxin' archidiaconus omnibus sancte ecclesie fidelibus, salutem. Notum vobis facio me dedisse in elemosinam ecclesie beati Iohannis de Godestowe decimam terre mee in dominio meo de Cudeslawe, ipsamque posuisse super altare in dedicatione ecclesie coram Alexandro Linc' episcopo et ceteris episcopis qui dedicaverunt ecclesiam. Valete.

At the time of the abbey's dedication (see no. 167n.). Cutteslowe is now in the northern suburb of Oxford (see *Oxon Place-Names*, ii, 267).

167. *Grant to the abbey and nuns of Godstow of exemption from archidiaconal jurisdiction.* [prob. Jan. 1139; poss. 1144 × 25 Aug. 1149]

B = PRO, E164/20 (Godstow cartulary), fo. 17r (5r). s. xv in. C = Bodl. ms Rawlinson B. 408 (Godstow cartulary, English calendar), fo. 16v (4v).[1] s. xv ex.
Pd from C, *Godstow English Register*, ii, 645, no. 867.

Walterus Oxinefordensis archidiaconus omnibus fidelibus sancte ecclesie, salutem. Notifico caritati vestre quod concessi ecclesie de Godestowe et monialibus ibidem deo servientibus omnem libertatem quam archidiaconus concedere potest, scilicet ut ab omni archidiaconali exactione sive aggravatione, ut in hospitiis exigendis aut capellanis implacitandis ceterisve ministris in causam ducendis, libera sit predicta ecclesia et prorsus quieta. Oleum quoque crisma et sanctum et infirmorum sine exactione habeat. Abbatissa etiam capellanos suos ponat et habeat ita ut, si ipsa noluerit, ad sinodos sive ad capitula non eant, nec [archidiacono nec]*a* decano aut eorundem ministris nisi voluntarie respondeant. Capellani quoque sui, si perverse egerint, convocet abbatissa ad ecclesiam suam vicinos quos elegerit presbiteros, quorum iudicio aut corrigat eos aut eiciat. Curam etiam monialium suarum absque scitatione alicuius archidiaconi sive decani habeat. Huius libertatis siquis temerario ausu molator aut destructor extiterit, perpetui anathematis sentencie subiaceat, nisi resipuerit et condignam satisfactionem*b* egerit. Huius rei existunt testes: Rodbertus Exoniensis episcopus, Ricardus*c* abbas Elemosine, Reginaldus abbas Eveshamie, Walt(erus) abbas Egenesh', Radulphus de Monem', magister Gaufridus Arturus, Rodbertus prior Oxinef', Rodbertus capellanus, Ansket' presbiter, Willelmus capellanus, Reginaldus filius com(itis) et filii sui, Willelmus de Keisn', Hunfr(idus) clericus, Andreas clericus, Hugo de Keisn', Willelmus filius Walt(eri), Simon de Gerard' molend(inarius), Nicholaus Basset, Nigellus del Broc, Radulphus de Broc, Willelmus filius Godef(ridi), Willelmus Luvel.

a Supplied conjecturally, implied by eorundem, B; C has at this point nother . . . to the archedecun ne to the dene   *b* satisfacionem B   *c Sic in B; ? error for* Reginaldus *(see note)*

Probably contemporary with the similar grant by Alexander, bp of Lincoln, made at the archdn's request on the occasion of Godstow abbey's dedication and witnessed, among others, by three of the present witnesses, the bp of Exeter and the abbots of Evesham and Eynsham (*EEA* I, no. 34; for the date, no. 33; Salter, *EHR* 34 (1919), 383). However, if 'Richard abbot of L'Aumône (*Elemosina*)' among the witnesses is correct, the date would be between 1144, when his predecessor, Reginald, occurs (*Gallia Christiana*, viii, 1397), and after 25 Aug. 1149, when abbot Reginald of Evesham died (*Heads*, 47), although the possibility that 'Richard' in the cartulary transcript is an error for 'Reginald' cannot be excluded. The presence of an abbot (or abbots) of L'Aumône in England is probably to be accounted for by the affairs of the abbey's daughter houses at Waverley (Surrey), founded 1128, and Tintern, founded 1131 (Knowles and Hadcock, 114–15). For abbot Walter (?II) of Eynsham among the witnesses, see *Heads*, 49. This important grant is discussed by Brett, *English Church under Henry I*, 208–9.

[1] The calendar is brief and lacks witnesses.

168. *Notification that, at the dedication of the church of St Giles outside the north gate of Oxford, his peasant tenants of Walton gave their tithes to that church with his assent, which he now confirms.*   [prob. 1149 × 1150]

A = Oxford, St John's College Muniments, V. A. 3. Endorsed: de Waltune (s. xii ex.). Size 115 × 73 mm. Seal on tongue (tie missing), fragment in stitched-up bag.
B = PRO, E164/20 (Godstow cartulary), fo. 99r (96r). s. xv in. C = Bodl. ms Rawlinson B. 408 (Godstow cartulary, English calendar), fo. 95r.[1] s. xv ex.
Pd from A with facsimile, *Oxford Charters*, no. 60; from C, *Godstow English Register*, ii, 422–3, no. 570.

Walt(erus) Oxin' archidiaconus omnibus fidelibus sanctę ęcclesię, salutem. Notum vobis facio quod rustici mei de Waltona in dedicatione ęcclesię sancti*a* Egidii, que est extra*b* portam de north*c* Oxinef', dederunt decimas suas eidem ecclesie assensu et voluntate mea, quod concedo et volo et ex parte dei sic esse precipio. Teste*d* Willelmo abbate de Egnesham, Rodberto priore sancte Friþesuid',*e* Godef(rido) priore de Egnesham, magistro*f* Galfrido Arturo,

Radulfo de Monumuta, Willelmo cappellano,^{g} Nigello presbitero, Iocelino clerico, Petro del Bar, Iordano, Radulfo de Melvernae,^{h} cum multis aliis. Valete.

a sancte *B*	*b Interlined in A*	*c* North' *B*	*d Sic in A,B*
e Freþesuid' *B*	*f* Magisto *A*	*g* capellano *B*	*h* Melverna *B*

The date is that proposed in *Oxford Charters,* no. 60n. Walter was provost and canon of the collegiate church of St George, Oxford, his prebend comprising three hides of land and tithes in Walton and the church of St Mary Magdalen, Oxford (ibid.; *Fasti Lincoln,* 35; Salter, *Medieval Oxford,* 115); the peasant tithes of Walton were transferred to the newly built church of St Giles when it was dedicated, before 1133, and passed with that church into Godstow's possession in 1139. In 1149 × 1150 St George's church was given to Osney abbey, against the archdn's wishes, and this was probably the occasion for the present act, which seeks to safeguard Godstow's rights (ibid., 114–16; *Oxford Charters,* no. 60n.).

¹ The calendar includes the first witness only.

169. *Notification that he has made Godstow abbey the heir of the land of Shillingford which Brityna his friend held by hereditary right and in which she made him her heir.* [? prob. 1149 × 1150]

> B = PRO, E164/20 (Godstow cartulary), fo. 145r (142r). s. xv in. C = Bodl. ms Rawlinson B. 408 (Godstow cartulary, English calendar), fo. 159r.¹ s. xv ex.
> Pd from C, *Godstow English Register,* ii, 535, no. 717.

Omnibus sancte fidelibus ecclesie Walt(erus) Oxin' archidiaconus, salutem. Sciatis quod hereditavi ecclesiam sancti Iohannis Baptiste de Godestowe de terra de Schillingford' quam Brityna amica mea hereditario iure tenuit et unde ipsa hereditavit me. Teste^a Galfrido Arturo, Radulfo de Monumuta, Willelmo capellano, Anschetillo de Wittona, Iocelino clerico, Randulfo de Chent, Petro del Bar, Iordano, pluribusque aliis. Valete.

> *a Sic B*

Probably contemporary with the preceding, with which it has six witnesses in common – see Salter, *EHR* 34 (1919), 384; it is dated (prob. wrongly) to 'about 1140' in *Godstow English Register,* no. 717.

¹ The calendar is without witnesses; for the Latin 'amica mea' (line 3 above) it reads 'his leman', i.e., his lover.

170. *Grant and approval, addressed to S(imon), bishop of Worcester, of the confirmation made at the request of his fellow canons of Warwick by the bishop, the pope, and T(heobald), archbishop of Canterbury, of [the settlement] between All Saints church, Warwick, and the priory of St Sepulchre's, Warwick.*
[8 Jan. 1139 × 20 Mar. 1150]

> B = PRO, E164/22 (St Mary's Warwick cartulary), fo. 17v (16v), no. 20. s. xv med.

Domino suo S. dei gratia Wigornensi episcopo W. Oxin' archidiaconus, salutem cum fidelitate servitii.^{a} Quod dominus papa et T. Cant' archiepiscopus et vos litteris vestris et sigillorum vestrorum corroboratione inter ecclesiam Omnium Sanctorum de Warrewich' et ecclesiam sancti Sepulcri eiusdem ville iustis postulationibus concanonicorum meorum confirmastis concedo et laudo et precor ut sic stabile et ratum permanere possit. Valete.

a Suggested reading; ms servitium

After Theobald's consecration as archbp and before the death of Simon, bp of Worcester (*Fasti Monastic Cathedrals*, 4, 99). Although the collegiate foundation in the church of All Saints in Warwick castle was transferred to St Mary's between 1125 and 1128 (Knowles and Hadcock, 419, 442; *VCH Warks*, ii, 125), the archdn clearly still thinks of it as at All Saints. The agreement must be the arrangement made by bp Simon of Worcester in 1125 × 1135 on the occasion of his consecration of a cemetery at St Sepulchre's (*Mon. Ang.*, vi (1), 602, no. 2), but no confirmation by the pope or by archbp Theobald is known; the latter's mandate, probably of 1157 (Saltman, *Theobald*, 501–2, no. 270), relates to a later dispute between St Mary's and St Sepulchre's. Cf. below, nos. 260–1.

171. *Confirmation, addressed to his fellow canons of Warwick, of the agreement between All Saints church, Warwick, and the priory of St Sepulchre's, Warwick, confirmed at their request by the pope, T(heobald), archbishop of Canterbury, and S(imon), bishop of Worcester.* [8 Jan. 1139 × 20 Mar. 1150]

B = PRO, E164/22 (St Mary's Warwick cartulary), fo. 17v (16v), no. 21. s. xv med.

Walt(erus) Oxin' archidiaconus fratribus et concanonicis suis de Warr', salutem et dilectionem. Conventionem quam dominus papa et T. Cant' archiepiscopus et S. Wig' episcopus inter ecclesiam Omnium Sanctorum de Warr' et ecclesiam sancti Sepulcri eiusdem ville vestris iustis postulationibus litteris suis confirmaverunt ex parte mea confirmo et laudo, et ut statuta summi pontificis et T. Cant' archiepiscopi et totius Anglie primatis*a* necnon vestri presulis decreta super hac re stabilia*b* et sic rata*c* permanere sinat(is) imperpetuum esse opto. Valete.

a Ms primati   *b Ms* stabile   *c Ms* ratum

Date as for no. 170.

Robert Foliot

172. *Notification to all clergy and faithful of Oxfordshire that he has confirmed the gift of all their demesne tithes of Piddington which Guy of Ryhall and his wife, Joan, of Piddington made in perpetual alms to the chapel of the Holy Cross of Muswell for the use of the canons of Missenden.* [early 1151 × 1152]

B = BL, Harley ms 3688 (Missenden cartulary), fo. 128v. s. xiv in. C = Aylesbury, Buckinghamshire R.O., Boarstall cartulary, Boarstall section, fo. 31r. s. xv med. Pd from B, *Missenden Cartulary*, iii, 65, no. 636; from C, Kennett, *Parochial Antiquities*, i, 104–5; *Boarstall Cartulary*, 103, no. 299.

Robertus archidiaconus Oxeneford'*a* omnibus clericis et fidelibus Oxenefordsirie,*b* salutem. Sciatis me, quantum ad officium meum pertinet, concessisse et confirmasse decimam illam quam Wido*c* de Ridala*d* et Iohanna uxor illius de Pidintona dederunt et concesserunt deo et capelle sancte Crucis de Musewelle*e* ad opus canonicorum Messendenensium*f* in perpetuam elemosinam,*g* omnem scilicet decimam de dominio suo de Pidintune*h* tam in blado quam in agnis et porcellis et omnibus aliis rebus domus sue decimandis. Et ut hec elemosina*i* rata et absque calumpnia sit in posterum, presentis scripti et sigilli mei attestatione predictis canonicis illam confirmo. Hiis testibus: magistro Gilberto de Bercestria,[j] Willelmo capellano de Bercestria, altero Willelmo sene de Bercestria, Radulfo[k] heremita,[l] et aliis.

a Oxon' *C*	*b* Oxenfordshir' *C*	*c* Guido *C*	*d* Rihala *C*
e Musewella *C*	*f* Missendeniensium *C*		*g* elimosinam *C*
h Pedyngton' *C*	*i* elimosina *C*	*j (and later)* Berecestria *C*	
k Radulpho *C*	*l* herimita *C*		

After the last occurrence of Robert's predecessor as archdn, prob. early 1151 (*Fasti Lincoln,* 35), and before Joan of Ryhall's second marriage (following Guy of Ryhall's death), which seems to have taken place before the end of 1152 (see *Boarstall Cartulary,* 69 and nos. 295, 297 and nn.). To the chapel of the Holy Cross, Muswell (in the manor of Piddington), was attached a hermitage inhabited by Ralph (one of the witnesses to this act), who had built the chapel by gift of Guy son of Payn, i.e., of Ryhall (see *Missenden Cartulary,* iii, no. 638; *Boarstall Cartulary,* no. 297). The second two witnesses here occur in Joan of Piddington's charter as 'Willelmus senex sacerdos de Berncestr' cum Willelmo capellano suo' (*Missenden Cartulary,* iii, no. 639). In 1236 × 1240 Missenden abbey granted its property in Muswell, except the chapel's tithes which it retained, to John de Plessis, and in 1279 the latter's son, Hugh, granted it to John son of Nigel, predecessor of the later lords of Boarstall (*Boarstall Cartulary,* 69 and nos. 303–4; *Missenden Cartulary,* iii, no. 640).

173. *Notification to all clergy of the archdeaconry of Oxford that W(illiam) of Aston and Osbert, his son, have given to Bradenstoke priory the church of [North] Aston, and that, at their presentation, he has received Prior Adam as parson of the same, to be held in perpetuity for the uses of the brethren there following the rule of St Augustine.*

[early 1151 × 27 Dec. 1166]

B = BL, Cotton ms Vitellius A xi (Bradenstoke cartulary), fo. 107r (106r). s. xiv med. Pd (calendar), *Bradenstoke Cartulary,* 192, no. 661.

R. archidiaconus Oxonford' universis clericis per archidiaconatum Oxeneford' constitutis, salutem. Noveritis W. de Estun' et Osb(ertum) filium eius deo et ecclesie de Bradenestok' ecclesiam de Estun' concessisse, et me priorem eiusdem loci venerabilem Adam illorum presentatione in personam iamdicte ecclesie perpetuo habende suscepisse in usus fratrum ibidem deo secundum regulam beati Augustini in perpetuum servientium. Valete.

After the last occurrence of Robert's predecessor as archdn, and before the death of Robert Chesney, bp of Lincoln, who confirmed the gift, as mentioned (along with the archdn's confirmation) in charters of William of Aston's grandsons (*Fasti Lincoln,* 35, 2; *Bradenstoke Cartulary,* nos. 497, 664; *EEA* IV, App. I, no. VII). The rubric identifies the church as North Aston.

174. *Notification of the settlement, in his presence and that of the chapter of the deanery of Stoke [Lyne], of the dispute between St Frideswide's priory and Cogges priory over two sheaves of the tithe of the demesne of Gilbert Pippard in Fritwell. St Frideswide's will pay annually to Cogges priory two shillings or a bezant.*

[early 1151 × 6 Oct. 1174]

B = Oxford, Corpus Christi College Lib., ms CCC 160 (St Frideswide's cartulary), p. 306, no. 466. s. xiii. C = Oxford, Christ Church, D. & C. Lib., vi. c. 1 (St Frideswide's cartulary), pp. 207–8. s. xv.

Pd from B, Kennett, *Parochial Antiquities*, i, 170–1; from B and C, *St Frideswide's Cartulary*, ii, 222, no. 974.

R.*ᵃ* archidiaconus Oxon' universis sancte matris ecclesie filiis, salutem. Noverit universitas vestra controversiam que diutius agitata est*ᵇ* inter ecclesiam Sancte Frideswide*ᶜ* et ecclesiam de Cogas super duabus garbis decime de dominio Gilberti Pippard*ᵈ* in Fretewll'*ᵉ* in presentia nostra et totius capituli de decanatu de Stokes tali transactione *ᶠ*in perpetuum*ᶠ* decisam esse. Ecclesia siquidem Sancte Frideswide*ᶜ* [Oxon']*ᵍ* annuatim persolvet*ʰ* ecclesie de Cogas*ⁱ* pro eadem decima duos solidos vel bisantium unum infra octabas sancti Michaelis. [Hiis]*ᵍ* testibus.

a Om. in C	*b Om. in C*	*c* Frid' *C*	*d* Pippard' *C*
e Fretwella *C*	*f–f Om. in C*		*g Om. in B; supplied from C*
h persolvent *C*	*i* Gokas *B*		

After the last occurrence of Robert's predecessor as archdn and before his own consecration as bp of Hereford (*Fasti Lincoln*, 35). The church of Fritwell was confirmed to St Frideswide's by bp Robert Chesney in 1148 × 1166 (*EEA* I, no. 218; *St Frideswide's Cartulary*, ii, no. 971, where the bp is wrongly identified as Robert Grosseteste). Two sheaves of the demesne tithe probably means two parts of the demesne corn tithes. Cogges priory, a dependency of Fécamp abbey, received a gift of such demesne tithe at Fritwell from its founder, Manasser Arsic, in 1103, confirmed by Henry I in 1110 (Kennett, *Parochial Antiquities*, i, 110; *Mon. Ang.*, vi, 1003).

175. *Notification that, at the presentation of Abbot Godfrey and the convent of Eynsham, he has received Ralph, clerk, as parson of the church of Souldern and has confirmed the* personatus *to him.* [early 1151 × 6 Oct. 1174]

B = Oxford, Christ Church, D. & C. Lib., vi. a. 2 (Eynsham cartulary), fo. 23v, no. 52. s. xii ex.

Pd, *Eynsham Cartulary*, i, 66, no. 52; (abbreviated), *Mon. Ang.*, iii, 21, no. 42.

Robertus archidiaconus Oxenef' universis sancte matris ecclesie filiis, salutem. Universitati vestre notum esse volumus nos recepisse Radulfum clericum in personam ecclesie de Sulthorna, presentatione Godefridi abbatis de Egnesham et totius conventus eiusdem loci. Nos vero personatum eiusdem ecclesie de Sulthorn' eidem Radulfo sigilli nostri testimonio confirmamus.

Date as for no. 174.

176. *Notification that Stephen de Ponsold and A(lice) de Gray, his wife, have given to the abbot and monks of Eynsham the church of Cornwell in perpetual alms; and that in the full chapter at Witney Walter, who had held the church, has surrendered it into the hand of the archdeacon, who has, at the said Stephen's presentation, assigned the* personatus *of the church in perpetuity to the abbot and convent.* [early 1151 × 6 Oct. 1174]

B = Oxford, Christ Church, D. & C. Lib., vi. a. 2 (Eynsham cartulary), fo. 23v, no. 53. s. xii ex.

Pd, *Eynsham Cartulary*, i, 66–7, no. 53; (abbreviated), *Mon. Ang.*, iii, 21, no. 43.

Robertus archidiaconus Oxenef' omnibus sancte matris ecclesie filiis, salutem in domino. Que coram personis ecclesiasticis recte statuuntur, dignum est memorie commendari, ne oblivione surrepente in posterum valeant in dubium devenire. Ideoque ad omnium notitiam volumus pervenire quod Stephanus de Ponsold' et A. de Grai uxor sua dederunt et concesserunt abbati et monachis de Egnesh(am) ecclesiam de Cornewella cum omnibus pertinentiis suis in perpetuam elemosinam libere et integre habendam et pro voluntate sua integre tractandam. Walterus quoque, qui eandem ecclesiam habuerat, eam in pleno capitulo nostro apud Witten' in manu nostra refutavit, et nos personatum eiusdem ecclesie, ad presentationem predicti Stephani, abbati et conventui in perpetuum assignavimus. Valete.

Date as for no. 174. For the gift of the church by Stephen de Ponsold and his wife Alice, daughter of Thomas de Gray, which is witnessed by Robert, archdn of Oxford, see *Eynsham Cartulary*, i, no. 116. The abbey already had the (demesne) tithes of Cornwell, however, and retained these for a time when the church was surrendered to Alice de Gray in 1201, the church eventually being given to Osney abbey (ibid., no. 7; ii, p. xxxix; *Oseney Cartulary*, iv, no. 287).

177. *Notification that, in the time of his predecessors, the abbot and abbey of Eynsham paid annually as Peter's Pence seven shillings for Eynsham, [South] Stoke, Shifford, Charlbury and [Little] Rollright.* [early 1151 × 6 Oct. 1174]

    B = Oxford, Christ Church, D. & C. Lib., vi. a. 2 (Eynsham cartulary), fo. 24r, no. 54. s. xii ex.
    Pd, *Eynsham Cartulary*, i, 67, no. 54.

Omnibus sancte matris ecclesie filiis Robertus archidiaconus Oxenef', salutem. Universitati vestre notum facimus abbatem et ecclesiam Egneshamie pro annua pensione sancti Petri, de Egnesham scilicet et Stoch' et Scipford' et Cherleberi et Rollendrith, tempore antecessorum meorum septem solidos et non amplius reddidisse, et ita omni administrationis mee tempore persoluisse.

Date as for no. 174. The amount of Peter's Pence due from the abbey, for a slightly different group of places, had risen to 8s by 1197 × 1200 (*Eynsham Cartulary*, i, no. 23A; *EEA* IV, no. 62). On the benefit accruing to the abbey from the collection of Peter's Pence, see *Eynsham Cartulary*, ii, p. lxii.

178. *Notification that, by gift of John de St John and Reginald de St Valery, and by confirmation of Robert, bishop of Lincoln, he has received Abbot Godfrey and the monastery of Eynsham into the perpetual* personatus *of the church of [North] Leigh.* [19 Dec. 1154 × 27 Dec. 1166]

    B = Oxford, Christ Church, D. & C. Lib., vi. a. 2 (Eynsham cartulary), fo. 45v, no. 177. s. xii ex.
    Pd, *Eynsham Cartulary*, i, 131–2, no. 177.

[O]mnibus sancte matris ecclesie filiis Robertus archidiaconus Oxeneford', salutem. Universitati vestre notum fieri volumus*[a]* quod ego Godefridum abbatem et monasterium de Egnesham in perpetuum personatum ecclesie de Legis suscepi, de donatione videlicet nobilium virorum Iohannis de Sancto Iohanne et Reginaldi de Sancto Walerico, sicut eorumdem carte testantur, et confirmatione domni*[b]* Roberti Linc' episcopi.

    a Plural sic   *b* Sic

After the accession of King Henry II, who is mentioned in Reginald de St Valery's charter

(*Eynsham Cartulary*, i, no. 175), and before the death of bp Robert Chesney, who confirmed the gift (ibid., no. 176; *EEA* I, no. 125). It is interesting to note that the bp's confirmation makes no reference to the abbey's reception as parson of the church, or the like.

179. *Notification that, acting on a mandate from the pope and with the consent of Hugh de Chastillon, lord of Leckhampstead, he has settled the dispute between the monks of Longueville priory and Richard Barro over the 'parish' of Akeley, which Richard claimed to belong to his church of Leckhampstead; on behalf of the monks the chaplain of Akeley will pay an annual pension of two shillings to the mother church of Leckhampstead, as Walter the chaplain has promised, and twice a year its parishioners will visit that church.* [early 1151 × 6 Oct. 1174]

B = Oxford, New College, Archive 9744 (Liber Niger), fo. 66v. s. xvi in.
Pd, *Newington Longeville Charters*, 21–2, no. 16.

Universis sancte matris ecclesie filiis Robertus archidiaconus Ox',[a] salutem. Universitati vestre presentibus litteris innotescat me, ex mandato summi pontificis, sollicitudinem suscepisse terminandi controversiam que vertebatur super parochia de[b] Acleia inter monachos monasterii de Longavill' et Ricardum Barro, quam idem Ricardus ad ius ecclesie sue de Lecamsted' pertinere asserebat. Tandem vero, post longam controversie ventilationem, amicabili compositione utriusque partis unanimi assensu necnon et consensu Hugonis de Chaveillen[c] tunc temporis domini de Lecamsted', negotium predictum domini pape auctoritate fretus terminavi hoc modo. Prefati monachi de Longavill' per manum capellani de Acleia de illa parochia duos solidos annuos matri ecclesie de Lecamsted' persolvent per eundem capellanum illuc deferendos, xii. d' infra octo dies Pasche et alios xii. d' infra octo dies post festum sancti Michaelis. Et ad hanc pensionem predicto modo solvendam Walterus tunc temporis capellanus de Acleia supranominate ecclesie de Lecamsted' sub fidei interpositione se obligavit, similem formam ex tenore compositionis successoribus suis ad cautelam et commodum sepedicte ecclesie de Lecamsted' prescribens. Insuper in eadem compositione convenit[d] quod parochiani de Acleia bis in anno, scilicet in Assumptione beate virginis Marie et in die Nativitatis eiusdem, debito iure parochiali[e] matrem ecclesiam de Lecamsted' visitarent et recognoscerent. Hanc autem compositionem more religionis in manu mea ad ipsius compositionis irrefragabilem stabilitatem utraque pars posuit; ultra[f] autem prescripte compositionis tenorem persone ecclesie de Lecamsted' a sepedicta capella de Acleia nichil exigent. Et ne in posterum alicuius machinatione inquietari valeat, ipsam presentis sigilli attestatione et delegata michi apostolice sedis auctoritate confirmo. Hiis testibus.

a Ms Ex'   *b* Ms ad   *c* *Sic; prob. error for* Chastillon   *d* Ms conen'
e *Reading uncertain*   *f* Ms utraque

Date as for no. 174. This act is unusually long for this archdn, but he was acting on a papal commission and is known to have been the bp's official (*Fasti Lincoln*, 35); moreover, the next Robert, archdn of Oxford, was Robert de Mariscis, *c.* 1254–59 (ibid., 37), by whose time the use of the first person singular and of the term *persona* had become much rarer. The places concerned lay in the neighbouring archdnry of Buckingham. The main manor in Leckhampstead had certainly been subinfeudated to Hugh (de) Chastillon by the later 12th century (*VCH Bucks*, iv, 182).

180. *Canonical reception and induction, by the authority of instruments of Robert, bishop of Lincoln, and at the presentation of Walter, Earl Giffard [of Buckingham], founder of Notley abbey, of the canons of the house into the church of Caversham; and confirmation of the church to the canons.* [*c.* 1162 × 1164]

B = Oxford, Christ Church, Archives, Notley Charter Roll, m. 3. s. xvi med.

R. archidiaconus Oxon' universis sancte matris ecclesie filiis, salutem. Noverit[a] universitas vestra nos, auctoritate instrumentorum Roberti Lincoln' episcopi et presentatione Walteri Giffard comitis, fundatoris abbatie de Nutel', recepisse canonicos eiusdem loci in ecclesiam de Caversham et introduxisse. Et [ut][b] quod a nobis canonice factum est in posterum in dubium venire non possit, presentis scripti et sigilli nostri munimine predictam ecclesiam eisdem canonicis confirmavimus.

a Ms Noverint   *b Conjecturally supplied*

Notley abbey was founded in 1162 or earlier (Knowles and Hadcock, 169), and Earl Walter died in 1164 (*Complete Peerage*, ii, 387). See also, *EEA* IV, App. I, no. XV.

181. *Notification to all the clergy of Oxfordshire that, at the precept of Robert, bishop of Lincoln, and in accordance with the charter of Earl Walter Giffard, he has received the canons of Missenden into the* personatus *of the church of Shiplake; in the synod of Oxford.* [prob. 1163 × early 1164]

B = BL, Harley ms 3688 (Missenden cartulary), fo. 135r. s. xiv in.
Pd, *Missenden Cartulary*, iii, 90, no. 679.

R. archidiaconus Oxon' universo clero per Oxenefordschir' constituto, salutem. Noverit universitas vestra me recepisse canonicos ecclesie de Messend' in personatum ecclesie de Siplac, precepto Roberti Lincoln' episcopi, secundum formam et tenorem carte comitis Walteri Giffardi. Hiis testibus: priore Dorkecestr', Willelmo decano de Stokes, Willelmo decano Wott', Waltero scriptore, Nigello decano, et multis aliis de sinodo Oxon'.

Earl William's charter, which is witnessed by bp Robert of Lincoln, is dated 1163 at [Long] Crendon (*Missenden Cartulary*, iii, no. 667), and the present act, though clearly at least a little later, since it relates to business in synod at Oxford, probably followed soon afterwards. The bp's confirmation of the gift is ibid., no. 668, but no other notice of his instruction to the archdn is known (see *EEA* I, no. 174).

Mr Walter of Coutances

182. *Notification of the settlement in his presence of the dispute between the canons of Osney and Robert de Sancto Remigio over the church of Iffley, namely, that Robert and his successors are to have the right of presentation in the church, and its parson is to pay one mark annually to the said canons.* [*c.* 1175 × 3 July 1183]

B = BL, Cotton ms Vitellius E xv (Osney cartulary), fo. 47r. ss. xii ex.–xiii in. Damaged by fire.
Pd, *Oseney Cartulary*, vi, 135–6, no. 1053.

Magister Walterus de Const(anciis)[a] Oxen' archidiaconus omnibus ad quos presens scriptum pervenerit, salutem eternam. Quoniam ea que compositione vel iudicio terminantur firma debent consistere, notum facere volumus universis quod controversia que inter canonicos Oseneie et Robertum de Sancto Remigio super ecclesia de Iveteleia vertebatur amicabiliter sopita est in hunc modum. Scilicet quod Robertus ipsiusque posteritas in prefata ecclesia ius presentationis semper habeat,[b] et persona ecclesie supradictis canonicis dimidiam marcam ad festivitatem sancti Michaelis et dimi[diam][c] ad Pascha solvat annuatim. Hanc autem compositionem in presentia nostra factam, [ne][c] possit in posterum malignitate convelli, isto brevi testimonio munivimus in perpetuum valituram.

    a Expansion from rubric   *b Singular sic*   *c Ms damaged; bracketed passage*
    supplied

After Walter became archdn (i.e., between (presumably) his predecessor's consecration as bp of Hereford, 6 Oct. 1174, and his own first occurrence as archdn, 14 Mar. 1176) and before his consecration as bp of Lincoln (*Fasti Lincoln*, 35).

183.   *Notification that, by the office of his archdeaconry, he has, at the presentation and grant of King Henry II, given and confirmed to the nuns of Godstow the church of Bloxham, and has instituted them in the* personatus, *saving the right of Roger de Clifford, who is to have the church in their name for life for an annual pension of one bezant.*   [Jan. 1182 × 3 July 1183]

    B = PRO, E164/20 (Godstow cartulary), fo. 26r (13r). s. xv in. C = Bodl. ms Rawlinson
        B. 408 (Godstow cartulary, English calendar), fo. 24v (12v).[1] s. xv ex.
    Pd from C, *Godstow English Register*, i, 228, no. 307.

Universis sancte matris ecclesie filiis ad quos littere presentes pervenerint Walt(erus)[a] Oxoneford' archidiaconus, salutem in Cristo. Notum esse volumus nos ex officio archidiaconatus nostri, ad presentationem et concessionem domini regis Angl(orum) Henrici filii Matildis imperatricis,[b] donasse et presenti carta mea confirmasse sanctimonialibus de Godestow ecclesiam de Bloxam cum omnibus pertinentiis, salvo iure Lincon'[c] ecclesie et nostro. Instituimus autem prenominatas sanctimoniales in personatum prefate ecclesie, salvo iure Rogeri de Clifford', qui nomine earum eandem ecclesiam in vita sua est habiturus pensione unius bisantii prescriptis monialibus annuatim reddendi ad Pascha. Testibus hiis: magistro Winemero, Iohanne de Const', magistro Radulfo de Const', Matheo et Rogero capellanis, Stephano, David clericis.

    a B inserts de Godestow *(sic)*   *b* impatricis *B*   *c Sic B*

The king's charter to Godstow is witnessed by the king's son, Geoffrey [Plantagenet], as chancellor, to which office he was appointed in Jan. 1182 (PRO, E164/20, fo. 26r; *Fasti Lincoln*, 2); Walter of Coutances was elected bp of Lincoln 8 May 1183, and consecrated 3 July (*Fasti Lincoln*, 35). The church had previously been held by Seffrid II, archdn of Chichester (above, no. 13).

 [1] The calendar lacks witnesses.

Mr John of Coutances

184. *As archdeacon of Oxford and treasurer of Lisieux, notification that, in his presence, Roger de St John, with the assent of William, his brother, has given in perpetual alms to the abbot and canons of Osney his church of [Steeple] Barton, which the archdeacon has confirmed.* [? late 1183 × 1 July 1190]

> B = BL, Cotton ms Vitellius E xv (Osney cartulary), fo. 48r. ss. xii ex.–xiii in. Damaged by fire.
> Pd *Oseney Cartulary*, iv, 154, no, 119B.

Universis sancte matris ecclesie filiis ad quos presens scriptum pervenerit Iohannes de Constanc' archidiaconus Oxon' et Lexoviensis thesaurarius, salutem in domino. Ea que perpetuam desiderant memoriam expedit litterali memorie commendare. Ea propter ad universitatis vestre notitiam pervenire volumus Rogerum de Sancto Iohanne, assensu Willelmi fratris sui, in presentia nostra concessisse et dedisse abbati de Osen' et canonicis ibidem deo servientibus ecclesiam suam de Bertona in perpetuam elemosinam. Et ne concessio quam idem R. fecit tractu temporis in irritum po[sset]*[a]* devocari, eam presenti scripto et sigill[i nostri]*[a]* appositione dignum duximus confirmandam. Testibus his: Iohanne Norwic' episcopo, *[b]*[Radulfo Foliot archidiacono]*[b]* Hereford', Roberto archidiacono Nothingeham, Stephano de Sancto Iacobo, magistro Ricardo de Ailesberi, Roberto capellano nostro, Rogero clerico, et multis aliis.

> *a Ms damaged: bracketed passage supplied ultraviolet light, but included in printed edn.*   *b–b Not now readable, even under ultraviolet light, but included in printed edn.*

After John became archdn (i.e., after Walter of Coutances, his uncle, was consecrated bp of Lincoln at Angers, 3 July 1183, and before the latter was confirmed as archbp of Rouen in Nov. 1184); and before Robert archdn of Nottingham was elected bp of Worcester (*Fasti Lincoln*, 2, 36; *Fasti Monastic Cathedrals*, 100). Roger de St John's charter is witnessed by the archdn and by Richard of Aylesbury, vice-archdn (*Oseney Cartulary*, iv, no. 119). William de St John was the incumbent of the church, which his brother, Thomas, had given him and in which he was confirmed by Abbot Hugh and the convent of Osney under an annual pension of 40s (ibid., nos. 119A, 119C).

185. *Confirmation, after inspecting their charters, of the gift by Henry de Noers and Juliana, his wife, to St Frideswide's priory, Oxford, of the church of Churchill.* [? late 1183 × 20 Oct. 1196]

> B = Oxford, Christ Church, D. & C. Lib., vi. c. 1 (St Frideswide's cartulary), p. 229. s. xv.
> Pd, *St Frideswide's Cartulary*, ii, 259, no. 1034.

Universis sancte matris ecclesie filiis ad quos presens scriptum pervenerit Iohannes de Constanc' Oxenford' archidiaconus, salutem in domino. Noverit universitas vestra nos inspexisse cartas Henrici de Noers et Iuliane uxoris sue quibus donatio ecclesie de Cercell' continetur, quam predicti H. et I. ecclesie Sancte Frid' de Oxenford' et canonicis ibidem deo servientibus concessisse et quantum ad eos pertinet dedisse predictarum cartarum serie protestantur. Et ne memorati H. et I. iamdicta concessione et donatione, quam ipsi predictis canonicis fecerunt, aliquo modo possint resilire, eam presenti scripto et sigilli mei*[a]* munimine roborare curavimus, salva in omnibus Lincoln' ecclesie dignitate, et iure restitutionis nobis et successoribus nostris reservato. Hiis testibus et c(eter)a.

> *a Sic*

After John became archdn (see no. 184n.), and before he was consecrated bp of Worcester (*Fasti Lincoln,* 36). The charters of Henry and Juliana are *St Frideswide's Cartulary,* ii, nos. 1025, 1027. The gift of the church was confirmed by archbp Richard of Canterbury in 1174 × 1181, the confirmation being confirmed by Pope Alexander III, 25 July 1181 (ibid., nos. 1032–3; *EEA* II, no. 180; *PUE* iii, no. 339).

Mr Walter Map

186. *Notification that he has learnt from the testimony of reliable men and from the inspection of instruments that the monks of Hereford have received from of old twenty shillings [annually] from the church of Mongewell; he himself knows that W. of Cornhill, the former rector of the church, paid this sum, to which he bound himself by oath in full synod before the archdeacon, and his successor, R. de Bosco, clerk, swore before the archdeacon that he would pay the sum annually to the prior and monks. The archdeacon now confirms the twenty shillings.* [*c.* Sept. 1196 × Sept. 1210]

> B = Oxford, Balliol College Lib., ms 271 (St Guthlac's Hereford cartulary), fo. 72v (55v). s. xiv in.

W. Map' archidiaconus Oxon', salutem in domino. Noverit universitas vestra quod tam ex testimonio virorum fidedignorum quam ex instrumentis nobis exhibitis ac diligenter inspectis sufficienter didicimus[a] priorem et monachos Hereford' xx. s' de ecclesia de Mungewell' antiquitus rationabiliter percepisse. Hoc etiam scimus pro certo quod W. de Cornhull', quondam rector ecclesie de Mungewell', quam diu fuit persona eiusdem ecclesie fideliter et sine omni contradictione statutis terminis predictos viginti solidos persolvebat, ad quorum solutionem iuramento interposito in plena sinodo coram nobis se obligavit. Postmodum simili modo R. de Bosco clericus, successor eius, rector illius ecclesie iuravit coram nobis quod predictos viginti solidos priori et monachis annuatim persolveret. Hec scimus et protestamur et karitatis[b] intuitu ad piam eorundem monachorum petitionem ipsis eosdem xx. s' confirmamus. In cuius rei testimonium presens scriptum sigillo nostro munitum eisdem priori et monachis tradidimus. Hiis testibus: magistro A. de Chenur' tunc officiali Oxon', magistro R. de Kenmiote, magistro R. decano de Hamma, Iohanne de Longeford, magistro Philippo Map', magistro Simone de Olopemm',[c] Waltero de Wylton', Philippo Map', Nicholao camerario, Iohanne de Mattesdun', et multis aliis.

> *a Ms* dedicimus   *b Ms* karitas   *c Reading uncertain; ?* Olopemin'

The dating limits are the widest possible for Walter's archidiaconate (*Fasti Lincoln,* 36). W. of Cornhill may be William of Cornhill, who became archdn of Huntingdon in June 1207 and was consecrated bp of Coventry in Jan. 1215 (*Fasti Lincoln,* 28), particularly since, as archdn, his official was Robert de Bosco (BL, Cott. ms Claud. D xi, fo. 227r). Mr Adam of Chinnor had become official of Oxford by 2 John, May 1200–May 1201 (*Thame Cartulary,* i, no. 13).

187. *Notification that, inquiry having been made in the chapter at Enstone, he has learnt that the chapel of the castle of Ascot d'Oilly, with the demesne tithes of the vill and half a hide of land, belongs to St Frideswide's priory, Oxford; and they have long been held at farm in the name of St Frideswide's, at one time by Roger of Shipton, afterwards by Robert of Kencot and then by Roger his son.*

[*c.* Sept. 1196 × Sept. 1210: ? 25 Mar. × Sept. 1210]

B = Oxford, Christ Church, D. & C. Lib., vi. c. 1 (St Frideswide's cartulary), pp. 222–3. s. xv.

Pd, *St Frideswide's Cartulary*, ii, 247, no. 1019.

Omnibus sancte matris ecclesie filiis ad quos presentes littere pervenerint W. Map Oxon' archidiaconus, salutem in domino. Noverit [p. 223] universitas vestra nos, diligenti capituli inquisitione apud Ennestan facta, cognovisse quod capella que vocatur de castello de Escot' Rogeri de Oilli, cum decimis de dominico totius ville de Escot' et dimidia hida terre cum pertinentiis, pertinet ad ecclesiam Sancte Frid' Oxon'; ita quod eas olim Rogerus de Sipton' et postmodum Robertus de Kenicote et deinde Rogerus filius eius, nomine ecclesie Sancte Frid', longo tempore visi*a* sunt ad firmam tenuisse, sicut ius et possessionem predicte ecclesie. Hiis presentibus et testibus et c(eter)a.

a Sic; the printed edn reads usi, *which is the reading of the rubric, but* visi *fits the syntax and is clearly correct*

Date in general as for no. 186, but this act may be closely connected with the settlement of a dispute over the tithes of Ascot between St Frideswide's and the rector of Shipton[-under-Wychwood], reached in the 3rd year of the General Interdict (25 Mar. 1210–24 Mar. 1211), the dispute having been committed to judges-delegate by Innocent III on 25 May 1210 (*St Frideswide's Cartulary*, ii, nos. 1017–18; *Innocent III's Letters*, no. 871); there is, however, no certain indication that this act was part of that settlement.

ARCHDEACONRY OF STOW ('WEST RIDING')

Roger de Almaria *or* Mr Richard de Almaria

188. *As precentor of Lincoln and archdeacon, notification to all the faithful of the archdeaconry of the 'West Riding' that he has confirmed the agreement between the canons and nuns of Bullington and Philip, canon of Lincoln, son of William, archdeacon [of Stow], concerning the church of Hackthorn; and, at the request of Hubert of Hackthorn, he has instituted the said canons in the church.*

[*c.* 1155 × late 1160 *or* late 1160 × *c.* 1187]

A = BL, Harley Charter 43 H. 21. Endorsed: Carta precentoris Linc' de ecclesia de Hachetorn (s. xii ex.). Size 145 × *c.* 68 + *c.* 11 mm (turn-up folded out). Seal in varnished white wax on tag (method 1), portion only, pointed oval; lower half of frontally standing figure of an ecclesiastic; fragment of inscription.

Pd, *Danelaw Charters*, 21–2, no. 31.

R. Linc' ecclesie precentor et archidiaconus omnibus fidelibus per Westrith' constitutis, salutem et dilectionem. Que rationabiliter facta esse noscuntur quanta possumus vigilancia promovere debemus, et ad eorum conservationem debitam diligentiam adhibere. Quoniam vero nostri officii ratione omnium debitores sumus, eis tamen propensius providendum esse censemus quos ad vite arcioris observanciam totis viribus assurgere contemplamur. Inde est quod venerabilium fratrum nostrorum canonicorum et sanctimonialium de Bulintun' indempnitati providere volentes, ne tractu temporis eorum condicio deterior fieri possit, conventionem inter eos et Philippum canonicum filium Willelmi archidiaconi factam super ecclesia de Haketorn ratam habemus et sigilli nostri munimine confirmamus, et ad peticionem Huberti de Haketorn predictos canonicos in prescriptam ecclesiam instituimus.

F. M. Stenton, perhaps following the Catalogue of Harley Charters in the BL, attributed this act to Roger (de Almaria), precentor of Lincoln and archdn of the West Riding (*Danelaw Charters*, no. 31); in 1962 Kathleen Major suggested that it was issued by Richard (de Almaria), Roger's successor as precentor (*Misc. D. M. Stenton*, 210, continuation of n. 4 from 209), but in 1968, since *Cirencester Cartulary*, ii, no. 669, shows Roger clearly to have been archdn of 'Lindsey' (i.e., Stow) in 1156 × 1158, she revised her opinion in favour of the view that the present act could have been issued either by Roger or by Richard (*Reg. Antiquissimum*, ix, 259–60), and that view is followed here. The date is therefore either *c.* 1155 × late 1160 (after Roger de Almaria's predecessor was still archdn of Stow and before Roger ceased to be precentor, *Fasti Lincoln*, 44, 12), or as for below, no. 189. For William the archdn and his son, Philip, canon of Lincoln, see *Fasti Lincoln*, 44–5, 103. For Hubert of Hackthorn, see *Danelaw Charters*, lvi n. Despite the reference here to the church of Hackthorn, Bullington priory in fact held only a moiety of the church, the other half belonging to St Catherine's priory, Lincoln, a Gilbertine house like Bullington (ibid., nos. 24, 30; Golding, *Gilbert of Sempringham*, 361).

Mr Richard de Almaria

189.   *As precentor of Lincoln and archdeacon, notification to all clergy of the 'West Riding' that he has confirmed the gift by Peter the knight of Coates to the brethren of St James, Welbeck, of the church of Coates.*   [late 1160 × *c.* 1187]

B = BL, Harley ms 3640 (Welbeck cartulary), fo. 125r. s. xiv med.

Ricardus Lincoln' ecclesie precentor et archidiaconus omnibus clericis per Westring' constitutis, salutem et dilectionem. Que canonice facta esse dinoscuntur in lucem venire desiderant et, ne in posterum *ᵃ*ob sui*ᵃ* vetustatem aliquo modo oblivioni tradantur, scripto commendari. Inde est quod, donationem quam Petrus miles de Cothes fecit sancto Iacobo de Well' et fratribus ibidem deo servientibus de ecclesia de Cothes ratam*ᵇ* habentes, auctoritate qua fungimur confirm(amus) et presentis sigilli nostri attestatione communimus. T(estibus): Alexandro canonico Linc', A. de Filingham.

a–a Reading uncertain   *b Ms ratum*

The dating limits are the widest possible limits for Richard as precentor and archdn; as precentor (and presumably also as archdn) his predecessor last occurs after Nov. 1160 and he himself occurs before 19 Apr. 1161; his successor in the archdnry first occurs *c.* 1187 (*Fasti Lincoln*, 13, 45).

190. *As precentor of Lincoln and archdeacon of the 'West Riding', notification that, having inspected the letters of gift by Thomas son of Richard of Cuckney to the canons of Welbeck of the church of Whitton, and the confirmation of the church by Robert, late bishop of Lincoln, he has confirmed the church to them.* [1167 × early 1184]

B = BL, Harley ms 3640 (Welbeck cartulary), fo. 125r. s. xiv med.

Omnibus sancte matris ecclesie filiis presentibus et futuris Ricardus de Alm(ar)io Linc' ecclesie precentor et archidiaconus de Westring', salutem. Que a patribus et pastoribus nostris canonice et rationabiliter facta esse dinoscuntur summa veneratione nos decet amplecti. Inde est quod, inspectis litteris Thome filii Ricardi de Cukeney super donatione ecclesie de Whiten' facta venerabilibus fratribus nostris canonicis de Well', necnon et confirmatione de eadem ecclesia pie recordationis Roberti Linc' episcopi, eandem donationem ratam habentes, prefatam ecclesiam eisdem canonicis auctoritate qua fungimur confirm(amus) et sigilli nostri attestatione communimus. Hiis testibus: Radulfo subdecano, Ylb',[a] Pag(ano), Alexandro presbiteris.

a Ms Ysb'

After the death of bp Robert Chesney of Lincoln, 27 Dec. 1166, and before Ralph of Caen's successor as subdean of Lincoln was in office (*Fasti Lincoln*, 2, 21–2). The three *presbiteri* in the witness-list were all canons of Lincoln (ibid., 129, 106, 120). Thomas of Cuckney founded Welbeck abbey in 1153, partly as a penance for his lawlessness during the 'anarchy' of Stephen's reign (Colvin, *White Canons*, 64–6).

191. *As precentor of Lincoln and archdeacon, confirmation of the gift made by John, constable of Chester, to the canons of Malton, in his presence and with his assent, of the church of Winterton.* [late 1160 × c. 1187]

B = BL, Cotton ms Claudius D xi (Malton cartulary), fo. 42v (40v). s. xiii med.

Ricardus de Am(ar)io Linc' ecclesie precentor et archidiaconus omnibus ecclesie dei fidelibus, salutem et dilectionem. Quo magis viros spirituales et artiori vite mancipatos agnovimus, eo diligentius a prelatis ecclesie eis in exterioribus provideri oportet. Hii namque cum Maria ad pedes domini sedent, Martha circa plurima occupata.[1] De talibus non dicitur, Si vis perfectus esse vade et vende omnia que habes et da pauperibus.[2] Inde est quod, venerabiles dominos et fratres nostros canonicos ecclesie beate Marie de Malton' omni devotione amplectentes, donationem ecclesie de Wintrinton' quam eis nobis presentibus et assensum prebentibus fecit Iohannes constabularius de Cest' ratam habemus, et quantum ad nos pertinet presenti carta confirmamus et sigilli nostri munimine roboramus, salva in omnibus dignitate Linc' ecclesie. Hiis testibus, et c'.

Date as for no. 189. The church was confirmed to Malton by Hugh of Avallon, bp of Lincoln, in *c.* 1189 × 22 Mar. 1194 (*EEA* IV, no. 117). The charter of gift by John, constable of Chester, is cartulary, fo. 209r.

[1] 'Hii namque cum Maria . . . occupata': cf. John 10: 39, 41.
[2] 'Si vis . . . pauperibus': Matth. 19: 21.

192.   *As precentor of Lincoln and archdeacon of the 'West Riding', notification that, at the presentation of Prior Geoffrey and the convent of Spalding, he has received and canonically instituted Hugh, clerk, in the* personatus *of the church of St Helen, [Gate] Burton, near Marton; Hugh will bear episcopal burdens.*

[*c.* 25 July 1176 × *c.* 1187]

B = BL, Additional ms 35296 (Spalding cartulary, part 1), fo. 392r–v (394r–v). s. xiv med.

Universis sancte matris ecclesie filiis presentibus et futuris ad quos presens scriptum pervenerit, Ricardus precentor ecclesie sancte Marie Linc' et archidiaconus de Westriding', salutem. Noverit universitas vestra nos, ad presentationem Galfridi prioris et conventus de Spald', recepisse H. clericum [fo. 392v] in personatum ecclesie sancte Helene de Burton' iuxta Martun'*ᵃ* et eundem canonice instituisse. Idem Hugo honera episcopalia sustinebit. Et ut hec institutio rationabiliter facta rata permaneat, sigilli nostri appositione corroboravimus. Hiis testibus.

a Exact reading uncertain

After the date when Prior Geoffrey's predecessor was still in office (*Heads*, 109) and before Richard ceased to be in office (*Fasti Lincoln*, 45). The identity of Burton is established by the church's dedication; the church was confirmed to Spalding by bp Robert Chesney in 1148 × 1166 (*EEA* I, no. 254), and, probably in the early 13th century, the archdn of Worcester recognised that he held the church of *Geiteburton'* of the priory (Spalding cartulary, fo. 393r).

193.   *As precentor of Lincoln and archdeacon of the 'West Riding', notification that, at the presentation of Abbot Robert and the convent of Bardney, he has received and canonically instituted Mr Richard of Hardres in the* personatus *of St John's church, Scampton, saving an annual pension to the monks of one mark; Richard will bear episcopal burdens.*

[late 1185 × *c.* 1187]

B = BL, Cotton ms Vespasian E xx (Bardney cartulary), fo. 199r (194r). s. xiii ex.

Universis sancte matris ecclesie filiis presentibus et futuris ad quos presens scriptum pervenerit Ricardus precentor sancte Marie Linc' et archidiaconus de Westriding', salutem. Noverit universitas vestra nos, ad presentationem Roberti abbatis de Bard' et eiusdem loci conventus, recepisse magistrum Ricardum de Hard' in personatum ecclesie sancti Iohannis de Scamtona et eundem canonice instituisse, salva pensione unius marce predictis monachis annuatim solvende. Idem Ricardus onera episcopalia sustinebit. Et [ut]*ᵃ* hec institutio rationabiliter facta rata permaneat, sigilli nostri appositione corroboravimus. Testibus hiis: magistro Roberto de Hardr' et c'.

a Supplied

Abbot Robert of Bardney was not appointed before Michaelmas 1185 (*Heads*, 27); Richard de Almaria had been succeeded as archdn by *c.* 1187, but probably not until after 29 Mar. (*Fasti Lincoln*, 45). Robert of Hardres, the first witness, became archdn of Huntingdon after 1189 and by Apr. 1192 (ibid., 27).

Mr Alexander

194. *Agreement, reached in his presence in the provincial chapter at [?East] Halton and fortified by his seal, by which the prior and convent of Nun Cotham have granted to the lady Matilda de Bayeux for life, on account of her infirmity and age, that she may have divine service for herself and her household celebrated three days each week in her chapel of Girsby by the nuns' chaplain who serves the parish church; all oblations and other proceeds will be reserved to the parish church and for the uses of the nuns. William, Matilda's brother, and Richard, his son, have given sureties for this, William swearing in the hand of the archdeacon, and Richard in the hand of Richard, dean of [West] Torrington, before the parish, that they will compel Matilda to abide by the agreement.* [1196 × c. 1200]

B = Bodl. ms Top. Lincs. d.1 (Nun Cotham cartulary), fo. 15r. s. xiii in. C = Ibid., fo. 38a v. s. xiii in.

[H]ec est conventio [facta]*ᵃ* inter priorem et conventum de Cotuna et dominam Matildem de Baius.*ᵇ* Videlicet quod prior et conventus de Cotuna concesserunt domine Matildi*ᶜ* ut habeat divinum officium in capella de Griseby tribus diebus per ebdomadam in vita sua tantum et*ᵈ* ipsa et familia domus sue quam diu ibi demorata fuerit*ᵉ* per capellanum monialium qui matrici ecclesie deserviet. Et hoc ei sola gratia pro sua imbecillitate et senectute concesserunt, nullo ipsius Matildis iure interveniente, ita quod nullus heredum eius ius reclamandi habeat super conventione ista nec exigendi ex debito quod moniales ei gratuito concesserunt. Oblationes autem vel beneficia que eidem capelle collata*ᶠ* fuerint matrici ecclesie et usibus monialium ex integro conservabuntur. Sciendum vero quod domina Matildis securavit in verbo veritatis et sub attestatione Cristianitatis sue quod ipsa pro posse suo providebit indempnitati matricis ecclesie ut nullum dispendium [monialibus]*ᵃ* per predictam capellam proveniat; et Willelmus frater eius et Ricardus filius eius huius conventionis tenende fideiussores sunt, ita quod Willelmus *ᵍ*iuravit et*ᵍ* affidavit in manu magistri Alexandri*ʰ* archidiaconi et Ricardus in manu Ricardi decani de Tirigtun*ⁱ* coram parochia quod ipsi pro posse suo facient dominam Matildem stare conventioni*ʲ* prescripte et secundum formam conventionis omnia conservari. Actum in provinciali capitulo apud Hautun, presidente magistro Alexandro archidiacono qui, ut prescripta omnia possint*ᵏ* inconcussa teneri, presentis conventionis paginam sigilli sui impressione munivit.*ˡ* Hiis testibus:*ᵐ* [Ricardo decano de Tiringt', Roberto suo capellano, Rogero iuvene, Willelmo presbitero de Rand, Iosep filio suo, Willelmo persona de Stayntun, Simone filio eius, Alano persona de Wullingham, Gregorio persona de Benyg', Roberto persona de Bischopt', Alano persona de Kevermunde, Achardo presbitero de Lissingtun, Willelmo presbitero de Hautun, Ricardo presbitero de Hautun, Galfrido presbitero de Burg', Michaele monacho de Parcho, Hugone presbitero de Benigwurth, Gilberto presbitero de Hautun, Iohanne presbitero de Pauntun, Ioce presbitero de Appelay, Ioce clerico de Ludeford, Radulfo presbitero de Barkewrth, Hugone de Mustrel, Stephano camerario].

a Om. in B; supplied from C	*b* Bayus *C*	*c* Matilde *B;* Matild' *C*
d Om. in C	*e* fuerat *B*	*f oblata C*	*g–g Om. in C*
h Alenandri *(sic) B*	*i* Tyringtun *C*	*j Placed before* stare *in C*
k possunt *B*	*l* munuit *B*	*m B ends; the remainder supplied from C*

Not earlier than 1196, when Hugh de Bayeux, presumably Matilda's brother and certainly brother of William de Bayeux, died (Sanders, *English Baronies*, 88), and before the first occurrence of Alexander's successor as archdn (*Fasti Lincoln*, 45). For William de Bayeux, brother of Hugh, see *Danelaw Charters*, nos. 255, 475. Though not formally in the name of the archdn, this is so closely connected with the exercise of archidiaconal authority as to warrant inclusion here. The parish church concerned was that of Burgh-on-Bain, whose parish includes Girsby and which was given to Nun Cotham in 1148 × 1166 (cartulary, fo. 13v; *EEA* I, no. 203). Since Burgh-on-Bain and all the benefices mentioned in the witness-list were in the rural deanery of Wraggoe in the archdnry of Lincoln, the archdn was here dealing with a matter outside his own archdnry, perhaps because of the absence of Peter, archdn of Lincoln (*Reg. Antiquissimum*, vii, 206–7); the archdn's 'provincial chapter' was therefore most probably at East Halton in Lincoln archdnry (rather than West Halton in Stow archdnry, as stated by D. M. Owen, *Church and Society in Medieval Lincolnshire*, Lincoln 1971, 29–30), since (a) so many clergy of one archdnry are unlikely to have agreed to attend in the neighbouring archdnry, and (b) when Adelelm, archdn of Dorset, was asked to hear a case in Wiltshire archdnry, he did so within that archdnry and not in his own (below, no. 235).

DIOCESE OF LONDON

Archdeaconry of Colchester

Richard Foliot I

195. *Notification to all 'prelates' of churches in the archdeaconry of Colchester that he has received the church of Beaumont from Prior W(illiam) of Hatfield [Regis] with the assent of the convent, for an annual pension of three marks, under specified conditions; after his death the church will revert to the monks.*   [*c*. 1167 × *c*. 1180]

> A = BL, Additional Charter 28334. Endorsed: De pensione pert' bello monte (s. xv). Hatfield (post-medieval). Size 131 × 225 + 17 mm. Seal and tag missing (method 1).
> Pd, with facsimile, *Facsimiles of Royal and other Charters in the British Museum*, i, no. 59.

R. archidiaconus Colecestrie universis ecclesiarum prelatis per archidiaconatum Colecestrie constitutis, salutem et dilectionem. Universitati vestre notifico me ecclesiam de Bellomonte a W. priore de Hatfeld', conventu suo ad id assensum prebente, sub annua pensione trium marcarum ipsi et monachis suis, xx. sciliced*ᵃ* solidis in festivitate beati Michaelis, xx. in Pascha solvendis, recepisse; meque etiam eis hanc pensionem soluturum, nec ecclesiam iam dictam alicui ad firmam vel alio modo citra voluntatem eorum et concessum concessurum, immo sollicitam me diligentiam adhibiturum, ut post meum decessum ecclesia cum suis ad eos redeat pertinentiis, tactis sacrosanctis euuangeliis firmiter promisisse. Et ut ecclesiam suam post me absque ulla dificultate*ᵃ* recipiant, hoc ipso sacramento adieci me nulli in iam nominata ecclesia vicariam concessurum, nisi primo iuraverit se, si quid humanitus de me acciderit, clavem ecclesie priori vel uni ex fratribus suis incontinenti traditurum. Et quia de consuetudine est ut hi quibus ecclesie ad firmam a monachis conceduntur pro ipsis tam episcopo quam archidiacono debeant respondere, me pro ipsis tam in his que episcopum quam que archidiaconum contingunt satisfacturum similiter obligavi. Et si forte ecclesia illa per me vel incrementum vel meliorationem aliquam receperit, de mea voluntate est ut ea cum sua recipiant ecclesia. Et ut hec conventio inter nos habita firma et illesa permaneat, eam presenti scripto et sigilli mei apposicione confirmare curavi. His testibus: Nicholao priore de Stokes et Adam monacho suo, Gaufrido capellano, Radulfo clerico, Hunfrido clerico, Michaele clerico, Michaele dapifero, Waltero, magistro Eustachio de Disce, Willelmo de blavinio,[b] Willelmo de Hledes, et multis aliis.

a Sic   b Reading uncertain; ? blauno

The archdn's predecessor last occurs after 21 Oct. 1166, and he himself first occurs as archdn, *c.* 1167 × 1168; he is not known to occur after *c.* 1180 at the latest and may have been transferred to Middlesex archdnry, *c.* 1181 (*Fasti St Paul's*, 18–19). This agreement was confirmed by Gilbert Foliot, bp of London, who instituted Richard as perpetual vicar under this pension, in an act which the editors suggested might date from *c.* 1179 (*Foliot Letters and Charters*, no. 376). In the printed facsimile it is dated *c.* 1175 × 1180.

196. *Notification to all 'prelates' of churches in the archdeaconry of Colchester that, at the request and presentation of Beatrice de Mandeville with the assent of Earl William de Mandeville, he has granted the church of Elsenham to Prior R(eginald) and the monks of Walden and, by the authority of G(ilbert), bishop of London, has solemnly instituted the prior as parson in the same.* [*c.* 1170 × 1180]

B = BL, Harley ms 3697 (Walden cartulary), fos. 38v–39r (21v–22r), no. 10. s. xiv ex.

Ricardus archidiaconus Colecestrie universis ecclesiarum prelatis per archidiaconatum Colecestrie [fo. 39r] constitutis, salutem et dilectionem. Universitati vestre presenti scripto notifico me, petitione et presentatione Beatricis de Mandevilla, comite Willelmo de Mandevilla ad id assensum prebente, ecclesiam de Elsenham R. priori de Waledena et fratribus ibidem deo servientibus concessisse, ipsumque priorem autoritate G. London' episcopi debita cum solemnitate personam in predicta ecclesia constituisse. Quod ne in dubium vel in irritum revocetur, sigilli mei appositione confirmare curavi. Hiis testibus: Willelmo priore de Athfeld', Waltero decano de Clavering, Godardo et Abel capellanis, Ricardo Aguilon, Galfrido de Dunam[a], Silvestro de Cestreford, Thoma de Rigling, Martino de Lutlebur', Gervasio capellano, et aliis multis.

a Reading of initial letter uncertain

Probably of the same period as Gilbert Foliot's confirmation of the gift of the church to Walden, which is witnessed by Henry (Banastre), treasurer of St Paul's, who was not appointed until after *c.* 1170, and by Hugh, dean of St Paul's, whose successor was elected at the latest, Jan. 1181 (*Foliot Letters and Charters*, no. 442; *Fasti St Paul's*, 21, 5).

Mr Ralph de Alta Ripa

197.   *Notification that he was present when G(ilbert), bishop of London, instituted the monks of St James, Walden, in the church of Arkesden and that, on the bishop's mandate, he inducted them into corporal possession of the same.*

[prob. 1180 × Sept. 1181]

B = BL, Harley ms 3697 (Walden cartulary), fo. 38v (21v), no. 7. s. xiv ex.

Universis sancte matris ecclesie filiis Radulfus de Altaripa archidiaconus Colecestr', salutem in domino. Universitati vestre notum fieri volumus nos fuisse presentes ubi venerabilis pater G. dominus Lundon' monachos monasterii sancti Iacobi de Waleden' in ecclesia de Arkesden' instituit, et nos de illius mandato eosdem in corporalem possessionem predicte ecclesie de Arkesden' induxisse. Hiis testibus: Ricardo et Thoma decanis, Simone Extraneo, Radulfo clerico de Binham, et multis aliis.

Gilbert Foliot's reception of the monks into the *personatus* of the church, which is witnessed by Ralph de Diceto as dean of St Paul's and therefore not earlier than 1180, is *Foliot Letters and Charters*, no. 446; archbp Richard's confirmation of the institution, as legate, can be dated not later than Sept. 1181 (*EEA* II, no. 221 and n.). The archdn's act most probably belongs in the same dating range. The church of Arkesden was given to Walden by William son of Ernulf and Eudo of Arkesden, whose separate charters are in the Walden cartulary, fo. 132v, nos. 6–7; William son of Ernulf also gave, by another charter, a moiety of all his demesne tithes in Arkesden, the other moiety of which belonged anciently to the church (ibid., fo. 132v, no. 5).

198.   *Notification that the dispute between himself and Mr Robert of Kent over the church of Ashdon has been settled before G(ilbert), bishop of Rochester, acting for the archbishop of Canterbury; Robert's right to the rectory has been proved before the bishop, and the archdeacon has received the vicarage, to be held of Robert as parson for an annual pension of one gold piece; the prior and monks of Lewes have given their consent.*   [29 Sept. 1185 × 1191]

B = BL, Cotton ms Vespasian F xv (Lewes cartulary), fo. 175v (204v). s. xv med.
Pd (transl.), *Lewes Cartulary*, iii, 33, no. 59.

Omnibus sancte matris ecclesie filiis ad quos presentes litere pervenerint Radulfus archidiaconus Colecestr', salutem in domino. Noverit universitas vestra controversiam que vertebatur inter me et magistrum Robertum de Kent super ecclesia de Essendun' coram domino G. Roffensi episcopo tunc agente vices domini Cant(uariensis) hoc fine fuisse sopitam. Iure siquidem magistri Roberti de Kent super personatu suo de ecclesia de Essendun' coram memorato episcopo declarato, vicariam ipsius ecclesie ab eodem magistro R. recepi imperpetuum possidendam [reddendo]*a* eidem magistro R. ut persone singulis annis aureum unum nomine ecclesie pro pensione in Natali domini. Et nos adinvicem hanc conventionem fideliter observandam fidei religione firmavimus, presentibus monachis de Lewes, scilicet M. camerario et W. constabulario, ex mandato prioris de Lewes et conventus assensum prestantibus. Hiis testibus: magistro Roberto Melden', et Thoma et Ricardo Agulun et Geroldo decanis de Samford' et de Depeden' et de Ulting', Willelmo capellano, magistro Fabiano, Silvestro de Cestreford', Ricardo de Bello campo, magistro Willelmo de Hactun' et Radulfo Ruffo, Roberto de Yffeld', Walkelino Turvill', et multis aliis.

a Gap in ms; supplied conjecturally

After Gilbert de Glanville was consecrated bp of Rochester (*Fasti Monastic Cathedrals,* 76) and before the archdn's death in 1190 or 1191 (*Fasti St Paul's,* 19). The editors of *Lewes Cartulary,* iii, date the act to *c.* 1185, as they do also an act of Gilbert Foliot instituting Robert of Kent as parson, which immediately precedes it in the cartulary, but the latter must be earlier, since it refers to a serving minister called Walter (*Foliot Letters and Charters,* no. 395, where dated 1163 × *c.* 1180).

199. *Notification that, at the request and presentation of the abbot and monks of Battle, he has granted to Robert de Funteney, clerk, the church of [Great] Sampford with the church of St Andrew,* Eston', *for an annual pension to the monks of two and a half marks, and with an agreement concerning hospitality for the abbot of Battle when in those parts; and notification that he has received Robert to these churches, the see of London being vacant.* [18 Feb. 1187 × 31 Dec. 1189]

B = San Marino, Huntington Library, Battle Abbey Papers, vol. 29 (Battle cartulary), fo. 96r–v. s. xiii ex.

Omnibus sancte matris [ecclesie]*ª* filiis ad quos presentes littere pervenerint Radulfus archidiaconus Colec', salutem. Noverit universitas vestra nos, ad petitionem et presentationem domini abbatis et fratrum de Bello, Roberto clerico de Funteneia ecclesiam eorum de Sanford' cum ecclesia sancti Andree de Eston' et omnibus aliis pertinentiis suis concessisse sub annua pensione duarum marcarum et dimidie ipsis monachis in festo sancti Martini per-solvenda. Hoc etiam inter eos ex nostra concessione convenit, quod predictus Robertus singulis annis bis abbatem, si totiens in partes illas venerit, in ecclesie possessione ex consuetudine hospitio [fo. 96v] suscipiet. Nos itaque tempore vacantis ecclesie Lond' Robertum ad predictas ecclesias suscepimus, et has ei nostre confirmationis litteras indulsimus. Hiis testibus: Radulfo abbate Sancte Oside, Moyse decano, Willelmo capellano, Silvestro de Cestreford', magistro Fabiano, magistro Reg(inaldo), Rogero camerario, Ricardo de Elnested', Roberto de Elnested', et multis aliis.

a Supplied

During the vacancy at London between the death of bp Gilbert Foliot and the consecration of bp Richard Fitz Neal (*Fasti St Paul's,* 2). In 1163 × 1171 Gilbert Foliot had instituted Thomas, clerk, as parson of Sampford at the presentation of abbot Walter of Battle (Huntington Lib., Battle Abbey Papers, vol. 29, fo. 96r; pd, *EEA* 15, no. 80). The church of *Eston'* has not been identified; by *c.* 1240 it was called a 'chapel' (Battle Abbey Papers, vol. 29, fo. 96v). Robert de Funteney was also instituted as parson of Great Thurlow, Suffolk, in Nov. 1189 × 1200 (see below, no. 220).

Archdeaconry of Essex

Robert Banastre

200. *Mandate and precept to Warin, knight of Purleigh, to make peace with the monks of [Monks] Horton concerning five acres of land which his father gave them in free and quit alms for the church of Purleigh; and, if he does not, precept to William, priest of Purleigh, to deprive him and his housefold of Christian service until he makes peace.*   [9 Apr. 1167 × ? *c.* 1200]

B = BL, Stowe ms 935 (Monks Horton cartulary), fos. 23v–24r (pp. 76–7). s. xv med.

Robertus archidiaconus de Essexia Warino militi de Purlai, salutem. Mando tibi et precipio ut facias pacem cum monachis de Hortuna de quinque acris terre quas pater tuus dedit illis in libera et quieta elemosina ad ecclesiam de Purlai. Quod si non feceris, [fo. 24r] precipio Willelmo presbitero de Purlai ut nullam Cristianitatem faciat tibi nec familie tue donec pacem facias cum predictis monachis. Vale.

Robert's predecessor as archdn died not earlier than 9 Apr. 1167; Robert first occurs as archdn, *c.* 1167 × 1168; his last certain occurrence is 1196, but he may not have died until *c.* 1200 (*Fasti St Paul's,* 12–13). As 'Mr Robert archdn of Essex', he witnessed Gilbert Foliot's inspeximus (1167 × 1174) of bp Richard de Belmeis II's confirmation (1152 × 1162) of the gift of the church to Monks Horton by Aubrey de Vere, Adelina his wife, and Henry of Essex (*Foliot Letters and Charters,* no. 420a). Henry of Essex, who lost his lands in 1163 after being convicted of treason in trial by battle, gave 12 acres of land for the lights of Purleigh church (cartulary, fo. 23r). On Purleigh, see Dodwell, 'Bacton Charters', in *Misc. D. M. Stenton,* esp. 150, 154–6.

201. *Notification to all faithful of the archdeacony of Essex that, having inspected the letters of the late Pope Lucius III, allowing the abbot and regular canons of Waltham to convert to their own uses the churches whose patronage belongs to them, he has inducted them into the vacant church of Nazeing, which belongs to their advowson, and put them into corporal possession of the same.*   [18 Feb. 1187 × 31 Dec. 1189]

B = BL, Harley ms 391 (Waltham cartulary), fo. 98r. s. xiii in.
Pd, *Waltham Charters,* 151, no. 232.

Omnibus sancte matris ecclesie filiis per archidiaconatum Essessie*ᵃ* constitutis Robertus Banastre archidiaconus Exex', salutem in domino. Ad communem vestri volumus devenire notitiam nos inspexisse litteras Lucii pape iii. pie memorie quibus indulsit abbati et canonicis regularibus de Walth(am) ecclesias suas, quarum ius patronatus ad eos spectare dinoscitur, in proprios usus convertere et earundem libere frui beneficiis. Cum vero ecclesia de Nasinges vacaret, que ad advocationem prescriptorum abbatis et canonicorum pertinebat, nos ipsos in predicta ecclesia de Nasing' introduximus et in corporalem possessionem eiusdem ecclesie misimus, salvo per omnia iure London' episcopi et eius officialium. Verum, quoniam id ratum et inconcussum in posterum permanere volumus, carte nostre attestatione et sigilli nostri appositione confirmamus. Testibus his: Roberto de Walda decano, magistro Radulfo de Alcrug', magistro Adam de Stokes, Gill(eberto) de Leit', Waltero de Berking', Edgaro de Wudeford', Stephano capellano de Walth(am), Radulfo de

Wanested', Fulcone de Berking', Herebert,[a] Roberto de Berking', Hai, Rogero clerico, et multis aliis.

a Sic

This was confirmed by Pope Celestine III in 1191, stating that Waltham's institution by archdns in the churches of Nazeing and Netteswell (see below, no. 211) had taken place while the see of London was vacant (*Waltham Charters*, no. 236; *PUE*, i, no. 291); the date is therefore as for no. 199.

ARCHDEACONRY OF LONDON

Nicholas

202. *Notification that Robert the Philosopher, having pursued by a royal writ a claim against the canons of Holy Trinity, London [Aldgate], that the parochial affiliation of Smithfield belonged to his church of St Peter in the Tower, both before the archdeacon and before G(ilbert), bishop of London, has now renounced his claim in the hand of the bishop and quitclaimed the parochial affiliation to the canons and their church of St Botolph without Aldgate.* [prob. 9 May 1166]

> B = Glasgow University Lib., ms Hunter 215 (U. 2. 6) (Holy Trinity Aldgate cartulary), fo. 172r. s. xv in.
> Pd (calendar), *Holy Trinity Aldgate Cartulary*, 191, no. 971.

Universis sancte matris ecclesie filiis Nicholaus Lond' archidiaconus, salutem. Ex precepto domini regis et cum litteris eiusdem Robertus philosofus adversus canonicos sancte Trinitatis Lond' litem instituit, petens et vendicans sue ecclesie sancti Petri in pedeplanis Turris parochiatum de Smethfeld'. Cumque utraque pars sepius ante me, aliquotiens autem coram domino meo G. Lond' episcopo, pro causa illa stetisset, Robertus, melius philosofatus et quod intellexerit canonicos iustam habere causam confessus, in manu domini mei episcopi liti et petitioni sue predicte pro se et pro ecclesia sua in perpetuum renuntiavit[a] et parochiatum predictum canonicis et eorum ecclesie sancti Both(ulf)i extra Algat', ad quam parochiatus ille iure parochiali pertinet, liberum et quietum omnino clamavit.

a Ms renutiavit

Probably of the same date as the settlement of the case, at which the archdn was present (*Holy Trinity Aldgate Cartulary*, nos. 969–70; *Foliot Letters and Charters*, 514–15, App. V, no. 5). The parochial affiliation had been in dispute between St Botolph Aldgate (in the priory's possession) and St Peter in the Tower (ad Vincula) for some time under different incumbents of the latter (see *Holy Trinity Aldgate Cartulary*, nos. 964, 966). For the priory's acquisition of St Botolph's in 1125, see ibid., xv, and no. 871; *Regesta*, ii, no. 1467.

203. *Gift to Nicholas, his nephew, of his houses in London and of his garden and land in Holborn after the death of Mr Richard, the archdeacon's brother; sealed with the seal of the chapter of St Paul's.*   [1169]

> B = London, Guildhall Lib., ms 25501 (St Paul's Cathedral cartulary), fo. 35v. s. xiii med. C = Cambridge, St John's College Lib., ms S. 25 (St Paul's Cathedral, almoner's cartulary, 1345), fo. 9v. s. xiv med. D = BL, Harley ms 4080 (transcript of C), fo. 9v. ss. xvii–xviii.
> Pd from B and D, *Early Charters of St Paul's*, 98–9, no. 134.

Sciant presentes et futuri quod ego Nicholaus archidiaconus Lond',*ᵃ* cum domino nostro Gilberto Lond' episcopo Romam iturus, dono et concedo Nicholao nepoti meo domos meas cum omnibus pertinentiis quas habeo Lond' et gardinum meum de Holeburn'*ᵇ* cum tota terra mea quam ibi habeo, de domino feudi*ᶜ* tenendum libere et quiete, salvo domini servitio, post mortem*ᵈ* magistri Ricardi fratris mei si idem Nicholaus ei supervixerit. Et ut firma hec mea habeatur donatio, ad maiorem huius donationis securitatem sigillum capituli Sancti Pauli Lond' huic presenti scripto feci apponere. Hiis testibus: Hugone decano nostro, magistro Nicholao filio Clementis,*ᵉ* [Alexandro de Saccavilla, magistro Ricardo fratre meo, Ricardo Ruffo, Willelmo de Beamieys, magistro David, et multis aliis].

> *a (and later)* London' *C,D*   *b* Holeburn' *C,D*   *c* feodi *C,D*
> *d Followed in C by* d *marked for deletion; in D by* D   *e B ends with* et aliis; *remainder from C,D*

The party set out for Rome at around Michaelmas (29 Sept.) 1169 (Diceto, *Opera Historica*, i, 335). For the relationship of the archdn to his nephew and brother, see A. Morey and C.N.L. Brooke, *Gilbert Foliot and his Letters*, 285.

204. *Notification that, at the presentation of Abbot Walter and the convent of Westminster, he has received and in general chapter instituted Geoffrey of Bedford, chaplain, in the church of St Margaret near London Bridge, whose gift belongs to the abbot and convent, for an annual pension of ten shillings to the chamberlain of the abbey, for in the same way and under the same pension Geoffrey the clerk, instituted by the archdeacon at their presentation, had previously held the church.*

          [1175 × 27 Sept. 1190; ? 18 Feb. 1187 × 31 Dec. 1189]

> B = BL, Cotton ms Faustina A iii (Westminster cartulary), fos. 290v–291r. s. xiii ex. C = Westminster Abbey Muniments, Book 11 (Westminster Abbey Domesday), fo. 477v (501v). s. xiv in.
> Pd from B and C, *Westminster Abbey Charters*, 212–13, no. 369.

Omnibus sancte matris ecclesie filiis ad quos presentes littere pervenerint Nicholaus dei gratia London' archidiaconus, eternam in domino salutem. Universitati vestre notum*ᵃ* facimus nos, ad presentationem venerabilis viri Walteri abbatis Westm' et eiusdem loci*ᵇ* conventus, recepisse et nullo contradicente in generali capitulo instituisse Galfridum de Bedeford' capellanum in ecclesia sancte Margarete de London' prope Pontem, que ad prefati abbatis et conventus donationem pertinere dinoscitur; ita ut nomine pensionis x. solidorum camerario Westm' singulis [fo. 291r] annis ad duos terminos anni reddere debeat, ad Pascha videlicet v. s' et ad festum sancti Michaelis v. s'; eodem enim modo et sub eadem pensione Galfridus clericus memoratam ecclesiam ex donatione abbatis et conventus et ex nostra concessione ante tenuerat, et in ea ad presentationem abbatis et conventus cum debita sollempnitate per nos institutus fuit. Ne igitur que in presentia nostra gesta sunt decetero possint*[c]* in dubium revocari,*[d]* ea sigilli nostri testimonio roboravimus. Hiis testibus:*[e]* [Radulfo cantore, Stephano camerario, magistro Ricardo fratre Nicholai archidiaconi, magistro Nicholao eiusdem nepote,*[f]* Nicholao capellano archidiaconi, magistro Silvestro, Roberto eius capellano, Iohanne capellano del Baille, Iohanne de Sancta Margareta, Rogero de Sancto Edmundo, Ernisio Bissope, Willelmo Aldelmanno, Ad(a) Camberletk', Andrea le Blunt, Iacobo le Want', et multis aliis].

a C repeats notum	*b Om. in C*	*c* possunt *C*	*d First syllable*
interlined in B	*e B ends with* et c'; *remainder from C*	*f* nepoti *C*	

The outside dating limits are those of Walter's abbacy at Westminster (*Heads,* 77), but the institution may belong to the vacancy at London after Gilbert Foliot's death (see above, no. 199n.). In Mar. 1184 Geoffrey of Bedford, priest, resigned his right to the church of St Margaret near London Bridge (Bridge Street) in a case heard by the prior of St Saviour's, Bermondsey, and archdn Nicholas, papal judges-delegate (*Westminster Abbey Charters,* no. 194; below, App. I, no. 5).

205. *Notification that, at the presentation of Abbot Walter and the convent of Westminster, to whom the gift of a moiety of the church of St Magnus the Martyr belongs, and at the presentation of Prior Henry de Soilli and the convent of Bermondsey, to whom the other moiety of the church with the right of gift belongs, he has received Mr Nicholas, his nephew, as parson of the church and, through his official, inducted him into corporal possession of the same.*

[*c.* 1186 × Sept. 1189; ? after 18 Feb. 1187]

B = BL, Cotton ms Faustina A iii (Westminster cartulary), fo. 246r–v. s. xiii ex. C = Westminster Abbey Muniments, Book 11 (Westminster Abbey Domesday), fo. 478v (502v). s. xiv in.
Pd from B and C (without collation), *Westminster Abbey Charters,* 211–12, no. 368.

Universis sancte matris ecclesie filiis ad quos presens scriptum pervenerit Nicholaus archidiaconus Lond', salutem in domino. Vestre notificamus universitati nos, ad presentationem Walteri abbatis Westm' et conventus eiusdem loci ad quorum donationem medietas ecclesie sancti Magni martiris de Ponte pertinet, et ad presentationem Henrici de Soliaco prioris Bermundeseye*[a]* et eiusdem loci conventus ad quos alia medietas prefate ecclesie pertinet*[b]* cum iure donationis, magistrum Nicholaum nepotem nostrum in personam ecclesie predicte recepisse, et ipsum per officialem nostrum in corporalem possessionem eiusdem induxisse. Unde, ut ea que a nobis gesta sunt firma habeantur, [fo. 246v] hoc presenti scripto cum sigilli nostri appositione roboranda duximus. Hiis testibus:*[c]* [Nicholao capellano nostro, Ricardo de Sancto Iohanne, Helia de Honilane, Gaufrido de Sancta Margareta de Ponte, Waltero de Sancto Botulpho de Ponte, Gregorio capellano, David filio eius, Swenone capellano nostro, Iohanne capellano eiusdem ecclesie, Willelmo filio Alexandri, Radulfo de Ulla, Hudone de Sancto Georgio].

a Beremundes' *C*	*b Placed after* donationis *C*	*c B ends with* et c';
remainder from C		

The outside dating limits are those of Henry de Soilli as prior of Bermondsey, who became abbot of Glastonbury in Sept. 1189 (*Heads*, 115), but the institution may have taken place during the vacancy in the see of London between 18 Feb. 1187 and 31 Dec. 1189 (see above, no. 199n.). This is a nice example of two patrons presenting the same clerk to the two moieties of a church.

Mr Alard of Burnham

206. *Notification that, in his presence, Agatha, daughter of Robert son of Ralph, and Bertram, son of William de Calverdon and husband of Agatha's sister Alice, have sworn to keep their agreement made with the canons of Otham [afterwards Bayham] concerning the land which belonged to Ralph de Dene, senior, in Tilton and in the marshes of Hailsham and Pevensey.*   [21 Apr. 1196 × May 1201; ? × c. 1200]

> B = BL, Cotton ms Otho A ii (Bayham cartulary), fo. 18r. s. xiii med. Damaged by fire, 1731. C = BL, Additional ms 6037 (transcripts by Sir Edward Dering, including extracts from same), fo. 85r (abbreviated text). 1627.[1]

*^a*Omnibus sancte matris ecclesie filiis ad quos presens scriptum pervenerit*^a* A. archidiaconus Lond', salutem. *^b*Noverit universitas vestra*^b* Agathen filiam Roberti filii Radulfi et Bertram filium Willelmi de Calverdon' maritum Alicie sororis predicte Agates*^c* nomine suo [et uxo]ris*^d* sue in presentia mea tactis sacrosanctis euuangeliis iurasse quod compositionem factam inter eos et canonicos de Oteham super terra que fuit Radulfi de Dene veteris in Teleton [et in]*^d* mariscis de Ailesham et de Pevenese *^e*et omnibus pertinentiis suis ipsi et heredes sui firmiter et fideliter et sine omni dolo tenebunt*^e* et servabunt, quod predictis canonicis de tenemento illo nullam questionem vel querelam movebunt unde eisdem canonicis dampnum aliquod vel amissionem prefati tenementi contingat incurrere. Ut autem hec conventio firma sit et stabilis in perpetuum duratura, utriusque partis petitione conventionem istam presentis scripti mei [   ]*^f* et sigilli mei appositione testificari curavi. H(is) testibus: magistro Nicholao, magistro Roberto Meldensi,*^g* Rogero de Moriston', Rogero de Cadendon'.

a–a Om. in C	*b–b* Notum sit omnibus *C*	*c* Sic in B,C	*d* B
damaged; supplied from C	*e–e* &c firmiter tenebunt &c *C; and C ends*		*f* B
damaged	*g* Reading uncertain		

Alard became archdn between 21 Apr. and 30 Dec. 1196, and had certainly become dean of St Paul's by May 1201, in which office he first occurs Mar. 1200 × May 1201 (*Fasti St Paul's*, 10, 6). The charters by Agatha and by Bertram son of William, both witnessed by the archdn, are Cott. Otho A ii, fos. 17v–18r, 14v. The Premonstratensian abbey of Bayham was established in 1205 × 1211 as the result of migrations from previous foundations at Brockley (Kent) and Otham (Sussex) (Knowles and Hadcock, 185–6; Colvin, *White Canons*, 109–115). For the family concerned here, see L. F. Salzman, 'Some Sussex Domesday tenants, II: the Family of Dene', *Sussex Archaeological Collections* 58 (1916), 171–89. Ralph de Dene was the founder of Otham and died *c.* 1187, and his son, Robert, gave Tilton, in Selmeston parish, to the canons (ibid., 176–7). Agatha and Alice were two of Ralph's nieces (see the genealogy, ibid., 189). Hailsham is near the site of Otham, and Pevensey was the honour of which Ralph was a tenant (Colvin, *White Canons*, 112–13). Why the oath was sworn in the presence of the archdn of London is unclear.

[1] A fair copy of C, made for Sir Edward Dering, is BL, Stowe ms 924, fo. 54v (p. 114).

ARCHDEACONRY OF MIDDLESEX

Richard de Belmeis II

207. *Letter to R(obert), bishop of London, written at the request of the canons of St Martin[-le-Grand], stating what he has heard as the truth regarding the chapel of Bonhunt. He was present in chapter at [Saffron] Walden before Ailward, archdeacon [of Colchester], when a certain Philip, having disputed at length with the canons over Bonhunt chapel and having come with few [supporters], requested an adjournment, but was opposed by the canons on the grounds that the case had long ago been settled by judgement and that their witnesses were present to give testimony; when the archdeacon refused to hear them, he (Richard), at the canons' request, listened to the witnesses apart and heard from two elderly priests, Aylmer of Newport and Turbert of Littlebury, that in chapter in Wenden church, before Cyprian the archdeacon, Bonhunt chapel had been judged to belong to Newport church and not to Wicken church.*

[July 1141 × Sept. 1150]

B = Westminster Abbey Muniments, no. 13167 (St Martin-le-Grand cartulary roll), no. cxxxii. s. xiii.
Pd (transl.), R. H. C. Davis, 'The College of St Martin-le-Grand and the Anarchy, 1135–54', 17–18.

Venerabili domino et patri R. dei gratia London' episcopo Ricardus de Belm(eis) archidiaconus, salutem cum fideli obsequio. Gravatos se asserentes canonici Sancti Martini de testibus suis corruptis et dolo ablatis, petitione illorum secundum quod audivimus et vidimus pro sola veritate hec vobis scribere curavimus.[1] Eram namque apud Waledonam cum priore ipsius ville in capitulo quando Ailwardus archidiaconus, convocatis*a* coram se partibus, quendam Philippum nomine de capella de Banhunt cum predictis canonicis contendentem diutius audivimus. Tandem idem Philippus, quia cum paucis ipse*b* venerat,*c* postulavit sibi respectum donari. Canonici autem contradixerunt, dicentes se per illum iniuste vexatos quoniam antiquitus hec eadem causa iudicio terminata fuerat. Et testes suos quos ibi presentes habuerunt in medium producere voluerunt, quos nollet audire archidiaconus. Nos ab ipsis canonicis rogati in partem secessimus ad audiendum quid testari voluissent testes eorum. Et audivimus duos venerabilis senectutis presbiteros, Eylmerum de*d* Neweport et Turbertum de Litilberia, testantes et testimonium probare paratos se audisse in ecclesia de*e* Wenden' in capitulo coram Cipriano archidiacono adiudicatam capellam de Bonhunt ecclesie de Neweport et abiudicatam ecclesie de Wica, tunc existente persona Ad(am) in ecclesia de Newep(ort) et Gaufrido persona in ecclesia de Wica. Et hec est veritas quam tunc ibi de testibus illis audivimus. Valete.

a Altered in ms from concovocatis   *b Ms* ipsa   *c Ms* venerant
d Followed in ms by Wenden' *marked for deletion*   *e Followed in ms by* N *marked for deletion*

During the pontificate of Robert de Sigillo, bp of London, who was nominated to the see in July 1141, consecrated before Apr. 1142, and died 28 or 29 Sept. 1150 (*Fasti St Paul's*, 2). On this remarkable document, which throws rare and interesting light on archidiaconal chapters and archdn's activities around the mid-12th century, see Davis,

'College of St Martin-le-Grand', 17–18. In connection with this dispute Henry of Blois, bp of Winchester and dean of St Martin's, complained against archdn Ailward to archbp Theobald, who ordered the archdn not to proceed in the case until bp Henry could be present (Saltman, *Theobald*, 390–1, where the order is dated *c.* 1144). Philip was evidently the incumbent of Wicken, for he seems subsequently to have reached an agreement with the canons whereby he and his successors would hold Bonhunt chapel of the canons for 5s annually, a sum which was still due in 1291 (Westminster Abbey Muniments, 13167, no. clii; *Taxatio*, 23). Bonhunt was in due course reckoned in the parish of Wicken, and the two names are combined in the parish's present name, Wicken Bonhunt (*Essex Place-Names*, 544). Newport church belonged to St Martin-le-Grand (*Regesta*, ii, no. 1362; iii, no. 538). For Ailward, archdn of Colchester, and Cyprian, his penultimate predecessor, see *Fasti St Paul's*, 18.

[1] The syntax in this and the following sentence is very awkward.

Mr Ralph de Diceto

208. *As archdeacon of the church of London, notification to the [rural] dean and chapter of Hinckford that, when he was appointed archdeacon by Richard, late bishop of London, and made inquiry as to who was the advocate, parson or vicar of each church, he learnt from the chapter of Hinckford that the prior and convent of Stoke[-by-Clare] had obtained the* personatus *of the churches of Ashen and Little Yeldham at the presentation and gift of the earls of Clare and by the authority of the bishops of London; and, as far as it pertains to him, confirmation of the cure and administration of these churches to the monks.* [4 May 1162 × Jan. 1181]

B = BL, Cotton ms App. xxi (Stoke-by-Clare cartulary), fos. 59v–60r. s. xiii med.
Pd, *Stoke-by-Clare Cartulary*, i, 100–1, no. 127.

Radulfus Lundoniensis ecclesie archidiaconus decano et toti capitulo de Haingford, salutem. Cum primo nobis curam archidiaconatus commisit Ricardus bone memorie quondam Lundonc'[a] episcopus secundus, et quis cuiusque esset ecclesie advocatus seu persona seu vicarius diligenter inquiremus, de communi totius capituli de Haingeford assertione didicimus quod prior de Stokes et conventus personatum ecclesie de Essa et personatum [fo. 60r] ecclesie de Parva Geldeham petitione, presentatione et donatione comitum de Clara et auctoritate Lundonencium episcoporum a retro temporibus obtinuerant. Quantum igitur ad nos spectat eisdem monachis memoratarum ecclesiarum curam et amministrationem, et ut eas libere, quiete, pacifice sine aliqua concussione teneant et possideant, concedimus. Valete in domino karissimi.

a Sic

After the death of bp Richard de Belmeis II and before the archdn became dean of St Paul's, Jan. 1180 × Jan. 1181 (*Fasti St Paul's*, 2, 15–16). The deanery of Hinckford (the name of the hundred) was later known as Hedingham (cf. *Taxatio*, 18). This valuable text provides rare evidence of an archdn's primary visitation of his archdnry and may suggest that he kept a record of his findings, perhaps a *scrutinium* or a *matricula* (see Kemp, 'Informing the archdeacon', 147–8).

Gilbert Foliot II

209. *Notification that the prior and monks of Walden have given to Mr P. de Waude, the archdeacon's clerk, the perpetual vicarage in the church of Edmonton which William the priest held, and have also granted him all lesser tithes of the parish, which they had been accustomed to have in their hands, under an annual pension of fifty shillings, all of which the archdeacon has confirmed.*

[11 June 1180 × 1 Aug. 1190]

B = BL, Harley ms 3697 (Walden cartulary), fo. 49r (34r), no. 25. s. xiv ex.

Universis sancte matris ecclesie filiis ad quos presens scriptum pervenerit G. Foliot archidiaconus Middelsex', salutem in Cristo perpetuam. Noverit universitas vestra dilectos nostros priorem et monachos de Waleden' dedisse et concessisse magistro P. de Waude clerico nostro perpetuam vicariam in ecclesia de Edelmeton', quam Willelmus sacerdos tenuit. Preterea etiam, amore et petitione nostra et predicti P. morum et meritorum exigentia, omnes decimas minutas predicte parochie, quas in manibus suis habere consueverant, eidem P. ad promotionis sue maius augmentum pie concesserunt, sub annua pensione quinquaginta solidorum eis a prefato P. singulis annis fideliter persolvenda. Nos itaque, donationem et concessionem ab eis factam ratam habentes et gratam, eam presentis scripti illibate memorie comendare*a* et sigilli nostri appositione roborare decrevimus. Valeat universitas vestra semper in domino.

a Sic

After the date when Gilbert Foliot was not yet archdn – he first occurs *c.* 1181 × 1183 (*Fasti St Paul's*, 16) – and before the elevation of Walden to abbatial status (*Heads*, 76). Mr P. de Waude is perhaps the Mr Peter, archdn's clerk, who wrote no. 210 and witnessed no. 211, and both may be the Mr Peter of Waltham, who became archdn of London, *c.* 1190 × Dec. 1192 (*Fasti London*, 9).

210. *Notification to the [rural] dean and chapter of Dunmow that he has confirmed the confirmation by G(ilbert) Foliot, bishop of London, of the church of Felsted to the abbey and nuns of La Sainte-Trinité, Caen.* [*c.* 1181 × 18 Feb. 1187]

B = Caen, A-D Calvados, H non classé 25/1 (inspeximus, by bps R(obert) of Bayeux, H(ugh) of Coutances and W(illiam) of Avranches, of charters concerning Felsted church (s. xiii in). C = PRO, PRO 31/8/140B, part 3 (transcripts by L. d'Anisy, 1836), p. 208. s. xix.
Pd (calendar) from C, *CDF*, 146, no. 434.

G. Foliot archidiaconus Meldens'*a* decano et capitulo de Donemawe, salutem in domino. Beneficiis que locis religiosis sunt assignata et auctoritate episcopali roborata ut perpetuum firmitatis robur optineant, benignum prebere tenemur assensum. Unde nos, venerabilis*b* patris nostri G. Foliot episcopi ʿLond' auctoritatem*c* sequentes, ecclesiam*d* de Felsted'*e* cum omnibus ad eam pertinentibus abbatie et monialibus sancte Trinitatis Cadom', quam eis idem episcopus, sicut ex inspectione litterarum eius plenius agnovimus, perpetuo possidendam concessit, auctoritate qua fungimur presenti carta benigne confirmavimus et nostri appositione sigilli communimus. Hiis testibus: Roberto decano, Iohanne de Marinn',*f* Ricardo persona de Beverston', David*g* capellano, Savarino de Estre, Symone de Cistan', Roberto de Felsted', capellanis,

Baldewino de Felested', et W. de Warlemund,[h] militibus, W. de Aveling',
Rogero de Graines,[i] le Briton', Roberto filio Briteve, W. London', Willelmo et
Baudewino de Offinton', et magistro Petro qui hanc cartam scripsit, et multis
aliis.

a Sic in all texts; ? rectius Middelsex' *(see note 1)*		*b* venerabili *C*
c–c Londoniensis auctoritate *C*	*d* ecclesia *C*	*e* Felsted *C*
f Marmiun' *C*	*g* Davide *C*	*h* Warlemont *C*	*i* G'ines *C*

The date is that of the confirmation by Gilbert Foliot, bp of London (*Foliot Letters and Charters*, no. 356).

[1] The archdn seems usually to have styled himself 'archdn of Middlesex' (see nos. 209, 211). 'Meldensis' is probably a scribal error, since Maldon (Essex) was not in that archdnry and had no connection with Dunmow.

211. *Notification to all faithful of the archdeaconry of Middlesex that, after the death of Turold, parson of the church of Netteswell, John, his son, brought a suit against the regular canons of Waltham, but has now resigned and quitclaimed what right he had in the church into the archdeacon's hands; and the latter, having inspected letters of the late Pope Lucius III allowing the canons to enjoy the benefits of their churches, has instituted them in the church of Netteswell in the person of Daniel, their subprior, and put them into corporal possession.* [18 Feb. 1187 × 31 Dec. 1189]

B = BL, Harley ms 391 (Waltham cartulary), fo. 103v. s. xiii in. C = BL, Cotton ms
Tiberius C ix (Waltham cartulary), fo. 156r. s. xiii med.
Pd from B and C, *Waltham Charters*, 154, no. 235.

Omnibus fidelibus per archidiaconatum Midelsexie[a] constitutis Gillebertus
Folioth archidiaconus Midelsex',[a] eternam in domino salutem. Ad communem
vestri volumus notitiam devenire quod, cum ecclesia de Netleswelle[b] vacaret
quia Turoldus, qui eiusdem ecclesie persona habebatur, in fata concessisset,
Iohannes filius eius, qui aliquando controversiam contra canonicos regulares de
Waltham moverat, maturiori usus consilio a proposito desistens, quicquid iuris
in predicta ecclesia habere se dixerat propria voluntate in manu nostra coram
multis resignavit et quietum clamavit. Nos igitur, inspectis litteris pie memorie
pape Lucii tertii quibus indulsit canonicis regularibus de Waltham frui
beneficiis ecclesiarum possessionum suarum, eos in prefatam ecclesiam de
Netleswelle[b] vacantem nullo reclamante per Danielem suppriorem[c] eorum
instituimus et in corporalem possessionem misimus, salvo per omnia iure
Lond' episcopi et officialium eius. Testibus his:[d] Gaufrido[e] decano de Hetfeld,[f]
magistro Alexandro de Torenei, magistro Petro clerico meo, Rogero capellano
de Hedham, Rogero et Anfredo sacerdotibus de Lattune, magistro Mauricio de
Hallingeb', Godefrido de Peridune, Willelmo de Redidune, Toma de Macinges
sacerdotibus, Hai, Roberto Pueir, Ricardo et Gaufrido servientibus abbatis de
Waltham, et multis aliis.

a Middelsexie *C*	*b* Nethleswell' *C*	*c* subpriorem *C*	*d* hiis *C*
e Galfrido *C*	*f C ends with* et c'		

The confirmation by Pope Celestine III states that this institution took place while the see
of London was vacant (*Waltham Charters*, no. 236; *PUE*, i, no. 291); it is therefore of the
same date as above, no. 201 (q.v.).

Ralph of Ely

212. *As archdeacon of the church of London, notification to all his clergy of Middlesex and Essex of the settlement, before him in the presence of the [rural] chapter of Hinckford at Wethersfield, of the dispute between Prior Hugh of [Stoke-by-]Clare and Robert, parson of Harefield, over the demesne tithe of Harefield, namely, that Robert has admitted that the tithe belongs to the right of the priory and surrendered it into the hands of the archdeacon, who has invested the prior with it; Robert, however, has received the tithe from the prior for life for an annual payment of seven shillings, which, if Robert sends the payment to the priory within the octave of St John the Baptist, will be reduced to half a mark, fourpence being deducted for the expenses of his messenger.* [1198 × Apr. 1205]

B = BL, Cotton ms App. xxi (Stoke-by-Clare cartulary), fo. 60r–v. s. xiii med.
Pd, *Stoke-by-Clare Cartulary*, i, 102, no. 129.

Radulfus Londoniensis ecclesie archidiaconus omnibus clericis suis tam de Midelsex quam de Essex, salutem. Noverit universitas vestra Hugonem priorem de Clara et Robertum personam ecclesie de Herrefeldia coram nobis in presentia capituli de Haingeford apud Werresfeld convenisse et de decima dominii [fo. 60v] de Herrefeld, super qua diu inter eos accitatum erat, composuisse hoc modo. Confessus est Robertus predictam decimam ad ius ecclesie sancti Iohannis Baptiste de Clara pertinere, eamque coram memorato capitulo in manus nostras refutavit. Nos autem tamquam ius suum ecclesie sancti Iohannis reddentes, sub testimonio eiusdem capituli prefatum priorem eadem decima investivimus. Robertus vero a manu ipsius prioris hanc recepit decimam omnibus diebus vite sue nomine ecclesie de Clara possessurus, annuum canonem predicte ecclesie solvendo, septem scilicet solidorum ad festum Nativitatis sancti Iohannis Baptiste. Conventumque est ut, si per nuntium suum infra octabas sancti Iohannis ad predictam ecclesiam de Clara hunc canonem miserit Robertus, soluta tantum dimidia marca quatuor nummi in expensam nuntii convertenter, sin[a] autem predicta ecclesia redditum septem solidorum integre recipiet. Post decessum autem predicti Roberti hec eadem decima libere et quiete ad ecclesiam sancti Iohannis de Clara revertetur, eamque integram recipiet in omnibus de quibus decima dari debet. Facta est autem hec compositio primum in capitulo de Haingeford', presentibus hiis eiusdem capituli clericis: Ernaldo decano de Finchingefeld, magistro Pagano, magistro Gilberto de Haustede, Willelmo presbitero de Ovitune, Nigello presbitero de Essa, Turstano presbitero de Redeswella, Iohanne presbitero de Stamburn', et aliis.

a Sic

After Ralph became archdn in 1198 (*Stoke-by-Clare Cartulary*, iii, p. xi) and before the first occurrence of Prior Hugh's successor, in Apr. 1205 (*Heads*, 110). The priory was entitled to two-thirds of the demesne tithe of Harefield (*Stoke-by-Clare Cartulary*, iii, 29).

DIOCESE OF NORWICH

ARCHDEACONRY OF NORFOLK

Roger of Calne

* 213. *As archdeacon of Norwich, grant in perpetual fee-farm to the monks of Norwich of his mills of Ringland.* [? *c.* 1125 × 1173]

> Listed only, in Norwich, Norfolk R.O., DCN 40/12 (Norwich Cathedral inventory of muniments), fo. 38v, section L. 35; pd, *Norwich Cathedral Charters,* ii, 111, no. 198.

Carta Rogeri de Calna Norwycensis archidiaconus de molendinis suis de Ringelond ad perpetuam feodi firmam monachis Norwyc' concessis.

Roger first occurs as archdn in 1126 × 1127, and may have owed his appointment to Everard of Calne, perhaps a relative, who became bp of Norwich in 1121; his successor in the archdnry occurs before Jan. 1174 (*Fasti Monastic Cathedrals,* 64–5, 55–6). This act and nos. 214–15 supply the archdn's surname, which he seems regularly to have used in his own acts, but which he is not given in episcopal witness-lists; he witnessed Norwich acts several times, but never as 'of Calne' (see *EEA* VI, index, *sub nomine* Roger; his surname is also omitted in *Fasti Monastic Cathedrals,* 64–5).

214. *As archdeacon of the church of Norwich, notification that Ulfketel the priest has renounced in his presence and that of his whole chapter two parts of the demesne tithe of Thelveton which, it was acknowledged, belonged to Crowland abbey; by agreement made before the whole chapter Ulfketel will hold the tithe of the monks for life by rendering annually five shillings.* [1146 × 1173]

> B = Spalding Gentlemen's Society, Crowland cartulary, fo. 199r. s. xv.

Rogerus de Calna dei gratia Norwic' ecclesie archidiaconus omnibus ad quos littere iste pervenerint, salutem. Notum vobis facimus quod Ulfketellus presbiter in presentia nostra et totius capituli nostri renuntiavit duabus partibus decime totius dominii de Thevelton' quas cognitum est et certificatum ecclesie de Croiland' pertinuisse, unde idem Ulfketellus, cum monachis Croylandie compositionem faciens coram omni capitulo de prefata decima, tenebit illam tota vita sua reddendo eis vel cui assignaverint v. solidos annuatim infra octabas sancti Michaelis. Cavit autem eis de rato coram omni capitulo per fidei interpositionem hanc conventionem sine dolo tenendam. Valete.

During the pontificate of bp William Turbe of Norwich, who confirmed this transaction, showing that it had taken place in the chapter of Diss (cartulary, fo. 199r; not in *EEA* VI; *Fasti Monastic Cathedrals,* 56).

215. *As archdeacon of the church of Norwich, notification to the abbot and convent of Crowland that Ulfketel, priest of Thelveton, has made an agreement before the whole chapter concerning two parts of the demesne tithe of Thelveton, by rendering to the abbot and convent five shillings annually, and has sworn to keep this agreement in the archdeacon's hand before the whole chapter.* [1146 × 1173]

> B = Spalding Gentlemen's Society, Crowland cartulary, fo. 199r. s. xv.

Domino abbati et conventui ecclesie de*ª* Croyland' Rogerus de Calna dei gratia Norwic' ecclesie archidiaconus, salutem. Notum vobis facimus quod Wlketellus presbiter de Telvetunia coram omni capitulo conpositionem fecit de duabus partibus decime dominii de Telvetunia, reddendo annuatim v. solidos infra octo dies post festum sancti Michaelis vobis sive alicui vestrum. Hanc autem conventionem*ᵇ* affidavit in manu R. archidiaconi tenendam coram omni capitulo. Valete.

a Interlined   *b Ms* convencione

Date as for no. 214.

Mr Steingrim

216. *As archdeacon of the church of Norwich, notification that, in his presence, Maurice of Barsham, knight, gave to the priory and monks of [Castle] Acre the patronage and [right of] presentation of [All Saints] church, Tattersett, and conveyed to the prior and convent in pure and perpetual alms all his right in that church.*

[Castle] Acre, 15 Aug. 1175

B = BL, Harley ms 2110 (Castle Acre cartulary), fo. 130r (124r). s. xiii med.

Omnibus sancte matris ecclesie fidelibus Tengr' Norwic' ecclesie archidiaconus, salutem. Ad universorum volumus pervenire notitiam quod Mauricius miles de Barsham in presentia nostra constitutus concessit et dedit deo et ecclesie sancte Marie de Acra et monachis ibidem deo servientibus et servituris patronatum et presentationem ecclesie de Taterseta, et omne ius quod in illa habuit ecclesia in priorem et conventum prescripte ecclesie in puram et perpetuam contulit elemosinam, anno ab incarnatione domini M.° C.° lxx.° v., mense Augusti, in die Assumptionis sancte Marie apud Acram. Huius etiam donationis sunt testes: Lodowicus clericus, Henricus decanus, Reg(inaldus) clericus Wimari, Eust' et Lamb' clerici, Gaufridus capellanus.

Maurice of Barsham's charter specifies the church as All Saints, Tattersett (cartulary, fo. 42v), which first appears in an episcopal confirmation to Castle Acre in that of bp John of Oxford in 1180 × 1182 (*EEA* VI, no. 184), whereas St Andrew's, Tattersett, had been in the priory's possession since at least the time of bp Everard (ibid., no. 27).

ARCHDEACONRY OF NORWICH

William I

217. *Notification of the settlement, now approved in his presence, of the dispute over parishioners between the churches of Wiggenhall St Mary Magdalene and Wiggenhall St Peter, which [Theobald], archbishop [of Canterbury], and Everard, late bishop of Norwich, confirmed.* [c. 1150 × 18 Apr. 1161]

B = BL, Harley ms 2110 (Castle Acre cartulary), fo. 130r (124r). s. xiii med.

Villelmus dei gratia Norwic' archidiaconus tam futurorum quam presentium universitati, salutem. Omnium memorie notum facimus controversiam super quibusdam parrochianis inter ecclesiam*ª* sancte Marie Magdalene et sancti Petri de Wigehale multo tempore habitam hac compositione esse terminatam: quod scilicet utraque ecclesia omnes in eadem intercurrentis aque parte qua ipsa sita est commanentes habeat parrochianos. Hanc autem compositionem sub nostra presentia legitimorum tam clericorum quam laicorum comprobavit testimonium. Eandem etiam, ut rata et inconcussa utrimque servaretur, litterarum suarum auctoritate cum sigillorum suorum impressione[b] et dominus archiepiscopus et bone memorie Ebrardus Norwicensis episcopus confirmaverunt.

   a Sic in ms; ? for ecclesias   *b Interlined*

After the date of Theobald's confirmation of the original settlement (Saltman, *Theobald*, 291, no. 66), but apparently before his death. The dates of William I, archdn of Norwich, are very uncertain; although he last certainly occurs in May 1148, his successor (whether Ralph or Philip) was not certainly in office before the death of archbp Theobald (*Fasti Monastic Cathedrals*, 62–3). For the act of bp Everard of Norwich (1121 × 1145), see Saltman, *Theobald*, 291, no. 66n. On the present act, see Kemp, 'Archdeacons and parish churches', 351.

William II

218. *Notification that the dispute between the monks of Norwich [cathedral priory] and the monks of Longueville over the tithes of the land of Buterus, Turold and William son of Sara at Witchingham has been settled; the parties agreed to abide by the decision of four selected men of good opinion, who have testified on oath that the three tithes pertained to the church of St Mary, [Great] Witchingham.*

[late May 1167 × 1182]

   B = Oxford, New College, Archive 9744 (Liber Niger), fo. 35r–v. s. xvi in.
   Pd, *Newington Longeville Charters*, 90, no. 117.

Omnibus Cristi fidelibus Willelmus dei gratia Norwicen' archidiaconus, salutem. Noverit universitas vestra controversiam que inter monachos Norwic' et monachos de Longavill' vertebatur super decimis de terra Buteri et Toroldi et Willelmi filii Sare apud Winchingeham hoc fine conquievisse. Elegerunt quatuor [fo. 35v] bone opinionis viros quorum testimonio post eorum iuramentum absque occasione se stare fide corporaliter prestita compromiserunt. Quattuor vero viri electi post sacramentum prestitum omnes unanimiter testati sunt tres decimationes prenominatas ad ecclesiam beate Marie de Winchingeham pertinere. Hiis testibus.

The dispute had been delegated by the pope (un-named) to Simon, abbot of St Albans, *c.* 21 May 1167–July 1183, whose act records the same settlement (*Newington Longeville Charters*, no. 116; *Heads*, 67); William II became archdn of Norwich before 1168 and had been succeeded in office by 1182 at the latest (*Fasti Monastic Cathedrals*, 63). For Longueville's holdings in Witchingham, including the churches of St Mary and St Faith, see *Newington Longeville Charters*, xxxviii–xl; for Norwich cathedral's claim to certain demesne tithes in Witchingham, see *Norwich Cathedral Charters*, i, 180, 193, 212.

Thomas

219. *At the presentation and request of Adam, prior of St Benet of Holme, on behalf of the convent, grant and gift to Wimar, the dean, of the perpetual vicarages of the churches of Neatishead and Irstead, for an annual pension of two marks to the altar of St Benedict or to the sacrist.*

[1178 × 14 Aug. 1200; ? 11 Sept. 1186 × *c.* 24 June 1187]

B = BL, Cotton ms Galba E ii (St Benet of Holme cartulary), fo. 46r. s. xiii ex.
Pd, *St Benet of Holme*, i, 57, no. 97.

Universis Cristi fidelibus T. dei gratia Norwic' archidiaconus, salutem. Ad universorum volumus pervenire notitiam nos*ª* concessisse et dedisse Wimaro decano perpetuam vicariam ecclesie de Neteshirde et ecclesie de Irstede, presentatione et petitione Ade prioris de Sancto Benedicto de Holm ex parte conventus, nomine pensionis annue altari sancti Benedicti vel sacriste de predictis ecclesiis duas marcas solvendo. Et ut hec nostra donatio perpetuum robur optineat, eam presentis scripti pagina et sigilli nostri appositione communimus. Testibus: Willelmo archidiacono, Roberto persona de Scothowe, Roberto pictore, et c'.

a In ms placed after volumus

After the latest occurrence of his predecessor as archdn and before the appointment of his successor (*Fasti Monastic Cathedrals*, 63–4), but, as the abbacy of St Benet appears to be vacant (since the prior makes the presentation), perhaps during the vacancy between abbots Thomas and Ralph (*Heads*, 68); Prior Adam had managed the abbey's ecclesiastical affairs during the abbatial vacancy of 1168–75 (*St Benet of Holme*, ii, 198) and was still alive temp. Abbot Ralph (ibid., i, no. 289). It is difficult to find an identity for the first witness other than Thomas' predecessor, William II; if that is right, it would appear that William had resigned the archdnry, while retaining the title. The cartulary rubric calls this act an 'institution'.

Archdeaconry of Sudbury

Roger

220. *Notification that, on the mandate of J(ohn), bishop of Norwich, he has put Robert de Funteney, parson of the church of Great Thurlow, into corporal possession of the church, having been present when Robert was instituted by the said bishop at the presentation of the abbot and convent of Battle.*   [Nov. 1189 × 2 June 1200]

A = PRO, E210/2154 (Ancient Deed D 2154). Endorsed: Magna Trillawe (s. xiii in.).
    Size 120 × 47 + 11 mm (turn-up folded out). Seal and tag missing (method 1).
B = San Marino, Huntington Library, Battle Abbey Papers, vol. 29 (Battle cartulary), fo. 91v (80v). s. xiii ex.

Omnibus Cristi fidelibus ad quos presentes littere pervenerint Rogerus Suberie archidiaconus, salutem in domino. Universitati vestre notum facere volumus nos, per mandatum domini I. dei gratia Norwic' episcopi, Robertum de Funteneio personam ecclesie de Magna Trillawia in corporalem misisse possessionem predicte ecclesie. Nos autem presentes fuimus ubi institutus fuit a predicto episcopo presentacione abbatis et conventus de Bello. Et in testimonium huius rei geste istas litteras sigilli nostri aposicione[a] firmavimus.

   a appositione *B*

After the latest occurrence of Roger's predecessor in the archdnry (*EEA* VI, no. 254) and before the death of bp John of Oxford (*Fasti Monastic Cathedrals*, 56). The bp's institution, written by the same hand, is pd, *EEA* VI, no. 166, where the parson's name is wrongly given as 'Robert de Sumeneio' (correct reading: 'de Funteneio'). The possibility that the bp's act is a forgery (discussed ibid., but rejected), on the grounds that the jurors in a dispute in the king's court in 1230 stated that the last parson, Robert, had not been instituted by the bp or inducted by the archdn (*CRR*, xiv, nos. 454, 456), is perhaps not dispelled by the fact that the originals of both the bp's and the archdn's acts are in very similar hands, and perhaps the same hand. Robert de Funteney also acquired the church of Great Sampford, Essex, in Feb. 1187 × Dec. 1189 (see above, no. 199).

ARCHDEACONRY OF SUFFOLK

Richard de Bello Fago

221. *Notification to Robert the sheriff and the king's ministers of Flegg [hundred] that, out of the alms which the king had given him, he has given the churches and tithes of Ormesby to [St Paul's] hospital for the poor in Norwich; and request that they cause Norman the monk, proctor of that house, to have the same.*   [c. 1115 × 1129]

   B = BL, Cotton Charter ii.19 (inspeximus by John Salmon, bp of Norwich, of nineteen charters to the hospital, 17 Mar. 1302), no. 3.

   Pd, *Mon. Ang.*, vi (ii), 699, no. 2 (3); *Norwich Cathedral Charters*, i, 157–8, no. 259 (3).

Ricardus archidiaconus karissimis suis Rodberto vicecomiti et ministris regis de Flego, salutem et orationes devotas. Dedi, de elemosina quam donavit michi gratia dei et regis nostri, ecclesias cum terrulis earum et decimas de Ormesby hospitali pauperum de Norwic pro salute regis et fidelium suorum. Unde precor vos quatinus domino Normanno monacho procuratori illius domus faciatis illam elemosinam habere plenarie tam de fructu ovium et animalium quam de fructu terre, ut deus vobis hoc retribuat.

Richard first occurs as archdn in *c.* 1115 × 1119 (*Fasti Monastic Cathedrals*, 67); and Robert Fitz Walter does not occur as sheriff of Suffolk after 1129 (Green, *English Sheriffs to 1154*, 77). Since the churches were of the royal alms, the gift was made with royal consent and confirmed by Henry I, Stephen, Henry II and later monarchs (*Norwich Cathedral Charters*, i, nos. 100–1, 35, 43); it was also confirmed by archbp Theobald (ibid., no. 259 (8); Saltman, *Theobald*, 411–12, no.188). For the four main churches in Ormesby, St Andrew, St Margaret, St Michael, and St Peter, see *Norwich Cathedral Charters*, i, no. 259 (11). The hospital of St Paul was founded by the cathedral priory of Norwich in the time of bp Herbert (d. 1119) and completed in 1121; Norman the monk was its first master (Knowles and Hadcock, 381).

Walkelin

222. *Notification that he was present when William, bishop of Norwich, received and instituted the canons of Blythburgh in the church of Blyford at the petition and presentation of Ralph de Criketot, who gave the church to them in pure alms; and was present when Ralph and the bishop confirmed the presentation and institution by charters to the canons.* [1146 × 1166]

B = BL, Additional ms 40725 (Blythburgh cartulary), fo. 16v. s. xiv ex.
Pd, *Blythburgh Cartulary,* i, 83, no. 125.

Omnibus sancte matris ecclesie filiis ad quos presentes littere pervenerint Walchelinus archidiaconus Suffolch', salutem in domino. Ad universitatis vestre notitiam indubitanter volumus pervenire nos interfuisse ubi Willelmus dei gratia Norwic' episcopus, ad petitionem et presentationem Radulfi de Criketot, recepit et instituit canonicos ecclesie sancte Marie de Blybur in ecclesiam de Blyford [quam idem Radulfus eis dedit]*ᵃ* in puram elemosinam pro salute anime sue et antecessorum suorum cum omnibus pertinentiis in perpetuum possidendam. Interfuimus etiam ubi predictus Radulfus de Criketot de presentatione sua, et dominus episcopus de institutione facta, eisdem canonicis super eadem ecclesia cartas suas confirmaverunt. Valete in domino.

a Passage in square brackets om. in ms; conjecturally supplied to make the sense

After William Turbe became bp of Norwich (*Fasti Monastic Cathedrals,* 56) and before Ralph de Criketot had been succeeded by his son Hubert, i.e., certainly by 1166 (*Blythburgh Cartulary,* i, 9). For Ralph's charter and bp William's confirmation, the latter witnessed by the archdn, see ibid., nos. 119, 124.

* 223. *Act showing that Mr Jordan de Ros was parson of the whole church of Hopton and that the clerk lately deceased was his vicar, who paid him an annual pension for a moiety of the church.* [1157 × 15 Nov. 1180]

Mentioned only, in the account of a dispute between Abbot Samson of Bury St Edmunds and Robert de Ulmo over the advowson of a moiety of Hopton church: *The Chronicle of Jocelin of Brakelond,* ed. H. E. Butler, London 1949, 61–2; R. C. van Caenegem, *English Lawsuits,* ii, 615–16, no. 569. A.

. . . Prosiliens ibi magister Iordanus de Ros, habens tam cartam H. abbatis quam predicti R. [*sc.* Robert de Ulmo] et hinc inde ut, uter eorum dirationaret ecclesiam [*sc.* Hopton], ipse personatum haberet, dixit se esse personam totius ecclesie et clericum proximo mortuuum fuisse vicarium eius, reddendo ei annuam pensionem de illa medietate, et inde ostendit cartam Walchelini archidiaconi. . . .

The dating limits are those of abbot Hugh's abbacy at Bury St Edmunds (*Heads,* 32).

Geoffrey

224. *Notification that, before him and many others, Gilbert Pecche gave and granted in pure and perpetual alms to the church and canons of St James, Northampton, a render of forty shillings from the tithes of his chapel of Sutton Hoo.*

[1188 × 2 June 1200]

> B = BL, Cotton ms Tiberius E v (St James Northampton cartulary), fo. 217r–v (203r–
> v). s. xiv in. Badly damaged by fire.

Omnibus Cristi fidelibus ad quos presens scriptum pervenerit Gaufr(idus) archidiaconus Suffolch', salutem in domino. Noverit universitas vestra quod dominus Gilbertus Pecch' concessit et dedit coram me et multis aliis ecclesie Sancti Iacobi de Norh(am)t' et canonicis ibidem deo servientibus redditum xl. s' de decimis capelle sue de Sugenho, que tunc libere et quiete [fo. 217v] ad eius spectaverunt donationem, in puram et perpetuam elemosinam [　　　]*a* antecessorum suorum. Et [　　] firma sit et stabilis, [　　] appositione quantum in me est confirmo. [?Hiis testibus:　　], Willelmo de Risinges, Simone clerico de Essefeld', Iohanne [　　], Gaufr(ido) clerico de Cloptun', magistro Rogero, et multi[s aliis].

> *a Square brackets indicate passages destroyed or illegible in ms*

After Gilbert Pecche succeeded to the barony of Great Bealings (Suffolk) and before the death of John of Oxford, bp of Norwich, who confirmed his gift (Sanders, *English Baronies*, 48; *EEA* VI, no. 261 and n.). Geoffrey, formerly bp's chaplain, became archdn after 13 Nov. 1188 (ibid., lxxxvi–lxxxvii) and last occurs in 1210 (*Fasti Monastic Cathedrals*, 67). Gilbert Pecche's charter, witnessed by the archdn, is BL, Cott. Tib. E v, fo. 216v.

DIOCESE OF ROCHESTER

ARCHDEACONRY OF ROCHESTER

Paris

225. *With Alexander de Saccavilla [both canons of St Paul's], notification that, in order to settle the suit brought against them by Dean Hugh and the chapter [of St Paul's] over the advowson of Caddington church, which they affirmed belonged to their prebends, they have publicly declared in chapter before Gilbert, bishop of London, that the advowson belongs to the chapter.*

[6 Mar. 1163 × c. 1180]

> A = London, Guildhall Lib., ms 25122/744 (St Paul's Cathedral Muniments, A 33/
> 744). Endorsed: De advocatione ecclesie de Cadendon' (s. xiii). Size 222 × 55
> +13 mm. Seal: originally two on tags (method 1), one seal missing, the other of
> green wax, circular, *c.* 25 mm diameter, design and legend unclear.
> B = Ibid., ms 25501 (St Paul's Liber A), fo. 29v (7a). s. xiii med.
> Pd, *Early Charters of St Paul's*, 55–6, no. 78.

Paris archidiaconus Roffensis et Alexander de Sacchevilla*a* omnibus in Cristo fidelibus, salutem. Cum venerabilis dominus et decanus noster Hugo et capitulum nostrum adversus nos de advocatione ecclesie de Kadendone*b* litigarent, nosque eam ad ius prebendarum nostrarum pertinere affirmaremus, sicque iam diu lis inter nos fuisset protracta, tandem in presentia domini nostri Gilleberti*ᶜ* episcopi Lond' vocati pariter convenimus in capitulo nostro; ibique, cum nichil certum haberemus quod de iure predicte advocationis pro nobis allegare possemus, consilio domini episcopi nostri et aliorum bonorum virorum pro bono pacis a lite penitus destitimus et predicte ecclesie advocationem ad ius capituli nostri pertinere publice in iure confessi sumus. Unde, ne litem tanta auctoritate sopitam nos vel successores nostri in posterum suscitare possint, quod publice confessi sumus scripti nostri manifestatione protestamur et sigillorum nostrorum impressione*ᵈ* communimus.

a Sakevill' *B*   *b* Kadindon' *B*   *c* Gilberti *B*   *d* inpressione *B*

After Gilbert Foliot's translation from Hereford to London, and before the death of Hugh de Mareni, dean of St Paul's, presumably June 1179 or 1180 (*Fasti St Paul's*, 2, 5). Paris and Alexander were prebendaries of Caddington Minor and Major, respectively (ibid., 34, 32).

Mr William son of Peter

226. *As archdeacon of Rochester and parson of Frindsbury church, notification that he has resigned the chapel of Strood, with all its appurtenances except corn tithes, into the hands of G(ilbert), bishop of Rochester, who has given the chapel in perpetual alms to the poor of the hospital of St Mary, Strood, establishing it as a parish church and dedicating a graveyard for it; the church and its clergy are to be free of all pecuniary exaction from the bishop, archdeacon or [rural] dean, and the steward of the hospital shall present to the bishop a suitable priest to minister in the church. With the archdeacon's assent, the bishop has established the same immunity for the churches of Aylesford, St Margaret's Rochester, and Halling, and has exempted the hospital and its poor from all power of the archdeacon and [rural] dean.*   [1192 × 14 Aug. 1193]

B = Maidstone, Centre for Kentish Studies, DRb/AR1/1 (Register of Hamo Hethe, bishop of Rochester, 1319–52), fo. 8r. s. xiv in.
Pd, *Registrum Roffense*, 639–40; (calendar), *Reg. Hamonis Hethe*, i, 10.

Omnibus Cristi fidelibus ad quos presens scriptum pervenerit W. Roffensis archidiaconus persona ecclesie de Frendesbery, eternam in domino salutem. Noverit universitas vestra me, ad promotionem commendabilem domus hospitalis sancte Marie de Strodes, resignasse*ᵃ* in manus domini G. Roffensis episcopi capellam de Strode cum oblationibus, obventionibus et omnibus aliis ad eam pertinentibus, exceptis decimis bladi. Idem autem dominus episcopus, de assensu meo et voluntate, assignavit et donavit eandem capellam cum memorata integritate sua pauperibus prelibate domus hospitalis de Strode ad sustentationem eorum in perpetuam elemosinam, et ipsam capellam constituit matricem ecclesiam et ei cimiterium dedicavit. Ita quidem ut tam ipsa quam in ea ministrantes clerici liberi sint et absoluti ab omni exactione pecuniaria, videlicet tallia et emenda, et omnibus aliis tam erga episcopum quam archidiaconum et decanum loci et omnes alios; et ut liceat iconomo domus hospitalis predicti providere quem voluerit presbiterum idoneum de suis sive de aliis ad ministrandum in eadem ecclesia et episcopo diocesano presentare. Et hanc emunitatem et ordinationem constituit, de assensu et voluntate mea, in ecclesiis

de Aylisforde et sancte Margarete apud Roff(a)m et de Hallynge et ministranti-
bus in eis observandam. Locum etiam ipsum hospitalem cum ambitu suo et
pauperes, clericos et laicos, ibi conversos sive aliter servientes exemit ab omni
potestate archidiaconi et decani loci, ut sint subiecti tantummodo sacrosancte
Romane ecclesie et Cant' archiepiscopo et episcopo loci. Ut igitur hec mea
resignatio et concessio firma et perpetua valitura permaneat, eam presentis carte
confirmatione et sigilli mei appositione communivi. Testibus hiis: magistro Elya
senescallo nostro, magistro Egidio, magistro W. de Caun', magistro Rogero de
Burned', Randulfo et Iohanne clericis, Waltero de Bro(m), Hugone fratre eius,
Roberto Marmi(un), Matheo de Capella, et multis aliis.

a Ms resingnasse

After the hospital was founded by Gilbert Glanville, bp of Rochester, in 1192 × 1193
(Knowles and Hadcock, 395), and before king Richard I's confirmation of the bp's gift of
the church of Strood to the hospital (*Registrum Roffense*, 640; Lander, *Itinerary of Richard I*,
79, 164). The bp's charter is witnessed by the archdn and by Mr Elias the steward and Mr
Giles; Elias was the bp's steward (*EEA* III, no. 623). The chapel of Strood, formerly
dependent upon Frindsbury church, is here raised to the status of an independent parish
church with its own graveyard.

227. *Notification that, from an inquiry held in the chapter of Dartford by mandate
of G(ilbert), bishop of Rochester, he is informed that the church of Lessness has
customarily paid only two shillings annually as archdeacon's aid.*

[*c.* 1192 × 24 June 1214]

B¹ = Bodl. ms Rawlinson B. 461 (misc. volume, including transcripts from lost
Lessness cartulary), fo. 56r. ss. xvii–xviii.

Omnibus sancte matris ecclesie filiis ad quos presens scriptum pervenerit
Willelmus archidiaconus Roffensis, salutem in vero*ᵃ* salutari. Noverit universitas
vestra quod, cum ad mandatum domini G. Roffensis episcopi facta fuisset
inquisitio in capitulo de Derteforde quantum ecclesia de Liesnes dare con-
sueverit archidiacono per annum auxilio suo, nobis*ᵇ* ex illa inquisitione innotuit
quod pretaxata ecclesia tantum duos solidos archidiacono per annum solvere
consuevit. Ego autem in huius inquisitionis testimonium sigillum meum duxi
apponendum. Hiis testibus: magistro Helya seneschallo, magistro Egidio, et
pluribus &c.

a Ms verbo   *b Plural sic*

After William became archdn and before the death of Gilbert de Glanville, bp of
Rochester (*Fasti Monastic Cathedrals*, 81, 76). Mr Elias and Mr Giles frequently witnessed
the bp's acts (e.g., above, no. 226n.; *Registrum Roffense*, 152, 161, 257–8, 529–30, 678) and
both, with the archdn, witnessed his complementary act concerning the same inquiry
(Bodl. ms Rawlinson B. 461, fo. 56r), but Elias and Giles are not certainly found at
Rochester after *c.* 1200.

¹ The classical diphthong 'æ' is here replaced by 'e'.

DIOCESE OF SALISBURY

ARCHDEACONRY OF BERKSHIRE

Geoffrey de Vernun

228. *Notification that William de Diva, son of Hugh de Diva, of [East] Haddon has orally informed him of his gift in free and perpetual alms to the Hospitallers of the church of Guilsborough, and that he, at William's presentation and having inspected his charters, has, by the authority of the archdeacon of Northampton for whom he was acting, instituted the Hospitallers as perpetual parsons of the said church and canonically assigned it to them in perpetuity.* [1175 × 1185]

B = BL, Cotton ms Nero E vi (Hospitallers cartulary for England), part 1, fo. 115r. s. xv med.

Galfridus archidiaconus de Berrecshire universis fidelibus sancte matris ecclesie ad quos presens scriptum pervenerit, salutem. Pervenit ad nos nobilis vir Willelmus de Diva filius Hugonis de Diva de Heddona viva voce attestans se divine caritatis intuitu dedisse et concessisse deo et sancto hospitali Ierl'm et fratribus*a* eidem hospitali servientibus in liberam et perpetuam elemosinam ecclesiam de Gildesburgh' cum omnibus pertinentiis suis, ad cuius presentationem audita viva voce eius et eiusdem cartis inspectis, auctoritate archidiaconi de Norhampton', cuius*b* vices tunc gessimus, instituimus memoratos fratres hospitalis perpetuas personas in ecclesia de Gildesburgh', et eis eandem ecclesiam cum omnibus ad eam pertinentibus libere et canonice imperpetuum habendam et possidendam assignavimus et concessimus et presenti scripto confirmavimus, salvo iure Lincoln' ecclesie. Hiis testibus: Warino [de]*c* Sanford' canonico Sar', Roberto decano, magistro Gregorio, Henrico de Heddona, Willelmo clerico, Radulpho de Esseby, Rad(ulpho) de Forda clerico.

a Ms adds que, *which is redundant*   *b Ms* eius   *c Supplied*

The archdn of Northampton for whom Geoffrey was acting was no doubt Savaric, who became archdn in 1175 (*Fasti Lincoln,* 31). The two were colleagues in the Salisbury cathedral chapter, where Savaric was treasurer (*Fasti Salisbury,* 20–1), and Geoffrey witnessed three of Savaric's archidiaconal acts (above, nos. 156, 159–60) and four of his acts as bp of Bath (*EEA* X, nos. 183, 230, 256, 263). His dates as archdn of Berkshire are very uncertain; his predecessor last occurs in 1155 × 1165, and he first occurs in Oct. 1173 (*Fasti Salisbury,* 29), but, since he was still in office in Feb. 1205 (*EEA* 19, 395), he may have been appointed in c. 1170. The later terminus here is supplied by the death of William de Diva (see above, no. 149, which in effect confirms this act).

229. *Notification that, on a mandate of the archbishop of Canterbury and at the presentation of Abbot G(eoffrey) and the monks of Lire, he has received Richard, chaplain, as parson of Basildon church and has confirmed this institution.*

[1177 × 1206]

B = BL, Egerton ms 3667 (Carisbrooke cartulary), fo. 27v (11v), nos. 28–9 (same text entered twice). s. xiii med.

Pd, *Carisbrooke Cartulary*, 29, no. 29 (second copy noted, 30, no. 30).

Omnibus Cristi fidelibus et c', G. archidiaconus Berch', salutem. Noverit universitas vestra nos, ad mandatum domini Cant' archiepiscopi et ad presentationem G. abbatis et monachorum Lirensium, recepisse in personam ecclesie de Bastend' Ricardum capellanum. Et ut hec nostra institutio firma perseveret, eam presentis carte attestatione confirmamus et sigilli nostri munimine roboramus. Hiis testibus et c'.

Geoffrey became abbot of Lire in 1177 and his successor occurs in 1206 (*Gallia Christiana*, xi, 646). There is no variation between the two copies of this act.

230. *Notification that, at the presentation of the abbot and convent of Lire, he had instituted parsons in the churches of their patronage in the archdeaconry of Berkshire, namely, Rocelin, clerk, in Ashampstead; Gilbert, chaplain of the late Roger, bishop of Worcester, in Shinfield and Swallowfield; and Richard, priest, in Basildon; and, after the said Gilbert's death, Mr Stephen of Reims in Shinfield and Swallowfield.*

[9 Aug. 1179 × 8 Oct. 1206]

B = BL, Egerton ms 3667 (Carisbrooke cartulary), fo. 27r–v (11r–v), no. 27. s. xiii med.

Pd, *Carisbrooke Cartulary*, 29, no. 28.

Omnibus Cristi fidelibus, et c', Gaufridus archidiaconus Berkesir', salutem. Quoniam ea que ad [fo. 27v] hutilitatem hominum fiunt a labili hominum memoria de facili excidunt, repertum est in rei testimonium scripture perhennis remedium. Inde est quod universitati vestre notum fieri volumus[a] nos, ad presentationem abbatis et conventus de Lira instituisse personas in ecclesiis quarum patronatum habent in archidiaconatu de Berchesir', videlicet Rocelinum clericum in ecclesia de Essehamested', et Gilibertum capellanum Rogeri bone memorie Wigorn' episcopi in ecclesiis de Siniggefeld et Swalewefeld, et Ricardum presbiterum de Bastlesden', et post decessum predicti Giliberti magistrum Stephanum Remensem in memoratis ecclesiis de Suniggefeld et de Swalewefeld. Et ne decetero cuiquam hominum in dubium venire possit quid iuris prenominati monachi in predictis habeant ecclesiis, hec caritati vestre dignum duximus notificare. Valete.

a Ms voluimus

After the death of Roger, bp of Worcester (*Fasti Monastic Cathedrals*, 99–100), and before Geoffrey had been succeeded in the archdnry by Alberic, who occurs, 8 Oct. 1206 (*EEA* 19, 395). That this is Geoffrey de Vernun is proved by the institutions of Gilbert at Shinfield and Swallowfield and Richard to Basildon (*EEA* 18, no. 79; above, no. 229).

231. *Notification, in chirograph form, of the settlement of the dispute between the prior and monks of Hurley and Ralph, parson of East Garston church, over the tithes of Maidencourt and Shortcombe, reached in St Mary's church, Reading, namely, that the prior and convent shall have a third of the grain tithes and of other [lesser] tithes of the demesne of Maidencourt and of Shortcombe.*

Reading, 1190: ? 25 Mar. 1190 × 24 Mar. 1191

A = Westminster Abbey Muniments, no. 7259. Endorsed: convencio (? s. xiii); Edgarestune (s. xiv). Size 186 × 110 + 14 mm. Seal missing, tag remaining (method 2).

Pd (calendar), F. T. Wethered, *Lands and Tythes of Hurley Priory*, 34–5; (facsimile), L. Harmer, *The Parish of S. Giles-in-Reading*, Reading 1946, facing 9.

CIROGRAPHUM

Omnibus Cristi fidelibus ad quos presens scriptum pervenerit G. archidiaconus Berkesir', salutem. Noverit universitas vestra controversiam que vertebatur inter priorem et monachos de Hurlea et Radulfum personam ecclesie de Esegareston' super decimis de Meidenecot' et de Sortescumb' tali concordia sopitam esse. Videlicet quod prior et conventus de Hurlea habeant terciam partem decimarum annone tocius dominii de Meidenecot' sine participatione et terciam partem de decimis agnorum, porcellorum, caseorum, lini et lane et pasnagii et de omnibus rebus in vivo et mortuo de quibuscumque decima dari debet; et similiter terciam partem omnium decimarum de tota terra de Sortescumb' tam culta quam inculta. Et si aliquid de dominio de Meidenecot' vel de Sortescumb' mutatum fuerit in villanagium a morte Osberti de Herlotera usque ad diem confectionis huius instrumenti, vel decetero mutetur, non *ᵃ*minus prior*ᵃ* de tali villanagio dictam terciam partem recipiet. Et similiter, si aliquid de villanagio ab eodem termino mutatum sit in dominium, nichilominus persona ecclesie de Esegareston' de tali dominio decimas suas plene percipiet. Hec autem conventio facta est in ecclesia sancte Marie de Rading', anno incarnationis dominice M.° C.° x°c, et corporali iuramento ab utraque parte firmata. Hiis testibus: magistro Roberto de Tacham, magistro Honorio de Hurlea, magistro Waltero de Widehaia, Philippo capellano de Etinged', Gilleberto capellano sancte Marie de Rading', Thoma capellano sancti Egidii de Rading', Roberto vicario de Hurlea, et aliis.

a–a Ms stained; legible only under ultra-violet light

The more specific dating assumes that the year began on 25 Mar. It is not stated that the archdn was present, but he may well have presided at this settlement, since at this time the diocesan bp, Hubert Walter, was overseas, initially with the king (*EEA* 18, xlviii; *EEA* 19, 407–8), even though Hubert appointed four ecclesistics to act as his *officiales* in his absence (*EEA* 18, xlix; *EEA* 19, 391–3).

232. *Notification that, at the precept of H., bishop of Salisbury, and at the presentation of the monks of Longueville, he has received Gilbert de Striginel, clerk, as parson of [Long] Wittenham church in general chapter at Harwell; Gilbert will pay annually a pension of six marks to the monks, who will possess the tithes of the earl's demesne* in proprios usus, *all of which Gilbert has sworn in the archdeacon's presence to observe.*   [prob. 5 June 1194 × 8 Oct. 1206]

    B = Oxford, New College, Archive 9744 (Liber Niger), fo. 35v. s. xvi in.
    Pd, *Newington Longeville Charters*, 58–9, no. 65; (extract only), *EEA* 18, no. 208a.

Omnibus Cristi fidelibus ad quos presens scriptum pervenerit Gaufridus archidiaconus Berquesire, salutem. Noveritis me, ad preceptum domini H. Saresbur' episcopi et ad presentationem monachorum de Longavil', recepisse Gilbertum de Striginel clericum in personam ecclesie de Wicheham in generali capitulo apud Harewell', ita quod idem G. solvet annuatim predictis monachis de eadem ecclesia sex marcas argenti, et idem monachi decimas de dominio comitis habebunt et in proprios usus possidebunt. Predictus autem G. in presentia nostra tactis sacrosanctis evangeliis de indemnitate supradictarum decimarum conservanda et de pensione memorata monachis fideliter solvenda corporaliter prestitit sacramentum. Ut autem hec perpetue firmitatis robur obtineant, ea presenti scripto confirmare dignum duxi. Hiis testibus.

The bp of Salisbury is almost certainly Herbert Poore, who was consecrated 5 June 1194 (*Fasti Salisbury,* 3), rather than his predecessor, Hubert Walter, who spent very little time in England and of whom no other act filling a parochial benefice is known. The archdn is almost certainly Geoffrey de Vernun, rather than a later Geoffrey, the successor of Alberic who last occurs in Nov. 1215 (ibid., 29–30), since the archdn's use of first person singular and of the verb *recipere* both favour Geoffrey de Vernun (see Kemp, 'Towards admission and institution', 161–73); the later terminus of this act is therefore 8 Oct. 1206, by which time Alberic was in office as archdn (above, no. 230n.). The church and demesne tithes of Long Wittenham were given to Longueville by (Earl) Walter Giffard before Sept. 1155 (*Newington Longeville Charters*, nos. 2, 3), but the demesne tithes were kept separate from the church (ibid., xxix, and no. 67; *EEA* 18, no. 209).

ARCHDEACONRY OF DORSET

Adelelm

233. *Notification that, in his presence and that of Alfred of Lincoln, Gervase of Watercombe has restored to the monks and brethren of Holme all the demesne tithe of Watercombe in the same way as Bardolf Bussel, his brother, had first given it in alms, except for a cartload of corn which the church of Warmwell ought to have.*
[? *c.* 1150 × *c.* 1180]

    B = Bodl. ms Trinity College 85 (Montacute cartulary), fo. 70r (58r). s. xiv in. C = BL,
        Additional Roll 24879 (charters relating to the priory of Holme, Dorset), no. 5. s.
        xiv ex.
    Pd (calendar) from B, *Bruton and Montacute Cartularies*, 165, Montacute no. 126.

Sciant tam presentes quam futuri quod Gervasius de Watercumba, coram me Adelelmo archidiacono Dorset' et domino Aluredo de Lincol', reddidit monachis et fratribus de Holna omnem decimam de dominio de Watercumba eo modo quo *a*Bardulfus Bussel*a* frater suus eis prius in elemosinam concesserat, excepta una carrata bladi quam ecclesia de Wermewulla*b* debet habere. Hiis testibus: Ricardo de Caln', Rodberto*c* de Gillefort,*d* Rainaldo decano, Willelmo capellano de Preston', Fulcone capellano de Corf, domina Albereda*e* de Corf, Ricardo Walensi, Andrea de Lincol', Rodberto*c* de Monasteriis, et multis aliis clericis et laicis.

> *a–a* Bardulphus Bussell' *C*   *b* Warmewulla *C*   *c* Roberto *C*
> *d* Gilford' *C*   *e* Albreda *C*

After the death of Alfred of Lincoln's father, Robert, which occurred before 1156 (Sanders, *English Baronies,* 99), and during the archidiaconate of Adelelm, who last occurs ? *c.* 1180 (*Fasti Salisbury,* 25). For the grant to Montacute of the whole demesne tithe of Watercombe by Bardolf Bussel (*alias* of Cheselbourne), a knight of Robert of Lincoln, see *Bruton and Montacute Cartularies,* 164, no.124. The Cluniac priory of Holme (Dorset) was founded in *c.* 1107 as a dependency of Montacute priory (Knowles and Hadcock, 97; but *VCH Dorset,* ii, 80, dates the foundation towards the mid-12th century). Watercombe lay within the parish of Warmwell, whose church was given to Montacute (and Holme) temp. William, prior of Montacute (? 1159 × before Sept. 1169 – see *Heads,* 122): *Bruton and Montacute Cartularies,* 166, no. 130; BL, Add. Roll 24879, no. 9.

* 234. *Act concerning the settlement in his presence, by mandate of the bishop of Salisbury, of a dispute between Reginald de Campo Florido, clerk, and Ailmer, parson of the church of Powerstock, over the same church; namely, that Reginald renounced what right he had in the church in the presence of the whole chapter, and promised not to raise a dispute over the church in the future.*   [1142 × 21 Mar. 1158]

> Mentioned only, in the settlement of a dispute between Reginald de Campo Florido and the abbot of Montebourg and William, his clerk, over the same church, made by Gilbert Foliot, bishop of London, papal judge-delegate, in probably 1163 × 1184: (A) Salisbury, D. & C. Muniments, Press I, Box 8, P-R/1; (B) Ibid., Liber Evidentiarum C, pp. 131–2, no. 155; (C) Trowbridge, Wiltshire R.O., D1/1/2 (Liber Evidentiarum B), fos. 41v–42r, no. 119; (D) Ibid., D1/1/3 (Registrum Rubrum), fo. 34r, no. 119; pd from A, *Foliot Letters and Charters,* 458–9, no. 421; from B, C and D, *Salisbury Charters,* 31–2, no. 38.

. . . proponentes [*sc.* the abbot of Montebourg's proctors and William, clerk] quod cum*a* Eilmero*b* eiusdem quondam ecclesie persone super [hac]*c* eadem ecclesia in presentia Alelmi Dorseten' archidiaconi, ex mandato domini Saresbiriensis*d* episcopi, iam pridem mota fuisset controversia, idem Reginaldus iuri, si quod*e* unquam in eadem ecclesia habuerat, in ipsius archidiaconi et totius capituli presentia sponte renuntiavit, et se nunquam super ecclesia hac moturum controversiam fidei interpositione firmavit. Nobis [*sc.* Bishop Gilbert Foliot] itaque super hiis que ab eis dicebantur, tam scripto ipsius archidiaconi quam viva voce testium omni exceptione maiorum fide sufficienter facta, . . .

> *a* causa *(sic) B*   *b* Elmero *B*   *c* Illegible in A through damp, supplied from
> copies   *d* Sar' *B, C;* Sarr' *D*   *e* Sic in all texts

The fact that Montebourg was apparently not involved in the dispute with Ailmer strongly suggests that the church of Powerstock had not yet been given to the abbey (see no. 236), while the form of reference to the bp of Salisbury suggests Jocelin de Bohun, Foliot's episcopal colleague (see *Foliot Letters and Charters*, no. 421n.).

235. *Notification to Jocelin, bishop of Salibury, that some thirty years ago a dispute arose between Roger, canon of Salisbury, and Walter of Hill over the church of Hill [Deverill]; that, because Walter did not trust the archdeacon, Azo [of Wiltshire], Roger's brother, the dispute was committed by Roger, late bishop of Salisbury, to him for settlement; and that, in the archdeacon's presence and that of the chapter of the 'province' in the church of [Longbridge] Deverill, it was adjudged on the oath of three priests, Roger's witnesses, that the church pertained to Roger's prebend of Heytesbury.* [? c. 1155 × 1165]

B = Trowbridge, Wiltshire R.O., D1/1/1 (Register of St Osmund), fo. 51r (p. 101). s. xiii in.
Pd, *Reg. S. Osm.*, i, 351–2.

Reverendo domino et patri karissimo Ioscelino dei gratia Sar' episcopo et omnibus sancte ecclesie fidelibus A. archidiaconus Dorset', salutem. Noverit paternitas vestra quod iam transactis triginta annis, ut credimus, orta fuit causa inter Rogerum canonicum Sar' et Walterum de Hull' super ecclesia de Hull; et quia Walterus suspectum habuit Azonem tunc archidiaconum fratrem Rogeri, eadem causa nobis commissa est cognoscenda et terminanda a Rogero bone memorie Sar' episcopo. Convocatis itaque ante presentiam nostram Rogero et Waltero, die statuto venerunt litigaturi super eadem ecclesia in ecclesia de Deverell', presente capitulo illius provincie. Rogerus autem asserebat ecclesiam illam adiacere prebende sue, et [ad]*ᵃ* hoc probandum produxit testes idoneos et sufficientes. Walterus autem e contrario allegabat ecclesiam illam numquam adiacuisse prebende sue de Hegtred(eberia). Accepto itaque sacramento trium presbiterorum testium Rogeri secundum ordinarium, adiudicata fuit ecclesia prefata prebende Rogeri.

a Supplied

This interesting and valuable act is very difficult to date. Adelelm was evidently archdn before the death of Bp Roger of Salisbury, 11 Dec. 1139 (*Fasti Salisbury*, 2), but for how long before is uncertain, although his occurrence as late as 'after 1173' perhaps suggests that he became archdn not earlier than *c.* 1130 × 1135 (ibid., 25). Roger, canon and prebendary of Heytesbury, known as 'of Ramsbury', became archdn [of Wiltshire] before Dec. 1139, in succession to his brother, Azo, who became dean of Salisbury (ibid., 9, 34, 74). Elias Giffard, possibly in *c.* 1130 × 1135, informed Roger, bp of Salisbury, of his confirmation of the same settlement before Adelelm, archdn of Dorset, indicating that Walter of Hill was Walter son of Osmund, one of his knights, who had originally agreed to the foundation of Hill [Deverill] church in his fee, and that the church where the 'provincial' chapter met was St Peter's church *apud Deverels de Glaston'*, i.e. Longbridge Deverill (*Reg. S. Osm.*, i, 349). For further discussion of this case, see Brett, *English Church under Henry I*, 206–7.

236. *Notification to all clergy of the chapter of Bridport that, in his presence, Roger Arundel gave in perpetual alms to the monks of Montebourg the church of Powerstock, and that afterwards, in his presence, Ailmer, who had earlier administered the cure as parson, received the church from the hand of the abbot of Montebourg, to hold for an annual payment of twelve pence; also that Hawise de Redvers, sister of Earl Richard, has informed him by her letters of her gift in perpetuity to Montebourg abbey of the church of Fleet, with the consent of Richard and her other brothers.*

[prob. late Mar. 1157 × 1158]

B = Salisbury, D. & C. Muniments, Liber Evidentiarum C, p. 147, no. 176. s. xiii ex.
C = Trowbridge, Wiltshire R.O., D1/1/2 (Liber Evidentiarum B), fo. 49r, no. 141.
s. xiv in. D = Ibid., D1/1/3 (Registrum Rubrum), fo. 41r, no. 141. s. xiv.
Pd from B, C, D, *Salisbury Charters*, 28, no. 33.

[A]delelmus de Dorset'[a] archidiaconus omnibus clericis capituli de Bridiport,[b] salutem. Notum sit omnibus vobis quod Rogerus Arundel dedit et concessit, me presente et concedente, ecclesie sancte Marie de Monteburg' et monachis ibidem deo servientibus ecclesiam de Porestok'[c] cum omnibus que ad eam pertinent in oblationibus et decimationibus et terris et pascuis et aliis consuetudinibus in perpetuam elemosinam. Ailmerus[d] vero sacerdos, qui retroactis temporibus in prefata ecclesia tanquam persona curam administrationis gesserat, in presentia mea eam de manu abbatis postmodum tenendam de ecclesia de Monteburg' suscepit, solvendo eidem ecclesie annuum canonem, videlicet xii. d'. Preterea domina Hatewysa de Rivariis, soror comitis Ricardi, literis suis mandavit michi se dedisse et concessisse prenominate ecclesie de Monteburg' et monachis in [e]ea deo[e] servientibus in perpetuum possidendam ecclesiam de Fluta[f] cum omnibus pertinentiis suis et consuetudinibus, fratre suo Ricardo comite[g] et aliis fratribus suis, ut asserebat, concedentibus. Valete.

a Dorseta *C*	*b* Brideport *C;* Brideport' *D*	*c* Powestok' *C,D*
d Aillmerus *D*	*e–e* eadem *C,D*	*f Sic in all copies*
C,D		*g* Gaunte *(sic)*

Roger Arundel gave Powerstock church to Montebourg abbey in the chapter at (? Maiden) Newton before the archdn on 21 Mar. 1157 × 1158, and invested Abbot Walter with the church 'by the archdn's hand'; the following day Ailmer, priest of the church, with his two clerks promised to pay 12d annually to Montebourg *in recognitionem*; and on 24 Mar., in the chapter at Dorchester, the archdn invested the abbot with the church *per clavem* with Ailmer's consent (*Salisbury Charters*, nos. 31–2); it seems likely that the present act belongs to this period. Both churches were confirmed to Montebourg by Bp Jocelin de Bohun of Salisbury in 1157 × 1162 (ibid., no. 34; *EEA* 18, no. 90), but Hawise de Redvers later claimed, after the bp's death, that she had originally given Fleet church to Quarr abbey (Isle of Wight) with his consent, but that Montebourg had unjustly acquired it through her brother, Henry de Redvers, i.e., Earl Richard's younger brother (*Redvers Charters*, 145–6, no. 113, and references there cited).

William

237. *Notification of the settlement in his presence, before the chapter of Bere [Regis] at Puddletown, of the dispute between the prior and canons of Christchurch, Twynham, and William de Vernun over the* ius et personatus *of the church of Puddletown, namely, that William has recognised the charter which he had given to the prior and canons but subsequently denied out of anger, and has given all his right in the church to the canons in perpetual alms. The archdeacon has, at his request, received the prior into the* personatus *of the church, as the bishop of Salisbury's charter witnesses, so that each prior shall institute whichever vicar he wishes in the church. The prior has instituted Richard, priest, as perpetual vicar, whom the archdeacon has received as such, and Richard has sworn before the archdeacon and the chapter to pay an annual pension of ten marks to Christchurch.*   [? *c.* 1180 × 18 Nov. 1184]

B = BL, Cotton ms Tiberius D vi, part I (Christchurch cartulary), fo. 137r–v (138r–v). s. xiv ex.

Universis sancte matris ecclesie filiis Willelmus archidiaconus de Dorset', salutem eternam in domino. Notum sit vobis quod lis que vertebatur inter priorem et canonicos Cristi ecclesie de Twynham et Willelmum de Vernoun super iure et personatu ecclesie de Pidelton' amicabili concordia in presentia nostra coram capitulo de Bera apud Pideltonam terminata est. Nam Willelmus de Vernoun recognovit cartam suam quam priori et canonicis fecerat, quamvis illam aliquando iracundia motus denegasset, et omne ius suum quod ipse in ecclesia illa de Pideltona habuerat ecclesie sancte Trinitatis de Twynham et canonicis ibidem [fo. 137v] deo servientibus atque servituris liberalissime dedit et concessit in perpetuam elemosinam pro salute sua et omnium parentum et amicorum suorum vivorum et defunctorum. Nos autem, ad petitionem ipsius Willelmi, priorem predicte ecclesie et omnes successores suos in personatum prefate ecclesie de Pudelton' recepimus, sicut carta[a] domini nostri Sar' ecclesie pontificis testatur; hoc videlicet modo quod quicumque fuerit prior Cristi ecclesie vicarium quem voluerit constituet in ecclesia de Pidelton', qui in ecclesia illa ministret [et][b] nobis de hiis que ad nos pertinent fideliter serviat et respondeat, salvo semper iure Sar' ecclesie. Sciatis quoque quod prior Cristi ecclesie instituit[c] Ricardum presbiterum vicarium perpetuum in illa ecclesia de Pidelton', et nos[d] quantum[e] ad nos pertinet[f] illum benigne in vicarium illius ecclesie suscepimus. Et ipse Ricardus iuravit coram nobis et capitulo quod ipse R. solvet annuam pensionem ecclesie sancte Trinitatis de Twynham, videlicet x. marcas argenti annuatim ad quatuor anni terminos reddendas, ad Natale domini duas et dimidiam, ad Pascha tantumdem, in Nativitate sancti Iohannis Baptiste tantumdem, ad festum beati Michaelis tantumdem. Et ne hec actio nostra maligno alicuius machinatione[g] de cetero possit infringi, hanc nostram cartam prefato priori sigilli nostri impressione munitam contulimus.

a Followed in ms by ipsius *marked for deletion*   *b Supplied*   *c Followed by illegible word marked for deletion*   *d Followed in ms by* quod *marked for deletion*   *e Ms* quod   *f Corrected in ms from* pertinent   *g Reading very uncertain*

After the latest occurrence of William's predecessor in the archdnry, Adelelm (*Fasti Salisbury*, 25), and before the death of Jocelin de Bohun, bp of Salisbury, who had confirmed Puddletown church to the priory in 1154 × 1170, declaring the prior to be the parson (ibid., 3; *EEA* 18, no. 57). For William de Vernun's charter recording this same settlement, see *Redvers Charters*, no. 67; no earlier charter by him is known, nor the reason for the anger which caused him to deny it. He succeeded his nephew, Richard de Redvers II, as 5th earl of Devon in *c.* 1191 (ibid., 4, 14). Christchurch priory was dedicated to the Holy Trinity (*VCH Hants,* ii, 152).

238. *Surrender to Simon son of Robert, to whom the churches of Lyme [Regis] and Halstock have been assigned as a prebend of Salisbury cathedral, of archidiaconal rights in these churches apart from Peter's Pence. In the Salisbury chapter.*

[20 Apr. × prob. 29 May 1193]

> A = Salisbury, D. & C. Muniments, Press IV, E5: Prebend of Lyme and Halstock/2. Endorsed: De Lym et Halgestok' (s. xiii); Tang' prebend' de Lym (s. xiv). Size 162 × 142 + 25 mm. Seal and tag missing (method 1).
> B = Trowbridge, Wiltshire R.O., D1/1/1 (Register of St Osmund), fo. 31v (p. 62). s. xiii in.
> Pd from B, *Reg. S. Osm.,* i, 243–4.

Universis Cristi fidelibus presentibus et futuris Willelmus archidiaconus Dorset', salutem. Noverit universitas vestra quod, cum ecclesie de Lim et de Halgestoke nobis sicut aliis archidiaconis Dorset' predecessoribus nostris in omnibus respondissent, sicut alie ecclesie parochiales eiusdem archidiaconatus, et ipse postmodum in prebendam Sar'*ᵃ* ecclesie fuissent assignate et Simoni filio Roberti in prebendam collate, nos spontanea voluntate, interveniente et*ᵇ* auctoritate domini H. Sar' episcopi, totum ius archidiaconale quod in eisdem habuimus ecclesiis et earum pertinentiis predicto Simoni et successoribus eius in perpetuum remisimus. Ita quod idem Simon vel eius successores nobis vel officialibus vel successoribus nostris in nullo respondere teneantur nomine predictarum ecclesiarum, preterquam in denariis beati Petri. Acta sunt hec in capitulo Sar' in presentia domini H. Sar' episcopi, presentibus et testantibus Iordano decano, Waltero precentore, Bald(ewino) cancellario, Rann(ulfo) thesaurario, Galfrido archidiacono Bercsir',*ᶜ* Willelmo archidiacono Wiltesir', Unfrido*ᵈ* archidiacono Sar', Wimundo subdecano, Iohanne succentore, magistro Simone de Scal',*ᵉ* magistro Iohanne de Bridiport,*ᶠ* Roberto de bella fago, Philippo de Havekeschirch', Willelmo de Cicestr', magistro Roberto de Linc', Willelmo de Wamberga et Ioscelino fratre suo, Ioscelino archidiacono Cicestr', Rogero de Basing', Roberto de Valeines, Thoma de Lond'.*ᵍ*

> *a* Sarr' *(throughout) B*   *b* etiam *B*   *c* Berkesir' *B*   *d* Hunfr' *B*
> *e* Scalis *B*   *f* Brideport' *B*   *g* London' *B*

This act is contemporary with another of Hubert Walter, bp of Salisbury, which dates from the few months between the latter's return to England and his election as archbp of Canterbury (*EEA* 18, no. 184; *Fasti Salisbury,* 3).

ARCHDEACONRY OF SALISBURY

Azo

239. *Notification to the master of the Templars in England that Joan, wife of Richard the knight of Chalfield, who proposed to become a Templar, has promised in the presence of the archdeacon's officials to preserve her chastity; and that he [Richard] has lately promised to accept the rule.* [? *c.* 1180 × May 1193]

> B = BL, Cotton ms Nero E vi (Hospitallers cartulary for England), part 2, fo. 267r. s. xv med.
> Pd, *Records of Templars*, 210, no. 5.

Karissimo sibi in Cristo S.*a* magistro fratrum Templi Ierl'm in Anglia Azo archidiaconus, salutem in domino. Noveritis quod Iohanna uxor presentium latoris Ricardi militis de Chaldef', qui se per dei gratiam iugo regule Templi subdere proposuit, licet confecta senio in tantum quod nulla*b* deinceps de ea poterit sinistra oriri suspicio, in presentia officialium nostrorum castitatem servare promisit; et ut ipse regule Templi subdat ultimo promisit. Unde et nos, veritati testimonium perhibere volentes, cum literis nostris extra pendentibus vos super hoc duximus certificare. Valete.

> *a Sic, but prob. error for G. (see note)*   *b Ms nullam*

Azo first occurs as archdn in ?*c.* 1180 and had been succeeded by May 1193 at the latest (*Fasti Salisbury*, 32). The master of the English Templars at this time was Geoffrey son of Stephen (*Records of Templars*, lviii–lix), the present transcript perhaps confusing 'Stephen' with 'Geoffrey'. Chalfield lay in the archdnry of Salisbury (see *Fasti Salisbury*, 32). Both the cartulary rubric, 'Receptio Iohanne Chaldefe in sororem Templariorum', and *Records of Templars*, lxii, misinterpret the text, since the masculine 'ipse' (line 6) clearly refers to Richard.

ARCHDEACONRY OF WILTSHIRE

Reginald fitzJocelin

240. *Notification that in his presence Margaret de Bohun has given to the canons of Llanthony the church of Chirton in perpetual alms, provided that he shall hold it for life, rendering thence to the canons one bezant annually; and that as archdeacon he has canonically invested the canons with the church.* [1167 × *c.* Apr. 1173]

> B = PRO, C115/K1/6679 (Llanthony cartulary), fo. 31v. s. xiii med. C = PRO, C115/K2/6683 (Llanthony cartulary), fo. 22v, i, no. 33. s. xiv med. D = Ibid., fo. 141r, viii, no. 6. s. xiv med. (extract only).

Reginaldus archidiaconus omnibus ad quos presens carta pervenerit, salutem. Noverit universitas vestra quod Marg(areta) de Bohun*a* dedit in presentia nostra canonicis *b*de Lanth'*b* in perpetuam elemosinam ecclesiam de Chyriton'*c* cum omnibus pertinentiis suis*d* et quicquid iuris in ea habuit ita libere et quiete sicut eam unquam aliquis liberius tenuit, eo tamen salvo quod ego Reginaldus eandem ecclesiam omnibus diebus vite mee teneam, reddendo inde annuatim eisdem canonicis unum bisantium ad festum sancti Michaelis. Et ego Reginaldus, sicut archidiaconus eiusdem loci, de ecclesia illa cum omnibus pertinentiis suis canonice eos investivi. Testibus: Willelmo senescaldo, Humfrido capellano, Elia Chokerel,*e* et aliis.

   a Boun *C,D*   *b–b Om. in C;* de Lanthon' *D*   *c* Chyritone *D*
   d D ends with et c'   *e* Chokel' *C*

After Margaret de Bohun's gift of the church to Llanthony in 1167 (Walker, 'Earldom of Hereford charters', no. 90) and before Reginald was elected bp of Bath (*EEA* X, 207). Reginald was an illegitimate son of bp Jocelin de Bohun and a relative of Margaret de Bohun; see also *EEA* 18, no. 81 and n.

Richard of Wilton

241. *Notification of the composition between himself and the monks of Gloucester in the presence of Roger, bishop of Worcester, over the demesne tithe of Robert of Ewyas at Clevancy; namely, that he will hold the tithe of the monks for life or until he changes his life, rendering to the prior of Ewyas one pound of incense annually at Gloucester.*

[1175 × 1178; ? 1178]

A = Hereford, Cathedral Archives, HCA 784. Endorsed: De decimis Rob' de Ewias de Cliva contra Ric' archid' (s. xii ex); Non indiget registrari (s. xiv). Size 200 × 115 + 21 mm. Seal in light brown wax on tag (method 1), pointed oval, nearly complete, *c.* 48 × 29 mm; obverse, frontally standing figure, tonsured and in deacon's vestments (dalmatic), hands folded in front, possibly holding a book to his chest; legend: + SIGILLVM: RICARDI [   ]DIACONI [   ]IENSIS.

Pd, W. St C. Baddeley, 'The early deeds of St Peter's, Gloucester', *Trans. Bristol and Glouc. Arch. Soc.* 37 (1914), 228, no. 13; D. Walker, 'Some charters relating to St Peter's abbey, Gloucester', *Misc. D. M. Stenton*, 261, no. 6; *Original Acta of Gloucester*, no. 36, with facsimile, plate VIIb; (calendar), M. G. Cheney, *Roger of Worcester*, 259, no. 26.

Universis sancte matris ecclesie filiis Ricardus archidiaconus Wiltesire, salutem in domino. Sciatis quod talis composicio facta est inter me et monachos Gloec' in presencia venerabilis domini nostri Rogeri Wigorn' episcopi super decima dominii Roberti de Ewias de Cliva: quod ego in vita mea tantum eandem decimam de prefatis monachis tenebo, reddens priori de Ewias singulis annis unam libram incensi in Assumptione sancte Marie apud Gloec'. Post decessum autem meum, vel vite mutacionem, predicta decima libera et quieta restituetur monachis Gloec' absque omni reclamacione alicuius. Quod quia ratum volo et immutabile permanere, presenti scripto sigillum meum apposui. His testibus: Symone archidiacono, magistro Moyse, magistro Silvestro, magistro Iohanne de Paris, Willelmo cantore.

Richard's predecessor, William, was still in office in 1175 (*EEA* 19, 395), and Roger, bp of Worcester, left England for the last time very early in 1179 (Cheney, *Roger of Worcester,* 222–3); this agreement may have been reached in 1178, however, when the abbeys of Gloucester and Lire reached a settlement over the tithes of Ewyas, Herefs (ibid., 259, no. 26n.). The role of Roger of Worcester is not explained, but it has been suggested that he was acting as a papal judge-delegate (ibid.).

242.　*Notification that, in his presence, Simon of Seagry, son of Alexander of Seagry, has confirmed to the priory and canons of Bradenstoke the church of Seagry in free, pure and perpetual alms in accordance with the charters of his father, himself and W(alter) de Clifford; and that, as far as pertains to his office, the archdeacon has confirmed the gift.*　　　　　　　　　　　　　　　　　　　　　　　　　[1175 × c. May 1193]

> B = BL, Cotton ms Vitellius A xi (Bradenstoke cartulary), fo. 81v (78v). s. xiv med. C =
> 　　BL, Stowe ms 925 (Bradenstoke cartulary), fo. 68v. s. xiv ex.
> Pd (calendar) from B and C, *Bradenstoke Cartulary*, 69, no. 170.

Omnibus Cristi fidelibus ad quos presens scriptum pervenerit R. dei gratia archidiaconus Wiltes', salutem in domino. Noverit universitas vestra Symonem de Segre filium Alexandri de Segre in presentia nostra concessisse et confirmasse deo et ecclesie sancte Marie de Bradenestok'*ᵃ* et canonicis ibidem deo servientibus ecclesiam de Segr' cum omnibus pertinentiis suis que in archidiaconatu nostro esse constituta dinoscitur; tenend' et habend' predictis canonicis in liberam, puram et perpetuam elemosinam secundum quod carte prefati A. de Segre et prenominati S. filii eius et W. de Clifford*ᵇ* eorum advocati eisdem canonicis testantur. Et ut hoc nullis imposterum*ᶜ* vertatur in dubium, presenti scripto sigilli nostri testimonium apposuimus, et quantum ad officium nostrum pertinet donationem et confirmationem predictorum advocatorum supradictis canonicis de iam dicta ecclesia de Segre rationabiliter factam corroboramus et confirmamus. Hiis testibus.*ᵈ*

> *a* Bradenestoke *C*　　　*b* Clifforde *C*　　　*c* in posterum *C*　　　*d Add* et c' *C*

Although the matter is not certain, this act is probably by Richard of Wilton rather than Richard Grosseteste, who became archdn of Wiltshire at the end of the century (*Fasti Salisbury*, 36). The members of the Seagry family cannot be precisely dated, and at least three of their Clifford overlords were called Walter (*VCH Wilts*, xiv, 189), but the present Clifford may be the Walter who died in 1190 (ibid.). Richard of Wilton's predecessor was still in office in 1175 (*EEA* 19, 395), and Richard had been succeeded as archdn of Wiltshire by Apr. × May 1193, in which months two successive archdns of Wiltshire occur, Humphrey of Bassingbourn and William of Ste-Mère-Eglise (*EEA* 18, nos. 183–4). For the charters of gift and confirmation by Alexander of Seagry, Simon, his son, and Walter Clifford, see *Bradenstoke Cartulary*, nos. 163, 165, 167.

* 243.　*Act concerning the annual payment of one mark from the incumbent of Wootton [Bassett] church to the prior and convent of [Monkton] Farleigh, until Alan Basset shall assign to them the same amount in definite rent.*　　　[?1182 × Apr. 1191]

> Mentioned only, in the renunciation by Prior Stephen and the convent of [Monkton] Farleigh to Alan Basset of their claim to the advowson of the church: PRO, E40/4861 (Ancient Deed A 4861); pd, *Basset Charters*, 163, no. 241; (calendar) *Cat. Anc. Deeds*, iii, 114.

. . . tali scilicet conditione quod predictus Alanus unam marcam argenti nobis [*sc.* the prior and convent] concessit et annuatim assignavit percipiendam de eo qui predictam ecclesiam habuerit quicumque fuerit ille . . . quousque pretaxatus Alanus . . . unam marcam argenti annuatim in certo redditu percipiendam nobis assignaverit, secundum quod carte Ricardi archidiaconi de Wiltescr' et sepedicti Alani testantur.

For the date, see *Basset Charters*, no. 241n.: Alan probably did not acquire Wootton

Bassett until after his father's death; and Prior Stephen's successor at Monkton Farleigh was deposed 21 Apr. 1191 (see *Heads*, 120).

244. *Notification that, at the instance of the abbot and monks of Malmesbury, he has confirmed the settlement between them and Hilary of Beckhampton over the demesne tithes of Beckhampton and* Stanmere. [1189 × c. May 1193]

> B = PRO, E164/24 (Malmesbury cartulary), fo. 173r, cap. 110. s. xiii ex. C = BL, Lansdowne ms 417 (Malmesbury cartulary), fo. 73r (67r). ss. xiv ex.–xv in.
> Pd from B, *Reg. Malmesburiense*, i, 441, cap. 110.

Omnibus Cristi fidelibus ad quos presens scriptum pervenerit Ricardus archidiaconus Wyltesir',[a] salutem in domino. Noverit universitas vestra nos, ad instantiam tam abbatis quam monachorum de Malm', compositionem super decimis de dominico de Bachampton'[b] et de Stanmer' inter ipsos et Hylarium de Bachampton' rationabiliter factam approbasse, et ipsam iuxta formam rescripti inter eos facti litteris nostris confirmasse. Et ut compositio predicta firma et inconvulsa [c]in posterum[c] permaneat, sigilli nostri appositione hanc confirmationem munivimus et corroboravimus. Hiis testibus: [d]magistro Vinc(entio),[d] magistro Thoma, Sampsone cappellan'.

> *a* Wiltesir' C   *b* Bachamton' C   *c–c* imposterum C   *d–d* Om. in C

The settlement was made by Abbot Robert II of Malmesbury, who was elected in 1189/ 90 (*Reg. Malmesburiense*, i, 443–4, caps. 115–16; *Heads*, 56); and Richard had been succeeded by Apr. × May 1193 (see no. 242n.). The archdn's confirmation of the settlement, which had been reached in the Malmesbury chapter house in the presence of Vincent, vice-archdn of Wiltshire (*Reg. Malmesburiense*, i, cap. 115), was perhaps called for in the absence of the diocesan, Hubert Walter, in these years (*Fasti Salisbury*, 3; see also Kemp, 'Archdeacons and parish churches', 350–1).

William of Ste-Mère-Eglise

245. *Notification that, at the presentation of the abbot and convent of La Trinité-du-Mont, Rouen, he has admitted Stephen, clerk, to the church of Easton [Royal] and canonically instituted him as parson in the same, saving an annual pension to the monks of twelve shillings.* [20 Apr. 1193 × 1198; ?June 1193 × 29 Apr. 1194]

> A = Trowbridge, Wiltshire R.O., 9/15/5 (Easton Priory deed). Endorsed: none medieval. Size 159 × 106 + 20 mm. Seal missing, tag remaining (method 1).

Omnibus sancte matris ecclesie filiis ad quos presens carta pervenerit Willelmus de Sancte Marie Ecclesia archidiaconus Wiltesir', salutem in domino. Noverit universitas vestra nos, ad presentationem abbatis et conventus Sancte Trinitatis de Monte Roth', divine pietatis intuitu admisisse Stephanum clericum ad ecclesiam de Estona, ipsumque in ea personam canonice instituisse, salva prefatis monachis debita pensione, videlicet duodecim solid(orum), quam eis ad duos anni terminos, scilicet sex solidos ad Purificationem beate Marie et sex ad Pentecosten, annuatim solvere tenetur. Quod ut ratum sit et firmum, presenti scripto sigilli nostri appositione munito duximus confirmandum. Hiis testibus: magistro Willelmo de Sumercot', magistro Reinerio de Stanf', Hugone Peverell', magistro Damiano, magistro Roberto Grosetest', magistro Nicholao de Hantona, et multis aliis.

After William became archdn of Wiltshire (between 20 Apr. and (prob.) 29 May 1193: see *EEA* 18, nos. 183, 184, both of which belong to this period, the first being witnessed by William de Ste-Mère-Eglise *not* as archdn, the second by him as archdn of Wiltshire, but without full name) and before his election as bp of London, 7 Dec. 1198, his successor in the archdnry, Richard Grosseteste, occurring 6 Jan. 1199 (*EEA* 19, 396; *Fasti Salisbury*, 35–6); but perhaps during the episcopal vacancy at Salisbury between Hubert Walter and Herbert Poore (ibid., 3), since on 18 Jan. 1197 the latter admitted and instituted the same clerk, styled Stephen son of Adam, in similar terms without reference to the archdn's action (*EEA* 18, no. 233; Kemp, 'Archdeacons and parish churches', 363).

246. *Notification that he has approved the form of the perpetual vicarage in the church of St Paul in the town of Malmesbury, namely, that whoever shall be received into the same, at the presentation of the abbot and monks of Malmesbury, shall pay to the abbey's sacrist six marks of silver annually.*   [20 Apr. 1193 × 1198]

> B = PRO, E164/24 (Malmesbury cartulary), fo. 173r, cap. 109. s. xiii ex. C = BL,
> Lansdowne ms 417 (Malmesbury cartulary), fo. 73r (67r). ss. xiv ex.–xv in.
> Pd from B, *Reg. Malmesburiense*, i, 440, cap. 109.

Universis ad quos presens scriptum pervenerit Willelmus de Sancte Marie Ecclesia de Wyltisir'[a] archidiaconus, salutem in domino. Noverit universitas vestra nos in hanc formam perpetuam vicariam in ecclesia beati Pauli, que est in villa de Malm', admisisse: ut quicumque in eam, ad presentationem abbatis et monachorum de Malm', susceptus fuerit reddet annuatim sacriste ecclesie sancti Aldhelmi vi. marcas argenti.

> *a* Wiltesir' C

Date as for wider limits of no. 245. This arrangement was no doubt a consequence of Pope Celestine III's grant in 1191 that, when St Paul's became vacant, the abbey might appropriate it 'to the lights of the abbey church' (*Reg. Malmesburiense*, i, 374–5).

Mr Richard Grosseteste

247. *Mandate to W., [rural] dean of Malmesbury, to induct the prior of Bradenstoke into corporal possession of the* personatus *of the church of Seagry, in accordance with the tenor of letters of Mr T(homas) of Chobham, the bishop's official, which he sends to the dean.*   [Jan. 1199 × 1216]

> B = BL, Cotton ms Vitellius A xi (Bradenstoke cartulary), fo. 81v (78v). s. xiv med. C =
> BL, Stowe ms 925 (Bradenstoke cartulary), fo. 68v. s. xiv ex.
> Pd (calendar) from B and C, *Bradenstoke Cartulary*, 69, no. 171.

R. archidiaconus Wiltes' dilecto sibi in Cristo W. decano Malmesbir',[a] salutem in domino. Mandamus vobis quatinus accedatis ad ecclesiam de Segre et priorem de Bradenestok'[b] in corporalem possessionem personatus eiusdem ecclesie inducatis, secundum tenorem literarum magistri T. de Cobbeham officialis domini episcopi nobis directarum, quas vobis inspiciendas transmittimus. Val' et c'.

> *a* Malmesbur' C   *b* Bradenestoke C

The archdn's predecessor was elected bp of London, 7 Dec. 1198 (*Fasti Salisbury*, 35), and he himself first occurs as archdn, 6 Jan. 1199 (*EEA* 19, 396). Thomas of Chobham (later subdean of Salisbury) was still bp Herbert Poore's official in Nov. 1215, but had been succeeded by another before bp Herbert's death, *c.* 7 Jan. 1217 (*EEA* 18, lxxvii). His letter to the archdn states that the bp has admitted the prior to the *personatus* of Seagry church, from which he will receive 40s annually, and orders the archdn to cause him to be inducted (*Bradenstoke Cartulary*, no. 169; see also no. 168).

DIOCESE OF WINCHESTER

Archdeaconry of Surrey

Mr Amicius

248. *Notification that, having inspected the charters of Savaric, archdeacon of Northampton [above, no. 151], the chapter of Salisbury, and Richard, late bishop of Winchester, he has confirmed the vicarage of the church of Godalming to Richard, clerk of Chiddingfold; and notification of the appurtenances of the vicarage, as discovered by inquiry in the [rural] chapter of Guildford, viz., the altar of the church with the graveyard, all kinds of obventions of the altar, all lesser tithes, all demesne tithes of the parson, the* redecime decimarum, *a messuage and curtilage, half a mark from the chapel of Hurtmore and half an acre of meadow in* Estmede.

[c. 1191 × prob. 20 Sept. 1192; poss. × Sept. 1215]

B = Trowbridge, Wiltshire R.O., D1/1/1 (Register of St Osmund), fo. 42v (p. 84). s. xiii in.
Pd, *Reg. S. Osm.,* i, 300–1.

Universis Cristi fidelibus ad quos presens scriptum pervenerit A. archidiaconus Surr', salutem. Noverit universitas vestra nos, inspecta carta Savarici archidiaconi Norhamton' de concessione vicarie ecclesie de Godelm(ing') quam fecit Ricardo clerico de Chidingef(aud'),[a] inspecta quoque carta capituli Sar' ecclesie hoc idem confirmantis, inspecta etiam carta bone memorie Ricardi quondam Winton' episcopi de confirmatione eiusdem vicarie, eandem vicariam cum omnibus ad eam pertinentiis[b] memorato R. clerico presenti carta nostra confirmasse, sicut carte predicte testantur. Sicut autem ex testimonio capituli de Gudeford' diligenti inquisitione facta plenius accepimus, hec sunt pertinentia ad vicariam ecclesie de Godelm': scilicet totum altare eiusdem ecclesie cum cimiterio et obventionibus altaris omnimodis et omnes minute decime, omnes quoque decime de dominio persone eiusdem ecclesie, et redecime decimarum et mesagium iuxta portam cimiterii cum curtillagio, et dimidam marcam argenti de capella de Hertmer' et dimidiam acram prati in Estmede. Quod ne futuris temporibus cuique veniat in dubium, presentis scripti munimine et sigilli nostri appositione duximus confirmandum. Test(ibus) et c'. *Addition:* Sigillum A. archidiaconi Surr'.

a For expansion, see above, no. 150   *b Sic; ? rectius pertinentibus*

After Amicius became archdn, *c.* 1191 × 5 Jan. 1192 (*Fasti Monastic Cathedrals*, 94; cf. *EEA* VIII, lvii and n. 18), and probably before Savaric, archdn of Northampton, was consecrated bp of Bath (*Fasti Lincoln*, 31); but the later terminus may possibly be the end of Amicius's archdnry, Jan. × Sept. 1215 (*Fasti Monastic Cathedrals*, 94; *EEA* IX, p. 175). The chapel of Hurtmore, in Godalming, is now lost (*VCH Surrey*, iii, 42).

249. *Notification that the prior and canons of St Mary, Southwark, have paid him all the debt which they owed him, and he has quitclaimed them of all debt.*

[*c.* 1191 × Sept. 1215]

   B = Northampton, Northamptonshire R.O., Montagu (Boughton) ms 87 (Fraunceys
      Register of Peterborough abbey: 'Registrum Fratris Georgii Fraunceys Sacriste'
      1404), p. 65. s. xv in.

Universis sancte matris ecclesie filiis ad quos littere iste pervenerint A. archidiaconus Surr', salutem in vero salutari. Noverit universitas [vestra]*ᵃ* priorem et canonicos sancte Marie de Suthwerk' michi omne debitum quod debebant persolvisse et plenarie satisfecisse, me etiam eos omnino quietos ab omni debito clamasse; ita etiam quod nec ego nec aliquis ex parte mea aliquod debitum de cetero ab eis possit exigere. Et ut hoc ratum et stabile sit imperpetuum, presens scriptum sigilli mei munimine corroboravi.*ᵇ* Hiis testibus: domino Symone capellano, Willelmo Alemanum,*ᶜ* Iohanne serviente domini episcopi, Thoma clerico, Radulfo clerico de Micham, Ricardo Tapinell', Gileberto Coco, et aliis.

   a Supplied   b Reading uncertain   c Final syllable uncertain

While Amicius was archdn (see above, no. 248n.). The folios in this section of the register are headed 'Paston' (Northants, now Cambs), to which chapel Amicius was presented by Peterborough abbey (*EEA* IX, 173–4). For other dealings between the archdn and Southwark priory, concerning the recovery of property held of the archdn needed for the rebuilding of St Thomas's hospital, Southwark, after the fire of July 1212, see *St Thomas's Chartulary*, nos. 17, 219; *EEA* IX, nos. 56–7.

250. *Notification that, by grant of B(enedict), late abbot of Peterborough, and the convent, he had certain tithes, anciently belonging to the almonry of Peterborough, namely, two thirds of the corn tithes of the whole parish of the chapel of Paston and two parts of the third sheaf of the tithes of four knights and two franklins [all named], all of which he had long before he acquired the chapel of Paston by their gift.*

[Oct. 1193 × Sept. 1215]

   B = Northampton, Northamptonshire R.O., Montagu (Boughton) ms 87 (Fraunceys
      Register – see no. 249), p. 66. s. xv in.

Universis Cristi fidelibus presens scriptum inspecturis A. archidiaconus Surr', salutem in domino. Noverit universitas vestra me, ex concessione bone memorie B. quondam abbatis Burgi et eiusdem loci conventus, habuisse et percepisse duas garbas*ᵃ* totius parochie capelle de Paston' et duas partes tertie garbe decimarum iiii.ᵒʳ militum, Yvonis videlicet de Gunethorp', Ascelini de Paston', Roberti Peverel, Roberti Grip, et duorum frankelanorum, Alurici scilicet de Wyderington' et Odonis de Wyderington', ad elemosinariam Burgi ab antiquo pertinentes, diu antequam ex eorundem dono capellam de Paston' habuissem. Et in huius rei testimonium huic scripto sigillum meum duxi apponendum. Bene valete.

   a ? insert decime *(cf. no. 251)*

While Amicius was archdn, but after Abbot Benedict's death, 25 or 29 Sept. 1193, poss. 1194 (above, no. 248n.; *Heads*, 61). These tithes were among the possessions confirmed to the almonry of Peterborough by King John in 1199 (*Rot. Chart.*, 32; *Northants Charters*, 46–7, no. 16).

251. *Notification in terms very similar to the preceding, but adding that he held the tithes of the almonry of Peterborough for an annual payment, and specifying that the tithes did not belong to the chapel of Paston.* [Oct. 1193 × Sept. 1215]

B = Cambridge University Lib., Peterborough, D. & C. Lib., ms 1 (Swaffham's Register), fo. ccxlix v. s. xiii med. C = Northampton, Northamptonshire R.O., Montagu (Boughton) ms 87 (Fraunceys Register – see no. 249), p. 66. s. xv in.

Omnibus Cristi fidelibus presens scriptum *ᵃ*visuris vel audituris*ᵃ* A. archidiaconus Surr', salutem in domino. Noverit universitas*ᵇ* vestra me, ex concessione bone memorie B. quondam abbatis Burgi et eiusdem loci conventus, habuisse et tenuisse*ᶜ* de elemosinaria Burgi sub annuo censu quasdam decimas, scilicet duas garbas decime totius parochie cappelle*ᵈ* de Paston' et duas partes tertie garbe decimarum iiii. militum, Yvonis scilicet de Gunetorp,*ᵉ* Ascelini de Paston', Roberti Peverel et Roberti Grip, et duorum frankelanorum, Aylrici*ᶠ* scilicet de Witherinton'*ᵍ* et Odonis de Witherinton', que de iure ad elemosinariam Burgi pertinent*ʰ* ab antiquo. Istas vero decimas diu antequam ex dono predictorum abbatis et conventus cappellam*ⁱ* de Paston' habuissem tenui, quia non spectant ad eandem cappellam.*ʲ* Et in huius rei testimonium huic scripto sigillum meum apposui.*ᵏ* Hiis testibus.

a–a inspecturis *C; the same word crossed through in B*		*b Interlined in B*
c concessisse *C*	*d (and later as appropriate)* capelle *C*	*e* Gunthorp' *C*
f Alrici *C*	*g* Witherington' *C*	*h Placed after* antiquo *C*
i cappelam *B*	*j Insert* de Paston' *C*	*k C ends*

Date as for no. 250. This is clearly a fuller and more satisfactory text than no. 250.

ARCHDEACONRY OF WINCHESTER

Roger I

252. *Grant to Prior G(uy) and the canons of Southwick that all their churches and chapels be free and quit of archdeacon's aid, payable by ancient custom at Christmas and Easter, namely, the churches of Porchester, Portsea, West Boarhunt, Nutley, [Preston] Candover and Wanstead, and the chapels of Empshott, Wymering and Walesworth, and, if it should come into their hands, the church of Shalden; grant also that the parish church of Southwick be free and quit of synodals as well as of archdeacon's aid; and that the canons may preach freeely in their parish of Portsea and receive the oblations, both on sea and on land. For this the canons will pay him twelve shillings annually, saving his hospitality, procurations and other customs in these churches.* [c. 1180 × 1208]

B = Winchester, Hampshire R.O., 1M54/1 (Southwick Priory Register 1), fo. 13v. ss. xii ex.–xiii in.

Pd (calendar), *Southwick Cartularies*, i, 47, no. I 83.

Sciant omnes ad quos presens scriptum pervenerit quod ego Rogerus Winton' archidiaconus divino intuitu concessi G. priori ecclesie de Suwic' et canonicis ibidem deo servientibus ut omnes ecclesie et capelle eorum, scilicet ecclesia de Porc', ecclesia de Portesia, *ᵃecclesia de Westburh',ᵃ* ecclesia de Nuthleia, ecclesia de Candevra, et capella de Ymbesiet', capella de Wimering', capella de Waleswrth', ecclesia de Wanested', libere sint et quiete a donis archidiaconi, que ex antiqua consuetudine in terminis Natalis et Pasche ab ipsis ecclesiis et capellis solvebantur; quod, si ecclesiam de Scaldeden' in manus eorum incidere contigerit, sub eadem libertate concludatur. Concessi etiam illis gratia loci religiosi ut parrochialis ecclesia de Suwic' libera sit et quieta a synodalibus et a predictis donis. Indulsi etiam quantum ad me spectat eisdem canonicis ut libere possint predicare in parrochia sua de Portes' et oblationes accipere tam in mari quam in terra. Ipsi vero canonici, in memoriam huius beneficii et pro hac concessione, solvent michi xii. solidos annuatim in duobus terminis, scilicet in festo sancti Michaelis vi. solidos et in Pascha vi. solidos. Hanc siquidem feci prefatis canonicis concessionem, salvis hospitiis meis et hospitiorum procurationibus et aliis consuetudinibus meis in prenominatis ecclesiis. Ut autem hec mea concessio firma et inconcussa permaneat, eam sigilli mei munimine duxi roborandam. Testibus: Audoeno decano, magistro Iohanne de Hechfeld', Radulfo clerico, Willelmo capellano, magistro Simone medico, Ricardo camerario, Henrico de Heling', Rogero de Montechan' clerico, Waltero clerico,ᵇ Ricardo de Limesia, Willelmo capellano eiusdem archidiaconi, Henrico de Burh', Henrico de Eling'.

a–a Interlined   *b The remainder is written on the next line, though over half the previous line is empty*

Roger's predecessor died before Sept. 1180, and Roger first occurs before 1181 (*Fasti Monastic Cathedrals*, 92); he last occurs Feb. 1206 and died Mar. 1207 or 1208 (*EEA* IX, 169). Guy, prior of Southwick, first occurs 1185 × 1187, but his predecessor, Philip, does not certainly occur after Aug. 1177 (*Heads*, 184). This rare and interesting act, releasing the priory's churches and chapels from ecclesiastical dues, may be compared with that of Savaric, archdn of Northampton, freeing a church and chapel of Canons Ashby from *cathedraticum* and other exactions and customs (above, no. 152). The problem involving Shalden church was that, although it was probably given by the priory's founder before his death in *c.* 1148, its possession was disputed by the de Mauduit family; nevertheless, William Mauduit III and his younger brother, Robert, each gave the church to the priory, the latter in a notification to Richard of Ilchester, bp of Winchester (*Southwick Cartularies*, i, nos. I 18 n. 3, I 111, I 31; E. Mason, 'The Mauduits and their Chamberlainship of the Exchequer', 18–19, App. IV, and see also 3, 6–7); it may be that the present act was given at a time when the Mauduit hold had not yet been finally extinguished. Walesworth 'church', which was already poor in 1291, was annexed to Widley church in 1426 (*Southwick Cartularies*, i, pp. liv–lv, n. 87; ii, no. III 1013). Wanstead church no longer exists.

DIOCESE OF WORCESTER

Archdeaconry of Gloucester

Gervase

253. *Settlement of the dispute between Prior William and the canons of Llanthony and the archdeacon over the tithes of the demesne at Southam and Sapperton, reached with the assent of Simon, bishop of Worcester, and Roger, earl of Hereford; namely, that all tithes of the demesne of Southam shall remain quit to Llanthony priory, and the tithe of Sapperton shall remain quit to the church of [Bishops] Cleeve and to the archdeacon and his successors.* [3 Sept. 1148 × 1150]

B = PRO, C115/K2/6683 (Llanthony cartulary), fo. 129v, vi, no. 62. s. xiv med.

Notum sit fidelibus Cristi presentibus et futuris dissensionem que fuit inter Willelmum priorem et canonicos de Lanthon' et Gervasium archidiaconum Gloec', videlicet de decimis dominii apud Sutham et Sapertonam quas utrinque calumpniabant, hoc amicorum consilio compositionis modo sedatam esse. Ab utraque parte spontanee concessum est quod ecclesie de Lanth' remanebit in perpetuum quieta decima de dominio de Sutham tota tam in blado quam in aliis rebus, de dominio videlicet quod tunc dominium erat, perempta deinceps calumpnia Gervasii et successorum eius. Ecclesie vero de Cliva et Gervasio ac successoribus eius remanebit decima de Sapertona prorsus quieta, perempta similiter deinceps calumpnia canonicorum tam illius decime quam aliarum possessionum omnium ad ius ecclesie de Cliva tunc pertinentium. Factum est hoc assensu domini Symonis Wygorniensis episcopi et Rogeri comitis Hereford', eodem episcopo compositionem hanc anathematis sententia confirmante, ne quis eam temere violare presumat, nisi forsitan utriusque partis spontaneo fuerit assensu mutata. Huius rei testes sunt: episcopi Robertus Bathon', Ylarius Cicestrensis, Gislebertus Hereford', Nicholaus Landav' et alii.[a]

a Ms aliis

After the consecration of Gilbert Foliot as bp of Hereford (Morey and Brooke, *Gilbert Foliot and his Letters*, 97), and before the death of Simon, bp of Worcester (*Fasti Monastic Cathedrals*, 99).

Matthew of Bayeux

254. *Gift in pure alms to the priory of Saint-Etienne de Plessis[-Grimould] of two tenements of land at Bayeux.* [1165 × 1178]

A = Caen, A-D Calvados, H non coté, 8/1. Endorsed: Matheus archid' (? s. xii ex.); de duabus man[suris] (? s. xiv); also post-medieval. Size: 123 × 123 mm (lower part damaged). Seal: no trace of turn-up or sealing left.

Universis sancte matris ecclesie fidelibus Matheus de Baiocis archidiaconus Glowecestrie, salutem. Noscat universitas vestra me dedisse ecclesie sancti Stephani de Peiss' duas mansuras terre apud Baiocas in remissionem peccatorum meorum et in remissionem patris mei et matris mee et Willelmi Anglici, in puram elemosinam perpetualiter tenendas, una scilicet mansuram que est iuxta domum Patricii archidiaconi et aliam mansuram quam Walchelinus camerarius emit ab Algoto Wetca et dedit prefato Willelmo nepoti suo et quam inde Willelmus dedit Galfrido servienti suo, a quo eandem mansuram legittime emi. Hii sunt testes: dominus Henricus Baioc' episcopus, et dominus Arn(ulfus) Lex' episcopus, et Rotb(ertus) subdecanus, et [   ]*a* [t]hesaurarius Lex' ecclesie, et Iohannes et Rotb(ertus) [   ].*a* Valete.

   a Ms torn or gnawed

After the consecration of Henry de Beaumont, dean of Salisbury, as bp of Bayeux (*Fasti Salisbury*, 9; *Foliot Letters and Charters*, 530), and before the archdn's death, 1177/8 (*Fasti Monastic Cathedrals*, 107). This is the only known source for the archdn's full name. Patrick the archdn witnessed a charter of Philip, bp of Bayeux, Henry's predecessor (*CDF*, 176, no. 496). The treasurer of Lisieux at this time was Silvester (*Arnulf of Lisieux*, lvi–lviii).

Mr William of Northolt

255.   *Gift to his servant, Robert Simple, of two hides of land of his inheritance in Cowley which belonged to Hugh of Colham, his grandfather, and to Hugh's son, Richard, his uncle, to be held in fee and inheritance by Robert and his heirs of the archdeacon and his heirs, by rendering to the abbot and convent of Westminster the service due, and to the archdeacon and his heirs one bezant annually.*

[15 May 1177 × 21 Sept. 1186]

   A = Westminster Abbey Muniments, no. 381. Endorsed: Covele (s. xiii); Carta Willelmi de Norhale archidiaconi Glouc' [de ii. hidis terre *interlined*] Roberto Simplici concessis (s. xiii ex.); Dupplicatur (s. xiii ex.); .j. (s. xiii ex.); Celar' (s. xiv). Size: 178 × 133 + 23 mm. Seal in black wax on plaited dark grey cords, pointed oval, 58 × 37 mm, repaired (original part *c.* 45 × 30 mm); obverse, frontally seated Virgin and Child, the latter on Virgin's right knee facing to front; to Virgin's right, suppliant kneeling on one knee: legend: + SIGILLVM WILLELMI ARCHIDIACONI GLOEC'; reverse plain.
   B = Ibid., Book 11 (Westminster Abbey Domesday), fo. 446r (459r). s. xiv in. C = Ibid., no. 371 (paper, inaccurate copy from B). s. xvi.[1]
   Pd from A and B, *Westminster Abbey Charters*, 289–91, no. 453.

Willelmus de Norhall'*a* archidiaconus Gloecestrie*b* omnibus amicis suis tam Francis quam Anglis,*c* salutem. Notum vobis facio me dedisse et hac presenti carta mea confirmasse Roberto Simplici servienti meo pro servitio suo duas hidas terre in Coveleia de hereditate mea, que fuerunt Hugonis de Coleham avi mei et Ricardi filii eiusdem Hugonis avunculi mei, in feudo et hereditate ei et heredibus suis post eum de me et heredibus meis tenendas ita libere et quiete et honorifice in bosco et plano, in viis et semitis, in pratis et pascuis, in aquis et in omnibus aliis locis, sicuti predecessores mei unquam melius et liberius tenuerunt, *d*faciendo inde omne servitium quod de eadem terra debetur*d* abbati et conventui ecclesie beati Petri de Westmonasterio, et preterea persolvet idem Robertus et heredes sui michi et heredibus meis in recognitionem iuris mei quod habeo in predicta terra singulis annis unum bisantium*e* infra*f* octabas sancti Michaelis. His testibus: Hugone de Ov, David de Iarponvill',*g* Osberto de Senleia, Rogero de Messendene,*h* Angoto *i*Duredent, Godefrido*i* de Tokinton',

Waltero [j]de Greneford', Rogero de la Dune,[k] Radulfo de Tokinton', Waltero[j] Duredent, Godefrido de Benchesham, Hamone de Roxeie, Hugone fratre eius,[l] Radulfo de Prestune, [m]Godefrido de Prestune,[m] Adam de Greneford', Iacobo, Ranulfo,[n] Adam de Essexe, Alexandro, Waltero et Ligerio servientibus meis, et multis aliis.

a Norhale B,C	b Gloucest' B,C	c Anglicis B,C	d–d reddendo
inde xxx. solidos pro omnibus servitiis B,C		e bizantium *followed by* vel duos	
solidos B,C	f Om. in B,C	g Gerponvill' B,C	h Messinden' B,C
i–i Om. in C	j–j Om. in C	k Doune B	l Om. in B,C
m–m Om. in B,C	n Ranulpho C		

After William became archdn, in 1177 (after 15 May) or 1178, and before his consecration as bp of Worcester, having been elected *c.* 25 May 1186 (*Fasti Monastic Cathedrals,* 107, 100). The variant readings at *d–d* and *e* should be noted; they may suggest either that the compiler of the Westminster Domesday had a different original before him or (perhaps) that he amended the text in line with other information available to him.

[l] The variants which this copy shares with that in the Westminster Domesday indicate that it was copied from the latter.

Mr Robert of Inglesham

256. *Notification that he has confirmed to his friend and colleague, Ernisius the chaplain, the vicarage of the chapel of Hardwicke, to which he has been presented to the archdeacon by the abbot of Gloucester.* [14 Oct. 1186 × Sept. 1191]

B = Gloucester, D. & C. Muniments, Register B (Gloucester cartulary), p. 179. s. xiv ex.

Omnibus sancte matris ecclesie filiis ad quos presens scriptum pervenerit R. de Inglesham Glouc' archidiaconus, salutem in domino. Noverit universitas vestra nos confirmasse dilecto amico et socio nostro Ernisio capellano vicariam capelle de Heredewyca cum omnibus ad eandem vicariam pertinentibus, secundum formam instrumenti abbatis Glouc' qui eundem nobis ad vicariam illam presentavit. Testibus hiis: magistro Iordano de Wykewan,[a] magistro Petro de Inglesham, et aliis.

a Sic; ? *rectius* Wykewar

Robert's predecessor was consecrated bp of Worcester, Sept. 1186; Robert occurs without title, 14 Oct. 1186, and first as archdn, Feb. 1187; his successor was in office by Sept. 1191 at the latest (*Fasti Monastic Cathedrals,* 107–8). The abbot of Gloucester was Thomas (Carbonel), 1179–1205 (*Heads,* 53), whose charter granting the vicarage to Ernisius, with the consent of the parson of Standish, was inspected by William (of Northolt), bp of Worcester (*Gloucester Cartulary,* i, 336–7; Gloucester, D. & C. Muniments, Register B, pp. 178–9, with witnesses, including Peter, archdn of Worcester; wrongly attributed to bp William of Blois in *EEA* 13, no. 10); the abbot's charter describes Ernisius as chaplain to William, bp of Worcester, thereby explaining the archdn's claiming him as a friend and colleague. For the presentation of prospective incumbents to archdns, see Kemp, 'Informing the archdeacon', 138 and n. 31.

Mr Richard II

257. *Notification that, at the presentation of Abbot Richard and the convent of Cirencester, he has admitted and canonically instituted Henry son of G(eoffrey) fitz P(eter), clerk, as parson in the church of Preston, the see of Worcester being vacant, saving an annual pension of forty shillings to Cirencester abbey.*

[May 1190 × 27 May 1199]

B = Bodl. ms Dep. C. 392 (Cirencester cartulary, Registrum A), fo. 111r (102r, p. 221). s. xiii med.
Pd, *Cirencester Cartulary*, ii, 339, no. 376.

Universis sancte matris ecclesie filiis ad quos presens scriptum pervenerit Ricardus Glouc' archidiaconus, salutem in domino. Noverit universitas vestra*a* quod nos, ad presentationem domini Ricardi abbatis et conventus Cyr', Henricum clericum filium G. filii P, ad ecclesiam de Preston' cum omnibus pertinentiis suis, salva annua pensione xl. solidorum ecclesie Cyr', vacante sede Wygornensi admisimus et eum in predicta ecclesia personam canonice instituimus. Et ut hoc in posterum ratum et inconcussum permaneat, sigilli nostri munimine corroboravimus. Hiis testibus: Willelmo decano Cyr', Milone de Cernay, magistro G. de Lant', Roberto de Stokes, Roberto clerico nostro, Henrico capellano nostro, Waltero persona de Colesburn', Roberto capellano de Preston', et multis aliis.

a Interlined

After the death of William of Northolt, bp of Worcester, 2 or 3 May 1190, his successor not being consecrated until 5 May 1191 (*Fasti Monastic Cathedrals*, 100); and before Geoffrey fitzPeter was created earl of Essex (*Complete Peerage*, v, 124). Richard first occurs as archdn, May × Sept. 1191, and died in 1200 (*Fasti Monastic Cathedrals*, 108), during which period there were four vacancies at Worcester (ibid., 100).

ARCHDEACONRY OF WORCESTER

Mr Godfrey

258. *Notification of the settlement before him in his chapter, on delegation from the archbishop of Canterbury, of the dispute between the canons of Cirencester and Osbert, clerk of Hatherley, over certain tithes of an assart belonging to Cheltenham; namely, that Osbert has admitted that the tithes belong to Cirencester abbey, from which he will hold them for life for an annual pension of two pounds of incense.* [1144 × 1168]

B = Bodl. ms Dep. C. 392 (Cirencester cartulary, Registrum A), fo. 121r (112r, p. 241). s. xiii med. C = Bodl. ms Dep. C. 393 (Cirencester cartulary, Registrum B), fo. 110v. s. xiv ex.
Pd, *Cirencester Cartulary*, ii, 375, no. 417.

Universis sancte matris ecclesie filiis et fidelibus Godefridus Wigorn' archidiaconus, salutem et orationes in domino. Quoniam solent sepenumero diuturnitate sua tempora temporibus rerum labentium*a* memoriam adimere, gestis nostri temporis litterarum nostrarum remedio consulendum esse decrevimus. Notum itaque presentibus facimus et ad maiorem ut ita dicam perpetuitatem quasi presentium manu posteritati porigimus quod controversia quedam inter canonicos Cirenc' et Osbertum clericum de Hatherleya versabatur super decimis quibusdam quas ipse habuerat de exsarto ad Chiltham pertinente. Ea autem congnitioni*b* nostre a domino Cantuar' delegata in facie capituli nostri in perpetuum est amicabili fine sopita.*c* Prenominatus enim Osbertus, in iure confessus quod decime ille sunt de iure Cirenc' ecclesie, eas a domino abbate Cirenc'*d* sub annua pencione duarum librarum thuris in vita sua tenendas suscepit, nisi infra sese religioni contulerit. Novissime vero, quoniam de pace in posterum volebamus esse securi, in presentia nostra et assessorum*e* nostrorum debita quadam solempnitate iuratoriam prestitit cautionem quod amodo predicte ecclesie et fratribus inibi deo servientibus et in decimis illis et in pencionis*f* solutione in alio tamen sic, et in alio sic, semet ipsum fidelem exiberet.*g* Testibus hiis.

a libencium *C*   *b* cognitioni *C*   *c* sapita *C*   *d* Cyrencestr' *C*
e *Altered from* antecessorum *B*   *f* pensionis *C*   *g* exhiberet *C*

After Godfrey's appointment as archdn in or after 1144 and before his death in 1167 × 1168, although he presumably did not hold office between his predecessor's restoration as archdn, by 1157, and the latter's death, *c.* 1158 × 1159 (*Fasti Monastic Cathedrals*, 105). It is not clear that the assart belonged specifically to the *church* of Cheltenham, as the heading of *Cirencester Cartulary*, ii, no. 417, states, but it evidently fell within the parish of Cirencester's church of Cheltenham.

259. *Notification to Pope A. [Anastasius IV, Adrian IV or Alexander III] that the original of the [enclosed] copy of a writing, in favour of the abbot and convent of Pershore, bears three seals — of King Edgar, Dunstan, archbishop of Canterbury, and Ælfhere, ealdorman of Mercia.*

[12 July 1153 × 1168; ? 31 July 1160 × 23 Aug. 1164]

A = BL, Cotton ms Augustus ii, no. 7. Endorsed: none medieval; Hic A. fuit Alexander 3 tempore Henrici 2*i* Galfridus Archidiaconus Wigorn' . . . . [etc.] (note by Cotton). Size 235 × 72 mm. Seal: no sign of sealing.
B = Cambridge, Corpus Christi College, ms 111 (Bath cartulary with additions), fo. 135r. s. xvi.

Reverentissimo*a* domino et patri A. summo pontifici minimus sanctitatis sue*b* servus Godefridus dictus Guigorniensis*c* archidiaconus, offerre domino incensum dignum in odorem suavitatis. Inter cetera virtutum indumenta que decent servum bonum et fidelem, presertim coram domino suo, valde necessarium estimo sinceritatis et veritatis ornamentum. Si quis enim huiuscemodi vestem nuptialem non habuerit,[1] non intromittetur ad nuptias, set eicietur foras[2] nec ascendet superius, ut sit honor ei coram simul discumbentibus, quia qui sine veritate est patrifamilias placere non potest. Ego itaque, ut tamen non loquatur os meum opera hominum, huius rei gratia veritatis emulator existens, ad veritatem vocatus, veritati testimonium perhibeo,*d* ut ex temporali veritatis exequtione*e* ab eo qui veritas est veritatem mereamini*f* mercedis eterne. Noverit itaque sanctitas vestra verum esse quod contrascripti*g* huius scriptum originale in virtute sancte Trinitatis sigilla tria trium personarum autenticarum ad veritatem triplici confirmatione commendant. Est autem sigillum primum illustris regis Edgari, secundum Dunstani Cantuariensis archiepiscopi, tercium Alferi ducis Merciorum, sicut ex diligenti litterarum*h* impressarum inspectione evidenter accepi. Operetur igitur, si vobis placet, filię vestrę sanctę Persoriensis ęcclesię detrimentum intolerabile, operetur inquam infra pietatis paterne viscera compassionem, compassio restitutionem, restitutio consolationem, et quę ex toto fere defecit, quia non erat qui adiuvaret, nunc nunc tandem cum acceperitis tempus iustitias iudicandi, sentiat prophetam esse in Israel,[1] eoque efficatius, quoniam et domnus[j] abbas et ceteri fratres inibi deo servientes per vitę quę coram deo est sanctitatem etiam ab hiis qui foris sunt testimonii sani meruere celebritatem. Valeat in perpetuum sanctitas vestra.

a Reverendissimo *B*	*b* tue *B*	*c* Wigornensis *B*	*d* exhibeo *B*
e executione *B*	*f* meriamini *B*	*g* conscripti *B*	*h* literarum *B*
i Israell *B*	*j* dominus *B*		

After the election or coronation of pope Anastasius IV and before the archdn's death (*Fasti Monastic Cathedrals*, 105), but excluding the period when his predecessor was restored (see above, no. 258n.); possibly during the vacancy at Worcester between bps Alfred and Roger (*Fasti Monastic Cathedrals*, 99). The supposed but probably spurious charter of Edgar for Pershore abbey (Cotton Augustus ii, 6; Sawyer, *AS Charters*, no. 786), to which the archdn's letter was attached in the 16th century (see Cambridge, Corpus Christi College, ms 111, fo. 135r), appears to have had three slits cut in its lower margin and later repaired. It is most unlikely, however, that seals would have been attached in this way to a tenth-century charter, but rather, if used at all, would have been employed to close and literally seal the document; see T. A. Heslop, 'English seals from the mid ninth century to 1100', esp. 2, 14–16. A bronze seal matrix of an ealdorman or thane of the later 9th century is known (ibid., 4–5 and plate IJ); and for a 12th-century forged seal of archbp Dunstan on a Westminster document, see T. A. Heslop, 'Twelfth-century forgeries as evidence for earlier seals', esp. 301–6 and plate 53. The precise nature of the archdn's involvement in the present case is unclear, but his letter provides a valuable insight into how pre-Conquest charters could be used in the 12th century, for help on which I am grateful to Professor Simon Keynes.

[1] 'vestem nuptialem non habuerit': cf. Matth. 22: 11.
[2] 'eicietur foras': cf. John 9: 34.

260. *Notification that the dispute between the canons of St Mary and All Saints, Warwick, and the canons of St Sepulchre's [Warwick] over parochial rights and a pension of thirty pence has been settled by himself and Gilbert, bishop of Hereford, judges-delegate of Pope Alexander [III], in favour of the canons of St Mary and All Saints, whom they have invested with the same; and that afterwards the latter, at the judges' request, have granted in person to Ralph, prior of St Sepulchre's, for as long as he remains prior, the parochial fruits, excluding baptism and sepulture, for an annual pension of ten shillings in addition to the payment of thirty pence.*

[prob. late 1161 × early 1162]

B = PRO, E164/22 (St Mary's Warwick cartulary), fo. 21r (20r), no. 30. s. xv med.

Universis sancte matris ecclesie filiis et fidelibus G. Guigorn' archidiaconus, salutem. Notum facio universitati vestre quod causam illam que vertebatur inter canonicos sancte Marie et Omnium Sanctorum de Warewich' et canonicos sancti Sepulcri super iure parochiali et xxx. denariorum pensione dominus papa Alexander domino Gilleberto Herefordensi episcopo et michi remoto appellationis subterfugio fine debito terminandam delegavit. Nos igitur, mandato apostolico pro debito obtemperantes, utriusque partis allegationibus patienter auditis et diligenter intellectis, veritatem et iustitiam canonicorum sancte Marie et Omnium Sanctorum, partim ex habundanti testium probatione, partim ex fideli instrumentorum inspectione, concipientes, eis et parochiam et annuam xxx. denariorum pensionem adiudicavimus et eos inde in publico apostolica auctoritate investivimus. Postmodum vero predicti canonici sancte Marie et Omnium Sanctorum, nostra interveniente petitione, persone Radulfi prioris non ecclesie sancti Sepulcri, salvo per omnia iure suo, fructus parochiales excepto baptismate et mortuorum sepultura pro annua x. solidorum pensione, et hoc supra pretaxatam xxx. denariorum solutionem, ad tempus indulserunt, scilicet quamdiu in ecclesia sancti Sepulcri gereret prioratum. Valete.

The act of the two judges-delegate is *Foliot Letters and Charters*, no. 345, q.v. for discussion of the date. Gilbert Foliot issued a separate act relating to the grant to Prior Ralph of St Sepulchre's, matching the present act of the archdn, and also a mandate to the archdn to instruct the (rural) dean to see that the agreement was implemented (ibid., nos. 346–7). The background to the dispute lies in the years 1125 × 1135, when bp Simon of Worcester had consecrated a cemetery at St Sepulchre's, within the parish of All Saints' and St Mary's, and reserved to the latter parochial rights and an annual payment of 30d from St Sepulchre's (*Mon. Ang.*, vi (1), 602, no. 2). See also above, nos. 170–1. Soon after the present settlement Henry II ordered St Sepulchre's to abide by it, and in 1163 × 1166 (poss. 1164) ordered Foliot, now bp of London, and the archdn to enforce its terms (PRO, E164/22, fos. 22v–23r, 22v).

261. *Mandate to Walter of Salford, his dean, to cause Prior Ralph [of St Sepulchre's] to restore to the canons of St Mary and All Saints, Warwick, in his presence and before the clergy of Warwick and the parishioners of St Mary and All Saints, the land for the burial of the wife of Gilbert le Nurric'; and to declare publicly in St Mary's church how the settlement between the two churches was made by the archdeacon and the bishop of Hereford, and to carry out before the people at Warwick the investiture which was made to the canons at Worcester.*

[prob. late 1161 × early 1162]

B = PRO, E164/22 (St Mary's Warwick cartulary), fo. 21v (20v), no. 32. s. xv med.

G. Guigorn' archidiaconus Galtero de Saltford' decano suo, salutem. Mandamus tibi et mandando precipimus quatinus coram clericis de Warew(ich') et parochianis sancte Marie et Omnium Sanctorum facias Radulfum priorem predictis ecclesiis et earum canonicis terram sepulture uxoris Gilleberti le Nurric' in presentia tua pro corpore restituere; et in ecclesia sancte Marie in publico omnibus exponas quomodo lis illa que vertebatur inter duas*a* ecclesias et earum personas a domino Herefordensi et nobis est apostolica auctoritate terminata, et investituram illam que prenominatis canonicis Guigorn' facta fuit eandem eis coram populo Warew(ich') facias. Vale.

a Ms dua

Date as for no. 260.

Mr Simon Luvel

262.   *With R(alph), prior of Worcester, notification that, by the authority of Roger, bishop of Worcester, and at the presentation of Prior A(nsketil) and the convent of Nostell, they have instituted Henry son of Peter of Northampton as parson of the church of Newbold [Pacey]; and that, in their presence publicly at Whitnash, Aytrop Hastang has renounced the* ius advocationis *of the church to the said prior and canons.*

[1167 × 1178; prob. Nov. 1167 × Aug. 1172]

B = BL, Cotton ms Vespasian E xix (Nostell cartulary), fo. 114r–v. s. xiii ex.

R. prior ecclesie Wigorn'[a] et S. eiusdem ecclesie archidiaconus omnibus Cristi fidelibus ad quos presentes litere pervenerint, salutem in domino. Notum sit universitati vestre nos, auctoritate domini Rogeri Wigorn' episcopi qua fungimur, instituisse personam ecclesie de Newebold Henricum filium Petri de Norhamtona per presentationem A. prioris et conventus Sancti Oswaldi de Nostl'. Preterea Aytrop Hastang universo iuri quod dicebatur habere in predicte ecclesie de Neubold advocatione publice in nostra presentia apud [fo. 114v] Wichin' sub fidei religione renuntiavit, et totum ius advocationis prefate ecclesie prenominato priori et fratribus Sancti Oswaldi de Nostl' libere et quiete sine omni reclamatione sui et heredum suorum in perpetuum concessit. Hiis testibus, et c'.

a Ms Wigon'

After the earliest possible date when Simon could have become archdn (*Fasti Monastic Cathedrals*, 105), and before Roger, bp of Worcester, left England for the last time (Cheney, *Roger of Worcester,* 222–3); probably while bp Roger was out of England during the Becket affair (ibid., 35, 54), when the prior of Worcester and the relevant archdn appear to have been entrusted with ecclesiastical business of this kind in the diocese (ibid., 99–100; Kemp, 'Archdeacons and parish churches', 357). Bp Roger subsequently granted the appropriation of the church to Nostell when it should become vacant after the death of Henry son of Peter of Northampton (ibid., 279, no. 48). Newbold Pacey church was given to Nostell by Aytrop's father, Aytrop, temp. Henry I, and later confirmed by the son (cartulary, fo. 114r; *Mon. Ang.,* vi (1), 93; *VCH Warks,* v, 123). For Whitnash, whose church was also given to Nostell, see *Mon. Ang.,* loc. cit.; *Warwickshire Place-Names,* 190.

* 263.   *Institution of Mr Roger in the chapel of Charlecote.*   [1167 × Feb. 1190]

Mentioned only, in the confirmation of the institution by Henry de Soilli, bishop of Worcester (1193–5): BL, Additional ms 47677 (Kenilworth cartulary), fo. 250r–v. s. xvi in.

. . . Notum facimus quod nos, inspecta carta Simonis quondam Wigorn' archidiaconi super institutione facta magistro Rogero de capella de Cherlecota, eandem institutionem ratam . . . [etc.]

After the earliest possible date when Simon could have become archdn, and before his death (*Fasti Monastic Cathedrals*, 105; *Worcester Cartulary,* lxv). This act was of interest to Kenilworth priory because Charlecote owed an annual pension to Wellesbourne church, which belonged to the priory (*VCH Warks,* v, 38, 197).

* 264. *At the presentation of Prior William and the convent of Great Malvern, and by order of B(aldwin), archbishop of Canterbury, the see of Worcester being vacant, admission and institution of Andrew, clerk, as perpetual vicar of St Andrew's church, Pershore.* [May 1185 × 21 Sept. 1186]

> Mentioned only, in the confirmation of the institution by William of Northolt, bishop of Worcester (1186–90): Westminster Abbey Muniments, Book 11 (Westminster Abbey Domesday), fo. 574v. s. xiv in.

. . . . cum ecclesia sancti Andree de Persora vacare contingeret, Willelmus prior et conventus Maioris Malvern', ad quos ius advocationis eiusdem ecclesie pertinere dinoscitur, Andream clericum ad ipsam presentaverunt. Cum autem, B. venerabili decessore nostro ad Cant' archiepiscopum electo, sedes episcopalis tunc temporis vacaret, quia institutiones diocesis nostre ad solos pertinent episcopos, Simon archidiaconus Wygorn' auctoritate et precepto prenominati archiepiscopi ipsum Andream ad prefatam ecclesiam admisit ipsumque pro tempore Wygorn' sede vacante perpetuum vicarium instituit. Nos [*sc.* Bishop William of Northolt] autem prefatam institutionem gratam habentes et acceptam . . . [etc.]

Between Baldwin of Forde's enthronement at Canterbury and the consecration of William of Northolt as bp of Worcester (*Fasti Monastic Cathedrals*, 5, 100). For Prior William of Great Malvern (*c.* 1177–? *c.*1190), who is omitted from *Heads*, 90, see Cheney, *Roger of Worcester*, App. III, 374–6. This is very probably (but not certainly) a reference to a written act.

Mr Peter de Leche

265. *Notification that, on making inquiry in the chapter of Warwick concerning the* personatus *of the church of Loxley, he has learnt from the testimony of the whole chapter that neither Roger Small nor anyone else other than the prior and convent of Kenilworth can claim any* proprietas *in the church.* [1189 × 1198]

> B = BL, Additional ms 47677 (Kenilworth cartulary), fo. 254v. s. xvi in.

Omnibus et c', P. archidiaconus, salutem in vero salutari. Ad universitatis vestre referimus notitiam nos diligenter in capitulo de Warwyk' fecisse inquisitionem super ecclesia de Lokesley utrum Rogerus Parvus aliquod ius in personatu ipsius sive aliquam*[a]* de iure, ut ipse asserit, debeat habere in ea *[b]*administratio-nem.*[b]* Ut autem rei veritas ex atestatione totius capituli nobis propalata vos de merit(is)*[c]* certos redderet, ex asertione prior(um) et maior(um) de capitulo in responsum suscepimus nec nominatum R. nec alterum aliquem*[d]* nisi priorem de Kenell' et eiusdem loci conventum in memorata ecclesia de iur(is)*[c]* ordine aliquam proprietatem posse vendicare, et c'.

a Ms aliqua   *b–b Suggested reading; ms* et ad ministrationem   *c Expansion uncertain   d Ms* aliquam

After Peter became archdn in 1189/90 and before his death, in or before 1198 (*Fasti Monastic Cathedrals*, 105).

* 266.   *'Ordination' of two parts of the church of Feckenham due to the abbot of*
Lire.   [1189 × 1198; ? 5 May 1191 × 1198]

   Listed only, in the Sheen inventory of charters: BL, Cotton ms Otho B xiv, fo. 25v. s.
   xv ex.

Item ordinatio P. archidiaconi Wigorn' super duabus partibus ecclesie de
Fekenham abbati de Lyra debit(is).

The wider dating limits are as for no. 265, but, since the list of charters in the Sheen
inventory appears to be in chronological order, and this item is preceded by another,
reading *Item provisio Roberti Wigorn' episcopi facta super resignacione ecclesie de Fekenham,*
possibly after that bp's consecration (*Fasti Monastic Cathedrals*, 100).

DIOCESE OF YORK

Archdeaconry of Cleveland

Hugh the Chanter (Sottovagina)

267.   *As precentor of York and archdeacon, letter to Prior Roger and the convent of*
Durham concerning the payment of chrism money from parish churches and its
remission by Archbishop Thurstan.   [1137 × prob. 4 July 1139]

   A = Durham University Lib., Durham Cathedral Muniments, 2. 4. Ebor. 6.
       Endorsed: Hugonis Sotewaine de ecclesia de Lythum. Quod nichil ab ea
       exigatur nisi den' crismales (s. xiii). Lethom (s. xiii). 2ᵃ. 4ᵉ. Ebor'. ff i. (s. xiv).
       Size 210 × 35 mm. Seal on tongue, white wax lightly varnished, pointed oval (*c.*
       62 × 50 mm); obverse, frontally seated ecclesiastical figure holding out a cross-
       staff in his right hand and a book in his left; reverse plain; legend:
       SOTTOVAGINE. COG[NOMINE] COGNITVS. HVGO.
   Pd, *Historians of the Church of York,* ed. Raine (RS), vol. ii, pp. xii–xiii; vol. iii, 68, no. 51.

Venerabili fratri Rogero priori et reverendo sancte Dunelmensis ecclesie
conventui Hugo Eboracensis ecclesie cantor et archidiaconus, sic in militia
dei currere per huius vite stadium ut milicie sue bravium accipiant ęterne glorie
premium. Ex antiqua consuetudine nulla parrochialis ecclesia reddebat pecu-
niariam consuetudinem Eborace metropoli nisi tantum vi. denarios, quos ipsi
vocabant denarios crismatis. Tempore Thome senioris archiepiscopi constitutum fuit dare denarios ad sinodum, maxime autem ad auxilium matricis
ecclesie destructe tunc et restaurande. Unde, consultus a presbiteris suis,
Willelmus qui tunc erat Dunelmensis episcopus, vir sapiens et in posterum
providens, interdixit*ᵃ* eis ne quicquam redderent nisi antiquam consuetudinem.
Ita vero extiterunt inde et solute et quiete. Predictos vi. denarios remisit
Turstinus archiepiscopus quia emptio crismatis videbatur. Testimonium perhi-
bui veritati. Nec nos plus quesivimus nec queremus de ecclesiis vestris. Valete.

   a Preceded in ms by a short erasure

After Roger became prior of Durham (*Fasti Monastic Cathedrals*, 33) and before the
probable date of the archdn's death (*EEA* V, 126). The seal is described and illustrated
in *Durham Seals*, no. 3285 and pl. 61.

Ralph Baro

268. *As archdeacon of the church of York, confirmation of the settlement between Rievaulx abbey and the church of Scawton, namely, that Rievaulx will pay to Scawton church twelve pence annually for the tithes of Staintuna and Oswaldesengas; witnessed by the 'universal' chapter at Thirsk.* [1139 × 1158; prob. 1157 × 1158]

B = BL, Cotton ms Julius D i (Rievaulx cartulary), fo. 157v (150v). s. xii ex.
Pd, *Rievaulx Cartulary*, 167, no. 226; *EYC*, iii, 443, no. 1831.

Radulfus Baro Eborac' ęcclesię archidiaconus universis ęcclesię filiis tam presentibus quam futuris, salutem. Ne pacta legitima aut oblivione depereant aut diversa assertione evanescant, quod pro utilitate ęcclesię actum est perpetua debet stabilitate vigere. Ea propter et nos pactionem inter ęcclesiam Rievall' et ęcclesiam de Scaltun' contractam, ut videlicet singulis annis prefata ęcclesia Rievall' ęcclesię de Scaltun pro decimis de Staintuna et Oswaldesengas xii. denarios persolvat,[a] nostra auctoritate corroboramus, et ne temere a quoquam violetur pro nostro officio interdicimus. His testibus: Gamaliele decano, Ivone persona de Sancto Felice, Suano presbitero de Boltebi, et universo capitulo apud Tresch.

a *Ms* persolvant

After Ralph became archdn (*Fasti York*, 36) and before the confirmation of the settlement by archbp Roger de Pont l'Evêque in 1157 × 1158 (*EEA* 20, no. 78), and probably shortly before the latter; the archbp reveals that the settlement had been made in the archdn's presence. 'Staintuna' and 'Oswaldesengas' are lost place-names (*Rievaulx Cartulary*, 17 n. 2; 43 n. 2). This agreement preserves the Cistercian abbey's privilege of tithe exemption (cf. above, no. 7n.).

Jeremy

269. *Notification that he was present when Henry de Riparia, in the presence of Roger de Mowbray, his advocate, granted the right of patronage of Brafferton church to the priory of Newburgh and renewed the gift he had previously made; and that he (the archdeacon) has confirmed it.* [c. 1170 × early 1186]

B = Bodl. ms Dodsworth 91 (transcripts of charters formerly in St Mary's Tower, York, 1636), fo. 13r, no. 21. s. xvii med.

Universis sancte matris ecclesie filiis Ieremia archidiaconus de Cleveland', eternam in domino salutem. Noverit universitas vestra nos interfuisse ubi Henricus de Riparia, in presentia nostri et advocati sui domini Rogeri de Mulbrai et filliorum suorum assensum prebentium, ius patronatus ecclesie de Braffertona ecclesie sancte Marie de Novoburgo concessit et hanc eandem donationem prius factam innovavit, necnon et cartam suam super hoc prenominate ecclesie prius collatam super altare obtulit. Hanc utique donationem quantum ad nos spectat de iure ratam habentes, pietatis intuitu presentis pagine testimonio communimus. Hiis testibus: Rogero de Albeneia, Alexandro decano, Iohanne clerico de Hovingham, Radulfo de Belvaria, Phillippo de Muntonium, Rogero de Gattenebi, Ricardo Golle.

After Jeremy became archdn, certainly by late 1171 (Clay, 'Archdeacons', 412–13; *Fasti York*, 37) and before Roger de Mowbray left on crusade to the Holy Land, where he was captured at Hattin in 1187 and died in 1188 (*Mowbray Charters*, xxxii). Roger de Mowbray's own charter, which is witnessed by Jeremy the archdeacon, is ibid., no. 209; Henry de Riparia's charter, which has no witnesses in common with either of the others, is Bodl. ms Dodsworth 91, fos. 12v–13r. See also Kemp, 'Archdeacons and parish churches', 349.

* **270.** *Notification that, when he demanded an annual procuration from the chapel of Hinderskelfe as from a mother church, and the canons of Kirkham objected, asserting that it was a chapel of the church of Crambe, he, learning the truth of the matter, has remitted the demand and publicly absolved the canons in respect of the procuration.* [*c.* 1170 × *c.* June 1189]

Abstracted in Bodl. ms Fairfax 7 (abstract of Kirkham priory's charters), fo. 74r. s. xv ex.

Carta Ier' archidiaconi de quiet' clam' procurationis capelle de Hyldyrskelf', in qua continetur quod, cum dictus I. exigisset de capella de Hyldr' unam procurationem per annum sicut a matrice ecclesia, quam procurationem canonici de K. debere dari omnino contradixerunt, asserentes ipsam esse capellam ecclesie de Cramb(u)n, cognita huius rei veritate huiusmodi exactionem indebit(am) et insolit(am) omnino remisit et imperpetuum relaxavit, dictos canonicos ab impetitione sua et successorum suorum super predicta procuratione puplice absolvens.

This cannot be dated more narrowly than the archidiaconate (Clay, 'Archdeacons', 412–13; *Fasti York*, 37). For Hinderskelfe, in Bulmer parish, see *Yorks N. Riding Place-Names*, 40.

ARCHDEACONRY OF THE EAST RIDING

Hugh du Puiset

271. *As treasurer of York, notification to the deans of his archdeaconry that he has inspected the royal and episcopal privileges confirming to the poor of the hospital of St Peter [i.e., St Leonard], York, one thrave of corn from each plough working in Yorkshire; and mandate that they induce detainers to pay the same.*
[*c.* 1143 × 20 Dec. 1153]

B = BL, Cotton ms Nero D iii (St Leonard's York cartulary), fo. 49r (47r). ss. xiv–xv.

H. Ebor' ecclesie thesaurarius dilectis sibi in Cristo decanis suis per archidiaconatum suum constitutis, eternam in domino salutem. Noveritis nos inspexisse privilegia tam regum quam pontificum quibus confirmatur pauperibus hospitalis sancti Petri Ebor' ut recipiant annuatim de qualibet caruca arante in Ebor'syra unam travam bladi. Quare vobis mandamus quatinus diligenter inducatis detentores predictarum travarum ad earum*a* solutionem. Et si quos resistentes inveneritis, sine dilatione eos ad condignam satisfactionem ecclesiastica censura compellatis. Valete.

a Ms eorum

After Hugh became treasurer and archdn of the East Riding, which two offices were held together until 1218 (*EEA* V, 122–3; Clay, 'Archdeacons', 277; *Fasti York*, 41), and before his consecration as bp of Durham (*Fasti Monastic Cathedrals*, 30). In 1276 the dean and chapter of York and the official of the archdeacon of Richmond referred in separate acts to these thraves, 'que vulgariter vocantur Petercorn' (Cott. Nero D iii, fo. 48r–v). St Peter's hospital became known as St Leonard's after king Stephen built a church of St Leonard for the existing hospital (Knowles and Hadcock, 407); it was among the largest and most important hospitals in England (ibid., 312, 407).

272. *As treasurer of York and archdeacon, notification that he has granted the church of St Mary, Swine, to the Benedictine nuns there by the grant of brother Robert de Verli.* [*c.* 1143 × 20 Dec. 1153]

> B = Bodl. ms Dodsworth 7 (Transcripts of charters formerly in St Mary's Tower, York, 1644), fo. 259r. s. xvii med.[1]
> Pd, *Mon. Ang.,* v, 494, no. 3; *EYC,* iii, 75–6, no. 1360; (calendar), G. Duckett, 'Charters of the Priory of Swine in Holderness', 123.

H. de Pusat dei gratia Eboracensis ecclesie thesaurarius necnon archidiaconus omnibus sancte ecclesie filiis tam presentibus quam futuris, cum dei benedictione salutem. Notum vobis sit ecclesiam sancte Marie de Suine, meo archidiaconatui attinentem, cum omnibus rebus eidem pertinentibus atque concessis sanctimonialibus secundum institutionem sancti Benedicti deo devote ibidem servientibus divine respectu remunerationis, ac concessione fratris Roberti de Verli, cuius ipsa ecclesia esse dinoscitur, me firmiter concessisse. Hoc itaque pie devotionis inceptum, quatinus ad honorem creatoris convenientius instituatur atque perficiatur, presentis scripture aminiculo ac proprio sigillo communiri feci. Valete.

Date as for no. 271. 'Brother' Robert de Verli was probably the parish priest of Swine, who founded the priory in association with his church; the priory was in some sense a double house, with Robert as perhaps its first master (J. Burton, *The Monastic Order in Yorkshire,*129, 140, 171, 173; see also S. Thompson, *Women Religious,* 69).

[1] Dodsworth provides a rough drawing of the seal, pointed oval (60 × 44 mm), frontally standing figure of an ecclesiastic, legend: + SIGILLVM: HVGONIS. EBORACENSIS THESAV:

ARCHDEACONRY OF NOTTINGHAM

Robert son of William (fitz Ralph)

273. *Confirmation to the canons regular of Darley of the gift in pure and perpetual alms by his father, William son of Ralph, of the church of St Michael, Derby, and the [dependent] chapel of Alvaston, paying the canons an annual pension of twelve pence.*
[*c.* Nov. 1181 × 5 May 1191]

> B = BL, Cotton ms Titus C ix (Darley cartulary), fo. 148r. s. xiii ex.
> Pd, *Darley Cartulary,* ii, 535, no. L 5.

Universis sancte matris ecclesie filiis tam presentibus quam futuris Robertus filius Willelmi archidiaconus Notingham, salutem. Noverit universitas vestra me concessisse et hac carta mea corroborasse canonicis regularibus sancte Marie de Derb' ecclesiam sancti Michaelis de Derb' et capellam de Alwaldeston' cum omnibus pertinentiis suis in puram[a] et perpetuam elemosinam, sicut Willelmus filius Radulfi pater meus eam eis donavit, reddendo predictis canonicis annuam pensionem xii. d'. Hiis testibus.

    a in puram *repeated in ms*

After the death of the archdn's predecessor, John son of Letold (*Fasti York*, 45), and before he himself was consecrated bp of Worcester (*Fasti Monastic Cathedrals*, 100). Darley abbey, founded in *c.* 1146 by Robert Ferrers II, earl of Derby, was also known as 'of Derby' in Henry II's reign (Knowles and Hadcock, 156; *Darley Cartulary*, i, iii–iv). Robert's father's gift of the church is ibid., ii, no. L 4. That Alvaston chapel was dependent on St Michael's church is clear from the latter's appropriation to the abbey in 1215 × 1223 (ibid., no. O 15).

Archdeaconry of Richmond

Osbert of Bayeux

274. *As archdeacon of York, notification to Hugh son of Gernagod, steward, and the ministers of the earl of Richmond that he and two others [named] were present when Godreda, daughter of Hermer, acknowledged and confirmed her father's gift in pure alms to Selby abbey of the land of Kelfield.*   [1136 × prob. 1146]

    B = BL, Additional ms 37771 (Selby cartulary), fo. 111r (110r). s. xiii ex.
    Pd, *Selby Coucher Book*, i, 341, no. 602; *EYC*, v, 68, no. 163.

[O]sb(ertus) Ebor' archidiaconus Hugoni filio Gernagodi dapifero et ministris comitis de Richesmund', salutem. Notum sit vobis me et Willelmum de Lac' et R. de Wysto' interfuisse audientes et videntes ubi Guderide filia Hermeri recognovit et testabatur donationem patris sui quam fecit deo et sancto Germano in pura elemosina, et nominatim de terra de Kelkefeld, et ipsa Guderide eandem donationem concessit ut heres et confirmavit. Et hoc scripto vobis significamus quod inde testes sumus. Valete. Et Unfea de Chipes testis est, et plures.

After the creation of the first earl of Richmond, Alan of Brittany, and, since he confirmed Godreda's act, probably before his death in Brittany in 1146 (*Selby Coucher Book*, i, no. 601; *EYC*, iv, 18, no. 16; *Complete Peerage*, x, 788–90). Godreda's charter is *Selby Coucher Book*, i, no. 600; *EYC*, v, 67, no. 162.

Godfrey de Lucy

275. *Notification of his confirmation of the gift by Alan, constable of Richmond, of the church of Stanwick with its chapels to the Premonstratensian canons of Easby, saving the ancient customs of the archdeacon of Richmond and provided that, when the church is vacant, the canons present to the archdeacon a suitable vicar, who will be maintained out of the church's goods, and who will answer to the canons in temporalities and to the archdeacon and his officials in spiritualities.*   [? *c.* 1184 × 22 Oct. 1189]

    B = BL, Egerton ms 2827 (Easby cartulary), fos. 289v–290r. s. xiii ex.
    Pd, *EYC*, v, 161, no. 270.

Omnibus sancte matris ecclesie filiis Godefridus de Lucy Rich' archidiaconus, salutem. Universitati vestre notum facimus quod nos donationem ecclesie de Staynwegg' cum capellis et omnibus pertinentiis suis per Alanum const(abular-ium) Richem' ecclesie sancte Agate et canonicis Premonstr(atensis) ordinis eiusdem loci factam pietatis intuitu ratam habemus, salvis in omnibus antiquis consuetudinibus archidiacono Richem' debitis, salvo etiam eo quod, cum prefata ecclesia vacaverit, predicti canonici vicarium idoneum archidiacono representent, cui de bonis ecclesie assignetur unde honeste possit sustentari et hospitalitatem exercere. Et predictis canonicis in temporalibus, archidiacono vero et suis officialibus de eorum iustitia in spiritualibus, valeat*a* respondere. Et ne donatio ista per oblivionis interitum revocetur in irritum, eam pagine presentis inscriptione et sigilli [fo. 290r] nostri appositione testificari pariter et confirmare curavimus. Test(ibus) et c'.

a Ms valeant

Godfrey had become archdn before 18 Aug. 1184, witnessing a charter of Clement, abbot of St Mary's, York, who died then (Clay, 'Archdeacons', 412; *Heads,* 84), and was consecrated bp of Winchester, 22 Oct. 1189 (*Fasti Monastic Cathedrals,* 85). The charter of Alan (son of Roald), constable of Richmond, is printed from the Easby cartulary in *EYC,* v, 161, no. 269, where it is dated 1171 × 1181.

* 276. *Confirmation of the gift of the church of Tunstall to the abbey of Croxton.*
[? *c.* 1184 × 22 Oct. 1189]

Mentioned only, in an account of Croxton abbey's acquisition of Tunstall church, in Belvoir Castle, Add. ms 71 (Croxton Abbey Register), fo. 86r. s. xiii med. (whence BL, Additional ms 4934, fo. 174v, being a transcript by F. Peck, 1731; BL, Stowe ms 928, fo. 74v, being a transcript by Dr Vernon, 1755); pd from Peck, Nichols, *Leicestershire,* ii (i), App. 82, no. 14 (5).

. . . Godefridus de Luci tunc temporis archidiaconus Richemundie*a* eandem ecclesiam [*sc.* de Tunstall] auctoritate sua nobis confirmavit et predictam donationem ratam habuit. . . .

a Richmundie Stowe 928

Date as for no. 275. This passage is preceded in the account by notices that Adam de Mundbegun (Yundbegun in BL, Add. 4934) gave the church, afterwards confirmed by his son, Roger de Mundbegun, and that afterwards William son of Cospatrick of Tunstall remitted his claim to the church; it is not absolutely clear, therefore, whether the archdn's confirmation related specifically to Adam de Mundbegun's gift.

William de Chemillé

277. *Confirmation of the confirmation by his predecessor, G(odfrey) de Lucy, to the canons of Easby of the church of St John, Stanwick.* [15 Sept. 1189 × 1196]

B = BL, Egerton ms 2827 (Easby cartulary), fo. 290r. s. xiii ex.
Pd, *EYC,* v, 162, no. 271.

Omnibus et c', Willelmus de Chymili Rich' archidiaconus, salutem. Noveritis quod ratam habemus concessionem et confirmationem venerabilis predecessoris nostri G. de Lucy quam fecit canonicis sancte Agate super ecclesia sancti Iohannis de Staynwegg' et pertinentiis suis. Quare et nos pro dei amore et pietatis intuitu eandem ecclesiam prefatis canonicis secundum cartam predicti domini G. de Lucy presenti scripto et sigilli nostri appositione confirmamus. Hiis testibus.

For the dating limits of William's archidiaconate, see *Fasti York*, 48; for his appointment by Richard I in 1189, see *Gesta* (Benedict), ii, 85; Howden, iii, 16.

278. *Notification that, at the presentation of the abbot and convent of Easby, he has received and instituted William, clerk, as perpetual vicar in the portion of St John Baptist's church, Stanwick, which he has canonically acquired by gift of the said abbot and convent.* [15 Sept. 1189 × 1196]

B = BL, Egerton ms 2827 (Easby cartulary), fo. 290r. s. xiii ex.

Universis et c', Willelmus de Chemile archidiaconus Richem', salutem. Noveritis nos, ad presentationem abbatis et conventus de sancta Agata, recepisse et instituisse Willelmum clericum perpetuum vicarium in illa portione ecclesie sancti Iohannis Baptiste de Staynwegg' cum omnibus pertinentiis suis quam canonice assecutus est ex donatione pred(ictorum) abbatis et conventus de sancta Agata. Et ut hec concessio et institutio rate permaneant et inconcusse, eas carte nostre attestatione et sigilli nostri corroboravimus appositione. Hiis testibus.

Date as for no. 277.

279. *Confirmation of the gift to the Premonstratensian canons of Easby by Thomas de Burgh and Ismania, his mother, with the assent of their lord, A(lan), constable of Richmond, of the church of St Wilfrid, [Great] Langton, saving the ancient customs of the archdeacon of Richmond and provided that, when it becomes vacant, the canons present to the archdeacon a suitable vicar, who will be maintained out of the church's goods, and who will answer to the canons in temporalities and to the archdeacon and his officials in spiritualities.* [15 Sept. 1189 × 1196]

B = BL, Egerton ms 2827 (Easby cartulary), fo. 295r. s. xiii ex.
Pd, *EYC*, v, 152, no. 261.

Omnibus et c', Willelmus de Chymili Richem' archidiaconus, salutem. Universitati vestre notum facimus quod nos donationem ecclesie sancti Wilfridi de Lang(eton') cum pertinentiis suis per Thomam de Burg' et Ysmenam matrem eius, assentiente et carta sua confirmante domino suo A. constabulario Richem', ecclesie sancte Agate et canonicis Premonstr(atensis) ordinis eiusdem loci factam pietatis intuitu ratam habemus, salvis in omnibus antiquis consuetudinibus archidiacono Richem' debitis, salvo etiam eo quod, cum predicta ecclesia vacaverit, predicti canonici vicarium ydoneum archidiacono representent, cui de bonis ecclesie assignetur unde honeste possit sustentari et hospitalitatem exercere. Et predictis canonicis in temporalibus, archidiacono vero et suis officialibus de eorum iustitia in spiritualibus, valeat respondere. Et ne donatio ista per oblivionis interitum revocetur in irritum, eam pagine presentis inscriptione et sigilli nostri appositione testificari pariter et confirmare curavimus.

Date as for no. 277. This act is *mutatis mutandis* identical with Godfrey de Lucy's confirmation of Alan the constable's gift of Stanwick church (above, no. 275). For other charters concerning this gift, see *EYC*, v, nos. 256–60, and below, no. 306.

280. *Notification that he has confirmed to the canons of the order of Sempringham, proctors of the house [hospital] and poor of Norton, the church of Marton in 'Boroughshire' and has instituted them as parson in the same to possess it* in proprios usus; *the canons will bear all burdens affecting the church.* [15 Sept. 1189 × 1196]

B = BL, Cotton ms Claudius D xi (Malton cartulary), fo. 60r–v (58r–v). s. xiii med.

Omnibus sancte matris ecclesie filiis, Willelmus de Chimelle archidiaconus[a] Richemund', salutem in domino. Noverit universitas vestra nos concessisse et hac presenti carta nostra confirmasse canonicis de ordine de Semplingh', procuratoribus domus de platea de Nort' et pauperibus ibidem procurandis, ecclesiam [fo. 60v] de Marthona in Burg'sire cum omnibus pertinentiis suis, et eosdem in eadem personam constituisse in proprios usus perpetuis temporibus possidendam. Ipsi vero canonici omnia honera ad eandem ecclesiam spectantia sustinebunt. Hiis testibus.

a Ms archidiach'

Date as for no. 277. For the original gift by Roger de Flamville of Marton church to the hospital of Norton, under the control of Malton priory, in the 1160s, see Golding, *Gilbert of Sempringham,* 368–9.

281. *As elect of Avranches, notification that Mr William de Flamville resigned into his hand as archdeacon of Richmond the church of Marton; and that, at William's request, he canonically 'assigned' the same church to the canons of Sempringham in pure and perpetual alms and instituted them as parson of the same.* [1196]

B = BL, Cotton ms Claudius D xi (Malton cartulary), fo. 60v (58v). s. xiii med.

Universis sancte matris ecclesie filiis Willelmus permissione divina electus Abrinc', salutem in vero[a] salutari. Noverit universitas vestra magistrum Willelmum de Flamevill' resignasse in manu nostra, qui tunc temporis archidiaconatum de Richemund' habebamus, ecclesiam de Marth(o)n', et nos, ad eius petitionem, intuitu caritatis et sancte religionis eandem ecclesiam canonice assignasse canonicis de Semplingh' in puram et perpetuam elemosinam et eos personam eiusdem ecclesie instituisse. Quod ut fidelius conservetur, scriptum presens sigilli nostri munimine dignum duximus roborare.

a Ms vere

The archdn was elected to Avranches in 1196, but translated to Angers before consecration (*Fasti York,* 48). The canons were specifically of Malton, to whom William de Flamville gave the hospital at Norton, which already had the church of Marton (see above, no. 280; Golding, *Gilbert of Sempringham,* 239). In *c.* 1202 × 1203, Honorius, archdn of Richmond, admitted and canonically instituted the canons of Malton in the church, and caused them to be inducted into corporal possession (cartulary, fo. 61r–v), carried out by the [rural] dean (ibid., fo. 61r).

282. *Notification that, with the authority of the chapter of York, he has exempted from all service and exaction pertaining to the archdeaconry of Richmond the churches which belong to the prebend of Masham within the archdeaconry by gift of Roger de Mowbray, namely, the churches of Masham and Kirkby [Malzeard]; and confirmation that they be as free of hospitality, chapters, aids, synodals and all other exactions as any prebend of York.* [Dec. 1189 × early 1194]

B = BL, Cotton ms Claudius B iii (York Minster cartulary), fo. 52r (50r). s. xiii ex.
Pd, *York Minster Fasti*, i, 82–3, no. 37; (transl.), Fisher, *History of Masham*, 532–3, App. C., no. 7.

[O]mnibus sancte matris ecclesie filiis has literas visuris vel audituris Willelmus de Sunelli archidiaconus de Richemund', salutem. Noverit universitas vestra me de mera voluntate mea absolvisse et ad utilitatem et honorem ecclesie nostre Ebor' de communi consilio et auctoritate totius capituli Ebor' exemisse*a* et ab omni servitio et exactione ad archidiaconatum de*b* Richemund' pertinente ecclesias illas que pertinent ad prebendam de Masham que sunt in archidiaconatu de Richemund' de donatione Rogeri de Moubrai, videlicet*c* ecclesias de Masham et de Kirkebi, cum omnibus earum pertinentiis. Unde volo et irrefragabiliter presenti carta mea confirmo ut predicte ecclesie ita libere et quiete a me et a successoribus meis in perpetuum remaneant tam de hospitiis quam de capitulis et auxiliis et sinodalibus et omnibus aliis exactionibus sicut aliqua prebenda liberior est in ecclesia sancti Petri Ebor'. Hiis testibus: Henrico decano, Radulpho archidiacono, magistro Simone cancellario, Galfrido archidiacono Cliveland', Roberto preposito Beverl', Stephano, Hugone Murdac, Ad' de Tornoure, Nicholao filio Hugonis, Reginaldo Arundel', Iohanne Morwic, Petro de Dinant, Willelmo de Mala Palude, Thoma filio Paulini, canonicis Ebor', magistro Milone de Beverlac', Petro de Ros, Willelmo filio Aldelini, Alexandro succentore, Alano de Sancto Wilfrido, Willelmo de Budthum, Arundello, presbiteris, Iohanne filio Galfridi, et aliis multis.

a Ms exmisse   *b Interlined*   *c Followed in ms by* ad *marked for deletion*

After Henry Marshal was confirmed as dean of York, Dec. 1189, having been appointed in the council at Pipewell, 15 Sept. (*Fasti York*, 9), and before Ralph d'Aunay, archdn of York, left England as a member of the delegation from the chapter of York to the pope in its dispute with Archbp Geoffrey, on which mission he died (Clay, 'Archdeacons', 421; Howden, iii, 272–3; *Historians of the Church of York*, iii, 92). Henry Marshal was elected bp of Exeter before 10 Feb. 1194 and consecrated by 28 Mar. (*EEA* XII, 303). The churches of Masham and Kirkby Malzeard were given first to Newburgh priory in *c.* 1145, but were transferred by Roger de Mowbray in 1154 × 1157 to York Minster, of which they became a prebend in *c.* 1163 × *c.* 1169 (*Mowbray Charters*, nos. 196–7, 325–6).

283. *Notification that, at the presentation of Theobald Walter, he has given in pure and perpetual alms to the abbot and monks of Wyresdale the church of St Michael's-on-Wyre, to be received* in proprios usus, *saving the right of the archdeacon of Richmond; the abbot and monks will sustain episcopal burdens and assign a permanent vicar in the same with a portion sufficient for his food and clothing.*
[June 1193 × 1196]

A = PRO, DL 36/1 (Duchy of Lancaster, Cartae Misc., vol. 1), fo. 6. Endorsed: Confirmacio archidiacon[i] de Richemund' de ecclesia sancti Mikaelis (s. xii ex.). Size 205 × 143 mm (no turn-up). Seal and cords missing; three holes at the foot.

Pd, *Ancient Charters*, 103, no. 63; *Lancashire Pipe Rolls and Charters*, 336, series viii, no. 1; *Furness Coucher Book*, ii, part 111, 733–4.

Omnibus sancte matris ecclesie filiis ad quos presens scriptum pervenerit Willelmus de Chimeilli archidiaconus Richemundie, salutem in domino. Noverit universitas vestra me, ad presentationem Theb' Walteri, dedisse et hac presenti carta mea confirmasse abbati et monachis de Wiresdal' ecclesiam sancti Michaelis super Wirum cum omnibus pertinentiis suis in puram et perpetuam elemosinam, in proprios usus percipiendam, salvo iure archidiaconi Richemund'. Predicti vero abbas et monachi de Wiresdale de ecclesia predicta omnia honera episcopalia sustinebunt, et certum vicarium in eadem assignabunt cum portione sufficiente ad victum et vestitum eiusdem vicarii. Et ut hec mea concessio rata permaneat in posterum, eam sigilli mei appositione dignum duxi corroborandam. Hiis testibus: H. Cant' archiepiscopo, H. episcopo Covintr', Theb' Walteri, Rann' thesaurario Sar', Gileberto de Kentewell', Simone de Camera, et multis aliis.

After Hubert Walter's postulation as archbp of Canterbury, 29 and 30 May 1193 (*Fasti Monastic Cathedrals*, 5), and before the archdn's election as bp of Avranches (above, no. 281n.).

284. *Notification that he has granted to the monks of Mont Saint-Michel an annual pension of five marks from the church of Wath, of which the monks are true patrons.*
[15 Sept. 1189 × 1196; prob. 1196]

[A = original, formerly at Saint-Lô, A-D de la Manche, destroyed in 1944 (but see facsimile noted below). Endorsed: unknown. Size, approx. 136 × 61 + 11 mm. Seal on tag (method 1), pointed oval; obverse, frontally standing figure in deacon's vestments holding a book in both hands; legend: + S' WILLELMI DE CHIMEL . . . ACONI.]
B = PRO, PRO 31/8/140B (Transcripts from Norman sources), part 2, p. 303, no. 96 (copy from A, with drawing of seal). 1835.
Pd from A, *EYC*, v, 225, no. 317, with facsimile, plate 22; (calendar) from B, *CDF*, 278, no. 765.

Universis sancte matris ecclesie filiis Willelmus de Chimelle archidiaconus[a] Rich', salutem. Noverit universitas vestra me concessisse et divine pietatis intuitu hac[b] mea confirmasse carta deo et beato Micaeli de Periculo Maris et monachis ibidem deo servientibus quinque marcas annuatim de ecclesia de Wath percipiendas nomine pensionis, [c]qui scilicet monachi[c] predicte ecclesie [d]iusti sunt[d] patroni. Hiis testibus: magistro Rogero de Rich' tunc officiali, Iohanne decano de Watlos,[e] magistro Roberto de Tuf',[f] et multis[g] aliis.

a *Insert* de B	b hec B	c–c cuiuslibet monachorum B	d–d qui
sunt iusti B	e Wirt' B	f Cestr' B	g Om. in B

Date in general as for no. 277, but perhaps contemporary with the gift of the church by abbot Jordan and the convent of Mont Saint-Michel to Mr Roger of Richmond, the archdn's official, witnessed by the archdn as both archdn and elect of Avranches, i.e., in 1196 (*EYC*, v, 226, no. 318; for the date, cf. above, no. 281n.).

Roger de St Edmund

285.   *Confirmation to the prior and monks of Durham of the gift in pure and perpetual alms by the late Richard son of Roger of the church of Lytham and land [there] with appurtenances.*   [May 1199 × ?1202]

> A = Durham University Lib., Durham Cathedral Muniments, 2. 4. Ebor. 8. Endorsed: C(arta) R. archidiaconi de Richem' (s. xiii in.); de ecclesia de Lithum (? s. xiv in.); 2ª. 4ᶜ. Ebor'. 1. H (s. xv). Size 164 × 192 + 25 mm. Seal on red and white cords through two eyelets in turn-up, in green wax, pointed oval, large portion surviving (*c.* 45 × *c.* 28 mm) but damaged and worn; obverse: frontally standing ecclesiastic (head missing) in alb and dalmatic, with maniple and amice, holding a book to his chest with both hands, his right hand on the top of the book, his left on the bottom; legend: . . . . .SCO EADMV. . . .
>
> B = Ibid., Cartuarium Vetus, fo. 171v. s. xiii med. C = Ibid., Cartuarium III, fos. 133v–134r. s. xv in.

Rogerus*ᵃ* de Sancto Edmundo archidiaconus Richemund' omnibus sancte matris ecclesie filiis ad quos presens scriptum pervenerit, salutem. Noverit universitas vestra me intuitu caritatis concessisse et presenti carta mea confirmasse deo et sancto Cuthberto et priori et monachis Dunelmen' predicto sancto servientibus et in perpetuum servituris donationem bone memorie Ricardi filii Rogerii,*ᵇ* scilicet ecclesiam de Lithum et terram cum omnibus pertinentiis suis, quas ipse Ricardus predictis monachis in puram et perpetuam elemosinam dedit, sicut in carta ipsius Ricardi continetur.*ᶜ* Hiis testibus: Emerico*ᵈ* archidiacono Dunl', magistro Roberto de Edinton', magistro Waltero de Hadinton', magistro Henrico officiali, magistro Willelmo Blesen', Waltero decano, Nigello capellano, Germano clerico, magistro Thoma de Kirtlinton', Henrico Pilat', et aliis multis.*ᵉ*

a Rogus *A*	*b* Rogeri *B,C*	*c B ends with* T'	*d* Emico *C*
e Om. in C			

After the death of Richard son of Roger, who was still alive shortly after the accession of King John (crowned 27 May 1199) but died before 26 Feb. 1201 (*VCH Lancs*, ii, 107), and probably not later than 1202, when Pope Innocent III ordered the dean and chapter of York to remove Roger de St Edmund from the archdnry in favour of Honorius, with whom he had been dispute since 1198 (Howden, iv, 52, 89, 176–85; *EYC*, iv, xxv–xxvi; *Fasti York*, 48–9); Mr William of Blois was elected bp of Lincoln before 6 July 1203 (*Fasti Lincoln*, 3). Richard son of Roger founded Lytham priory as a dependency of Durham after 1191 (*Heads*, 94 and n. 1); for discussion of his charter(s), see *VCH Lancs,* ii, 107. It is curious that the monks of Durham should have kept this confirmation from Roger de St Edmund and not obtained one from Honorius, the eventual victor in the dispute; the mystery is heightened by the fact that the only other early archidiaconal act at Durham concerning this gift is an early 13th-century original, with its seal, in the name of Morgan, archdn of Richmond, otherwise unknown as archdn (Durham Cathedral Muniments, 2. 4. Ebor. 9; copied into ibid., Cartuarium Vetus, fo. 171v, and Cartuarium III, fo. 134r).

VICE-ARCHDIACONAL ACTA

DIOCESE OF LINCOLN

Mr Robert of Hardres

286. *Notification that, at the presentation of the prior and monks of St Andrew's, Northampton, he has received Alan, brother of Laurence archdeacon of Bedford, into the church of Newton [in Aveland] and canonically instituted him as parson in the same.* [Apr. 1175 × early 1184; ? *c.* 1180]

> B = BL, Royal ms 11 B. ix (St Andrew's Northampton cartulary), fo. 37v. s. xiii ex. C = BL, Cotton ms Vespasian E xvii (St Andrew's Northampton cartulary), fo. 248r (233r). s. xv med.

Omnibus sancte matris ecclesie filiis Robertus de Hard'e[a] vicearchidiaconus Linc', salutem. Noverit universitas vestra me, ad presentationem prioris et monachorum sancti Andree de Norh(am)t',[b] suscepisse Alanum fratrem domini [c]archidiaconi Laurentii Bedeford'[c] in ecclesiam de Neuton',[d] et ipsum in eadem personam instituisse. Et ut hec institutio solempniter satis et canonice facta firma sit et stabilis, eam presenti carta confirmavi et pendenti sigilli mei testimonio communivi. Hiis testibus: Radulfo subdecano Linc', Ricardo precentore, Alexandro, Adam de Amundevile,[e] Ricardo de Kileseia,[f] Pagano, Samsone,[g] presbiteris et canonicis, Galfrido de Torpell', Philippo, Alexandro Malabiss',[h] Radulfo de Virin',[i] et Hugone, canonicis.

> a Harder' *C*　　　　b Northampton' *C*　　　　c–c Laurentii archidiacononi
> Bedford *C*　　　　d Newenton' *C*　　　　e Amundervyll' *C*　　　　f Keleseia *C*
> g Sampsone *C*　　　　h Malebyss' *C*　　　　i Vyryn *C*

For the date, see *Fasti Lincoln*, 161, App. 30, where this act is discussed; Ralph of Caen had been succeeded as subdean by late 1183 or early 1184 (ibid., 21–2). Peter, archdn of Lincoln in this period (ibid., 25), was a notorious absentee, necessitating the vice-archdn's action.

287. *Notification, without title, that when he had care of the archdeaconry of Lincoln he found the abbot and monks of Bardney in possession of the church of Edlington, except that they had assigned a vicarage in the church to William of Stainby, clerk, for an annual pension of three marks; this was ratified by G(eoffrey), elect of Lincoln, who ordered him to ratify it; he therefore demitted them in tranquil possession.* [? *c.* 1175 × 6 Jan. 1182]

> B = BL, Cotton ms Vespasian E xx (Bardney cartulary), fo. 32r–v (28r–v). s. xiii ex.
> Pd, *Registrum Antiquissimum*, vii, 206.

Robertus de Hard' universis has litteras visuris et audituris, salutem. Universitati vestre innotescat quod, cum archidiaconatus Linc' curam gererem, possessionem ecclesie de Edlington' in manu abbatis et monachorum de Bard' liberam et quietam cum omni integritate sua inveni, excepto quod quandam vicariam in eadem ecclesia Willelmo de Stigedebi clerico [fo. 32v] suo assignaverunt, pro qua annuam eis pensionem trium videlicet marcarum persoluit. Hoc totum dominus electus Linc' G. ratum habuit et michi precepit ut ratum haberem. Statui ergo eos decetero auctoritate qua fungebar cum omni tranquillitate possidendi in pace dimittere. Hiis testibus: Willelmo decano de Hagwrthingham, Hugone de Strattune, magistro R. de Kima, Willelmo de Stiherbi, Eudone de Wadingwrd', Hervi de Horsington', Willelmo de Hereford', Simone de Insula.

Robert is here probably acting for the absent Peter, archdn of Lincoln, who was appointed by his half-brother, Geoffrey, bp-elect of Lincoln, in *c.* 1175 (*Fasti Lincoln*, 25); the act implies that Geoffrey is still elect of Lincoln, from which position he resigned, 6 Jan. 1182 (ibid., 2). It has been suggested, however, that Robert de Hardres may have hard charge of the archdeaconry before Peter was appointed (*Reg. Antiquissimum*, 206). For Geoffrey's appropriation of the church to Bardney, see *EEA* I, no. 285.

288. *Notification that, in his presence at Lincoln, the canons of Bridlington proved their right to the church of Baumber, and that consequently he has allowed them their possession of the church.*   8 May 1182

B = BL, Additional ms 40008 (Bridlington cartulary), fo. 273r (269r). s. xiv in. C = Ibid., fo. 327v (323v). s. xiv in.
Pd (calendar) from B and C, *Bridlington Chartulary*, 355–6, 434–5.

Omnibus visuris sive audituris litteras has Robertus de Hard' vicearchidiaconus Linc', salutem. Noverit universitas vestra quod eo tempore quo gerebam vices archidiaconi in ecclesia Linc' inveni canonicos de Bridl' possidentes ecclesiam de Bamburgh*[a]* cum omni integritate sua. Propter cuiusdam tamen*[b]* interpellationem qui adversus eos qualemcumque moverat questionem super eiusdem ecclesie quibusdam portionibus, non permisi eos omnino inconcusse possidere donec in ecclesia Linc' die eis constituto sub audientia sollempni*[c]* in presentia mea*[d]* sufficientem et canonicam exhiberent probationem. Videlicet adhibitis sacrosanctis ewangeliis*[e]* et iurantibus sacerdotibus quamplurimis ceterisque personis ydoneis quod predicti canonici hanc*[f]* ecclesiam ex quo eam adepti sunt cum omni integritate possiderint, percipiendo ex eadem omnes fructus et obventiones absque diminutione, capellanos ibidem ponendo et ammovendo pro suo arbitrio. Ego autem, ex habundanti probatione iure eorum cognito, statui eos de cetero auctoritate qua fungebar cum omni tranquillitate possidendi in pace dimittere, salva dignitate Lincolniensis ecclesie. Hiis testibus: *[g]*Radulfo abbate de Bardeneya, Hugone abbate de Revesby,*[g]* Radulfo abbate de Tupeholm, Lamberto priore de Kime, magistro Alexandro sacerdote, et magistro Alexandro Malebisse,*[h]* et Rogero filio Willelmi, canonicis Linc' ecclesie, Rogero canonico de Kyme,*[i]* Willelmo capellano de Burrathe,*[j]* Roberto capellano de Marum, Hugone decano de Stratton, Ivone et Willelmo capellanis de Bamburg', Thoraldo clerico de Edlingtone,*[k]* Hugone clerico de Scamelesby, Baldewino capellano de Sancto Petro, Radulfo capellano de Hosberneby.

a Bamburg *C*	*b Om. in C*	*c* solempni *C*	*d me C*
e evangeliis *C*	*f* habent *C*	*g–g Om. in C*	*h* Melebisse *C*
i Kime *C*	*j* Burrache *C*	*k* Edelington' *C*	

The date is derived from the cartulary rubric to the C text: 'Probatio possessionis ecclesie de Bamburg facta anno domini M° C° lxxx° ii°, viii° idus Maii . . .' The presence of so many heads of Lincolnshire monasteries and canons of Lincoln is notable.

289. *As canon of Lincoln and vice-archdeacon, notification that Alexander, clerk of Auburn, brother of Alfred of Haddington, has renounced into his hand the church of Auburn, before B(aldwin), archbishop of Canterbury, G(ilbert), bishop of Rochester, G(odfrey) de Lucy, William of Northolt, Mr H(enry) of Northampton and P(eter) of Blois; and that, with the archbishop's assent, and at the presentation of Ralph de Albini, to whom belongs the* ius patronatus, *he has canonically instituted the prior and convent of Belvoir as parson in the said church, vacant, and put them into corporal possession.* [29 Sept. 1185 × 21 Sept. 1186]

B = Belvoir Castle, Add. ms 105 (Belvoir cartulary), fos. 26v–27r. s. xv in.
Pd (calendar), *HMCR Rutland,* iv, 114.

Universis sancte matris ecclesie filiis ad quos presens scriptum pervenerit Robertus de Haydr' Linc' ecclesie canonicus et vicearchidiaconus, salutem in domino. Ad universitatis vestre volumus devenire notitiam quod eo tempore quo vices archidiaconi Lincl' gessimus Alexander clericus de Aburn' frater Alvredi de Hadint', in presentia B. domini Cant' et in conspectu G. Rofens' episcopi et G. de Luci et Willelmi de Norhala et magistri H. de Norhant' et P. de Bleis et aliorum multorum, quicquid iuris in ecclesia de Ab(urn') et eius [fo. 27r] pertinentiis habebat sponte et sine aliqua coactione in manu nostra resignavit et ab prefata ecclesia et beneficiis eius penitus se deposuit. Nos igitur divine pietatis intuitu et assensu et consilio B. domini Cant' ad presentationem et iusta petitione domini Radulfi de Albenei, ad quem ius patronatus predicte ecclesie pertinere dinoscebatur, priorem et conventum de Belver in supradictam ecclesiam vacantam personam canonice instituimus et in corporalem eiusdem ecclesie possessionem misimus, salva in omnibus Linc' ecclesie dignitate. Ne igitur institutio ista in processu temporis in irritum revocetur, eam scripti nostri munimine et sigilli appositione corroboravimus. Hiis testibus: magistro Emm' subdecano Linc', magistro H. de Lund', et Ricardo de Kima, canonicis Linc', cum ceteris aliis.

After Gilbert de Glanville was consecrated bp of Rochester and before William of Northolt was consecrated bp of Worcester (*Fasti Monastic Cathedrals,* 76, 100). For archbp Baldwin's letters, see *EEA* II, no. 234, in the note to which the editor, following *HMCR Rutland,* iv, 114, states wrongly that the present act includes the phrase 'vacante personatu'. A., [rural] dean of Swinderby, subsequently 'instituted' (i.e., inducted) the priory as parson (*sicut personam*) on the vice-archdn's instruction (*HMCR Rutland,* iv, 114). For Ralph de Albini's original gift of the church to Belvoir, its confirmation by archbp Richard in 1174 × 1177, and an institution of the priory in the church by Alexander, acting for the archdn of Lincoln, in 1174 × 1181, see ibid., 113–14; *EEA* II, no. 57.

290. *As canon of Lincoln and vice-archdeacon, ratification to the monks of Crowland of their possession of the church of Whaplode, having inspected the charters of archbishops of Canterbury, of Robert, late bishop of Lincoln, and of the lords of the fee, namely, Emecina and her heirs, Fulk and Waleran de Oyri; and notification that, at their presentation, he has received Hugh the chaplain and Fulk and Geoffrey in the said church, under an annual pension of 100 shillings to be paid by the three proportionately; when any portion [of the church] is vacated, it shall fall to the monks' use.*   [*c.* 1187 x 4 Apr. 1192]

B = Spalding Gentlemen's Society, Crowland cartulary, fos. 76v–78r.[1] s. xiv med.

Universis sancte matris ecclesie filiis presentibus et futuris Robertus de Hardr' Lincoln' ecclesie canonicus et vicearchidiaconus, salutem. Noverit universitas vestra nos, inspectis cartis mona[fo. 78r]chorum de Croiland' tam archiepisco-porum Cantuar' et Roberti Lincoln' quondam bone memorie episcopi super confirmatione ecclesie de Quappelad' quam dominorum fundi, scilicet Emecine et heredum suorum, Fulconis et Walranni de Oyri, illam[a] ratam habentes, eam pacifice possidere sustinuimus sicut debuimus, salva in omnibus Lincoln' ecclesie dignitate; ad quorum presentationem recepimus Hugonem capellanum et Fulconem et Galfridum in predicta ecclesia sub annua pensione centum solidorum assignata unicuique portione sua tam in ecclesia quam in pensione reddenda. Ita quod, cum quelibet pars vacaverit, cedet usui monachorum secundum autentica et scripta eorum. Et ut hec confirmatio ipsis a nobis facta rata permaneat, eam sigilli nostri appensione corroboravimus. Testibus, et c'.

a Ms illud

After Robert was made a canon, i.e., following Hugh of Avallon's consecration and certainly by *c.* 1187 (*Fasti Lincoln*, 81; *EEA* IV, xxvi), and before Robert's first occurrence as archdn of Huntingdon (*Fasti Lincoln*, 27). No. 291 shows that Fulk (the younger) and Geoffrey were sons of Waleran. The church was first given to Crowland by Emecina, widow of Walter de Cantelu, in 1148 × 1161 (*EEA* I, no. 102); the archiepiscopal confirmations were by Theobald and Richard (cartulary, fo. 76r; *EEA* II, no. 118). For further discussion, see *EEA* IV, no. 44n.

[1] The cartulary's foliation omits number 77.

291. *As canon of Lincoln and vice-archdeacon, notification that, at the presentation of the abbot and convent of Crowland, he has received and canonically instituted Geoffrey son of Waleran de Oyri and Fulk his brother in the perpetual vicarage of the whole church of Whaplode, saving the right of the monks of Crowland; the said clerks will answer for the church concerning all temporalities and customs.*   [*c.* 1187 × 4 Apr. 1192]

B = Spalding Gentlemen's Society, Crowland cartulary, fo. 78r. s. xiv med.

Universis sancte matris ecclesie filiis ad quos presens scriptum pervenerit Robertus de Hardr' Lincoln' ecclesie canonicus et vicearchidiaconus, salutem. Ad universitatis vestre notitiam volumus pervenire nos, ad presentationem abbatis et conventus Croiland', ad quos ecclesia de Quappelad' spectare dinoscitur, Galfridum filium Walerandi de Oyri et Fulconem fratrem suum in perpetuam vicariam totius ecclesie de Quappelad' recepisse et canonice instituisse, salvo iure monachorum Croiland', et salva in omnibus Lincoln'

ecclesie dignitate. Et predicti clerici pro predicta ecclesia de omnibus temporalibus et consuetudinibus respondebunt. Et ut hec institutio rata sit et illesa
permaneat, eam scripti nostri munimine et sigilli nostri appositione corroboravimus. Hiis testibus et c'.

Date in general as for no. 290, but presumably later than it, since one of the three
portioners has now disappeared.

292. *As canon of Lincoln and vice-archdeacon, notification that, at the presentation
of the prior and monks of Spalding, he has received H., chaplain, to the perpetual
vicarage of the church of Moulton, to be held for an annual pension of seven marks.*
[*c.* 1187 × 4 Apr. 1192]

> B = BL, Additional ms 35296 (Spalding cartulary, part 1), fo. 321r. s. xiv med.

Omnibus Cristi fidelibus Robertus de Arderne Linc' ecclesie canonicus et
vicearchidiaconus, salutem. Noverit universitas vestra me, ad presentationem
prioris et conventus de Spald', suscepisse H. capellanum in perpetuam vicariam
ecclesie de Multon', tenendam sub annua pensione vii. marcarum, salva in
omnibus Linc' ecclesie dignitate.

Date as for no. 290. The text is evidently truncated

293. *As canon of Lincoln and vice-archdeacon, notification that, at the presentation
of Eustace de Merk, he has received and canonically instituted the canons of Royston in
the* personatus *of the church of [North] Owersby.*
[*c.* 1187 × 4 Apr. 1192; ? × 18 Nov. 1189]

> B = PRO, E41/237 (transcript of Royston priory charters), m. 2. s. xiii ex. C = BL,
> Additional ms 46362 (T) (leaf from Royston cartulary), numbered p. 151, no. 3. s.
> xiv.

Universis sancte matris ecclesie filiis[a] ad quos presens scriptum pervenerit
Robertus de Hardres Lincoln' ecclesie canonicus et vicearchidiaconus, salutem
in domino. Noverit universitas vestra nos, ad presentationem nobilis viri
Eustachii de Merk, canonicos de Cruce Roys ad ecclesiam de Ouerisbi[b]
vacantem cum omnibus pertinentiis suis recepisse et in personatum eiusdem
canonice instituisse, salva in omnibus Lincoln' ecclesie dignitate. Et ut hec
institutio rata sit et illesa permaneat, eam scripti nostri patrocinio et sigilli
appositione duximus coroborandam. Hiis[c] testibus: magistro Wynemaro[d] subdecano, magistro Hugone[e] de London',[f] magistro Alexandro,[g] magistro Alano,
Ricardo de Kelesey, canonicis Lincoln', Willelmo de Barden', magistro Radulfo
de Kyme, magistro Gerardo Hoylondie,[h] magistro Ricardo, magistro Luca,
Waltero de Horkestowe,[i] Rogero de Kokewald,[j] Alano presbitero de Tofte,
Rogero de Stikeswald, Willelmo de Paris.

a filliis *C*	*b* Ouresbi *C*	*c* His *C*	*d* Wynmaro *C*
e Followed in B by Lincoln' *deleted*	*f* Lund' *C*	*g* Allexandro *C*
h Hoilandie *C*	*i* Horkestou' *C*	*j* Cukewald *C*

Date in general as for no. 290, but possibly before the date of Richard I's general
confirmation to Royston, which includes Owersby church (*Cartæ Antiquæ Rolls 11–20*,
no. 508; *Mon. Ang.,* vi, 405, with wrong date), especially since bp Hugh of Lincoln's
institution of the canons may be as early as 1186 × 1188 (*EEA* IV, no. 162). Eustace de

Merk's charter, and the confirmation by his nephew, Ralph of Rochester (Rovecestre), are in PRO, E41/237, m. 2, and Eustace's charter also in BL, Add. ms 46362. Richard I's charter calls Eustace the founder of the priory, but, although he built the original chapel at Royston, the foundation was mainly due to his nephew, Ralph of Rochester (Knowles and Hadcock, 172; *VCH Herts*, iv, 436).

R. de Insula

294. *Notification of the settlement of the dispute between the church of Barkston and the church of Honington over certain tithes and other obventions from ten bovates of land formerly of Robert son of Walter in Barkston, as follows. The corn tithes of five and a half bovates of the demesne of the nuns of Stixwould shall belong to Honington church, and the corn tithes of four and a half bovates cultivated by the peasants shall be divided between the churches of Honington and Barkston, the latter receiving also all lesser tithes from the four and a half bovates; the children of the peasant parishioners are to receive baptism at Honington, where also their wives are to go for purification; and, if any of them makes a will, the first bequest shall go to Honington church, the second to Barkston church; burial of the dead and confession shall be at Honington; this church will also receive wax-scot at two times in the year, the church of Barkston at a third time; on Easter day, on the feast of St Wilfrid and Christmas day man and wife from each house shall visit Honington church with their oblations, their households going to Barkston church.* [*c.* 1190 × 24 Aug. 1203]

B = BL, Additional ms 46701 (Stixwould cartulary), fo. 102r–v (pp. 203–4). s. xv.

Omnibus [sancte]*[a]* matris ecclesie filiis R. de Insula vicearchidiaconus Lincoln', salutem. Noverit universitas vestra querelam que vertebatur inter ecclesiam de Barkeston' et de Honyngton' super quibusdam decimis et aliis obventionibus de decem bovatis terre que fuerunt de feodo Roberti filii Walteri de Barkeston' sub hac forma compositionis conquievisse. Decime siquidem de blado quinque bovatarum et dimidie*[b]* de dominio monialium de Stikeswald' ad ecclesiam predictam de Honyngton' spectabunt. Medietas autem decimarum de blado de quatuor bovatis terre et dimidie*[b]* quas rustici colunt spectabit ad predictam ecclesiam de Honyngton' et altera medietas ad ecclesiam de Barkeston'. Et omnes alie decime a parochianis predictas quatuor bovatas et dimidiam*[c]* colentibus persolvende sunt ecclesie de Barkeston', videlicet de lano, de agnis, de ortis etiam si bladum in ortis venerit,*[d]* et generaliter de omnibus minutis decimis et obventionibus. Parochianorum rusticorum parvuli apud Honyngton' sacramentum baptismatis percipient, et illuc uxores eorum ad purificationem venient. Si vero contigerit aliquem illorum testamentum facere, primum legatum cedet ecclesie de Honyngton',*[e]* secundum ecclesie de Barkeston'. Mortui vero apud Honyngton sepulturam accipient, et confessionem in quadragesima, scilicet*[f]* de domo vir et uxor dumtaxat. Ceragium autem in duobus terminis ecclesia de Honyngton recipiet, scilicet*[f]* in die Pasche et in die Purifi[fo. 102v]cationis beate Marie, ecclesia autem de Barkeston' tertium recipiet*[g]* ceragium, scilicet in festo omnium sanctorum. In die vero Pasche et in die sancti Wilfridi et in die Natalis domini vir et uxor de domo cum oblationibus suis ecclesiam de Honyngton visitabunt, familia vero ecclesiam de Barkeston'. Et ut hec transactio rata et illibata*[h]* permaneat, dignum duxi eam sigilli mei appositione roborare. Hiis testibus: Rogero de Graham et Hugone*[i]* decanis,^{j} et Roberto de Wyvelforde decano, Alano de Lawyngton, Adam de Carlton, Roberto de Stokys clerico, Roberto filio Walteri, Thoma de Lunderthorpe, Hugone^i Skott,^{k} Osberto Baswyn', Hamone filio Ivonis, Hamone filio Radulphi, et c'.

a Supplied	*b Ms* dimidii	*c Ms* dimidium	*d Reading uncertain*
e Ms Honygton	*f Ms* silicet	*g Ms* recipient	*h Ms* illebata
i Ms Heugone	*j Ms* decanus	*k Reading uncertain*	

The suggested dating depends upon the assumption that the vice-archdn is Mr Robert de Insula, who had become archdn of Shropshire (Coventry diocese) by 5 Apr. 1201 × 24 Aug. 1203 (*EEA* 17, lv), and who may have been made vice-archdn of Lincoln after Robert de Hardres, vice-archdn, became archdn of Huntingdon after 1189 and before 4 Apr. 1192 (*Fasti Lincoln*, 27). The details of parochial dues given here are remarkable for this date.

ARCHDEACONRY OF OXFORD

Mr Nicholas of Lewknor

295. *Notification of the settlement before him of the dispute, delegated to him by the archbishop of Canterbury, between the abbot and canons of Osney and the abbot and monks of Bruern over two-thirds of the demesne tithes of 'Treton' [i.e., Bruern], which the former claimed anciently belonged to the church of St George, and of the dispute between the same parties over the whole church of 'Treton', namely, that the abbot and monks of Bruern will pay four shillings annually to the abbot and canons of Osney, who have renounced their claim to the tithes and to the church.*

[*c.* 1175 x 3 July 1183]

A = PRO, E327/48 (Ancient Deed Madox 48); right side slightly gnawed in two places. Endorsed: Inter Bruer' et Osene de decimis Treton' (s. xii ex.). Size 141 × 117 + 15 mm. Seal: originally two, both missing; two tags remaining (method 2).
B = BL, Cotton ms Vitellius E xv (Osney cartulary), fo. 158v. ss. xii ex.–xiii in. Damaged by fire. C = Oxford, Christ Church, D. & C. Lib., vi. a. 1 (Osney cartulary), fo. 169v. s. xiii ex.
Pd from A, Madox, *Formulare*, 27–8, no. 48; from B and C, *Oseney Cartulary*, iv, 530, no. 510.

CIRO GRAPHVM

Nicholaus vicearchidiaconus Oxeneford'^{a} universis sancte matris ecclesie filiis, salutem. Ad omnium vestrum noticiam volumus pervenire controversiam inter abbatem et canonicos de Oseneia^b et abbatem et monachos de Brueria super duabus portionibus decimarum dominii de Treutona,^{c} quas idem canonici proponebant antiquo iure ad ecclesiam beati Georgii pertinuisse, que ad eos^d spectare dinoscitur, auctoritate domini Cantuariensis nobis delegatam, et preterea causam quam idem canonici [pre]dictis^e monachis coram nobis de tota ecclesia de Treutona^f moverunt, tali fine conquievi[sse]. Siquidem abbas et monachi de Brueria^g persolvent ecclesie de Oseneia^b pro bono pacis iiii.^{or} solidos annuatim reddendos ad Pascha, et ipse abbas et canonici de Oseneia^b toti controversie quam adversus abbatem et monachos de Brueria^g tam super memoratis decimis quam super prefa[ta] ecclesia instituerunt renuntiaverunt. Et ut hec composicio rata sit et firma, eam sigillo nostro et utriusque ecclesie sigillis munire curavimus. His*^{h}* testibus:*^{i}* Roberto priore de Kinildewurth'*^{j}* Philippo priore de Sancta Fritheswith',*^{k}* magistro Waltero de Londoniis,*^{l}* magistro Roberto de Bedeford, magistro Roberto Aaron, magistro Gaufrido de Lard',*^{m}* Nigello decano, magistro Adam de Langedona,*^{n}* Albino canonico, magistro Laurentio, Henrico filio Petri, Radulfo capell(ano), et *^{o}*aliis pluribus.*^{o}*

a Oxen' *B;* Oxonef' *C*	*b* Osen' *B, C*	*c* Treotuna *B;* Treton' *C*
d ipsos *B, C*	*e All letters in square brackets lost from A; supplied from B, C*	
f Treuton' *B;* Treton' *C*	*g* Bruera *C*	*h* Hiis *C* *i C ends*
j Kenildewrd' *B*	*k* Frideswida *B*	*l* Lond' *B* *m* Lardier *B*
n Langedone *B*	*o—o* multis aliis que affuerunt *B*	

While Walter of Coutances, whose vice-archdn Nicholas was, was archdn of Oxford (above, no. 182n.; *Oseney Cartulary*, ii, 189 n. 1). For the lost name, 'Treton', replaced by 'Bruern', see *Oxon Place-Names*, ii, 337. For St George's church (in Oxford castle), see above, no. 87n.

Mr Richard of Aylesbury (*alias* Grim)

296. *Notification to all [rural] deans, parsons, priests and clergy of the archdeaconry of Oxford that he has inspected the charters of Peter de Mara, Walkelin Hareng and Alexander of Barton, granting to the abbey and monks of Eynsham, respectively, a moiety of [Lower] Heyford church, the church of [Brize] Norton and the church of [Westcot] Barton in perpetual alms; and has confirmed the same by the authority conferred upon him by John of Coutances, archdeacon of Oxford, while in the schools.*
[? late 1183 × 20 Oct. 1196]

B = Oxford, Christ Church, D. & C. Lib., vi. a. 2 (Eynsham cartulary), fo. 24r, no. 55. s. xii ex.
Pd, *Eynsham Cartulary*, i, 67–8, no. 55.

Ricardus vicearchidiaconus Oxenef' omnibus decanis, personis, presbiteris et universo clero per archidiaconatum Oxenefordie constituto, salutem in domino. Ad universitatis vestre notitiam volumus pervenire quod cartas nobilium virorum Petri de Mara et Walchelini Hareng et Alexandri de Berton' inspeximus, quibus tam ex ipsarum inspectione quam proborum virorum fide dignorum assertione nobis indubitanter innotuit quod iamdicti P. de Mara medietatem ecclesie de Heiford' et W. Hareng ecclesiam de Norton' et A. ecclesiam de Berton' deo et sancte Marie et monachis de Egnesham in perpetuam elemosinam concesserunt. Ut igitur concessiones eorundem per diuturniora tempora in sua firmitate permaneant, nec alicuius malignitate in posterum perturbentur, auctoritate a domino I. de Constantiis archidiacono Oxenef' nobis indulta dum in scolis moratur presenti scripto et sigilli nostri appositione corroboravimus. Testibus: Rogero decano de Langef', Martino presbitero, Roberto de Oxenef', Adam de Walingef', Gilleberto grando, Henrico Banastre, et multis aliis.

The dating limits are those of John of Coutances' archidiaconate (see above, no. 185n.). For the charters of the grantors here confirmed, see *Eynsham Cartulary*, i, nos. 134, 103, 117, respectively. Of the witnesses here, Martin the priest was presumably the parson of [Westcot] Barton who gave his assent to the grant (ibid., no. 117). For John of Coutances, who spent time in the schools at Oxford and was described as *magister* when elected bp of Worcester in 1196, see Emden, *Biog. Reg. Oxford*, i, 504–5.

297. *Notification to the same that he has inspected the charter by Alan son of G(eoffrey) of Aston granting to the abbey and monks of Eynsham four marks of silver annually in the church of [Steeple] Aston in perpetual alms, saving the right of patronage to Alan and his heirs; and has confirmed the same by the same authority as in no. 296.* [? late 1183 × 20 Oct. 1196]

B = Oxford, Christ Church, D. & C. Lib., vi. a. 2 (Eynsham cartulary), fo. 24r, no. 56. s. xii ex.

Pd, *Eynsham Cartulary*, i, 68, no. 56.

Ricardus vicearchidiaconus Oxenef' omnibus decanis, personis, presbiteris et universo clero per archidiaconatum Oxenef' constituto, salutem in domino. Ad universitatis vestre notitiam volumus pervenire quod cartam nobilis viri Alani filii G. de Estona inspeximus, ex cuius inspectione et proborum virorum fide dignorum assertione nobis indubitanter innotuit quod iamdictus A. filius G. de Eston' iiii.ᵒʳ marcas argenti annuas in ecclesia de Eston', salvo iure patronatus in eadem ecclesia sibi et heredibus suis, deo et sancte Marie et monachis de Egnesham in perpetuam elemosinam concessit. Ut igitur concessio eiusdem per diuturniora tempora in sua firmitate permaneat, nec alicuius malignitate in posterum perturbetur, auctoritate a domino I. de Constantiis archidiacono Oxenef' nobis indulta dum moratur in scolis presenti scripto et sigilli nostri appositione corroboravimus. Testibus: Martino presbitero, Adam de Walingef', Gilleberto grando, Henrico Banastre, Willelmo blundo, Radulfo clerico, Roberto scriptore, et multis aliis.

Date as for no. 296. For the charter here confirmed, see *Eynsham Cartulary*, i, no. 155.

298. *Notification to the deans, parsons, vicars and all clergy of the archdeaconry of Oxford that Lercelina of Glympton with the assent of Bertram her son, and afterwards Bertram himself, have given in perpetual alms to the canons of Kenilworth their church of Hethe, as appears from inspection of their charters in full chapter at Stoke [Lyne].* [? late 1183 × 20 Oct. 1196]

B = BL, Additional ms 47677 (Kenilworth cartulary), fo. 356r. s. xvi in.

Magister Ricardus vicearchidiaconus Oxon' decanis, personis ecclesiarum, vicariis et universo clero per archidiaconatum Oxonie constituto, in domino salutem. Ea que perpetuam desiderant firmitatem expedit per literas memorie commendare. Ea propter ad universitatis vestre volumus notitiam pervenire Lercelinam de Glinton', consensu Bertramᵃ filii et heredis sui, primo et postea ipsum Bertramᵃ ecclesiam suam de Hethra, in patrimonio videlicet ipsorum sitam, canonicis de Kenell' in perpetuam elemosinam concessisse et cartis suis confirmasse, sicut ex inspectione ipsarum cartarum in pleno capitulo apud Stoches celebrato manifeste cognovimus, et c'.

a Sic

Date as for no. 296. Stoke Lyne (Stoke Insula) was the next parish to Hethe in the same rural deanery (*Taxatio*, 31).

Mr Nicholas of Lewknor and Mr Richard of Aylesbury

299. *As former vice-archdeacons, notification that they have heard that the dispute between the abbot and canons of Osney and Thomas, parson of Ewelme, over two-thirds of the demesne tithes of Humphrey Pigace was settled in synod at Oxford, namely, that Thomas should receive the tithes for so long as he held the church; and declaration that at the time of the settlement the said tithes were in sequestration in the hand of John of Coutances, archdeacon of Oxford.* [Oct. 1192 x 20 Oct. 1196]

> B = Bodl. ms Twynne 23, p. 67 (transcripts of St Frideswide's and Osney deeds formerly at Christ Church, Oxford). s. xvii.
> Pd, *Oseney Cartulary*, iv, 446, no. 414A.

N. de Leuecanor et R. de Ailesberi quondam vicearchidiaconi de Oxeneford omnibus ad quos litere iste pervenerint, salutem. Noverit universitas vestra nos audivisse in sinodo Oxeneford controversiam que fuit inter abbatem et canonicos Osneye et Thomam personam de Lewelm' super duabus portionibus decimationum dominii Humphredi Pigace de omnibus rebus que decimari solent hoc fine sopitam fuisse. Predictus T. dictas decimas percipiet quamdiu ecclesiam de Lewelm' possidebit, salvo tamen iure utriusque ecclesie, scilicet de Osney et de Lewelme, &c. Sed ne quis dubitare possit in quo statu fuerunt decime ille illo tempore, universitati vestre in veritate que deus est protestamur memoratas decimas tempore huius concordie facte in sequestro fuisse, scilicet in manu Iohannis de Constanc' archidiaconi Oxeneford.

Nicholas of Lewknor and Richard of Aylesbury were successively vice-archdns of Oxford under, respectively, Walter of Coutances and John of Coutances (above, nos. 182–5; *Oseney Cartulary*, ii, 189 n. 1). However, since John of Coutances seems here still to be archdn, this declaration is evidently before his consecration as bp of Worcester (*Fasti Lincoln*, 36); the earlier terminus is provided by Richard's occurrence as vice-archdn in Oct. 1192 (*Oseney Cartulary*, iv, no. 401B).

ARCHDEACONRY OF STOW

Mr Alexander

300. *As canon of Lincoln and vice-archdeacon, notification that, by the mandate of Geoffrey, the king's son and elect of Lincoln, and at the presentation of Eudo of Mumby, he has instituted the canons of Bullington in the church of St Peter, Burgh[-le-Marsh], and inducted them into corporal possession.* [c. May 1173 × ? c. 1180]

> A = BL, Harley Charter 43 C. 37. Endorsed: Carta Alex' Archid'. De institutione [*space*] ecclesie de Burc (? s. xii ex.). Size 145 × 69 + 16 mm. Seal on tag (method 2), in red wax, circular, nearly complete (*c.* 35 mm diameter); frontally seated tonsured figure with arms outstretched, very worn; legend: SIGILLVM. SECRETVM.; perhaps a counterseal, on the reverse of an otherwise plain lump of wax (see also *BM Cat. Seals*, i, nos. 1815–16).
> Pd, *Danelaw Charters*, 8–9, no. 11.

Universis sancte matris ecclesie filiis ad quos littere iste pervenerint A. Lincolniensis ecclesie canonicus et vicearchidiaconus, salutem. Universitati vestre notum facere volumus nos, de mandato Gaufridi domini regis filii et

Lincolniensis ecclesie electi, et ad presentationem Eudonis de Mumbi, canonicos de Bulinctun in eclesiam sancti Petri de Burc instituisse et in corporalem possessionem induxisse. Et quia volumus ut hec illorum institutio in posterum firma et illibata permaneat, hanc presentis scripti nostri munimine et sigilli nostri appensione corroborare dignum duximus. His testibus: Alelmo decano Linc' ecclesie, Alexandro Malebisse, magistro Petro de Melide, Pagano canonico, Aluuredo[a] decano de Fordintun, Ricardo capellano de Calesbi, Ranulfo capellano decani, Alano capellano de Hocgestorp, Rogero Arsi, Drogone filio Rad(ulfi), Arnisio de Nova Villa.

a *Sic*

While Geoffrey Plantagenet was elect of Lincoln and before Adelelm ceased to be dean (*Fasti Lincoln,* 2, 9; *Fasti Salisbury,* 25, for Adelelm, who was also archdn of Dorset). For Alexander, who became archdn of Stow in succession to Richard de Almaria in *c.* 1187 (after 29 Mar.), see *Fasti Lincoln,* 45. The church of Burgh-le-Marsh was to prove quite a valuable asset to the priory (Golding, *Gilbert of Sempringham,* 358).

Since the church was in the archdnry of Lincoln, the vice-archdn was evidently acting here outside his own archdnry by commission of the bp-elect of Lincoln. In the same period, *c.* Aug. 1174 × 23 Jan. 1181, he carried out an institution in Aubourn church, acting in place of the archdn of Lincoln (the habitually absent Peter), though not calling himself vice-archdn (*HMCR Rutland,* iv, 114); and he did so again in Low Toynton church in 1184 × 1186 *sede vacante,* apparently in the capacity of 'official of the church of Lincoln' (see below, no. 301).

As archdn (from *c.* 1187) Alexander was called 'Mr', and there can be no doubt that he is also to be identified with the Mr Alexander, official of the West Riding (i.e., Stow), who issued a notification in *c.* 1180 that, on the precept of Richard de Almaria, archdn of the West Riding, and at the presentation of the monks of Durham, he had inducted Robert, clerk of Blyborough, into corporal possession of Blyborough church (*Misc. D. M. Stenton,* 209, no. 6, with facsimile, plate XVII); he is not called 'canon' here, however, and the seal used is different from that on no. 300.

* 301. *As canon of Lincoln and vice-archdeacon, [canonical][1] institution of Roger [or Richard] [clerk] in the church of Low Toynton at the presentation of Robert of Sausthorpe [the see being vacant].* [late 1184 × 21 Sept. 1186]

> Calendared in a list of institutions *sede vacante* in the diocese of Lincoln: Lincoln, Lincolnshire Archives, D. & C. Muniments, Dij/62/1/1a. s. xiii med., badly eaten away in places; pd, C. W. Foster, 'Institutions to Benefices in the Diocese of Lincoln', 186.

Alexander canonicus Lincoln' vicearchidiaconus[a] instituit Rogerum in ecclesiam de Minori Tynton ad presentationem domini Roberti de Sauthorp'. Hiis testibus: [   ][b] de Baginburg', Thoraldo decano, Eudone de Wadingwrd, Waltero capellano de Thymelby, Waltero capellano de Tynton, W[   ] [capellano][c] de Bardn', [   ] clerico de Winceby, Willelmo clerico de Luceby, et Radulfo de Stawenby, et residet litera super hoc confecta penes [   ].

a *Ms* vice archid'   b *Square brackets indicate words or passages lost through damage*   c *Suggested reading from remaining letters :* [   ]ll'o

During the vacancy at Lincoln between the election of Walter of Coutances as archbp of Rouen and the consecration of Hugh of Avallon as bp (*Fasti Lincoln,* 2–3). As in no. 300, the church concerned lay in the archdnry of Lincoln. This is almost certainly the act produced in an assize of darrein presentment in the king's court in Michaelmas term, 1219, between Robert of Sausthorpe and Osbert, parson of Horncastle, although the instituted clerk is there called Richard (*CRR*, viii, 171). The Curia Regis roll reads: '. . . et inde profert [*sc.* Robert of Sausthorpe] cartam Alexandri officialis Linc' ecclesie, que testatur quod ipse canonice instituit Ricardum clericum in ecclesiam de Minori Tinton' ad presentationem Roberti de Saucestorp' vacante sede. Profert etiam cartam Hugonis quondam Linc' episcopi, que testatur quod ratam habuit et confirmavit institutionem quam Alexander archidiaconus Westrithing' tunc officialis Linc' fecit Ricardo clerico de ecclesia de Minori Tinton' ad presentationem Roberti de Saucestorp.' This makes it clear that Alexander was regarded as acting as official of Lincoln *sede vacante,* and a strict reading of the passage reveals that he was not yet archdn of Stow when he made the institution, but had become so by the time of Hugh of Avallon's confirmation (cf. *EEA* IV, no. 203).

¹ Square brackets in the heading indicate information derived from *CRR*, viii, 171 (see note).

DIOCESE OF SALISBURY

ARCHDEACONRY OF BERKSHIRE

Richard of Shrivenham

302.   *Notification that, following the death of Mr Philip of Calne, parson of [West] Hendred, during the absence overseas of G(eoffrey), archdeacon of Berkshire, he attempted to take the church into the archdeacon's hands, but was resisted by the prior of Wallingford, who in the presence of the abbot of Abingdon appealed to the pope, much to the indignation of Jocelin, bishop of Salisbury. Subsequently the latter, learning of the prior's right, and by the intervention of the bishop of Bath, was placated; and by his order the vice-archdeacon, in general chapter at Kingston [Bagpuize], has received the prior as parson of [West] Hendred, it being clear to the vice-archdeacon and the chapter that no one had entry into the church after the death of Philip of Calne but the prior of Wallingford.*

[23 June 1174 × 18 Nov. 1184]

>   A = Oxford, Corpus Christi College, Archives, B. Cap. 1, Ev. 11 (surface damaged in places). Endorsed: Henreth'm. (? s. xiv). Size 178 × 84 mm (70 mm to tongue). Seal: very small fragment in white wax on tongue (repaired); no wrapping tie.
>   Pd, J. G. Milne, 'Muniments of Holy Trinity Priory, Wallingford', 54, no. 4.

Ricardus de Scriveham omnibus has litteras videntibus, salutem. Domino meo G.ᵃ archidiacono Berchesir' in transmarinis agente et me vices eius in Berchesir' gerente, decessit magister Philippus de Calna persona ecclesie de Henred, quam cum ex ratione officii mei tanquam vac[an]temᵇ in manum domini mei archidiaconi suscipere voluissem, restitit michi prior de Walingeford' et in presencia domini abbatis Abendon' appellavit ad p[resenciam]ᵇ domini pape et indignationem domini Saresb'r Iocelini hoc facto plurimum provocavit. Qui tamen postmodum temporis beneficio placatus factus est, domino Bat[hon']ᶜ interven[ie]nte, iure quoque cognito quo prior utebatur. Unde fuit ut ex mandato domini Sar' supramemorati vice domini archidiaconi [i]n gen[era]li [c]apitulo apud Chingestun' predictum priorem in personam ecclesie de Henred susciperem nullo penitus reclamante, presertim cum michi et capitulo constiterit nullum hominum omnino preter priorem de Walingeford' in ecclesiam iam dictam usque in presens habuisse ingressum post decessum magistri Philippi de Calna, qui proximum in ecclesia illa gerebat personatum ante priorem prefatum. Hec omnibus scribenda duximus ut omnibus rei geste veritas innotescat et ordo. Valete.

a Milne reads C. *(in error)*   *b Surface of ms damaged; bracketed letters supplied*
c Milne inserts J., for which there is no evidence

After the consecration of Reginald, bp of Bath, son of Jocelin, bp of Salisbury, and before the latter's death (*Fasti Salisbury*, 34–5, 3). On this act and no. 303, see Kemp, 'Informing the archdeacon', 143–4. In this case some sort of inquest had evidently been held in the chapter to establish the prior of Wallingford's claim. Another very early example of such an inquest took place not later than 1189 in the rural deanery of Maidstone over the church of Chart (Kent); it was held by Nicholas, the (rural) dean, and the chapter in the presence of Mr John, vice-archdn (of Canterbury): Canterbury Cathedral Lib., ms Chartae Antiquae C408 (I owe this reference to the kindness of Professor Nicholas Vincent).

303. *Notification that, on the precept of Jocelin, bishop of Salisbury, he has received the prior and convent of Holy Trinity, Wallingford, as parson of the church of West Hendred, which the bishop has granted to them so that its obventions may be converted in usus proprios. This institution was made in the general chapter of Abingdon at Kingston [Bagpuize].*   [23 June 1174 × 18 Nov. 1184]

A = Oxford, Corpus Christi College, Archives, B. Cap. 1, Ev. 8. Endorsed: Institucio ecclesie de Henreda (s. xii ex.). J. Amberl' (s. xiv). m. .X. (? s. xiv). Size 147 × 91 mm (no sign of turn-up). Seal and tag missing; possible trace of one slit in foot.
Pd, Milne, 'Muniments of Holy Trinity Priory, Wallingford', 55, no. 5.

Omnibus sancte matris ecclesie filiis ad quos presens scriptum pervenerit Ricardus vicearchidiaconus Berkesir', in domino salutem. Noverit universitas vestra quod nos, ad preceptum domini mei Iocelini dei gratia Sar' episcopi, recepimus priorem et conventum ecclesie sancte et individue Trinitatis Walingeford' personam ecclesie de Weshenr'. Dominus vero Sar' ecclesiam illam cum omnibus pertinenciis suis libere et quiete et absque omni indebita vexatione priori et conventui ibidem deo servienti pro salute [anime]*ᵃ* sue concessit, ita ut in usus proprios omnes obventiones convertere possint. Hec institutio facta est in generali capitulo Abendunie apud Cingest(un') celebrato. His testibus: Amone de Wittenham, Henrico de Enneneia, Willelmo de Dengestwor'. Willelmo de Sancta*ᵇ* Helena, Rodberto de Fifhida, Osberto de Arewell', Stephano de Hachberna, et multis aliis clericis, Rodberto de Bachepuz, Henrico de Cingestuna, Rogero de Fifhida, Galfrido fratre suo, Henrico d[e] Peseia, militibus, et multis aliis tam clericis quam laicis.

a Supplied; hole in ms   *b Ms* Sancto

Date as for no. 302. The witness-list illustrates very well the attendance of laity as well as clergy at rural chapters.

DIOCESE OF WORCESTER

ARCHDEACONRY OF GLOUCESTER

Mr Peter de Leche

304. *Notification of the settlement in his presence of the dispute between Prior R(oger) of Llanthony and Amiot of Woodstock, king's serjeant, over the advowson of the church of Windrush, namely, that Amiot presented a clerk, R(alph), to the church, as it had previously been recognised in the king's court that he could do, which presentation the prior confirmed; and Amiot, at the request of many, granted that the church would henceforth belong to the church of [Great] Barrington, as a chapel to its mother, as the prior had earlier claimed, and also that R(alph) would hold it of the mother church as a perpetual vicarage, rendering annually two gold pieces. Amiot placed the key of the chapel on the altar of the mother church, and the prior took it and handed it to the vice-archdeacon, who, at the prior's presentation, [? instituted in the chapel] R(alph) the clerk, the see of Worcester being vacant, and he himself exercising the cure of the archdeaconry.* [1185 × 21 Sept. 1186]

B = PRO, C115/K2/6683 (Llanthony cartulary), fo. 71v, iii, no. 49. s. xiv med.

Omnibus ad quos presentes littere pervenerint P. vicearchidiaconus Glouc', salutem in domino. Noverit universitas vestra quod controversiam que diu vertebatur inter R. priorem Lanthon' et Amisium de Wodestoke servientem domini regis super advocatione ecclesie de Wenrich hoc modo me presente conquievit. Predictus A. presentavit quendam*^a* clericum R. nomine ad prefatam ecclesiam, sicut prius recognitum fuit in curia domini regis quod hoc de iure facere potuit, cuius presentationem predictus prior concessit et ratam habuit; et predictus Ami(sius) pro dei amore et petitione multorum concessit eam ab eo die pertinere ad ecclesiam de Berninton', tanquam capellam ad matrem, sicut ipse prior prius eam vendicaverat, et quod predictus R. clericus teneret eandem [a]*^b* matrice ecclesia in perpetuam vicariam, reddendo i. aureum annuatim, et pro fructibus alium aureum, ita quod ii. annuatim solvet. Ipse vero A. clavem predicte capelle super altare matricis ecclesie posuit, quam prior ibi recepit et michi tradidit. Ego vero R. clericum, ad ipsius prioris presentationem [? institui in predicta capella],*^c* ecclesia Wygornensi tunc vacante. Hiis vero, quia me presente facta sunt et tunc curam archidiaconatus gessi, per litteras meas sigillatas testimonium perhibeo.

a Ms quoddam   *b* Supplied   *c* Bracketed passage conjecturally supplied

Mr Peter de Leche, who was not yet a vice-archdn in May 1177 (BL, Add. Charter 7013), became archdn of Worcester in 1189/90; the episcopal vacancy at Worcester was therefore almost certainly that between the translation of Baldwin to Canterbury and the consecration of William of Northolt (*Fasti Monastic Cathedrals*, 100), particularly since Amiot of Woodstock renewed his renunciation of the chapel in the latter's presence (PRO, C115/K2/6683, fo. 71v). Peter de Leche, vice-archdeacon, witnessed Amiot of Woodstock's first renunciation of his right in the chapel to the mother church of Great Barrington; and, in another confirmation, by William son of Baldwin, Amiot's uncle, the clerk is identified as Ralph (ibid., fo. 71r, 71r–v). Llanthony priory acquired both the church of Great Barrington and the chapel of Little Barrington, which was dependent upon it (ibid., fo. 70v). For the identification of *Wenrich* as Windrush, see *Gloucestershire Place-Names*, i, 209.

DIOCESE OF YORK

ARCHDEACONRY OF THE EAST RIDING

William Gerold

305. *With dean Roger of Lockington and the chapter of Buckrose, notification that William Noble, with the assent of Geoffrey, his son and heir, gave the church and advowson of Burythorpe to the canons of Kirkham and afterwards, before the chapter, ratified his gift while the parson, Robert Wacelin, was yet living; and that, on the latter's death, the canons of Kirkham presented Mr Richard of Perth to Archbishop G(eoffrey) of York, who admitted and instituted him, for an annual pension to the canons of one mark.* [18 Aug. 1191 × May 1205; ? not before 1198]

B = Bodl. ms Dodsworth 7 (Transcripts of charters formerly in St Mary's Tower, York, 1644), fo. 211r. s. xvii med. C = Bodl. ms Fairfax 7 (Kirkham cartulary), fo. 33v (calendar only). s. xv ex.

Omnibus sancte matris ecclesie filiis visuris vel audituris literas has Willelmus vicearchidiaconus de Oustriding et Rogerus decanus et capitulum de Bucchorossire, salutem. Quia audivimus quosdam iniuste vexare canonicos de Kirkaham super ecclesia de Bergetorp, ne per suppressionem veritatis in hac causa possit falsitas optinere, rei veritatem quam super hoc novimus universitati vestre presentibus literis insinuamus. Sciatis itaque quod Willelmus Nobilis ecclesiam de Bergetorp in libero tenemento suo fundatam et ad ipsum iure hereditario pertinentem cum ipsius ecclesie advocatione deo et canonicis de Kirkaham, assensu Gaufridi filii*a* et heredis sui, dedit et carta sua confirmavit, et ipsam donationem suam postea coram capitulo de Bucchrossire concessit et ratam habuit, vivente Roberto Wacelin, eiusdem ecclesie persona. Quo defuncto, predicti canonici de Kirkaham ad prefatam ecclesiam de Bergetorp vacantem presentaverunt magistrum Ricardum de Pert domino G. Eboracensi archiepiscopo. Idem vero Ricardus, ad eorum presentationem ab eodem archiepiscopo, cum constaret ei de iure ipsorum, admissus et in eandem ecclesiam institutus, tenet eam nomine eorundem canonicorum et de eadem ecclesia solvit eis annuatim pensionem unius marce voluntate prefati Eboracensis archiepisciopi. Ut autem super hiis fides certissima vobis fiat, in testimonium veritatis huic scripto appendimus sigilla mea*b* ego Willelmus vicearchidiaconus de Oustriding, et ego Rogerus de Lochington decanus de Bucchros, et ego Robertus prior de Wattun.

a Followed in ms by sui *deleted*   *b Sic; ? rectius* nostra

After the consecration of Geoffrey, archbp of York, and while Robert was prior of Watton: he occurs in ?1198 × 1204, June 1200 and Nov. 1202, and had been succeeded at the latest by Easter term 1205, when his successor occurs (*Heads*, 205). A charter by Geoffrey Noble, confirming his father's gift and witnessed by William Gerold, vice-archdeacon of East Riding, is Bodl. ms Dodsworth 7, fo. 210v. It is possible that the present act is not earlier than 1198, when the advowson was in dispute between Geoffrey Wacelin (perhaps a relative of Robert Wacelin) and another, and Kirkham had to make its claim (*CRR*, i, 49). Subsequently, during the northern eyre of winter 1198–9, Geoffrey Wacelin confirmed to Kirkham the advowson of the church of *Berkerthorp*, which he had claimed against the priory in the king's court (see his charter, witnessed by the eyre judges: Dodsworth 7, fo. 207r; cf. *Pleas before the King*, iii, pp. cxxxv, cxliv), and archbp Geoffrey received and instituted Mr Richard of Perth at the priory's presentation (Bodl. ms Fairfax 7, fo. 63v). For Buckrose, see *Yorks E. Riding Place-Names*, 19–20.

ARCHDEACONRY OF RICHMOND

Mr Roger of Melsonby (*alias* of Richmond)

306. *With Geoffrey, dean [of Richmond],*[1] *notification that, when the canons of Easby asserted before them in full chapter at Richmond that the church of St Wilfrid, [Great] Langton, belonged to them by gift of T(homas) de Burgh, former patron of the church, and Ismania, his mother, and by confirmation of W(illiam), archdeacon of Richmond – T(homas) being present and confirming that he had conveyed to the canons his right in the patronage of the church – there were also present Elias of Bedale, who admitted that he was due to pay the canons one gold piece [annually] from the church, and the parson of Witton, who admitted that he had no right in the church save through Elias of Bedale.* [15 Sept. 1189 × 1196]

B = BL, Egerton ms 2827 (Easby cartulary), fo. 274r. s. xiii ex.

Universis et c', magister Rogerus vicearchidiaconus Rich' et Gaufridus decanus, salutem. Universitati vestre significamus quod, cum canonici de sancta Ag(ata) protestati essent coram nobis in pleno capitulo apud Richem' ecclesiam sancti Wilfridi de Langeton' cum pertinentiis suis ad ipsos pertinere, tam ex don(atione) T. de Burg' quondam patroni eiusdem ecclesie et Ismene matris eius quam ex concessione et confirmatione W. archidiaconi Richem', presente prefato T. de Burg' et publice confitente se in prefatos canonicos intuitu pietatis contulisse quicquid[a] iuris et patronatus ipse et antecessores sui in prefata ecclesia habuerunt, presente etiam nichilominus Helia de Bedale et sollempniter confitente se esse obligatum ad solvendum prefatis canonicis unum aureum de prefata ecclesia; affuit etiam persona de Wytton', qui et ipse publice confessus est in iure se nichil iuris habere in prefata ecclesia nisi per Helyam de Bedal'. Quia igitur dignum est et legibus consentaneum ut unicuique iura sua integra illibataque serventur, dignum duximus predicta que audivimus presentis scripti attestatione et sigillorum nostrorum appositione notitie vestre manifestare, ne ius canonicorum in prefata ecclesia quacumque malignantium[b] machinatione periclitetur in posterum. Test', et c'.

a Ms quicquit   *b* Ms malingnantium

While William de Chemillé was archdn of Richmond (see above, no. 277n.); for the archdn's confirmation of the gift by Thomas and Ismania, and for other charters concerning it, see above, no. 279 and n. Elias of Bedale was incumbent of the church (*EYC*, v, no. 259).

[1] For his identity, see *EYC*, v, page viii.

APPENDIX I

ARCHDEACONS ACTING AS PAPAL JUDGES-DELEGATE BEFORE 1200

1. John, archdn of Exeter (named first), with H(enry), prior of Hereford (St Guthlac's), and W(illiam), precentor of Hereford, delegates of Innocent III in the dispute between Walter of Cormeilles, knight, on one side, and the prior of Monmouth and M., clerk of Tarrington, over the patronage of Tarrington church. [After 15 Feb. 1199]. PRO, E210/3242 (Anc. Deed D 3242).

2. Mr Robert (of Hardres), archdn of Huntingdon (named second), with P(ayn), abbot of Warden and W(alter), prior of Chicksands, delegates of Celestine III, in the dispute between the nuns of Harrold priory and B(aldwin), son of the count of Guines, over the church of Stevington. [1192 × 1199]. C. R. Cheney, 'Harrold priory: a twelfth-century dispute', *Bedfordshire Historical Record Society*, 32 (1951), 13–15, nos. 3–5. (Robert was too busy to act.)

3. Mr Wimar, archdn of Northampton (named second), with Hugh [of Avallon], bp of Lincoln, and H(ugh), prior of Pontefract, delegates of Celestine III in the dispute between Geoffrey, archbp of York, and the canons of York. [Jan. 1195; c. Jan. 1196]. Three acts. *EEA* IV, nos. 214A–C.

4. Nicholas, archdn of London (named third), with G(ilbert), bp of London, and Ralph [de Diceto], dean of London, delegates of Lucius III in the dispute between Prior Alan and the brethren of St Bartholomew's Hospital, London, and Peter of Wakering over the church of [Little] Wakering. [c. 1182 × 1186]. N. Moore, *History of St Bartholomew's Hospital*, i, 147n., with facsimile of original opposite; *Foliot Letters and Charters*, no. 416.

5. Nicholas, archdn of London (named second), with the prior of Bermondsey, papal delegates in the dispute between Geoffrey of Bedford, priest, and Geoffrey de Turre, clerk, over the church of St Margaret near London Bridge. [Mar. 1184]. *Westminster Abbey Charters*, no. 194.

6. Mr Peter [of Waltham], archdn of London (named third), with Richard, bp of London, and Ralph [de Diceto], dean of London, delegates of Clement III in the dispute between the Hospitallers and Barking abbey over tithes and parochial rights in Handley. [1190 × 1191]. Chelmsford, Essex R.O., D/DP T1/693; cal., Fisher, 'Petre Documents', 80; see also *EEA* 15, no. 79n.

7. Mr Peter [of Waltham], archdn of London (named second), with R(ichard), prior of Bermondsey, papal delegates in the dispute between the monks of Hatfield Regis (Broad Oak) and the canons of St Botolph's, Colchester, over certain demesne tithes at Hatfield Regis. A.D. 1194. BL, Additional Charter 28336.

8. Thomas, archdn of Norwich (named first), with the priors of Westacre and Buckenham, delegates of Innocent III in the dispute between the monks of

Warden and the canons of Holy Cross, Thetford, over the ninth sheaf of thirty-six acres in Barham. [1199]. *Wardon Cartulary,* no. 223; cf. no. 224.

9. Walkelin, archdn of Suffolk (? named second), with H(ugh), abbot of Bury (St Edmunds), papal delegates in the dispute between Mr Gilbert of Sempringham and the brethren of Alvingham (priory), on one side, and Mr Stephen, on the other, over the church of Keddington. [1157 × 1180]. Bodl. ms Laud misc. 642 (Alvingham cartulary), fo. 122r. s. xiii ex. (In this case Walkelin was too busy to act.)

10. Walkelin, archdn of Suffolk (named first), with Gilbert, prior of Butley, delegates of Lucius III in the dispute between Wim(ar), parson of Grimston church, and G. clerk of Bawsey, over tithes and obventions of parishioners of Wendling and of ?Rudham. A.D. 1184. *Eye Cartulary,* i, no. 78.

11. Paris, archdn of Rochester (named third), with G(uerric), abbot of Faversham, and the abbot of Boxley, papal delegates in the dispute between the church (cathedral priory) of Rochester and John *de Blachemore* over the church of Stifford. [1177 × 1188/9]. BL, Cotton ms Domitian A x (Rochester cartulary), fo. 153r–v. s. xiii in. (Revocation of a judgement by an earlier panel of delegates.)

12. Mr Godfrey, archdn of Worcester (named second), with Geoffrey, dean of Hereford, Mr Rannulf, canon of Hereford, and Mr Simon of Bromyard, clerk of David, bp of St Davids, delegates of Alexander III in the dispute between Hamelin, abbot of Gloucester, and Hugh, clerk of Aberllynfi, over the tithes and parochial obventions of Tregoyd and Pipton. [1159 × 1168]. Two acts. Gloucester Cathedral Lib., Register A, fos. 100v–101v, fo. 101v; pd (calendar), 'Register of Gloucester churches', nos. 42–3.

13. Mr Godfrey, archdn of Worcester (named second), with Gilbert, bp of Hereford, delegates [of Alexander III] in the dispute between the canons of St Mary's, Warwick, and the canons of St Sepulchre's, Warwick over parochial rights and a pension. [prob. late 1161 × early 1162]. *Foliot Letters and Charters,* nos. 345–6. Cf. above, no. 260.

14. Adam [de Thorner], archdn of York (named third), with Simon, dean, and Hamo, treasurer of York, papal delegates in the dispute between Alexander the clerk and Rievaulx abbey over certain corn tithes in [East] Bolton. [?1196 × 1201]. *Rievaulx Cartulary,* no. 145u; *EYC,* iv, no. 99.

See also above, nos. 179, 260–1.

Delegate of Archbishop Hubert Walter

15. Geoffrey, archdn of Suffolk (named first), with E(gelinus), prior of Snape, delegates of Hubert, archbp of Canterbury, in the dispute between the prior and canons of Butley and the prior and monks of Mendham over certain lands belonging to the church of Weybread and their tithes. [1198 × 1205]. *Leiston Cartulary and Butley Charters,* no. 130; *EEA* III, no. 364.

See also no. 130, where the archdeacon acts as delegate of a bishop, and no. 258, where he acts as delegate of an archbishop.

APPENDIX II

TWELFTH-CENTURY ENGLISH VICE-ARCHDEACONS: A PROVISIONAL LIST

For an earlier list, see C. R. Cheney, *English Bishops' Chanceries 1100–1250,* Manchester 1950, 143–5. The normal title of the archdeacon's deputy in the twelfth century was 'vice-archdeacon', but the title 'sub-archdeacon' existed as a much less common alternative for the same office. The known occurrences of sub-archdeacons are given separately below, for the sake of clarity and in order to highlight the extreme rarity of the form. The Appendix ends with a small selection of references to individuals acting as representatives of archdeacons without employing the title of vice-archdeacon or sub-archdeacon.

Sub-archdeacons

Diocese of Exeter

Exeter diocese
Alfred, ?1133 × 1136 (*EEA* XI, no. 15 – suspicious)
Ralph de Leu, ?1133 × 1136 (*EEA* XI, no. 15 – suspicious)

Cornwall
John, *c.* 1171 × 1184 (1177 × 84) (*EEA* XI, no. 97)

Exeter
Ralph, 1177 × 1184 (*EEA* XI, nos. 95, 97)

Diocese of York

Cleveland
Robert son of William, *c.* 1160 × 1174; ?*c.* 1165 × 67 (*EYC,* ix, no. 131)
Reiner, *c.* 1170 × 1185 (*EYC,* i, no. 577)

Vice-archdeacons

Diocese of Bath and Wells

Bath
Un-named, *c.* 1180 × 1191 (*Petri Blesensis . . . Opera Omnia,* 173, no. 58) [Peter of Blois, archdeacon of Bath, addressed G. his *vicarius,* ?*c.* 1189 × 1191; ibid., 450–2, no.157; *Fasti Bath and Wells,* 28, no. 100.]

Taunton[1]
  Mr Richard de Feny, ?*temp.* Henry II (*St Mark's Cartulary*, no. 237 and p. 275)
  Richard de Herlem', 1185 × 1191; *c.* 1186 × 1187 (*EEA* X, no. 171; *HMCR Wells*, i, 40)
  Richard of Spaxton, ?1186 × 1204; 1203 × 1205 (above, no. 1; *Storgursey Charters*, no. 51(8); *Select Canterbury Cases*, 12)

Wells
  Samuel, 1136 × 1158 (*EEA* X, no. 37)
  W., ?*c.* 1180 × 1191 (*HMCR Wells*, i, 42)

Diocese of Canterbury

Canterbury
  William, ?*c.* 1155 × *c.* 1165 (*Cal. Chart. R.*, ii, 298)
  Robert, 1168, 1169 (*Materials*, vi, nos. 432, 500) [In 1169 Robert was twice addressed as *vicarius* of Geoffrey (Ridel), archdeacon: ibid., nos. 488, 499.]
  Mr John, ?1176 × 1181 (Canterbury Cath. Lib., Chart. Ant. C408)
  Mr Ralph, 1182, 1184, 1188 (*Canterbury St Augustine's Cartulary*, ii, 553, 543, 544)
  R., 1189, *c.* 1190 (*Epp. Cant.*, 298; *Canterbury St Augustine's Cart.*, ii, 503)
  Mr Everard, ?1195 × 1200; ?late 12th cent; 1198 × 1204 (*CDF*, 490, no. 1348 – with Henry archdn; = *Arch. Cant.*, iv, 213, no. 15; Bodl. ms Rawlinson B. 336, pp. 146–7, 165)
  E., 1199 (*Epp. Cant.*, 467)

Diocese of Chichester

Chichester diocese
  Mr Thomas, 1174 × 1180; 1181 × 1182 (*Chichester Acta*, no. 64; = *Chichester Cartulary*, no. 1016; *Chichester Acta*, no. 119)

Diocese of Coventry and Lichfield

Coventry
  John, 1186 × 1187 (*EEA* II, No. 297B)
  Mr J., ?*c.* 1200 (Stratford-upon-Avon, Shakespeare Birthplace Trust, DR 10/208)

Diocese of Exeter

Cornwall
  Ralph, 1171 (*EEA* XI, no. 140)
  John, 1170 × 86; dead by 3 June 1190 × 1 June 1191 (?by late 1190) ('Tavistock Charters', no. 30; above, no. 37)
  Robert, *c.* 1177 × 96 (*Launceston Cartulary*, no. 96)

---

[1] It is very difficult to distinguish and date the following three vice-archdns, or indeed to be certain that they were all separate individuals, but all occur in the context of churches, etc., in the archdnry of Taunton.

Exeter
  Ralph, *c.* 1185 × ?1187 (*EEA* XII, no. 158)
  William of Axmouth, 1190 × 1191 (*CDF,* 16, no. 60)

Totnes
  Ivo, *c.* 1170 × 1186 (BL, Add. Ch. 27527)

Diocese of Hereford

Hereford
  William de Stokes, 1186 × 1193 (*EEA* VII, no. 221; for date, see *Reading Abbey Cartularies,* i, no. 358)

Diocese of Lincoln

Huntingdon
  Mr Peter of Paxton, 1183 × 1195 (BL, Add. Ch. 15470)

Leicester
  (Mr) Gerard (son of Baldric de Sigillo) (BL, Cott. Vesp. E xviii, fo. 181v)

Lincoln
  Mr Robert of Hardres, 1175 × 1184; 1182; 1183; 1185 × 1186; *c.* 1187 × 1192 (above, nos. 286–93; BL, Add. ms 46701, fo. 47r–v; *Pinchbeck Register,* i, 425)
  R. de Insula, *c.* 1190 × 1203 (above, no. 294)

Northampton
  Mr Richard, 1175 × 1192; 1176 × 1180 (above, no. 153; App. III)

Oxford
  Mr Philip, 1174 (*Oseney Cartulary,* ii, 224–6, nos. 783–4; *Foliot Letters and Charters,* 462, no. 426; *EEA* II, 153–4, no.178)
  Nicholas of Lewknor, *c.* 1175 × 1183 (above, no. 295)
  . . . . (former), 1192 × 1196 (above, no. 299)
  Mr Robert Aaron, 1177 × 89 (PRO, E164/20, fo. 40r–v)[2]
  Mr Richard of Aylesbury (*alias* Grim), 1174 × 1193; ?1183 × 1196, *c.* 1187; 1192 (PRO, E164/20, fo. 143r; above, nos. 296–8; *Oseney Cartulary,* iv, nos. 63A, 119, 401A–B)
  . . . . (former), 1192 × 1196 (above, no. 299)
  A(dam of Chinnor), 1201 (Bodl., Laud. Lat. 17, fo. 224v)

Stow
  Mr Alexander, *c.* May 1173 × 1186; 1175 × 1190 (above, nos. 300–1; *Danelaw Charters,* no. 425; *Foliot Letters and Charters,* no. 467)

Diocese of Salisbury

Berkshire
  Un-named, 1142 × 1184 (*Cirencester Cartulary,* ii, no. 479; = *EEA* 18, no. 52)

[2] He appears to have become vice-archdn later than Nicholas of Lewknor, since he witnesses without title an act of the latter (above, no. 295).

Richard (of Shrivenham) 1174 × 1184; 1183 × 1184; 1184 × 1187 (? × 1185) (above, no. 303; *EEA* 18, no. 114; Oxford, Christ Church, Notley Roll, m. 4; papal judge-delegate)

Dorset
Mr Hamo, 1190 × 1193 (*EEA* 19, App. II, no. 1)
Mr Alfred, 1198 × ? early 13th cent. (BL, Add. Ch. 74468)

Wiltshire
Mr Vincent, 1189 × 1190; 1189 × 1205 (*EEA* 18, 140–1, no. 179; *Reg. Malmesburiense*, i, 443–4; *Cirencester Cartulary*, ii, no. 487)

Diocese of Worcester

Gloucester
Mr Peter de Leche, 1175 × 1190; 1185 × 1186 (*Gloucester Cartulary*, ii, no. 559 – for date, see Walker, 'Earldom of Hereford charters', no. 103; *Landboc Winchelcumba*, i, 85; PRO E164/20, fo. 40r–v; PRO, C115/K2/6683, fo. 71r, no. 47; above, no. 304)
Drew (?), ?late 12th. cent.[3] (*Flaxley Cartulary*, 137, no. 13)

Diocese of York

York diocese
Angot, *c.* 1119 × *c.* 1138 (*EYC*, ii, no. 1073; for date, see above, lii n.)

Cleveland
Robert (son of William), 1161 × 1167; 1174 × 1180 (*EYC*, i, no. 562; *Guisborough Cartulary*, ii, no. 718; = *Chichester Acta*, no. 67)

East Riding
Mr William of Gilling, 1154 × 1180 (*EYC*, iii, no. 1397; *St Bees Register*, no. 20)
William Gerold, *c.* 1180 × 1190; 1191 x 1205 (?1198 × 1205) (*EYC*, i, no. 623; above, no. 305)

Richmond
Mr William, ?*c.* 1160 × 1171; × ?*c.* 1175 (*EYC*, v, no. 297; *Fountains Cartulary*, i, 175, no. 10)
Robert, *c.* 1180 × 1190 (*EYC*, v, no. 307; *Fountains Cartulary*, i, 176, nos. 17–18)
Mr Theobald, 1180 × 1199; 1187 (*Lancashire Pipe Rolls*, 360–1; *EYC*, v, no. 148)
Mr Roger of Melsonby (*alias* of Richmond), ?1187 × early 13th cent.; 1189 × 1196; *c.* 1191 × 1203 (*Coll. Top. et Gen.*, v, 119, no. 7; ibid., 106, nos. 1–2, and 224–5 (= *EYC*, v, nos. 275, 277–8), 228; above, no. 306)

[3] Both the date and the association with this archdnry are uncertain; the reference is to a charter by Gilbert Talbot, witnessed by 'Drew at that time vice-archdn', giving to Flaxley abbey 12d annually from the mill of *Ruddekeshale*, which is possibly (but not certainly) Ruddle in Newnham (Glos).

York
> William, 1154 × 1181; 1160 × 1170; 1160 × 1180; 1170 × ?*c.* 1180 (*Fountains Cartulary*, ii, 487, no. 9;[4] ibid., i, 273, no. 20; *EYC*, i, nos. 443, 233; Bodl., ms Rawlinson B. 455, fo. 232r)
> Robert, *c.* 1164 × 1175 (*EYC*, xi, no. 253, and cf. no. 107)
> Nicholas of Tadcaster,[5] *c.* 1185 × 1193; 1185 × 1200 (*EYC*, iii, nos. 1652, 1868)

VICES ARCHIDIACONI

Exeter
> Un-named – *me qui tunc vicem gerebam H. archidiaconi,* 1161 × 1188 (BL, Harley 3660, fo. 76r; wrongly cal., *Canonsleigh Cartulary*, no. 145)

Colchester
> Robert, dean of [West] Bergholt, *qui . . . archidiaconi vices gerebat,* 1168 × 1184 (*Colchester Cartulary*, ii, p. 540)

Berkshire
> Mr Rannulf of Calne, *quondam vices archidiaconi gerentis in Berkesira,* ?*c.* 1150 × *c.* 1170 (*EEA* 18, no. 103)
> Richard of Shrivenham – *me vices eius in Berchesir' gerente,* 1174 × 1184 (above, no. 302)

Richmond
> Mr William – *vicem archidiaconi tunc tenente,* 1168 or slightly later (*EYC*, v, no. 244)

---

[4] The reference is to 'William nephew of William the vice-archdeacon'.

[5] There can be no reasonable doubt that he is to be identified with the Nicholas of Tadcaster who was parson of Tadcaster (York archdnry) from before 1160, in succession to his father Ernald, and rural dean (*EYC*, xi, nos. 10, 28, 50, the last dating from 1189); in 1164 × 75 he occurs as rural dean with two chaplains (ibid., no. 23), and was clearly of sufficient standing in the archdnry to be made vice-archdn late in his career.

APPENDIX III
ADDITIONAL ACTUM
(This actum was discovered while the present edition
was in the press)

DIOCESE OF LINCOLN

Archdeaconry of Northampton

Savaric

*Notification that, at the presentation of King Henry II, he has granted to abbot
William de Pavily and the convent [of St James, Northampton] the church of
[Rothers]thorpe, vacant, and has instituted them as parson in the same by Richard, his
vice-archdeacon.*   [late Jan. 1176 ×17 Sept. 1180]

> B = BL, Cotton ms Tiberius E v (St James Northampton cartulary), fo. 128v (116v). s.
> xiv in. Badly damaged by fire, 1731; some words readable only under ultra-violet
> light. C = Bodl. ms Top. Northants, c. 5 (abbreviated transcripts from B made
> before the fire), p. 406. s. xviii in.

Omnibus sancte matris ecclesie filiis Salvaricus*a* archidiaconus de Norh',
salutem. N[overit]*b* universitas vestra nos, ad petitionem et presentationem
domini nostri Henrici [secundi regis]*c* Angl(orum), abbati Willelmo de Pavely
et conventui eiusdem loci ecclesiam de [Throp] liberam et vacantem cum
omnibus pertinentiis et libertatibus eiusdem ecclesie concessisse [et per]
Ricardum vicearchidiaconum nostrum eos personam in predicta ecclesia
instituisse. Ne a[utem] nostra rite facta institutio possit vel debeat iritari, eam
sigillo nostro communivimus. *d*Hiis testibus: Radulfo priore de Broc, magistro
Ricardo [vicearchidiacono]*e*, [Henrico] de Haddon', magistro Roberto Temprenoise, Willelmo persona, Rog(ero) de Midelton', [   ] [pres]bitero de Colintre,
Ilberto presbitero, Ad(am) presbitero, Radulfo de Plumton', et aliis.*d*

> *a Sic in B, C   b Words in square brackets either supplied from C or, if omitted there,
> supplied conjecturally where possible   c 2R^s C   d–d The abbreviated list in C
> reads:* Test' Radulfo prior' de Broc. Hen. de Haddon. Will' p^a. de Midelton, Rad' de
> Plumton & al.   *e Reading uncertain*

After 14 Jan. 1176, when abbot William de Pavily's predecessor died, and before the
abbot's own death (*Heads*, 178), i.e., during the period when Geoffrey Plantagenet was
bp-elect of Lincoln, 1173–1182 (*Fasti Lincoln*, 2). The manor of Rothersthorpe was held
of the king in chief by the de Chocques family until *c.* 1186, after which it came to the
de Bethune family (Sanders, *English Baronies*, 141). Although Anselm de Chocques
(died 1150 × 1161) gave lands in the manor to Rothersthorpe church, possibly soon
after its dedication (BL, Cott. Tib. E v, fo. 129r; Bodl. ms Top. Northants, c. 5, p. 406),
the gift of the church to St James's abbey was due to Henry II and must have occurred

when the manor was for some reason in the king's hands. It was confirmed to the abbey by Hugh of Avallon, bp of Lincoln, and by William de Bethune, who died in 1213 (*EEA* IV, no. 133; BL., Cott. Tib. E v, fo. 128v; Bodl. ms Top. Northants, c. 5, pp. 405–6; Sanders, 141).

INDEX OF PERSONS AND PLACES

Arabic numerals refer to the numbers of the acta in this edition. Small Roman numerals refer to the pages of the introduction. The letter W following a number indicates a witness. Conventional abbreviations for the English counties have been used. All county locations are in accordance with the pre-1974 boundaries. In addition the following abbreviations for religious orders have been used:

Aug.   Augustinian
Ben.   Benedictine
Cist. Cistercian
Clun. Cluniac
Gilb. Gilbertine
Prem. Premonstratensian

A., canon of Missenden, 83W
    clerk of Ashendon, 84W, 85W
    dean (rural) of Langford, 66
    dean (rural) of Swinderby, 289n.
    Mr, official of Carlisle, 12W
    ?priest, 24W
Aaron, Robert, Mr, 295W; vice-archdn of
    Oxford, App. II, p. 201
Abbots Bromley, *see* Bromley, Abbots
Abel, chaplain, 196W
Aberllynfi (Breconshire), clerk of, *see* Hugh
Abingdon, Abendon', Abendunia (Berks),
    abbot of (Ben.), 302
    chapter of (rural), xlviii, 303
    and see St Helen
Abrinc', *see* Avranches
Aburn', *see* Aubourn
Acard, Achard, priest (*presbiter*)/chaplain (of
    archdn Baldric de Sigillo of
    Leicester), lii, 131W, 132W, 133W,
    134W
    priest (*presbiter*) of Lissington, 194W
Aclaia, Acleya, *see* Oakley
Acleia, *see* Akeley
Acre, Castle, Acra (Norfolk), priory of
    (Clun.), 216
Acton Reynald, Actona (Salop), chapel of,
    dep. on Shawbury church, 23n.
    parochial affiliation of, xlv, 23
Adam (de Hele), 128W
Adam, abbot of Cirencester, 154n.
    abbot of Evesham, papal judge-delegate,
    154–5
    butler (*pincerna*), 147W

clerk of Leighton Buzzard, 48W
    monk of Stoke-by-Clare, 195W; *cf.* Stokes,
    Adam de, Mr
    nephew of Nicholas archdeacon of
    Bedford, 51W
    parson of Newport, 207
    priest (*presbiter*), App. III W
    prior of Bradenstoke, made parson of
    North Aston, 173
    prior of St Benet of Holme, 219
Adam son of Cospatrick, of Dunbar, 31
    son of Cospatrick son of Orm, parson of
    Camerton, xlvi, 7
    son of Hugh, chaplain, 161W
Adam, Stephen son of, *see* Stephen son of
    Adam
Addington, Little (Northants), church of, 165
Adelelm, Alelm, Alelmus, archdn of Dorset,
    xlviii, 194n., 233–6, 237n.; dean of
    Lincoln, 300W
Adrian IV, pope, ?259
Adrinth', *see* Alderton
Adstone, Attiniston' (Northants), chapel of,
    dep. on Canons Ashby church, 152
Ælfhere, ealdorman of Mercia, 259
Agatha, daughter of Robert son of Ralph,
    206; sister of, *see* Alice, wife of
    Bertram
Aguilon, Agulun, Richard, 196W; dean
    (rural) of Debden, 198W; ? =
    Richard, dean (q.v.)
Ailbrictus, Ailbrittus, Ailbryttus, *see* Albrict
Ailesberi, Ailesbiri, *see* Aylesbury
Ailesham, *see* Hailsham

Ailmer, Aylmer, Eilmer, Eylmer, parson of
    Powerstock, 234, 236
  priest (*presbiter*) of Newport, 207
Ailriches, *see* Arlesey
Ailward, archdn of Colchester, xliv, 207
Aimeric, archdn of Carlisle, 12; chaplain of,
    see Roger; archdn of Durham, 285W
Aishell, *see* Ashill
Akeley, Acleia (Bucks), chaplain of, *see*
    Walter
  parochial affiliation of, xlv, 179
Alan, almoner of Ramsey, incumbent of
    Warboys church, 125a, 125b
  archdn of Stafford, xlvii, 28
  brother of Laurence archdn of Bedford,
    parson of Newton in Aveland, 286
  Mr, canon of Lincoln, 62W, 293W
  chaplain of Hogsthorpe, 300W
  constable of Richmond, 275, 279
  parson of Kirmond-le-Mire, 194W
  parson of Willingham, 194W
  priest (*presbiter*) of Toft, 293W
  prior of St Barthlomew's, London, App. I,
    no. 4
Alan son of Geoffrey, of Steeple Aston, 296
  son of Meinfelin, 74W
  son of Torphin, 6n.
Alan, Geoffrey son of, *see* Geoffrey son of
    Alan
Alard, Mr, *see* Burnham, Alard of, Mr
Alard Fitz William, *see* Fitz William, Alard
Alban son of Gervase, 31W
Albenei, Albeneia, *see* Albini
Alberic, archdn of Berkshire, 230n., 232n.
Albini, Alben', Albenei, Albeneia, Ralph de,
    289
  Robert de, 47
  Roger de, 269W
Albinus, Mr, 28W
  canon, 295W
  clerk, 3W
Albrict, Ailbrictus, Ailbrittus, Albrittus, dean
    (rural), li, 114W, 128W
  priest (*presbiter*), 130W
Alcrug', Ralph de, Mr, 201W
Aldbury, Aldeberia (Herts), Fulk of, 110W
Aldelin, William son of, *see* William son of
    Aldelin
Alderman, Aldelmannus, William, 204W;
    and cf. Alemanum?
Alderton, Adrinth' (Northants), priest of, *see*
    William
Aldetheleg', *see* Audley
Aldgate, Algat', *see* London
Aleinton', *see* Allington
Alelm, Alelmus, *see* Adelelm
Alemanum?, William, 249W; *and cf.*
    Alderman
Alexander, 255W

Mr, 125bW
Mr (?same), 159W, 160W
Mr, archdn of Stow, 194, 300n., 301n.; as
    canon of Lincoln acting for the
    archdn of Lincoln, 289n.; as canon of
    Lincoln and vice-archdn (of Stow),
    liii, 300, App. II, p. 201; as official of
    Stow, liii, 300n.; as official of church
    of Lincoln, 300n.
bp of Lincoln, 32n., 70n., 72n., 88, 100n.,
    141n., 142n., 166, 167n.
brother of Alfred of Haddington, *see*
    Alexander, clerk of Aubourn
canon and *presbiter* of Lincoln, 189W,
    190W, 286W
Mr, canon and *sacerdos* of Lincoln, 288W,
    293W; ? = Alexander archdn of Stow
    (q.v.)
canon of Osney, 27W
canon of Ruxox, 52, 53
clerk, App. I, no. 14
clerk of Aubourn, 289
Mr, ?clerk of Godfrey, bp of Winchester,
    41W
dean (rural), 25W
dean (rural; another), 269W
III, pope, 27, 99, 154n., 185n., ?259, 260,
    App. I, nos. 12, 13
prior of Canons Ashby, 126W
prior of Ely, 33n., 106
Alexander, William son of, *see* William son of
    Alexander
Alfred, bp of Worcester, 259n.
Mr, canon of Exeter, 37W
dean (rural) of Fordington, 300W
priest (*presbiter*) of Hardingstone, 130W
sub-archdn in Exeter diocese, App. II, p. 199
Mr, vice-archdn of Dorset, App. II, p. 202
Algat', *see* London, Aldgate
Alice, daughter of William Clement,
    runaway nun of Ankerwyke, xlvi–
    xlvii, 22, 139
  wife of Bertram son of William of
    Calverdon, and sister of Agatha, 206
Allington, ?East, Aleinton' (Devon), Randulf
    of, 44W
Almaria, Richard de, Mr, archdn of Stow
    and precentor of Lincoln, 73n., 115n.,
    188–93, 286W, 300n. *bis*
  Roger de, archdn of Stow and precentor of
    Lincoln, 188
Alnei, *see* Hannah
Alricheseie, *see* Arlesey
Alspath (Warks), church of (now Meriden),
    18
  Ivo of, 18n.
Alta Ripa, Ralph de, Mr, archdn of
    Colchester, 194–6; vicar of Ashdon,
    198

Blunham, Bluham (Beds), parson of, *see* Hugh

Blunt, Andrew le, 204W

Blyborough, Bliburch (Lincs), church of, 300n.; clerk of, *see* Robert

Blybur, *see* Blythburgh

Blyford (Suffolk), church of, 222

Blythburgh, Blybur (Suffolk), priory of (Aug.), 222

Boarhunt, West Boarhunt, Burh', Westburh' (Hants), church of, 252
Henry of, 252W

Boarstall (Bucks), 172n.

Boby, Hugh de, 137

Bodin, Boiderus, parson of Upper Stondon and rural dean, 57n., 61W, 62W

Bohun, Jocelin de, bp of Salisbury, xxxix n., 150n., 234n., 235, 236n., 237, 302–3; son of, *see* FitzJocelin, Reginald
Margaret de, 240
Robert de, prior of Newport Pagnell, 88W

Boiderus, *see* Bodin

Bolingbroke, Bolingbroc (Lincs), chapter of (rural), 143

Bolonia, Richard de, 31W

Boltby, Boltebi (Yorks N.R.), priest of, *see* Sweyn

Bolton, East *or* Low (in Wensley, Yorks N.R.), App. I, no. 14

Bonhunt, Banhunt (Essex), chapel of, xliv, 207 *and see* Wicken Bonhunt

Bootham, Budthum (York), William of, priest (*presbiter*), 282W

Bordesley, Bordesl' (in Redditch, Worcs), abbey of (Cist.), monk of, *see* Robert

'Boroughshire', Burg'sire (Yorks N.R.), 280

Bosco, R. de, clerk, rector of Mongewell, 186
Robert de, official of William of Cornhill archdn of Huntingdon, 186n.

Bowel', *see* Bueles

Boxley (Kent), abbot of (Cist.), papal judge-delegate, App. I, no. 11

Braci, William de, and son Gilbert, 88

Bradenstoke, Bradenestoke (Wilts), priory of (Aug.), 173, 242, 247
prior of, *see* Adam

Bradwell, Bradewelle, prior of (Ben.), *see* Nigel; William

Brafferton, Braffertona (Yorks N.R.), church of, 269

Brafield-on-the-Green, Brachafeldie, Bragefeld (Northants), church of, 130

Brampton, Brampton' (Cumb.), church of, 12

Brampton, Brampton', Branton' (Hunts), John of, 128W
John of (?another), 103W
John of, vicar of Godmanchester, 123
Osmund of, 103W

Bray, Brai, William de, kt., lord of Shenstone fee, 27, 27W

Brian, Brien, William son of, *see* William son of Brian

Bridlington, Bridl' (Yorks E.R.), priory of (Aug.), 288

Bridport, Brideport, Bridiport (Dorset), clergy of chapter of, 236
John of, Mr, 3W, 238W

Brigham (Cumb), Walter of, 10W

Brigstock, Brikestoch', Brikestok' (Northants), church of, 154; chapels of, *see* Oakley, Little; Slipton

Briteva, Robert son of, *see* Robert son of Briteva

Brito, William, archdn of Ely, xlvii, 32

Britollio, Ralph de, Mr, 130W

Briton', Le (*sic*), 210W

Brittany, 274n.
Alan of, earl of Richmond, 274; steward of, *see* Hugh son of Gernagod

Brityna, friend of Walter, archdn of Oxford, 169

Brize Norton, *see* Norton, Brize

Briueton', *see* Bruton

Broc, Broch, Humphrey de, 155W
Nigel del, 167W
Ralph de, 167W
Richard de, 79W
Walter de, 81W, 86W
and see Brooke

Brockley (Kent), 206n.

Brom, Walter de, 226W; brother of, Hugh, 226W

Bromley, Abbots, Bromleia (Staffs), lands in, 28

Bromyard, Simon of, Mr, clerk of David, bp of St Davids, papal judge-delegate, App. I, no. 12

Brooke, Broc (Rutland), prior of (Aug.), see Ralph

Broy, Robert de, clerk, 68

Brudos, Roger, 6W

Bruern, Bruera, Brueria, Bruiera (Oxon, formerly 'Treton'), abbey of (Cist.), 295
prior of, *see* Wibert
church and tithes of, 295

Bruges, Walter de, Mr, 28W

Bruiera, *see* Bruern

Bruton, Briueton' (Som.), Bucchros, priory of (Aug.), 1

Bucchorossire, Bucchros, Bucchrossire, *see* Buckrose

Buchcastre, Buchecastre, Buthcastre [etc], *see* Bewcastle

Buchintun' (? High Bickington, Devon), Joel de, knight, 37W

Buckenham (Norfolk), prior of (Aug.), papal judge-delegate, App. I, no. 8

Cambo, Camboc, Gilbert de, 8W, 9W
Cambridge, Cantebrige, Cantebrigge,
    Cantebrigia, archdn of (Ely), *see*
    Nicholas
  Geoffrey of, official of archdn Richard
    Barre of Ely, 34, 34W
  Reginald of, Mr, 161W
Camera, Rocell' de, 111W
  Simon de, 283W
Camerton, Camertona, Camberton'
    (Cumb.), church of, 7
  chapel of, *see* Flimby
  parson of, *see* Adam son of Cospatrick
Campellis, Robert de, ?knight, 37W
Campo Florido, Reginald de, clerk, 234
Candover, Preston, Candevra (Hants),
    church of, 132
Canons Ashby, *see* Ashby, Canons
Cantebrige, Cantebrigge [etc], *see*
    Cambridge
Cantelu, Walter de, 290n.
Canterbury, Cantuariensis (Kent), archbp
    of, xxxiii, 198, 226, 229, 258, 290,
    295, *and see* Becket, Thomas; Dover,
    Richard of; Dunstan; Forde,
    Baldwin of; Theobald; Walter,
    Hubert
  archdn of, *see* Becket, Thomas; Castilion,
    Henry de; Poore, Herbert; Ridel,
    Geoffrey
  archdnry of, 2–4
  diocese of, 2–4
  vice-archdn of, *see* Everard; John; Ralph;
    Robert; William
  St Mary's church of, xxxiv
Capella, Matthew de, 226W
Carbonel, Thomas, abbot of Gloucester,
    256n.
Carlisle, Carliolensis, Karleolum, Karliel'
    (Cumb.), 7; chapter at, 6; synod at,
    xlvii, 7n.
  archdn of, *see* Aimeric; Robert; Ros, Peter
    de
  official(s) of, 8–9, *and see* A.; Thorp,
    Thomas de; William
  archdnry of, 5–12
  bp of, *see* Æthelwulf; Bernard; Hugh
  bpric of, custodian of, *see* Ros, Peter de
  cathedral priory of (Aug.), canons of, 7
    prior of, *see* John; Walter
  dean of (rural), *see* Kirkbride, William of
  diocese of, xxxviii *bis*, xlvii, lii, 5–12; clergy
    and laity of, 8–9
Carlton (?Carlton Scroop, Lincs), Adam of,
    294W
Castilion, Castellione, Henry de, archdn of
    Canterbury, 4; brother of, Robert, 4
  and see Chastillon
Castle Acre, *see* Acre, Castle

Castletown (Cumb.), library at, 8n.
Caun', *see* Calne
Cave, Robert de, 10W
Caversham (Berks, formerly Oxon), church
    of, 180
Cawston (Warks), *see* Dunchurch
Cawthorpe, Little, Calethorp (Lincs), church
    of, 140
Celestine III, pope, 22n., 201n., 211n., 246n.,
    App. I, no. 3
Cercell', *see* Churchill
Cestrefeld, *see* Chesterfield
Cestreford, *see* Chesterford
Cestreham, Cestresham, *see* Chesham
Cestretona, *see* Chesterton
Chadwell, Chaldewel (Leics), priest of, *see*
    Robert
Chalfield, Chaldef' (Wilts), *see* Richard, kt,
    and wife, Joan
Chalfont St Peter, Chalfhunte, Chalfunda,
    Chalfunta (Bucks), church of, 82
  rector of, *see* Ralph
Chambas, Odo de, 114W
Chapem', Ralph de, 149W
Charlbury, Cherleberi (Oxon), 177
Charlecote, Cherlecota (Warks), chapel of,
    263; incumbent of, *see* Roger, Mr
Chastillon, 'Chaveillen', Hugh de, lord of
    Leckhampstead, 179
  and see Castilion
Chatteris, Chartriz (Cambs), abbey of (Ben,
    nuns), 33
'Chaveillen', *see* Chastillon
Chebsey (Staffs), church of, 26
Cheddington, Chettend' (Bucks), church of,
    93; incumbent of, *see* William son of
    Fulk
Cheinna, William de, ?knight, 37W
Cheltenham, Chiltham (Glos), 258
  church of, 258n.
Chemillé, Chemile, Chimeilli, Chimelle,
    Chymili, Sunelli, William de, archdn
    of Richmond, xxxviii, 277–84, 306;
    official of, *see* Richmond, Roger of;
    bp-elect of Avranches, 281, 283n.,
    284n.; bp of Angers, 281n.
Chenduit, Cheneduit, Ralph, 110; son of,
    William, 110n.
Chent, *see* Kent
Chenur', *see* Chinnor
Cherleberi, *see* Charlbury
Cherlecota, *see* Charlecote
Cheselbourne (Dorset), *see* Bussel, Bardolf
Chesham, Cestreham, Cestresham (Bucks),
    chapter at, xlviii n., 79
  chaplain of, *see* Peter
  church of, moiety of, 78n., 79n., 98;
    chaplain of, *see* William
  dean of (rural), *see* Laurence

Forde (Dorset), Baldwin of, bp of Worcester, 304n.; archbp of Canterbury, xxxix n., 15, 92n., 264, 289, 304n.

Fordington, Fordintun (Lincs), dean of (rural), *see* Alfred

Forewoda, Forwode, Forwud', *see* Farwood

Forton (in Montford, Salop), tithes of, 24n.

Fountains, Fontes (Yorks W.R.), abbey of (Cist.), 65
  abbot of, *see* Haget, Ralph; Robert

Franc(o), brother of Savaric, archdn of Northampton, 149W

Freiston, Frestunenges (Lincs), meadow in, 134

Fretewll', Fretwella, *see* Fritwell

Frindsbury, Frendesbery (Kent), church of, 226
  parson of, *see* William son of Peter

Fritwell, Fretewll', Fretwella (Oxon), tithe in, xlv, 174

Frumentyn, William, vicar of Fenny Compton, 20

Fulcher, William son of, *see* William son of Fulcher

Fulk, chaplain of Corfe, 233W

Fulk, William son of, *see* William son of Fulk

Funteney, Funtenela, Funteneio, Robert de, clerk, incumbent of Great Sampford church with Eston', 199, 220n.; parson of Great Thurlow, 199n., 220

Fyfield, Fifhida (Berks), Geoffrey of, kt, brother of Roger, 303W
  Robert of, clerk, 303W
  Roger of, kt, 303W

G., clerk of Bawsey, App. I, no. 10
  dean (rural) of Newport, 24W
  vicarius of Peter of Blois, archdn of Bath, App. II, p. 199

Gaddesden, Little, Parva Gadesdena (Herts), church of, 126

Galo, Richard son of, *see* Richard son of Galo

Gamaliel, dean (rural), 268W

Gant, Robert de, 141n.
  Walter de, 141n.
  Walter de, abbot of Waltham, 34

Garendon, Gerold', Gerunden' (Leics), abbey of (Cist.), xlvi, 131–3
  abbot of, papal judge-delegate, 96; *and see* Thurstan

Garinus, prior of Spalding, 142

Garston, East, *see* East Garston

Gate Burton, *see* Burton, Gate

Gatenby, Gattenebi (in Burneston, Yorks N.R.), Roger of, 269W

Gaubert, Mr, 156W

Gave, Ralph, 37W

Gayhurst, Giherst (?Bucks), Hugh of, clerk of

bp Godfrey de Lucy of Winchester, 41W

Geiteburton, *see* Burton, Gate

Geldeham, *see* Yeldham

Gelstona, Nicholas de, 46W

Geoffrey, Mr, 149W
  abbot of Lire, 229
  archdn of Berkshire, 232n.; *and see* Vernun, Geoffrey de
  archdn of Cleveland, *see* Muschamp, Geoffrey
  archdn of Suffolk, xl, xlii n., 224; judge-delegate of archbp, App. I, no. 15
  brother of abbot Robert de Gorron of St Albans, 31W
  chaplain, 195W
  chaplain (?another), 216W
    and see Geoffrey, clerk/chaplain
  chaplain of King Henry II, 13W
  clerk/chaplain of archdn Nicholas de Sigillo of Huntingdon, l–li, 111W, 114W, 118W, 126W, 127W
  clerk of Clopton, 224W
  clerk, incumbent of St Margaret near London Bridge, 204; ? = Tower, Geoffrey of the (q.v.)
  deacon, 128W
  dean (rural) of Hatfield (Broad Oak), 211W
  dean of Hereford, papal judge-delegate, App. I, no. 12
  dean (rural) of Richmond, 306
  official of Ipswich (=Suffolk) archdnry, liii
  palmer, 97
  parson of Wicken, 207
  priest (*presbiter*), 147W
  priest (*presbiter*) of Burgh-on-Bain, 194W
  priest (*presbiter*) of Little Missenden, 69W
  prior of Spalding, 192
  scribe (*scriptor*), 81W
  servant of the abbot of Waltham, 211W
  servant of William English, 254

Geoffrey FitzPeter, *see* FitzPeter, Geoffrey

Geoffrey son of Alan, 97W
  son of Stephen, master of Templars in England, xlvi, 239

Geoffrey, Alan son of, *see* Alan son of Geoffrey
  Henry son of, *see* Gorhambury
  John son of, *see* John son of Geoffrey

Ger', prior of Huntingdon, 113W

Gerard, Girard, (Mr), son of archdn Baldric de Sigillo of Leicester, lii, 131W, 132W, 134W; vice-archdn of Leicester, App. II, p. 201

Gerard', Simon de, miller, 167W

Gerinus, ?incumbent of Great Gransden church, 101

German, clerk, 285W
  prior of Durham, 31

Halstock, Halgestoke (Dorset), church of, xxxiv, 238

Halton, East, Hautun (Lincs), chapter at, 194

priest of, *see* Gilbert; Richard; William

Halton, West (Lincs), 194n.

Hamelhamsted, *see* Hemel Hempstead

Hamelin, abbot of Gloucester, App. I, no. 12

dean (rural) of Yarburgh, 140

Hamelin, Walter son of, *see* Walter son of Hamelin

Hamma (unidentified), dean of, *see* R.

Hamo, Mr, *see* Winchester, Hamo of, Mr

clerk (another), 126W

dean of Lincoln, xlvii, 139

treasurer of York, papal judge-delegate, App. I, no. 14

Mr, vice-archdn of Dorset, App. II, p. 202

Hamo son of Ivo, 294W

son of Meinfelin, 74

son of Ralph, 294W

Hamt', Roger of, constable, 127W

Hamtona, Hantona, Nicholas de, Mr, 245W

Ralph de, 111W

Handley (in Ingatestone, Essex), App. I, no. 6

Hannah, Haneya, Alnei (Lincs), dean of (rural), *see* Robert

Robert of, 140; prob. = Robert, dean of Hannah (q.v.)

Hanney, Enneneia (Berks, East *or* West), Henry of, clerk

Hantona, *see* Hamtona

Haranc, Hareng, Ralph, 30W

Walkelin, 296

Harbin, George., 1n.

Hardingstone, Hardinstor', Hardyngystou (Northants), priest of, *see* Alfred

Hardres, Aderne, Harder', Hardere, Hardr' (?Kent), Richard of, Mr, parson of Scampton church, 193

Robert of, Mr, 193W; canon of Lincoln, 289–93; vice-archdn of Lincoln, liv, 286–93, App. II, p. 201; archdn of Huntingdon, xl, 193n., 290n., 294n., App. I, no. 2

Hardwick, Herdewik, Herdwyc (Northants), church of, 159

Hardwicke, Heredewyca (Glos), chapel of, dep. on Standish church, 256; vicar of, *see* Ernisius

Harefield, Herrefeld, Herrefeldia (Middx), church of, 212; parson of, *see* Robert

tithe of, xlv, 212

Hareng, *see* Haranc

Harewell', *see* Harwell

Harewold', *see* Harrold

Harlington, Herlingedun' (Beds), church of, 63; possessor of, *see* Philip, clerk

lord of fee of, *see* Pirot, Ralph

Harrington, Harintun' (Northants), clerk of, *see* Simon

Harrold, Harewold' (Beds), priory of (Aug. nuns), 67, App. I, no. 2

Harrowden, Great, Harwedon' (Northants), church of, 163

parson of, *see* Sulby, abbot of

vicar of, *see* Elias

Hartona, *see* Hayton

Hartwell, Hertwella (Bucks), clerk, parson of, *see* Benedict

Harundel, *see* Arundel

Harwedon', *see* Harrowden

Harwell, Arewell', Harewell' (Berks), chapter at, 232

Osbert of, clerk, 303W

Hastang, Aytrop I, 262n.

Aytrop II, 262

Hastings, Hasting', Nicholas de, Mr, 23W

Richard de, parson of Barwell church, 135

William de, mother of, *see* Erenburga

Hatfield Broad Oak (Hatfield Regis), Athfeld', Hatfeld' (Essex), App. I, no. 7

dean of (rural), *see* Geoffrey

priory of (Ben.), dep. on St Melaise, Rennes, 103n., 195, App. I, no. 7

prior of, *see* William

Hatherley, Hatherleya (Glos), clerk of, *see* Osbert

Hatley Cockayne, Hattele (Beds), church of, 57, 66; parson of, *see* John; vicar of, *see* William

Hattin (Palestine), Battle of, 269n.

Haughmond, Haghem' (Salop), abbey of (Aug.), xlv, 23; ?canon of, *see* Herbert

Haustede, *see* Halstead

Hautun, *see* Halton

Hawkchurch, Havekeschirch' (Devon), Philip of, 238W

Hawnby (Yorks N.R.), church of, xlvi

Hayling, Heling' (Wight), Henry of, 252W

Hayrun, Alban, 107

Hayton, Haitona, Hartona (Cumb., near Brampton), Richard of, 8W, 9W

Heckfield, Hechfeld' (Hants), John of, Mr, 252W

Heddenham, *see* Haddenham

Heddona, *see* Haddon

Hedham, *see* Hadham

Hedingham (Essex), deanery of (rural), *see* Hinckford

Hegtred(eberia), *see* Heytesbury

Heiford', *see* Heyford

Hele, Adam de, *see* Adam

Heliensis, *see* Ely

Heling', *see* Hayling

Hella, Richard de, 51W

Helmesl' (?Helmsley, Yorks N.R.), Robert de, dean (rural), 10W

Hemel Hempstead, Hamelhamsted (Herts), Alfred of, 110W

Helto, brother of, *see* William

Hemingford Grey, Hemmingeford' (Hunts), 100

Hendred, West, Henred (Berks), church of, 302–3; parson of, *see* Wallingford, priory

Henefeld, *see* Enfield

Henlow, Henlawe (Beds), priest of, *see* Hugh

Henry I, king of England, xliv, 5, 15, 174n., 221n.

Henry II, king of England, 2n., 5n., 15n., 52, 60–1, 79, 100n., 116, 129n., 178n., 183, 221n., 260n., 300; App. III; chancellor of, *see* Becket, Thomas; Plantagenet, Geoffrey; chaplain of, *see* Nicholas; Roger

Henry VI, emperor, xlix n.

Henry, abbot of Crowland, 120n.

  archdn of Huntingdon, *see* Huntingdon, Henry of

  chaplain of Ralph Foliot, archdn of Hereford, 46W

  clerk, son of Peter of Northampton, incumbent of Alspath church, 18

  dean (rural), 110W

  dean (rural; another), 216W

  dean of East Haddon (Henry of Haddon), 62W, 155W, 161W, 228W; App. III W; parson of Guilsborough, 149

  Mr, official (?of Richmond), 285W

  priest (*presbiter*), 27W

  priest (*presbiter*) of Loddington, 146W

  prior of St Andrew's, Northampton, 46

  prior of St Guthlac's, Hereford, papal judge-delegate, App. I, no. 1

  son of Geoffrey FitzPeter, parson of Preston, 257

  treasurer of St Paul's, *see* Banastre, Henry

Henry FitzHarding, *see* FitzHarding, Henry

Henry son of Geoffrey, *see* Gorhambury

  son of Peter, 295W

  son of Peter, of Northampton, parson of Newbold Pacey, 262; vicar of St Giles', Northampton, 161

  son of Richard, *see* Oxendon

  see also Robert, son of the priest

Herbert, 201W

  canon (? of Haughmond), 23W

  chaplain, 161W

  prior of St Martin's, Richmond, 5

Herbert, William son of, *see* William son of Herbert

Herdewik, Herdwyc, *see* Hardwick

Heredewyca, *see* Hardwicke

Hereford, Hereford', Herfordensis, archdn of, xxxiv n., *and see* Foliot, Ralph

  archdnry of, xxxiii, 45–6

bp of, *see* Foliot, Gilbert I; Foliot, Robert

cathedral of, canon of, *see* Rannulf

  dean of, *see* Geoffrey

  precentor of, *see* William

  diocese of, xxxiii, xxxiv n., 45–6

  earl of, *see* Roger

  vice-archdn of, *see* Stokes, William de

St Guthlac's priory of (Ben.), dep. on Gloucester, 24, 186

  prior of, *see* Henry; Osbert'

Hereford, William of, 287W

Herlem', Richard de, vice-archdn (of Taunton), App. II, p. 200

Herlingedun', *see* Harlington

Herlotera, Osbert de, 231

Hermer, daughter of, *see* Godreda

Herrefeld, *see* Harefield

Hertford, Hertford' (Herts), All Saints church in, 127

Hertfordshire, xlviii n.

Hertmer', *see* Hurtmore

Hertwella, *see* Hartwell

Hervey, Mr, 156W

  bp of Ely, 32

  marshal (?of earl of Leicester), 131n.

Hervey, Osbert son of, *see* Osbert son of Hervey

Hesseburne, *see* Husborne

Hethe, Hethra (Oxon), church of, 298

Heyford, Lower, Heiford' (Oxon), church of, 296

Heytesbury, Hegtred(eberia) (Wilts), prebend of in Salisbury cathedral, 151n., 235

Hibaldstow, Hiboldeston', Hibolestou' (Lincs), Robert of, Mr, 62W

Hida, *see* Hyde

Hide, Ralph de, 81W

Hideshale, *see* Idsall

Higford (in Stockton, Salop), tithes in, 24n.

Hilary, bp of Chichester, 14, 253W

Hill, Hill wapentake, Hillewapp' (Lincs), dean of (rural), *see* Ralph; *and see* William, dean of Hagworthingham

Hill Deverill, Hull (Wilts), church of, 235

  Walter of, 235; = Walter son of Osmund, 235n.

Hillesden, Hildesdon, Hill'don' (Bucks), church of, 86; clerk of, *see* Martin

  Martin of, *see* Martin, clerk of Hillesden

Hinckford (*alias* Hedingham), Haingeford, Haingford (Essex), chapter of, 208, 212

  dean of (rural), 208

Hinderskelfe, Hyldr', Hyldyrskelf' (in Bulmer, Yorks N.R.), chapel of, 270

Histon, Histona, Huston (?Cambs), Simon of, Mr, 1 *bis*, 111W, 112W, 114W, 121W, 123W, 125aW, 125bW, 126W, 127W

clerk of Babraham, 34W
clerk of Hovingham, 269W
clerk of Langford, 34W
clerk, incumbent of Amersham, 81
constable of Chester, 191
dean (rural) of Preston Bissett, li, 74W,
    75W, 84W, 85W, 86W
dean (rural) of Thornton Watlass, 284W
monk of Crowland, 121W
parson of Hatley Cockayne, 66
parson of Walkern, 99
priest (*presbiter*) of Panton, 194W
priest (*presbiter*) of Stambourne, 212W
prior of Huntingdon, 123n.
prior of Luffield, 74
prior of Missenden, 82W
servant (*serviens*) of bp (unidentified), 249W
son of Turold the parson of Netteswell, 211
sub-archdn of Cornwall, lii, App. II, p. 199
succentor of Salisbury, 238W
Mr, vice-archdn of Canterbury, 302n.,
    App. II, p. 200
vice-archdn of Cornwall, lii, liv, 37, App.
    II, p. 200; brothers of, *see* Jordan;
    Reginald; William
vice-archdn of Coventry, App. II, p. 200
John son of Geoffrey, 282W
    son of Letold, archdn of Nottingham,
    273n.
    son of Nigel, 172n.
    son of Mr Ralph, 34W
    son of William, of Rollright, 95
John, Walter son of, *see* Walter son of John
Jordan, 168W, 169W
    Mr, l, 109W, 125bW, 127W, 128W
    abbot of Mont Saint-Michel, 284n.
    brother of John vice-archdn of Cornwall,
    37
    dean of Salisbury, 238W
Jordan son of Avenell, *see* Avenell
Jordan, Hugh son of, *see* Hugh son of Jordan
Josce, Joce, clerk of Ludford Magna, 194W
    priest (*presbiter*) of Apley, 194W
Joseph, *see* William, priest of Rand
    William son of, *see* William son of Joseph

Kaain', *see* Keynes
Kadendone, Kadindon', *see* Caddington
Kainoto, *see* Chesney
Karent', Bartholomew de, clerk, 42W
Karleolum, Karliei', *see* Carlisle
Karn, John de, 71
Keddington (Lincs), church of, App. I, no. 9
Keisn', Hugh de, 167W
    William de, 167W
    and see Chesney
Kelfield, Kelkefeld (in Stillingfleet, Yorks
    E.R.), land of, 274
Kelsey, North, Keleseia, Kelesey, Kileseia

(Lincs), Richard de, canon of
    Lincoln, 286W, 293W
Kencot, Kenicote (Oxon), Robert of, 187; son
    of, Roger, 187
Kenebella, *see* Kimble
Kenilworth, Kenelingwrthe, Kenell',
    Kenildewrd', Kinigwrtha,
    Kinildewurth' [etc] (Warks), priory of
    (Aug.), 20, 90, 263, 265, 298
prior of, *see* Robert
Kenmiote, R. de, Mr, 186W
Kent, Chent, Randulf of, 169W
    Robert of, parson of Ashdon, 198
Kentwell, Kentewell' (?Suffolk), Gilbert of,
    283W
Kevermunde, *see* Kirmond-le-Mire
Keynes, Kaain', Ralph de, 35
    William de, 35
Kileseia, *see* Kelsey
Kima, Kime, *see* Kyme
Kimble, Kenebella (Bucks), Richard of, kt,
    83W; brother of, William, kt, 83W
Kingesfeld iuxta Offordeslawa (?in Great
    Gransden, Hunts), tithes of, 101
King's Sutton, *see* Sutton, King's
Kingston Bagpuize, Chingestun', Cingestuna
    (Berks), chapter at, xlviii, 302–3
    Henry of (Kingston), kt, 303W
King's Walden, *see* Walden, King's
Kinigwrtha, Kinildewurth', *see* Kenilworth
Kirby, Monks, Kirkebi (Warks), priory of
    (Ben.), 15, 134n.
Kirkbride, Kirkebride (Cumb.), William of,
    dean (rural) of Carlisle, 8W, 9W
Kirkby Malzeard, Kirkebi (Yorks W.R.),
    church of, 282
Kirkebi, *see* Kirby; Kirkby
Kirkham, Kirkaham (Yorks E.R.), priory of
    (Aug.), 270, 305
Kirklington, Kirtlinton' (Yorks N.R.),
    Thomas of, Mr, 285 W
Kirkstead, Kirke(stede) (Lincs), abbey of
    (Cist.), 134, 144
Kirmond-le-Mire, Kevermunde (Lincs),
    parson of, *see* Alan
Kirtlinton', *see* Kirklington
Kokewald, *see* Cuxwold
Kymba, Simon de, justice-in-eyre, 11
Kyme, Kima, Kime (Lincs), priory of (Aug.),
    prior of, *see* Lambert; canon of, *see*
    Roger
    Ralph of, Mr, 287W, 293W
    Richard of, canon of Lincoln, 289W

Lac', William de, 274
Lambert (?), clerk, 216W
Lambert, prior of Kyme, 288W
Lamerton, Lamerton' (Devon), corn and
    tithes of, 37

Lilleburn', Hugh de, 41W
Lilleshall, Lilushull' (Salop), abbot of
	(Arroasian Aug.), *see* W.
Lillingstone (Bucks), Philip of, Mr, 75W
Lilushull', *see* Lilleshall
Lim, *see* Lyme
Limesia, Richard de, 252W
Linces, Linc', Robert de, Mr, 238W
Lincoln, Lincol', 288
	archdn of, 73, 194, 289n., *and see* Peter;
		Robert
	archdnry of, xlviii, 140–5, 286–94, 300n.
	bp of, 123n., *and see* Alexander; Avallon,
		Hugh of; Blois, William of; Chesney,
		Robert; Coutances, Walter of;
		Plantagenet, Geoffrey; Sutton, Oliver
	official of, *see* Bedford, Robert of; Foliot,
		Robert; Rolleston, Roger of
	cathedral of, 61–3, ?141, 142n., 143, 159–
		60, 183, 191, 228, 288, 290–3
	authority of, 53, 64, 83, 86, 88, 90–1
	canons of, *see* Alan; Amundeville, Adam
		de; Hardres, Robert of; Hugh; Ilbert;
		Kelsey, Richard of; London, Hugh
		of; Kyme, Richard of; Malebisse,
		Alexander; Payn; Philip; Roger son
		of William; Samson; Torpell',
		Geoffrey de; Virin, Ralph de;
		Winchester, Hamo of
	chancellor of, *see* Swafeld, Stephen de
	dean of, *see* Adelelm; Hamo; Rolleston,
		Roger of
	prebend of, *see* Scamblesby; Sutton-
		cum-Buckingham
	precentor of, *see* Almaria, Richard de;
		Almaria, Roger de; Bedford, Robert
		of
	subdean of, *see* Caen, Ralph of; Wimar
	treasurer of, *see* Martin
	church of, official of, *see* Alexander, Mr,
		archdn of Stow
	diocese of, xxxiii, xxxvii–xxxviii, xlvii–
		xlviii, lii, 22, 47–194, 286–301
	archdns of, 139
	vice-archdn of, *see* Hardres, Robert of;
		Insula, R. de
	St Catherine's priory of (Gilb.), 188n.
Lincoln, Alfred of, 233
	Andrew of, 233W
	Robert of, father of Alfred, 233n.
Lincolnshire, Linc'sire, clergy and laity of, 141
Lindebonia, *see* Lillebonne
Lindent', Nicholas de, 146W
Lindsey (Lincs), archdn of, *see* Stow
Lire, Lira, Lyra (Eure), abbey of (Ben.), 229–
		30, 241n., 266; abbot of, *see* Geoffrey
Lisieux, Lexoviensis (Calvados), bp of, *see*
		Arnulf
	subdean of, *see* Robert

treasurer of, *see* Coutances, John of;
		Silvester
Lissington, Lissingtun (Lincs), priest of, *see*
		Achard
Lithum, *see* Lytham
Littlebury, Litilberia, Lutlebur' (Essex),
		priest of, *see* Turbert
	Martin of, 196W
Little Addington, *see* Addington, Little
Little Barrington, *see* Barrington, Little
Little Cawthorpe, *see* Cawthorpe, Little
Little Gaddesden, *see* Gaddesden, Little
Little Houghton, *see* Houghton, Little
Little Missenden, *see* Missenden, Little
Little Oakley, *see* Oakley, Little
Little Paxton, *see* Paxton, Little
Little Rollright, *see* Rollright, Little
Little Wakering, *see* Wakering, Little
Little Yeldham, *see* Yeldham, Little
Llandaff, Landav' (South Glamorgan), bp of,
		see Nicholas
Llanthony, Lant', Lanthon' (Glos), priory of
		(Aug.), 240, 253, 304; prior of, *see*
		Norwich, Roger of; Wycombe,
		William of
Lockington, Lochington (Yorks E.R.), Roger
		of, dean of Buckrose, 305
Loddington, Lodinton' (Northants), priest of,
		see Henry
Lodewicus, Lodowicus, *see* Lewis
Lokesley, *see* Loxley
London, London', Londoniis, Lund',
		Lundon', houses in, 203, land in,
		129
	archdn of, xliv n., *and see* Belmeis, William
		de; Burnham, Alard of; Nicholas;
		Waltham, Peter of
	archdnry of, 202–6
	bp of, 201, *and see* Belmeis, Richard de II;
		Fitz Neal, Richard; Foliot, Gilbert I;
		Sigillo, Robert de; Ste-Mère-Eglise,
		William of
	cathedral of St Paul of, 129, 203, 225
	canons of, *see* Paris; Ruffus, Richard;
		Saccavilla, Alexander de
	dean of, *see* Burnham, Alard of; Diceto,
		Ralph de; Langford, Ralph of;
		Mareni, Hugh de
	treasurer of, *see* Banastre, Henry
	church of St Botolph Aldgate, 202
	church of St Magnus the Martyr, 205;
		chaplain of, *see* John; parson of, *see*
		Nicholas, nephew of Nicholas archdn
		of London
	church of St Margaret near London Bridge
		(Fish Street Hill; Bridge Street), 204,
		204n., App. I, no. 5; incumbent of, *see*
		Bedford, Geoffrey of; Geoffrey, clerk;
		and cf. St Margaret, John of

Malton, Malton' (Yorks N.R.), priory of (Gilb.), 107–8, 138n., 191, 280–1

Malvern, Melverna, Melvernae (Worcs), Ralph of, 168W

Malvern, Great, Maior Malvern' (Worcs), priory of (Ben.), dep. on Westminster, 264; prior of, *see* William

Mandeville, Mandevilla, Beatrice de, 196
   William de, earl of Essex, 196

Map, Map', Philip, 186W
   Philip, Mr, 186W
   Walter, Mr, archdn of Oxford, 186–7

Mara, Peter de, 296

Mareham le Fen, Marum (Lincs), chaplain of, *see* Robert

Mareni, Marinn', Hugh de, dean of St Paul's, London, 203W, 225; papal judge-delegate, 27
   John de, 210W

Mariscis, Robert de, archdn of Oxford, 179n.

Market Stainton, *see* Stainton, Market

Marmiun, Robert, 226W

Marshal, Henry, dean of York, 282W; bp of Exeter, 42n., 282n.

Marston, Merstoun' (?Bucks), Simon of, 78W

Martin, chaplain, 10W
   clerk of Hillesden (Martin of Hillesden), 84W, 86
   priest (*presbiter*), 147, 296W, 297W; parson of Westcott Barton, 296n.
   treasurer of Lincoln, 104n.

Martin, William son of, *see* William son of Martin

Marton, Martun' (Lincs), 192

Marton, Marthona (?Yorks N.R.), church of, 280–1; holder of, *see* Flamville, William de

Marum, *see* Mareham le Fen

Masham (Yorks N.R.), church of, 282
   prebend of (in York minster), 282
   churches of, *see* Kirkby Malzeard; Masham

Matching, Macinges (Essex), priest of, *see* Thomas

Matilda, wife/widow of Robert Grimbald, 159–60; 2nd husband, *see* Pek, Richard de

Mattesdun' (?Matson, Glos), John de, 186W

Matthew, chaplain, 183W

Mauduit, family of, 252n.
   Robert, 252n.
   William II, 252n.

Maureward, family of, 133n.

Maurice, Mr, priest (*sacerdos*) of Hallingbury, 211W

Meidenecot', *see* Maidencourt

Meinfelin, Alan son of, *see* Alan son of Meinfelin
   Hamo son of, *see* Hamo son of Meinfelin

Melden', Meldensis, *see* Maldon

Meldens' (prob. error for Middlesex), 210

Melebisse, *see* Malebisse

Melhuish, Melewis (in Tedburn St Mary, Devon), Henry of, Mr, canon of Exeter, 37W; archdn of Exeter, xli n.

Melide, Peter de, Mr, 300W

Melsonby (Yorks N.R.), Roger of (*alias* Roger of Richmond), Mr, official/vice-archdn of Richmond, liii, 284W and n., 306, App. II, p. 202

Melton Mowbray, Meultonia (Leics), church of, chapter at, xlvii n., xlviii, 133

Melverna, Melvernae, *see* Malvern

Mendham (Suffolk), priory of (Clun.), App. I, no. 15

Meppershall, Meperteshale (Beds), Adeodatus of, 61W

Mercia, Merciorum, ealdorman of, *see* Ælfhere

Meriden (Warks), church of, formerly Alspath, q.v.

Meriet, *see* Merriott

Merk, Eustace de, 293

Merriott, Meriet (Som.), Nicholas de, 1

Merse, William de la, kt, 83W

Merstoun', *see* Marston

Merton, Merton' (Surrey), priory of (Aug.), 123; prior of, 35, *and see* Robert; Walter; canon of, *see* Roger

Messendena, Messinden', *see* Missenden

Meultonia, *see* Melton Mowbray

Michael, 128W
   clerk, 195W
   Mr, clerk of William de Longchamp, bp of Ely, 34W
   dean (rural) of Bletchley, 75W
   monk of Park (?Louth Park), 194W
   Mr, parson of Haddenham, 34W
   steward (*dapifer*), 195W

Micham, *see* Mitcham

Middelton', *see* Milton Ernest

Middlesex, Middlesexia, Midelsex, Middelsexia, archdn of, *see* Belmeis, Richard de II; Diceto, Ralph de; Ely, Ralph of; Foliot, Gilbert II
   archdnry of, 207–12, 195n.
   clergy of, 212

Midelton', *see* Milton Malsor

Miles, Mr, 44W

Milton Ernest, Middelton' (Beds), church of, 59–60; vicar of, *see* Bedford, John of
   Cecily of, and sons, 59
   Robert of, 59–60

Milton Malsor (?), Midelton' (Northants), parson of, *see* William
Roger of, App. III
Missenden, Messendena, Messendene, Messinden', Missendienenses (Bucks), abbey of (Arroasian Aug.), 69, 82–3, 172, 181; canons of, *see* A.; P.; Richard; prior of, *see* Anketil; John
land in, 69
Hugh of, 69W
Roger of, 255W
Missenden, Great (Bucks), priest of, *see* Ralph
Missenden, Little, alia Messend' (Bucks), priest of, *see* Geoffrey
Mitcham, Micham (Surrey), clerk of, *see* Ralph
Modbury, Motberi (Devon), Adam of, chaplain, 44W
Molesho, Moleshou, *see* Moulsoe
Monasteriis, Robert de, 233W
Monemuta, *see* Monmouth
Mongewell, Mungewell' (Oxon), church of, 186; rector of, *see* Bosco, R. de; Cornhill, W. of
Monks Horton, *see* Horton, Monks
Monks Kirby, *see* Kirby, Monks
Monkton Farleigh, *see* Farleigh, Monkton
Monmouth, Monemuta, Monumuta, prior of (Ben.), App. I, no. 1
Ralph of, 129W, 167W, 168W, 169W
Montacute, de Monte Acuto (Som.), priory of (Clun.), 38–9, 233n; prior of, *see* William
priory of, *see* Holme
John de, 38–9
Monte, Gilbert de, 147
Montebourg, Monteburg (Manche), abbey of (Ben.), 236
abbot of, 234, *and see* Walter; clerk of, *see* William
Montechan' *see* Munchensy
Montford (Salop), *see* Forton
Mont Saint-Michel, beatus Micael de Periculo Maris (Manche), abbey of (Ben.), 284
abbot of, *see* Jordan
Morborne, Morbourne, Moreburn' (Hunts), church of, 121; incumbent of, *see* Richard
John of, 113W
Moreton, Maids (Bucks), chapter at, xlviii, 96n.
Morgan, archdn of Richmond, 285n.
Moriston', Roger de, 206W
Mortuna (?Moreton, Staffs), William de, clerk, 25W
Theoderic de, 25W

Morwic, John, canon of York, 282W
Moses, Mr, 241W
dean, 199W
Motberi, *see* Modbury
Moubrai, *see* Mowbray
Moulsoe, Molesho, Moleshou (Beds), parson of, *see* Roger son of William
tithes in, 92
Moulton, Multon' (Lincs), church of, 292; vicar of, *see* H.
Mowbray, Moubrai, Mulbrai, Roger de, 269, 282
Mumby, Mumbi (Lincs), Eudo of, 300
Munchensy, Montechan', Munchanesi, Agnes de, 89
Ralph de, 89n.
Roger de, clerk, 252W
Warin de, 89n.
Mundbegun, Yundbegun, Adam de, 276n.; son of, Roger, 276n.
Mungewell', *see* Mongewell
Muntonium, Philip de, 269W
Murdac, Hugh, canon of York, 282W
Mursley, Muresle (Bucks), church of, 76n.
deanery of (rural), xlix n.
Gilbert of, ?incumbent of Mursley church, 76 and n.
Murton (in Hawnby, Yorks N. R.), tithe of, xlvi
Muschamp, Muschamp', Geoffrey, archdn of Cleveland, 65W, 282W; bp of Coventry, 65n.
Mary de, 163
Mustrel, Hugh de, 194W
Muswell, Musewella, Musewelle (in Piddington, Oxon), Holy Cross chapel of, 172
hermitage attached to, 172n.; *and see* Ralph

Nazeing, Nasinges (Essex), church of, 201
Neatishead, Neteshirde (Norfolk), church of, 219; vicar of, *see* Wimar, dean
Netteswell, Nethleswell', Netleswelle (Essex), church of, 201n., 211; parson of, *see* Turold
Neuport, *see* Newport Pagnell
Neutone, *see* Newton
Neville, Nevill', Novavilla, Novill', Ernis de (Arnisius, Hern'), 296W; justice, 11
Walter de, 66
Walter de (?another), 107–8; son of, Walter, 107
Newbold Pacey, Newebold (Warks), church of, 262; parson of, *see* Henry son of Peter
Newburgh, Novoburgum (Yorks N.R.), priory of (Aug.), 269, 282n.
Newnham, Newenham (Beds), priory of,

vicar of Puddletown, 237
Mr, vice-archdn of Northampton, 153W,
  App. II, p. 201, App. III, ?App. III W
Richard Fitz Neal, *see* Fitz Neal, Richard
Richard son of Galo, 118
  son of Osbert, brother of Hugh Barre, 129
  son of Pichot, 23W; brother of, John, 23W
  son of Reiner, of London, 110n.
  son of Richard (*alias* Richard of
    Chiddingfold), 150–1; vicar of
    Godalming, 151, 248
  son of Roger, founder of Lytham priory,
    285
  son of Wale, 158
  son of Wale, jnr, 158
  son of William, 111W; *cf.* William son of
    Richard
Richard, Thomas son of, *see* Cuckney
  William son of, *see* William son of Richard
Richmond, Richemund', Richemundia,
  Richesmund' (Yorks N.R.), chapter
  at, 306
  archdn of, xxxvii, *and see* Bartholomew;
    Bayeux, Osbert of; Chemillé,
    William de; Honorius; Lucy,
    Godfrey de; Morgan; St Edmund,
    Roger de; official of, 268n.
  archdnry of, 5n., 274–85, 306
  constable of, *see* Alan
  dean of (rural), *see* Geoffrey
  earl of, 274, *and see* Brittany, Alan of;
    steward of, *see* Hugh son of Gernagod
  official of, *see* Henry; Melsonby, Roger of
  vice-archdn of, *see* Melsonby, Roger of;
    Robert; Theobald; William
  St Agatha's church of, 5
  St Martin's priory of (Ben.), dep. on St
    Mary's York, 5 and n.; prior of, *see*
    Herbert
  Roger of, Mr, *see* Melsonby, Roger of
Rickling, Rigling (Essex), Thomas of, 196W
Ridala, *see* Ryhall
Ridel, Geoffrey, archdn of Canterbury, App.
  II, p. 201; bp of Ely, king's justice, 21
  Hugh, dean (rural), 146W
Ridgewell, Redeswella (Essex), priest of, *see*
  Thurstan
Rievaulx, Rievall' (Yorks N.R.), abbey of
  (Cist.), xlvi, 268, App. I, no. 14
Rigling, *see* Rickling
Rihala, *see* Ryhall
Ringland, Ringelond (Norfolk), mills of, 213
Riparia, Henry de, 269
Rippingale, Reppinghala (Lincs), Alan of,
  115
Risborough, Riseburgh' (Bucks, Monks *or*
  Princes), priest of, *see* Nigel
Rising, Risinges (Norfolk, Castle *or* Wood),
  William of, 224W

Rivariis, *see* Redvers
Robert, 128W
  (another), 254W
  Mr, 130W
  abbot of Bardney, 193
  abbot of Crowland, 121–2
  abbot of Fountains, *see* Robert, abbot of
    Pipewell
  II, abbot of Malmesbury, 244n.
  abbot of Pipewell, 19n.; abbot of
    Fountains, 19n.
  abbot of Ramsey, *see* Trianel, Robert
  archdn of Carlisle, xxxix n., 5–7
  archdn of Lincoln, 73n., 140–2
  archdn of Nottingham, *see* Robert son of
    William
  Mr, archdn of Shropshire, 24n.
  archdn of Stafford, 28n.
  archdn of Wells, xxxviii n.
  bp of Bath, 253W
  II, bp of Exeter, 36n.
  brother of Richard Fitz Neal archdn of Ely,
    33
  canon of Notley, 86W
  chaplain, 167W
  chaplain of Felsted, 210W
  chaplain of [ ]indune, 88W
  chaplain of archdn John of Coutances of
    Oxford, 184W
  chaplain of Mareham le Fen, 288W
  chaplain of Mr Silvester, 204W
  chaplain of Richard dean of West
    Torrington, 194W
  chaplain of St Thomas's (?chapel,
    Northampton), 159W, 160W
  chaplain of Sawston, 34W
  clerk, 125bW
  clerk of Audley, 20
  clerk of Blyborough, 300n.
  clerk of Newnham priory, *see*
    Wilshamstead, Robert of
  clerk of Scamblesby, 142
  cook, 147W
  dean, *see* Robert, dean of Northampton
  dean (rural) of ?Dunmow, 210W
  dean (rural) of Hannah, 140n.; prob. =
    Hannah, Robert of (q.v.)
  dean (rural) of Northampton, 149W,
    155W; = Robert, dean, 228W
  dean (rural) of South Weald, 201W
  dean (rural) of West Bergholt, liii, App. II,
    p. 203
  dean (rural) of Wilsford, 294W
  janitor, 31W
  monk of Bordesley, 27W
  painter (*pictor*), 219W
  parson of Biscathorpe, 194W
  parson of Harefield, xlv, 212
  parson of Scottow, 219W

Stoke-in-Teignhead, Stokes (Devon), church of, 40

Stoke Lyne (Stoke Insula), Stoches, Stoke (Oxon), chapter at, xlv, 298
   deanery of (rural), xlviii, 174
   parish of, 298n.

Stoke-upon-Tern (Salop), tithes in, 24n.

Stoke, South, Stoch' (Oxon), 177

Stokes, Adam de, Mr, 201W
   William de, vice-archdn of Hereford, App. II, p. 201

Stondon, Upper (Beds), parson of, *see* Bodin

Stone, Stanes (Bucks), church of, 88; clerk of, *see* Luke

Stone, Stan' (Staffs), 25
   church of, 25
   priory of (Aug.), 25

Stow, Lindsey, Westriding, Westring', Westrith' [etc] (Lincs), archdn of, *see* Alexander; Almaria, Richard de; Almaria, Roger de; William son of Osbert
   archdnry of, xxxvii, 115n., 188–94, 300
   clergy of, 189
   official/vice-archdn of, *see* Alexander

Stowe (Bucks), chapter at, xlviii, 94
   chaplain of, *see* John

Stratford, Water, Stratford, Stratfort (Bucks), church of, 94
   William son of William of, 94

Stratton, Strattune, *see* Sturton

Strensall (Yorks N.R.), prebend of (in York minster), 65n.

Strigenel, Gilbert de, parson of Long Wittenham, 232

Strood, Strode (Kent), chapel/church of, 226
   St Mary's hospital of, 226; *iconomus* of, 226

Studham, Stodham (Beds), church of, 51; parson of, *see* Dunstable, prior of
   Alexander of, 51; John son of, clerk, 51

Stukeley, Stiveclai, Stivecle, Stiveclea [etc] (Hunts), Adam of, clerk, son of Henry of Huntingdon, 104, 107–8, 113W; parson of Kings Walden, 107n., 108
   Jocelin of, 103W

Sturton, Stratton, Strattune (Lincs), dean of (rural), *see* Hugh

Stuteville, Estotevill', Robert de, 4
   William de 11W

Sudbury, Suberia (Suffolk), archdn of, *see* Roger
   archdnry of, 220

Suffolk, Suffolch', archdn of, *see* Bello Fago, Richard de; Geoffrey; Walkelin
   archdnry of, 221–4; called 'of Ipswich', liii; official of, *see* Geoffrey
   sheriff of, *see* Fitz Walter, Robert

Sugenho, *see* Sutton Hoo

Suine, *see* Swine

Sulby, Suleby (Northants), abbey of (Prem.), 149n.; abbot of, 163–5; parson of Great Harrowden, 163

'Sumeneio', error for 'Funteneio': *see* Funteney

Sumercot', William de, Mr, 245W

Sumeri, *see* Somery

Sunelli, *see* Chemillé

Suniggefeld, *see* Shinfield

Suntorp, *see* Swinthorpe

Surrey, archdn of, *see* Amicius
   archdnry of, xxxiv, 248–51

Sutham, *see* Southam

Suthcroxt', *see* Croxton, South

Suthwerk', *see* Southwark

Suthwick, Oliver, bp of Lincoln, 163

Sutton, Oliver, bp of Lincoln, 163

Sutton, King's (Northants), church of, 97n.

Sutton-cum-Buckingham, Sutton', prebend in Lincoln cathedral, 97; canon of, *see* Swafeld, Stephen de

Sutton cum Duckmanton (Derbys.), 21n.

Sutton Hoo, Sugenho (Suffolk), chapel of, 224

Sutton Scarsdale (Derbys.), parish of, 21n.

Suwic', *see* Southwick

Swafeld, Stephen de, Mr, archdn of Buckinghgam, 75n., 87n., 94–8; chancellor of Lincoln, 75n., 87n., 93n.; prebendary of Sutton-cum-Buckingham, 97

Swallowfield, Swalewefeld (Berks), church of, 230; parson of, *see* Gilbert, chaplain of bp Roger; Reims, Stephen of

Sweyn, chaplain of archdn Nicholas of London, 205W
   priest (*presbiter*) of Boltby, 268

Swinderby (Lincs), dean of (rural), *see* A.

Swine, Suine (Yorks E.R.), church of, 272; priest of, *see* Verli, Robert de
   priory of (nuns, ?Cist.), 272; master of, *see* Verli, Robert de

Swinthorpe, Suntorp (in Wragby, Lincs), tithes of, 144

Swynnerton, Swinvertona (Staffs), church of, 25; clerks of, *see* Osbert (two)
   lord of, *see* Robert son of Eelen

Sywell, Siwell', Siwellia (Northants), Hamo of, 130W

T., Mr, clerk of earl David of Huntingdon, 46, 62n.

Tacham, *see* Thatcham

Tadcaster (Yorks W.R.), parson of, *see* Ernald; Tadcaster, Nicholas of
   Nicholas of, parson of Tadcaster and [rural] dean, and vice-archdn of York, App. II, p. 203

Tailebois, Elias, 128W

Tamesford, *see* Tempsford

Tamworth (Staffs), Ralph of, archdn of
Stafford, 26–7
Tapinell', Richard, 249W
Taplow, Tappelawa, Tappellawa (Bucks),
church of, 83; patron of, *see* Turville,
Wiiliam de
Tarrington (Herefs), church of, App. I, no. 1;
clerk of, *see* M.
Tathwell (Lincs), dean of (rural), *see* Thorald
Tattersett, Taterseta (Norfolk), All Saints
church of, 216
St Andrew's church of, 216n.
Taunton (Som.), archdn of, *see* Guildford,
Robert of; Lechlade, Ralph of;
Wrotham, William of
archdnry of, xxxiv, 1
vice-archdn of, *see* Feny, Richard de;
Herlem', Richard de; Spaxton,
Richard of
Tavistock, Tavistoc', Tavistoch' (Devon),
abbey of (Ben.), 37
Teleton, *see* Tilton
Telvetunia, *see* Thelveton
Templars in England, master of, *see* Geoffrey
son of Stephen
Temprenoise, Robert, Mr, 156W, App. III W
Tempsford, Tamesford (Beds), church of, 54
Tengr', *see* Steingrim
Terfeld', *see* Therfield
Testard', Geoffrey, Mr, 156W
Tetfort, *see* Thetford
Teyssun, Ralph, 161W
Thatcham, Tacham (Berks), Robert of, Mr,
231W
Thelveton, Telvetunia, Thevelton' (Norfolk),
priest of, *see* Ulfketel
tithe in, 214–15
Theobald, archbp of Canterbury and
primate, xlv, 2n., 28n., 32, 54n.,
100n., 101, 116n., 125a, 125b, 128n.,
170–1, 217, 221n., 290n., legatine
title of, 32n.
steward (seneschal) of abbot of
Westminster, *see* Feering, Theobald
Mr, vice-archdn of Richmond, App. II,
p. 202
Therfield, Terfeld', Therefeld (Herts), Walter
of, 125bW
Thetford, Tetfort (Norfolk), priory of Holy
Cross (? = Holy Sepulchre) (Aug.),
App. I, no. 8
priory of St Mary (Clun.), 136
Thimbleby, Thymelby (Lincs), chaplain of,
see Walter
Thirsk, Tresch (Yorks N.R.), chapter at, 268
Thomas, Mr, 130W
Mr (another), 244W
archbp of York, *see* Bayeux, Thomas of
archdn of Norwich, 219, App. I, no. 8

chaplain (of archdn Robert of Burnham of
Buckingham), li, 81W, 89W
chaplain of Amersham, 79W
chaplain of St Giles', Reading, 231W
clerk, 109W
clerk (another), 249W
deacon, of Warwick (Cumb.), 9W
dean (rural), 197W; ? = following
dean (rural) of Great Sampford, 198W
parson of Ewelme, 299
parson of Great Sampford, 199n.
priest (*sacerdos*) of Matching, 211W
Mr, vice-archdn in Chichester diocese,
App. II, p. 200
Thomas son of Paulinus, canon of York,
282W
son of Richard, *see* Cuckney
Thomas, Robert son of, *see* Robert son of
Thomas
Thorald, clerk of Edlington, 288W
dean (rural), 301W
dean (rural) of Tathwell, 140
Thornborough, Thorneberg', Torneberg'
(Bucks), church of, 74
Thomas of, 74W
Thornedale (unidentified, ?Yorks N.R.), 5
Thorner, Tornoure, Adam de, canon of
York, 282W; archdn of York, papal
judge-delegate, App. I, no. 14
Thorney, Thorneia, Thorneye, Torneye
(Cambs), abbey of (Ben.), 32, 113–15
abbot of, *see* Prunelai, Robert de
Thornton, Thorton' (Lincs), abbot of (Aug.),
see Benton, John
Thornton Watlass, Watlos (Yorks N.R.),
dean of (rural), *see* John
Thorp, Thomas de, official of archdn Peter
de Ros of Carlisle, liii, 8W, 9W, 10W
Thorton', *see* Thornton
Throp, *see* Rothersthorpe
Throwley (Kent), church of, xxxiv
Thurlow, Great, Magna Trillawia (Suffolk),
parson of, *see* Funteney, Robert de
Thurstan, abbot of Garendon, 131
archbp of York, 167
priest (*presbiter*) of Ridgewell, 212W
reeve (?of Chichester), 14
Thymelby, *see* Thimbleby
Tilen', Peter de, Mr, 62W
Tilton, Teleton (in Selmeston, Sussex), land
in, 206
Tinemutha, *see* Tynemouth
Tintern (Mon.), abbey of (Cist.), 167n.
Tinton', *see* Toynton
Tirigtun, Tiringt', *see* Torrington
Tockington, Tokinton' (?Glos), Godfrey of,
255W
Ralph of, 255W
Toft, Tofte (Lincs), priest of, *see* Alan

INDEX OF SUBJECTS

Arabic numerals refer to the numbers of the acta in this edition. Small Roman numerals refer to the pages of the introduction.

abbey, abbot, *see under names* Abingdon;
    Bardney; Barking; Battle; Bayham;
    Bec; Boxley; Bruern; Burton; Bury St
    Edmunds; Byland; Caen, Sainte-
    Trinité; Chatteris; Cirencester;
    Colchester; Combe; Crowland;
    Croxton; Darley; Easby; Edinburgh,
    Holyrood; Eynsham; Faversham;
    Flaxley; Fountains; Garendon;
    Glastonbury; Gloucester; Godstow;
    Grimsby; Haughmond; Holm
    Cultram; Kirkstead; Leicester;
    Lessness; Lilleshall; Lire; Louth
    Park; Malmesbury; Missenden;
    Mont Saint-Michel; Montebourg;
    Northampton St James; Notley;
    Osney; Otham; Pershore;
    Peterborough; Pipewell; Polesworth;
    Quarr; Ramsey; Rennes; Revesby;
    Rievaulx; Rouen, La Trinité-du-
    Mont; St Albans; St Benet of Holme;
    Saint-Bertin; Selby; Shrewsbury;
    Sulby; Tavistock; Thorney;
    Thornton; Tupholme; Valmont;
    Waltham; Warden; Welbeck;
    Westminster; Whitby; Wyresdale;
    York St Mary's
abbey church, 32
'abjudication' (*abiudicare*), 207, 260
adjudgement (*adiudicare, adiudicatio*), 70, 101,
    207, 235
administration (of church), 86, 208, 236, 265
admission, of parsons, etc., 38–9, 55, 58a,
    58b, 62, 88, 90, 125b n., 145, 161, 165,
    245, 247n., 257, 264, 281n., 305;
    canonical, 8
advocate, of church, 27n., 49, 208
    of priory, 242
    and see patron
    (overlord), 269
advowson, 8, 18n., 19n., 47, 55n., 60, 82n.,
    110n., 128n., 138, 145, 201, 223, 225,
    243, 304, 305; *ius advocationis*, 262,
    264; *and see* patronage; presentation
affidation, 131n., 194, 215, *and see* oath
age, old age, 194

agreement, xlvi, 36, 37, 83, 95, 132, 136,
    154–5, 171, 188, 194–5, 199, 206,
    214–15, 241, *and see* settlement
aid (*auxilium*), archdn's, 227, 252, 282
    ecclesiastical, 12, 123 (*dona et auxilia*)
    sheriff's, 33
almoner, almonry (monastic), 250–1, *and see
    under names* Alan
alms, gift, grant, confirmation, possession in,
    69, 140, 166, 233
    free and perpetual, 146, 228
    free and quit, 200
    free, pure and perpetual, 63, 77, 242
    perpetual, 1, 7, 13, 16–18, 33, 47, 73, 104–
        5, 109, 115, 129, 151, 159–60, 172,
        176, 184, 222, 226, 236–7, 240, 296–8
    perpetual and free, 4
    pure, 254, 274
    pure and perpetual, 14, 45, 94, 120, 133,
        216, 224, 273, 281, 283
alms, king's, 221
altar, of abbey, 115, 124, 166, 219
    of church, 13, 25, 248, 304
    of priory, 100, 102
anathema, excommunication, by archdn,
    xlvii, 22, 67, 101
    by bp, xlvii, 139, 253
    by dean (rural), 91
    by ecclesiastical judges, 22
    by monastery, 115
anniversary (of death), 14
appeal, to the pope, 302
appropriation, of churches, xxxviii, 165n.,
    246n., 262n., 287n.
    grant, conversion, possession *in proprios
        usus*, 12, 21n., 143, 201, 280, 283; in
        future, 61
    grant *in usus*, 64, 173
    obventions of church converted *in usus
        proprios*, 303
    and cf. 117, 120, 194, 266
appropriation, of tithes, *in proprios usus, in usus
        suos*, 79, 114, 232
archbishop, *see under names* Canterbury;
    Rouen; York
archdeacon, archdeaconry, *see under names*

PERCEPTUAL TRAINING IN THE CURRICULUM

GEORGE H. EARLY

Achievement Center for Children
Purdue University

PERCEPTUAL TRAINING IN THE CURRICULUM

Illustrations by CAROL STERLING
Line Diagrams by LESTER DAVIS, JR.

CHARLES E. MERRILL PUBLISHING COMPANY

Columbus, Ohio   *A Bell & Howell Company*

738

Standard Book Number: 675-09537-9 (hardbound edition)
675-09536-0 (paperbound edition)
Library of Congress Catalog Card Number: 69-12182

1 2 3 4 5 6 7 8 9 10 — 73 72 71 70 69

Printed in the United States of America

THE SLOW LEARNER SERIES
edited by
NEWELL C. KEPHART, Ph.D.

For Peter

Editor's Introduction

The primary responsibility of the public schools is to teach — to develop in the child a body of skills, attitudes, and knowledge which will permit him to adjust to his environment and contribute to the society in which he lives. The slow learner presents a challenge to this basic educational task. Certain learning procedures and processes are disturbed in the slow learner so that the normal presentations by which teaching is customarily accomplished do not function, or function to a greatly reduced degree.

The difficulty lies in the child. His learning processes deviate from the normal either in kind or amount or both. Since learning is an all-embracing problem which transcends the specialized tasks of the school, the major concern should be directed toward therapeutic procedures which will reduce the learning problem and permit the child to learn from the great mass of experiences both in and out of the classroom. When research and clinical investigations began to reveal specialized therapeutic techniques which could ameliorate the learning disability, educators were naturally eager to provide such opportunities for the children under their care.

The result has been the development of a large number of excellent programs for the treatment of slow learners. The assumption is that, after remedial help, the child can learn from the typical classroom presentations or at least can profit from these presentations to a greater degree. Experience is beginning to indicate that, at least in many such cases, this assumption is correct.

In some programs, virtually all attention has come to be devoted to remedial techniques, and the teaching function of the school is delayed until remediation is complete. If the remediation period is extensive, as it frequently is, the child sometimes finds himself deprived of information which is offered to his peers. While therapy is occurring, he drops further and further behind in his general fund of information to the point where, when therapy is complete, he finds he has only exchanged one problem for another.

The amount of information required by the child in our modern civilization is staggering. From year to year as he grows, both the amount and the acceleration with which it must be assimilated increase. Any interruption in the process of assimilation throws him further behind. Exclusive attention to therapeutic activities, often rather remote from the stream of learning, represents such an interruption. We seem to say to the child in effect, "When you can learn like other children, then I will teach you what you need to know." Sometimes the resulting delay is costly.

The apparent dichotomy between therapy and teaching need not exist. The slow learner characteristically shows marked discrepancies in ability. In one area of performance the child may function very poorly. In other area, however, he may function very well. This fact suggests that probably in one or more areas he can be taught rather well and can absorb the informational data which he needs. Therefore teaching is possible through one set of learning functions at the same time that remediation is being attempted in less adequate areas.

Furthermore, informational presentations, by incorporating therapeutic techniques, can provide therapy as well as teaching. Strong areas can be used to bolster weak areas. Therapeutic activities can be directed so that they result in the discovery of information. Skills being taught therapeutically can be applied, as they develop, to the gathering of information. Thus, the teaching function and the therapeutic function can proceed side by side. Some of the most effective therapy has resulted from such a coordination of these two functions.

The present volume presents some examples of such coordination. Therapeutic procedures in the perceptual-motor area have been incorporated into classroom processes so that information is provided to the child along with activities to aid in the development of basic learning skills. At the same time, the teaching function has been made more flexible so that intact abilities in the child can bolster and encourage weaker functions. The whole is based upon units of study which can provide organized bodies of information. Thus, the demands both of therapy and of teaching are served.

Although the material presented represents only examples, it can be used to guide the teacher in the development of similar classroom procedures. Units of study prescribed by the curriculum can be altered to introduce perceptual-motor and other therapeutic procedures and can be liberalized to permit more efficient learning in the face of the child's handicap. In this way, the overall efficiency of the classroom activity, from the point of view of its basic objective, learning, can be increased.

N. C. KEPHART

Glen Haven Achievement Center
Fort Collins, Colorado

Contents

738

PERCEPTUAL TRAINING IN THE CURRICULUM

chapter 1

The Problem and
an Approach

Teachers and other educators are showing increasing concern for children who have learning problems. Concern is warranted, and most welcome. A highly developed society is making increased demands upon its members. Those who cannot meet the demands, who cannot keep up, are finding that hardly any place exists for them in the bright, brave world which is mushrooming into being before our eyes. Generally speaking, children who do well in school will be able, as adults, to meet the demands of this complex world, but those who do poorly will not be able to keep up later. The school experience becomes an ever more important factor in equipping children for functioning in the world. Since school achievement is such a crucial matter, every method for helping the slow learner should be explored thoroughly.

Many children who do not achieve their full potential in school have perceptual problems. Such children do not see, hear, feel, and otherwise experience the world about them in the same way most people do. Perception involves both receiving information from the world and organizing that information into some meaningful pattern or form. If a child does not receive the correct information through his senses, or if he receives correct information but cannot organize it properly, perceptual difficulties occur and, quite understandably, he will have problems in school. Children with per-

3

ceptual problems typically achieve below their potential in one or more academic areas. Further, their perceptual problems often make it difficult for teachers or other professionals to determine just what their potential might be.

Perceptual training can help many children who have perceptual handicaps. This training consists of remedial activities designed to correct a child's basic perceptual difficulties. Where a perceptual problem is interfering with learning, perceptual training deals with the root of the problem. Many schools are conducting perceptual training and, as information on the subject becomes more widely known, many others are planning similar efforts. Some schools have special classes exclusively for children with perceptual handicaps. Others conduct perceptual training as a regular part of their remedial programs in a variety of special-education classrooms. In still others, teachers have been using these training techniques with slow learners in regular classrooms. While as yet no single pattern for conducting perceptual training has emerged, awareness is rapidly growing that many children have perceptual deficits, that these deficits can result in lack of school achievement, and, most important of all, that something can be done to improve the situation.

Introducing perceptual training into a classroom confronts the teacher with a very large problem: How shall he conduct perceptual training with some children without neglecting the main task of teaching the regular academic subject matter to the whole class? In attending to the primary academic task, he finds that time for basic remedial work is often limited. On the other hand, if remedial procedures are attempted, the academic work may suffer. Many teachers have recognized the need for perceptual training, have discovered the rich resources available for such training, but have been discouraged by the conflicting demands of the academic and the remedial tasks.

This book presents an approach to the problem which should help resolve the dilemma. It suggests ways of using certain aspects of the academic curriculum itself as activities for perceptual training. This suggested approach involves teacher modifications of some curricular activities so that those activities result in perceptual training. If modifications can be made, then academic and perceptual training often can be combined, and perceptual training will not be an entirely isolated group of activities which compete with academic training.

The suggestion to modify some curricular activities does not in the least mean that all perceptual training should be done in this fashion. Perceptual training in the curriculum is presented as one more technique for making it available to those children who need it. If no perceptual training program is available, then use of the modified curriculum may make this training accessible to some children who otherwise would be denied it. If some ongoing program of perceptual training is available, it may be enriched and supplemented by perceptual training through these suggested curriculum modifications.

At present, the regular classroom is the place where perceptual training is needed most urgently. The vast majority of children with learning disorders are in regular classrooms. If they get help they will get it there. Most of these children do not have problems which are so severe that they should be placed in special classrooms even under ideal conditions, and present conditions are far from ideal. Not enough special classes exist to meet even the needs of children with severe problems, and this situation is likely to prevail for years to come. No one knows how many children in regular classrooms need some form of perceptual training, but no doubt these children are in our classrooms and they are there in large numbers; estimates range from one-tenth to one-third of the school population. If the regular classroom does not provide help, most of these children will go without it.

The use of certain modified curriculum activities for perceptual training should be helpful also to special-education teachers, for these teachers face the same problem as the regular teacher where perceptual training is concerned: The academic training and perceptual training tend to compete for time. Two of the four sample curriculum units in the book, therefore, have been designed primarily for a special-education classroom setting; both of the other units, with only slight modifications, would be suitable for special-education classes. Conversely, the special-education material illustrates techniques which could be adapted to regular classes.

The latter part of Chapter 1 consists of a statement of a theory of perceptual development and a discussion of principles for modifying curriculum activities to promote perceptual training. The four chapters which follow are presented as applications of the theory and principles. Each contains a unit of study which is designed to convey academic subject matter along with related perceptual training activities. These units are for illustrative pur-

poses only. Each unit is for a different grade level and academic
area as follows:

Chapter 2:   5th Grade, *Social Studies* (This chapter contains
             a special social-studies project; it is not properly a
             unit of study.)

Chapter 3:   1st Grade, *Language Arts*

Chapter 4:   Intermediate Elementary Educable Mentally Re-
             tarded, *Science*

Chapter 5:   Secondary Educable Mentally Retarded, *Vocational
             Training.*

The unit activities are concrete examples of modifying the presentation of typical curriculum material to provide the student with
academic learning experiences and remedial activities simultaneously. Explanations of how a given activity leads to remediation
accompany the description of that activity, except where repetitions would be merely tiresome.

*That the teacher view the four curriculum units as examples of
applications of theory and principles is extremely important.* You,
the teacher, should make your own curriculum modifications out
of your own insights into children's needs and from your own
knowledge of just what remediation a given activity may contribute
to those needs. A teacher should not attempt perceptual training
on a "cookbook" basis; rather, he should know what a given
activity is expected to accomplish and how it accomplishes it. The
four units are aids to demonstrate how theory and principles may
be applied. The units will have served their purpose for you, the
teacher, whenever they illustrate principles which you will come to
use when you yourself plan or modify other units.

The approach presented in this book is offered only as a beginning step toward combining perceptual training with curriculum
activities. The intention is to suggest how such a combination can
be brought about, rather than to prescribe specific programs.
Hopefully, the ultimate goal of extracting perceptual training from
the curriculum will be realized as creative teachers set their
imaginations to the task. The purpose of this book will have been
achieved if it stimulates those teachers to attempt the task, and
if it offers a few guidelines along the way.

A THEORY OF PERCEPTUAL DEVELOPMENT

For a comprehensive theoretical basis of the approach to perceptual training used in this book, the reader is referred to *The Slow*

Learner in the Classroom (Kephart, 1960) and "Motor Generalizations in Space and Time" (Dunsing and Kephart, 1965). Only a broad outline of theory is attempted in this chapter. Emphasis is placed upon those aspects which seem especially important to classroom teachers.

THE STRUCTURED SELF AND THE STRUCTURED WORLD

If a child is to receive and organize information from the world about him, he himself must be organized or structured internally. A child who is disorganized internally cannot be expected to organize information which comes from some source outside himself. If, for example, he has not developed an inner awareness of "left" and "right," he will have trouble distinguishing the letter "b" from the letter "d," because the only difference between these two letters is a difference in direction. If he has a poor internal awareness of "up" as different from "down," he may be unable to tell the letter "p" from the letter "d" or to distinguish "b" from "q." Without inner organization, the child's world will be confused, and the information he receives from that world will not be dependable or meaningful. For this reason, it is often said of children with perceptual problems, "They do not see what we see, hear what we hear, or experience the world as we experience it." Perceptual difficulties arise when the child's internal structure is missing, incomplete, or distorted. He must develop an internally structured self in order to function in a structured world.

Structure, in general, denotes an orderly arrangement of interrelated parts to make up a whole. In any structure, each part must perform its function in relation to all other parts and their functions. An automobile, for example, is a highly structured piece of equipment. It is made up of many parts which must function together if the whole car is to do its work of transporting you along the road. It has a frame and four wheels which roll. An engine produces the power for movement, and a power train (transmission, drive shaft, differential, axles) connects the power to the wheels. An accelerator varies the speed, and a brake stops the movement. A steering system controls direction. All these elements have particular functions to perform if the car is to operate properly, and each part must perform its function in relation to the others: The engine must be started before the wheels turn; the car must be in motion before the steering system can control direction; the brake is not applied when the accelerator is increasing speed, and so on.

The driver controls the automobile; he makes it do his bidding. Drivers are made, not born. As a driver must learn to drive, as he must learn to monitor and control the complex automobile with all its dynamic and flexible potentialities, so must the child learn to monitor and control the far more complex equipment of his body. The development of the structured self may be compared to the training of a driver: When the structured self has developed, the child is "in the driver's seat" with respect to his body. The structured self is that internal awareness whereby the child knows his body and its potentials and limitations, and controls that body so that it functions to serve him.

The automobile is a structured piece of equipment because it is put together on the assembly line in such a way that all the parts function together. In a similar manner, the child must structure himself into a functional whole. He begins with the parts; his task is to put the parts together into his own unique but structured self.

The child structures himself by interacting with the orderly world in which he lives. From this interaction he receives information about the world and about himself in relation to the world. He uses this information to develop an inner awareness of his own body in relation to space and time. This inner awareness lets him know where and what his body parts are, how they work together, and what they can or cannot do. His structured self becomes the reference point, the starting point, the "zero-point," from which he relates and orders the elements of the space-time world.

When this inner structure or organization is well developed and functioning, the child is in charge of a magnificent instrument — his own body. He can cause his hand to perform highly skilled tasks without concentrating on the movements; he can keep his attention on the task itself. He can vary the tasks over an astounding range, because he can bring to bear literally an infinite number of specific manipulations out of a vast storehouse of flexible movement patterns. He can look at an object some distance away and know in which direction his eyes are pointing, and also how far the object is from him. In a split second he can comprehend its shape, color, and texture, and he has some idea about how heavy it is and what kind of sound it would make if he struck it with his hand. He can move from place to place with smooth and rhythmic motions without thinking about or planning each motion, because these actions, too, come out of his storehouse of flexible patterns. He can listen, and in the process gain information from the sounds which come from a friend's mouth. He can bring into a harmonious whole the air in his lungs and the muscles in his vocal cords, tongue, lips, jaws, cheeks, with a precision of timing that staggers the imagination; and he can use the end product to tell you of the things he sees, knows, loves, and fears. He can do these things and a million more because he is a structured self in a structured world.

The child who is this well structured internally is able to take part in the perceptual process. He can receive information through his various sense avenues, and he can interpret it, because his own internal structure gives him a basis for organizing the information.

As a simple example of how internal organization is used to organize incoming information, consider a child as he looks at a tree some 50 or so feet from himself. He knows the direction to the tree only because he knows the direction in which his own head and eyes are pointing. He knows the direction of his head and eyes only from his internal structure. His neck muscles produce information about the location of his head; the muscles which control eye movements produce information about the location of his eyes with respect to his head. Since he is organized internally, this information from these particular muscles tells him the direction of his gaze. Without this internal organization he will not know with accuracy where his eyes are pointing, and so will lack essential information for learning relationships among objects in space.

His internal structure tells him more about the tree than its direction. From this same internal structure, he can make fairly accurate estimates of the distance to the tree and the time needed for him to walk that distance. His previous interactions with the world have helped him develop internalized information about relative distances and times. Visual information from the tree can thus be measured against his internal scale of distance and time.

From the educator's point of view, the development of internal structure is a matter of the highest importance. In reading, a child must receive and organize complex visual information from printed symbols on a page. Successful performance of this task demands a highly developed internal structure. Similarly, arithmetic involves the vicarious manipulation of relationships among objects in space. Listening to a story being read requires receiving auditory stimulation and translating that stimulation into meaningful patterns. Drawing a simple form requires the ability to organize the form internally and to translate this internal organization into a series of movements which take place in both time and space. Writing demands a similar but more complex ability. In all these and countless other school tasks, successful achievement depends directly upon the child's internal structure.

This all-important internal structure does not occur automatically; it develops in an orderly way as the child interacts with his environment, and as he receives and processes information from his interactions. The development begins at birth and is generally fairly complete at around 8 years of age. If the development is hampered in any way, the internal structure is likely to show some deficits, and perception may be impaired. For example, an understaffed children's institution may result in lack of opportunity to interact with the environment, and development may suffer. Or the environment itself may be so impoverished that it offers restricted opportunities for meaningful interactions, as is often the case in culturally deprived areas. On the other end of the socio-economic scale, a toddler may be forced to restrict his explorations of his environment because he is a lively threat to prized or fragile ornaments or household furnishings. Anything which interrupts or interferes with a child's explorations and interactions can affect adversely the development of the structured self. An extended hospital confinement, a slight injury to the central nervous system, too much confinement to the playpen, or any other restrictions upon free movement and spontaneous exploration may impede the development of internal structure.

THE MOTOR BASIS OF INTERNAL STRUCTURE

The infant's interactions with his environment produce information about that environment and about the infant himself. This information which comes from his explorations and interactions must be processed in some fashion. Without processing, it is nothing more than a mass of raw sensory stimuli. The interactions produce both internal information about what is happening to the infant and external information about what is going on outside of him. In interacting with the world, therefore, the infant is alternately and progressively learning about his own body and the world in which his body is functioning. Initially, he is thought to learn something of his body; this initial body knowledge gives him a basis for learning something from the world at large.

The infant's earliest learnings are motor learnings. The first information he learns to process is motor information; that is, the internal information which is produced by his own movements. Motor information comes from the vestibular sense (equilibrium) and kinesthetic receptors inside the body. These kinesthetic receptors are in the muscles, tendons, and joints. They provide a continuous feedback to the central nervous system about movement and position of the body parts.

Motor information is also the first information which is organized as part of the internal structure. Furthermore, as motor information becomes structured it provides a basis, or frame of reference, for organizing information from the senses. Visual information and auditory information are organized and structured as they are matched to previously organized motor information.

This internal organization of motor information will be called the *motor base*. Motor base refers to an internal and organized awareness of the body which develops from processing motor information; the parts of the body, their relative location and interrelatedness, and their movements and possibilities for movements. The motor base is the primary internal structure to which other sensory information is subsequently matched and structured. This matching of other sensory information to the motor base is discussed more fully later.

The motor base does not become fully developed before it is used to organize visual and auditory information. It develops in stages. Vision, for example, may be organized by matching visual information repeatedly to the motor base at progressive stages; however, a partially organized motor base will result in a similar partial organization of vision. Both motor base and vision will develop together in progressive stages, but at each stage the organization of the motor base normally precedes visual organization. The important point is that the motor base is the foundation structure upon which all other perceptual information is in turn structured. For this reason, certain motor activities often play an important role in remediation of perceptual problems.

DEVELOPING THE MOTOR BASE

The infant's beginning movements are total movements, usually involving the whole body. Typically, a sweep of movement from head to foot occurs. Such total movement is called undifferentiated movement; no one part makes distinctive and purposeful movements. The movement of an arm, for example, is not distinguished as separate and distinct from the total movement of the body as a whole. The general effect is a mass of unorganized movement where everything seems to "go off at once." Obviously, this mass of undifferentiated movement is of little value for exploring the world and obtaining information.

The first step is to differentiate, distinguish, or separate out the individual body parts and their movements from the total or undifferentiated mass of movement. Coghill (1929) has shown that the differentiation of body parts proceeds in sequence and in two directions: (1) the proximo-distal direction (from the center of the body outward), and (2) the cephalo-caudal direction (from head to toe). In the proximo-distal sequence, the infant first distinguishes those parts which are closest to the vertical midline of his body; then he differentiates in order the other parts lying progressively farther from his center. Thus, he first differentiates his trunk, next his shoulders, then his upper arms, elbows, forearms, wrists, hands, and finally his fingers — all in sequence and in a direction from the midline outward. In the cephalo-caudal sequence, he first differentiates his head and neck, next his shoulders and trunk, then his knees, legs, ankles, feet and toes — again, all in sequence and in a head-to-foot direction.

Kephart (1960), drawing upon Coghill's work, has emphasized the importance for the educator of this sequential development. In many children with learning disorders, the development has either not been completed, or some parts have not been differentiated in the proper sequence. Without realizing it, a teacher may even complicate and increase the problem. In kindergarten or first grade, a child may be required to use his fingers in complex manipulation of crayons or pencils before he has differentiated his hand, wrist, elbow, or even his whole arm. Under these conditions, what skill he manages to force upon his fingers develops as an isolated or "splinter" skill. Such isolated skills are termed "splinter" skills because they are not part of a flexible pattern of movement; they are said to be "splintered off" from the motor base, and they tend to be highly restricted movements which are capable only of specific and rigid operations.

The problem of splintering is intensified when the fingers are forced into action before the preceding parts are differentiated and organized into flexible movement patterns. Motor problems may persist beyond the early grades because the splintering may prevent completion of the sequential differentiation. The writer has a vivid recollection of a 9-year-old boy with learning disorders who, in writing at the chalkboard, kept his entire arm rigid while making all movements for writing from the shoulder only. His arm, elbow, wrist, and hand all moved as one stiff unit. This boy had scarcely differentiated any parts of his arm beyond his shoulder. Incomplete or improperly sequenced differentiation of body parts can result not only in such specific school problems as the foregoing, but can also interfere with the development of the motor base itself.

As the child differentiates his body parts and their movements, as he becomes better acquainted with his body and how the parts move, he must next recombine, or integrate, the parts into flexible, purposeful, and generalized movement patterns. In integrating the separate movements, he must also deal with the reflexes, combining them into the flexible patterns. Reflex movements are specific movements caused by specific stimuli; they are therefore restricted and rigid in their patterns. To be useful, they must be broadened and incorporated into functional patterns. Starting with a mass of unorganized movement, the child first separates movements from each other; he then combines these movements with the reflexes, and puts them back together as organized patterns. Most important, the new patterns must be *generalized movement patterns* rather than specific, narrow and rigid skills.

A generalized movement pattern is highly flexible. It may make use of an unlimited variety of muscular movements. In the simple act of reaching for an object, one may begin reaching no matter what the starting position of the hand. If the hand is at the side, reaching forward from that position will require the activation of certain specific muscles; if the hand happens to be elevated, an entirely different set of muscles will be brought into play. If a child has developed generalized movement patterns, he has an inner awareness of all the possibilities for movement at any given moment. Generalized movement patterns enable him to draw upon this inner awareness and to bring into action whatever specific muscles are needed for a given task. He does not need to rely only upon one set of muscles for a particular task; he can set the generalized pattern in motion, and the specific muscles are activated as elements of the pattern. For a given movement, then, the well-developed child does not have to make a detailed analysis of which muscles need activating; instead, he brings the pattern into play, and the muscular activity follows naturally and smoothly.

Generalized movement patterns let a child focus his attention upon the goal of his movements; he is not distracted by the necessity of attending to the production of each specific movement. A well-organized child can walk without attending to moving first one foot and then the other. He can keep his attention on where he is going instead of on the movements he must make to get there. Furthermore, he can vary the manner of locomotion as he wishes or as the situation demands: He can walk, run, hop, skip, or lope, and he can detour obstacles in his path without having to reorganize his movements with each break in the pattern.

The difference between generalized movement patterns and splinter skills may be illustrated by examining the manner in which children write. Some children seem to learn writing as a collection of detailed and highly specific splinter skills. Each element of each letter is made as if the specific movement to make that element were memorized. At the chalkboard, the wrist is rested on the board, duplicating as nearly as possible the position of the hand when the child was seated at a desk or table. Writing movements typically are slow and jerky, each movement requiring recall and planning before it is executed. With so much attention demanded by the movements for writing, one can easily see that the child can give little attention to what is being written.

The child with a well-developed motor base, on the other hand, can employ generalized movement patterns in writing, and can keep his attention on what he is writing rather than on how he makes the movements for writing. For the task of writing, he has available a generalized pattern of movements from which he can draw an unlimited number of specific movements as needed. This child can write at the chalkboard with a radically different set of muscles and movements from those he uses at his desk. The movements will flow smoothly because each movement is part of an organized pattern of movement; any individual movement does not have to be planned and executed separately. The development of generalized movement patterns is so important for learning that it can hardly be overemphasized.

Development of generalized movement patterns arises directly out of the following conditions:

1. Greatly varied interactions with a rich and varied environment.
2. Differentiation of body parts in the proper sequence (proximo-distal and cephalo-caudal).
3. Integration of the separate parts and their movements into generalized movement patterns.

In interacting with his environment, the child is, in effect, conducting countless experiments which help him learn what his body can do. A variety of experiments in a rich environment reveals to him the enormous range of movements which is possible with his body parts, either as individual parts or in combination. From this experimentation comes differentiation and integration of parts as the child discovers the parts and experiments with the wide range of movements they make.

In summary, developing the motor base means developing an inner awareness of all the possibilities for movements that are available for each body part and for all possible combinations of parts. The motor base develops as the child makes a wide range of experiments with a rich and diverse environment. From these experiments, the child differentiates his body parts in proper sequence and then integrates the parts into generalized movement patterns. From this differentiation and integration comes an inner awareness of the body and all its potential for movement. The organized inner awareness is termed a motor base because it is the base upon which subsequent organization is built. To the extent that the motor base is truly an inner awareness, to the extent that it is "wired in" so to speak, further movements and explorations can be made without requiring the child to focus his attention on the movements themselves. He is free to attend to the goals of movement and exploration, and thus is better able to receive and process information.

STRUCTURING SPACE

In the entire universe, no object is right or left, up or down, before or after, *in and of itself*. These terms denote relationships, and relationships require a point of reference in order to have meaning. If two people face each other, what is "right" for one is "left" for the other. For these directional terms to have meaning, they must be referred to an observer who becomes the reference point. The child structures the universe initially by referring objects to his own body. By using his body as a reference point, he is able to impose his internal structure upon the external world and thus to determine relationships among the objects and events in that world.

The child develops an internal awareness of left and right from his internal awareness that his body has two sides. The inner awareness is called *laterality*, and laterality is part of the motor base. It should be emphasized strongly that laterality is an inner awareness of left as different from right. It is therefore something more than just knowing the names of the two sides. A child may be able to name the sides accurately and still not possess laterality.

Laterality develops as the infant solves the fundamental problems associated with maintaining the posture and balance of his body. In shifting his body to assume various postures and in maintaining his balance, he comes to grips with the one constant in his world: the force of gravity. This force is always in the same direction ("down"), and this constant direction serves as a dependable reference for sorting out the various parts of the body. In fighting with gravity to maintain balance and posture, the child must continuously activate sets of opposing muscles. If he sways to the left, he tenses muscles on the right side of his body to prevent a fall. From many similar experiences he becomes aware that his body has two separate sides, and that the two sides work together.

In similar fashion, the relative location of body parts along a vertical line promotes an inner awareness of "up" as contrasted to "down." The feet become associated with "down," and parts closer to the head are associated with "up." This inner awareness of up and down is termed *verticality*. In like manner, parts in front of the body are distinguished from parts behind. The net effect is as if the body were bisected by three planes as follows:

1. One vertical plane dividing the body into two lateral halves: left and right.
2. One horizontal plane dividing the body into two parts: upper and lower.
3. One vertical plane dividing the body into two parts: front and rear.

The internal awareness of left as different from right, up as different from down, and front as different from rear has the effect of giving the child his own personal set of three-dimensional space coordinates. Information coming from the world can be located in terms of the child's three-dimensional awareness of his own body. The child first learns to organize that part of the world which is within arm's reach. An object is touched, and from the internal organization it is determined that the object is, for example, on the child's right front and that it is about chest-high. Touching an object will give information about where that object is located only if the child knows where his hand was when the object was touched. His internal organization lets him know where his hand is, and from this knowledge he knows the relative position of the object he touched. In this experience of locating by touch, the child is locating objects outside himself by projecting his own internal organization outward upon objects in space. Through such projections, the near space within arm's reach becomes structured. As he learns to match the visual information from looking at an object to the tactual experience of touching the object, he comes to locate objects at near point from visual information alone. When this development has taken place, he then can expand his near-point organization, and can locate objects beyond arm's reach. In this way, he begins to structure space by structuring the objects that fill space. The child's structuring of space, then, depends upon his development of his own internal structure and the projection of that structure outward upon the world around him.

Space is organized as the child receives information from the world and matches that information to his internally organized motor base. This matching of information is known as the *perceptual-motor match*. According to the theory presented here, the incoming information for perception is matched to the motor base; as incoming information is matched to a structured motor base, the incoming information itself becomes structured. The information comes in a variety of forms through the various sense avenues. Through the perceptual-motor match, all this information becomes structured into meaningful wholes. Without structure, the information is little more than a jumble of sensory stimulation.

Visual information, auditory information, and tactual-kinesthetic information are the major types of incoming information with which the perceptual-motor match is concerned. Exploring just one object may produce information simultaneously from eyes, ears, and muscles. The information from each of these three sources is different information, because sight is different from sound, and muscles are different from both. However, each source gives its different information about the same object. A child may *see* the corners, surfaces, and edges of a block, and he may *feel* the corners, surfaces, and edges at the same time. His hands and eyes give him distinctly different information, but a connection exists between the two: The information comes from the same source. An edge "looks sharp" because it "feels sharp," and the child has learned that certain aspects of "feeling" give a corresponding aspect of "looking." Similar obvious comparisons may be made with respect to how objects "sound."

Through countless experiments, a child learns to organize incoming information from the three major sources by relating this information to his motor base. From his motor base he knows where his hand is located at a given moment. If his hand touches an object and explores the object, he knows where the object is located because the tactual-kinesthetic information is referred to the motor base. From these explorations he determines both the location of the object in space and also the internal relationships of the elements which make up the object. If the child explores the object visually at the same time, the movements of his eyes come in time to correspond to hand and finger movements; in this fashion eye movements and hand movements become coordinated. The visual impression of the object becomes organized as the visual information is matched to the information simultaneously referred to the motor base through the hand and fingers. If, in exploring the object, the child bangs it on the floor and makes a sound, auditory information is produced. As sound becomes related to visual and tactual-kinesthetic impressions, more information about the object is matched to the motor base. The location of the object becomes determined from auditory clues as well as tactual-kinesthetic and visual clues, and tactual and visual impressions of relative "hardness" become associated with the sound the object makes. Visual, auditory, and tactual-kinesthetic impressions thus become organized by being matched to a previously organized motor base; in the process, the sensory avenues become coordinated and interrelated.

If perception is understood as organizing or structuring incoming information into meaningful patterns, then the role of the motor base in the perceptual process becomes of fundamental importance. The motor base provides the initial structure. Incoming sensory information is structured as it is matched to the structured motor base. A child's structured motor base provides him with an accurate knowledge of what is happening to his body, the parts of his body, and the movements the parts make. The movements he makes in exploring his world are now organized movements. Visual information and auditory information become organized by matching to organized movements; the organized movements provide a means of linking visual and auditory information to the motor base. Through countless repetitions of the perceptual-motor match, the visual and auditory sense avenues themselves become structured; at this point, the motor base need no longer be involved directly in each and every act of seeing and hearing. The motor base is used to structure vision and hearing; once this has been done, the eyes and ears are able to receive and organize information directly.

If the sense avenues are not structured, they do not give the child consistent, dependable, or veridical information about the world. If a child is to function in school, he must be able to perceive form. Words are composed of letters, and each letter is a visual symbol. To recognize the symbols, the child must be able to receive organized information through his eyes. If his vision is not organized, he will not be able to organize the visual information which the symbols are supposed to convey to him. Arithmetic demands that he be able to perceive relationships among objects in space, but if his vision lacks structure, he will be unable to perceive the basic relationships among objects which are right in front of his eyes, to say nothing of the more abstract perception of relationships when concrete objects are removed.

The coordination of eye and hand is of such importance to educators that special note of this aspect of the perceptual-motor match will be made here. This development is in two stages: The hand-eye stage develops first and the eye-hand stage follows later. In the hand-eye stage, the movements of the hand tend to attract the attention of the eyes. The hand will be moving, and the eyes, almost by accident, will be attracted by and begin to follow this movement. In time, the child realizes that the motor information from hand movements and the visual information from his eyes as they follow those movements are actually two sources of information about the same event: the movement of the hand. The information from the eyes is matched to the information from the movements of the hand. In this hand-eye stage the hand leads the eye; that is, the eye merely follows hand movements. Eye-hand coordination develops after hand-eye coordination. In this latter stage, the eye can now fix upon a certain object, and the hand can be brought to the object.

From the foregoing it can be seen that the motor base serves as a vehicle for organizing the information for perception during the time when perception is developing. Once perception has developed, the motor aspect can drop out, and information can be organized more directly. As you read these printed words, you are receiving visual information which you readily combine into meaningful information. You are organizing visual symbols into forms and patterns which give you information about concepts which the writer is trying to convey. As you read these lines, you no longer need be aware that they read from left to right. These words consist of lines in space, and you readily organize the lines which make up each letter. You do this without going through the laborious process of comparing each bit of visual information to your internally organized motor base. You do not, for example, need to refer each letter of each word to your motor base to determine whether it is rightside up or upside down. You are able to do all this, however, because you did develop a stable motor base, and you did learn to use that motor base to organize the information you received through your various sense avenues.

Because your sense avenues are organized or structured, you are able to organize your surroundings readily and with astonishing efficiency. You can take a quick glance around you, and everything fits together. You can lift your eyes from this book and look at the table or desk at which you are sitting. You perceive it as a table or desk. You know how the surface will feel without touching it. You know that the corners are sharp or round simply by looking; you need not touch them to know this. You know by looking that the material in the desk or table is solid and will not sag if you press your hand down on it; you need no longer experiment to discover it. You know that if you drop this book on your desk a certain sound will occur, and that if you set a coffee cup on it a different sound will be forthcoming. Merely by looking, you can know all this and much more about what is before you at this moment. You can shut your eyes and retain a good mental picture of the location of most of the objects in the room. You can organize your surroundings this efficiently because when you were a child you performed a thousand experiments where you matched incoming information to your motor base. The child who has not succeeded in structuring his sense avenues has trouble organizing his surroundings. Space, for him, does not hold together consistently as it does for you.

STRUCTURING TIME

Space and time are related. As a child must learn to structure space, so must he learn to structure time. The relationship between space and time is such that the child must learn to move readily from one to the other and to interchange one for the other. A simple example may point up the relationship between space and time, the need to structure both of these worlds, and the necessity for moving back and forth from one to the other.

A child who has developed a structured space world and a structured time world can, among other things, perceive and draw a square. A square consists of four equal lines in specific relationship. Perceiving the form called "square" requires the ability to deal with lines and relationships as they exist in *space*. On the other hand, if the child draws a square, he cannot draw all four lines in the same instant; *he must, therefore, transfer the form in space into the world of time* if he is to draw it. He draws the first line, then the second, third, and fourth lines; each line is produced at a time which is different from the time in which any other line is produced. As he draws any one line he must hold onto the form as it exists in space. He must function in the time world while holding onto a form which he perceives in the space world. To accomplish even this simple task, a child must have both a structured space world and a structured time world, and he must be able to move freely from one world to the other.

The behavior of many children suggests strongly that their time world lacks structure. A child may attempt copying tasks at great speed as if he is trying to do the task in "zero time," and in this way avoid the necessity of functioning in the time world. Seemingly, he can deal with only one element of the task at a time; in dealing with this one element he "loses" the other elements. In drawing a square, he may produce one line, but lose the other three as he deals with the one. He tries to solve the time problem by making extremely rapid movements, as if by moving rapidly he can finish the task before the elements elude him.

The same lack of temporal structure is seen in a child who cannot perform a sequence of activities. Johnny may be told to do three things: erase the board, empty the wastebasket, and take a note to the principal. If all these instructions are given to him before he starts any one task, he may do the first (or the last), and then be at a loss as to what comes next. Events take place in time; time must be structured if those events are to hold together or have dependable relationships.

Dunsing and Kephart (1965) point out three aspects of time, and compare each aspect to a corresponding aspect of space. The three aspects of time are synchrony, rhythm, and sequence. These terms are defined as follows:

1. *Synchrony* is "controlled simultaneity of movement designed for a purpose."
2. *Rhythm* is "a regular succession of repeated synchronous acts designed for a purpose."
3. *Sequence* is "an ordering in time of dissimilar objects or events."[1]

---

[1]Permission granted by Special Child Publications, Inc., 4535 Union Bay Place N.E., Seattle, Washington 98105, for the use of quotations from Jack D. Dunsing's and Newell C. Kephart's chapter, "Motor Generalizations in Space and Time" printed in Vol. 1 of the annual series *Learning Disorders,* edited by Jerome Hellmuth.

These three "dimensions" of time are developed and structured in much the same way that space is developed and structured: Both time and space structures grow out of the developing motor base.

Synchrony is related to "nowness"; that is, if the terms "before" and "after" have meaning, that meaning can only be in relation to a point in time we call "now." Synchrony provides such a point in time ("now") to which other events may be related. This awareness that a "now" exists in time develops initially from synchronous body movements. The earliest awareness of "now" arises from the child's efforts to balance himself as he assumes various postures. If, in attempting any given posture, his body tends to become unbalanced, he can maintain balance by making corrective movements. Such corrective movements to maintain balance must be made at the precise moment when balance is threatened; they must be made "now" and not "later." In this way, a starting point on the child's time scale develops from his body movements. *Just as his body becomes the starting point for ordering objects in space, so his body becomes the same kind of starting point for ordering events in time.*

If synchrony provides a starting point or "zero point" on the time scale, rhythm may be said to furnish the scale itself. From rhythmic movements the child develops an awareness of time divided into units which correspond to the inches on a yardstick. In creeping on hands and knees, for example, the infant is moving from one point to another in space. His movements typically are rhythmical, smooth, and beautifully coordinated. As he negotiates a given amount of space he also negotiates a given and corresponding amount of time. Both space and time are measured in terms of the movements he makes to cover that much space and that much time. Perhaps no example is clearer than this to point up the close connection between space, time, and body movements.

As synchrony has been presented as the starting point on the time scale, and rhythm has been compared with the scale itself, so sequence may be described as the form, or pattern, of time which corresponds to form perception of objects in space. Objects exist in space, and their relationships to one another form patterns. Events exist in time, and, in a somewhat similar fashion, their relationships in time form patterns. It has been shown that the child's initial location of objects in space is made possible by his own internal body structure. A similar point can be made with respect to his locating and structuring events in time. As objects are first located in space by movements from one object to another, so events are located and organized in time in terms of the body movements which intervene between one event and another.

FROM THEORY TO REMEDIATION

As an infant, the child began functioning at the first, or *motor level,* where his main source of information about the world was from his motor interactions. He then began to develop a motor base, and to move to the second, or *motor-perceptual level* where incoming data for perception were matched to the motor base. At this second level, for example, the hand leads the eye. Next, he advances to the third level, where incoming perceptual data can lead motor activities; in one instance, the eye now leads and guides the hand. The third level is known as the *perceptual-motor level.* The fourth level is the *perceptual level,* where incoming sensory data are organized into meaningful patterns without overt reference to the motor base.

Once a child is functioning adequately at the perceptual level, he is ready to proceed to the development of *concepts.* He begins building concepts from a number of percepts; in this fifth or *perceptual-conceptual level,* concepts depend upon percepts. The sixth level is the purely *conceptual level,* where conceptualizing may take place independently of any overt perceptual activity. The seventh, and final, level is the *conceptual-perceptual level,* where perception is conditioned by previously developed concepts.

Children with learning disorders often demonstrate, upon careful diagnosis, certain behaviors which clearly indicate that they have not developed a solid internal structure, and that this lack of structure adversely affects their ability to organize their world and the information which comes from that world. Failure to achieve adequate structure may occur at any level of development. At the lowest level, the motor development may be inadequate, thus affecting the structure of higher levels. The perceptual-motor match may be faulty, resulting in inadequate structuring of one or more of the sensory avenues: visual, auditory, tactual-kinesthetic. Development of structure also may be adequate up to a point, and fail to take place beyond that point. Wherever the development of the internal structure breaks down, a corresponding inability to organize the external world may be expected. Children who fail to develop a functioning inner structure and project that structure outward upon their environment are truly "perceptually handicapped." To the extent that they can be helped to develop an internal structure, they may be released from their handicap, and be made more susceptible to the typical academic demands placed upon them.

Stated in its baldest form, the theory outlined would hold that the fundamental problem in many children with learning disorders is a lack of inner structure, and that this lack of structure prevents a child from receiving and/or processing information in a dependable way. Inadequate structure shows up in a variety of ways in the classroom. Copying from the chalkboard is extremely difficult for many children with poor visual-motor structure. Shifting the eyes from chalkboard to desk involves rapid movement of eyes and prompt refocusing. In attempting this quite basic task, a child may search for the place on his paper, and, in the act of searching, forget what he saw on the board. He shifts back to the board, finds again what he just lost, shifts again to his paper, begins a new search for the proper place, and possibly loses the copy again. Such a child may have visual acuity of 20/20 and still lack an adequately structured and functional vision.

Other children are in trouble whenever they must add motor activity to any task. Writing requires of these children an excessive effort and concentration merely to produce the characters. With so much attention upon the production of the writing movements, little is left to concentrate upon what is being written. For others the reverse is true; they must still add the motor to guide the visual. These children may need a hand or finger to guide their eyes while reading; without this crutch their eyes cannot sweep smoothly over the page.

The problems associated with inadequate structure are complex and endlessly varied. The examples given suggest only a few of the difficulties. By careful observation of a child's behavior, a teacher may, however, make some dependable judgments regarding just where structure seems inadequate, and what remediation is in order. The school psychologist may have information which would help locate areas of functioning which need attention. Various standardized test instruments often yield information which will suggest specific deficits of structure. The following tests are especially helpful, and may be administered by teachers:

The Purdue Perceptual-Motor Survey (Roach and Kephart, 1966)

The Marianne Frostig Developmental Test of Visual Perception (Frostig, 1963)

Screening Tests for Identifying Children with Specific Language
Disability (Slingerland, 1964)
Durrell Analysis of Reading Difficulty (Durrell, 1955).

In using these tests to assess areas of structural difficulty, the
teacher should analyze the subtest scores and the child's pattern
of performance on each subtest. Total scores on any one test will
not be too helpful in the type of analysis suggested here. Rather,
a comparison of performances on several subtests often will point
to specific areas where structural deficits are causing trouble. For
example, one Frostig subtest is named "Spatial Relations." The
test items require the child to reproduce configurations of increasing complexity; the configurations consist of short connected lines
with abrupt changes in direction. If a child scores low on this test,
his problem could be a lack of directionality (caused by poor
laterality), inadequate visual structure, inadequate motor coordination (which interferes with his ability to reproduce the figures),
poor visual-motor coordination, difficulty with form perception,
or a combination of these. By comparing performance on this
subtest with that on other subtests, certain items will come to the
fore as indicators of the basic structural problem. If the Frostig
"Figure-Ground" test is passed, one may eliminate tentatively
the possibility that form perception is the main problem. If laterality items on the Purdue Perceptual-Motor Survey are scored
low, then further checking on directionality is indicated. If "Eye-
Motor Coordination" (Frostig) and "Perceptual-Motor Match"
(Purdue) are low, then a lack of visual-motor structure is suggested. By checking clues from one subtest against clues from
other subtests, a pattern begins to emerge.

The Durrell and Slingerland tests have many helpful subtests.
The Durrell gives grade norms for comprehension on oral and
silent reading as well as listening. If a child is much higher on
listening comprehension (where vision is eliminated from the
task) than on reading (where vision is basic to the task), a further
check on vision obviously is indicated. The "Ocular Control" items
on the Purdue Survey may give some decisive information in this
case. The Slingerland test includes reading at both far-point and
near-point, and it also has some extremely helpful items where
reading and writing are deliberately interrupted by gross motor
activities.

The various subtests contain a variety of items where tasks are
designed to involve different sensory and motor activities. Following the clues from these test items will help the teacher locate the
areas where structure has broken down and is causing learning

problems. Teacher observations of behavior patterns are essential to analysis. The tests discussed above are suggested as aids to systematic observation, but not as a substitute. The teacher may prefer other test instruments than these listed; many tests will yield much the same information. Regardless of the method of assessment, the key suggestion is that the child's pattern of performance be studied in an effort to discover the basic problems in his structure of himself, his structure of his environment, and his structure of the avenues through which his environment is perceived.

In those cases where lack of structure is interfering with learning, the remediation logically should focus upon the fundamental problem: the lack of structure. If the teacher takes this assertion seriously, then the remediation of some academic problems will involve activities which are bound to seem strange or even out of place in the classroom. An almost unspoken assumption is that the business of education is conducted only through books, words, paper, pencils, chalk, audio-visuals, field trips, and the like. The suggestion to employ activities to promote balance, posture, laterality, body image, eye-hand coordination, and similar perceptual training carries with it the faint suspicion that one is proposing something that is not quite academic. Nevertheless, the assertion still is made: If lack of structure is causing learning problems, the obvious remedy is to introduce activities which will promote structure.

All that has been presented so far has been described as theory, but this theory is buttressed by a wealth of clinical experience and solid research. From the considerable literature on the subject, the study of Hagin, Silver, and Hersh (1965) will be summarized as a fairly typical and rather dramatic example of the results of perceptual training.

Hagin, Silver, and Hersh conducted an experiment with forty boys (ages 8-11 years), all of whom were referred to the Bellevue Mental Hygiene Clinic because of behavior and school learning problems. The boys were divided into two groups, and each child was paired with a corresponding child in the other group in terms of age, IQ, psychiatric diagnosis, and neurological status. The experimental group received 6 months of training in "perceptual stimulation"; the control group received individual sessions of conventional teaching from a basal reading series. Each child in each group received training or teaching for two 45-minute periods each week during the 6-month period. Test-retest measures revealed that the experimental group (which received perceptual training) made significant gains on the Jastak Wide Range Achievement Test and on the Reading Section of the appropriate levels of the Metropolitan Achievement Tests. The control group (which received individual conventional teaching) did not make significant improvement on either of these measures. In addition, the experimental group made significant improvement on the Bender-Gestalt Test and the Right-Left Discrimination Test; however, no significant improvement was made on Wepman's Test of Auditory Discrimination, Goodenough Drawing, or the Finger Schema Test. The control group did not make significant improvement on any of the psychological measures. In discussing their experiment, these authorities offer the following significant comment: "It is suggested that perceptual training stimulates neurological maturation to a level appropriate for reading. This implies a relationship between perception and language abilities. If we look for a common denominator in our methods of perceptual stimulation, *we are impressed that problems in spatial and temporal orientation underlie them all*, be they visual, auditory, tactual, or kinesthetic." (Italics mine)[2]

From this study, the point which should be underscored is this: Perceptual training, a "nonacademic" set of activities, resulted in statistically significant academic gains. Equally important, perceptual training resulted in significant gains on various psychological tests. On the other hand, strictly academic training by the same teacher who conducted the perceptual training failed to produce significant gains in either academic performance or on psychological measures. From the theoretical position maintained in this book, the perceptual training is seen as the means whereby the internal structure of the experimental group was enhanced; the improved structure thus enabled these boys to deal more effectively with the demands of the academic task. From the same theoretical position, the failure of the academic training is seen as a failure to attack the problem at its roots.

THE CURRICULUM AS A SOURCE OF PERCEPTUAL TRAINING

Certain types of curriculum activities can be modified by the teacher to promote or provide perceptual training. The chapters

---

[2]Reprinted with permission of Rosa A. Hagin and the International Reading Association.

which follow are, in effect, examples of how this can be done. The remainder of Chapter 1 will be devoted to general principles which underlie the modification of curriculum activities in order to provide perceptual training in the ongoing school experience.

The broad goal of perceptual training is to help the child structure himself and structure the space-time world in which he functions. Perceptual training activities should aim at developing the motor base and promoting the perceptual-motor match. The motor base and the perceptual-motor match are developed progressively and interdependently; often the same activity is promoting both at the same time.

The motor base is developed and refined by differentiation of the body parts and their movements, and by a subsequent integration of these parts into smooth, flexible, and generalized movement patterns. In general, differentiation develops as a child becomes aware of each part of his body as separate and distinct from the whole body, and as he learns the movements which each part is capable of making. In promoting differentiation, the teacher plans activities to help a child become aware of the individual parts of his body, and to help him move a single part without setting off excessive movements of other parts. Activities should be planned in light of the proper sequences of differentiation. Integration involves organizing the separate parts into flexible movement patterns where the parts work together. Integration develops as the child experiments with the almost unlimited possibilities for using the different parts in combination. To promote integration, the teacher plans a wide variety of activities so that as many parts as possible are brought into play. Further, any one activity should be performed in many different ways so that generalized movement patterns may develop instead of splinter skills.

The perceptual-motor match involves receiving incoming information from eyes, ears, and muscles, and organizing this information by referring it to the motor base. Through countless matchings of "outside" information to "inside" structure, the child comes, in time, to organize his world. To promote perceptual-motor matching, curriculum modifications should call for learning tasks where eyes, ears, and muscles all work together, and where information received through one sensory avenue is reinforced and verified by matching it to the motor base. Stated another way, the perceptual-motor match enables a child to experience the learning task with his body; at the perceptual-motor level the child is still learning from concrete experience. Perceptual-motor match-

738

ing is thus seen as a remedial activity for children who failed to develop the ability to structure information from their environment.

From the chapters which follow, one example may illustrate curriculum modifications which provide activities to develop the motor base and to promote the perceptual-motor match. In Chapter 2, one suggested project is the construction of a large globe map of the earth. The globe is a 3-foot diameter sphere, mounted on a suitable base, and so made as to have a fairly rough surface. The activity calls for the children to construct the globe and to draw in the lines of latitude and longitude as well as the outlines of the major land masses. Assume that the globe itself has been constructed, and that a child is now drawing the appropriate lines on the globe. The following discussion will indicate how the activity of drawing the lines contributes to the two-fold purpose of developing the motor base and promoting the perceptual-motor match.

Consider first the development of the motor base. The large size of the globe is all-important. As the child works at the top of the globe, he must assume one position for drawing; as he works at the bottom of the globe (or even at the midportion) he must assume a radically different position. Each different position demands that he utilize a separate and distinct set of muscles; however, with each different set of muscles he accomplishes the same basic task of drawing lines. By using different muscles at different times to accomplish the common goal of drawing, the child is building his motor base by developing generalized movement patterns. Here is an example of curriculum modification enhancing the development of the motor base. In addition, as the child draws on the large globe, he is learning to differentiate the parts of his body through clues provided by certain aspects of the task itself.

An activity to promote differentiation of body parts should be designed to provide a variety of simultaneous clues to the location and movements of the body parts. The activity of drawing lines on the globe is structured to provide for drawing on a rough surface with a charcoal pencil. As the child performs this task, the design of the task is such that clues to the activity of his hand are magnified. The charcoal pencil on the rough surface makes a louder sound than usual; this sound is a clue to the movement and momentary location of the hand. The charcoal pencil moving over the rough surface of the globe also produces a characteristic and magnified "feel" (or tactual-kinesthetic feedback); this "feel" is another clue to the movement and momentary location of the hand. Finally, the charcoal pencil produces a fairly broad line as it moves over the globe surface; this line is a magnified visual clue to the movement and momentary location of the hand. Thus, it can be seen that in drawing a line with a charcoal pencil on the rough surface of the globe, the child is receiving magnified clues to the movement and momentary location of his hand, and he is receiving these magnified clues simultaneously through his visual, auditory, and tactual-kinesthetic sensory avenues. Each clue helps him differentiate the hand and arm movements which produced that clue, to distinguish these parts and their movements as separate and distinct from other body parts and their movements. By such curriculum modifications, the differentiation of body parts and their movements is promoted and improved.

In addition to promoting development of generalized movement patterns and differentiation of body parts, the activity of drawing on the rough globe surface with a charcoal pencil is promoting the development of the perceptual-motor match. The stimuli which produce the visual, auditory, and tactual-kinesthetic clues to hand and arm movements all originate from the outside world. The clues to these movements all come from the environment and they all come through the appropriate sensory channels. All the clues bring information about what is going on in the outside world. As these clues come in and are matched to the motor base, the outside world progressively takes on more structure. So it can be seen that this same curriculum modification not only helps develop the motor base; it also helps the child organize his environment.

Of course, not all curriculum modifications will contribute to all the basic tasks of developing generalized movement patterns, developing differentiation, and promoting the perceptual-motor match. Some modifications will promote one or more of these aspects, while others will represent a combination. Furthermore, it should be noted that function may overlap; to some extent no one aspect functions in complete isolation from the others. A particular curriculum activity, however, may be designed to emphasize one aspect (such as differentiation) apart from the other two.

In these activities, development of the motor base and the perceptual-motor match is given practical assistance. As differentiation and integration develop more fully, the child builds a more adequate internal structure. Through the perceptual-motor match, the world of space and time comes to have a better structure. Since information from the environment comes through visual, auditory, and tactual-kinesthetic channels, these channels also take on more structure and become more interrelated. In this way, perceptual training assists the child in his struggle to become a structured self functioning more adequately in a structured world.

Finally, the use of the curriculum as a tool for perceptual training must be set in larger perspective. It should be emphasized strongly that perceptual training in the curriculum is not seen as replacing perceptual training which might not be related to curriculum activities. In general, the proposals in this book are presented more as a supplement to, rather than a replacement of, a sound program of perceptual training which is aimed at remedying the child's fundamental perceptual problems. Any program of perceptual training ideally should be planned after careful diagnosis has determined the particular perceptual deficits of the individual child. Once this diagnosis has been made, the perceptual training program will consist of a number of specific activities. The main thrust of this book is to suggest ways in which the ongoing curriculum may be modified to produce some of these specific activities which a sound diagnosis might indicate as being helpful. With experience, the teacher may come to use creative curriculum modifications more and more as a means of providing those activities which a particular child needs for structuring himself and his world.

chapter 2

Perceptual Training with Social Studies

This chapter will present a specific example of perceptual training designed to accompany a social-studies curriculum, for use with a fifth-grade class. The whole project ideally should be carried out mainly by the "lower group," the "under-achievers" or "slow learners." What is presented is not a unit of study, but a project which should be considered as enrichment for the slow learners. The classroom is assumed to be a normal one engaged in a typical fifth-grade social-studies curriculum. All members of the class, including the slow learners, are assumed to be involved in the usual social-studies activities. The activities suggested in this chapter may be woven into the class program by using one or a combination of the following procedures:

1. If social-studies projects are assigned by groups, assign the project in this chapter to the slow learners.
2. Substitute the project for regular activities which may be beyond the capabilities of the slow learners.
3. Assign the project to the entire class, but give special attention to parceling out perceptual training activities to the slow learners.

In a typical fifth-grade social-studies program, the children are soon involved with history and geography. They are learning about things that happen in many different places and in many different times. The events they are studying take place thousands of miles from each other, and are also separated from the learner and from each other by centuries of time. To further complicate matters, children must move vicariously over great spans of time and space without moving themselves and without experiencing the flow of time. At one moment in class they may be "doing arithmetic," and a few moments later they are centuries away, sailing the high seas with Columbus. Within the social-studies curriculum itself, they often cover thousands of miles and many years in the same day. If their learning is to have meaning, the events, the time, and the space must all hold together.

The learning problem, then, is a complicated one, involving a high degree of structure or organization. Each event must be related to the individual child and his momentary location in time and space, and each event must be placed in its proper relation to a host of other events. If adequate structuring does not take place, some events will be jumbled together, some will not even exist for the learner, and some may float around vaguely. Solving the structure problem is quite a task for all children; for the slow learner the task is almost insurmountable. As previously noted, many slow learners are, themselves, not structured. They do not have that internal awareness which lets them know where they are in time and space; they have not established their own bodies as a zero point from which events and objects in our space-time world can be located reliably.

The project will aim at these broad goals:

1. Using the social-studies subject matter to provide visual, tactual, auditory, and kinesthetic experiences for slow learners, in such a way that these experiences will take place concurrently with the academic learning. The goal is to involve the eyes, ears, hands, muscles, and the whole body in the learning process. In this area, the project is deliberately designed to provide remediation for the slow learner while offering him academic training.

2. Using the social-studies subject matter to structure the space-time world and to relate the learner to that world. The social-studies curricula by their very nature offer rich and unique possibilities for unfolding for the child the world about him and helping him place himself in that world.

3. Motivating the slow learner by means of experiences which will give him a feeling of success. The project involves construction, mainly by the slow learners, of several items. These items, when constructed, can be used as learning aids for the whole class. Success experiences for slow learners could consist of letting them be the ones to demonstrate the items to the rest of the class. Other success experiences for slow learners will come from the actual construction of the items.

This project is presented as *one approach* to integrating perceptual training with academic subject matter. It is presented as *a solution* rather than *the solution*. It is meant to be an example of how integration can be achieved rather than a prescription. Hopefully, it will be suggestive rather than definitive. The perceptive teacher can accomplish the goals by developing a wide variety of quite different projects. Those who use this project are encouraged to make their own creative variations.

THE PROJECT: AN OVERVIEW

Basically, the project consists of constructing and using a globe map, a floor map, and a time line, all three items made on a very large scale. These items are basic ingredients of a fifth-grade social-studies curriculum, and are used as learning tools with nearly all social studies. The project, therefore, will not be confined to a particular unit, but will be used with all those social-studies units where events are to be located in time and place.

The project should be started as soon as practicable after the class begins social studies, at least as soon as times and places are encountered. Since the construction phase will involve the use of some basic mathematical concepts, the slow learners might begin on the project during time allotted to arithmetic. Much of the project, and especially the construction phase, will be of real help to those slow learners whose difficulties with mathematics are related to poor concepts of objects in space.

The project is designed so that perceptual training will be provided both while the items are being made and while they are being used as aids for classroom study. Perceptual training will come naturally as the children go through the project; however, this training can be increased greatly if the teacher will take advantage of spontaneous situations which inevitably will arise. It is impossible to point out all the training opportunities in a project such as this, but the teacher can see them as the project unfolds. The project description, therefore, will indicate the major aspects of perceptual training offered, realizing that the teacher will add many elements on his own initiative.

The perceptual training offered by each major element of the project is presented in outline form below.

I. *Construction Phase*

    A. Constructing the Globe Map

        1. Making styrofoam rings (which will be formed into the sphere).

            a. *Perceptual-motor Matching:* Sawing concentric rings from styrofoam gives simultaneous visual, auditory, and tactual-kinesthetic feedback.

            b. *Differentiation:* Feedback promotes awareness of parts used in the task.

            c. *Integration:* Coordinated movements are developed. Control of movement is developed.

            d. *Generalization:* Different sizes of rings are made, thus varying the movements involved.

        2. Assembling styrofoam rings into outline of sphere.

            Form Perception: Parts are assembled into a whole. Motor and visual activity are both involved; the child *experiences* the whole coming together from the parts.

        3. Making the globe surface with papier-maché clay.

            a. *Perceptual-motor Matching:* Visual and tactual-kinesthetic feedback comes from hands spreading clay.

            b. *Differentiation:* Clay gives unique tactual-kinesthetic feedback which promotes awareness of those parts involved in the task.

            c. *Integration:* Two hands and arms work together in spreading clay; coordination and control are developed.

            d. *Generalization:* Working on top, bottom, and sides requires different body positions and much variety of muscle combinations to do the same task.

        4. Locating North and South Poles.

            a. *Directionality, Spatial Relations:* North Pole is located by children observing (from a distance) and pointing to high point on globe; motor is involved with visual in indicating relations.

b. *Generalization:* South Pole location involves same task, but radically different body positions and movements.

5. Locating and drawing equator, lines of longitude and latitude, and outlines of land masses.

a. *Perceptual-motor Matching:* Globe surface is rough sand finish; drawing is done with charcoal pencil. Drawing thus provides visual, auditory, and tactual-kinesthetic feedback.

b. *Differentiation:* See preceding sections on differentiation.

c. *Integration:* See preceding sections on integration.

d. *Generalization:* Task requires variety of body movements and muscle combinations.

e. *Form Perception:* Whole is *experienced* from visual, auditory, and tactual-kinesthetic involvement of child with parts.

B. Constructing the Time Line.

The construction phase for the time line provides relatively little perceptual training. The children will divide a very long line into centuries and decades, and will thus experience a whole being broken down into parts. The "Use Phase" will offer considerably more perceptual training (see below).

C. Constructing the Floor Map.

1. Tracing over a large United States map which is projected onto a 9 x 13 foot plastic sheet. The plastic sheet is placed on a wall, and the map is projected with an opaque projector; children trace map with charcoal pencils.

a. *Perceptual-motor Matching:* See preceding sections.

b. *Differentiation:* See preceding sections.

c. *Integration:* See preceding sections.

d. *Generalization:* Large size of map involves many different body positions and muscle combinations. Projection of trace offers opportunity to work with midline problems.

e. *Form Perception:* Whole is first perceived visually; then parts are experienced through all major sensory-motor avenues. Finished product is a whole from experienced parts.

2. Inking over pencil lines (map on floor; use felt-tip pens).

   a. *Generalization:* Entirely different body positions and muscle combinations. Work previously done in vertical plane is now done in horizontal plane.

   b. *Perceptual-motor matching, differentiation, integration,* and *form perception* are promoted also.

3. Orienting the Map.

Orienting marks are placed on the floor and map, so that "map North" may be oriented readily with "ground North." Training in spatial relations and directions results. This learning utilizes motor activity along with visual. Directions and relations are thus experienced motorically as well as visually.

Use Phase

A. Using the Globe Map.

Once constructed, globe map may be used as would any other. Size, rough surface, and initial absence of national boundaries make possible the following major types of perceptual training:

1. *Relations among objects in space:* Graphic demonstrations of objects moving over horizon are possible because of size. Large size also makes possible concrete demonstration of latitude determination.

2. *Spatial and temporal orientations:* National and state boundaries are drawn as events involving map locations are studied; children are helped to correlate events in time with map locations. Sensory-motor activity in drawing thus adds additional dimensions to associating temporal events with spatial locations of those events.

3. *Perceptual-motor matching and form perception:* Rough surfaces of globe may be exploited in many ways. Example: children trace outlines of continents, routes of explorers, and the like with fingers moving over rough surface.

B. Using the Time Line.

Time line is quite long (20 to 30 feet) and divided into centuries and decades. Children hang cards listing events studied at proper time locations on line. All events studied to date are placed on line *each day*, and removed at end of day. Major perceptual training:

Temporal-spatial relations: Time is translated into a visible scale located in space: the time line. Visual-motor activity is required to place a card indicating an event in time; thus time unfolds and is organized (relatively) in terms of the activity involved in hanging a card at a particular place. Further, the time line represents a chronological outline of social-studies activities to date. Each day the child experiences an expanding block of time he has given to social studies; he experiences this in terms of his visual perception of the time line and the cards on it and by the visual-motor experience of building the block of time anew each day. Training is also given in form perception as locations are determined in relation to location of events on the line.

C.   Using the Floor Map.

Large map size is the key to perceptual training with the floor map. Major perceptual training is in *spatial relations*. Locations of events studied may be experienced in terms of motor activity in moving from one place to another on the large map.

The main emphasis in the foregoing outline has been to suggest how perceptual training results from project activities. The project activities themselves will be presented now in more complete form. The outline may be consulted whenever project activities need relating to perceptual training goals. Many variations of activities may be planned to add additional training.

CONSTRUCTION PHASE

a. Constructing the Globe Map

The globe itself should be approximately 3 feet in diameter. If it is made much smaller than 30 inches its effectiveness will be decreased. Two different methods for making the globe are suggested. The method described in this section is easy; a harder method is described in the Appendix.

Before presenting the easy method, let a word be said in behalf of the harder one. It offers many more opportunities for perceptual training. It will not add to the academic aspects of social studies, but it should certainly be remedial for arithmetic. If the time can be made available, the harder method will more than repay the extra effort required. Briefly, this method consists of using sheets of styrofoam 1 inch thick, cutting progressively smaller rings from these sheets, and stacking the rings on top of each other to form a rough hemisphere; the process is repeated for the second hemisphere, and the rings are glued together. The surface is made smooth by filling in the gaps at the outer edges of the rings with a suitable filler. Figure A-1 in the Appendix illustrates the construction procedure. Cutting the rings gives a wealth of experience in matching visual data to tactual, kinesthetic, and auditory data. The cutting instrument is a bare hacksaw blade; styrofoam is so easy to cut that no handle is needed for the blade. A child can cut the material quickly and easily, and with very brief instructions can attain competence. The writer has seen a first-grader cut a 36-inch circle with more than acceptable accuracy and with no previous experience.

The easy method is to obtain a large plastic beach ball, the kind which is made with segments of plastic bonded together leaving only very fine seams when inflated. Inflate the ball and paint it with two coats of latex base paint; the first coat is applied as it comes from the can, but a "sand float finish" material (obtainable at paint stores) is added to the paint before the second coat is applied. The finished surface is identical to the "plastered" finish put on interior wallboard in homes, and gives the rough texture needed.

The following additional construction details apply to the globe map regardless of whether the sphere is made by the hard or by the easy method.

After the globe itself has been made, the next step is to add the lines of longitude and latitude. Explain to the group what these lines are, and how they are used to locate any position on the earth. A regular classroom globe should be used for this explanation. Since the regular classroom globe will be used frequently as a model during construction, it would be well to obtain one which has the lines of longitude and latitude marked quite clearly. Tell the group they will put these lines on the globe, and that the first task is to locate the North Pole.

Explain that the North Pole will be at the top of the globe; they must find the highest place on the globe. (Ignore the tilt of the earth to simplify construction.) Tell them that their eyes may fool them if they try to find the high point by looking. To demonstrate this, place four or five dots randomly in the near vicinity of the top of the globe, and ask each class member to indicate which one he thinks is the top or closest to the top. A difference of opinion probably will arise. The random dots should then be removed.

To locate the North Pole accurately, use a team of three children. One child stands by the globe and holds a pencil touching the approximate location of the pole; a second child stands several steps away from the globe and facing it; the third child also stands several steps away from and facing the globe, but at right angles to the other two and in such a position that the pencil forms the vertex of a right angle (see Figure 2-1). The child holding the pencil moves the pencil either right or left as each child tells him. He first takes directions from one child, moving the pencil either right or left, until the point of the pencil is on the topmost point of the globe *as that child sees it*. Then, without moving the pencil, he turns to the other child, and moves the pencil right or left *as the other child sees it*. He repeats this process, taking directions

FIGURE 2-1. **Locating the North Pole**

from first one child and then the other, until both see the pencil point at the very top without further moves. This point is the North Pole, and should be marked plainly. To increase accuracy, go through the entire procedure several times, using different children. Several dots quite close together should be obtained, and the final location of the pole should be made in the center of the group of dots.

The South Pole should be located in the same manner, but the team of three children should lie on the floor. To turn the globe upside down would, of course, be easier, but lying on the floor will add to the variety of positions and encourage more generalized movements.

The next step is to locate the equator. Remind the group that the equator is halfway between the North and South Poles, and show them on the classroom globe how it goes around the earth like a belt. Tell them they should start by finding just one point which is halfway between the two poles, and ask if anyone can think how to find the point that is exactly in the middle. If they have trouble responding (and they probably will), show them a piece of stout string about 6 feet long, and ask, "Can you use this?" If they still have trouble, have one child hold the string on the North Pole while another stretches it down to the South Pole. Have them fold the measured length in half, and tie a short piece of string at the midpoint. One end can then be placed on the North Pole and stretched to the midpoint, and a mark can be made which is one point on the equator.

Now point out that the North Pole is at the *highest* part of the globe and that the equator goes around the *widest* part. Suggest that they could have used the wall to find the widest part, and they would not have had to use the string. Ask if anyone knows how to use the wall to find the widest part. If they have trouble with this question, ask one of them to move the globe close to a smooth section of vertical wall. Have them look at the globe and the wall, and ask if they can now see how the wall shows which part is the widest. Then have them move the globe until it barely touches the wall, and mark the contact point on the globe (see Figure 2-2). This point is on the equator. Next, have them find the point which they measured with the string, and turn the globe so that this point faces the wall. Have them move the globe until it again just touches the wall, and mark the contact point on the globe. The two marks (one from string measure and one from wall contact) should be quite close to the same height from the floor.

FIGURE 2-2. Locating the Equator

While the globe is at the wall it will be convenient to mark a number of points so that the equator can be drawn by connecting these points. The globe is placed against the wall (barely touching), a mark is made on the globe, the globe is then shifted and again placed against the wall and marked; this process is continued until a series of marks outlines the equator. The children can then draw in the equator by connecting the marks. All drawing and marking should be done with soft-lead pencil or charcoal pencil at this point. When the entire globe map is finished, the pencil lines can be gone over with felt-tip pens or some other suitable instrument.

Now the North and South Poles and the equator are located on the globe. The next step is to add the lines of latitude and longitude. It is important that the constructed globe have the same divisions between the marked lines as does the classroom globe. The children will use the classroom globe as a guide to mark off the outlines of the major land masses, and if the lines of latitude and longitude are marked off in different units the children will become confused when they come to this stage. So have the group examine the classroom globe carefully. They should count the number of latitude "spaces" around the whole globe. Explain that they will divide the globe they make into the same number of "spaces," and will number the spaces in the same way as they are on the regular globe.

Latitude lines will probably be drawn on the globe for each 10 degrees. Nine equal divisions must be made from the equator to the North Pole, making a total of 90 degrees in this arc. Have someone run a string from the North Pole straight down to the equator, and mark this distance on the string. The problem is to divide this distance into nine equal parts. Measuring and dividing by use of arithmetic will most likely result in unwieldy fractions. A simpler way is to draw on the chalkboard parallel lines 2 inches apart, marking off nine spaces 2 inches wide (the teacher should do this). Then stretch the measured length of string at an angle across the lines until each end of the string is on one of the outside lines. Mark the string where each line crosses it, and the string is divided into nine equal parts (see Figure 2-3).

FIGURE 2-3.   **Using Parallel Lines to Divide a String into Equal Parts**

Have the children take the divided string and place one end on the North Pole and run the other end straight down to the equator. Two children should hold the string in position while a third makes a mark on the globe opposite each mark on the string. Then lift the end lying on the equator until that end is at least as high as the end on the pole, and shift the string slightly to one side and again run it straight down to the equator. Now another set of latitude divisions can be marked on the globe opposite each mark on the string (see Figure 2-4). Repeat this until the string has been worked all around the globe. Repeat the process for the South Pole, removing the globe from its base if necessary. Put the globe back on the base and have the children draw in the lines of latitude by connecting the marks. The children should take turns working the string and marking, and as many as possible should be at work at the same time drawing in the latitude lines. In parceling out the work, try to see that each child does some work on the top, middle, and bottom of the globe. Do not permit turning the globe to make the drawing more convenient; the drawing should be done from different and unusual body positions.

To lay out the lines of longitude, begin by making an arbitrary mark at any point on the equator, and label this point "0." Place one end of a long piece of string on the point and run the string

FIGURE 2-4.   Marking Points for Lines of Latitude

all around the globe, keeping the string on the equator. Several children will be needed to keep the string in place. When the circumference of the globe has been measured with the string, remove the string and fold it in half, marking the midpoint. Place the end of the string on the "0" mark again, and this time run it around the equator only halfway. Place a mark on the equator at the midpoint of the string, and label this point "180." In similar fashion, locate 90-degree (east and west) points on the equator, and label them. The equator is now divided into four equal quandrants. If the classroom globe is divided into 10-degree intervals of longitude, then each 90-degree quandrant will be divided into nine equal parts. If the intervals are 15 degrees, then the quandrants will have six equal divisions. When these divisions have been marked on the equator, a line of longitude may be located by running a string from the North Pole through a division mark on the equator and on down to the South Pole (see Figure 2-5). The string should be kept straight, and the longitude line may be marked by using the string as a guide. The children, of course, should do all the measuring, marking, and drawing of lines.

The globe now has both poles and the lines of latitude and longitude drawn in with pencil or charcoal. Before outlining the

FIGURE 2-5.   Drawing Lines of Longitude with String Guide

land masses, it would be well to go over the light lines with a brightly colored felt pen or other instrument to make the lines stand out. Also, at this time the lines should be labeled, using the classroom globe as a guide.

Take time to explain the major features of latitude and longitude to the group while only these lines are on the globe. Show them how these lines are used to locate a position on the map. Write several positions on the board, giving latitude and longitude of each position, and have the children point to the position on the globe. Spend as much time as necessary so that everyone in the group is able to handle these relationships. The procedure can be varied and enriched by having the children locate a certain city on the classroom globe, determine its latitude and longitude, and then locate it on the globe they have made.

Interpolating within a section of the globe marked off by lines of latitude and longitude will represent a real step forward for many slow learners. For example, if they can learn to visualize 24 degrees latitude as "not quite halfway between 20 and 30 degrees," and can make such estimates consistently, they will have made a significant gain. Those who cannot do this by visual inspection should use a finger or stylus to trace the distances from one division to another, repeating this until they get the "feel" of the distance. They can then practice moving one-half, one-third, one-fourth of the distance; they can do this for different parts of the globe, which will involve doing it from different body, arm, and hand positions. The tactual-kinesthetic experience will have additional reinforcement if the child will say aloud "one-half" or "one-fourth" as he moves the corresponding distance.

The next step is to have the children draw in the land areas on the globe, using the regular classroom globe as a model. Each child should be assigned a major area so that he has a complete figure to deal with. One could draw North America, another South America, another Africa, and so on. In this phase, form perception can be trained: First the child should experience his assigned area as a whole figure. Then he should experience the various elements of that figure as he reproduces it on a larger scale. Finally he should experience the whole figure coming together from its elements. In effect he will be getting a whole figure, breaking it up into smaller elements which will be easier for him to handle, and then reassembling the whole from the elements. By having him do this on a different scale, generalization has been added.

The following procedure should help the child do this task:
Use the regular classroom globe to assign the child his area. Have
him trace the outline with his finger. Ask him to look at the globe
and pick out the lines of latitude and longitude which are just
outside the total figure, and which form a rough boundary for
his whole area (see Figure 2-6). Have him write down his boun-

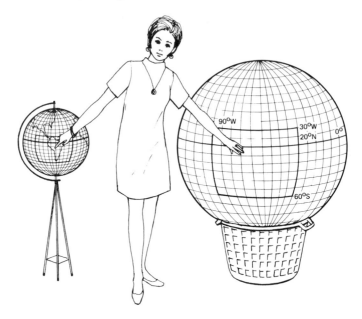

FIGURE 2-6.   An Assigned Area Marked Off for One Child

daries in some such fashion as this: "South America is between
latitude 20 degrees north and latitude 60 degrees south. It is
also between longitude 30 degrees west and longitude 90 degrees
west." Now have him locate these same "boundaries" on the
globe being constructed, and mark in charcoal along each boundary so that he can readily identify the rough area in which he
will be working. By now, he should have the whole figure fairly
well in mind, and he should be aware of its relative location with
respect to the globe.

To divide the whole figure into more manageable parts, take
advantage of the crisscrossing lines of longitude and latitude. Ask
the child to point out on the regular globe the place where he
would like to start his drawing. When he has done this, show him
that his starting point is inside a small figure of four sides made
up of longitude and latitude lines (see Figure 2-7). Then go to

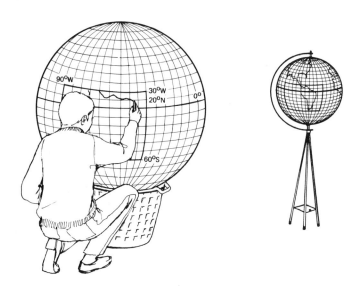

FIGURE 2-7.   **Drawing the Assigned Area in Segments**

the other globe, locate the same small segment of the globe, and have him mark where he will start his drawing. Now go back to the regular globe, and point out how every part of the outline is in one of these small segments of the globe. Ask him to draw his outline one part at a time, but to draw each part as it follows the one before it. He should do this drawing with pencil or charcoal so that errors may be corrected. When the child has completed the drawing, he has experienced the figure as a number of parts in orderly sequence.

The whole figure can be brought together again simply by having the child trace over his own lines with a felt pen or other marker. Have him start at a different point and draw this time in the opposite direction from the one he used to outline his area. Do not let him follow the "segmenting" by which he originally produced the figure; he should draw with a much freer and more sweeping movement now.

The globe map is now virtually complete, except for any refinements the teacher may wish to make, such as coloring the oceans and lakes and labeling the continents. Borders of nations and states should not be added until such times as these places are studied; they can be added one at a time as they are encountered.

b. Constructing the Time Line

The time line can be made in a variety of ways, depending upon the arrangement of the classroom and the teacher's preference. It consists only of some form of a straight line divided into centuries and decades, arranged so that labels can be added and removed easily. What is recommended is the usual time line made larger and more flexible. It should be nearly as long as the classroom (at least 20 feet long). It could turn a corner if necessary to obtain the desired length.

The time line should be laid out on a scale of ¼ inch to 1 year. A line 20 feet long would therefore represent a span of time of some 960 years, which would embrace the times of the Viking explorers to the present. If the teacher does not intend to deal with this large a time span during the school year, the scale could be made ½ inch to 1 year. In this case a 30-foot line would cover 720 years or a 20-foot line would cover 480 years. Basically, a long line is suggested which will represent the total span of time studied during the school year.

The line itself could be a length of stout cord stretched taut along a wall, along the top of the chalkboard, under the chalk tray, or even in the middle of the room; any convenient place will do. It should be parallel to the floor, and its height should be such that a child must reach, stoop, or squat (or get into some other unusual position) in order to touch the line. If a small ladder or sturdy chair is available it would be well to have the line high enough that one of these would be needed in order for a child to get to the line. The slow learners will be using the line frequently, and it should be necessary for them to assume unusual positions as they do so. In planning for this aspect, safety should be underscored, especially since some slow learners have unusual and often unnoticed problems in balance, coordination, and vision.

The line may also be made of a strip of masking tape running along a wall, or a background of butcher's paper running along a wall with a narrower strip of paper or tape fastened to this background. Whatever type line is used, provision should be made for attaching and removing all labels. Clothespins, paper clips, and similar fasteners will work well with labels on a cord, but if a tape line on a wall is used, then some other means of fastening must be provided.

After selecting the size, type, and scale of the line, have the children divide the line by measuring with a ruler. This work could best be done by working at a table and measuring the line before it is installed in its permanent location. The children should first measure off the centuries (25 inches is one century if the ¼-inch scale is used). If the line is made of cord, the divisions could be marked by tying a short piece of colored string or yarn around the cord at the proper place. After the centuries have been marked, each century should be divided into 10-year intervals. These decades should be marked with a different color string. Labels should then be made on cards (at least size 5 x 7) for each century and each half century (1500, 1550, 1600, and so on). The century labels should be written in one color and the half-century labels should be in another color.

When all the labels have been made, let the children stretch the string (or put up any other kind of line which may have been selected), and attach each label at its proper place. Explain that the line represents time, and that they have divided the time into centuries and decades. After the children have inspected the finished product, remove the labels and put them away for future use. A supply of blank labels should be obtained; this completes the equipment needed for use of the line. The blank labels will be used for writing in events as they are studied, and these should be larger than the time labels. All labels should be of sturdy stock which will not curl unduly when the labels are suspended.

c. Constructing the Floor Map

The floor map of the United States should be made quite large; large enough, in fact that a child in walking on it would experience a noticeable amount of movement as he crosses several states. If possible, it should be as large as 9 x 13 feet; every effort should be made to have it no smaller than 6 x 9 feet. These dimensions are suggested because they are roughly proportional to the length and breadth of the nation, and also because the recommended materials can be used in· their standard width with only one seam. If these dimensions seem to make excessive demands upon classroom floor space, remember that the map need be on the floor only while it is being used; at other times it can be folded or rolled into a small bundle for storage.

The recommended material is plastic upholstery material, available in the dime store in widths of 54 inches (4½ feet). Two widths can therefore be joined to make a 9-foot dimension. One side has a pattern, but the other side is plain; the map should be constructed on the plain side. To make the map "sheet" in the 9 x 13 size, obtain two pieces of the material, each piece being 13 feet long, and join them together with a strip of 3-inch surgical tape or masking tape. The tape should be applied on the reverse side of the map, which would be the patterned side of the material. The 6 x 9 size can be made the same way, except that in this case each of the two pieces need be only 6 feet long. This material is inexpensive and quite tough, and will take much rough wear from walking, turning, shifting position, as well as from folding and rolling.

An overhead opaque projector should be used to project a map of the United States onto the large map sheet, and the children should trace over the projected lines with charcoal pencils. The opaque projector is the type which will project from a printed page; however, if a transparency map is available, the overhead transparent projector will do as well. For this part of the construction, the large plastic map sheet should be tacked temporarily to a wall. The projector should be at right angles to and centered on the sheet to avoid distortion, and the projected image should be as large as the sheet will allow. With the image on the sheet, have the children trace the outline of the United States and the boundaries of the individual states (omitting Alaska and Hawaii unless the teacher wishes to add them as an "inset"). The map obtained for this purpose should be clear, and the lines of latitude and longitude need to be marked on it in 5-degree intervals. In selecting the map, see that the latitude and longitude lines are printed across the map itself (on some maps these lines stop at the boundaries), and have the children trace these lines as well as the boundaries. Number each line of latitude and longitude.

Several children can trace at the same time. Note that in tracing they will be working in many different body positions as they attack the lower and upper portions of the projected map. This variety of body positions is highly desirable. Furthermore, the children must trace from beside the line they are working on at a given moment, or else their bodies will cast a shadow and obscure the projected pattern. This problem will necessitate still more variation of body movement. You will probably find that right-handed children will tend to stand to the left of the spot they are working on, while left-handed children will stand to the right. If a child does this consistently he is probably avoiding crossing his vertical midline; in such a case he should be corrected and required to alternate so that his hand will work across the midline as well as on the side of the working hand. The upper portions of the map will be out of reach of the children, and short ladders or other safe standings will be needed. To avoid requiring the children to work from undue heights, try taping a charcoal pencil to a pointer for extra "reach," for this will add to the training considerably, and at the same time will solve a practical problem.

When the tracing is completed, put the map on the floor and have the children go over the traced lines with a felt-tip pen. The national boundaries should be in a dark color and the state boundaries should be made very pale. Explain to the children that we did not always have the same states, and that boundaries changed from time to time. Tell them that they will trace in the state lines in darker colors when they study about them.

Let the children locate their school on the map, using road maps to compare with the floor map. Mark and label this location, and draw a North line from their school location all the way to the north edge of the sheet, making this line parallel to the longitude lines, and using the longitude lines as a guide. Then place the map in the location where it will be used, and let the North line on the map point roughly to north. Have one child stand on the map at the point where the school location was marked, and determine as accurately as possible which direction is north from this point. When this has been determined, shift the map until the North line is actually pointing north. Without moving the map, extend the line from the school location south until the line is at the south edge of the sheet. When this extension is made, a North-South line will run through the school location, and across the entire sheet. With the map still in place, put a piece of tape on the floor in such a place that the tape is next to the north end of the line; do the same at the south end. Make a short extension of each end of the line so that the line goes off of the sheet and on to the tape. Label these short extensions "North" and "South" respectively. Move the map a short distance and show the children that they can get the map pointing north again by matching the line on the map with the two marks on the tapes.

Explain how the map is oriented whenever the North line on the map is pointing to north on the ground. Also tell them that when the map North line is pointing at north on the ground, then all the places on the map are in their "real" direction from the school location and from each other. Demonstrate this fact by having one of the children stand on the school location; then tell him, "You want to go to Texas. Show us Texas on the map. Which direction would you go if you went straight to Texas?" Have him walk to Texas on the map; then have him walk back to school. Several variations of this should be made until the children begin to experience the relative directions. Be sure that they see not only the "map directions," but also the "ground directions" as related to real directions in the classroom itself. Choose several places so that they can look out a window and visualize directions extending beyond the room itself. When everyone understands that the map directions are the same as the "real directions" on the ground, the construction phase of the floor map is then complete, and the map can be stored until needed for instruction.

II. USE PHASE

After the children have made the three items, they can use them whenever the class is studying events which happened at a given time and place. The unobtrusive selection of slow learners to work with these materials is suggested.

a. Using the Globe Map

The globe map may be used in several ways which its large size makes possible. The children can see how men began to think the earth was curved as they watched ships come over the horizon and noticed that the taller parts were sighted first and then, progressively, the lower parts. Make a sighting device about $\frac{1}{2}$ inch in diameter from a rolled piece of paper, and tape it to the globe. For realism, one end could be located on the west coast of Portugal so that the "lookout" is looking west over the Atlantic Ocean. Let one child sight through the tube while another moves a piece of chalk toward him slowly, sliding the chalk vertically along the globe surface as the mast of a ship would appear (see Figure 2-8). The chalk should be started over the horizon from the lookout, and he should tell when he first sees the top of the chalk. The chalk can then be moved closer to him and stopped; he then can mark with a pencil the lowest part of the chalk which is visible to him through the tube; the chalk is then moved closer, stopped, and marked again. As a variation, other objects can be

FIGURE 2-8. **Using the Globe to See an Object
Over the Horizon**

moved and the viewer required to sketch the parts he sees at various distances. Still another useful variation can be obtained by letting the viewer move the object himself.

Any globe can be used to demonstrate how a ship determines its longitude by knowing Greenwich Mean Time at high noon at its position. Demonstrating how latitude is determined is another matter, and is more effective if a large globe, such as the one the children made, is available. The navigator measures the angle from the horizon to the sun at high noon, and this angle is known as the altitude. The greater the angle, the smaller the latitude. To demonstrate this relationship, use a chalkboard eraser as a ship. Use a piece of string about 20 feet long, and tape the string to the eraser about 2 feet from one end, the tape being wound around the eraser several times at the "amidships" point. The short end of the string will represent the line of sight to the horizon; the longer end, the line of sight to the sun. Use three children in the demonstration: one to move the ship, one to stretch the short line to the horizon, and one to hold the long end and to represent the sun. Have the three children take their places, with the ship slightly north of the equator (Figure 2-9).

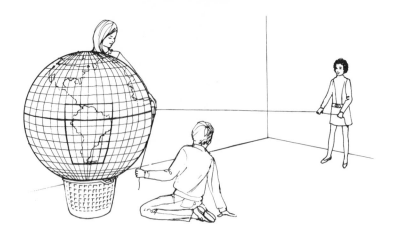

FIGURE 2-9.   Demonstrating Latitude Relationships

When the short line has been stretched downward until one point
touches the globe, the horizon has been determined. When the
long line is stretched, it represents a ray from the sun. Point
out the angle between the horizon and the sun, and explain that
this angle is called the altitude angle; also point out that the
ship is close to the equator and that therefore its latitude is small.
Then move the ship north, stop, and observe the latitude and the
size of the altitude angle. The decrease in altitude angle and
increase in latitude should be noticeable. This demonstration is
not completely accurate, because the sun's rays are parallel. The
teacher may not want to add this refinement lest the children
become confused with too much technical data. Should the teacher
wish to add the refinement, the child representing the sun must
keep the long line parallel to the floor at all times.

b. Using the Time Line

The time line may be used in this manner: Each session should
start with the line bare of all labels; even the labels for the centuries and half centuries should have been removed at the close
of the previous day. Assume the class is studying the signing of
the Declaration of Independence. As the session starts, one child
should put the century and half-century markers up, so that all

the time to be covered during the whole school year is marked out anew for each session. Then another child should put up the labels of all the events studied before the present session on the Declaration of Independence. One label with a color different from all the rest and bearing a legend such as "Today we are here" is placed on the time line at "1776." Some time during the session, one child should make a new label proclaiming "1776—Declaration of Independence signed" and any other information the teacher wishes. Toward the close of the session, the "Today we are here" label is replaced by the newly-made label. By the end of the school day all labels should be removed and stored for use at the next session.

In using the time line in this fashion, the teacher is providing many different opportunities for movements to be associated with points in time, the flow of time, and the fact that events occur in a time dimension where there is a "before" and an "after" and a "during." Only centuries and half-centuries are labeled, and decades are marked but not labeled; therefore, each time a label is put at a point on the line, it involves coping with a space measurement as well as a time location. To locate 1776, a child must find 1750 (which is labeled), count off two more decades beyond this, estimate six-tenths of the distance into the third decade, and put the label at this point. To put up different labels at different times, he must move over significant distances because of the scale of the line. As he puts the century and half-century markers in place (they should be put up in chronological order), his perception of the flow of time should be aided by his movements from 1400 to 1450 to 1500, for example. The time line permits adding body movements and manipulations of labels on a line to the visual and auditory experience of reading and hearing about events.

c. Using the Floor Map

As an example of class use of the floor map, assume the same learning situation about the signing of the Declaration of Independence. It soon will be established that this happened in Philadelphia on July 4, 1776. A child should be asked to locate Philadelphia, first on the globe and then on the floor map. The floor map is oriented so that "north on the map" is pointing to "north on the ground." The location of the school is a permanent fixture of the floor map, so another child should be asked to stand on the

map at the school location, and from this point show where Philadelphia is on the map. He should then walk on the map from
school to Philadelphia and back to school from Philadelphia. When
he is again at school, ask him to show the group the actual direction he would travel if he were going straight to Philadelphia (the
"ground direction" and not just a "map direction"). Then point
out the fact the direction on the map is the same as the
actual direction to Philadelphia. Have another child give the name
of the direction. Have others pretend that they live in different
cities, and let them discover the directions from their cities to
Philadelphia by actually standing on the different map locations,
walking to Philadelphia, pointing out actual directions, and naming those directions.

Some slow learners have difficulty translating from a horizontal
to a vertical plane; therefore, it would be well to use a wall map
of the United States in conjunction with the floor map. A child
may be able to handle directions on the floor map and still become
confused with a wall map on which north is now "up" instead
of "over there," east is "right" instead of "that way," and the like.
The wall map should be used at least as long as any child is experiencing this difficulty.

CONCLUSION

Additional use of the time line and the globe and floor map,
along with added perceptual training, is provided by drawing internal boundaries at the times when particular nations, states,
territories, and the like are first studied in the class program.
Whenever a boundary is drawn on the floor map of the United
States, the same boundary should be drawn on the globe. The
dates associated with new boundaries often may be identified on
the time line. If construction is completed progressively by drawing boundaries as the corresponding places are studied, the two
maps would provide, at any given moment, a graphic record of
every place studied to date, and this record would correspond to
that provided by the time line.

In addition to these specific recommended uses of the materials,
it is assumed that the two maps and the time line would provide
the teacher with three visual aids of a type commonly used with
social-studies curricula. They could be used in the same manner

as any other maps and time lines are used. The fact that the visual aids were constructed by the children should result in added enthusiasm and increased motivation.

This project weaves perceptual training in with academic training. It consists of a construction phase and a use phase. Each phase contains both academic and perceptual training. In designing the project, an attempt has been made to translate the academic structure into meaningful activities which represent perceptual training.

chapter 3

Perceptual Training with the Language Arts

This chapter will present a unit on reading for first grade, and will suggest ways of including perceptual training as an organic part of the unit.

An excellent and frequently recommended supplementary tool for teaching reading in first grade is the experience method described by Kirk (1940, pp. 80-81). Curriculum-makers use varying terms to describe the process; in this unit, the term "experience chart" will be used. In making an experience chart, the children first share some common experience such as a trip to a farm, a nature walk, or a visit to a supermarket. Later, in the classroom, the teacher and the children discuss the experience, and the teacher suggests that they write a story about the different things they did. In an informal way, the children compose short statements about what they saw and otherwise experienced, and the teacher writes these down on a large chart in the children's own words. The children read from the chart with the teacher's help. A common variation is to construct the experience chart from spontaneous or even individual experiences: a party, a holiday, a fire drill.

The experience chart is usually recommended for use during the child's earliest reading experiences (Harris, 1961, pp. 77-79). This use seems wise, for some children have difficulty connecting words on a printed page with events in their active world; how much better to have their earliest encounter with words flow from their own experience. The experience-chart approach has drawbacks, however. Vocabulary is not controlled and is not repeated sufficiently, and some children memorize the chart without learning the words. For this reason Harris (p. 79) recommends that experience charts be " . . . used as an introduction to reading and as a supplement to basal readers rather than a substitute for them. . . . " The unit presented is therefore recommended for the period of beginning reading.

THE UNIT: AN OVERVIEW

This unit proposes that the children learn to play "kickball," that they play each day until they have mastered the game and its structure, and that they compose stories about their experience. The teacher will write each story on a chart, and the children will read from the charts, using them as part of their stock of beginning reading materials. Involvement with the game itself could take place during recess and/or the time for physical education. The unit also will offer some suggestions for remediation of basic perceptual problems which probably will be noted as the children play kickball. The teacher may wish to begin some of the remediation while unit activities are still in progress; some remediation may extend past the time allotted for the unit. The recess and physical education periods can provide opportunity to help children overcome many perceptual problems.

The game of kickball is a variation of baseball. It has four bases, and players make runs as in baseball. The game is played by two sides, and each side is "up" until it makes three "outs." Instead of using a bat to start the ball in play, a player kicks the ball which is rolled toward him by the pitcher. The ball can be a volleyball or a sturdy inflated rubber or plastic ball of approximately the same size. The baseball rules for fouls, fly balls, runs, outs, and the like all apply, except that in kickball a player may be put out by being hit with the ball, in addition to the other ways he may be put out. Kickball does not require the precision necessary for baseball or softball, and the only equipment needed is a ball and four bases. The number of players can vary; two teams can be formed by dividing the first-grade class into two equal groups. Extra players can be added to the outfield.

Why kickball? Mainly because children who are playing this game are getting a great deal of perceptual training in the process. A lot of sheer activity is taking place, and this activity is quite varied. Many children from all strata of society do not routinely engage in vigorous and varied activities which help develop flexible movements, body awareness, and motor coordination. Kickball and similar games can help alleviate some of these deficits, and can help that basic development which is essential for good perception.

Consider some of the activities the game involves. Children kick, run, stop and start, catch, throw, dodge. All these activities help develop coordination. A rolling ball comes toward a child and he kicks it. Another child runs to catch it. Both are developing an internal synchrony, for their movements, to be effective, must mesh in time and place with the changing position of the ball. A child who consistently kicks too soon or too late or a child who consistently misses catching a ball is going to need help. The same can be said of the child who throws awkwardly, stiffly, or erratically. The perceptive teacher may be able to watch a group playing kickball, and pick out some who will have learning problems.

Furthermore, the game has a structure, and children who play it are experiencing this structure with their own muscles. Some events can take place only in relation to other events. A player must kick the ball (within a designated area, lest it be a foul) before he may start running the bases. He may start from one base and run to another base only if he estimates that his chances of arriving safely outweigh his chances of being put out; and he may be put out in several ways. A player's relationship to the structure of the game is a dynamic relationship: At any given moment he must keep in mind where he is, where he wants to go, where certain of his teammates are and what they are doing, where the ball is in relation to himself and to other players, and where all the opposing players are and how their locations and future actions affect his immediate situation. Still more structure derives from the fact that the arena in which his activity takes place is a geometric pattern: a "ball diamond," which is more accurately labeled a square. In playing the game, he negotiates this geometric pattern. Thus, the structure is made up of elements which embody time, space, dimension, and form. In playing the game, the player experiences all of these elements, and has opportunities for developing and refining his own internal structure.

The game of kickball, then, will serve a dual purpose in this unit of instruction. It will be the experience upon which the experience chart is based, and it will provide some fundamental activities which should develop or enhance those perceptual-motor abilities which are essential to good reading. The main thrust toward perceptual training, however, will come through the teacher's use of specific perceptual-motor training activities which form an integral part of the unit. The teacher's observation of the children playing kickball probably will reveal some perceptual deficiencies which will require remediation. The unit offers guidance in detecting these deficiencies, and presents some remedial measures.

If the game itself provides perceptual-motor activities, why bother with additional perceptual-motor training? The answer lies in the fact that a game offers opportunities for development, but does not assure that a child will take advantage of those opportunities. A child with perceptual problems may perpetuate those problems in playing a game. Even more significant is the fact that a particular problem is not always solved in what seems the most obvious fashion. For example, if a child lacks rhythm in his movements, his basic need may be for adequate balance and posture; in this case, merely to encourage him to move smoothly will do little good. Children with perceptual problems typically have trouble mastering games. They experience frustration in attempting to cope with the demands for structure and skill which most games impose. Often they hang back because of repeated failures, and this practice becomes self-defeating. The unit therefore contains suggestions for certain specific perceptual-motor training activities designed for remediation of basic problems. These activities are so structured that they will provide far better perceptual training than does the game itself. A conscious effort has been made to present these extra training activities as a logical part of the unit itself, so that from the child's point of view they do not seem an artificial addition.

An experimental study by Rutherford (1965, pp. 294-296) tends to justify the addition of perceptual training *per se* to play experiences. In this study, forty-two boys and thirty-four girls in a church-sponsored kindergarten were divided through random assignment into experimental and control groups. Both groups played for 30 minutes each day under supervision of the investigator. For the controls, the period was spent in almost completely free play on typical playground equipment. The experimental group played on special equipment designed to aid development of perceptual-motor skills; this group spent approximately two-thirds of the period in free play and the rest in directed use of the equipment and activities. The activities for the experimental group were designed to develop the following basic skills: laterality, directionality, accurate body image concepts, visual-kinesthetic matching, and binocular and monocular control. The study investigated the effects of the training program on the readiness development of kindergarten children as measured by their performance on Metropolitan Readiness Tests. The study covered a period of 11 weeks.

Rutherford reports gains in reading readiness for both groups; however, the experimental group made significantly greater gains than did the control group. The following mean gains in reading readiness for each group as measured by Metropolitan Readiness Tests are reported:

Total experimental 4.3571
Total control 1.7857

The difference between the total groups was found to be significant at the 1-per cent level of confidence.

For purposes of presentation, the unit is organized into three broad areas:

1. Experience Activities (the kickball game).
2. Perceptual-Motor Training Activities.
3. Reading Activities.

While the unit will be presented and discussed in this order, it should be conducted in a different order. Soon after the Experience Activities have begun, the Perceptual-Motor Training Activities should be added and continued throughout and perhaps beyond the whole unit. Reading Activities (that is, preparation and use of experience chart or charts) may be added as early as the teacher thinks best, and continued as long as they prove useful. Once the unit is under way, therefore, activities from all three areas may be employed in a given day. This flexible organization for conduct of the unit should permit its use in a wide variety of teaching situations.

Under each of the above three areas, the recommended activities will be presented and discussed. In a separate but parallel column the teacher will find suggestions for detecting some basic problems and procedures for their remediation. Since the remediation is described in the second area, Perceptual-Motor Training Activities, the first area typically will contain references only to remediation which can be found in the second area; thus much repetition can be avoided.

UNIT: BEGINNING READING WITH EXPERIENCE CHARTS
Area 1: Experience Activities

EXPERIENCES	PROBLEMS AND REMEDIATION
Opener:	*Note:* Remedial activities will be indicated by roman numerals according to the following key:
1. Ask the class if anyone knows how to play kickball. Try to get a general, unstructured discussion going. The discussion should not bog down in details of rules, but should keep to the main elements: two teams, four bases (names of bases), runs, players, outs. If the game is known only to a few, tell them it is "like baseball"; this definition may widen the circle of those who have knowledge to contribute. Tell them they will be playing kickball, and that the class will write a story about things that happen in the game. Avoid detailed instructions; at this point they should be getting, through their discussion, a general picture of the game. Their later learning of the game should come about naturally as they involve themselves in it, rather than as a response to verbal structuring. This discussion should take place shortly before the game is played for the first time.	I. Activities for BALANCE AND POSTURE II. Activities for BODY IMAGE AND DIFFERENTIATION III. Activities for PERCEPTUAL-MOTOR MATCH IV. Activities for OCULAR CONTROL V. Activities for FORM PERCEPTION. In Area 1, typical problems indicating need for these remedial activities will be described so the teacher may be alerted for observation of certain behaviors. The key will be used to link problems to remedial activities; the remedial activities themselves are described in Area 2. As used here, the term "problem" refers to consistent behavior. Perhaps all behaviors described will occur at some time with nearly all children. Behaviors should be considered as problems to be dealt with only when they appear consistently.
2. *Dividing into Two Teams.* Division should be random, and the following procedure should be used: Form the class into a line facing the teacher. Have them count off in twos from left (teacher's right) to right. The first child says "one," the next child says "two," the next says "one," and so on. Strive for a smooth rhythm to the counting. With the children still facing in the same direction, go	2. In counting off, each child's contribution to the total rhythm is, for him, a combined individual problem of synchrony and rhythm. If the sweep of sound along the line is to be smooth, each one must call his number at the right moment. Calling the number at the right moment is a problem in synchrony. Knowing just when the right moment has arrived requires the child to sense the

EXPERIENCES

behind the line and, using a clear and normal tone, say something like the following: "I will say 'one, two, three, go.' When you hear 'go' all number ones will go one step to the front. Number twos will not move. Ready? One, two, three, go." Counting should set a rhythm so that the children will be able to anticipate when the "go" signal will come. Point out that the class is now divided into two teams. Now re-form them into one line by giving the same signal for number twos to step forward. Up to this point the children have moved only in response to an auditory signal, since the teacher was behind them.

With the children again in one line, move to the front of the line, and have the teams separate at a visual signal. With this visual signal a visual rhythm (corresponding to the auditory rhythm of "one, two, three, go") should be developed. For example, teacher's right hand could be used for "go," and left hand could be waved three times as preparation. Or, three sheets of white paper and one of red could be placed in a line on the wall; teacher points to all four in rhythmical sequence, with pointing to red (last) being signal to move.

Children should divide into different teams each day. When most children have mastered the counting off and are able to move into teams readily on signal, variations should be introduced. Such variations are extremely important in that they aid the development of generalizations. Patterns of activities develop instead of isolated or splinter skills. Counting off may be varied in many ways. Teams can have any of a variety of names instead of team

PROBLEMS AND REMEDIATION

rhythm of sound before it reaches his position in the line. Only by sensing the rhythm can he anticipate the moment when he must sound his number. Children who speak too soon or too late, or who are otherwise confused by this activity, probably have not developed synchrony and rhythm and/or have failed to match auditory information to the motor base. REMEDIATION I and III.

As teams move by command, be alert for hesitation, awkwardness, and directional confusion. Hesitation may indicate lack of synchrony; however, it may indicate vision or hearing problems. Note especially the child who responds markedly better to either visual or auditory signals. If a child has trouble only with auditory signals, help from the speech and hearing therapist should be sought, or another appropriate attempt made to determine if he has problems with auditory acuity. Poor response only with visual signals may suggest poor vision, or it may be due to consistent failure to integrate visual information with the motor base. Some children may have good visual acuity and still not have developed the ability to match the visual to the motor. Such children perform well until visual information is added to the ongoing activity, at which point confusion enters. For example, a child may be able to tie his shoelaces until he looks at his hands; looking then throws him off, and his performance loses smoothness. If acuity problems in both vision and hearing are ruled out, hesitation in moving on signal quite possibly is due to lack of synchrony (REMEDIATION I), poor body image (REMEDIA-

EXPERIENCES

PROBLEMS AND REMEDIATION

one or team two; the children would then sound out the team name instead of a number (red team, blue team; Dodgers, Giants; tigers, lions). The military method of counting off is a good variation: Every one turns his head to the left, and snaps his head to the front at the moment he calls his number or team name. Or the line can be changed to a column, and the children can count off from front to rear or rear to front. When they are in a column, the movement into teams can be varied by having them step left or right, or having one team step right while the other steps left (or, if in line, by having one step forward and the other back at the same time). Instead of stepping, the teacher may call for hopping (both feet, left, right). These variations and many others should be used.

3. *Preparation of the Playing Field:* Let the children place the four bases in locations where they think they should go. The so-called "diamond" is actually a square; distances between bases are all equal and each corner is a right angle. Begin by having one child place the bases. Ask others if they think the bases are placed correctly. If anyone thinks they are not, ask him to shift those which are in the wrong place.

When the children are satisfied with the arrangement, show them how to check the locations. To do this, one line is needed as a reference line. The line between home base and first base can be this reference line. The location of these two bases can therefore be arbitrary be-

TION II), or (in case of visual signals) poor ocular control (REMEDIATION IV). The problem could lie in one, several, or all these areas; the routine perceptual training outlined in Area 2 should shed more light upon which areas need attention.

General awkwardness in moving suggests that balance, posture, and body image and differentiation of body parts all have some developmental lack. REMEDIATION I, II.

Consistent movements in the wrong direction may indicate lack of directionality due to lack of laterality. REMEDIATION I, II.

3. Laying out the bases involves the child in a number of perceptual problems. He must have an internal awareness of a square, and be able to visualize a large square on the ground where no guidelines exist. He must also have some idea of equal distances between bases and the angles at the corners. If he actually puts the bases in their locations, he must be able to translate all these inner awarenesses into appropriate movements organized into a sequence of events.

If a child cannot cope with any part of the operation, he may not be able to perceive the figure itself. REMEDIATION V.

If a child shows confusion in directions, he may have

EXPERIENCES

cause they determine one line from which all other lines can be located.

The first problem is to find the direction from first base to second base. The desired direction is one which will be at right angles with the line from home to first. Have one child stand at home base simply to mark the location. Another child should stand at first base; this child will be the controller. A third child stands at the approximate location of second base, and will move right or left as directed by the controller on first base. While standing on first base, the controller raises both arms straight up and out from his sides until they are horizontal. He then shifts his body around until his arms are parallel with the line from home to first base. He can check this orientation by sighting along his left arm, aligning it with the child who is standing at home. He should shift his feet and not twist his trunk in making these adjustments; the arms should be at right angles to the feet at all times. When the controller's arms are oriented properly, he should turn his head directly to his front. He is then looking generally in the direction of second base. The controller signals with the appropriate arm to tell the child in front of him to move right or left until that child is located in the proper direction of second base.

At this point, the proper direction to second base has been determined, but the actual location of second base requires that the distance from first to second be the same

PROBLEMS AND REMEDIATION

a basic problem in balance and posture or differentiation. REMEDIATION I AND II.

If verbal counting cannot be matched to stepping, the problem may involve balance, body image, and the perceptual-motor match. REMEDIATION I, II, III.

PROBLEMS AND REMEDIATION

EXPERIENCES

as the distance from home to first. The child standing at home can step off the distance to first base. He should walk with even steps, and should count his steps aloud. He steps the same number of steps in the direction to second base; at the end of his stepping will be the location of the second base. The procedure is repeated to locate third base; the controller now stands at second with one child at first and another at the approximate location of third. When all bases have been positioned, a check on accuracy may be made by stepping the diagonal distances from home to second and from third to first; these two distances should be equal. The pitcher should stand halfway between home and second base and also halfway between first and third. Whenever a pitcher takes his place, he should be required to align himself with respect to the diagonal lines; this aligning will provide valuable experience in spatial orientation.

The bases should be laid out in this manner each time the game is played. Rotate the tasks of positioning bases so that all will have an opportunity to be the controller and to perform the tasks of stepping off distances. The distance between bases has not been specified; the teacher should adjust this to suit needs of the children.

For the first few times the game is played, or until the children have an adequate grasp of the game's structure, the bases should be in the same general area of the playground (or gym). After this initial period, different areas for playing should be selected each time, and the orientation should also be varied. Variation will aid generaliza-

EXPERIENCES

tion. Thus, after learning the structure of the game in a particular setting and against a constant background, a child will experience the same structure against varying backgrounds as the field is changed from day to day. As he stands at home base on a given day, the school building (a major feature in the background) may be behind him; on another day the same building may be on his left, right, or front, as variations are introduced.

4. *Playing the Game:* The two teams should start play with a minimum of guidance from the teacher. They should learn the structure of the game from their own playing and their interaction with one another, with the teacher intervening only when they are in trouble. The teacher should give ample opportunity for some children to learn from other children.

While the game is in progress, frequent changes of player positions should be made. Such shifting of players should be according to a preset pattern, and each player should begin his movement to his new position on a common signal given to the whole team by the teacher. The following is a good pattern. At the signal from the teacher, the pitcher goes to the fielder's position farthest from first base. The fielder nearest first base goes to first base. The first baseman moves to second, second baseman to third, third baseman becomes catcher, and catcher becomes pitcher. All other fielders should shift slightly closer to first base to fill the gap left by the fielder who moved to first base. The children should be taught to

PROBLEMS AND REMEDIATION

4. In suggesting a somewhat inductive approach for the children's initial learning of the game's structure, the aim is to encourage exploratory activity. Some children will involve themselves in new activities more readily than others. The child who consistently holds back will need encouragement. Holding back may be a signal to the teacher that a child has perceptual problems. Typically, the perceptually handicapped child has trouble with games; he does not grasp the structure, he makes gross mistakes, and incurs the displeasure and even the scorn of his playmates. For such a child the game can become a threat, and he may react by holding back or engaging only in the most peripheral aspects where he is not challenged to use abilities he does not possess. Children who exhibit this pattern of behavior probably will profit from the entire spectrum of perceptual training activities outlined in Area 2. Their performance in these training activities may indicate specific areas of difficulty which will in turn indicate specific emphasis in remediation.

Changing the player positions also should help screen

EXPERIENCES	PROBLEMS AND REMEDIATION
move immediately when the teacher gives the signal, each child starting his move without waiting for other children. The teacher should give the signal with practically no warning. The signal could be: "Change positions! One, two, three: scramble!" This systematic changing of positions gives the child a varying task of moving with relation to the structure imposed by the game. He must not only cope with his present position, but must also be prepared to change that position in an orderly way. He must be aware, then, of the overall structure of the game, and not just the one element represented by his present position. Before the activity of changing positions is started, the children should have a good general grasp of the game's structure from their play experience. When this activity is first introduced, have them make the changes several times as practice. While the game is being played, the teacher will want to be alert for the following performances which indicate possible developmental problems underlying perceptual difficulty: a. Stiffness and awkwardness in general movements. b. Excessive attention to the movements themselves. The child should focus his attention on where he is going rather than on how he is producing movement. c. Erratic throwing. d. Eye-blink and ducking when catching the ball. e. Kicking at the ball too soon or too late as the ball rolls toward the child; overshooting or undershooting	those children who have general perceptual problems, but this activity also will not be too helpful in pinpointing the specific developmental lacks. It should serve rather to alert the teacher to those children needing closer observation during perceptual training in Area 2. The child whose general movements are stiff and awkward probably has not solved the basic problem of dynamic balance and posture, nor has he developed body image and the ability to differentiate his body parts. REMEDIATION I, II. The child who must give excessive attention to movement *per se* has these same problems, and will profit from the same remediation. Erratic and awkward throwing suggests poor body image and differentiation, deficits in perceptual-motor matching, and possible lack of ocular control. REMEDIATION II, III, IV. Consistent eye-blink and/or ducking when catching the ball point to a lack in integrating primitive reflexes with other generalized movement patterns. The generalized patterns themselves may not have developed, or the integration may not have taken place. Activities under REMEDIATION I, II should reveal whether the problem lies in the area of lack of generalized movement patterns; activities under REMEDIATION III, IV should aid integration. Kicking too soon or too late and overshooting fly balls suggest problems in synchrony, rhythm, perceptual-motor match, and ocular control. REMEDIATION I, II, III, IV.

EXPERIENCES	PROBLEMS AND REMEDIATION
when trying to catch a fly ball. f. Response only at the instant the ball makes contact with the player. Sometimes it is obvious that a ball moving toward a child is producing little or no visual anticipation of its arrival. The response takes place only at the instant of contact, and this response is more exaggerated and explosive because the child did not expect contact. The child seems surprised and the contact appears to startle him.	Response only when the ball makes contact suggests problems in perceptual-motor match and ocular control. The key problem is that the incoming visual stimulation is not triggering a preparatory motor response. This problem points to poor perceptual-motor match. The problem is more complicated, of course, if poor visual acuity or poor ocular control results in distortion of the incoming stimulation itself. REMEDIATION III, IV.

The Experience Activities, or the kickball game, could take place on the playground or possibly in the gym. The Perceptual-Motor Training Activities are presented under two headings: one for those activities which require the gym, and another for classroom activities. The Reading Activities, of course, take place in the classroom, although, in a larger sense, all the activities in all the other areas are actually reading activities in that they are aimed at improving readiness.

A number of references to *The Slow Learner in the Classroom* by N. C. Kephart appear in Area 2. To avoid repetition, reference to this work has been abbreviated as "SL" followed by a parenthetical notation of page numbers. This unit may be enriched by using additional training activities described by Dr. Kephart in Part III of his book.

Area 2: Perceptual Training Activities

Perceptual training activities should begin soon after the children have started playing kickball. It is highly desirable that these training activities appear to the children as a means of increasing their skill at kickball and as a means of helping them learn reading. Some of the activities will be interesting to the children, but others may seem pointless to them and will require motivation in the form of tying training to kickball and reading.

One obvious way of connecting training to the kickball game is to remind the children that all athletic teams must train for playing. Start a discussion about the different ways teams train, and make a definite point that training means doing many things other than just playing the game. The children may have some background knowledge about spring training of professional baseball teams, training activities of local football teams, and the like. The main point is that many training activities are different from playing activities, and that the class will have some things to do as training which are not the same as the things they do while playing kickball. Most children also are eager to read, and the knowledge that the training will help them read should aid motivation.

The perceptual training activities are divided into two subareas: One part of the training is designed to be conducted in the gym (Area 2a); the other part is designed for the classroom (Area 2b). A daily gym period devoted to the activities described in Area 2a is considered to be crucial to the success of this unit. The gym period should last for about 50 minutes each school day. If the class has a daily physical education period, the perceptual training (Area 2a) might be conducted during that time. If this cannot be arranged, an additional gym period for perceptual training should be attempted. If neither of these alternatives is possible, perceptual training activities under 2a may be attempted, with modifications, in the regular classroom. However it is done, the Area 2a activities should be conducted; they should not be omitted.

The children should wear gym suits or clothing which will permit them to move freely and to function on the floor or gym mats where they undoubtedly will get dirty. Old clothes which still fit well would be ideal, because the training activities in the gym will involve much wear and tear on clothing. Girls should wear slacks or shorts for the gym period. An advance note about clothing from the teacher to the parents will be helpful, and may even avoid some parental misunderstanding.

All children in the class should benefit from perceptual training activities; however, those with developmental lacks or whose performance of the suggested activities is poor will profit from additional individual activities. The teacher will notice some children who are having difficulty either playing kickball or engaging in the perceptual training. Such children will need additional time with those specific training activities which are designed to overcome their particular perceptual deficits. Some major problems were anticipated in Area 1, and the roman numeral key system ties observed problems to suggested remediation in Area 2. Additional problems will come to light as the teacher observes performance of the training activities themselves. From both areas, therefore, a number of children will be identified as needing additional training beyond the organized group routines in Area 2.

Providing more of certain activities on an individual basis for some children while the majority of the class proceeds with the group program is a problem. Those activities conducted in the gym will make heavy demands upon the teacher for supervision and coordination; little opportunity will be available for individual training. If a teacher's aide or other responsible adult is available for the gym activities, the teacher may be freed for individual work with children who need it. Older or more advanced children may be used to supervise some of the simpler routines, once the teacher has started them. If the teacher must conduct gym activities unaided, it probably would be better to work on individual problems during classroom time. Individual work will not require the large gym area needed for the group program. The teacher should review the gym program carefully in advance, and organize the activities around his immediate situation.

The trampoline is indicated for use in the gym program. This device is excellent for developing dynamic balance, coordination, and muscular control. Its use in this unit will require special planning. No danger exists if an adult is present and if certain simple safety rules are followed. An adult should be present, however, and this adult should give his full attention to supervising the trampoline activities. Another difficulty is that in a 50-minute gym period only a few children, perhaps six or seven, can be accommodated by the trampoline; if more are "run through" they will not have enough time to get the full benefit. The trampoline should therefore be viewed as a separate project requiring a block of time and an adult to supervise. Admittedly, this complicates the teacher's problem of organization. The trampoline offers such unique and highly desirable training that it is well worth the extra effort.

The writer has first-hand knowledge of a gym program for perceptual training which was conducted with first-graders substantially as presented in this unit. The children were enthusiastic about the activities. Their interest was keen and sustained. On the other hand, as one sets down in words a systematic presentation of the program, the descriptive details most likely will come over to the reader as a rather dull and depressing business. Perhaps nothing reads with more dreary monotony than an account of body movements, positions, activities, and the like. But when the details of the program, tiresome as they seem to our adult eyes, are translated into action on a gym floor, the children have a thoroughly delightful experience. What is more, they get good perceptual experiences.

Area 2a: Perceptual Training Activities, Gym

ACTIVITIES	KEY	NOTES AND VARIATIONS
1. *Daily Warm-ups*		1. All activities should be varied each day.
a. Jumping: Children jump several times each foot and both feet.	I	a. Vary by using rhythmic patterns such as LR, LLR, RRL, LRRR, RLLL, and so on. While jumping is mostly for balance and posture, addition of rhythmic patterns will promote perceptual-motor match.
b. Body parts: Teacher says: "Touch your ears. Touch your knees. Touch your shoulders, and so on." Proceed through all body parts (eyes, nose, mouth, ankles, feet, hips, elbows, head, wrists). Child should use both hands for touching.	II	b. Vary order each day; children should not memorize an order, but should solve the problem of locating and touching a part on command. Watch for hesitation in moving to any part. Elbows and wrists may cause initial confusion because touching these requires child to "cross over" and touch right part with left hand and vice versa.
c. Imitation of movement: Teacher says: "Watch me and do what I do." Teacher then makes a variety of body movements, and children copy. Teacher may use movements in b, above, as one group of movements for children to copy. Use arm movements shown in SL, page 132, and vary by adding movements of arms horizontal and forward. Avoid duplicating the sequence, but be sure to include all three types of movements: unilateral, bilateral, and crosslateral.	II	c. Children should make prompt and sure movements. A child may mirror teacher's movements or may make one-for-one correspondence. Vary order each day, and vary content.
d. Differentiation exercises: Have the children move specified parts, performing specified movements	II	d. The goal here is to provide experience in the great variety of movement which is possible with

ACTIVITIES	KEY	NOTES AND VARIATIONS
with each part. Examples: Arms horizontal and out from sides, make circles by rotating entire arm; make large and small circles; repeat with arms to front. Raise one foot and move toes up and down; rotate foot by making vertical circles with toe, then horizontal circles. Touch each finger to thumb; move each finger independently; rotate each finger; flex each finger; make fist and open hand. Move head back and forth, side to side, and rotate head. Rotate hand at wrist; move hand up and down and side-to-side with wrist as the pivot point.		the parts of the body. The variations are practically unlimited, and only a very few examples are given. The teacher should plan for this activity by considering a given body part and all the different movements of which that part is capable. If a child has problems in moving his body extremities smoothly and flexibly, be careful in making corrections. Corrections should take into consideration the proximo-distal and cephalocaudal developmental sequence. Thus, if a child cannot produce flexible finger movements, teacher should first check to see if the hand as a whole moves properly from the wrist; if this movement is not satisfactory, check his ability to move his forearm; if forearm movements still give problems, check movement of arm as a whole from shoulder; then finally check ability to move the shoulder itself. This direction of checking is the reverse of the proximo-distal direction, and should enable the teacher to identify that point beyond which the child has not differentiated portions of his body. In making corrections, the teacher should start at this point and work outward. If the teacher attempts to correct finger movements without regard to the developmental sequence, the danger exists that the fingers will be "splintered off" from the sequence, and will develop in isolation from the other parts to which it has close relationships. If a child has not differ-

ACTIVITIES	KEY	NOTES AND VARIATIONS
		entiated his hand as a whole from his arm, then he should be helped with movements of the whole hand before attention is given to the fingers; similarly, if the arm has not been differentiated from the shoulder, then attention should focus on the arm before working with the hand. This precautionary note is most appropriate in the case of first-graders. Some of the earliest tasks which the school requires of the child involve his using his fingers and hands in ways which demand a high degree of precision. All too often, he is required to concentrate on his fingers and the movements they make in drawing, copying, or writing, without regard to whether he has differentiated in an orderly way those parts which are developmentally prior to his fingers. In trying to cope with these demands, he may come to use his fingers in a stiff and awkward fashion, and he may not develop adequately a functional use of wrist, or arm, or shoulder.
e. Exercises on the floor:		e.
(1) Lie on back, arms crossed over chest. Raise head and shoulders only, and look at parts of body which teacher designates.	I, & II	(1) Vary by having children look at designated places in the room. Designate places which require looking right, left, up, down.
(2) Lie on back, raise leg. Make geometric patterns with toes outlining patterns; leg straight. Make circle, cross, square, triangle, rectangle, diamond.	II, III, V	(2) Do with both legs. Vary size of patterns. Vary angle to which leg is raised. Letters of alphabet may be added to geometric figures if children know the alphabet.

ACTIVITIES	KEY	NOTES AND VARIATIONS
(3) Same as (2), except child points to toes as toes move in geometric patterns. In pointing, arm should be extended fully, and the entire arm moves as finger follows moving toes.	II, III, IV, V	(3) Same variations as in (2), but add this important variation: Child points first with right hand to right toe; left hand to left toe. Vary by crossing sides: left hand to right toe and vice versa.
(4) Lie on back, hands under hips with palms to floor. Raise both legs, keep legs together, and move both legs as one unit in making patterns. Eyes follow toes.	II, III, IV, V	(4) Vary by having each leg move separately to form two simultaneous patterns. Vary directions of patterns; change from parallel to opposite directions.
(5) Lie on side, shoulders elevated and supported by elbow, legs outstretched. Raise top leg and make same patterns as above. Eyes follow toes.	II, III, IV, V	(5) Vary size and directions of patterns.
(6) Lie on stomach, hands clasped behind at small of back. Raise chest as high as possible, hold for a few seconds.	I, II	(6) With chest elevated, look right, left.
(7) Sit with knees drawn up to chest, arms clasping legs slightly below knees. Lean back until feet are off floor and balance on bottom. Rock slightly back and forth and maintain balance.	I, II	(7) Rock to sides; rock with rotary motion.
(8) Sit with legs crossed, hands under knees and grasping feet. Roll all the way back until back is on floor. Come back to original position, all the while maintaining knees to chest and hands to feet.	I, II	(8) While on back, roll right, roll left; maintaining knees to chest and hands to feet.
(9) Sit with legs outstretched and apart; lean back slightly and support trunk on out-	I, II	(9) Raise one hand or one leg at a time as teacher designates.

ACTIVITIES	KEY	NOTES AND VARIATIONS
stretched arms with hands slightly to rear and palms flat on floor. Raise body off floor, keeping trunk and legs in a straight line. Hold a few seconds.		
(10) Sit with legs outstretched and feet apart, hands resting in lap. Pretend top of head is a pencil, and move trunk, neck, and head as a unit, with top of head forming geometric patterns.	I, II, III, V	(10) Vary size of figures; vary directions.
(11) Angels-in-the-Snow: For instructions on conducting this training see SL (230-233).	II	(11) To supervise a group in this activity it may be necessary to form pairs; one child to perform while the second child passes visual signals from the teacher to the performer. This pairing is suggested in case all children cannot see the teacher while lying on their backs.
2. *Obstacle Course.* The obstacle course should be conducted daily. Various obstacles, described below, make up the course, and each child negotiates each obstacle, going from one to the next without waiting for the group to assemble. Thus, at a given moment some children will be on each part of the entire course. Several children should be designated teacher's assistants, and one assistant should be stationed at each obstacle to pass on information about the obstacle and to assist where needed. These assistants can go through the course when the other children have finished. While most of the class is on the obstacle course, the teacher		2. The obstacle course should be varied in the following ways: Use a different sequence for the obstacles each day. Each child should vary his own manner of performance each time he goes through the course. He may, for example, go through forward one time, backward the next, sidewise next, on hands and knees, and so on. Each child should go through the entire course several times each day, using a different manner for each trip. Children should be encouraged to discover different ways of attacking an obstacle, the assistant offering

ACTIVITIES	KEY	NOTES AND VARIATIONS
may be able to work with those children who need individual help.		suggestions only when they have exhausted their own resources. The obstacles described below may suggest others to the teacher; such variations by the teacher will enrich the experience.
Elements in the obstacle course:		
a. Walking boards: Three or four boards can be used in the obstacle course to prevent a pile-up of children waiting their turn. They could be laid parallel, and a child would negotiate only one board for each trip. The walking board is a standard 2″ x 4″ board and from 8 to 12 feet long. Each end is fitted into a bracket which raises the top edge 6 inches off the floor.	I	a. See SL (217-221) for use and variations of the walking board. Begin with 4-inch side up and turn 2-inch side up on some boards as the children begin to master the larger side. Remember the goal is not to teach a highly developed skill, but rather to provide a variety of experiences where the child must solve the balance problem. Additional variations are stepping over or under a ruler held above board; walking with objects of different weight in each hand; balancing light objects on backs of hands; balancing book on head; changing from forward to sidewise, sidewise to backward, and so on; catching and throwing ball while walking the board.
b. Balance boards: Three or four of these also will prevent pile-ups.	I	b. See SL (222-224) for construction, use, and variations.
c. Climber: The climber can be any one of a number of climbing devices such as a climbing ladder, a dome-type climber, a climbing house, or similar device available from manufacturers in varied designs. The object is to provide an obstacle which requires the child to use hands, arms,	II	c. Have the children experiment with different ways of getting over the climber. Insist upon variations.

ACTIVITIES	KEY	NOTES AND VARIATIONS
legs, feet, and many muscle pairs in going over.		
d. Tunnel: This item can be as simple as a long box made of corrugated paper board. A steel drum with both ends removed (edges smoothed for safety) will serve as well. A cloth mesh fastened to round wire hoops which fold in an accordian fashion is available commercially. The child goes through in a prone position, and gains an awareness of the space his body occupies, and an awareness of his body in relation to a definite amount of enclosed space.	II	d. Vary by having child go through head-first, feet-first, on back, on stomach, on sides, on hands and knees. He should discover these variations for himself if possible.
e. Barriers: The course should contain a minimum of three barriers: (1) A low object which the child steps over; (2) a higher object which he ducks under; (3) an object which he must avoid by going around. These barriers should be negotiated while the child is in motion; he should therefore begin his movement prior to his arrival at the barrier. This activity helps him develop generalized movement patterns in that he should learn to cope with the barrier without undue attention to the movements themselves.	II	e. Vary the means of locomotion used as the child approaches the barrier; that is, walking, running, skipping, loping, hopping, and so on. Some children will stop at the barrier before negotiating it; some will hesitate and break the movement pattern. Such children have not developed generalized movement patterns. They lack the ability to focus their main attention on the goal of movement and give too much attention to the movements themselves. These children will need extra help in all the movement activities in Area 2a; the teacher should therefore help them with phases other than the barriers alone.
3. *The Trampoline.* If the trampoline is available, it is suggested that one child at a time be working on it under adult supervision. In this way, an individual	I II III	3. See SL (224-230) for use of trampoline and variations.

ACTIVITIES	KEY	NOTES AND VARIATIONS
child may have some time on the trampoline several times each week, depending upon the size of the class. As children finish their turn on the trampoline, they could join the rest of the class in the ongoing activities. As previously noted, this excellent device for developing coordination should be used in this unit if at all possible.		

Area 2b: Perceptual Training Activities, Classroom

ACTIVITIES	KEY	NOTES AND VARIATIONS
Each activity in Area 2b is a small-group activity. A number of these group activities could be taking place simultaneously. The teacher may want to assign a child to a particular group, and move him from group to group, upon the basis of teacher observations of the child's perceptual problems and his progress in training.		
1. *Movement and Form.* Mark out a kickball "diamond" on the floor, using tape to outline the field. The "diamond" is actually a square, and should be made with each side about 10 feet in length. Put a book on each corner to represent bases.		
a. Space relations: Designate one base as "home," and put a child at this base facing second. Have him point to first, second, and third bases, and have him tell which direction each is from himself (right, left, front, as the case may be).	II	a. Vary by designating different bases as "home," thus varying the child's orientation to the room. Reverse the procedure by asking him, for example, "Which side of you is closest to third base?"
b. Auditory space: Station five children in the following player positions: pitcher, catcher, three numbered basemen. Place a sixth child at home plate facing second. When he has seen all the players, blindfold him. At a visual signal from the teacher (pointing will do), one player claps his hands once. The blindfolded child is asked to identify the player by sound.	II III	b. Let the children take turns being blindfolded. Vary by leading the blindfolded child to first base, facing him toward second, telling him where he is and where he is facing; then have children make sounds for identification. Also vary sounds by having players stamp foot, whistle, groan, and the like. A child should engage in this activity at all bases.
c. Form through movement: Have the child walk through the "diamond," keeping his feet on the	I, III,	c. Vary by changing means of locomotion: heel-toe while walking lines, sidewise while keeping toes

ACTIVITIES	KEY	NOTES AND VARIATIONS
lines. He names each base as he comes to it. All members of the group can use the "diamond" at the same time; one following behind another. Variations are essential, and all should be used.	V	on line, sidewise while keeping heels on line, and walking backwards. Reverse order of walking bases (from home to third, second to first, and back to home); however, emphasize that base numbers do not change.
d. Form through movement and auditory clues: Station a child at each of the four bases, and assign a distinctive sound for each child to make at the proper time. Place a fifth child at "home," and let him look in turn at each child on a base while the latter makes his distinctive sound. Blindfold the fifth child, face him toward first base, and have him walk to first guided only by the sound being made by the child at first base. As soon as the blindfolded child arrives at first base, the child at first base stops his sound, and the child at second base begins his sound. This signal tells the blindfolded child to change directions and start to second. He continues until he reaches home base.	III V	d. Children take turns being blindfolded. Reverse order of walking to bases. Start at base other than "home," and have child tell name of each base as he reaches it. Stop the child at any point, and while he is still blindfolded, have him point to designated players. He should identify players from his internal awareness of where he is in relation to the total form; only one player continues to make his sound while identification is in progress.
2. Experiences with Form and Direction		2.
a. Have each child in the group draw a square on a piece of paper; this drawing is done while seated at desk or table. Point out that we can use the square as a picture of the kickball field, and have each child choose where he would like home base to be on his picture. He should put a mark	III V	a. Vary by changing location of teacher's mark. Set up situations where one or two children are on base when the hypothetical ball is kicked, ask to which base the fielder would throw the ball, and have the child draw line to that base. After variations such as these with child seated, repeat the

ACTIVITIES	KEY	NOTES AND VARIATIONS
next to home base. Teacher then goes to each child, places a mark on his paper in any location which would represent right or left field, and says, "You kicked the ball and the fielder caught it here (teacher's mark). He will throw the ball to first base. Draw a line from the fielder to first base."		entire activity with child at chalkboard; then with child on floor drawing with crayon or felt-tip pen on newsprint. For children who have trouble drawing the square in any of these positions, see SL (202-205) for remedial techniques.
b. Point out that the children have been drawing a square to make a picture of the kickball field, but that we call the field a "diamond." Show them how the square looks like a diamond if they turn their papers so that one corner of the square is pointing toward the chest. Have everyone do this. Now have them draw a "square diamond," shifting the paper so that they must use all diagonal lines instead of the vertical and horizontal lines used in the previous drawing of the square. No child should attempt to use diagonal lines until he has mastered the use of the vertical and horizontal lines of the square. Repeat activity of 2a, using the diamond as the picture of the field.	III V	b. Present same variations as in 2a.
3. *Ocular Training.* In SL (146-150), specific procedures for assessing the child's ability to control his ocular movements are set forth. Training techniques are presented in SL (241-257). Because of the extreme importance of functional vision in the school program, the teacher is urged to include both assessment and	IV	

ACTIVITIES

training of ocular control in this unit of perceptual training. The techniques are described in detail in SL. The teacher should study the above references carefully. Assessment of all children in the class should be made; training activities should be used where indicated.

KEY

NOTES AND VARIATIONS

Area 3: Reading Activities

Construction and use of experience reading charts should be started soon after the children have learned the kickball game and are playing it with some degree of confidence.

As the children discuss some of their experiences with the game, the teacher should suggest that they make up their own story about what they have been doing. The children tell the story in their own words, and the teacher writes their sentences on the chart. This work should be a group effort with several children contributing different elements. As new experiences emerge, additional charts are made. The teacher can control, therefore, the number of charts and the times when their use is most appropriate in relation to other classroom activities.

In the early stages of the unit, a typical experience chart might look like this:

Today we played kickball.
We take turns.
We ran to the bases.
Jim made a home run.
The Tigers won.
We had fun.

When a chart has been made, the teacher reads what is written. The teacher's hand should sweep along smoothly under the line being read, not stopping under each word. Voice and hand, of course, should be synchronized with the written words.

When the teacher has finished reading, children who volunteer may read. A child may wish to read only one sentence, or perhaps only one word. The teacher may lead the discussion to a particular event and ask if someone would like to read about it from the chart. Children who may not be able to read a sentence may pick out some of the words, or they may be able to point out which sentence describes a certain event.

At a later time, the teacher should make a second copy of the chart on stiff paper. The second copy can be cut into lines or phrases or single words, forming cards for vocabulary building.

In writing the story from the children's own words, the teacher probably will need to do some slight editing, but this should not be so extensive that the finished product becomes the teacher's story instead of the children's. One problem with the experience method is that the children will use words beyond grade level. To offset this problem to some extent, the teacher may suggest simpler substitutes. Another difficulty with the method is lack of repetition of vocabulary. By unobtrusive editing, the teacher may be able to increase repetition. It is best not to strive for orderly structuring of sentences into paragraphs, but to write the sentences in the spontaneous order in which they come from the children.

Whenever the children read from the chart, every effort should be made to get the hand into the activity along with eye and voice. The experience method can be most helpful in emphasizing the left-to-right progression of reading. Children who have difficulty with this progression should have extra attention on activities for balance and differentiation (I and II) during perceptual training. The same activities, along with activities for perceptual-motor match (III), will help those children who are unable to synchronize the eye, voice, and hand.

chapter 4

Perceptual Training
in a Science Unit

This chapter sets forth a unit in science for use in a special education class for educable mentally retarded children (EMR) of intermediate grade school age. The unit is designed to provide academic training in the science area of "Force, Energy, and Power," and concurrently to provide perceptual training as an integral part of this academic training. It can be adapted to the regular classroom if desired.

CONCEPTUAL BACKGROUND

The goal is to provide learning experiences on these five learning levels: (1) motor, (2) motor-perceptual, (3) perceptual-motor, (4) perceptual, and (5) perceptual-conceptual. The concepts of force, energy, and power have elements which lend themselves naturally to helping a child structure himself and his world. A discussion of these elements and how they will be used with the five learning levels follows.

Force is experienced by a child through his muscular efforts as he moves, changes direction and/or speed, and interacts with persons and objects in his environment. Such muscular effort produces data which the child comes to use as part of his motor base.

In many ways, the child *experiences* force; he has many and varied inner awarenesses of force.

Every force has two elements: magnitude and direction. A 10-pound object at rest is exerting a force in the magnitude of 10 pounds and in a direction named "down." Any force can be conceived of as a straight line with an arrow on one end to show the direction; the length of the line will represent the magnitude of the force. Forces act together in predictable relationships governed by logical laws; therefore, several interacting forces can be pictured as geometrical patterns made up of straight lines which go in various directions and even form angles. Force, then, is not only something which a child experiences; it is also something which can be pictured. The unit takes advantage of this fact by beginning with force which is *experienced*, and from this starting point leading the child to force which is *conceptualized*. The unit moves progressively through five learning levels as it goes from experienced force to conceptualized force.

Since magnitude and direction are fundamental aspects of the space-time world in which the child must function, forces can be used to inform his data-processing mechanism about some aspects of that world. At the same time, he can be helped to build a firmer base from which to make relative judgments concerning his future encounters with his world.

Other phenomena are often associated with forces: Sometimes a visual experience occurs along with a force, sometimes an auditory experience, sometimes a tactual-kinesthetic one. The unit attempts to capitalize on these concurrent experiences so that more than one sense avenue is used to obtain data concerning the same event.

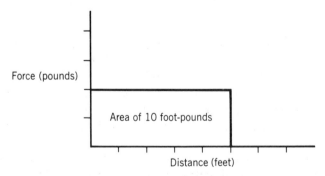

FIGURE 4-1.   An Energy Graph

If force can be conceptualized as a straight line, *energy* can be conceptualized as an *area*. Energy is force acting through a distance; it is the product of force and the distance through which that force acts. If a child raises a 5-pound brick 2 feet off the floor he has exerted 10 foot-pounds of energy. A graph of this results in an area (see Figure 4-1).

In dealing with energy, then, a new element is added: distance. Distance also has magnitude and can be experienced. In exerting energy, in having energy exerted upon him, or in perceiving the expenditure of energy, a child is exposed to the magnitude and direction of force, and to the magnitude of distance. Each of these elements varies, but all are interrelated. They do not vary haphazardly; they vary in patterns. Reliable relationships can be experienced, perceived, and conceptualized. Patterns can be manipulated to set up many different situations for experience, perception, and conception; the unit offers some of these variations for the different learning levels.

The element of time is added explicitly when dealing with *power*. Power is energy expended in a given unit of time. Thus, dealing with power involves dealing with magnitudes, directions, and times. Situations may be structured where these elements are experienced as realities of the space-time world, where they are experienced in pattern and in relationship, and where each element can be varied at will and the variation experienced in the total situation.

The unit provides for unfolding these concepts of force, energy, and power hierarchically through the five levels of learning. At the *motor* level, the main interest is in providing opportunities for motor exploration which will increase the child's internal awareness of his body, and which will help build his motor base into a well-organized whole. At the *motor-perceptual* level, interest focuses upon opportunities to match the incoming perceptual data to the motor base. At the *perceptual-motor* level, the goal is to help the child project his internal structure outward upon the external data of perception so that he can structure that part of the world which is not immediately available to him. At the *perceptual* level, the motor can begin to drop out, and he can perceive without overt exploration. At the *perceptual-conceptual* level, he begins to deal with relations between perceptions without manipulating the individual percepts. In the unit outline, the content and the learning experiences are numbered from one through five to indicate the learning level. The divisions between levels are not sharply defined, and many activities will involve some overlapping.

CONDUCTING THE UNIT

The teacher should not expect that every child in an intermediate class for educable mentally retarded children will reach the higher levels developed in the unit; indeed, in many classes it is possible that none of the children will progress this far. However, children who cannot go all the way need not be dropped by the wayside. Even at the highest levels of learning as developed in the unit, tasks can be assigned so that all may share in the experience and gain perceptual training. The perceptual training in this sense can be had even if the corresponding higher level is not attained from this unit of study. What is unique about the unit design is this: The child interacts with a structured set of experiences, bringing into play a variety of sensory-motor mechanisms in the process. Interacting with this set of structured experiences provides opportunity for development of coordination. At the same time, the experiences are designed to teach the child something about the functions of force, energy, and power. He may not attain the latter goal, but attaining the former can aid his future learning of subject matter other than that in his unit.

The unit is presented in recommended chronological order. Three basic ideas are developed at the following learning levels:

Basic Idea I: Force tends to change the speed or direction of objects.
Learning levels:
1. Motor
2. Motor-perceptual
3. Perceptual-motor
4. Perceptual
5. Perceptual-conceptual

Basic Idea II: Energy is force acting through distance.
Learning levels:
3. Perceptual-motor
4. Perceptual
5. Perceptual-conceptual

Basic Idea III: Power is the rate at which energy is produced or consumed.

Learning levels:

4. Perceptual
5. Perceptual-conceptual

A simple numbering system for unit activities indicates the learning level which is most prominent for a given activity. The three "Basic Ideas" are designated by roman numerals. Each Basic Idea is subdivided into content areas and designated as "Content A," "Content B," and so on. Each content area is made up of unit activities, and each activity has a two-digit number with a decimal point separating the digits. The first digit indicates the learning level, as outlined above. The second digit merely designates the position of a given activity at a given level and content. For example, four activities under Basic Idea II, Content A, are at learning level 3 (perceptual-motor). These activities are numbered 3.1, 3.2, 3.3, and 3.4; in each instance the first digit indicates the learning level (3), and the second digit serves as a numerical listing of the activities at that level.

A SCIENCE UNIT: FORCE, ENERGY, AND POWER

Basic Idea I: Force tends to change the speed or direction of objects

LEARNING EXPERIENCES	EXPLANATORY NOTES
CONTENT A: *We use force to stop and start, to change from running to walking, and so on.*	

Opener:

Tell the children, "We are going to begin a science project. We will do many things scientists do. (Classroom will be a laboratory at times, we will make measurements, do experiments, and the like.) Scientists study many things. Many times they study force and energy and power; we are going to study these things, too. We will start with *force*."

Development:

1.1 Have one child *push* a chair a short distance, then *pull* the chair back. By questions and discussion, establish that pushing and pulling are examples of force. Force was needed to start the chair moving. Let each child push and pull a chair, and ask if he can "feel" the force. Try to get several descriptions of what it feels like to push or pull; where the feeling is located and what it is like.

Materials: Basic need is space for walking, running; gym would be ideal, or outdoors if weather permits; if in classroom, clear large area. Several chairs (not folding).

Perceptual Training: Pushing and pulling an object gives training in differentiation (the muscular activity emphasizes that the arms are separate and distinct from other body parts, and that their movements are special to the arms), synchrony (starting, stopping, and reversing movements teach about "now"), and integration (to do the task, different parts must be coordinated in their movements to accomplish the goal):

LEARNING EXPERIENCES	EXPLANATORY NOTES
1.2 "Let's do an experiment. How many different body parts can we use to make a force that will move the chair?" (Hands, fingers, wrist, elbow, shoulders, head, back, leg, knee, ankle, heel, toe, and so on.) Another experiment: Demonstrate body positions from which force may be developed to move chair. (Lying on back, stomach, sides; sitting, and the like.)	*Perceptual Training:* The major emphasis in this activity is generalization. By using many different movements to accomplish the same task, the children are helped to develop generalized movement patterns instead of "splinter skills." Movement of many individual parts also aids differentiation.
1.3 "We used force to start the chair moving; we use force to start ourselves moving." Have child walk a few steps, stop, and start walking again. Discuss: What "pushed" the child and got him moving? Could he feel the force in his legs? Could he feel the extra force in starting and stopping? (Avoid a precise locating of muscles; we want to avoid "splintering.")	*Perceptual Training:* Synchrony (starting and stopping) and differentiation (awareness of specific movement).
1.4 Use one child to demonstrate these four "speeds": standing still (zero speed), slow walk, fast walk, and run. Have each child change from one speed to another on command. Vary by using verbal commands, visual signals with teacher's hands, or four different colored sheets of paper (each sheet representing a command to change to a different speed).	*Perceptual Training:* Development of generalized movement patterns by varying means of locomotion. Development of synchrony by changing speeds upon command. Development of rhythm through rhythmical movements. Development of sensory-motor coordination by use of auditory and visual commands to control movements.
2.1 "We used force to change our speed; we use force to change the speed of moving objects." Roll a bowling ball, a volleyball, and a beach ball to each child, keeping the speed of each ball the same at this stage. Have the child use his hands to change the speed of	*Materials:* Bowling ball, volleyball, and beach ball (or other objects of different weights which can be rolled). *Perceptual Training:* Generalization (different weight balls are used), eye-hand coordination (hand movement must

LEARNING EXPERIENCES

each ball (slow it, stop it, or make it go faster). Discuss which ball needs the most force to change its speed and why each is a different weight). Let each child feel the difference in weights by lifting the balls from the floor (watch toes with the bowling ball).

2.2 Roll each ball several times at different speeds. Discuss difference in forces at different speeds. Vary by having children use different body parts to change speed of balls.

2.3 Instead of teacher rolling ball, let children pair off and roll the balls to each other, varying speeds and body parts. (Because of weight of bowling ball, children should stand while manipulating it, standing and stooping to reach it, for sake of safety). At this stage, try to get across the idea that a big starting push requires a big changing or stopping push; that what we do to start and what we do to stop or change are connected.

3.1 At 2.1, we held speed constant and discovered that balls with differing weights required differing forces to change their speeds. Now attempt the more difficult task of having the child produce consistently the same force (by striking the balls with the heel of his hand, and developing the same speed at moment of impact each time), and observing the different effects this

EXPLANATORY NOTES

be coordinated with the visual monitoring of the moving ball).

Perceptual Training: Primarily generalization. Different weight balls are now rolled at different speeds. Added generalization from use of different body parts.

Perceptual Training: Synchrony (starting and stopping), generalization (different weight balls are still being used), directionality (child must determine proper direction and roll ball in that direction), eye-hand coordination (required in starting ball).

Perceptual Training: Muscular control, monitoring of tactual-kinesthetic feedback.

LEARNING EXPERIENCES

same force produces on balls of differing weight. First have the children practice making the same force each time. They may use the heel of one hand to strike the other, practicing a "feel" of the same force. They may also strike the hands of fellow students and get verbal feedback regarding how consistently they produce the same force with each striking motion.

3.2 When the children have developed a reasonably constant striking force, have them pair off and let each one use his constant force to propel the balls to his partner. The partner notes the receiving force (that is, the force he must apply to stop the balls), and in turn uses his constant force to send them back. Each child tells what happens to the balls when he uses the same force to make them move (some go faster than others). Each child describes how much force he used to stop each ball (this should be about the same).

CONTENT B: *We use force to change our directions and the directions of objects.*

1.1 Explain that we used force to change our speed and we also used force to change the speed of balls. Tell the children that we also use force when we change our direction and when we change the direction of objects like balls. Have each child walk and make

EXPLANATORY NOTES

Perceptual Training: Visual monitoring of varying speeds, together with concurrent monitoring of tactual-kinesthetic feedback from the muscular effort to produce the speeds. Generalization.

Perceptual Training: Directionality through changing directions. Directional changes develop synchrony and aid in differentiation of those body parts which are activated in changing directions. Rhythm is developed through rhythmical movements.

LEARNING EXPERIENCES	EXPLANATORY NOTES
changes of direction, (left, right, reverse, half-left, and half-right) as he wishes. Each discusses what force he feels as he changes direction.	
1.2 Each child now walks in a circle. After all have done this, let the group discuss which side pushed with the most force. Now change directions of circles, and again discuss which side pushed the most. (In going in a circle, a child is continually changing directions, because he is moving away from a straight line at any given instant; hence, with each step he takes he is changing his direction).	*Perceptual Training:* Differentiation (muscles used are emphasized). Form perception (form is experienced through kinesthetic feedback from muscular effort in walking in a circle.)
1.3 Vary the two preceding experiences by having the child change directions as he runs, walks fast, walks slowly; do these variations by changing speeds in walking, in line, and in circles. A most interesting variation (and one which will aid the development of synchrony) is this: With the child standing still, have him start moving and make a change of direction at the same moment he starts.	*Perceptual Training:* Different movements help develop generalized movement patterns. Speed changes are for synchrony; direction changes are for directionality.
2.1 Use the bowling ball, volleyball, and beach ball for experiences of using force to change directions of moving objects. One child can start a ball rolling, and another can push it in a new direction. Children should learn that more force is needed to change direction of a heavier object and that, for a given	*Materials:* Bowling ball, volleyball, beach ball. *Perceptual Training:* Eye-hand coordination, generalization, synchrony, directionality, visual-motor monitoring.

LEARNING EXPERIENCES

object, more force is needed for greater changes in direction.

3.1 We now want the child to learn how to control his application of force so that he can propel a moving ball in a desired direction. Several targets can be set on the floor; one child rolls a ball to another, and the second child pushes the moving ball toward one of the targets which the teacher designates. A child uses only one pushing motion for each assigned target. Use all three balls.

3.2 Have four children stand so that they form a square; each child represents a corner. Each ball is rolled around the "square," the children keeping the ball in motion by pushing (one push) from one child to another. If they cannot form the square by keeping the ball in continuous motion, let each child stop the ball when it reaches him, and then send it on its new direction to the next child. Give each child in the square a piece of newsprint and a crayon, and have him draw the square with the paper on the floor. Then have him go to the board and draw the square. Repeat the procedure with other geometric figures: rectangle, triangle, diamond.

EXPLANATORY NOTES

Perceptual Training: Eye-hand coordination, directionality, generalization, muscular control, monitoring of visual information from a moving object, synchrony, and monitoring of kinesthetic feedback from muscles which propel ball.

Materials: Newsprint, crayons.

Perceptual Training: The major perceptual training in this activity is form perception and generalization. Form is first *experienced* (rolling ball around the outline of the form), and then it is *produced* from two different body positions. A variety of generalization is provided in the activity: Drawing the form with newsprint on the floor and then drawing the same form on the chalkboard requires two radically different sets of muscular activity for the same task, thus promoting generalized movement patterns. More generalization is provided by drawing in two distinct planes; horizontal (floor) and vertical (chalkboard). (Many children cannot move easily from one plane to another.) Still more generalization comes from dealing with the same form in different settings: The form is first encountered as children forming the corners, next as a drawing on paper, and finally as a drawing on the

LEARNING EXPERIENCES

3.3 "We use force to make our bodies go where we want them to go." Use masking tape to lay out several large patterns and geometrical figures on the floor. Have the children follow the tape markings by walking on the tape. When a child has completed one figure by walking through the complete figure (or pattern), have him draw that figure on newsprint and then on the chalkboard. Have the child label the figures he draws (circle, square, and the like), and engage him in conversation so that he says the name of the figure.

EXPLANATORY NOTES

chalkboard. In addition to the major training in form perception and generalization, the activity offers several other obvious aspects of perceptual training.

Materials: Masking tape figures on floor: Square, triangle, rectangle, diamond. Masking tape patterns as follows:

FIGURE 4-2.   Masking Tape Patterns

LEARNING EXPERIENCES	EXPLANATORY NOTES
4.1 Draw a figure or pattern on the chalkboard, and have the children identify the corresponding figure (or pattern) on the floor. Children walk through the pattern after they have identified it.	*Perceptual Training:* This variation of 3.2 adds more of the same type training.
4.2 Draw a figure on the board, and have the children walk through the figure or pattern *without* using the masking tape lines as guides.	*Perceptual Training:* Previous activities have helped the child experience forms and produce those forms, both perception and production being aided by motor involvement. This activity offers training in perception of form through vision alone, with the opportunity to confirm visual perceptions with subsequent visual-motor experience of walking through the form which is outlined on the floor. Walking through the form also aids visual-motor coordination. Children who are unable to perform this activity should have additional experiences similar to those in activities 3.2 and 3.3.
4.3 Draw the figures on the chalkboard, and have the children draw the same figures on paper and then on the board. Then draw the figures on the board and erase. Tell the children to reproduce the figures on paper and then on the board. Next tell them to draw a figure as you call its name. Have the children reproduce these figures also on paper and then on the	*Perceptual Training:* Visual perception of form is confirmed by motor activity to produce the same form. This activity is to help tie the visual and motor avenues together. All the foregoing activities involving forms also aid generalization, since any one form is experienced in a variety of ways. *Perceptual Training:* This activity is mainly to provide more generalization. Having children draw after teacher erases copy is to add experience in recall (and gives the teacher a check on this performance). Note the variety of ways in which the children deal with form.

LEARNING EXPERIENCES

board. If children have trouble with any figures at this stage, have them walk through the figures and then attempt to reproduce them.

CONTENT C: *We use different forces to move objects which have different surfaces in contact. This is the concept of friction.*

2.1 Explain that round objects like balls move by rolling over the floor, but some objects are flat and must be moved by sliding. We will call the contact surface the "sliding part." Sliding parts can be made of many different materials; different materials need different forces to make objects slide. Demonstrate this by having the children put their palms down on a table top and slide their hands while pressing down; repeat with handkerchief between palm and table top. Discuss differences in forces needed to move the hand in the two instances. Emphasize that the different surfaces (skin and cloth) made them use different forces to slide their hands.

EXPLANATORY NOTES

Perceptual Training: Mainly differentiation and eye-hand coordination. Insist that they watch hands while performing. The increased muscular activity will emphasize the arm and hand as distinct parts of the body. Some children will tense the whole body on activities such as this. Try to encourage those who do this to relax as much of the body as possible except for the parts which are exerting force. Careful observation of children on this activity will help pinpoint those who tend to tense the whole body whenever they activate any set of muscles. This general tensing of the whole body is most undesirable, because the movement of parts does not stand out sufficiently from the overall tension; thus differentiation is hampered. Training in differentiation will be much more effective if the child is taught to tense only those muscles needed for the task, while keeping other muscles as relaxed as possible. In this way, tension in the muscles which are working will contrast with, or stand out in bold relief from, the muscles which are relaxed and not needed in the task. If this contrast can be experienced, the child is better able to become aware of the movements of the differ-

LEARNING EXPERIENCES

2.2 Have one child sit on a piece of cloth, while another child grasps one end of the cloth and pulls with just enough force to move the first child. Change to different materials and note difference in force needed for each material. Take turns. Point out the two surfaces, the floor and the material we sit on, and that the material slides over the floor.

2.3 Vary the preceding experience by using combinations of different materials as sliding surfaces. One cloth can be anchored to the floor by two children standing on it; the second piece of cloth is then laid on top of the anchored cloth and the child sits on the second piece. The child who pulls does so by pulling on the top cloth and making it slide with respect to the anchored cloth. Children should always pull the same child, lest the differences in weights introduce a confusing variation.

2.4 Have children slide bricks with different surfaces over a table top by pulling on strings tied around bricks.

EXPLANATORY NOTES

ent body parts, and thus to differentiate those movements from each other.

Materials: Several pieces of sturdy cloth, at least 18 inches wide and 3 or 4 feet long; each piece to have different texture (burlap, carpeting, drapery material, plastic, or the like).

Perceptual Training: Generalization, differentiation, and control of movement. The activity involving the hand in 2.1 is generalized by involving the whole body in the same type experience. Generalization also takes place as the task is varied so that the children experience different forces with different materials in the same task.

General: This variation is most important. The children should experiment with these different surfaces until they can agree which is the easiest, second easiest, and so on, to the very hardest combination.

Perceptual Training: Mainly generalization.

Materials: Six ordinary bricks, the kind used in buildings, without holes in bricks if possible. Glue six different ma-

LEARNING EXPERIENCES

Then vary by placing one brick on top of another, holding bottom brick, and sliding top brick by pulling on its string. Keep string horizontal and parallel to brick edges so that force needed for sliding will not be distorted. Determine relative gradients of forces needed to move bricks with different surfaces in contact. Have children feel all surfaces and identify by touch and by name of surface. Children should exert just enough force on string each time to barely start brick moving.

EXPLANATORY NOTES

terials (sandpaper, construction paper, plastic, cloth of different textures, or the like) to the two large surfaces of each brick. Each brick should have two different sliding surfaces for variation; for example, glue sandpaper to one surface of a brick and another piece of sandpaper to one other brick. Tie string between the two prepared surfaces and around the brick, thus:

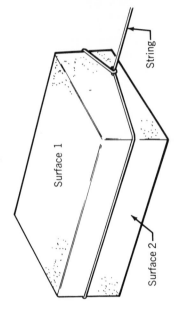

Surface 1

Surface 2

String

FIGURE 4-3.   Brick with Two Prepared Surfaces

Perceptual Training: Experience in previous activities is generalized by changing to the new type activity with bricks. Experience within this new activity is further generalized by varying the surfaces to provide different forces from the same type of activity. In addition, some perceptual training takes place in differentiation of arm

LEARNING EXPERIENCES

3.1 Weigh each brick and write weight on brick. Use spring scale for weighing. Explain that the *weight* of a brick is the *amount of force* that brick exerts when it is put on top of a table or floor; that is, a brick weighing 4 pounds pushes down with a force of 4 pounds, and it pushes down with this much force on a table or any other object we put it on. We can tell how much force the brick is exerting by measuring the force we must exert to lift it straight up. Let each child attach the scale to a brick, raise the brick from its resting place, and read on the scale how much force he exerted to do so. Let each child also feel this force by placing a brick on his hand as the hand is resting on a table.

CONTENT D: *We can draw a picture of a force by using a line. The size of the force is shown by the length of the line, and the direction of the line is the direction of the force.*

4.1 Explain that we can draw a picture of a force by drawing a straight line; the length of the line shows

EXPLANATORY NOTES

and hand as well as hand-eye coordination. In this and similar activities, children should watch the parts which are performing in the tasks.

Materials: Spring scales. A convenient scale for this purpose is the kind sold by sporting goods stores for weighing fish. One popular model is known as a "Fisherman's De-Liar," and contains a flexible steel tape which rolls into the scale itself when not in use. This steel tape feature will be useful for later portions of the unit. The "Fisherman's De-Liar" comes in two sizes: one will weigh up to 16 pounds; the other up to 8 pounds. The smaller size should be adequate for most of the experiences outlined here, and is somewhat easier to read.

Perceptual Training: Generalization and differentiation. Children are also helped to learn about the visual symbols which indicate weights; experiencing a connection between the symbol and the muscles needed to lift the brick. The unit offers many similar opportunities which are considered extremely important for children with learning disorders.

Perceptual Training: The major training in this activity is for the child to generalize from an experience of a force

LEARNING EXPERIENCES

how much force, and the direction of the line shows the direction of the force. Draw a vertical line 4 inches long on the chalkboard, and explain that we will let this be a picture of 1 pound. Draw a long vertical line close to the "1-pound" line, and have one child read the weight of any one brick. Then, have a child measure the weight of the brick on the long line by marking the length of the 1-pound line on the edge of a piece of paper, and marking this length on the long line as many times as there are pounds in the brick. If the brick weighs 4 pounds, he would have four lengths of 4 inches each marked off on the long line. Erase the excess of the long line, and put an arrow at the bottom to show "down." Underscore the fact that the long line with the arrow is a picture of the force of the brick pushing down on the table. The line is drawn with an arrow pointing down to show the direction of the force, and we made the line "4 pounds long," for example, by measuring the weight of the brick on the line. We cannot see the force but we can feel it when we pick up the brick. We can feel how much force and we can feel the direction of the force. (See Figure 4-4.)

EXPLANATORY NOTES

to a visual symbol of the force. His experience of various forces has been in terms of the kinesthetic feedback from muscles as they encountered various forces. This con-

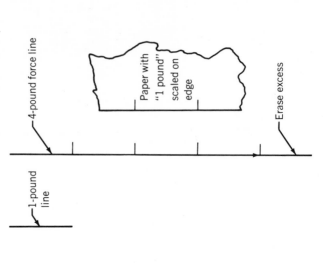

FIGURE 4-4.   **Scaling Force**

LEARNING EXPERIENCES

4.2 Have the children draw force lines representing the weights of the five other bricks, leaving a space of 3 or 4 feet between each line. Draw a "1-pound" line as a scale for each of the lines.

4.3 Now demonstrate the fact that more than one force can act on an object at the same time. When the children slid one brick with respect to another by pulling on a string, two forces were involved: one vertical force (the weight of the brick), and a horizontal force (the force of friction, or the force of the pull on the string). To demonstrate this, set a table close to the chalkboard next to the force line of one of the bricks. Use only the brick whose force line is next to the table in the demonstration. Place the brick directly in front of its force line, and have a child attach the spring scale to the string, move the brick by pulling on the scale, and read the force needed to barely move the brick. The direction of the pull should be parallel to the chalkboard, so that the relationship of forces can be shown on the board more clearly. Now draw a horizontal line, beginning at the point of the arrow on the force line, and measure the amount of force

EXPLANATORY NOTES

crete experience is now linked to the visual symbol. Many children seem to have difficulty connecting symbols with experience. It is important that each child be helped to make these most fundamental associations.

Perceptual Training: Additional experience of the same type as 4.1. Drawing and measuring gives training in eye-hand coordination.

Materials: Spring scale and bricks.

Perceptual Training: In pulling the brick along a horizontal surface, two separate forces are acting together: the weight of the brick is down, and the pull on the string is horizontal. The child can experience the size and direction of each of these two forces. He thus, in effect, can develop a kinesthetic figure in space through the information which comes through his muscles. The present activity helps him translate the "experienced figure" into a visual symbol of that figure. His muscles experience a relationship in space, and he translates this relationship into a visual figure in space. Along with this experience, he is receiving other perceptual training from muscles, eyes, and hands working together.

LEARNING EXPERIENCES

EXPLANATORY NOTES

needed to move the brick. At the end of this new horizontal line, place an arrow to show its direction. (See Figure 4-5.)

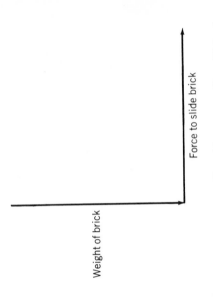

Weight of brick

Force to slide brick

FIGURE 4-5.   Two Forces on One Object

4.4 We have now demonstrated two simultaneous forces operating upon the same object. For any one brick, its vertical force will be the same, but the horizontal force needed to move it will vary as the sliding surfaces are changed. Have the children measure the sliding forces and draw force diagrams for the different forces needed to slide the bricks with varying surfaces in contact.

Perceptual Training: Mainly generalization. Some differentiation (from muscles in activities) and eye-motor coordination.

LEARNING EXPERIENCES

CONTENT E: *Forces acting together can be pictured as different shapes or patterns.*

5.1 Each force diagram consists of a vertical force (weight of brick) and a horizontal force (sliding force). Each of these force diagrams are actually two sides of a right triangle. (See Figure 4-6.) Ask if anyone can see the two lines as part of a figure. When they see this figure, have them complete the triangles for all the force diagrams by drawing in the hypotenuse on each diagram. The figures should be left on the board or, if inconvenient, the triangles should be transferred to scale on large sheets of paper.

EXPLANATORY NOTES

Perceptual Training: The children are now definitely into the perceptual-conceptual level; that is, percepts are used to help develop concepts. Force was first experienced through the muscles, then through visual symbols which represented relationships between forces. Through manipulations of a variety of mutually related forces, the child has the opportunity to form concepts of forces forming patterns.

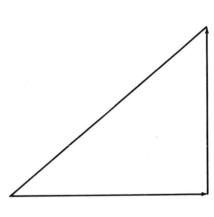

FIGURE 4-6.   **A Force Triangle**

LEARNING EXPERIENCES

5.2 Possibly by now the children are beginning to conceptualize the two forces as forming a triangle. However, a much more important relationship can be demonstrated quite easily. Arrange a simple inclined plane so that the slope may be varied at will, and so that the vertical and horizontal components may be measured on the device itself (see Figure 4-7 for one way of doing this). Have the children set the board to the various slopes indicated by the various force triangles which they previously drew. For each slope, the surfaces corresponding to the force triangle should be set up on brick and board, and the angle at which the brick barely slides should be noted and compared with the corresponding angle of the force triangle. A very important variation is as follows: Set up two surfaces on the brick and board, and *without measuring* simply tilt the board to the position where the brick barely slides. Use the cord to fix the board in this position, and then measure the slope of the board and compare with the angle in the force triangle. (See Figure 4-10.)

EXPLANATORY NOTES

General: Each "force triangle" contains an angle which is the slope of an inclined surface, down which the brick will slide of its own free weight. For example, consider a brick

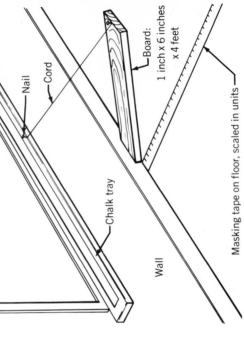

Nail

Cord

Board:
1 inch x 6 inches
x 4 feet

Chalk tray

Wall

Masking tape on floor, scaled in units

FIGURE 4-7.   Making an Inclined Surface. In the example, the board is the inclined plane and its slope is changed by changing the length of the stout cord which suspends one end of the board in mid-air. A length of masking tape is stuck on the floor; the edge

LEARNING EXPERIENCES

EXPLANATORY NOTES

of the tape is placed next to the edge of the board when the board is lying flat on the floor. The tape can be marked off in pound units (1 pound equal to 4 inches is a convenient scale) and each pound is marked off into ¼-pound divisions (¼ pound = 1 inch if the suggested scale is used). The zero-point on the tape is the point where the tape touches the wall (or baseboard).

with a sandpaper surface resting upon a horizontal surface of paper. Assume that we pull the brick until it barely slides, and we find that it required 3 pounds to slide the brick. We weigh the brick and find that it weighs 5 pounds. We draw its force triangle:

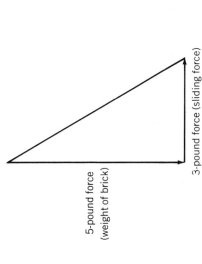

5-pound force
(weight of brick)

3-pound force (sliding force)

FIGURE 4-8. Force Diagram of 5-Pound Brick Which Requires 3 Pounds of Force to Slide It.

LEARNING EXPERIENCES

EXPLANATORY NOTES

We can then set up an inclined plane so that the slope of the plane is *three units vertically* for every *five units horizontally*, and we will find that the brick with sandpaper sliding against paper will barely slide down this slope. Note that each force triangle can be rotated 90 degrees, and the slope of the inclined surface is shown by the hypotenuse.

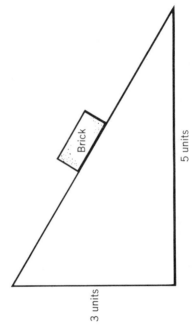

3 units

5 units

FIGURE 4-9.   Inclined Plane from Force Diagram; Brick Will Slide of Its Own Weight

Assuming the brick weighs 5 pounds and required a sliding force of 3 pounds, first measure the 5-pound force on the scaled length of masking tape, and place a chalk mark on the floor at this 5-pound point. From this point,

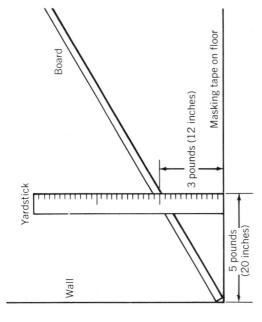

FIGURE 4-10. **Measuring on the Inclined Surface. To illustrate the procedure, assume that we have a brick weighing 5 pounds which requires a sliding force of 3 pounds. We first measure the 5-pound force on the scaled length of masking tape, and place a chalk mark on the floor at this point. From this point, we measure 3 pounds straight up, and we adjust the cord so that the board is raised to the 3-pound (or 12-inch) point.**

LEARNING EXPERIENCES

5.3 Have the children set the board to correspond to one of the force triangles they have already dealt with, put the brick on the board (with proper surfaces on contact) so that the brick barely slides. Explain now that the brick slides because the slope of the board makes part of the weight of the brick shift downward in the direction of the board. This force is just enough to overcome the friction of the two surfaces, and so the brick will slide. But all the force of the brick's weight does not make it slide; some of the brick's weight is still pushing on the board. Tell them we will draw a picture of the brick's weight and the two forces it divides into on our sloping board. Draw a sloping line on the chalkboard,

EXPLANATORY NOTES

measure 3 pounds straight up, and adjust the cord so that the board is raised to this 3-pound (or 12″) point. Since we assumed our force diagram was for a brick with sandpaper surface sliding on paper, we can thumbtack a piece of paper to the board and place the brick on the paper with the sandpaper surface in contact with the paper. The brick should barely slide. Bear in mind that our measurements of weights and distances are not as accurate as laboratory conditions would allow; therefore, it probably will be necessary to make a slight adjustment in the slope of the board to find the precise point at which the brick will barely slide. Our measurements are of sufficient accuracy, however, that the slope of the board will approximate quite closely the angle of the force triangle.

Materials: Carpenter's square, string, spring scales.

General: When an object such as a brick rests on a sloping surface, the weight of the object divides into two components: One component is parallel to the sloping surface and the other component is perpendicular to the same surface. The size of the two component forces depends upon the weight of the object and the slope of the surface. These two component forces can also be pictured as a force triangle, and the triangle will be a right triangle and will contain one angle equal to the slope of the surface. This relationship is illustrated by Figure 4-11. If the weight of the brick is drawn to scale, then the two components will also be to scale.

EXPLANATORY NOTES

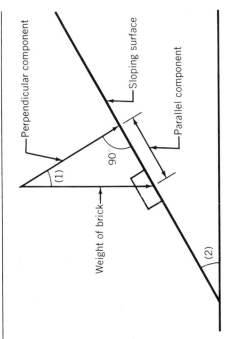

FIGURE 4-11. An Object on a Sloping Surface Divides Its Weight into Two Components — One Parallel to the Slope and One Perpendicular to the Slope: Angle (1) = Angle (2)

LEARNING EXPERIENCES

with the slope of the line equal to the slope of the inclined board. Draw a vertical line to scale representing the weight of the brick, and let this vertical line end on the sloping line as illustrated in Figure 4-12. Erect a line perpendicular to the sloping line and from a point at the very top of the vertical line representing the brick's weight. This line is the perpendicular component, and its scale length is the actual amount of force which pushes perpendicular to the sloping surface. The horizontal component is the distance from the perpendicular to the vertical line. The children should measure both of these component force lines, and should label each one according to the force its length represents. Now go back to the sloping board, and set the brick on the board. Put two thumbtacks (or other obstacle) into the board so that the brick cannot slide down, but so that it can be slid upward. Attach a string and a spring scale to the brick and have one of the children pull upward and parallel to the sloping board until the brick just begins to move; read the force on the scale at this point. Have the child then attach the scale to the brick so that he can pull in a direction which is perpendicular to the sloping board. He should pull in the perpendicular direction until the brick begins to lift from the board (the point of pull should be as near the center of the brick as possible). Measure the perpendicular force at the point where the brick begins to move from the board. The perpendicular and the parallel forces measured on the

LEARNING EXPERIENCES

spring scales should be quite close to the amount of force measured on the chalkboard. Taking these measurements is illustrated by Figures 4-13a and b. Remember that the slope of the board should be consistent with the force triangle for a particular set of surfaces, and that the same set of surfaces should be used in this demonstration.

EXPLANATORY NOTES

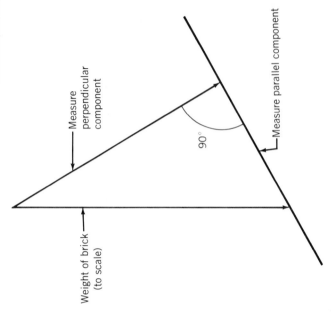

Weight of brick (to scale)

Measure perpendicular component

90°

Measure parallel component

FIGURE 4-12. Constructing the Force Triangle for the Two Component Forces. Use large carpenter's square to draw the perpendicular line.

LEARNING EXPERIENCES

EXPLANATORY NOTES

General: Use large carpenter's square to draw the perpendicular line.

Perceptual Training: Note that in this activity the children must stoop over or sit down or perhaps even lie on one side in order to do the tasks outlined. These unusual positions mean that they do tasks in unaccustomed positions, and therefore they use different sets of muscles than usual. Most of their eye-hand activities, for example, are usually from a sitting position at their desks. Putting

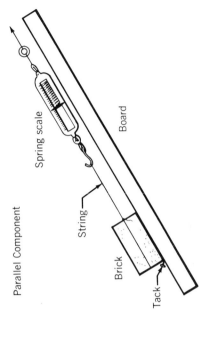

Parallel Component

Spring scale

String

Brick

Tack

Board

FIGURE 4-13a. **Determining the Components.**

LEARNING EXPERIENCES

EXPLANATORY NOTES

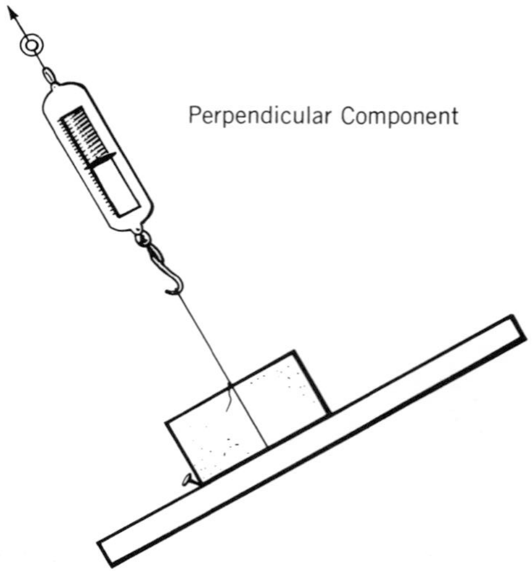

Perpendicular Component

FIGURE 4-13b.   Determining the Components.

them in new positions for working puts new sets of muscles into play and helps promote generalized movement patterns. Other perceptual training has been explained in preceding sections.

General: Of course the teacher will not use terms such as "parallel component" in discussing these relationships with the children. Simpler terms such as "the force

LEARNING EXPERIENCES

5.4 Explain to the children that when forces act together there is a balance; that is, all the forces in one direction are equal to all the forces in the opposite direction. For example, all the "up" forces must equal all the "down" forces, and all the "left" forces must equal all the "right" forces. To demonstrate this, suspend a brick of known weight from two spring scales, using string, and anchor the ends of the two scales to two table legs as shown in Figure 4-14. Point out the point of suspension, and tell the children that the brick is pulling down on this point with its whole weight of 5 pounds, for example. Now point to the two supporting strings, and tell them that each string is pulling up and to one side. Tell them that the suspension point is now not moving; all the forces on that point are in balance. The "up" forces in the two strings add up to the weight of the brick, and the "left" force in the left string is the same as the "right" force in the right string. Explain that we will draw a picture of the forces acting on the suspension point. Place a large piece of paper behind the strings, and trace in the three lines and the suspension point formed by their intersection. At this point, we are interested only in the angles and the suspension point. Remove the paper and tape it to the

EXPLANATORY NOTES

along the board" (parallel) and "the force *on* the board" (perpendicular) are recommended both here and other places where technical terms would be confusing.

Materials: Two spring scales, string.

General: Now it has been established that a given force can split off into components, and that these components have interrelationships and can be conceptualized as forming geometric patterns. Applications of this simple fact are

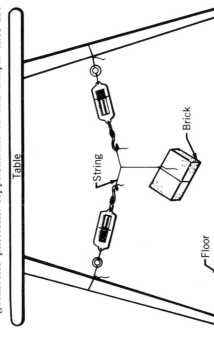

FIGURE 4-14.   Brick Suspended So That Forces of Suspension Can Be Measured.

EXPLANATORY NOTES

limitless. The remainder of this section will consist of a few applications.

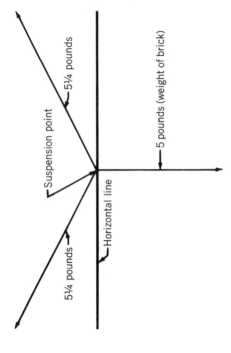

Suspension point

5¼ pounds

5¼ pounds

Horizontal line

5 pounds (weight of brick)

FIGURE 4-15.   Force Diagram Drawn to Scale

General: Children need not add with numbers to find any of the forces; they can measure them all and apply the measured lengths to a scale such as the masking tape on the floor.

LEARNING EXPERIENCES

chalkboard; the lines are in the same relationship as the strings from which they were drawn. Use a straightedge and go over the three lines to make them more uniform. Draw a horizontal line through the suspension point, and explain that the forces above this line are pulling up and the forces below it are pulling down. Have the children read the two spring scales, and measure off the number of pounds on the corresponding lines on the paper. Have them measure the weight of the brick on its line on the paper. A relationship to scale is shown by Figure 4-15. Call attention to the fact that the two supporting forces in the two strings add up to more than the weight of the brick, because only *part* of each force in each string is pulling *up;* another part of each of these two forces is pulling to the side. We can find out how much of the force in each of the two strings is pulling up, by drawing perpendiculars from the two supporting forces to the horizontal line as shown in Figure 4-16. Note that the two "up" forces of 2½ pounds each total the one and only "down" force. The amounts of forces in the supporting strings will vary as the angles are changed, but if the forces are measured to scale and marked out as this example has shown, then the "up" and "down" forces will be in balance. To complete our picture of all the forces acting on the suspension point, we need only measure and record the "left" force and the "right" force as shown in Figure 4-17. Have the children vary this procedure by using different angles of suspension.

EXPLANATORY NOTES

LEARNING EXPERIENCES

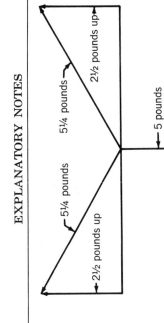

FIGURE 4-16. Determining the "Up" Forces; "Up" Forces = "Down" Forces (2½ + 2½ = 5)

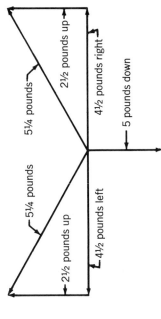

FIGURE 4-17. The Complete Force Picture with "Left" and "Right" Forces Added to the Previous Diagram

LEARNING EXPERIENCES

5.5 As a variation of the foregoing, fasten a heavy spring scale to each end of a 10-foot length of rope. Position a child at each end of the rope; each child is prone (back on floor), and reaches over his head to grasp the scale. Each child pulls as hard as he can to put as much tension on the rope as possible. Have other children grasp the ankles of the two "operators" to keep them from sliding. A third "operator" is placed midway of the rope, lies prone and fastens his scale to the middle of the rope, pulling at right angles to the rope to deflect it. (See Figure 4-18.) This third child will cause the rope to deflect in the middle, thus forming the same kind of pattern of forces which was used in the preceding section. Read the forces on the scales, and mark the angles on the floor with masking tape. Measure the forces on the masking tape; a scale of 1 inch equal to 1 pound will work better with the larger forces now in use. Discuss with the children how easy it is for one child in the middle to deflect the rope at first, and how much harder he must pull when the angle in the middle gets smaller. Repeat this procedure several times, and show with the masking tape how the forces working against the No. 3 child will get stronger as the middle angle gets smaller. This relationship is illustrated by Figures 4-20a and b.

EXPLANATORY NOTES

Materials: Three heavy spring scales, each of which will register 50 pounds; one rope, at least 10 feet long.

FIGURE 4-18.   **Forces Acting on a Rope**

EXPLANATORY NOTES

LEARNING EXPERIENCES

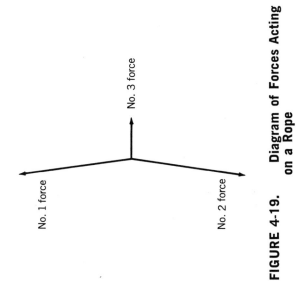

FIGURE 4-19.   Diagram of Forces Acting on a Rope

LEARNING EXPERIENCES   EXPLANATORY NOTES

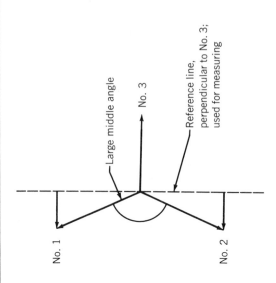

Large middle angle

No. 3

Reference line, perpendicular to No. 3; used for measuring

No. 1

No. 2

FIGURE 4-20a.   Effect of Angle Size. Assuming that number 1 and 2 always pull with the same force, then the components of their pulling forces which are opposing the pull of number 3 become greater as the middle angle becomes smaller.

EXPLANATORY NOTES

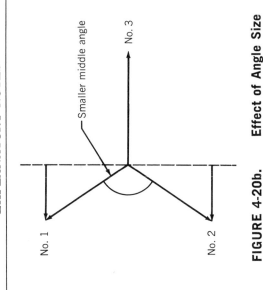

FIGURE 4-20b.   **Effect of Angle Size**

LEARNING EXPERIENCES

5.6 A most important variation can be had by reversing the procedures; that is, by observing only the force which No. 3 exerts, laying out the angles on the floor with masking tape, and measuring off the forces which No. 1 and 2 must exert to balance with No. 3. To do this, lay out the angles with masking tape, and scale off the distance of the No. 3 force. Use a string to find one-half of the No. 3 force, and move the line along the No. 1 force line until a point is reached where the

EXPLANATORY NOTES

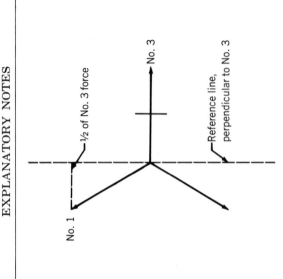

No. 3

½ of No. 3 force

No. 1

Reference line,
perpendicular to No. 3

**FIGURE 4-21.   Using Number 3 Force to Find
the Other Two Forces. Finding number 1 force
is illustrated. Repeat for number 2 force.**

Materials: Rope, three spring scales.

LEARNING EXPERIENCES

one-half length of line will exactly equal the perpendicular distance from the reference line. Measure the
length of the No. 1 force line; the scaled distance in
pounds is the force No. 1 must exert. Repeat for No. 2.
(See Figure 4-21.) Check measurements by using
spring scales to read forces for Nos. 1 and 2.

5.7 Still other variations can be provided by setting up
hypothetical problems. Lay out only the three angles
and a reference line, and assign an arbitrary value to
the No. 3 force. Then have the children measure (as
in 5.6) to find the Nos. 1 and 2 forces. Use the rope

LEARNING EXPERIENCES

and spring scales to check the measured forces. This checking is done by having the children pull the rope until the rope conforms to the angles laid out in the problem. Nos. 1 and 2 pull until the assigned force is read on the No. 3 scales; then read the scales for Nos. 1 and 2. Have the children assume different positions as they pull the scales; sitting, squatting, and the like.

EXPLANATORY NOTES

Basic Idea II: Energy is force acting through distance

LEARNING EXPERIENCES	EXPLANATORY NOTES
CONTENT A: *Energy (or work) is the product of force and the distance through which the force acts.*	*Materials:* Various objects which the children can lift and slide short distances; scales and measuring tapes for weighing and measuring. Be sure to use the bricks and strings from the previous section. Chairs, tables, and other items in the classroom will serve.

Opener:
Under Basic Idea II the children will be moving forces through distances, thus *using up energy* from their bodies. They can *experience* the energy output and they can *see* what this energy has accomplished. This relationsip between their internal experience and the observable external results should be discussed during each activity under Basic Idea II.

General: If multiplying numbers is beyond most children, do not spend undue time on arithmetic, since a different approach to this aspect of energy will come later on in the unit.

Perceptual Training: Previous explanatory notes on perceptual training should make clear how such training is obtained from the activities outlined in the remaining portions of the unit. In order to avoid needless repetition,

Development:
3.1 Tell the children that we are now going to learn about *energy.* Energy is force moving through a distance. Have someone weigh a brick and lift the brick 2 feet straight up (a second child can hold a measuring tape so that the first knows where to stop). Assume the brick weighed 4 pounds. Now explain that the one who lifted the brick produced a 4-pound force which moved a distance of 2 feet; therefore he used up 8 *foot-pounds* of *energy.* Have the children lift or slide a number of different objects various distances, each time measuring the force and distance.

LEARNING EXPERIENCES

3.2 One child sits on a piece of sturdy cloth and another child pulls him along the floor. Measure sliding force and distance pulled; compute energy in foot-pounds, teacher doing arithmetic for those who cannot do this. If weight of child on cloth is known, force triangles can be drawn as was done with bricks and string. Children take turns.

3.3 Weigh each child on school scale, and record weight on chart. Post chart in semipermanent location where it will be available to children for reference. Tell children we will find out how much energy it takes to jump. Place a child next to chalkboard and mark his height. Have him jump as high as he can, and mark topmost height of his head. His weight multiplied by the distance jumped is the amount of energy (in foot-pounds) expended in one jump. Repeat with several children. Vary by computing energy for jumping on right foot, left foot.

3.4 Now find how much energy it takes for a child to walk up a stair. Take children to a stairway, and measure the vertical distance from floor to landing. If this is not convenient due to construction of the stairway, measure the height of one stair riser, count the risers and multiply to find height. Have a child walk from floor to

EXPLANATORY NOTES

notes on perceptual training do not appear after this point.

Materials: Large spring scales, rope, measuring tapes, and cloth which was used in *Learning Experiences* 2.2, preceding section. Tie rope to cloth and scale to end of rope.
General: Once force necessary to start child has been measured, scale is no longer needed. This applies to all similar force measurements that follow; the starting force is the only essential force measurement.

Materials: School scale (nurse's scale), chart paper.

Materials: Stairway (8 or 10 feet from floor to landing), measuring tape.

General: This computation will result in some impressive sounding figures, for if Johnny weighs 70 pounds and walks a stair 10 feet high, he has put out 700 foot-pounds

LEARNING EXPERIENCES

landing; multiply his weight by the vertical height (in feet) and the result is the energy he produces to walk up.

CONTENT B: *We can draw pictures of energy.*

4.1 It is possible to arrange many different ways for the children to cause forces to operate through distances. A simple way to begin is to have them slide a brick by pulling horizontally on its string. They can measure the distance pulled and they can measure the force by using the spring scale. Explain how we can draw a picture of the energy, and let them measure off rectangles which will show how much energy they used. Note that now we are concerned only with *how much* force; we are no longer picturing the direction of the force.

EXPLANATORY NOTES

of energy. Some children may be encouraged to learn that they can produce something which sounds so grand.

General: In this section the children will, in effect, be drawing graphs indicating the energy expended or absorbed in various activities. These graphs will be in the form of rectangles (and combinations of rectangles). The unit will follow the engineering convention of measuring force in a vertical direction, and distance in a horizontal direction. The amount of energy is therefore shown by the *area* in a given rectangle, because energy is the product of force and distance and area is the product of height and length. At first use a scale of 4 inches to 1 foot; a square 4 inches on a side would thus represent 1 foot-pound of energy. For example, if a child lifts an object weighing 4 pounds and he raises it 3 feet in a vertical direction, he has expended 12 foot-pounds of energy. This task can be represented graphically by drawing a rectangle 16 inches (or 4 pounds) high and 12 inches (representing 3 feet) in length:

LEARNING EXPERIENCES	EXPLANATORY NOTES

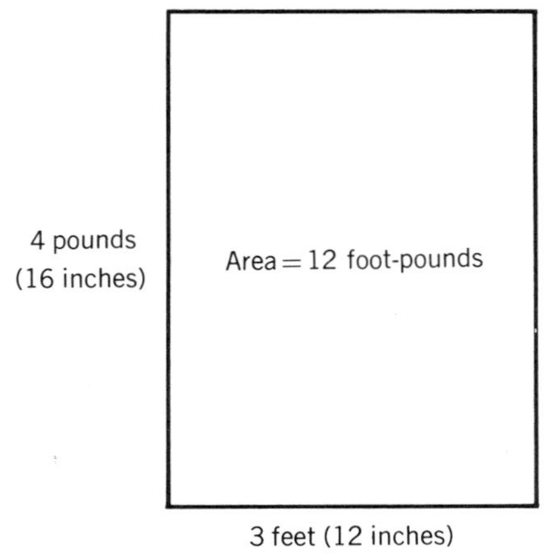

4 pounds
(16 inches)

Area = 12 foot-pounds

3 feet (12 inches)

**FIGURE 4-22.　Example of Scaling Energy:
4 Pounds x 3 Feet = 12 Foot-pounds**

The area of the rectangle would show the energy: 4 pounds times 3 feet equals 12 foot-pounds. In the earlier stages of this procedure, it will be much simpler if forces are measured in whole pounds and distances in whole feet, thus avoiding cumbersome fractions.

4.2 Vary the procedure by having them pull one brick a few feet, stop and put another brick on top of the first one, pull both bricks a few feet, add still a third brick,

EXPLANATORY NOTES

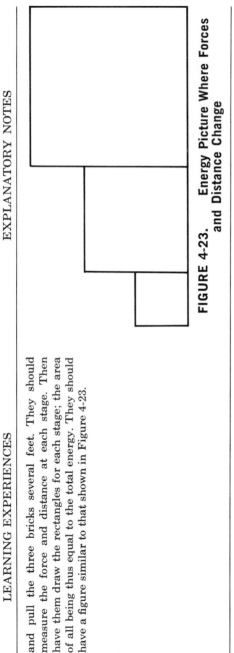

FIGURE 4-23.   Energy Picture Where Forces and Distance Change

LEARNING EXPERIENCES

and pull the three bricks several feet. They should measure the force and distance at each stage. Then have them draw the rectangles for each stage; the area of all being thus equal to the total energy. They should have a figure similar to that shown in Figure 4-23.

4.3 Explain to the children that the same amount of energy can have different energy pictures, depending upon how the forces and distances combine. Twelve foot-pounds of energy can be made up of 6 pounds and 2 feet, 2 pounds and 6 feet, 3 pounds and 4 feet, 4 pounds and 3 feet, 1 pound and 12 feet, and so on. Have them pull two bricks for 4 feet, then four bricks for 2 feet, and draw the energy picture. The areas should be approximately the same, but the rectangles will look different. (See Figure 4-24.)

LEARNING EXPERIENCES	EXPLANATORY NOTES

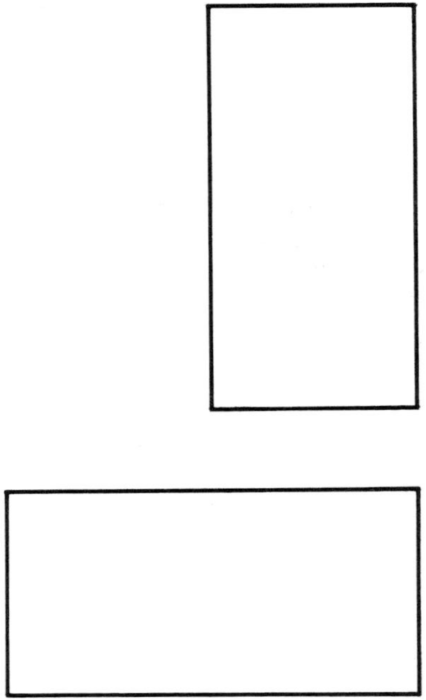

FIGURE 4-24. Two Bricks 4 Feet and Four Bricks 2 Feet (Not to Scale)

LEARNING EXPERIENCES

CONTENT C: *We can change the form of energy, but we cannot create energy or destroy it.* (This is a crude statement of the law of conservation of energy.)

5.1 Explain to the children that when we put out energy, only the amount of the energy we put out is available to work for us; we cannot get more work done than we produce with our own energy. To demonstrate this idea, use an ordinary playground seesaw. Have one child (we know his weight from the chart) sit halfway between the fulcrum and one end of the seesaw. Have another child use a spring scale to measure the force which must be used on the other end to lift the child clear off the ground. (See Figure 4-25.) Once this force has been measured, the scale may be set aside. Have a child pull down on the free end until he raises the seated child 1 foot vertically. Measure also the vertical distance which the free end moved; this distance should be 2 feet if the seated child is at the midpoint of his end of the seesaw. The force needed to pull the free end should be one-half the weight of the seated child; it will actually be slightly more than one-half due to the small amount of force necessary to overcome the friction at the fulcrum. If the seated child weighs 70 pounds and is raised 1 foot, then 70 foot-pounds of energy was necessary to raise him. If he is seated at the midpoint, then the force on the free end would be 35 pounds which moved through a distance of 2 feet; this expenditure is also 70 foot-pounds. Have the children lay out large energy rectangles on the floor, using masking tape

EXPLANATORY NOTES

Materials: Playground seesaw, measuring tapes, heavy spring scales.

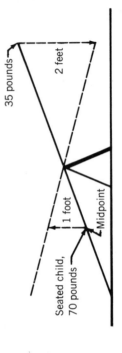

FIGURE 4-25. The Same Amount of Energy Is Produced on Each Side of a Seesaw, Even Though Forces and Distances Are Different.

LEARNING EXPERIENCES

to outline them. A scale of $1'' = 1$ lb. $= 1'$ will work best for this. Point out that the energy is about the same in both rectangles. (See Figure 4-26.)

5.2 Point out to the children that on the seesaw we used only 35 pounds of force to raise a child weighing 70 pounds; thus we multiplied *force*. We saw, however, that the energy was the same on both sides of the seesaw; the smaller force moved through a larger distance, keeping the energy in balance. Since we have seen how

.EXPLANATORY NOTES

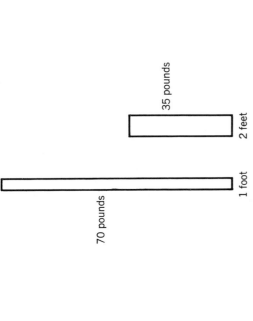

FIGURE 4-26.   Energy Rectangles for Seesaw.
Each rectangle contains 70 foot-pounds.

Materials: Tagboard or heavy construction paper, scissors, rulers.
General: For small forces such as bricks, the scale $4'' = 1$ lb. $= 1'$ is recommended; for larger forces such as weights of children, a scale of $1'' = 1$ lb. $= 1'$ will be more convenient.

LEARNING EXPERIENCES

energy is made up of force and distance in many different combinations, we need a way to measure the space (or area) in our energy rectangles. Have the children make a number of "energy units" to scale from tagboard or heavy construction paper. To make an energy unit for the small forces, have the children cut out 4-inch squares, labeling a vertical edge "1 pound" and a horizontal edge "1 foot." (See Figure 4-27.) Energy rectangles can then be built by placing the units in the appropriate columns (for force) and rows (for distance). (See Figure 4-28.)

EXPLANATORY NOTES

General: For example, if a force of 6 pounds operates through a distance of 3 feet, we could make the energy rectangle by arranging the units as shown in Figure 4-28. *General:* Determining the area (18 foot-pounds) can be done several obvious ways at the teacher's discretion. For the larger forces, make the energy "units" 10 inches long

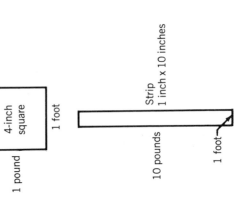

FIGURE 4-27.   **Energy Units**

EXPLANATORY NOTES

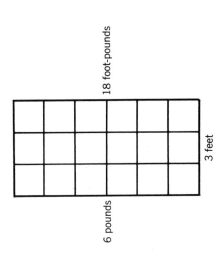

FIGURE 4-28.   Using Energy Units with Small Forces

(10 pounds) and 1 inch wide (1 foot). Several of these strips should be divided into inches so that forces less than 10 pounds may be scaled. Use of those is shown in Figure 4-29.

LEARNING EXPERIENCES

EXPLANATORY NOTES

LEARNING EXPERIENCES

Scaled strips
placed underneath
long strips

66 foot-pounds

10 pounds	10 pounds
10 pounds	10 pounds
10 pounds	10 pounds

3 feet

22 pounds

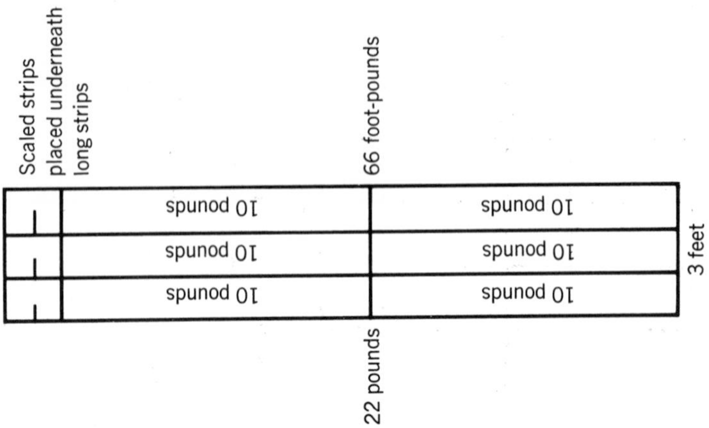

FIGURE 4-29. Using Energy Units with Larger Forces

LEARNING EXPERIENCES

EXPLANATORY NOTES

5.3 Have the children use the energy units to make energy rectangles for various combinations of actual energy expenditures; actually measuring the forces and distances as they slide bricks, slide one another, or perform the energy balance with the seesaw. Many other variations of using forces and distances will occur to the teacher. Include several instances where the same energy is developed with different combinations of force and distance, and have the children use the energy units to see how energy rectangles of different dimensions can have the same area. Counting the energy units in a given rectangle should conform to the teacher's preference for using these to aid in teaching multiplication. Vary by assigning hypothetical problems for the children to solve with the energy units.

Basic Idea III: Power is the rate at which energy is produced or consumed.

LEARNING EXPERIENCES	EXPLANATORY NOTES
CONTENT A: *Power is a measure of how fast we exert energy.*	
4.1 Have the children measure various energy outputs and the number of seconds for each one. They can slide bricks, slide one another on the cloths, walk and run up a stair, and the like, each time measuring the force, the distance, and the time in seconds. For each such measurement the teacher should divide the energy by the number of seconds and announce the amount of power: "Let's see, Jim; you pulled 20 pounds 10 feet. That makes 200 foot-pounds. You did it in 5 seconds. That's 40 foot-pounds every second."	*Materials:* Stop watch, sturdy cloth for sliding children, stairway, bricks and strings for pulling, ropes, large and small spring scales. General: So far, the unit has dealt with energy as a quantity without regard to how fast or how slowly we produce it. In dealing with power, it is necessary to bring in the time element. Power is the amount of energy exerted (or consumed) in a unit of time. If a force of 50 pounds is exerted through a distance of 2 feet in 1 second, we can specify the amount of power simply by saying "100 foot-pounds per second."
4.2 Have each child perform one energy operation at two distinctly different rates; first slowly and then rapidly. Measure the energy and the time. Point out and discuss with the children that different amounts of power must be used to do the same amount of work when we change the *time.* They can experience this; that is, they must work "harder" to do a given task when they speed up their efforts.	*General:* One child can pull another on a cloth for 6 feet with a force of 30 pounds. If he does this slowly the first time, it might take 10 seconds. On his second try (pulling the same child the same distance) he might do the same task in 3 seconds. Power for the first try is 18 foot-pounds per second; for the latter, power is 60 foot-pounds per second.
5.1 Have the children make a number of new energy units to a new scale, using a different color paper or tagboard from that used previously. Let each unit repre-	*Materials:* Tagboard or heavy construction paper, rulers, straightedges, scissors.

LEARNING EXPERIENCES

sent 10 foot-pounds, and make each square 5 inches on a side; labeling each square "10 foot-pounds." Four of these squares can then be arranged so that they make a larger square. This larger square will then represent 40 foot-pounds, the amount of energy per second in our *manpower unit.* (See Figure 4-30.) To use these new unit squares to determine power output, have a child make the usual measurements of force, distance, and time, for an activity involving energy output. Have him use the "old" energy units first to determine only the energy. At this point, he will have a number which represents the number of foot-pounds of energy. Round off this number to the *nearest 10 foot-pounds* (762 would round off to 760; 766 would round off to 770, and so on). Now have him count out enough "new" units to total the amount of energy in the rounded-off number. He would count out 76 "new" units if his rounded number was 760 (each "new" unit is 10 foot-pounds). He then picks up all the new units and sorts them into equal piles; the number of piles corresponds to the number of seconds of time. At this point, each pile represents the number of foot-pounds per second. He then takes the unit squares *from one pile only,* and makes as many large 40-foot-pound squares from these as possible; the number of these large squares is the *manpower* developed in the original activity. Have each child measure the data for several activities, and determine the amount of "manpower" as outlined above.

EXPLANATORY NOTES

General: The unit will present now a means of determining graphically the amount of power developed in an operation involving energy output. The most common unit by which power is measured is *horsepower;* 1 horsepower is 550 foot-pounds per second. This unit is awkward; it vexes engineers, and it is much too large for present purposes, since it would require dealing with small fractions. Let us, therefore, invent our own unit of power. We will call it the *manpower,* and we will define 1 *manpower* as *40 foot-pounds per second.* This unit is strictly arbitrary, and does not necessarily bear any relation to the power which a man can develop.

General: To illustrate with a concrete example, assume a 70-pound child runs up a 10-foot (vertical distance) stair in 5 seconds. He would first use the "old" units to determine that the energy expended was 700 foot-pounds. He would then count out 70 of the new units (each one is 10 foot-pounds) to represent the energy of 700 foot-pounds. Since the time is 5 seconds, he would sort the 70 units into five piles, each pile being made as nearly equal to the others as possible. The sorting can be done in the same manner as one deals from a deck of cards. In this case, there would be fourteen units in each pile. He would then know that he had developed 140 foot-pounds of energy per second. He can arrange the fourteen new units into as many large squares (each large square being made up of four unit squares) as possible; in this case he could make three large squares with two small unit squares left over. By counting, he could determine that he had developed 3½ "manpower" as illustrated in Figure 4-31.

EXPLANATORY NOTES

LEARNING EXPERIENCES

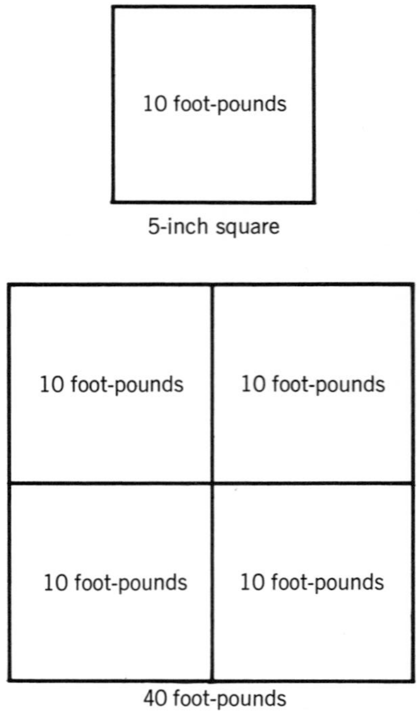

FIGURE 4-30.   New Energy Units. One 5-inch square represents 10 foot-pounds.

EXPLANATORY NOTES

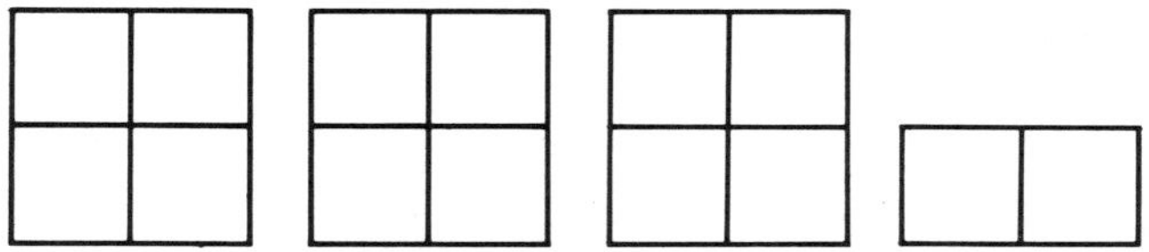

FIGURE 4-31.   Fourteen New Units Form into 3½ "Manpower" Units

General: In sorting the units into piles, they will not, of course, always come out even. If the teacher wishes to avoid fractions, simply use a pile which is most typical. If the teacher wishes to deal with fractions, the extra units in some piles may be removed, cut up appropriately and distributed so as to equalize piles.

LEARNING EXPERIENCES

chapter 5

Perceptual Training
in an Industrial Arts Unit

One general characteristic of the school program is the abstract, symbolic, and highly verbal nature of the academic process. This characteristic becomes more pronounced as the student advances to higher grade levels. More and more he is led away from manipulations of concrete objects, and is forced to deal with abstractions. Conceptualizing requires no overt involvement with the concrete. The academic process, therefore, offers progressively fewer occasions for promotion of developmental activities at the motor, motor-perceptual, and perceptual-motor levels.

Industrial arts studies and activities represent an exception to the foregoing observations. Most industrial arts training brings the student into active involvement with the concrete as opposed to the abstract. In planning perceptual training in conjunction with industrial arts, seldom does any need arise for introducing artificial or unusual activities. Abundant activities for perceptual training are present in the ongoing program. The teacher's task becomes one of utilizing opportunities which are naturally available — organizing, structuring, and highlighting certain aspects of the learner's experience to insure that the desired perceptual training arises from a given typical program.

CONDUCTING THE UNIT

Almost invariably, industrial arts subjects possess an inherent structure. Furthermore, the nature of the structure permits learning of that structure through direct involvement of a variety of sensory avenues. The structure may be experienced by the learner as he sees, hears, feels, and moves various elements in the learning situation itself. The goal of perceptual training in the industrial arts is to convey the inherent structure through the learner's various sense avenues in such a way that he is helped toward an inner structuring of himself as he interacts with concrete elements in the learning situation. Thus, a student who has some lack in his internal structure is brought into sensory-motor involvement with structured elements. The assumption behind this approach is that the slow learner's basic problem is some lack of inner structure, and that his basic learning problem can receive remediation through sensory-motor interaction with a structured situation.

Consider, for example, a student who experiences directional confusion. One simple activity to help remedy this basic problem is work with a socket wrench and ratchet handle in tightening and loosening bolts. Nearly all bolts and nuts have a "right-hand" thread; that is, in facing the bolt or nut a clockwise turning causes tightening and a counterclockwise turning causes loosening. When a student faces a bolt and attaches a socket wrench with ratchet handle, the handle becomes, in effect, the radius of a circle with the bolt at the center. The ratchet has two settings, one for tightening and the other for loosening. In tightening or loosening, the student receives visual, auditory, and tactual-kinesthetic feedback which is related to the direction of movement. The structure of the situation is such that each direction of turning provides its corresponding and distinctive feedback. When the student tightens a bolt he cannot avoid interacting with the inherent structure. His interaction produces feedback which in turn may be used to help him develop further his own internal structure.

Perceptual training will not come about automatically merely by arranging for the student to interact with a structured situation. The teacher must plan for developing activities which are generalized; without planning, the student will develop splinter skills instead of the internal structuring which he needs. In the preceding example, the student may come to approach all bolt-tightening tasks in a rigid way, using almost identical movements each time he engages in this activity. This practice is most undesirable. He needs, rather, to develop that flexibility which will let him bring to a given task a rich variety of generalized movement patterns from which he may draw as needed

Varying the movements by which any task is accomplished will increase flexibility and will help develop a more generalized internal structure. If the task is tightening a bolt with a socket wrench and ratchet handle, the student should be required to do this task from many different body positions. He should change hands occasionally. He should operate the ratchet handle from different positions relative to the location of the bolt; a movement of the handle at the "three o'clock" position, for example, requires an entirely different set of muscles than does the "nine o'clock" position. By introducing these and other variations, the structure of a bolt, with its built-in directional demands, provides an infinitely varied feedback to the student. The structure of the task does not change, but the student's interaction with the task changes greatly. True perceptual training arises from the student's internal organization of varied feedback from a given external structure.

The industrial arts teacher, therefore, has unique opportunities for combining perceptual training with the subject matter he is teaching. His task in this connection is not to devise activities for perceptual training. The activities are always close at hand in the form of the ongoing program. To provide perceptual training, the industrial arts teacher can analyze a particular task in terms of the student's interaction with that task—the sensory-motor avenues employed, the feedback which results, means of amplifying the feedback, and the possibilities for variation. From such an analysis should come new ways of involving the student so that the perceptual training is assured.

The unit of study in this chapter is presented as an illustration of how typical activities in industrial arts classes may be used for perceptual training. The unit title is: "Small Gasoline Engines: Disassembly, Assembly, Nomenclature, and Functioning." The assumed classroom situation involves a group of educable retarded teenagers in either a vocational training program or an industrial arts class in school. This group of students has been selected in order to illustrate maximum use of perceptual training in the unit. With only slight modifications by the teacher, the unit may be used with a regular class, emphasizing, in this case, the perceptual training aspects for those slow learners who need specific help.

The following materials and instructional aids for ten students and one instructor will be needed:

Two complete engines (air-cooled, one-cylinder, L-head, four-stroke cycle).

Two cylinder-block assemblies (engines, less head, carburetor, manifolds, tank, and other accessories).

Four hand cranks, approximately eight inches long and fabricated to replace engine drive pulleys or drive gears. These cranks are simple to construct, and will be used in turning engines by hand.

Four engine mounts, constructed of wood, to be used in mounting of engine to work bench. Use clamps to attach engine mount to bench. Construct mount so that engine may be clamped to bench in two different positions: piston vertical and piston horizontal.

One set of mechanic's tools, including socket wrench set (six-point sockets are preferred) with flex and ratchet handles.

One chalkboard.

One large wall chart showing the four strokes of the engine cycle. If a chart is not available, an appropriate filmstrip and projector may be substituted.

Two workbenches or tables.

The engines and the cylinder-block assemblies need not be in operating condition. If they are not immediately available, they may be purchased secondhand. In fact, items which are worn beyond normal use will be quite suitable for this unit. Engines and block assemblies in this condition are often discarded as junk by repair shops; often these discards will be given to the school without charge. It is recommended, however, that the two complete engines can be put in running condition without purchase of major parts. Putting two engines in running shape will provide a highly desirable success experience.

Each of the two work benches should have one complete engine and one cylinder-block assembly mounted on top and near one edge of the bench. Mount the engines with pistons vertical at first. The hand cranks should be attached so that when the piston is at top-dead-center the crank handle is at its highest point. A student should be able to turn the crank handle in a complete circle. Mount the engines and block assemblies so that two students can turn cranks at the same time without mutual interference. The chalk-board should be visible from each work bench.

The unit is divided into three major sections:

Section I: Functioning of the Engine
Section II: Disassembly, Nomenclature, and Assembly
Section III: Training in Sequencing and Sensory-Motor Integration

Unit activities are suggested under each section, with a parallel column noting concurrent perceptual training.

AN INDUSTRIAL ARTS UNIT:
SMALL GASOLINE ENGINES: DISASSEMBLY, ASSEMBLY, NOMENCLATURE, AND FUNCTIONING

Section I: Functioning of the Engine

ACTIVITIES	PERCEPTUAL TRAINING
1. Divide the class into two groups, one around each cylinder-block assembly. Explain that some parts have been removed to show how the main parts of the engine work together. Call attention to the complete engines and have students identify parts which are not on the block assemblies. Have students turn hand crank on block assembly, and point out that as the crank goes in a circle, the piston moves up and down. Have each one turn the crank while he uses his other hand to feel the simultaneous linear movement of the piston.	1. The major perceptual training at this stage is the tactual-kinesthetic experience of the interrelated and simultaneous rotary movement of the hand crank and the linear movement of the piston. Emphasize that when the engine is working, the piston makes the crankshaft turn, and that in turning the crank by hand the students are reversing the normal operation of the engine. Make clear that when the crank is at its topmost position, the piston is also at its topmost position. Let the students experience this operation by closing eyes, turning the crank, and feeling the piston move with other hand.
2. Use the block assembly to demonstrate the four strokes of the cycle: intake, compression, power and exhaust. Point out the interrelationships of parts for each of the strokes. The crank may be stopped at each stroke as the details are explained. Have each student feel the parts to further discover relative positions for each stroke. All explanations should be in terms of the dynamic functioning of the engine. For example, the intake valve is open on the intake stroke to let in the mixture of gasoline and air, while the downward motion of the piston causes this mixture to be drawn inward;	2. The emphasis should be upon synchrony. In the engine, as it operates, many events take place simultaneously and in relation to each other. The intake valve must open at the instant the piston is in a certain position, and so on. On most small engines, the size of parts will permit a student to place the heel of his palm on both valves, and at the same time keep several fingers of the same hand in contact with the top of the piston. His other hand can then be used to turn the crank. In this way he can feel the synchronous movements of major elements. This tactual-kinesthetic experience can be iso-

ACTIVITIES

both valves are closed on compression and power strokes to seal in the mixture, and so on.

3. Have each student demonstrate the four strokes beginning with the intake stroke, and explain all major events as he moves the crank from one position to another. At first the student should turn the crank to the intake stroke, stop, and then tell about the events that happen during the stroke; next, he should turn to the beginning of the compression stroke and describe the corresponding events, proceeding in this fashion through the entire cycle. When most of the group have mastered this activity, have everyone repeat the exercise, except this time the crank should be turned with a slow, continuous motion while the student describes appropriate simultaneous events. A typical description might begin, "The intake valve is open; the piston is moving down; the gas and air are coming in; now both valves are closed and the piston is coming up on the compression stroke; now the piston is at the top and the spark plug fires; the explosion is pushing the piston down. . ."

4. Have each of the two groups gather around the complete engine. Remind them that everything which took place in the block assembly happens inside the complete engine, except that now they can see only the crank

PERCEPTUAL TRAINING

lated by having the student perform with eyes closed, adding the visual later when he has mastered the total experience tactually and kinesthetically. Let students feel the alternate vacuum and compression by placing palms over the cylinder while turning the crank.

3. Verbal activity is now being added to the total situation. Data from speech mechanisms and auditory feedback are added to visual and tactual-kinesthetic data. When all these data come together at once, some students may not be able to keep them organized. First, try to have such a student slow down the process. Then have him try to perform with eyes closed; incoming visual data may be causing confusion. If removing the visual data brings no improvement, the motor activity involving speech may be interfering with other body activities. This interference may be checked by having someone other than the student slowly describe the cycle aloud while the student tries to turn the crank to correspond with the verbal description. These procedures may help isolate the problem; use of the engine for remediation will be discussed in Section III of this unit.

4. This activity provides excellent training in perceptual-motor matching. The following data are arriving simultaneously for processing:
a. Visual data obtained from visual monitoring of

ACTIVITIES	PERCEPTUAL TRAINING
movements. *Disconnect the spark plug wire to avoid accidental starting, and caution against touching the terminal.* Have students turn the crank on the complete engine, and see if some of them can feel movements and listen to sounds which will tell them where the piston is at a given moment. Point out that the position of the crank will tell them where the piston is, and that by listening carefully they can find out how the sound of the intake stroke differs from the sound of the exhaust stroke. Also, the crank will turn hardest when the piston is moving up on the compression stroke, and it will turn easiest when it is moving down on the power stroke. From these clues, they should be able to determine where the now invisible piston is at all times; knowing this, they should also be able to determine which valves are open or closed at all times. The teacher should help those who have difficulty, giving help mainly in the form of bringing more of the student's data-processing mechanisms into play. When the class is able to determine and to describe the internal activity in the complete engine, have them take turns describing what happens while turning the crank.	movements. The location of the crank is established partly from visual data as the student observes both the crank and his hand turning the crank. b. Tactual-kinesthetic feedback from the muscular activity in turning the crank. These data help establish crank position, and provide the same information as is received through the visual channel. In addition, tactual-kinesthetic feedback is a clue for determining when the piston is moving up on compression (this stroke requires the most turning effort) or down on the power stroke (this stroke requires the least turning effort). c. Auditory data from the sound of air rushing in during the intake stroke and rushing out during the exhaust stroke. Students should be given ample opportunity to experience the simultaneous arrival of the three types of data. Insist that they watch the hand as they turn the crank. This activity should extend well beyond the point where the student is able to identify each stroke; he should overlearn. Provide generalization by clamping the motor to the bench in different positions: piston horizontal and pointing left, then right; piston down; crankshaft vertical with hand crank turning in a horizontal plane, first with crank on top, then with crank on bottom. Put motor on floor, and operate from varied positions.
5. Remove the spark plug from each complete engine. Place a pencil through the hole left by the spark plug, and	5. These activities are for further generalization. Perceptual data are still received, but they come more indirectly

PERCEPTUAL TRAINING

ACTIVITIES

let the end of the pencil touch the top of the piston. Have a student hold the pencil steady while turning the crank. Call attention to the up and down movement of the pencil, and emphasize that the piston is moving the pencil. Have students take turns cranking. Next, remove the pencil, and have a student turn the hand crank while all listen to the new and distinctive sound of compressed air rushing out of the spark plug hole during the compression stroke. Have the student distinguish the sounds peculiar to each stroke in this new situation. While spark plug is removed, connect ignition wire to spark plug and place plug on engine. Turn crank to let students see spark. Point out that the spark occurs at the top of the compression stroke. Let the student press a thumb over the spark plug hole and feel the force of compression as the piston comes up on the compression stroke. The student should be able to differentiate the compression stroke from all others by using only this clue. Have the student perform this last activity with ears plugged and eyes closed. Students should take turns on all activities.

than in previous experiences. For example, the student still feels the movement of the piston, but only indirectly through the related movement of the pencil. He cannot see the piston move, but he can see the pencil which the piston causes to move. The same type of indirect experience arises from putting the thumb over the spark plug hole and feeling the pressure during the compression stroke.

For certain children, such activities, involving indirect perceptual experience of unseen objects and events, can be extremely important. It appears that for some children an object or event ceases to exist whenever the object or event is no longer visible. Such a child may look at an object and comprehend it as part of his world. When he turns his back on the object, however, that object seems to pass from his world. It is as if the object no longer exists for the child when he cannot see it. Piaget (Hunt, 1961, pp. 129-130)[1] notes that objects normally begin to acquire permanence for the infant from 4½ to 8 or 9 months; a search for an object which is removed from his vision will occur. Before this development, when the object vanishes from vision it does not elicit searching. Some older children with learning problems seem not to have developed a sense of object permanence when the object is not seen.

[1]J. McV. Hunt, *Intelligence and Experience.* Copyright© 1961. The Ronald Press Company, New York.

PERCEPTUAL TRAINING

ACTIVITIES

The teacher should be alert for students who show indications of this pattern of behavior. The following activities will provide extra help for these students:

a. Begin with the student operating the block assembly (the piston is visible). Have him turn the crank with one hand while fingers of the other hand remain in contact with the moving piston. See to it that he watches closely the hand on the piston, and looks occasionally at the hand on the crank. Have him describe only the movement of the piston while he turns the crank, saying something similar to this: "On top . . . going down . . . on bottom . . . coming up . . . on top. . . ." Have him do also with eyes closed.

b. When he has mastered this assignment, have him hold a pencil on top of the piston (that is, the piston in the block assembly) and turn the crank while watching the hand on the pencil, the pencil, and the piston. He describes the movement in the same fashion as before. Have him do also with eyes closed.

c. When the foregoing performance is satisfactory, tape a piece of paper over the cylinder of the block assembly so that the piston is no longer visible. Punch the pencil through the paper, and have him hold the pencil in contact with the piston while turning the crank. Again he watches hand and pencil movements while describing the movements aloud. Have him perform with eyes closed.

d. Now have him go to the complete engine, place the pencil through the spark plug hole so that the pencil

ACTIVITIES

6. Show the wall chart to the class. The wall chart should consist of four schematic diagrams showing the four strokes of the cycle. Volunteers may explain each stroke, pointing to applicable portions of the chart as they speak. All should attempt the explanation from the chart. For those who have trouble, go back to the block assembly, then back again to the chart.

7. Position the chalkboard so that each student can see one of the block assemblies and can look at the chalkboard without changing his position unduly. Have one student operate each block assembly. The student operator sets the piston at the beginning of the intake stroke. Members of the class then describe everything which takes place during that stroke, and the teacher writes their descriptions on the board under the heading, "Intake Stroke." The procedure is repeated for each stroke, in order. Students then copy what is written on the board. After this activity, some students may be able to write

PERCEPTUAL TRAINING

touches the piston, hold the pencil against the piston while turning the crank, watch the hand and pencil, and describe at the same time the movement of the *piston.* Have him close his eyes, turn the crank, and tell where the piston is. Vary by having him stop on teacher's command, and then say where the piston is.

e. Vary by having him hold the pencil while someone else turns crank; he tells where the piston is.

6. With the wall chart, the student moves a small step away from concrete experience and takes a small step toward a symbolic representation of the concrete. Note, however, that a foundation of concrete experience and perceptual organization of that experience was provided before the symbolic representation was added.

7. This activity is presented as only one example of connecting the symbolic activity of reading and writing to the perceptual activity associated with concrete experience. The teacher should add reading and writing to the unit activities whenever possible. For many children, little or no connection seems to exist between words on a page and concrete experience. Industrial arts subjects provide a unique opportunity to help the student make this important connection.

ACTIVITIES	PERCEPTUAL TRAINING
descriptions in their own words. Such assignments should be made at the teacher's discretion. 8. Explain the ignition and carburetion systems to the class.	8. In presenting the carburetion system, low pressure can be experienced by having the student place his palm over the cylinder while the piston is moving down. Show how the intake valve makes an opening between the cylinder and the carburetor. On the complete engine, let him feel the low pressure at the carburetor (air cleaner removed). In presenting the ignition system, the main relationship which can be perceived directly is the interrelatedness of the spark, the ignition points, and the ignition cam.

Section II: Disassembly, Nomenclature, and Assembly

ACTIVITIES	PERCEPTUAL TRAINING
1. Divide the class into four groups, each group to work with an engine or a block assembly. Each group should disassemble its engine or block assembly under supervision of the teacher. At appropriate stages of the disassembly, the teacher may point out relationships which could not be seen clearly while the engine was assembled. The most important of these is the relationship between the camshaft and the valves. Students should learn the correct names of the more important	1. Before disassembly begins, the teacher might explain the importance of direction in tightening the loosening bolts. Use socket wrenches and handles for student experience. Point out how a clockwise direction tightens a bolt only if the student faces the bolt; the direction reverses if the bolt faces away from the student. Students should also practice estimating the size socket needed for a particular bolt or nut, checking each estimate by trying to fit the wrench to the bolt or nut.

ACTIVITIES

parts, and they should learn to write them and to recognize the written names.

2. With the engine (or block assembly) disassembled, have students select parts which can be fitted together on the basis of form or patterns of holes. Have them pair off, with one student of a pair selecting a part for the other to match through clues from form or pattern. When a student thinks he has found a match, he should try it for fit.

3. Assembly of the engine and block assemblies should have detailed supervision from the teacher. Each group should select the parts which that group thinks should be assembled first. They should explain to the teacher what they plan to put together and point out exactly how they propose to do so. Then another logical group of parts is selected, and the process is repeated until the engine is complete. If the teacher notes that the students' plan will result in problems, he may tell them that they are making a mistake, but he should let them discover the mistake, checking new plans with him before proceeding.

PERCEPTUAL TRAINING

2. The perceptual training here is obvious. The teacher should note, however, that matching of form or pattern in this instance involves the student with unfamiliar shapes and configurations, but that an involvement with the perceptual organization of the whole has preceded involvement with the parts.

3. Whereas disassembly helps the student perceive the parts which make up the whole, assembly helps him perceive the whole as coming together from the parts. In suggesting a detailed supervision pattern, the aim is to provide experience in dealing with the logical sequence in which elements must come together. For example, one group may want to put the cylinder head and crankshaft on before installing the piston and connecting rod. In most small engines, this order will not work. Usually, either the cylinder head or the crankshaft may be installed before installing the piston and connecting rod, but not both. Students should be exposed to this kind of problem in assembling the engine.

Each student should make at least one gasket for use on the engine. Making a gasket is excellent perceptual training. The method which offers maximum perceptual training is the one used frequently by mechanics: Gasket material is held firmly against the part surface, and a

ACTIVITIES

PERCEPTUAL TRAINING

shop hammer is used to tap around the part outline. The tapping is concentrated at the edges, and forces the gasket material against the edge. The edge cuts through the gasket material, and when all edges have been tapped sufficiently the gasket is in proper form. Tapping out bolt-holes should be done with the rounded end of the hammer. This task requires the student to feel the outline of the part through the gasket material, and to use the feel to guide his tapping. Thus, the major sensory-motor avenues are involved.

Section III: Training in Sequencing and Sensory-Motor Integration

ACTIVITIES

PERCEPTUAL TRAINING

1. All activities in Section III use the two cylinder-block assemblies; complete engines will not be needed. Begin with piston vertical.

   With eyes closed, a student turns the crank with one hand. With the other hand he maintains continuous contact with valves and piston (heel of palm on valves and fingers touching piston). As he turns the crank, he describes what is happening, just as he did previously in Section I, 3. When he can perform this activity, the teacher has him stop, then move both hands clear of the engine, but keep eyes closed. The teacher then turns the crank several times, and stops the crank in any arbitrary position. The student explores the various parts

1. If the student has truly acquired a grasp of the sequence of events in the four cycles, he should be able to deal with isolated elements of the sequence. At any point in the sequence he should be able to relate that point to preceding and succeeding events, and to the sequence as a whole. With his eyes closed, he uses only the tactual-kinesthetic feedback from exploratory movements to gain information about relative locations of engine parts. He can discover the valve positions, and from the position of the crank he can determine whether the piston would be moving up or down. This information is all he needs to know to determine the stroke and activities related to this position. He should perform this activity

ACTIVITIES	PERCEPTUAL TRAINING
with his hands only, and tells which stroke is operating and what is happening in this position. He opens his eyes afterward to check his performance.	with the engine in various positions, and with his body in various relations to the engine.
2. Repeat the preceding activity, but with eyes open. The student turns his back to the engine while the teacher sets the crank in an arbitrary position. When the teacher has set the crank, the student looks at the engine. He is to explore it only with his eyes now. He then announces the stroke, and describes what is happening at this instant represented by the setting. Repeat activity with settings from all four strokes, varying not only the stroke, but also varying positions within a given stroke.	2. For most students, this activity should not be attempted until the student has mastered the one immediately above. However, if a student can perform with eyes open, but cannot do so when he closes his eyes, he may be helped by reversing the usual order. In this case, he should first describe the sequence while someone else turns the crank (thus eliminating all sensory channels except the visual); then he should turn the crank while watching and feeling all movement; finally he should close his eyes and perform as in III, 1. In the more typical situation, it is expected that the visual organization will follow the motor. Thus, this activity begins with the student who has mastered the motor organization, adding training in visual organization to the motor organization.
3. Have the students stand or sit facing the chalkboard. Place a block assembly behind the students, and place a screen between them and the block assembly. Write the name of one of the strokes on the board ("exhaust stroke," for example). Have a student go behind the screen and turn the crank to correspond with the stroke written on the board.	3. This activity requires the student to perform a sequence of activities. He must (1) read the name of the stroke, (2) remember what he has read while he walks to the block assembly, (3) solve the problem of the sequence of events within the engine, and (4) return to his place. Many children with learning problems cannot organize such a sequence of events in time; in dealing with one element, the others become lost or disorganized. The overt activity of walking to the block assembly will

ACTIVITIES

4. Reverse the activity in 3 by setting the block assembly on a position; a student looks at the block assembly and writes the name of the stroke on the board. Vary by having the student explore the block assembly with eyes closed, and then write the name of the stroke on the board.

5. Vary 3 by giving an oral command instead of writing the name of the stroke. ("Set the block assembly on the compression stroke.") Vary 4 by setting the block assembly on a certain position, and have the student announce the name of the stroke.

PERCEPTUAL TRAINING

distract some to the point that they will not remember what they are to do when they arrive. This activity also helps connect written symbols with concrete experience.

5. The teacher should be alert for the student whose performance of activities 3, 4, or 5 reveals marked differences. This clue may suggest that one or more sensory-motor avenues are functioning at a lower level than others. For example, if performance on activity 5 is much better than on 3, vision may be functioning at a lower level than audition. The teacher may modify activity with the block assembly to help isolate a particular sensory-motor avenue which is causing trouble. Activities 3, 4, and 5 require use of vision, audition, and motor activity. By selective modification of these activities, the teacher may remove first one and then another to determine relative functioning.

Appendix

Constructing a Styrofoam Sphere

The sphere is made from 1-inch thick sheets of styrofoam. The sheets are the type sold by building supply firms for home insulating purposes; this variety is a lower grade and much less expensive styrofoam than that sold for craft and hobby use.

The foundation of the sphere is formed by stacking progressively smaller styrofoam rings on top of each other until a rough hemisphere is built. The procedure is repeated for a second hemisphere, and the two are joined to make a rough sphere. The surface is completed by applying papier-maché clay to the outside, forming a smooth and continuous surface. See Figure A-1 for cross-section view of one hemisphere.

To cut rings from styrofoam sheets, the inner and outer diameters of each ring must be determined. The following procedure will give these diameters by direct measurement and without the necessity of making mathematical computations:

1. On a large sheet of paper draw full-scale a half-circle of the same radius you wish the finished sphere to have. Draw the diameter and one radius perpendicular to the diameter (Figure A-1).

2. Measure the thickness of one styrofoam sheet (it may not be exactly 1 inch). Beginning at the center of the half-circle, measure *along the radius* and make marks on the radius, dividing

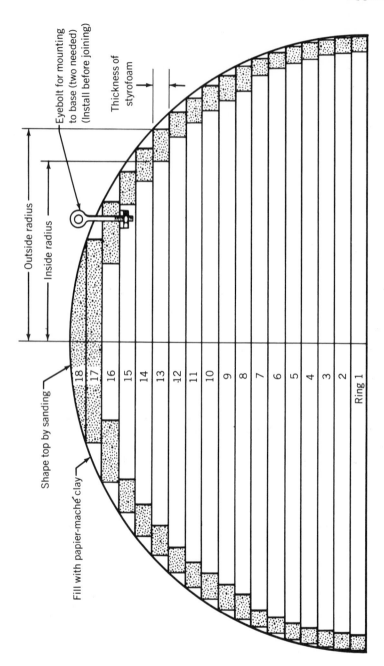

Eyebolt for mounting to base (two needed) (Install before joining)

Thickness of styrofoam

Outside radius

Inside radius

Shape top by sanding

Fill with papier-maché clay

18
17
16
15
14
13
12
11
10
9
8
7
6
5
4
3
2
Ring 1

FIGURE A-1. **Cross-section of Styrofoam Rings Forming Hollow Sphere**

the radius into short lengths equal to the thickness of one styrofoam sheet. Draw lines through these marks, making the lines parallel to the diameter line; each line should extend to the edge of the half-circle.

3. The outside radius of each ring can now be measured directly. Measure from the half-circle radius line to the edge of the half-circle, measuring along the parallel lines (Figure A-1).

4. The inside radius of each ring should be such that each ring will have adequate contact surface to join with and support the immediately adjacent smaller ring. Examine Figure A-1 carefully, and note that as outside diameters become smaller the widths of the rings must increase in order to make contact. If a 36-inch diameter sphere is being made, the following information will apply to inner radii of rings 1 inch thick (Figure A-1).

Rings 1 through 7: Make inside radius 1-inch smaller than outside radius.

Rings 8 through 12: Make inside radius 1½ inches smaller than outside radius.

Rings 13 through 15: Make inside radius 2 inches smaller than outside radius.

Ring 16: Make inside radius 4 inches smaller than outside radius.

Note: Cover (No. 17) and Top (No. 18) are solid.

5. When inside and outside radii for all rings have been determined, the rings may be marked out and cut from styrofoam sheets with a hacksaw blade. To start a cut, push one end of blade through the styrofoam sheet at a convenient starting point on the ring outline and begin sawing. Side of blade should be kept as nearly perpendicular as possible to the styrofoam sheet, so that sawed edges will not be slanted.

6. Glue rings together to form two hemispheres. Toothpicks may be pushed through rings to hold them while glue dries. *Important*: Use type glue recommended by your supplier, since some types react chemically with styrofoam. Let glue dry. Use rough sandpaper to form top into spherical shape (Figure A-1). Insert two eyebolts (with washers and nuts) into ring 16 of *one hemisphere* only, before joining hemispheres (Figure A-1). These eyelets are for anchoring to base.

7. Fill in the outer spaces with papier-maché clay, smoothing the clay into a uniform spherical surface.

8. When the clay has dried, use sandpaper to smooth and shape any rough or uneven areas. Paint with two coats of latex-base paint, using heavy sand-float finish with second coat.

9. A fairly large plastic laundry basket will make a good base. Place the globe on the basket with the eyebolts down (Figure A-2). Shift the globe so that the eyebolts are approximately the same distance from the sides of the basket. Tie stout cords from each eyebolt to the side of the basket, tying cord ends well below the eyebolts. Neither eyebolt should be in the location of the South Pole.

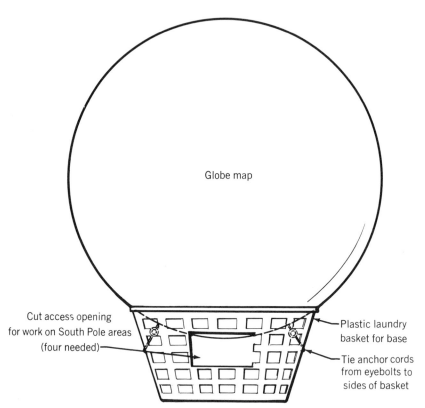

FIGURE A-2.   **Mounting the Globe Map on a Base**

10. Cut four openings in the basket for future access to lower part of globe. Openings should be equally spaced, and should be large enough to permit inserting arms for drawing in South Pole areas.

Bibliography

Coghill, G. E., *Anatomy and the Problem of Behavior,* Cambridge: Cambridge University Press, 1929.

Dunsing, Jack D., and Newell C. Kephart, "Motor Generalizations in Space and Time" in *Learning Disorders,* ed. Jerome Hellmuth (Seattle, Washington: Special Child Publications, 1965), I, 77-121.

Durrell, Donald D., *Durrell Analysis of Reading Difficulty,* New York: Harcourt, Brace & World, Inc., 1955.

Frostig, Marianne, *Developmental Test of Visual Perception,* Palo Alto, California: Consulting Psychologists Press, 1963.

Hagin, Rosa A., Archie A. Silver, and Marilyn F. Hersh, "Specific Reading Disability: Teaching by Stimulation of Deficit Perceptual Areas," in *Reading and Inquiry,* ed. J. Allen Figurel, Newark, Delaware: International Reading Association, 1965, X, 368-70.

Harris, Albert J., *How to Increase Reading Ability* (4th ed., rev.), New York: David McKay Company, Inc., 1961.

Hunt., J. McV., *Intelligence and Experience,* New York: The Ronald Press Company, 1961.

Kephart, Newell C., *The Slow Learner in the Classroom,* Columbus, Ohio: Charles E. Merrill Books, Inc., 1960.

Kirk, Samuel A., *Teaching Reading to Slow-Learning Children,* New York: Houghton-Mifflin Company, 1940.

Roach, Eugene, and Newell C. Kephart, *The Purdue Perceptual-Motor Survey,* Columbus, Ohio: Charles E. Merrill Books, Inc., 1966

Rutherford, W. L. "Perceptual-Motor Training and Readiness," in *Reading and Inquiry,* ed. J. Allen Figurel, Newark, Del.: International Reading Association, 1965, X, 294-296.

Slingerland, Beth H., *Screening Tests for Identifying Children with Specific Language Disability,* Cambridge: Educators Publishing Service, 1964.

Index

Index

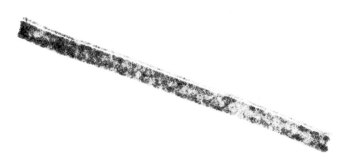